D1524259

INTERNATIONAL AND DOMESTIC POLITICS IN GREECE DURING THE CRIMEAN WAR

by
JON V. KOFAS

EAST EUROPEAN MONOGRAPHS, BOULDER
DISTRIBUTED BY COLUMBIA UNIVERSITY PRESS
NEW YORK

1980

EAST EUROPEAN MONOGRAPHS, NO. LXI

to
Helen Kofas

PREFACE

The primary focus of this work is Greek foreign policy during the Crimean War period. The domestic and foreign developments of Greece are traced from 1844, the beginning of the Kolettes administration, to 1857, the ending of the Anglo-French occupation of Greece. The Kolettes administration which lasted three years, 1844-1847, was responsible for setting the foundation for an expansionist foreign policy. John Kolettes as Prime Minister introduced the *Megali Idea* to Greece and Otho I, king of Greece, faithfully followed this policy which called for the annexation of the Greek populated Turkish Provinces of Epirus, Thessaly and Macedonia. The result of this policy was antagonism not only between Greece and the Ottoman Empire, but also between Greece and the Western European Powers, who supported a policy of the Ottoman Empire's integrity.

This study has been made possible by the assistance of many. I should like to thank Professor Walter Gray who supervised the dissertation on which this book is based. I am also grateful to Professors Franklin Walker and Margaret O'Dwyer for their thoughtful comments and contributions to this study. I am especially thankful to the Loyola Gradute School for granting me financial assistance during my Ph.D. program.

During my research in Athens I was privileged to be assisted by Dr. Domna N. Donta, Director of the Historical Archives of the Greek Foreign Ministry, and by Mr. Constantine Diamante, Director of the General State Archives. Also I wish to thank the Public Records Office which was very helpful in providing me with all the material I requested and the Quai d'Orsay in Paris which sent me a number of useful documents for my research. Finally, I wish to express my gratitude to Professor John A. Petropoulos for his kind advice and encouragement.

TABLE OF CONTENTS

INTRODUCTION

The country in southeastern Europe known as "little Greece to its inhabitants of the nineteenth century[1] had a population of one million just before the Crimean War[2] and its territory amounted to 47,000 square kilometers.[3] The newly formed nation became a kingdom in 1832 when Great Britain, France and Russia, the three Protecting Powers of Greece, appointed a Bavarian Prince, Otho I, to reign over the country.[4] Otho came to Athens early in 1833 but the king did not assume his responsibility as a ruler until he was twenty years of age in 1835. The man who dominated the scene and exerted much influence in the government was Count Joseph von Armansperg.[5] After February 1837 Otho became the absolute ruler of Greece as he dismissed Armansperg from his position as Arch-Chancellor. The king ruled without a constitution for about seven years after the Armansperg dismissal, but not without opposition. During that time he managed to accomplish nothing more than hatred from his subjects, rivalry from the Greek political parties and the three Protecting Powers, all elements which contributed to the weakness of the young nation. As Professor Tzivanopoulos points out:

> Instead of exerting himself to consolidate the freedom which the Greeks had conquered, the efforts of King Otho were all directed toward the complete extinction of that freedom. The Bavarian ruler, forgetful that he was an elected Monarch, and that his subjects had won their independence by their own swords, thought that he was called to govern after the fashion of his ancestors . . . The people who had preserved their institutions entirely under the weight of Ottoman dominance, now saw their country transformed into the likeness of a German duchy.[6]

Othonian absolutism was too unpopular among the freedom-loving Greeks who in 1843 revolted and demanded that a constitution be drawn up so that the people would have some form of representation in their government.

The principal leaders of the September revolution[7] were military officers who had much of the public support in the capital. The 1843 revolution was bloodless and more important it was successful in driving the Bavarian bureaucracy from Greece and persuading Otho to agree to the formation of a constitution. The French constitution of 1830 was used as the model for the Greek constitution of 1843 which was to change the political system and hopefully bring economic relief and general progress to "little Greece." In the field of religion, the Greek Orthodox Church was recognized as the official national Church but all religions would be tolerated. (Articles 1 & 2).[8] In the area of civil rights important accomplishments were achieved. "All Greeks are equal under the law . . . " (Article 3.) "The press is free, and censorship is not allowed." (Article 10.) The new Constitution secured certain legislative rights for the representatives of the people as it stated that the legislative power belongs to the king, the Boule[9] (Parliament), and the *Gerousia* (Senate). (Article 15.) "The official interpretation of the laws belongs to the Legislative authorities." (Article 19.)

Even though the Constitution did provide many political and civil rights for the people, it was still a Constitution which fell short of creating a liberal form of government such as enjoyed by Great Britain at the time. The king was guaranteed such powers that if put to use, as they were, would in fact make him an absolute monarch. The king had the right to appoint and dismiss ministers at will. (Article 24.) He had the right to declare war and conclude treaties of peace, alliances and commerce. (Article 25.) He also had the right to dismiss the Parliament, (Article 30) , appoint senators, (Article 70) and judges, (Article 86). The most important accomplishment of the revolution of 1843 and the constitutional achievement was the elimination of the Bavarian bureaucracy which had administered the affairs of the country since 1832, and the theoretical limitation of the monarchical power.

There were three political parties; the "French" party or *moshomanga* as it was commonly known, the "Russian" party or *napist* and the "English" party. All were in a position to share in the power of governing their country.[10] As the names of these parties indicate they were set up and supported by individuals who were convinced that the Protecting Power, after which they modeled their party, had helped the Greeks in the past and would help Greece more than any other in the future. The parties also designated the internal policy supported by their followers. Those who were affiliated with the "Russian" party wanted the government of Greece to be modelled after that of Tsarist Russia and to be as friendly as possible to that Power. Those who followed the "English" tended to be constitutionalists and were opposed to the Bavarian dynasty in Greece as long as it would insist on absolutist principles. The "French" party was somewhere in between the two extremes, although it tended to side with the "Russians" more so than with the "English." Naturally the three Protecting Powers infiltrated the political parties of Greece in order to exert the maximum possible influence in the governing process of the country. According to the treaty of 7 May 1832[11] drawn up by the Protecting Powers, Greece would be under the constant surveillance of Great Britain, France and Russia until it had discharged its financial obligations to these countries. Article XII of the Treaty states that Greece was guaranteed a loan of 60 million francs by the three Powers for which:

> The sovereign of Greece and the Greek state shall be bound to appropriate to the payment of the interest and sinking fund of such instalments of the loan as may have been raised under the guarantee of the three Courts, the first revenues of the state in such a manner that the actual receipts of the Greek treasury shall be devoted, first of all, to the payment of the said interest and sinking fund, and shall not be employed for any other purpose, until those payments on account of the instalments of the loan raised under the guarantee of the three Courts, shall have been completely secured for the current year. The diplomatic representatives of the three Courts in Greece shall be especially charged to watch over the fulfillment of the last mentioned stipulation.[12]

Under such conditions it was clearly impossible that the Protecting Powers would not interfere in the internal affairs of Greece. The stage for foreign political dominance was set therefore by the Treaty of May 1832 when the Bavarian Prince, Otho, was elected to rule over the Greek people and when strict measures were set up by the Powers to influence the government of Greece.

The history of the Othonian period in the political sphere is marked by rivalries among the parties and therefore among England, France and Russia. From 1837 when Otho dismissed Armansperg and assumed the role of absolute monarch until 1840 the "Russian" party was the dominant faction in Greece.[13] From 1841 until 1850 the "French" party enjoyed political supremacy, leaving the "English" party with a brief period of four months in 1944 to play the dominant role in the political sphere. The importance of controling or having a good deal of influence in the Greek government was immense for the Great Powers. There were economic, strategic and political reasons which made Greece an attractive nation to control in the Near East.

The dominance of one party in the government meant the alliance of Greece with that party's patron nation and her opposition to the patron nations of the other two parties. During the 30-year period of "foreign party" rule Greece became victim of such politics which continuously placed her under the antagonisms of the Protecting Powers. The worst of all the devastating consequences suffered by the young nation was in the period during the Crimean War when her foreign policy antagonised that of the Allied Powers and favored Russia. In this work the development of foreign and domestic Greek policy as well as international incidents which occurred in Greece from 1844 until 1857 will be traced to unfold the whole story of the insurrection of 1854 and the Franco-British occupation of Greece which followed. The reason that this study begins with the Kolettes administration in 1844 and not with the Menshikov mission in 1853 is because the causes which gave rise to the events of 1854 are to be found in the earlier decade. First, the government of Kolettes, founder of the "French" party,[14] supported a policy of irredentism, as opposed to internal development, second, it supported brigand chiefs who were a potential threat to the neighboring Turks, third, it opposed constitutionalism in Greece, and fourth, it created a very hostile environment for Greek-British relations which led to a number of confrontations between the two countries, Greece always coming out as the loser.

At the opening of Greek-Turkish hostilities in 1853 the British minister at Athens, Thomas Wyse, felt that the era of the Kolettes administration was responsible for the problems which were currently facing Greece.

> "Place" and "Religion," "Hellenic Nationality" and "Eastern Church" against the Proselytism and Anti-hellenism of the Western Religions and Politics, is the cry put forward in plain terms, in all their recent publications. This cry might have been resisted some years ago with every prospect and probability of success, by the

counter cry of Commerce and Constitution and by a cordial cooperation in support of both, on the part of the two great Western
Powers, England and France. But these claims have of late years
much diminshed principally owing to the narrow and purely personal policy pursued by France since the Administration of Mr.
Coletti (Kolettes), surrendering for the illusory influence derived
from ephemerel Portofolios and Court favors that solid power,
now required, which can only be attained by honest and preserving
exertions for the true interests of the people.[15]

As the Kolettist era was linked with the rise of the events of 1854, the
Greek-British hostilities from 1847 to 1850 were also responsible for
harsh measures adopted by the Allied Powers against Greece during the
occupation. The three-year Franco-British occupation, the persistent
attempts by the king to carry out a policy of irredentism, and the
socio-economic consequences of the war and occupation will all be
discussed in order to determine what the role of Greece was during
the Crimean War.

CHAPTER ONE

THE KOLETTES ADMINISTRATION AND ANGLO-FRENCH RIVALRY IN GREECE

A. The Nature of the Kolettes Government

John Kolettes, the founder and leader of the "French" party, was appointed Prime Minister of Greece by the king on 6 August 1844 after he had contributed a great deal to the disturbances which led to the resignation of the Mavrokordatos Government. Alexander Mavrokordatos, leader of the "English" party, was elected Prime Minister on 30 March 1844. Besides the political opposition pressures from Kolettes and Andreas Metaxas, founder and leader of the "Russian" party, several other incidents occurred which contributed to the downfall of Mavrokordatos on August 4th. The press accused him of "becoming an English organ for a British conquest of Greece according to the method applied by the British in the conquest of India and presently applied in Greece."[1] Another factor which damaged the image of the Prime Minister was the publication of the Londos, Minister of Justice, letter which ordered the authorities of Patras to "secure his election at any price." Finally, the illegal election of Dimitrios Kallergis, the General who led the military against the absolutist regime of Otho in the revolution of September 1843, helped to bring the resignation of Mavrokordatos.[2]

The new Prime Minister's sympathy with the Crown influenced the royal decision. In a message sent to Desages, the French Charge d'Affaires, dated 29 February 1844, Kolettes expressed his real views about the constitutionalists of 1843. He claimed he had to infiltrate the National Assembly "in order to neutralize the influence of the revolutionary sector," so that the King, the monarchy, and the country would be saved.[3]

Kolettes became one of the most notorious dictators in the history of modern Greece when he realized that his affection for the Crown would give him unlimited power to act at will instead of following the Constitution. Even though he declared in public that he was a firm believer in justice, impartiality, and constitutional principles,[4] he acted in a dictatorial manner and disregarded the laws of the land. Most of his contemporaries as well as modern historians agree that Kolettes abused the constitution (of 1843). Nicholas Dragoumes, affiliated with the "English" party, described Kolettes as a liar, a man who suppressed public authorities, persecuted the press, intervened in elections, and systematically eliminated political opposition.[5]

Another contemporary—a French writer—wrote:

> The manner in which Kolettes attempted to wipe out the Parliament, is all new, alien to Greek ethics. . . . The last struggle of the government against the island of Hydra in the election recognized by the examining committee as perfectly legal was cancelled. This struggle proclaims . . . the first step toward the establishment of a system of dictatorship.[6]

Scholars of modern Greek history, whether they are leftists like Kordatos,[7] liberal like Douglas Dakin,[8] or monarchists like Aspreas,[9] all characterize the Government of Kolettes as "Parliamentary Dictatorship."

Born in Epirus and educated in Italy, Kolettes became the doctor of Ali Pasha of Janina which may explain his attitude about government. Bower and Bolitho, biographers of Otho I, write that:

> His (Kolettes) idea of ruling Greece was founded on the principles of his former master Ali Pasha; bribery, corruption and malversation of public funds. His party was composed of the least stable elements of the country and he deliberately set out to assimilate as many of these as possible into the administration in order to prevent them from making trouble.[10]

At the beginning of his appointment "the Prime Minister of the 6th of August," as Kolettes was known by his contemporaries, had the support of Metaxas and the "Russian" party otherwise he would not have been able to maintain a majority needed to form a government.[11] Metaxas was in charge of the Ministries of Navy and Economics, and the Prime Minister reserved for himself the Ministries of Foreign Affairs, of Internal Affairs and of Ecclesiastical Affairs. The Kolettes-Metaxas coalition was designed to eliminate the threat of constitutionalism in Greece. By the time of the first elections, "having at its disposal the military and political authorities, using force and intrigue, the allied government almost anihilated the "English" party in all of Greece."[12]

It was not the intention of this dictator, however, to share his power with the "Russian" party and Metaxas. By 30 December 1844 Piscatory, the French Minister at Athens, could write to Guizot that, "the success of Kolettes is continuing. Metaxas until now is following an honest policy. And he sees that his party is disintegrating under the sun of Kolettes' [party]."[13] On July 26th Metaxas gave his written resignation to the King and so Kolettes and the *Moschomanga*, as the "French" party was commonly known, monopolized political power.[14]

With the Napists out of the picture Kolettes had concentrated his power in his own hands but he was also fearful of the political opposition which was building as a result of the government's inability to accomplish anything other than corruption. On 2 September 1845 *Aion* (Century), the Russian newspaper, published an article exposing the unconstitutional practices of the government. "Greece is ruled constitutionally and Kallergis, Spiro-Melios, Skarveles, Rodites and other "Septemberists" officers are being ostracized, mourning away from their families, and Makrygiannes is considered suspect of discovering the plot against the Constitution."[15] John Makrygiannes, a military hero affiliated with the "French" party, was one of the leaders who fought for Constitutionalism in 1843. In his memoirs Makrygiannes recalled the determination of Kolettes to annihilate the "Constitutionalists" of 1843, and do away with the constitution itself and its influence on the public mind. In March 1845 Kolettes ordered that the inscription of the Constitution should *not* be displayed in the public ceremony of the 25th March national celebration. He further had plans to disperse the "Constitutionalists" at the ceremony by the military forces. "They were determined," writes Makrygiannes, "to destroy the Constitution. They make an Association at first, to assassinate at one time all the "Septemberists" all who did not shut up on their own . . ."[16] The Prime Minister's plans were never carried out for they were discovered by Makrygiannes and his friends, but this one particular case of Kolettist tactics exemplified how his government operated while in power.

Kolettes would not have been able to emerge as the dynamic dictator that he was in a country whose monarch was known for his absolutist tendencies even after he accepted the constitution unless he had the solid support of the Crown. In a letter to Metternich, Otho expressed his greatest satisfaction with his prime minister and his achievements.

My present Government for the happiness of Greece has faced fortunately all the storms, which threaten it. I say for the happiness of Greece, for I doubt seriously whether another Government would be in position to insure tranquility in the country. I have also reason to be pleased from the devotion of Kolettes to me.[17]

Royal support for the administration of Kolettes secured an unchallenged government in power whose major task was to stay in power. The major opponent of the "French" party was the Mavrokordatos faction which was weakening considerably under the increasing power of the existing administration. Elections were conducted in an openly illegal manner by the use of force exercised by the government in power on the voters in order to secure the re-election of the party member.[18] The result of course was the lifetime Prime Ministership of John Kolettes and the dominance of the "French" party in politics for the decade of the forties.

Such was the nature of the Kolettes administration; brutal, corrupt, dictatorial, all elements which contributed to the degradation of the young Greek nation in need of economic growth and development. If the word "favlokratia" (government by villains) is applicable to any Greek administration in the nineteenth century, it is certainly a fair label for that of Kolettes. His government set out to achieve the following goals: (1) The restoration of prestige to the Crown, (2) the permanent establishment of his Prime Ministership, and (3) the expansion of the country's boundaries. The first two goals were accomplished; as a result the work of the Constitutional revolution was wasted as Greece once again after the Kolettes administration became in practice an absolute monarchy.

B. *The Expansionist Foreign Policy of Kolettes and the Mousouros Incident*

Kolettes' foreign policy has been described by historians by the terms *Megali Idea* (Great Idea). This concept owes its origin to prerevolutionary thought and dreams of those Greeks who believed that one day they would free themselves from the Ottoman Empire and restore in its place the immortal Byzantine Empire. This was a dream which kept the Greek spirit alive amidst a Muslim conqueror. For many Greeks including Kolettes this dream was taken very seriously. In 1844 the "Prime Minister of the 6th of August" conceptualized the *Megali Idea* in the following manner:

> Greece, by her geographical location is the center of Europe; with the East on her right and the West on her left she was destined through her downfall to enlighten the East. Our forefathers executed this task, the second is assigned to us. In the spirit of our oath and

this great idea we saw always the delegates of the nation assembling to decide not for the fate of Greece but for the entire Greek race. A nation which through its own downfall enlightened so many other nations, is reborn today, not divided into many small states, but consolidated, with one government and one religion . . . . What do all the Orthodox Christian peoples in Europe, the East, and elsewhere do? All wait to hear whether we still possess the Greek Idea.[19]

In opposition and as a practical alternative to the foreign policy of irredentism of Kolettes and the Crown the "English" party with Mavrokordato offered a policy of internal development and economic growth.

Mavrokordatos was a liberal whose main concern was the economic strengthening of the weak young nation. He believed that the Greek government should not be looking to free the remaining Greek occupied territories of Thessaly, Epirus, Macedonia, Thrace, and Crete but rather it should concentrate on developing internally its economic sector. Once the country was strong enough internally it could take up the challenge of the Ottoman Empire in order to regain its desired territories. Kolettes on the other hand was convinced "that the first and major goal of the young country should be boundary expansion and that the work of internal revival was unattainable with the poor means of the free fragment of Greek land. He felt that the creation of the Kingdom was a condition of truce, not peace, and this truce should be broken as soon as possible."[20] Even though, as Tatsios remarks, "the solution to the nation's internal and external problems were identified with two antithetical political groups, ..."[21] namely that of Kolettes and that of Mavrokordatos, it was clear to most people in the government and to those comprising an educated public opinion that a policy of internal development was more urgent than a policy of irredentism which antagonized not only the Sublime Porte but the Great Powers' Near Eastern policy as well.[22]

The only opposition to the *Megali Idea* foreign policy came from the "Russian" and "English" parties. In a series of articles published in the *Aion*, the "Russian" organ, (on the 10th, 13th and 17th September 1847) the *Megali Idea* was bitterly attacked as a treacherous policy dangerous to the interests of Greece.[23] The Western Powers, namely France and Great Britain, also criticized the expansionist policy of Kolettes. The French foreign minister of Louis-Philippe, Francois Guizot, a long time friend of Kolettes,[24] and his most faithful European political supporter, opposed the personal policy of expansion entertained by Kolettes.

The Near Eastern policy of Guizot during the Kolettes administration was parallel to that of England, namely, the integrity of the Ottoman Empire and maintenance of the status quo in the Balkans.[25] In a letter to Kolettes before the new minister took office, Guizot made it clear that France supported the integrity of the Ottoman Empire. .

> You are much preoccupied with the future of the Greek race, but don't be deceived; this will not come tomorrow. It is very far. Be certain as to this. Europe, and when I say Europe I mean the good as well as the bad European policy, our friends as well as our enemies, Europe does not want the near falling of the Ottoman state. . . . Europe had made a firm decision and Greece will not blackmail the hands of Europe. . . direct your attention to the domestic affairs of Greece, in order to restate her simply as a country governable domestically.[26]

Kolettes, who had found it convenient to lie about his beliefs and convictions concerning the constitution and the idea of justice for all, also found it convenient to lie to a European statesman about the foreign policy which he had designed to carry out. He wrote to Guizot that the present administration in Athens had no intentions or plans to antagonize the Ottoman Empire even though he was firmly convinced of the injustice of a "little Greece" carved out by the will of the Great Powers.

> This is my belief; but never was it meant that this destiny should be fulfilled by an invasion in the Ottoman state of by a forced conversion (propaganda). I am therefore a devotee of the status quo. This is why from the beginning of my entrance into the government I seriously struggled to curb the forceful excitement of the small prudent and small provident of the Parliamentarians who push the government on a dangerous and anti-rational road. The measures which I have taken have pleasant results; the frontier relations between the Greeks and the Ottoman authorities are perfectly friendly; and thy give cause for mutual help to each other. I declare my respectable friend that for as long as I am Prime Minister Turkey will have nothing to fear for my part. Every unfriendly movement against the neighboring frontiers I regard least political and very dangerous.[27]

These promises made to Guizot were never kept nor were they meant seriously. Kolettes knew what the policy of Europe in the Near East was but he had to choose between following the wishes of Europe or following his own policy and become popular with the King as well as with the majority of the people. By raising the flag of the *Megali Idea* the "Prime Minister of 6 August" appealed to the nationalist sentiments of the masses who were eager to see all Greeks in the Ottoman provinces join the mother country. On the one hand the Prime Minister was promising to Europe to support the status quo in the Near East and on the other he was promising the people of Greece expansion of territories. This contradictory policy of Kolettes had as its purpose the popularity of his own government both with Europe and with the Greek people.

Some of his astute contemporaries, however, who were involved in political life could see this contradition in the government's policy and criticized it as a deceptive policy. "But because the disappointment against the authorities," wrote Dragoumes, "inflamed openly by foreigners, was general, the government was fearful of the springing up of general disturbances, the *Megali Idea* was forwarded, electrifying the people distracting and altering their attention from the domestic to the foreign grandeur of the country."[28] In this passage Dragoumes explains that the Prime Minister used the *Megali Idea* policy to distract the people's attention from the domestic to the foreign problems giving them hope of national expansion. It cannot be maintained, however, that the Kolettes administration went no further than verbal promises about national expansion. One of the practical steps that the government which believed in the *Megali Idea* adopted was the support of brigandage. Throughout Greece as well as in the Greek-Turkish borders the "warparty" of Kolettes (as it was labeled since they supported war), allowed brigandage to continue to grow and actually supported it. The Prime Minister viewed the brigandage chiefs as valuable warriors who would be used in an event of a Greek-Turkish war.[29] "Always the domestic questions were small and secondary," writes Kyriakides, "commerce and industry never occupied his thoughts and his conceptions; about transportation, about road planning he never thought, because he conceives one and only road to plan, that toward Thessalonika, and toward Constantinople; about Brigandage he is never concerned, because the brigands are his future soldiers. . . ."[30] The Ottoman Empire as well as Great Britain[31] criticized the government in Athens for its support of Brigandage.[32] In the House of Lords, Lord Beaumont crticized the domestic as well as the foreign policy of Greek aggression against Turkey.

> Not only had Athens become the scene of the deepest and strangest intrigues . . . but even beyond the internal affairs of Greece, beyond the frontiers, had that country already shown a total disrespect, not only for treaties, but for the common law of nations—for the common practice of international friendship; and set a defiance at the common laws of humanity, by establishing on the frontiers of Turkey an absolute system of Brigandage.[33]

The *Megali Idea* propagated through the government newspapers caused Chekib Effendi, the Turkish minister for foreign affairs, to complain to the ambassadors of the three Protecting Powers on 17 March 1845. Chekib Effendi accused the Greek Government of exciting revolutionary activities in Thessaly and Epirus, Turkish provinces, populated mostly by Greeks. He warned that if support to revolutionary intrigues continued in these provinces the Sublime Porte would resort to strong measures of repression.[34] Under the pressure of the Turkish Government as well as of the Great Powers Kolettes was forced to adopt measures less hostile to the neighboring nation.

The most faithful supporter of the Sublime Porte at this time was the British foreign secretary, Lord Palmerston, who reacted with extreme anger toward the government of Athens when informed of Greek anti-Turkish schemes. Influenced by reports from the Constantinople embassy as well as the Legation at Athens, the British Foreign Secretary accused Kolettes of encouraging disorder and granting amnesty to bands of brigands.[35]

The government in Athens hoped to counter the British antagonism to Greece by using France, the supporter of the *Moschomanga*, as its protector. Kolettes was convinced that he needed to counterbalance the power of Lord Palmerston, who opposed the Greek administration in power, with that of French Foreign Minister, Guizot, and the French Legation in Athens who supported the administration.[36] Since France had stood solidly behind Kolettes ever since he took power, the Greek Prime Minister believed that his patron nation would once again come to his rescue.

The situation was not as simple, however, as Kolettes viewed it at the time. Guizot had an obligation to support the pro-French government in Athens but he was also committed to support Mustafa Reshid Pasha, the progressive Turkish statesman who had served as ambassador to Paris after he was dismissed as Foreign Minister in 1841[37] and was as much pro-French as Kolettes.[38] If Guizot would have decided to support the Kolettes administration his country would have risked losing both Great Britain and the Ottoman Empire as important allies. So it was impossible for the French foreign minister to sacrifice the interests of his country by opposing Palmerston and the Ottoman Empire in order to satisfy the expansionist dreams of a petty Greek politician. As the observations made in the House of Lords in 1845 by Lord Beaumont indicate, the Near Eastern interests of both Western Protecting Powers were identical and not conflicting as Kolettes and many other Greeks believed.

> The interests of the two countries were essentially the same in both quarters—their object was, and ought to be identical. England and France alike were deeply interested in preserving the independence, integrity and due influence of the Ottoman Empire, who was and could be the only safe keeper of the Dardanelles; for should the key of that gate be wrenched from her, and the opening and shuting of the Dardanelles and Bosphorus be at the discretion of the Northern Power, the trade and possessions of England and France in the Mediterranean be at the mercy of Russia.[39]

Since England and France shared common interests in the Mediterranean against Russia it would have been logical for Kolettes to appeal to the Tsar for help but since the revolution of 1843 Russia had taken a back seat in the affairs of Greece. First, the napists were not in control of the government, and second, Russia disapproved of the constitutional change which had taken place in Greece.[40] Furthermore, the Tsar had "made it clear" to the British government in the summer of 1844, "that he would oppose control of Constantinople and the Straits by any one of the Great Powers (including Russia) or by an enlarged and strengthened Greece."[41] Considering that none of the Powers were ready to support expansion of Greece at the cost of upsetting the status quo in the Near East, it would be realistic for Kolettes to abandon his immediate plans of *Megali Idea*. No force, however, was large enough to control the germ of expansionism in the Prime Minister's mind so he continued searching for an opportunity to strike at Turkey. Such an opportunity presented itself during the crisis of the Mousouros incident.

The Mousouros Incident

Greek-Turkish relations continued to deteriorate even after the warnings of the British government to Greece and the complaints of the Sublime Porte to the Great Powers. In 1847 the "Mousouros Incident" was responsible for the total break in diplomatic relations between the government of Athens and the Ottoman state. This affair, which was to have far greater consequences than any one in the Kolettes ministry could foresee, began in January 1847 when Tsames Karatasos, asked for a Turkish visa to visit Constantinople. The Turkish embassy denied Karatasos the granting of a visa because he was involved in insurrectionary schemes against the Porte.[42] When the secretary of the Turkish embassy, Komenou Bey, told Karatasos that he could not renew his passport without the proper authorization from the Turkish government,[43] the latter replied that such a rejection was insult to the king of Greece,[44] and proceeded to report the incident to the Prime Minister. Kolettes seized upon this incident and chose to blow it out of proportion in order to create friction with the Sublime Porte.[45] The reasons that the Greek Prime Minister acted in such a manner was first because he needed public support and second because he desired to open hostilities in the Near East for the purpose of gaining the adjacent Turkish provinces of Thessaly and Epirus. As Professor Karolides explains:

That Kolettes through these and other aggravating internal and foreign diversions, precisely in order to rid himself from these diversions inventing a great and more serious foreign matter, he asked to provoke a rupture in the Ottoman state, in order to domestically direct the attention of the Greek people to the Megali Idea while externally to provoke a clash and a Greek-Turkish war, extending it very likely to an Anglo-French and possibly converting it into a general European , so that in the general confusion of everything he would rise as a great political man, a great Greek patriot.[46]

The king was informed of the affairs involving Karatasos and the Turkish embassy at a palace dance which Mousouros, the Turkish charge d'affairs in Athens, attended.[47] Otho approached the Turkish representative and angerly said, "J'esperais, que le roi de la Grece meritait, plus de respect que vous n'avez pas montre monsieur," and he returned his back on Mousouros. When Mousouros related the incident to Edmund Lyons, the British minister at Athens, the latter advised the Turkish minister to leave the Palace with his entire personnel.[48]

Two days later, (15 January) after further instructions from Lyons, Mousouros blamed the king's attitude towards him on Kolettes.[49] The Turkish government[50] and all the representatives of the Powers—except for the French—in Constantinople sympathized with the Turkish minister in Athens. When Kolettes refused to personally go to the Turkish embassy and apologize on behalf of his government's conduct, as Aali, the Turkish Foreign Minister had demanded, diplomatic relations between Greece and Turkey broke off and were not to resume for an entire year. There was a long correspondence between Otho and the Sultan during 1847 which was a rather fruitless attempt to restore relations between the two countries since the Great Powers behind the scenes exercised a great influence in the major foreign policy decisions made by either Greece or Turkey. The incident therefore remained unresolved and the two were only to resume diplomatic relations after the death of Kolettes, the man responsible for the entire affair.

C. Anglo-French Rivalry in Greece

Anglo-French rivalry in Greece existed before the pro-French government of Kolettes as a result of conflicting interests and power politics among the Great Powers.[51] When Mavrokordatos resigned and Kolettes became prime minister in 1844, however, the antagonism between France and England over political influence in Greece was greatly accentuated. Kolettes made no particular efforts to hide his antipathy for Great Britain and, especially, for Edmund Lyons. Both Lyons and Palmerston, who supported Mavrokordatos' policy of internal reform and development, despised Kolettes' policy of irredentism. Palmerston described Kolettes in a letter to Lord Normanby as follows:

> I have no doubt that Coletti would, as Wallenstein says, prefer France to the gallows, but I do not see why he should be reduced to that alternative. To be sure, St. Aulaire said to me the other day that Coletti was a necessary minister, for that he is the chief and leader of all the robbers and scamps of Greece, . . . Otho loves him as a second self, because he is as despotic as Otho himself; and as long as a majority can be had for Coletti in the chambers, by corruption and intimidation, by the personal influence of the king and by money from France, Coletti will remain minister.[52]

Guizot, however, felt that Kolettes was a good Prime Minister for Greece and supported him against the British government's attacks.[53] During his administration Kolettes made numerous attempts to have Lyons replaced as minister to Athens. In August 1845 Kolettes persuaded the king to use his influence in removing Lyons from Athens. When Otho was informed that the Queen of England would visit Germany accompanied by Aberdeen he wrote to his father:

> ...quite pleased I was informed that the Queen of England will travel to Germany....I hope therefore, that you will have no difficulty in meeting her...then perhaps the Queen since she has a will power of her own may be won over by your politeness dear Father, and that she will believe in your guarantee of my friendly feelings toward England and realize the necessity of recalling Lyons without jeopardizing his career. One can't ignore the danger of Lyon's violent prejudices, and no order even from his government, would prevent him from intriguing in secret. You most probably know yourself that recently, when he was talking to your minister, he said that if Greece was not able to pay its foreign debts, then it was apparent that the country was too small for a monarchy.[54]

The conflict between the *Moschomanga* and the "English" parties did not have an effect on the Anglo-French rivalry or the Kolettes-Lyons power struggle but its influence extended to the people of Greece who fell victims to power politics. As Aspreas explains:

> As the parties evolved, Greeks fought against Greeks, but the flags under which they were fighting were not Greek. Piscatory was no longer behind Kolettes and Lyons behind Mavrokordatos. The representatives of the two rival Great Powers had openly come to the arena. They were the opposing party leaders under whose inspiration the Greeks fought, wearing out their strength, paralyzing the country and giving a pitiful view of political ideology.[55]

Piscatory, who was devoted to Guizot, and Lyons "who had begun his diplomatic career as a protege of Palmerston," were not on speaking terms and were constantly attacking each other in the Greek press.[56]

The continuing support of Guizot to the Greek government[57] forced Aberdeen to order Lyons to break off all relations with Piscatory.[58] The ascendancy of the "French" party in Greece not only presented a political threat to the British interests in the Near East but an economic threat as well. One of the instructions by the British government to Edmund

Lyons was to promote British economic interests in Greece.[59] As Thouvenel wrote to Desages:

> England has interests in Greece. The neighboring Ionian Islands, the between Syra and Patra's commerce, the London based colony of Chios' merchants, the totally profitable grain transport executed under the Greek flag, finally the commerce of imports, all these elements give England a material place in Greece.[60]

In 1854 the total imports of Greece amounted to 22.3 million drachmas and total exports to 11 million. Corinthian raisin (which British merchants exploited) amounted to 3.5 million. The major importing ports were Syros and Patras, and the following countries contributed the majority of imports to Greece: Great Britain amounted to 7.3 million, Turkey 4.3 million, Austria 4 million and France and Russia 2 million.[61]

One of the ways by which England exerted its influence and protected its interests in the Near East was by making continuous demands on the Greek government to pay the interest on the guaranteed loan of 1832.[62] When Kolettes became prime minister he inherited an empty treasury and a payment of 6.3 million drachmas due to the Protecting Powers. Considering that there was a budget deficit every year but one, 1836, since 1832 interest payments were repeatedly postponed. In 1845 the Prime Minister tried again to postpone payments due to the Powers, and Lord Aberdeen as well as Cochrane[63] criticized Greece in Parliament for not making its payments. Lord Aberdeen stated that:

> We have also guaranteed the payment of the interest of a loan contracted by the Greek State, which we have been called upon to discharge ourselves for the last two or three years. This, therefore, gives us undoubtedly a right to interfere so far in the internal affairs of this State as to see that we should be released from these obligations as rapidly as possible. And the Greek Government would do well to recollect that, by the provisions of the Treaty, we are enabled to enter into possession of such of the revenues of Greece as we think proper for the repayment of the debt so contracted.[64]

The concern of the British government over the payment on the loan kept increasing as did their dissatisfaction with the pro-French Kolettes administration. The British wanted the Greek Prime Minister and his government to know just how disappointed the Aberdeen government was with the state of affairs in Greece so Lyons was instructed to send a letter from the Earl of Aberdeen informing the Greek government of its negligent financial practices. The British Foreign Secretary stated that Greece had violated the terms of the Treaty of May 7th 1832 by not making complete efforts to discharge its financial obligations to the three Protecting Powers. Aberdeen further noted that Great Britain was determined to insist on administrative reform and a reduction in the armed forces of Greece.

> The expenses of the war department continue to absorb one-third of the revenues of the state. Brigandage has increased. The tranquility of the conterminous Turkish provinces has been repeatedly troubled by acts of rapine; and the Ottoman territory has been repeatedly violated by armed Greek bands. Out of respect for the independence of Greece, Great Britain is unwilling to interfere in her internal affairs. But it is manifest that if Greece desires to be exempt from external control, she must place herself in a position to discharge her own financial obligations without having recourse to the aid of the guaranteeing Powers.[65]

Interest payment on the loan was the strongest, although not always the most effective means used by the Peel administration, by Palmerston and by the Earl of Clarendon to pressure Greece to yield to British demands. The British Parliament and certain historians favorable to Palmerston and Great Britain maintained that the concern of the Foreign Office was with the growth and development of the Greek nation and that Great Britain stood for constitutionalism against the absolutism of the Bavarian monarchy in Greece and the corrupt and dictatorial Kolettes administration.[66] Nothing could be further from the truth. As Palmerston's letter to Prince Albert will reveal below, the concern of the British government was not the internal development of Greece and her general economic and social progress, but rather the dominant influence exercised by the French in that country which diminished British influence in the Near East.

Palmerston made it clear to Prince Albert that his nation had nothing against the people of Greece but only against Kolettes. He hinted that Trikoupis, the pro-English politician, was far more capable of governing Greece in a constitutional manner, and that the royal support of Kolettes was resented by the Foreign Office. Most strongly the British Foreign Secretary objected to the French influence in the Kolettes administration.

> In the foreign relations of the country Mr. Koletti seems to have had three leading objects in view, aggression towards Turkey, subserviency of Mr. Koletti toward France, and insult towards England. The subserviency of Mr. Koletti toward France is too notorious, too evident, and has been too publicly boasted of by the French Government to be now denied.[67]

Throughout the month of April 1847 Lyons kept asking for the 700,000 drachmas which the English government paid to the Greek nation for the guaranteed loan.

In Parliament the heat was building against Greece which could not make the payments to the Protecting Powers.[68] At the same time domestic political opposition to the Kolettes administration was building as a result of the Prime Minister's mishandling of the Mousouros incident. In panic, Kolettes consulted with Otho and then dismissed Parliament—the *Boule*—and called for elections.[69] The elections which took place were conducted in the same corrupt and unconstitutional manner which suited Kolettes' purposes. The leaders of the "Russian" and "English" parties decided to form a coalition in order to be able to stop the present administration from getting reelected. Their plan, however, failed as the government was too well prepared and determined to meet the oppostion. Makrygiannes described the misfortunes of the elections and how Kolettes was able to retain power as follows:

> Grivas went to Bonitsa and raised the flag. They (the partisans of Kolettes) attacked him, not even having fired at them, and dumped him in the sea. He would have been lost if the English had not saved him. Mamoures took 35,000 drachmas from Metaxas and Mavrokordatos, which they had collected to help the movement; he cheated them and turned on the side of the government . . . Kolettes began his elections. Everywhere in the nation there were murders and disappearances of residents. Kolettes won all of the electorates out of one hundred.[70]

This process was called "elections" in mid-nineteenth century Greece. A young nation in need of honest progressive political leaders was subjected to rule by villains.

The loss of the "English" party created bitter reaction in England against the existing government. Lord Palmerston openly accused Kolettes in the House of Lords for his Francophilism.

I cannot understand the great value placed by France in maintaining in Greece a ministry which is regarded representative of French interests. If the French Government believes that it is the advantage of France and the French nation to regard this as its triumph, that the Prime Minister of Greece is their chief. . . .I cannot say anything more . . .no one in England wants to think of bothering the French dominated events.[71]

The Anglo-French rivalry was not destined to last in Greece, for Kolettes, leader of the "French" party, died on 1 September 1847. The Revolution of 1848 which brought an end to the government of Louis Philippe also brought an end to the dominating French influence of Greek politics. Even though the struggle for power never stopped, the tensions between France and England tended to ease as they both realized that the foreign policy of the *Megali Idea* was in conflict with their policy of the Ottoman Empire's integrity. The other factor which eased the tensions between French and English policy in Greece was that Otho was not really favorable to either France or England and tended to be drawn towards Russia after 1850.

During the three years of his dictatorial rule Kolettes was successful in accomplishing in the domestic sphere: (1) the alienation of the "Russian" and "English" parties, (2) the violation if not total rejection of the Constitution, and (3) the establishment of the Prime Minister-King dictatorship. In the external sphere, (1) the antagonism of England against Greece, and (2) the support of brigandage against the Ottoman State, and as a result the antagonism of Turkey against Greece. This is the Kolettes' legacy. The tragedy of it was that its influence extended beyond the decade of the 40's to the war period of the 50's. The king would follow Kolettes' foreign and domestic policies to plunge Greece into a senseless conflict involving Turkey and the Western Powers.

CHAPTER TWO

ANGLO-GREEK HOSTILITIES AND THE RISE OF RUSSOPHILISM IN GREECE

A. Foreign Policy and Anglo-Greek Hostilities 1847-1850

The period from the death of Kolettes to the Anglo-French occupation of 1854 in Greece was characterized domestically by monarchical tyranny, and in the field of foreign affairs by expansionist schemes directed against the Ottoman Empire. Kolettes reinstated the king's prestige in 1844 after it was downgraded and limited by the Constitutional revolution. When Kolettes was out of the political scene the Greek monarchy was determined to absorb all the powers of the government into its own hands.

The only two powerful leaders, Metaxas and Mavrokordatos, who were likely candidates to replace Kolettes, would not be acceptable to the pro-French Parliament (*Boule*) and much less to the Crown which both politicians had fought against. From 1847 to 1853, therefore, absolute monarchy was reinstated in practice though not in theory in the background of viod in political leadership. The governments which were in power during these seven years were known as "court governments" or "court ministries," since the prime ministers were puppets of the king.[1]

During the period of the "court ministries" the constitutional rights of the citizens were abused by the king and his court whose ultimate goal was the full reinstatement of absolutist powers to the Crown. The Kolettes administration had already set the stage for a political system which would give all the governmental powers to the king and create a monarchical dictatorship behind the disguise of puppet ministers.

The first "court ministry" was headed by an illiterate man, Kitsos Tsavellas, who served as Minister of the Army in the administration of Kolettes.[2] Kitsos Tsavellas was the grandson the infamous Lambros Tsavellas, a hero in the War of Independence. He was not a politcally minded man but his devotion to the Crown made him the best candidate for the position of Prime Minister. The primary concern of the Tsavellas government was the suppression of legitimate political opposition to the government which had begun while Kolettes was in power,[3] as well as revolutionary activities throughout Greece which presented a serious threat to the Crown. In the summer of 1847, there was a wave of opposition to the government of Kolettes. Under the leadership of Makrygiannes and other prominent military figures a coalition of peasants, military officers and politicians of the opposition was formed and called for the restoration of the constitutional principles in government. Otho and his court managed to silence Makrygiannes and his followers by armed force but the wave of revolution which swept Europe in 1848 had too great of an effect on Greece even for Otho to control.[4]

As long as the tide of unrest remained free from implicating the Protecting Powers, the Tsavellas government could control it. There were two incidents, however, of major importance which implicated Great Britain in the revolutionary activities of 1847-1848. The first incident involved Theodore Grivas, inspector in the army during the Kolettes government, and Nicholas Kriezotes, Province Inspector in Euboia. Both men were supporters of Kolettes up to the April 1847 elections when the "Prime Minister of the 6th of August" dismissed the Parliament. At that time Grivas and Kriezotes decided to fight against the dictatorship of Kolettes even though the latter had promised both of them seats in the senate. Kolettes sent an armed force against Grivas and his rebels but with the help of the British, Grivas escaped to Prevesa where he received assistance and cooperation from the British Consulate and ultimately resorted in the Turkish province of Janina.[5]

The second incident involved Merendites, a Captain in the army during the Kolettes administration. Merendites was dismissed from the army by the Tsavellas government for suspicion of being in the opposition. This tragic occurence in the captain's life prompted him to resort to brigandage. He robbed the Patros Branch of the National Bank of Greece of 25,000 drachmas, the Customs House of 32,000 and he took 92,000 from the Public Fund. He then sought refuge in the Austrian embassy but was not accepted so he went to the British who were eager to give help to anyone in the opposition.[6]

In both instances, one with Grivas and the other with Merendites, the Greek government found itself in another confrontation with the British authorities. When Greek officials became aware that the British took part in aiding rebels such as Grivas and brigands such as Merendites they became infuriated. Glarakes, the Greek Foreign Minister, complained to

Lyons about the role of the British authorities in Greek internal affairs and Lyons reported the incident to Palmerston. The British statesman who had little to be sympathetic about with the government in Athens wrote a very aggressive and degrading letter against the Greek authorities which he sent to Lyons. He maintained that:

> Mr. Glarakes will do well to abstain in the future from unfounded accusations against her Majesty's government and her personnel . . . and if this government showed the slightest sympathy towards him (General Grivas) it did this only because he has been a victim of tyranny, oppressing and agitating the Greek people all over, where the activity of this system is now felt: a system provoking natural consequences and evident revolt.[7]

This letter came as a shock to everyone and, especially, the king, who ordered the Foreign Ministry to respond to Lord Palmerston in a "very declaratory manner."[8] The irony of this entire affair was that Great Britain the defender of liberty and constitutional principles, the only one of the Great Powers really to speak out against brigandage in Greece, turned to aid rebels and brigands, which proves that all the talk of Palmerston and the debates in the House of Commons and House of Lords against brigandage was just talk and nothing more.[9] When it came to making a choice between the pragmatic interests of their nation and ideology the British put aside their ideological jargon.

As Anglo-Greek relations continued to deteriorate the Greek government was half-heartedly trying to restore relations with the Sublime Porte. The Musouros incident, which occurred during the administration of Kolettes, was unresolved when Tsavellas took power. A solution to this incident was imminent not only because it represented a possible threat to Greek economic, that is to say, commercial interests which were threatened by such a break of relations between the two countries, but also because the Great Powers sympathized with the Turkish position on this matter. On October 4, the Greek Foreign Minister sent a memorandum to the five Great Powers—Britain, France, Russia, Austria and Prussia—stating the Greek government's concessions to the Sublime Porte's demands and the latter's unwillingness to accept these.[10] In response to this memorandum the Sublime Porte charged that Greek brigands were organizing to invade Turkish territories. The Turks maintained that the Greek position was irreconcilable and should therefore be regarded as hostile by the Great Powers.

Otho realized that unless a friendly power intervened in support of Greece the Turkish demands would have to be met and this would mean diplomatic defeat for the Greek Court and humiliation for the Crown. The Greek Court decided, therefore, to appeal to Tsar Nicholas, who Otho felt, would be more sympathetic to Greece than to the Ottoman Empire. The Tsar answered Otho on 18 October 1847 not at all to the satisfaction of the Greek monarch. ". . . it always seemed essential to me that Greece, in the delicate position which she is should observe wherever possible, mostly a policy of abstention from displeasing the Porte and England. It was the only way not to fall into extreme tensions which was produced successively in the relations with these two Powers and Greece."[11] The Tsar went on to blame the Kolettes administration for the existing tensions between Greece and the Porte and England, and did not commit himself to helping Greece resolve her existing problems with Turkey.[12] It should have occurred to Otho that Russia would not side with Greece for a minor incident and jeopardize her friendly relations with England.[13]

In the face of political opposition and social unrest domestically, and diplomatic opposition from practically all of the Great Powers the Greek government gave in to the demands of the Sublime Porte. Glarakes wrote a letter expressing the apologies to his government to Aali; on 25 January Mousouros returned to his post and diplomatic relations between Greece and the Sublime Porte resumed.[14] This incident marked the end of Greek-Turkish hostilities which were not to reoccur in the Turkish provinces until 1853.[15]

The revolution of 1848 in Europe had a decisive influence in Greece. Throughout the country there were sporadic revolts expressing the peoples' dissatisfaction with the monarchy, the continuing foreign intervention in Greek internal affairs, the poor economy, and the corruption at all levels of government.[16] Under the pressure of revolutionary activity, the Tsavellas government fell in March and was replaced by the Koundouriotes administration.[17] Before Koundouriotes was chosen to head the ministry by the king, Lyons used his offices to pressure Otho to form a pro-British government.[18] Otho would not give in to British pressure even though he knew that he no longer had the support of the French government[19] and that the Russian Court continued to maintain a policy of abstention from Greek internal affairs.

The principal preoccupation of the Koundouriotes ministry in the domestic field was to silence the political opposition and put an end to the sporadic revolts. In the field of foreign relations, the settlement of the disputed Greek-Turkish frontier[20] and the establishment of friendly relations with the Powers, took precedence. Domestically, therefore, the same problems which faced Kolettes and Tsavellas also threatened the ministry of Koundouriotes. In the area of foreign affairs also the problems were the existing tensions between Greece and the Ottoman Empire and the Great Powers—particularly Great Britain.

It was to be expected that any government which could not be influenced by the British would make Lyons and Palmerston adopt a hostile policy towards Greece. In a dispatch to Palmerston on 29 March 1848 Lyons expressed his disappointment with the king's influence in government. He charged that the current administration in collaboration with the Crown was responsible for abusing the constitution and robbing the people of their rights. If there were any ministers in power who wished to alter the course of things for the better, they were prevented from acting out their wishes by a *Boule* which was at the disposal of the king and the *camerilla* which actually governed the nation. Further the British minister wrote,

> I am informed that the ministers are determined to resign in case the king would continue to reject the measures which they would like to employ and it is regarded possible that the king will make certain concessions because the news from Paris, Vienna and Munich have created here great disturbance.[21]

Lyons was eager to keep his position in Athens as he had engaged in a personal war with the "French"party. Even though he had at one point told Piscatory, "there is only one good policy—for France and England to act together," he never acted on this principle himself, and as Seton-Watson maintained, he "treated the Greeks as inferior mortals."[22]

In 1848, however, Lyons had more than just personal feelings against the "French" party to complain about to the Foreign Office. The European revolutions of 1848 intensified the existing political opposition to the Greek government during the early months of that year. The British charge d'affaires at Athens, fearful of further French dominance of Greek domestic politics, welcomed revolutionary activity in Greece[23] which might weaken the government to the point where the king would have to dismiss the Koundouriotes ministry and look to the British for support.

Lyons was not successful in persuading Otho to call for the formation of an "English" government so Stratford Canning[24] was sent to Athens in May of 1848 to achieve this task. Canning's mission proved unsuccessful[25] for the king was determined to keep members of the "English" party out of the government. Finally, after immense domestic and foreign pressure the *camerilla*[26] came to its senses and dismissed the unpopular Koundouriotes government; this time Otho was ready to give Mavrokordatos a chance to form a ministry. Before he was summoned, however, the king had an interview with him concerning his domestic and foreign policy. The first question put to Mavrokordatos was, "Which places can and must Greece take?"[27] The answer given was unsatisfactory to Otho. Mavrokordatos felt as he had in 1844 when he was prime minister that the internal development of Greece was a far more essential matter to deal with and deserved all the attention of the government, whereas the question of territorial expansion was an issue of the future. Otho's foreign policy was basically identical to that of Kolettes, namely, territorial expansion should be the primary issue of the government. A greater Greece, Otho felt, would mean prosperity for the nation: the domestic problems—economic and social—would be solved as the goal of territorial expansion was realized. This basic disagreement on domestic and foreign policy between the two resulted in the rejection of Mavrokordatos as a likely candidate for prime minister.

Once again Lyons asked that Mavrokordatos be summoned to form a government but the king went along with the wishes of Thouvenel and in October 1848 appointed Admiral K. Kanares.[28] The French influence in Greece and the refusal of the king to accept Mavrokordatos or Trikoupis in the government made Palmerston so furious that he declared that he would never approve a government in Greece unless its leader was from the "English" party.[29]

Greek-British relations continued to deteriorate even further as a series of incidents occurred in the next five years which contributed to the existing friction of relations between the two countries.[30] The first incident involved the British claim to the two islands Elaphonese and Sapientza, at the southern tip of Peloponnese.[31] The importance of these islands was commercial—they were used as loading bases—but to the Greek nationalists the sentiamental value was far greater than the commercial.

There were three more demands made by Palmerston's government all which were intentionally used to exert pressure on the *camerilla* so that Otho would welcome British influence in Greek internal and foreign affairs. The first of these three demands was indemnity for piracy by Greeks of six Ionian ships in September 1847. In this affair Greece was blamed for the acts of priacy committed by Greek citizens. The government of Greece declared that it could not be held responsible for all wrongdoings of its citizenry.[32] Secondly, the British demanded indemnity for damages commited against Dom Pacifico, a Portugese Jew who was a citizen of England residing in Athens.[33] The damage to Pacifico's property was claimed at 886,736 drachmas, an unrealistically high figure considering the value of the money at the time.[34] The British embassy would under normal circumstances turn this matter over to the Greek authorities to handle. They chose, however, to make an incident out of it blowing it out of proportion and interpreting the abuse of the property of a British subject, Dom Pacifico as an act of hostility by the Greek government against the British government. When the claim of Pacifico was handed over to the Greek authorities by the British officials, naturally the reaction of the Greeks was the same as it had been in the case of the pirates who plundered the six Ionian ships, namely, that they could not pay for damages committed by irresponsible individuals and that the matter should be taken to the Greek Court to be settled.[35]

Finally, there was a claim of the Scottish historian George Finlay to be settled.[36] In 1842 Finlay wrote to the Earl of Aberdeen complaining that part of his property had been incorporated into the Royal Garden and he was not indemnified for this property by the Greek government.[37] Aberdeen instructed Lyons to proceed to represent the claim of Finlay but the matter was not resolved and in 1846 Lyons began to pressure Kolettes for indemnification of Finlay's property.[38] The Greek government felt that the 45,000 drachmas which Finlay demanded for his property was enormous and it refused to meet these demands.[39]

All of the incidents mentioned above started before September 1847 but they were all compiled by Palmerston to form a series of charges against Greece at the end of 1849. The main reason for this as explained by a prominent Greek historian was British fear that Otho might provoke anti-Turkish activities in the provinces adjacent to Greece.

Besides the grave political anomalies of Europe the relations between Russia and Turkey were seriously irritated as a result of Walachia and Moldavia Principalities which were occupied by a large number of Russian soldiers and fears existed concerning an explosion of war between the two powers. Knowing Otho's intentions and fearing the Greek call for disturbances in Turkey, regarded opportune the situation in order to attack Greece during the occasion when the complication of the Powers did nto allow them to distract themselves with Greek affairs.[40]

The British government received intelligence reports to the effect that in case of a Russo-Turkish war Greece would side with Russia.[41] The Near Eastern crisis of the fall of 1849 was the primary reason for the severe demands of Palmerston on the government of Otho, but the desire to teach Greece a lesson in discipline and British dominance in the European community was another reason for what was to follow. At the end of 1849 the threat of a Russian attack on Turkey was no longer in existence as the British ambassador in Russia reassured Palmerston. "I think we may reasonably expect that at all events during the reign of the emperor Nicholas no attempt will be made by Russia to subvert the Ottoman Empire."[42] In spite of this reassurance of Russia's peaceful intentions towards Turkey, Palmerston sent the following dispatch to the Admiralty.

> I have to signify to your Lordships the Queen's commands that Sir William Parker should be instructed to return to Athens or Salamis on his way back from the eastern end of the Mediterranean, and that he should, on arriving on the coast of Greece, place himself in communication with Mr. Wyse, Her Majesty's Minister at Athens, who has been instructed to require a final settlement of certain claims which have been long pending the Greek government. . . . Sir William Parker should support Mr. Wyse in his demands for an immediate adjustment thereof.[43]

On January 3, 1850 the British Fleet of Admiral Parker set anchor at Piraeus. The admiral did exactly as he was instructed by Palmerston; he went to the British embassy in Athens and together with Wyse they visited the Greek Foreign Minister. They gave an ultimatum of twenty-four hours for their demands to be met otherwise they would be forced to execute the orders received from their government.[44] When the Greek

Foreign Minister told Wyse that the presence of the other two representatives of the Protecting Powers was required in order for the Greek government to come to a final decision, the British minister simply granted another twenty-four hour ultimatum.[45] The Greek government did not meet the ultimatum so Admiral Parker's fleet proceeded to blockade the port of Piraeus and to place under arrest all Greek vessels. Londos, the Greek foreign minister, immediately informed Thouvenel, the French minister at Athens and Persiany, the representative of Russia in Greece.

> Thouvenel wrote, without delay, to Wyse:—According to Article IV of the Treaty of 7 May 1832, Greece is an independent monarchy under the guarantee of the three Powers. The interdiction which made her dispose freely of her war-vessels must be considered as a first blow to her independence. Without doubt independence equals responsibility and the British government has the right to pursue the recovery of her grievances. But the question does not present itself only in these simple terms. For the Greek government demands an arbitration which conforms with the terms and the spirit of the article aforementioned.[46]

Persiany also sent a note of complaint to the British embassy at Athens and both ministers—of France and Russia—urged Wyse that Londos' suggestion to settle the Greek-British dispute in the presence of all three representatives of the Protecting Powers be accepted.[47]

Europe was shocked at Palmerston's actions. The Tsar wrote a letter to Otho expressing his dissatisfaction with British policy towards Greece. He stated that he was very displeased with the actions of the British government in Greece and he had made his formal protest to the Foreign Office. Nicholas advised the king of Greece not to yield to the British demands for to do so would mean yielding his legitimate claim which belonged to every independent sovereign. "It only remains to heal the country's wounds and also to make good the losses which recent events have caused to the commerce of Greece and Your Majesty can count upon my willingness to lighten, for some period of time the pecuniary burden which your finances have to bear."[48] The press in Greece as well as in Europe criticized the actions of Lord Palmerston as severe and hostile towards a friendly small nation.[49] Popular poetry was written and recited by A. Soutso against the British imperialists while praises were heard of Russia who was assuming the role of the supporter of Greece.[50] The public mind turned to Russian favoritism and away from the Western

Powers who seemed always to interfere in the internal affairs of Greece for their own interests. The layman as well as the politically minded Greeks could see that the national interest of Russia as well as of Greece was the disintegration of the Ottoman Empire. The Western Powers had a policy of supporting the integrity of the Ottoman state. Their policy, therefore, ran counter to Greek national interests. Furthermore, the Russians viewed the blockade of Piraeus as an indirect British display of power to Russia. As Professor Karolides explains:

> Russia regarded the Parker events in Greece as a continuation of the British fleet's display of Hellespont, and somehow as reprisal to the failure thereof the intended British activities; she took from the beginning of the crisis a hostile position at British action.[51]

On February 7, Nesselrode announced that his government was displeased with the hostile activities of the British fleet in Greece. The Count criticized Great Britain for reassuring the Russian government of the harmonious Anglo-Greek relations just before Admiral Parker's fleet entered the Port of Pireaus. He also denounced the secrecy of British operations in Greece and its insistence on leaving France and Russia, the other two Protecting Powers in ignorance of British intentions. He ended his remarks about British involvement in Greece with a strong warning against the illegal blockade of Admiral Parker:

> The Imperial Government, commands her ambassador to direct towards the British Government serious remarks, asking her very seriously to quickly put an end to matters in Greece, which are neither necessary and by no means justifiable. The prompt acceptance of this measure would indicate to the Imperial Government in what manner Great Britain wishes to regulate the rest of her relations with the Imperial Government.[52]

This announcement of the Russian government motivated France to act in the same respect and denounce Palmerstonian diplomacy in Greece just as harshly as had Russia, out of fear that French influence in Greece might be in danger of being overshadowed by that of Russia. Wisely, the Russian government allowed France to take the upperhand in the matter since French opposition to English policy in the Near East could only mean the weakening of the Anglo-French alliance which resulted from the Near Eastern crisis of October 1849.[53]

On February 7 Drouyn de Lhuys sent a dispatch to Palmerston expressing his government's disapproval of the hostile actions taken by Britain against Greece without previous consultation with the French government.[54] Palmerston's answer to Drouyn de Lhuys was very friendly and it revealed his fear that France was drawn away from the recent Anglo-French alliance, siding on the issue of the Piraeus blockade with Russia. He agreed that a French negotiator should be appointed to mediate between Britain and France.

> In order to leave the freest scope to the action of the French negotiator, Her Majesty's Minister at Athens shall be instructed not to mix himself up with the negotiation of the French Agent, except in so far as he may be requested by the Agent to do so.[55]

Palmerston's kindness to the French in the Greek crisis was due not only to the diplomatic reality of a possible Franco-Russian alliance but also to the internal pressure against his mishandling of the British grievances in Greece. The British Minister for Foreign Affairs was attacked by the press, from both Houses and from the Queen for jeopardizing the role of Great Britain by mindless actions and by what seemed to many a personal foreign policy. In the House of Lords, Lord Stanley not only criticized the "ill-advised expedition to the Dardenelles," but he felt that "we had proceeded to acts of injustice and violence against a friendly foreign Power, or rather, a weak friendly foreign State, the very weakness of which state should have been the strongest inducement upon our part to exercise that greatest forbearance, whose peculiar position rendered any misunderstanding with regard to the affairs of Greece a matter of more importance of the state itself."[56] Palmerston's secrecy regarding his proceedings in the Near East and the official communication between the Powers and England was also criticized by Lord Stanley as well as by the House of Commons.[57]

By the middle of February, the blockade in Greece had become a major international matter which was to do the greatest damage to the career of Lord Palmerston. "This Greek question," wrote Charles Greville, "is the worst scrape into which Palmerston had ever got himself and his colleagues. The disgust at it here is universal with those who think at all about foreign matters; it is past all doubt that it has produced the strongest feelings of indignation against this country all over Europe, and the ministers themselves are conscious what a disgraceful figure they cut, and are ashamed of it."[58]

It was agreed by England, Russia and Bavaria that France should send a negotiator to Athens in hope of a settlement. Baron Gros was chosen to mediate on behalf of Greece and arrived in Athens on 6 March. He began negotiations but found progress impossible due to British determination to collect full indemnities and to concede nothing.[59] Drouyn de Lhuys in London also tried to negotiate a settlement for the Anglo-Greek dispute but with no results. In early May, the Greek government in Athens informed the French government that Lord Palmerston used the demands for indemnity payments to the British subjects in an extortionist manner to humiliate and ridicule the Greek government. This gave cause to the government of Prince Louis Napoleon to recall its ambassador from London and cause a near Anglo-French diplomatic rupture.[60] Palmerston believed that the recalling of Drouyn de Lhuys was carried out by the French government as a display to the public in France of Louis Napoleon's strong abilities and determined leadership in challenging English policy.[61] The House of Lords, however, had a different interpretation on the matter. Apparently it was announced that Drouyn de Lhuys left London of his own free will when he was actually recalled by his government. Upon the news of the truth concerning the recalling of the French minister Palmerston was blamed for keeping secret the facts from both Houses and he was once again criticized for jeopardizing the position of England in the European community. Lord Brougham stated:

> It turns out that the French government, in the exercise of its undoubted discretion, has deemed it to be its duty to take a step which has not been taken since the year 1803 . . . . The complaint of the French government is, that London is made to focus of all intrigues against its existence—that it is source from which all communications are made to the "Parti Rouge"—so called because it takes the colour of Blood as its appropriate ensign. Yes the "Parti Rouge" takes its orders from the Caussidieres and the other era-pulous leaders and miscreants who now infest this country after they had been forced to desist from infesting France.[62]

The French government, which felt that Great Britain was exceeding its power in Greek affairs as granted in the Treaty of 1832, was really concerned with its own power which was threatened by the presence of the British fleet, but out of a Franco-British diplomatic quarrel Greece benefited, if not in anything more than the removal of the blockade. On July 6th the negotiating parties reached a settlement in Athens and the nightmare which had brought instability to Franco-British raltions and deplorable conditions to Greece was over.[63]

The blockade of Piraeus cost Greece more than the 180,068 drachmas indemnity damages. The Greek commerce suffered greatly and as a result the already weak economy of Greece was seriously damaged. It would be no exaggeration to maintain that by far the most damage was inflicted in the minds of the Greek people.[64] England, one of the nations which once fought for the independence of Greece and signed the treaty which made that country legitimately recognized in the European community, came to a point of doing her great damage.

The only one in Greece who really benefited politically from the blockade was the king. He was viewed as the defender of the national rights of the people against the interventions of foreign powers.[65] Of the three parties, the "French," the "English" and the "Russian," the last benefited the most from the crisis. France was viewed with suspicion by many Greeks for her role in Greece seemed to be purely selfish, namely, the curbing of British influence in the country,[66] whereas Russia was regarded as the only true defender of Greek interests.[67] As far as relations with England were concerned, Greece got off to a friendly start after the settlement of the British grievances but it was not very long before another issue, that of brigandage, was to create friction in Anglo-Greek relations. After Trikoupis was sent to London as the representative of the Kriezes government, Palmerston wrote the following letter to Delygiannes, the Greek Foreign Minister:

> I have the honor to assure Your Excellency that Mr. Trikoupes has been received and treated with all the consideration and regards due to a representative of a sovereign with which the Queen desires sincerely to maintain relations of the most friendly character. I avail myself to this occasion to offer to Your Excellency the assurance of the distingushed consideration with which I have the honor to be.[68]

This letter was written in December 1850. Nine months later the Foreign Office invited the Powers to use their influence in Athens to pressure the Greek government to put an end to brigandage.[69] Even though brigandage was at a considerably low level, only to reach its peak in 1854, there was a good deal of concern in London with regard to the potential threat of brigandage to the Ottoman Empire.

At the same time that the issue of brigandage was brought up there was another crisis developing which was to drive Greece even further away from both England and France and bring it closer to Russia.

B. Russophilism 1850-1853

The Synodal Tomos

After the British blockade the attention of the Greek public was shifted to ecclesiastical matters. The Greek church had been declared independent and autonomous in 1833 and had remained so until 1850.[70] As a result of this the Patriarch of Constantinople broke off all relations with the Church. By 1850, however, it was becoming apparent to most Greeks that the Patriarchate desired to reestablish relations with Athens and the reason behind this factor was primarily political. Tsar Nicholas was opposed to an autonomous Greek Orthodox Church in 1832, and he resented the fact that a Roman Catholic king would assume the role of the ceremonial head of an autonomous Orthodox Church.[71] After the Anglo-Greek hostilities of 1850, the Tsar urged the Synod and the Patriarch in Constantinople to "soften their position toward Greece in its moment of crisis."[72]

The change of attitude toward Otho and the Greek government was due, therefore, to the Tsar's interest in penetrating the higher clergy in Greece and in capitalizing on the recent anti-British movement in the country.[73] Although the Tsar maintained a cool attitude toward the king and the Greek government from 1833 to 1850 the "Russian" party was won over by Kolettes and his anti-Turkish foreign policy.[74]

By 1850 a great number of people in Greece desired to see an end to the existing schism of the Greek Orthodox Church and the Patriarchate. The king of Greece also desired the same thing but for political and not religious reasons. Otho hoped that a resolution to the Church controversy would bring him into closer cooperation with the Tsar whose support he needed.[75] Missael Apostolides was sent to the Patriarch Anthimos IV delivering a message written by the Holy Synod of the Church of Greece with the desired goal that the Patriarchate would recognize the Church of Greece.[76] Anthimos IV rejected the message but the Russian minister to the Porte, Titov, who participated in the discussions concerning the subject of recognition of the Greek Church, supported it.[77] The Holy Synod met again and decided to ask recognition from the Patriarch once more, only this time they would present an official letter of support to the Synod by Otho. The Patriarch accepted the second request and the king of Greece as well as the "Russian" party achieved a great political victory. Nicholas was also quite satisfied with the realliance of the Greek Orthodox Church and the Patriarchate. He wrote the following letter to Otho as soon as he was informed of the recognition of the Church by Anthimos IV:

> Sir my Brother, it is with real satisfaction that I received from the hands of Archimandite Missael the letter of Your Majesty by which it announces to me the canonical recognition of the Church of the Greek Kingdom and from this Synod by the Patriarchical Ecumenical Throne of Constantinople. It delights me, just as Your Majesty, this event, that it responds so well to the desires of the people and fulfills one of their spiritual needs, the most legitimate so far as it restores the unity and the evangelical brotherly relations between her (Greek) Church and the other venerable chairs of Orthodox Churches of the East and of Russia. It was most particularly pleasant to learn that my instructions to my minister at Constantinople have contributed to this happy result, to which the solicitude of Your Majesty wisely prepared the way.[78]

Not everyone, however, was as happy as Nicholas, Otho and the "Russian" party about the results of the Synodal Tomos. Many progressively minded individuals in Greece opposed the late recognition of the Patriarchate of the Greek Orthodox Church and believed that it was an insult to the Greek nation that the Patriarchate had acted as though no independent Greece existed between the period of 1833 to 1850.[79] The British government was also displeased with the actions of the Synodal Tomos. The British Minister, Wyse, at Athens was stunned about the reestablishment of relations between the Greek Church and the Patriarchate. He interpreted the recognition of the autocephalous Church as a means which Russia used in order to exert her influence in the affairs of Greece. The French Minister, Sabatier, reacted in the same manner as Wyse.

> It is certain today that M. Titov was the grand agitator of this affair at Constantinople and that Russian influence has dictated the Patriarchical Bull. M. Deliany was fooled or seduced but Otho, however, fully accepted the results of the Tomos and as a result the Church of Greece received the recognition it sought from the Patriarch and the the Greek government received the moral support of the Tsar.[80]

The alliance of the Greek Church with the Patriarchate marked the beginning of friendly Greek-Russian relations and the end of French support to Greece. The solidarity of the Anglo-French alliance in October 1849 which was shaken by the British blockade in Greece was restored when Greece chose to side with Russia against the Western Powers. This alliance was only to become stronger in the following years when the Holy places controversy broke out.

The Role of Greece in the Holy Places Question

At the same time that the Greek Church was requesting recognition from Constantinople, developments leading to one of the major crisis in the Nineteenth Century were taking place in the Middle East. The affair known as the "Holy Places Question" began in the middle of 1850 when Louis Napoleon decided to demand from the Ottoman Porte Catholic dominion in the Holy Places.[81] The Sublime Porte decided, for purely political and not religious reasons,[82] to grant the wishes of the Emperor risking a possible Russo-Turkish conflict. The Religious policy of Turkey towards the various millets, or religious groupings in the Empire, was very lenient as all regions were treated with equal respect.[83] Traditionally, the Orthodox who were the majority in the Empire dominated the Holy Places as a privileged religious group. So when the Latins requested what seemed to the Sultan's government religious rights in the Holy Places their wish was granted for it was in accordance with the law. "By a note February 9, 1852, it (the Sublime Porte) directed that the keys of the north and south gates of the great church at Bethlehem and of the grotto of the Holy Manger 'must be given' to the Latins, 'as of old' and they were allowed to erect a silver star adorned with the French arms in the shrine of the nativity."[84] The French had not counted on direct Russian interference in the Holy Places Question:[85] they thought instead that since this was a matter of religion it would be handled by the Patriarchate in Constantinople which represented the Orthodox millet.[86] Napoleon III used a religious matter for diplomatic reasons, namely, to harm "Russia and the Holy Alliance, surely normal activity for a Bonaparte ruler."[87] Due to the religious controversy over the Holy Places, Franco-Russian relations deteriorated considerably to the point that neither side was total satisfied with the Turkish settlement of the affair.[88]

During this crisis the Greeks and the "Orthodox" party, composed of radical pro-Russian elements, sided with Russia against the Roman

Catholic French. Russophilism was constantly increasing in Greece and the spirit of revolt and war against the Turks was once again haunting the country. A rising in Montenegro which began as an internal strife contributed to the existing anti-Turkish atmosphere in Greece. Prince Danilo, the ruler (*vladika*) of Montenegro, attempted, after he succeeded his uncle Peter II in 1851, to make Montenegro more independent from the central control of the Ottomans.[89] A minor incident between Montenegrins and Turkish authorities was turned into a major Ottoman invasion at the request of Omer Pasha, a military leader who become governor of Bosnia Hercegovina and Montenegro in 1850.

The revolutionary activity in Montenegro, whose cause was supported by Austria, and the events of the Holy Places set the atmosphere for revolution in Greece. Forth-Rouen, the French charge d'affaires in Athens wrote to Paris that the conflict in the Holy Places had brought the "Russian" party in Greece real strength. He noted further that the flag of religion which had often been used in Greece, was brought out again. "Religion is in danger and its children are called once more to run to its defence. . . . Religion is in Greece a powerful element of intrigue, and in representing Catholicism as invading, as menacing Orthodoxy. . . one is sure to move the spirits profoundly."[90] France and England became increasingly worried when Otho appointed Stavro Vlahos, a prominent member of the "Russian" party, Minister of Worship. Wyse and Forth-Rouen were concerned with the Russophilism of the king as well as of the public. The "Orthodox" party which was totally devoted to Russia was becoming more powerful by 1850 and its activities were widely publicized. The Papoulakos movement[91] became an instrument of the "Orthodox" party openly to express its hostilities against the Catholics, the Liberals—"French" and "English" parties—as well as the Catholic King.

The representatives of France and England, in Athens, mostly blamed the king for the Russian extremism among the public. They felt that Otho was reflecting Tsarist policy against the interests of the Western Powers in the Near East. Upon the appointment of Vlachos, Wyse commented that the man whom Otho chose to be his Minister of Worship, "is little qualified by his want of religious moderation for the onerous duties of an office become lately of peculiar responsibility."[92] Neither the British nor the French would reaize that Otho was not acting as an agent of the Russians against the Near Eastern interests of the Western

Powers but that he was acting in accordance with the *Megali Idea* policy which he hoped would bring him personal glory.

C. The Menshikov Mission and Greek Reaction

On January 14, 1853 Nesselrode worte to Brunnow:

> To the indignation of the whole Greek population following the Greek rite, the key of the Church of Bethlehem has been made over to the Latins, so as publicly to demonstrate their religious supremacy in the East. The mischief is done, and there is no longer any question of preventing it. It is now necessary to remedy it.

Nesselrode added:

> The (Russian) emperor is very irritated with the Sultan and thinks it necessary to intimidate him to avoid being obliged later to come seriously and actually to war, which according to him must at all costs be avoided, whether in the East or West.[93]

The measure taken by the Tsar to put an end to the Holy Places controversy was to send Prince Sergeevich Aleksandr Menshikov, head of the Naval Ministry, to Constantinople with a set of Russian demands to present to the Ottoman government. The Menshikov mission was doomed to failure for its purpose as revealed in the Russian demands was one which invited hostilities by the Great Powers and the Sultan's government.[94]

As was anticipated by Nesselrode the negotiations of Prince Menshikov and the Turkish authorities were a failure when it was apparent that the Sublime Porte refused to comply with a number of the Tsar's requests and especially the request "for a note from the Sultan to the Tsar, pronouncing his intentions with reference to Greek Christians and guaranteeing Russian rights in Turkey."[95] The government and most Greeks anxiously awaited developments of a Russo-Turkish conflict. They would then be able to strike at the Turks in the provinces of Thessaly, Epirus and Macedonia in order to free all Greeks from the Ottoman yoke and also expand the national boundaries of Greece. Then the unexpected occurred. Prince Menshikov's aide-de-camp, Admiral Kornilov arrived in Athens on 15 March 1853 on the war steamer, "Bessarabia." The visit, the Russians explained publicly, was due to the Admiral's archeological and historical interests. For the Western Powers, the Greek government and the people of Greece, the Kornilov visit was somehow politically connected to the Menshikov mission. On 17 March, the day the Russian war vessel departed from Athens to Constantinople the British Minister at Athens wrote to the Earl of Clarendon about the Kornilov visist to Athens expressing his dissatisfaction and suspicions about it.[96] Forth-Rouen was even more apprehensive about the unexpected visit of Kornilov to Greece. He expressed his fear that a visit such as the one the Admiral made would have grave consequences in the public mind especially when Russo-Turkish negotiation settlements were prepared for the rights of Christian subjects in the Ottoman Empire.[97]

Five days after the "Bessarabia" had left the port of Pireaus, Wyse had met with the Turkish charge d'affaire, Nechid Bey, in Athens to discuss the Kornilov visit. Wyse wrote to Clarendon that:

Nechid Bey said that whatever might be given to the contrary he was convinced that the visit was political. He brought dispatches for Mr. Persiany with whom he was in continual communication and had on the day of his arrival a private audience with the king for two hours. The "Bessarabia" war steamer which brought him here, left Constantinople after midnight, and her departure and destination were kept so secret, that it was not known that she had gone till the next day, and then it was believed for exercise to the sea of Marmora. It is also to be added that the Admiral returned to Constantinople in utmost speed, though Prince Menshikov it is understood remains there for some months. Mr. Persiany denied all this; he stated to me the other day that the Admiral came for personal objects only, *that he had no private interview with the king*, and that he leaves Prince Menshikov and the mission for Russia immediately on his return to Constantinople.[98]

If the French and British representatives were suspecting the Russian government's intentions concerning Greece they had every right to do so since events made the Russian position a suspicious one. Contrary to the suspicions of Forth-Rouen and Wyse, however, the Russians had no intention of arousing excitment against Turkey in Greece since the Tsar was determined to avoid war[99] and as long as Prince Menshikov was in Constantinople there was a chance of a peaceful settlement. "Persiany," writes Dr. Donta, "tried to convince the Greek government to prevent the press from presenting to the people a misleading picture of Russia pressing for war against Turkey."[100] The Menshikov mission, however, was interpreted in Greece by the people as well as by the authorities as an indication of increased Russian power in Constantinople.

The king and the Greek government thought that the Tsar's plans did not include a Russo-Turkish war nor did they include the reestablishment of a Byzantine Empire with Otho as the emperor.[101] Even though Paicos, the Greek foreign minister, tried to reassure the representatives of France and England that no hostilities would be undertaken against the Turks, and even though Forth-Rouen strongly urged the Greek government to suppress the anti-Turkish and pro-Russian propaganda in the press,[102] the public mind was prepared by the "Russian" party propaganda and by the nationalist press, which continuously exalted the *Megali Idea*, for a Greek-Turkish conflict. In a dispatch on the state of the public mind in Greece, Wyse reported the following:

> "Religion" and "race" the two great objects from principle and passion, of Greek devotion, are used as watchwords to stimulate the popular enthusiasm. Heterias never extinguished are again rising. Their organization has been long familiar to every Greek and it requires not time nor discipline but opportunity to bring them into action.[103]

Wyse went on to report that the only ones in Greece who were against Russia and did not support a policy of irredentism and Greek-Turkish conflicts were the professional and commercial classes, but that the king and the "Russian" party were in favor of territorial expansion.[104] The commercial class[105] was against Russia and a policy of expansion for the simple reason that a war against Turkey on the side of Russia would be inviting another blockade as in 1850, if not an actual war by the Western Powers against Greece. Such a conflict would have a disastrous outcome for the commercial class which did a great deal of business with the West. The idea of a Greek-Turkish war appealed to the masses, however, who were constantly under the propaganda machine of the Greek religion and press. These people knew nothing of power politics and were not, as Wyse and Forth-Rouen presented them, more inclined to favor Russia than the Western Powers for any other reason than perhaps the common religion and common enemy—Turkey. As one prominent historian of Greek diplomatic history explains:

> The unofficial Greece, however, in the exhortation of Russian extremists, had as its only purpose the dynamic realization of the *Megali Idea*, because as it proclaimed, the existing suffocating restricted boundaries did not permit Greece to evolve into a contemporary and organized state.[106]

CHAPTER THREE

GREEK-TURKISH HOSTILITIES IN 1853 AND
ANGLO-FRENCH REACTION

A. Causes of the 1854 Greek-Turkish Conflict and Anglo-French Reaction to Greek Foreign Policy

The Turkish provinces of Thessaly and Epirus were predominately populated by Greeks at the outbreak of the Crimean War. According to one French official[1] in 1850 the population of Thessaly ranged from 350,000 to 400,000 inhabitants. From the total population only 70,000 were Turks. In Epirus the population was approximately 450,000 with two-thirds Christian and one-third Moslem.[2]

In a part of the world where religion and common heritage were regarded as the binding forces of all Greeks it was only natural that after the War of Independence nationalist uprisings would take place in a effort to "liberate" all Greeks from Turkish domination. The geographical position of Thessaly and Epirus as well as Macedonia facilitated the attempt of the Greek nationalists to revolt against the Turks in 1854. These provinces which were predominately populated by Christians and were adjacent to Greece were subject to constant raids from brigands ever since the War of Independence.

The brigandage acts carried out by Greeks on Greek soil as well as on Turkish—Thessaly and Epirus—were not entirely acts of looting but were primarily intended to stimulate insurrection in the Turkish provinces. Such acts led to the break of relations between Greece and Turkey and eventually into a war in 1854. There is a complexity of reasons as to how and why brigands were turned into professional revolutionaries and brigandage became a means of expressing the nationalist commitments of the Greek people. Although many brigand chiefs who took part in the rising of Epirus, Thessaly and Chalcidice in 1854 were determined nationalists who needed no external agitation to drive them to fight the Turks, many were recruited by the Greek government either directly or indirectly, and still others joined the brigand bands after they came under the enormous propaganda of the "Russian" party and the Greek Court.[3]

A recent study of the insurrection of 1854 in Thessaly entitled *The Insurrection of 1854 and the Thessaly Undertaking*[4] presents the events which led to the war of 1854 as purely acts of liberation on behalf of the Greek people who sought to free themselves and their brothers who were living in the Ottoman provinces. As it will become apparent towards the end of this chapter there is a certain amount of truth to this thesis, but to go as far as equating the revolution of 1854 with the War of Independence as not only Professor Koutroumbas has done but other Greek historians as well, is misleading if not biased. The reality of the Greek-Turkish conflict and the events which led to it are too complex to be dismissed as another war of independence.

The Montenegro rising, the Holy Places controversy, the Menshikov mission, and the Kornilov visit to Athens were all elements which contributed to an already critical situation between the Turks and Greeks. Naturally, tensions ran just as high on the Turkish side as they did on the Greek. The Porte feared that serious trouble on the Greek-Turkish frontiers would be stirred up by the Greek brigands. On March 2, 1853, Metaxas, Greek minister to Constantinople and a member of the "Russian" party, informed Paicos that Rifaat Pasha, the new Turkish foreign minister, informed him that the Ottoman government threatened to take possession of two villages on the Greek-Turkish frontier which were legally occupied by the Greeks.[5] The Turkish foreign minister claimed in a dispatch to the Greek government that the villages[6] legally belonged to the Ottoman Empire. Furthermore, the Porte claimed the villages under its authority because of the universal brigandage which threatened the peace of the Ottoman Empire. Rifaat further asserted that the Porte had no desire to go through another struggle with revolutionaries as it had recently in Montenegro.[7]

The Turkish occupation of villages, which the Greeks claimed legally belonged to them, triggered a number of incidents which intensified hostile feelings between the Greeks and the Turks. The Greek government, which really sought an opportunity for confrontation with the Porte made no effort to compromise, that is to say, to take measures to repress brigandage on the frontiers in order to relieve tensions and reassure the Turkish authorities of their peaceful intentions. Instead Paicos wrote the following letter to Metaxas challenging the latest Turkish acts in the Provinces:

> The Ottoman Porte has forgotten it seems, that the separate Ottoman State's boundaries in Greece stretched under the terms of the three Great Powers under whose guarantee Greece remains, and therefore the present question cannot be solved by taking the law into one's own hand arbitrarily but the consent of the three Guarantors is required.[8]

Paicos proceeded to inform the Greek people of the presence of Turkish troops on the frontiers which intended to take over the Greek villages. By thus provoking the anti-Turkish sentiments of the public, Paicos and the Greek government hoped to gain public support in order to justify sending troops to the Epirus-Thessaly frontiers to counter the action of the Sublime Porte. Nothing could be more dangerous and explosive than the presence of both Greek and Turkish troops on the frontier, for immediately the Greeks in Thessaly and Epirus thought that the time for a showdown had finnaly arrived and they were preparing for war.[9]

Neshid Bey, the Ottoman charge d'affaires at Athens complained to both representatives of the two Western Powers about the action taken by the Greek government on the Greek-Turkish frontier. On March 23 he informed Wyse that Greek emissaries in Albania and neighboring provinces had been active. He further complained that the Greek emissaries had brigands who were on the frontier and in the provinces of Epirus, Albania and Thessaly were connected with the parties in Greece and acted under the watchful eye of Greek authorities. Neshid Bey also complained about the brigands in Asia Minor and the islands and especially Crete. All these events were taking place under the eyes of Greek authorities who allowed them to continue.[10]

Wyse informed Clarendon, the British foreign secretary, that Neshid Bey related these complaints of his government to Paicos but,

> Mr. Paicos in answer to these remonstrances had promised nothing: nor did he (Nehid Bey) expect from what he had already seen anything really effective from the Greek government. At the same time he was convinced that if his representations continued to be disregarded, this indifference sooner or later would infallibly lead to open dissensions and disturbances in the Turkish villages and to consequences he need not say, the most disastrous.[11]

Forth-Rouen also reported to Paris that even though Paicos reassured him that the mission of Scarlato Soutzo and his troops to the frontier was to put an end to brigandage, the Greek troops were there for security reasons only. Forth-Rouen explained to Drouyn de Lhuys, that in spite of these reassurances the presence of Greek troops gathered on the frontier could only have negative consequences and leave an impression of tensions among the Greeks of the provinces.[12]

The Greek government was well aware of British, French and Russian policy in the Near East and especially Greece. All three Powers maintained that Greece should not be enlarged at the cost of Turkish territory. Greece had experienced devastating consequences as a result of her long antagonism with Great Britain during the Kolettes ministry and later during the "Court governments" with the Pacifico and Finlay claims. After the Holy Places question her good relations with France deteriorated as both the court and the people sided with Russia. At the opening of the Menshikov negotiations the Greek government was composed primarily of Russophiles and royalists,[13] an indication that the king was blind to Near Eastern policy of the Western Powers.

Otho and his Russophile ministers chose to disregard all realities of international politics and pursued a risky policy of antagonizing the Porte. In the first week of April, reports showed that regular and irregular troops numbering one thousand two hundred were sent from Athens to the frontier near Lamia by orders of the government. This action was taken on behalf of Greek authorities without informing the representatives of France and England and Neshid Bey. This arbitrary action greatly alarmed both Wyse and Forth-Rouen who immediately requested a conference with Paicos and demanded an explanation of the Greek government's hostile moves towards the Ottoman Empire. Paicos explained that the reason the troops were sent to the frontier was because Rifaat Pasha had threatened forcibly to take the two villages which were rightfully inhabited by Greeks. Forth-Rouen and Wyse warned Paicos of the damaging consequences a Greek military occupation of the villages could have but Paicos reassured the two ministers stating that Greece would abstain from any military advances on the frontier.[14] Wyse in a private meeting with Forth-Rouen found that the French minister was as worried about the turn of events in Greece as he was. When the British minister visited Persiany to find out what his feelings about the late developments on the frontier were, he was surprised to hear that the Russian minister also was not informed about the Greek military operations. Persiany sympathized with his French and British colleagues and pledged his full support and cooperation to them in this crisis.[15]

The cooperation between the Protecting Power's representatives and Paicos reassurances to maintain peace on the frontiers left Wyse, Rouen and Persiany optimistic about the future conditions in Greece although they all expressed concern about the revolutionary and warlike state of mind of Greek public opinion. Reacting to the presence of the three Powers and fearing another blockade such as the one that had taken place in 1850, the Greek government temporarily retreated from any further agitation with the Turks. Public opinion, however, influenced by the propaganda of the press, and especially *Aion*, the organ of the "Russian" party, openly expressed its anti-Turkish and pro-Russian sentiments; it was ready for a conflict. An article, which appeared in *Aion* written as an address to the English state reveals the nature of propaganda to which the Greek public mind was exposed.

> We love Russia because she crushed the head of the Turk which you want to lift again and to last forever. The all powerful and magnificant eagle of the North, which possesses seven parts of Europe, who has advanced to the new frontiers, the Emperor Nicholas occupied Dacia and Moldavia in the end forcing the English to renounce their protection over the Ionians in favor of the future Hellenic Empire, which it will restore in opportune time Dacia and Moldavia.[16]

The Greek Court took no measures to curb propaganda in the press for it wished that the public be indoctrinated with ideas which conform to the *Megali Idea*. Demonstrations and protest gatherings directed against Turkey were allowed to continue in Athens, in spite of solemn promises made to Wyse and Forth-Rouen and to Turkey by Paicos that Greeks desired peace.[17] Not only were the anti-Turkish demonstrations and propaganda allowed to continue, but the Greek government encouraged and supported them.[18]

After the Sultan, Abdul-Mejid, had made up his mind not to give in any more to Russia's demands even if it meant going to war, the Ottoman Empire was determined to take strong measures to deal with Greece, Rifaat Pasha who replaced Fuad as foreign minister demanded from the embassy in Constantinople that the Greek troops on the frontier be removed, otherwise the Turkish government would resort to armed force.[19]

The last thing France and England wanted was another Greek-Turkish conflict over two insignificant villages, during the time when Russo-Turkish relations were becoming more strenous. Both Clarendon and Drouyn de Lhuys instructed their ministers in Constantinople to intervene between the Porte and Greece in order to settle the dispute diplomatically.[20]

The Greek troops by the middle of April numbered two thousand. A firm indication that Greece was no more looking for a peaceful settlement than was Turkey. Paicos insisted, however, that the troops were to suppress brigandage and not to begin a war.[21] When a conference took place in Constantinople between the Greek and Ottoman legations "the three Protecting Powers provided that the Greek govermment on its side would immediately withdraw the troops lately concentrated on the frontier and thus obviate the necessity on the part of the Sublime Porte of augmenting its force in the same direction."[22] In spite of the efforts of the three Powers (Turkey, France and England) to have the Greek troops removed from the frontier, the Greeks did not recall a single soldier back to Athens.[23] This indicated that the Greek government was not at all serious about maintainng peace with Turkey. In reality Greece was looking for an opportunity to start a war.

The break in diplomatic relations between Russia and Turkey on May 17th[24] and the four-hundredth anniversary of the Fall of Constantinople on May 29, 1853, helped to set the stage for great expectations by the Greek people and, especially, by King Otho.

> Now that the Russians had struck at the Turks, the long-awaited moment for increasing his dominions seemed at hand; greater men than Otho might be excused for yielding to this temptation. He would never remember that the guarantee of Greek independence by the Protecting Powers was, in a sense, a two edged weapon. These Powers, or at any rate England and France would be as anxious to protect the existing frontiers of Turkey as those of Greece.[25]

If the king was blinded by the expansionist ideas which he formulated largely under the influence of Kolettes, his ministers and many politicians who embraced the foreign policy of *Megali Idea* were deceived by looking back at the position of France and England during the War of Independence. Many Greeks felt that, in case of Russo-Turkish conflict,

Greece should strike in the Northern Provinces, and if the takeover of the Provinces was successful they argued, the Western Powers would not try to intervene. A similar situation had occurred during the War of Independence, with the only difference being that there was no Greek state to fight against Turkey, only Greeks. In 1853, however, if Greece would strike against Turkey this would mean official declaration of war of one country against another, which could very well mean that Turkey's allies would come to her aid in case of war. Many chose not to follow this course of reasoning and rely on history instead hoping that it would repeat itself in their favor. The realities of international politics, however, were quite different than the reality conceived by most officials in the Greek government.

The Western Powers had a much greater problem to solve in order to allow Greece to become an obstacle in their Near Eastern policy. On May 7 Wyse sent a formal letter to Paicos expressing "the regret of her Majesty's government that at a moment when it was so manifestly desirable to preserve the public tranquility, measures should have been adopted by the Greek government which could not fail to produce the greatest public excitement."[26] The efforts of the "Russian" party continued to press for open hostilities against Turkey. With the exception of the small professional class and the classes of merchants and businessmen, the majority of the country supported the "Russian" party and the king.[27] The actions, military or brigandage, taking place in the Provinces against the Turks were wholeheartedly supported by the masses in Greece. Towards the end of May a band of brigands from Lamia murdered the exdemarch (mayor) of Eubea and wounded several persons while the two thousand troops of the Greek government were stationed in the frontiers with their only purpose being to suppress brigandage, and maintain tranquility.

During the time that hostile actions were taking place on the Greek-Turkish frontiers and were allowed to continue under the watchful eye of the Greek local authorities, the government in Athens placed an order for twenty-five thousand to twenty-seven thousand rifles from France which were to be shipped without delay to the National Arsenals.[28] The French government obviously turned down the request but the fact that the Greeks ordered arms from the French with the covert intention of using them against the Turks shows their naivite about international politics. The irony of this entire affair is that Paicos continued to reassure

Wyse of the Greek peaceful intentions towards the Ottoman Empire[29] while the intelligence reports of the British Legation in Athens indicated that Greece was indeed preparing for war or an organized revolt in the provinces of Thessaly, Epirus and Chalidice.

The efforts of the Western Powers after the month of May to neutralize Greece in case of a possible open war between Russia and Turkey became more intense. On June 4th Wyse sent a dispatch to Paicos pointing out the determination of the Western Powers to maintain the integrity of the Ottoman Empire.

> I have the honor to inform you that I am instructed by the Earl of Clarendon to state to you that her Majesty's Government have had much reason to complain of the Greek Government for sending troops to the Frontier and keeping their intentions secret from the representatives of the three Powers at Athens; that at a moment, when it was important to allay invitation these troops were sent under circumstances calculated to increase and to turn to account the pressure of Prince Menshikoff and Constantinople and the unfounded rumors currently respecting the object of his mission; that in thus causing excitement, and creating false hopes, in the minds of the Greek people the Greek Government have displayed a want of judgement as well as knowledge of the policy of the Great Powers of Europe, who have never been more firmly determined than at the present time, to maintain the integrity and independence of the Turkish Empire.[30]

Even though this warning dispatch came as a shock to the Greek government and took by surprise both Persiany and Forth-Rouen, it cannot be argued that the British government had not warned Greece before about its hostilities towards Turkey and that Clarendon was not justified in taking such extreme measures to warn Greece about any anticipated plans for war against its neighbor.[31] The British suspicions about Greek anticipation of war were well founded. The British and Ottoman intelligence had discovered that, as early as June, Greeks from London, Vienna, Trieste collected funds in order to aid the Greek population in Turkey in case of war.[32]

France was as concerned about the developments on the frontiers as England. The Quai d'Orsay had been informed that the Orthodox, pro-Russian Greeks, identified with the Russian cause and that Greece would find herself in danger if she followed a policy which endangered the interests of the Western Powers in the Near East.[33]

At the same time troubles and incidents among the irregular troops stationed on the Greek-Turkish frontier and the residents began to annoy the Turkish authorities. Also the Greek press kept increasing its anti-Turkish propaganda and was not at all discouraged by the government's injunction to refrain from attacking a friendly neighboring nation. Finally, Nechet Bey complained about the developments in Greece which placed the Ottoman Empire in a defensive position and jeopardized the peaceful coexistence of the two nations. Paicos replied to the Turkish charge d'affaires that he would endeavor to maintain tranquility in the border provinces. He stated, however, that he could not regulate or suppress the press which was engaged in a press war with Turkey. "Permettez-moi, tout-fois de vous faire observer qu'il n'est pas à son pouvoir de corriger le languge de quelques journalistes, ni de régler les idees et les pensées de tout le monde."[34] He went on to charge that bands of brigands were supported by Turkish authorities and "were admitted to the public service" of the Ottoman Provinces.

The Paicos communique was obviously not intended to soften Neshid Bey but he was correct that there were brigands used by the Turks to run the provinces and, as the inter-Legation correspondence concerning the frontier indicates, Greek subjects under Ottoman rule in the provinces were harshly treated throughout 1853 (another reason why so many Greeks of the Provinces of Thessaly and Epirus joined the insurrection as will be shown in the following sections).[35] The maltreatment of Greeks by the Ottoman authorities was due partly to the rise of Russophilism in Greece and anti-Turkish propaganda, and partly to the recent developments on the frontiers which made the Turks very apprehensive as they very well knew that liberation of all of Greece—from Crete to the gates of Constantinople—was the goal which they had to confront.

The Greek government sought the opportunity to capitalize on the cruel treatment of Greek subjects in the provinces and on the use of brigandage by Turkey. On July 8, the Greek ministers in London, Paris, St. Petersburg and Munich expressed to the Protecting Powers and to the European community the Greek government's grievance against the irregular Albanian troops, and the government's desire to maintain Greek troops on the frontiers for the sake of keeping order in the troublesome areas.[36] All the Protecting Powers advised the government in Athens and ans the king to retain order and not to step out of line.[37] The plan to gain the sympathy of Europe—as during the War of Independence—did not work for it was obvious that Otho and his Court had more in mind than keeping peace in the provinces.[38] While the government in Athens promised Europe that her plan for the future only included peaceful coexistence with Turkey, there were undergoing secret preparations for war.[39] On September 19, Wyse wrote to Paicos that he had been instructed by the Earl of Clarendon to bring to the attention of the Greek government several incidents involving ammunition transport on Greek vessels. Gun powder was transported from Syra to the ports of Prevesa and Arta for use by the Greek brigands. The transportation of gun powder and other war supplies were carried out with a prior knowledge by the Greek authorities, Wyse charged and further:

> It has been stated to the Lord High Commissioner (of the Ionian Islands) that a large depot of powder and other military stores had been framed at Syra by persons in connection with the Greek Hetaerias,[40] and Signor Posali, a responsible merchant at Corfu, while he denies any connection with the present cargo admits that to his knowledge many similar consignments have been made from Syra to Prevesa and Arta during the last few weeks, the object of which can be easily understood.[41]

While preparing for war the Greeks searched desperately for allies who would support their expansionist policy. Obviously, England and France would never support Greece since its foreign policy stood in opposition to theirs. Russia would have no part in supporting Greece in extending its territory since Nicholas feared that the creation of a strong state in the south would mean limitation of his country's power in the Aegean Sea. Greece therefore appealed to Bavaria for help but the Bavarian Court would not support an expansionist policy since the Tsar had declared that he opposed Greek territorial expansion.[42] The situation for Greece and especially for Otho who was the most devoted supporter of the *Megali Idea* was critical. He had to make a difficult decision: either go to war with Turkey and thereby risk an Allied blockade of Greece, even an occupation, or to give up all immediate plans for expansion and wait for the propitious moment in the future.

B. Otho's Support for Greek-Turkish Hostilities

Historians of contemporary Greek history agree that Otho and the Greek Court were responsible for pressing a Greek-Turkish war and territorial expansion. Even though the king has been praised by some scholars for acting on behalf of the nation's interests,[43] most agree that the foreign policy executed by him during the Crimean War period was disastrous to the welfare of the nation. "Otho and Amalia," writes Philaretos, "nursed under Kolettes in the *Megali Idea*, were thirsty for greater ambitions in which they found consultation from the bitterness of their childlessness and weariness from the domestic convulsive wailing. Thus Otho became the leader of the war policy himself assuming the direction of every operation."[44] Another prominent Greek historian writes:

> The war-like psychology of the Greek people as we saw, was adopted by Otho and Amalia, not because they were patriots and wished to free Epirus and Thessaly, but so that they could strengthen their throne which was shaky. And they succeeded by pretending to be warlike. So for a period they succeeded to win the sympathies of the greater mass of the people.[45]

King Otho was confronted with a very peculiar situation in 1853. He remembered how he became popular with the masses in 1850 during the British blockade for not giving in to the demands of a Great Power. Now he had once more the opportunity to become popular by posing as a Greek nationalist and if everything went his way he would be popular aı d a king of a "Greater Greece." At the same time, however, he was confronted with serious warnings from the Western Powers against any undertakings in the Turkish provinces.

In June Otho wrote to his father that he had to postpone his trip to Germany due to the developments in the Near East. "The latest events," he wrote, "have irritated the Great Powers to the point that in order to calm them I have to remain here."[46] A month and a half later the situation in Greece was much more critical and the king expressed his thoughts about it as follows:

> Conditions here are stretched at the highest level, as a result of the Russo-Turkish dispute. I believe that the matter will result in war . . . And this because the fanaticism of the Turks has reached such a point that the Sultan is afraid of the question of retreat because of the possible disastrous consequences. I am trying to calm the minds of my faithful subjects . . . . But at the same time I am convinced that Divine Providence has decided the enlargement of Greece.[47]

The need to increase and secure his power became increasingly urgent for Otho.

In September 1853 the king called for elections because he feared the power of the opposition would diminish his popularity in the country.[48] Very few people participated in the elections and the general public apathy caused rumors that the king was preparing a *coup d' état* and ultimate suppression of the Constitution. The day before the elections Wyse sent the following report to the Foreign Office:

> It is unnecessary to point out the consequences if such (*coup d'état*) a movement is successful; suppression of all freedom of the press and of all publicity, personal liberty placed at the mercy of a party; of finances levied, and applied at their caprice and for their purposes;...the military occupation of the kingdom would be exclusively in the hands of the king.[49]

Wyse went on to urge to the Foreign Office that English policy and intentions in the Near East should be spelled out to the Government in Athens.

> Our best means of standing against Russia or other influences, is the just confidence we inspire that we shall always continue to in the cause of national liberty, good administration, public order, commerce and industry in a word Western civilization against Eastern barbarism. The least semblance even, of a departure from such a policy would be not only an infringement of our former engagements, but I am quite convinced a manifest sacrifice of our most solid and important interests here, and would *amount* to little less that a wholesale transfer of the sympathies of a large body of this people in our favour, to Russia or France on the other.[50]

Among other things, this dispatch of the British Minister reveals that although British Near Eastern policy paralleled French policy, British interests were naturally the primary objective of the Foreign Office. Besides the economic interests, which England had in Greece,[51] it was also essential to develop a machinery, through the "English" party of course, of political control. All the talk of "liberty," "justice" and "western civilization" was not to be taken seriously for the purpose of the Foreign Office was to secure and promote British interests and not to teach the world a lesson in liberalism. Greece was nothing more than a tool for England, at times a tool which was difficult to cntrol for other Powers had a share of it. The main obstacle to exert Brtish political control in Greece was the king. In 1853, however, the king was left with no one major power to support his policy so at his moment of weakness it would be easier for the British government to intervene in Greek affairs than in the past.

Otho, however, did not bend as easily as the Foreign Office would have liked. Clarendon warned him three times in 1853 of the English determination to uphold the Ottoman Empire's integrity[52] but the king who was the main architect and supporter of the aggressive acts taking place on the frontiers against the Turks,[53] chose to disregard them. In early October additional troops were being armeḍ to be sent to the frontier and once again Paicos did not inform Rouen, Wyse and Nechet Bey about this matter. When questioned by Nechét Bey as to when the new troops were to be sent to the frontier, Paicos replied that he did not know and that he had to ask the minister of war. Finally, when pressed for an explanation the Greek Minister of Foreign Affairs wrote to Wyse that, "as far as the marching of additional troops to the frontier from Nauplia is in question his colleague, the Minister of War, inform him that a single soldier has not quitted that fortress, a company only of artillery with four pieces of cannon left Athens within these last few days to replace another at Lamia."[54] The intelligence reports of Nachet Bey and the British Legation in Athens, however, indicated that "an *Hetaeria* is in full operation in Lamia and in communication, with sympathizers on both sides of the frontier, under the eyes of the Greek authorities and without any effectual means having been taken to their repression."[55] It was no secret to any one that ever since brigand chiefs were affiliated with the Court they were used as weapons to manipulate events in domestic and foreign affairs.[56] Wyse feared, as had Lyons before him and many British statemen before 1853, that brigandage in Greece was a threatening element to the stability and peace in the provinces for it was bands of brigands who were converted into revolutionaries and fought for an independence in 1821.[57] The king knew this just as well and this is the reason he liked to patronize chieftains. In November he addressed the following letter to his father:

A few days ago I said to an elderly Epiriot who gives great significances to a prophetic book, *The Good Angel*, that we in the

period of one year will be in Constantinople. If this book deter-
mines time or not I do not know. But it is known to me . . . that
a Bavarian is about to reign there.[58]

After the garrison from Nauplia moved to the frontier, Otho wrote to
his brother Maximilian that he "was convinced that providence had
decreed the expansion of Greece" and pointed the necessity for replacing the old weapons with new ones. Maximilian disapproved of Otho's
activities and intentions, and Otho appealed to him again, saying "that
it was the duty of all Christians in Europe to fight for their co-religionists
who were downtrodden by the Crescent."[59]

Otho was determined to carry out his dream of a greater Greece even
though his own relatives discouraged him from engaging in acts which
could endanger his throne. In February 1854 Napoleon III wrote a letter
to the King of Greece trying to discourage him from going too far with
his plans to antagonize the Turks.

The recent attitude of Your Majesty's Government has shown me
that its intentions are very different from what I expected. Instead
of enlightening Your Majesty's subjects on the situation, the Government has allowed them to be misled; and through the weakness
and connivance of the authorities, matters have come to such a
point that the insurgents in Epirus are openly recruiting supporters,
not only among Your subjects, but even among Your troops. Under
any conditions I would regret bitterly if Greece were to compromise
her destiny by provoking distrubances in the Near East, but Your
Majesty will understand that today I should be forced to consider
any attack directed against the Ottoman Empire as being directed
against France herself.[60]

After Baron Forth-Rouen delivered Napoleon's letter to Otho, the king
was taken by surprise never expecting such strong warnings to come
from France, a nation, unlike England, with which Greece had had fair
relations for most years since its existence. The king answered Napoleon
in a very touching letter pointing out that he could not conceive that
French soldiers who once fought by the side of Greeks would now turn
their guns against them. He went on to add that the crisis in the Near
East was not to be blamed on the Crown of Greece and that even though
there were sympathies in Greece for the Christian subjects of the Provinces,
there was no attempt on the part of the kingdom to promote a revolt or
engage in war against Turkey.[61]

It has been argued that Otho was convinced that the expansion of the Greek kingdom would work not only to the advantage of his own country but also to that of the Western European countries as well. He felt that a greater Greece would be able to maintain the balance of power in the Near East by checking the Russian power.[62] Otho did not entertain an expansionist foreign policy because he was concerned with the problem of balance of power in the Near East. Among other sources, the memoirs of Spiridon Pelikas,[63] Minister of Justice during the Kriezes administration, unfold the full implications of the king's involvement in planning, triggering and wholehearted support of the insurrection of 1854, for more reasons than that of his own egotistical goals.

When the revolution broke out in Epirus, Soutsos, confident of Otho, informed the Ministerial Council which was convening with the king about the events in the Turkish provinces. The matter of the insurrection was then opened for discussion by the ministers and all agreed to support it secretly but they agreed not to allow the Sublime Porte to become suspicious of the government's involvement. The king agreed that the meeting of the Ministerial Council was secret and he dismissed the council.

> All of us unhesitantly were waiting, as was natural and expected to return again to the Ministerial Council so that the matter can be determined and to set the grounds which we were supposed to keep in mind in order to conduct the manner of our activities. Unfortunately the King, distrustful as it seems, not unjustly of certain ministers did not give us the necessary information, if he had from Europe and from the outer Provinces. Therefore as the public, neither did we at the beginning think that the King would have positive hopes either from France or Germany. Only after two or three months I learned from outside sources various data, which led met to believe that the insurrection was not genuine, but was instigated from within (the Court).[64]

This indicated that the king did not take the advice of the Powers in regard to his foreign policy and deliberately kept the Ministerial Council ignorant of the facts so one can only conclude that the greater part of responsibility for the Greek government's actions in the insurrectionary developments in Northern Greece lies with the Greek Court and Otho himself. Otho used the patriotic movement of the Greek people for his own goals. Otho ignored the interests of Greece and went ahead to side with the Russians and hoped that they would be victorious in the Crimean

War so that he would benefit from their victory. In April 1854 he wrote
to Tsar Nicholas:

> As a Christian and as King of Greece, I follow with the greatest
> interest everything Your Majesty wished to do in the final cause to
> protect in an effective manner the religious rights of the Eastern
> Church in Turkey to which belong the great majority of my sub-
> jects and to which will belong my children, if God gives me any,
> and in any case, the heirs to my throne. The decision which Your
> Majesty is to take in favour of the Christians who, pressed to drive
> out, grabbed the arms for the defence of the Church and their
> homes, not a less noble and loyal manner by which Your Majesty
> has announced his eminent and firm will coming in aid to introduce
> a summit to all the wishes of these populations. . . . And I do not
> act either to satisfy the general sentiment of the deepest acknow-
> ledgement in addressing Your Majesty my most sincere gratitude.[65]

This eulogy to Russia and devotion to the Tsar by Otho was naturally
understandable since Russia was the only possible ally Greece could
have which would approve its foreign policy.

C. *"Internal" and "External" Causes of the Insurrection*

As has already been stated there were a number of complex causes
for the insurrection of 1854. From the study of the insurrection, its
nature, its beginnings, and its direction, it can be concluded that its
causes were of two types, "internal" and "external." In the "internal"
causes can be included the social, economic, religious and political problems facing the Christian subjects of the Turkish provinces who chose
to join the revolution. In the "external" causes can be listed the foreign
elements which were to be found in the insurrection, namely, the involvement of the king and the Greek government, and also the contribution of fanatic nationalists who took part in the insurrection but were
not part of the community of Christians under Ottoman rule.

One of the most firm supporters of a Greek revolt against Turkey
was the "Russian" party. Their newspaper *Aion* had been publishing
severe critiicisms of Turkey and eulogies of Russia ever since the Menshikov mission and in 1853 this newspaper was so blunt as to publish
an article which openly expressed hostility against the Turkish government.[66] The article was signed by P. Soutzo, a poet, and N. Bambas,
professor of philosophy at the University of Athens. Wyse felt that it

was an outrage that a public servant was allowed to write such an article against a friendly power. Naturally Nechet Bey went immediately to Wyse after he read the article and complained that the Greek government did not refute the article in the government press and took no action against Professor Bambas, the co-signer of the article. Wyse immediately brought this to the attention of the Greek Foreign Minister who promised to take appropriate action in the matter.[67] The relations between Greece and Turkey were on a steady decline in the Fall. The Porte had been hoping to avoid confrontation with Greece which would result if carried to extremes in a war, and a two-front war was an adventure the Sultan's government could do without. Nechet Bey wrote to Paicos on December 3 accusing Greece of actively seeking deterioration of relations with the Porte. He stated that the Sublime Porte wanted to maintain good relations with Greece but the latter showed no effort of good-will by continuing to send troops to the frontier.[68]

As the Turkish authorities felt threatened by the presence of the Greek troops on the frontier, Greek authorities constantly complained about the mistreatment of Christians by the Ottoman authorities. It was only to be expected that the sympathies of the Greek Orthodox subjects with the Russian cause would create alarm among the Turks. On October 7, three days after the announcement of *Aion* that the war between Russia and Turkey was under way, Lambros Beikos, an officer of the Greek army, entered Epirus with a company of three hundred men. This was an obvious sign that the Greek government had every intention of capitalizing on the Russo-Turkish war. Suleiman Bey Frasare, General Derven Aga of Epirus, was forced to gather two hundred men from the Turkish provinces and five hundred irregulars from Albania to go after one of the Greek military leaders, Koutsonika, who was known to engage in revolutionary activity. The Greek ambassador in Epirus upon receiving this news called on the Lieutenant Commander of Western Greece to concentrate his troops on the frontier as "a display of strength."[69]

This movement caused great concern to the European community as well as to the governments of the involved parties. The Greek government realizing the danger involved in the consequences, Anglo-French threat, of such activities sent to the frontier lieutenant Skylodemo to disperse the rebels, and immediately placed the blame for the entire incident on the *Nomarch* (Governor) of Aitolia and Akarnania for allowing it to take place. The Turkish authorities having the full support and cooperation of the Allied Powers did not take the incident lightly especially when later another Greek rebel, Theodore Ziakas entered Thessaly.[70]

Wyse sent the following report informing the Foreign Office of the incidents on the frontier:

> This, however, is not the only instance, I regret to say of disposition on the part not only of the Government but of the Court to add to the unsatisfactory nature of the relations between the two governments. Neshid Bey complained to me a few days since that the lately appointed ministers had alone omitted him among their round of visits, and that on several occasions of late, their Majesties had passed him by, though close to them, without the honor of the usual salute.[71]

Wyse advised Nechet Bey to communicate with the Greek Foreign Minister before he officially notified the Porte.

Paicos was in a real dilemma. On the one hand he was overtly trying to prevent a war or revolution from breaking out for he feared the Anglo-French threats to Greece and on the other hand the Greek government was too deeply involved in the events on the frontier and provinces. In a dispatch to Trikoupes, Paicos expressed his fear that if Greece dared to engage in a conflict with Turkey, France and England would support the Sultan not only by their moral but with their armed force as well.[72]

The majority of Greek statemen had a difficult time understanding that the two Western Powers which contributed to their independence and fought for the creation of the Greek nation would fight to prevent that same country from expanding its borders and taking territories which, in their view, were rightfully Greek. The decision had to be made, however, whether Greece would follow a policy of expansion or stay neutral. The dilemma could only be resolved by Otho; the king chose to glorify his Crown.[73]

The external causes of the Greek-Turkish war were reinforced by the internal causes which did not play as important a role in international politics but did contribute to the explanation of the beginnings of the revolution in the provinces. One could easily understand why the representatives of the Allied Powers would not admit the "internal" causes of the insurrection even if they were looking for them. Wyse denied any possibility of the existence of "internal" causes for an insurrection and in December he wrote:

> I do not perceive any immediate probability of such, [internal causes] nor do I think it at any rate time likely to make much way, unless originated or continued by the Greek Government or stimulated by reports of Russian success.[74]

This reflects to a great extent the official British governmental attitude concerning the causes for the insurrection. They placed all emphasis on the influence and actions of the Greek Court and government, the "Russian" party, and the propaganda of both Greece and Russia concerning the condition of Christian subjects in the Ottoman Empire. All of these are "external" causes which are applicable but only partially explain the reasons behind the insurrection. There was no place allowed for Greek Christian subjects of the Ottoman Empire who did not want to be ruled by the Porte for religious and ethnic reasons, and Greeks living in Turkey or other Christians were mistreated or murdered many a time when there were strained relations between Greece and Turkey. Legation reports from the Northern provinces and other accounts indicate that the events of 1854 were triggered partially by socio-economic, religious and ethnic causes. The pressures of the Turkish officials on the Christian subjects was one of the reasons many Greeks welcomed the opportunity to strike back.[75] One of the first villages to revolt was Radovishi. The reasons for this were: (1) there was jealousy among Albanians because Greeks from Radovichi were on the payroll of the Porte used as troops to maintain order in the provinces,[76] and (2) they objected to the heavy taxes imposed upon them by the Ottoman authorities.[77]

The movement of Radovici was known to the Greek authorities and it was allowed to continue. What is astonishing, however, is when the news reached Athens that the villagers of Radovici took up arms against the Turks, there was a general enthusiasm all over Greece and the events were compared in many minds to 1821.[78] To many the time had arrived for the liberation of all Greek subjects and territory.

One Greek writer[79] maintained that the insurrection was doomed to failure before it even began for lack of money needed to carry out a successful attack against the Turks. Despite an empty treasury in Greece the chieftians were urged to continue their venture against the Turks not only by the government sector but also by the private sector. When the

Roumeliotes asked for a loan of 30,000 drachmas early in 1854, the President of the National Bank of Greece, G. Stavrou, replied that he did not have the funds available but they should continue their struggle against the Turks with his blessings. He clearly implied that the loan could and would become available to them in the near future.[80] Such reassurances from the top in both private and public sources left the insurgents confident that they had more than just the moral support of Greece.

The greatest mistake the government for its part could commit in the insurrection, as Metaxas pointed out,[81] was to support such a movement (in Radovichi) after the Western Powers had decided on a policy which would call for the suppression of such a mission,[82] and before the Russians crossed the Danube.[83] Nevertheless, the revolution of 1854 began in Radovichi and it provided the spark needed to cause other Christians in the Northern provinces to revolt. The spirit of 1821 lived among the leaders of the revolution since many of them had seen or participated in the War of Independence and others were sons of chieftains. Two of the most prominent leaders were Spyridon Karaiskakes and Demitrios Grivas, the son of Lieutenant-General Theodore Grivas.[84] On January 29 all the revolutionaries met at the villages of Peta, Neochori and Kombote to organize new attacks against Arta. Karaiskakes delivered the following historic message to his men on January 30th:

Greek! While dying my father cried: Redeem Athens! Leaving as the only inheritance to me his sword, he died. Taking the inheritance of my father and finding Athens free, the land of his birth is enslaved. . . . Oh people of Epirus! The flag of freedom I raised among us. Greeks! The second Turkish war is coming; the revolutionary flame has started and the holy spirit of freedom and faith has descended from heaven and is increasing the flames of the fire. Look at the Heptanesos (seven islands—Ionian Islands) as a seven-headed serpent it hisses, Epirus is moving, Thessaly is shaking, Macedonia is stirring, Thrace is waiting; Courage, then Courage! During the first Turkish war (that of Independence) the Greeks with 50,000 soldiers defeated 500,000 men from Asia, Europe and Africa. Today autonomous Greeks, Epirotes, Thessaloi, Macedonians and Thracians, six million we are fighting a weak kingdom which is been fought at the Danube by multi-numerous and threatening armies. . . . Forward. The cross on the one hand, the sword on the other. . . . Freedom or death. This is the voice of 10 million

Greeks, Serbians and Bulgarians in Europe and 4 million Greeks in Asia.[85]

It was apparent from this speech that the spirit, at least some of it, of 1821 was once again being recreated in 1854. In many ways 1854 was the year that many hoped to see bring the War of Independence to a full cycle and free all Greek Christians from the Turks.

The historian who relies solely on British and French sources for the causes of the insurrection can be mislead a great deal for Western European sources only reflect the partial observations of Western Europeans who did not have access to the Greek documents and were also under the influence of the political biases and policy of the Allied Powers. It was impossible, therefore, to come to the conclusion that any "internal" factors existed in the revolution if one does not review the Greek ones. A typical view of a contemporary Western European concerning the causes of the insurrection is that of the Scottish historian, George Finlay. "But in spite of Greek and Russian encouragement," he maintains, "the Christian subjects of the Sultan refused to take up arms the public administration was so bad in Greece, that independence offered few attractions when the result on the value would be subjection to Greek misgovernment."[86] Even though the observations of Finlay—a *misehellene*, hater of Greeks, as labelled by Greek historians—are to a certain extent correct since not every Greek took up arms and marched to fight the Turks, there is ample evidence of a great number of people who joined and did so for they had political, economic and social reasons.[87]

After Mehmet Fuad Pasha, former minister of foreign affairs (1852-53), who was entrusted by the Sultan with suppressing the revolts in northern Greece, had published the warning to all Christians who joined the insurrection,[88] the Greeks of Epirus and Thessaly sent him the following message:

> To the brightest Fuad Effendi. We former *ragiades* etc. cursed by the Sultan, until yesterday were sitting on glass and nails and on our *rahati* (back) as you would say. And seeing that from the taxes on the value of products, from instalment taxes, from taxes on sheep, from taxes on trade, from fire taxes, from luxury taxes and from commerce taxes . . . not even saliva was left in our mouth. The irregular Turks of our territory and the *Nizamledes* sent by Ali Osman . . . have stripped us . . . . They'll slaughter us

like goats. . . . There is no other way but to ask for help from our King Otho. Farewell till we meet at the Byzantium, if you haven't left there before we come. The Greeks of Epirus and Thessaly.[89]

The Greek subjects of Thessaly and Epirus had fallen victims to a semi-feudal system of Turkish government which could nto reform fast enough for the liberal and nationalist demands of the Greek people. The *Tanzimat* came to these provinces in the mid-1840's[90] and its effects were insignificant since, as Bailey maintains[91] it was not a radical reform program to satisfy the rebelling spirit of the Orthodox subjects of the Ottoman Empire. On June 2, 1853, a letter of the British Consul at Prevesa reported to his government that the Christian subjects of Thessaly and Epirus were "oppressed by fiscal exations, and subjected to intolerable acts of violence and injustice. . . ."[92] He further noted that these people would readily take up arms in support of an insurrection against Turkey. In another report by Lord Stratford on July 4, 1853, the Turkish authorities were charged with treating the Christian subjects with "cruelty, rapine and murder."[93] A "proclamation to all Greeks and Philhellenists, believers of Christ,"[94] dated January 9, 1854, is not only a good indication of Greek propaganda before the insurrection of 1854 but it also serves as an example of Turkish tyranny and reflects the nationalist and liberal spirit of the Greek people. Europe, at least Western Europe, had progressed economically, politically and socially. Greece and the Greek subjects of the Ottoman Empire were aware of this progress and compared their devastating condition to that of Western Europe so they desired to abolish all form of oppression.

Such were the internal causes of the revolution and it is really difficult to determine their weight in the entire scheme of things. As they present themselves, the facts tend to incriminate the Greek government and especially the Greek Court for the insurrection of 1854, but this does not mean that the effect of the "internal" factors must be minimized since it took the combination of both "external" and "internal" factors for the creation of what was intended to be the second War of Independence for Greece.

CHAPTER IV

WAR AND OCCUPATION

A. War in Thessaly, Epirus and Chalcidice

The Radovichi occurrences obviously created much excitement not only among the Greeks but also among the Turkish and European governments. Turkey was always fearful of facing a two front war, one at the Danube and the other at the Greek frontier. The Porte knew that the enemy at the Danube was much too strong to be held back by the Turkish forces, so all troops had to be concentrated in the Russian front. Aware of their shortage of manpower the Ottoman authorities wanted to end the revolution before it spread into a major war. Accordingly, they adopted severe measures in dealing with the Christians in order to discourage them from engaging in any adventurous revolutionary activities.[1]

On February 9, about one thousand men were sent to take Pente Pegadia (Five Wells) held by Greek insurgents. Pente Pegadia was a village between Arta and Janina which the rebels had taken along the Peta. It became one of the main headquarters for the insurgents. The Greeks forced the Turks to defend themselves from Arta. When the latter were unable to emerge victorious in their struggle, reinforcements were sent but they too failed to defeat the insurgents and retreated to Janina.[2] The Greeks were left free to attack the neighboring Turkish villages and possibly take Arta, the village still held by Turkish forces after the rebels unsuccessfully tried to capture it on February 12.

Another attempt was made by the Turkish military forces to send help to Arta, this time eight hundred men in addition to the seven hundred regulars and two hundred armed police.[3] Like the previous reinforcements these also met with defeat as they were stopped by the bands of Greek chieftains led by Rago, Strato and Karaoules.

On February 16 the Greeks scored another victory against a group of three hundred Turks who attempted to rescue those at Arta.[4] In Epirus, at the village of Peta, the rebels defeated the Turks as they had in Thessaly. Theodore Grivas with three hundred men scored a victory at Koutsoulio,[5] and on February 28 he was a few miles outside Janina. In the early days

of March many villages fell into the hands of the Greeks and it seemed
that the revolutionaries were successful in their task. After the outbreak
of the insurrection the notables in Agrafa made the following announcement:

> Patriots, a cry had been poured in our hearts, that our Epirotes
> compatriots have taken arms asking for their freedom against the
> centuries long tyrannt. Grab, therefore, fellow-patriots your arms,
> place your hands in your heart,. . .imitate our predecessors, and
> cast your black for the honor of religion, the honor of your
> freedom.[6]

Epirus came under the leadership of Kitsos Tsavelas, former Inspector
General of the Greek army, who had left the military along with a number
of others to join the revolution. Peta was the headquarters for the insurgents in Epirus and it was from where Tsavelas and Karaiskakes
operated. In the eparchy of Janina Grivas and his son were in control
and headed for the town of Janina. Still other insurgent bands operated
from Paramethia.[7]

The revolution spread from Thessaly and Epirus to Macedonia where
Ziakas with two hundred men from Lamia entered into Turkish territory.

> They occupied the strategic position of Spileon and the passage
> between Melia and Drania in the area between Metsovo and Grevena.
> Ziakas' plan was to bar the crossing of Turkish troops from Epirus
> to Western Macedonia, and to unite the insurrection in Epirus,
> Thessaly and Macedonia through Grevena.[8]

The reaction from the people of Greece to these sporadic uprisings in
the north was alarming. Many who were indoctrinated in the beliefs
of "religion" and "nation" took up arms and ran to the troubled provinces feeling they had a holy mission to carry out. Wyse wrote that:

> Recruiting, I am informed, is going on in the open day and under
> the very eyes of the Government officials and local authorities, not
> only in Missolonghi, but in many other Provinces, even so far down
> as the Peloponesos. . . . A still more daring spirit is conspicuous at
> Athens. Four committees have been regularly formed and are in
> permanent sitting here, for the purpose of receiving subscriptions
> and enroling recruits, presided by Deputies and others of authority
> in touch, one of these immediately opposite Neshid Bey's house.
> Another similarly organized for the same purpose at Patras.[9]

It was not only the indoctrinated masses who applauded the revolts but the king as well. He wrote to his father when the Epirus uprising occurred that the Christian subjects of Turkey were mistreated by the officials and they desired to free themselves from the Turkish yoke so they could join the mother country, Greece. He added that even though the uprising was not timed rightly for it broke out in the middle of the Russo-Turkish war, it did, however, prove that it was not caused by Russia, as the Western Powers suspected, but was indeed genuine.[10]

The Turkish authorities did not take any serious measures against the repression of Christian subjects in the Ottoman Empire until after the Tsar announced that the war against Turkey was fought on behalf of the "repressed brothers."[11] Fuad Effendi, the former minister of Foreign Affairs, who became commissioner extraordinary in charge of all operations in Thessaly and Epirus,[12] was entering Prevesa with three thousand men as T. Grivas and N. Zervas were making advances toward Janina. Fuad Effendi landed with three war ships accompanied by a British frigate, an obvious indication that Great Britain had taken the role of an advisor to Turkey in military operations.[13] Seinel Pasha, who was assigned as General Dervend in Thessaly and Epirus was sent to Volos with one thousand five hundred to two thousand five hundred men[14] one two steamers which were also escorted by a British and a French steamers.[15] The Turks also sent troops by land to stop the spreading of the insurrection. Fuad Pasha published a proclamation holding forth a general amnesty for all those who were willing to return to their duty and effective protection to the peaceable and well disposed.[16] The publication read as follows:

> Though you were staying in your homes inside our borders men came . . . and destroyed our lands. Those who desire to remain under the authority of the Sultan, Kotsombasedes ect. disassociate yourselves from the insurgents and come with me. (1) Those who did not participate in this stirring of events will be treated kindly by our Sultan. (2) Those who remain armed will be punished and with a different treatment. (3) Villages which did not accept the revolution, will be paid by other villages who did. (4) Those, will not be tolerated and will immediately be punished.[17]

On March 1 Lieutenant General A. Hatzi-Petros, an aide de camp of Otho, entered Thessaly with five hundred men. Another aide de camp of Otho, Lieutenant General Dimitris Tsames Karatasos, also joined the revolution which of course was converted into a full scale war after the Turkish troops from Constantinople had arrived in the provinces. Dimitrios or Tsames Karatasos, son of Athanasios Karatasos, fought with his father in Macedonia and other parts of Greece during the War of Independence.[18] Many observers in Greece believed that the revolutionaries had a good start and the chances of a Turkish victory were slim since they needed their forces to hold back the Russians. Wyse explained the situation to the Foreign Office as follows:

> In Greece the impression is, that the forces as yet sent is too feeble, to stop the current, and that even twice that number would still be inadequate to oppose any effective resistance to a movement which they believe will become before another month, *Pan hellenic*. The passage of volunteers from the border Provinces, is every day increasing, nourished by these hopes and reports of a constant succession of victories.[19]

The Turkish offensive, however, began to build up gradually as more help from France and England came to assist them in fighting the Russians. General Grivas suffered a defeat on March 23 at Metsovo by Abdi Pasha, who commanded two thousand five hundred men.[20] Grivas retreated to Peta with the other chiefs and after a long battle with the Turks, which the Greek insurgents lost they dispersed[21] and this marked the end of the revolutionary effort in Epirus. Abdi Pasha in conjunction with "Fuad Effendi, followed up his (Abdi Pasha's) victory by taking Pente Pigadia, and reopening the communications between Arta and Ioannina (Janina)."[22] Thessaly also was ready for Turkish hands as a force of three thousand men stationed at Almiro were determined to put an end to the advance of Papakosta at Platanon. Even though the forces of Papakosta proved to be much more effective in holding back the Turks than Grivas' forces, the internal disputes among the chiefs resulted in the general weakness of the movement.[23] Disputes among the chiefs were not, however, the only cause which lost the war for the Greeks. One of the worst loses suffered by the rebels was at Volos. By March 30 six thousand Egyptians and a French steamer, "Heron" came to the aid of the Turks and for all practical purposes the undertaking was well on the way to being crushed under such military power.[24]

The next important battle was fought on May 10 at Kalambaka. Before this battle took place, Soutso, Minister of War, gave orders on his own accord without consulting the Minister of Justice, Pelikas, that prisoners from Chalcidice should be allowed to go free so that they may join the insurrection.[25] The Kalambaka battle between Hadji-Petro and Selim Pasha marked the height of insurgent victories in the North.[26] The Macedonian revolts were inspired by those of Epirus and Thessaly but started late in March.

The two men responsible for organizing the Macedonian movement were N. Filaretos and Tsames Karatasos. The grievance of the Christians of Macedonia had against the Turks was about land which was granted to them by the Turkish Court but was not obtained by them.[27] A Secret revolutionary group of three hundred and ten men were organized by the two Greek chiefs, and on March 23 Filaretos started from north Eubioa to Pelio. By the end of the month the effort was completely demolished by a combination of factors. (1) Filaretos felt that the people of Pelio were not ready for revolution and war, (2) disputes among the insurgent leaders, and (3) one Demitrios Gabriel announced everywhere that "ten thousand British were coming to Prevesa to punish the rebels,"[28] which obviously scared everyone involved in the insurrection.

The revolts in the provinces were unsuccessful for a variety of reasons. One of them, the most important, was that Turkey had the support of Western Europe whereas Greece had only Russian moral support during the entire affair. The Foreign Office instructed Wyse on March 23 that:

> If it should turn out that the Greek troops have violated the Turkish territory, in the name of Her Majesty's Government, strongly to protest against the act and the unworthy attempt of the Greek Government to accuse the Turkish troops (of crossing the Greek frontier).[29]

The Greek Court and the expansionists in the government would not listen to threats of the Allied Powers. When the Turks captured Chrone Nasdeke at the Battle of Berivolia, of Volos, they found on him documents incriminating the Greek government in the revolution. They immediately sent these documents to Constantinople as official evidence of the Greek government's aggression against Turkey.[30] This caused the Turks and their allies to become even more serious and determined in their efforts to extinguish the revolution. Great Britain and France warned that the conduct of the Greek Court and government and, eespecially, the king and queen, had brought the two Powers to the point where they were seriously considering breaking off diplomatic relations. They further warned, "that the coasts of Greece would be blockaded, Greek commerce put an end to, and that ulterior measures would then be determined on."[31]

Paicos and the Court were not about to give in to demands of the Allied Powers as long as they knew that the insurrection still had a chance of accomplishing something. Furthermore, it was too late to pull out and stop everything as though nothing had happened. The people burned with nationalism, the king was more determined than ever to give full support to the movement until it was successful, and the press kept the war propaganda stronger than ever before.

There were other factors, however, besides pressure from the Allied Powers which resulted in the failure of Greeks to capture the Turkish provinces. First, there was no fully organized effort on behalf of the Greek government to engage in war. The authorities in Greece allowed the revolt to occur, supported it morally and materially, but as a result of British and French threats and pressure the Greek government abandoned the effort of the insurgents while it was still flourishing. If there was more determination on the part of the king and those in government who supported the revolution of 1854, a greater effort could have been made to risk everything in order to win the designated Turkish provinces.

There was also another factor which has already been mentioned, namely, disputes among the leaders of the insurgents which made the movement very weak in its internal organization. The following letter of Grivas to Georgandas reveals much about internal feuds among the chiefs:

After the battle of historic fame at Metsovo, of which I send you the description and plan today, seeing the greatest conspiracies and treacheries existing against me on the part of my companions in arms, I was compelled to retreat from thence and take the direction of Thessaly. On my arrival there I found the same divisions prevailing between the different chiefs, and I came to the resolution to remain quiet in Agrapha, until I could come to some understanding with the Government of His Majesty . . . . The struggle which we have undertaken is great; it is higher than that of 1821, in as much as we aim at the restoration of the Greek Empire. But such a struggle requires union, subordination, order, primary means in abundance, and a Commander in Chief, otherwise there is an end to all hope . . . . The Government ought either at once to take up the struggle appointing publicly the proper persons to a regular army at a regular pay or let us sit down quietly at home, so that we may not be the causes of destruction of our fellow Christians.[32]

Considering these elements, Anglo-French opposition, no organized Greek governmental support to the revolutionaries and internal feuds among the chiefs, the movement which ambitiously began as a repeat of 1821 ended in failure. All this much to the disgrace and devastation of the people who in the name of religion and nation had taken up arms to free themselves from the backward Ottoman Empire.

B. Rupture of Greek-Turkish Relations and Anglo-French Reaction to the Insurrection

Western Europe was convinced that there was a definite connection between the Russo-Turkish disputes and the Greek uprisings in 1854. There can be little doubt that fragile relations between Russian and Turkey provided a strong reason for the Greeks to go through with an uprising in the south-western front of the Ottoman Empire since it would have been necessary for the Turks to concentrate their forces on the northern front. That the insurgents were taking direct orders from the Russians was untrue. Nesselrode made an announcement on March 18 dispelling all such accusations. He stated that the Tsar sympathized with Greece and with the Christians who were trying to free themselves from the Turkish yoke, as they had once before in 1821.[33] There was little doubt in the minds of Western Europeans, however, that the Greek revolts were indeed used by the Russians as strategic tools of distraction against the Turks. During the month of January the reports received at the Foreign Office were mostly about the widespread propaganda influence of *Aion*, the "Russian" party newspaper. The press propaganda received more attention than the real causes of the revolution, so obviously the British government and British public opinion were influenced by what were in many respects the effects of the insurrection and further the pro-Russian Greek newspaper *Aion* which had primarily the following only of those who sympathized with the "Russian" party.[34]

In February, Wyse sent a report to his government expressing his fears of Russian influence in Greece and he linked the uprising on the frontier entirely to this influence. According to him when Kornilov visted Athens in 1854, he charged that the present ministry had radical pro-Russian elements which were dominant in the government and that the Foreign Minister allowed Greek government officials to contribute money for the *Megali Idea*. Further, Colonel Soutso deliberately substituted old officers of the army with young pro-Russian ones who favored Russian interests. Wyse went on to write:

> The simple impression of the whole case (however it may be disguised is thus: a Russian government prepared to take advantage under Russian protection, for purposes of aggrandisement, of any contingency which in the course of events may chance to arise. Should such a contingency occur, should war for finstance, become inevitable and be followed by any decided success on the part of Russia, or insurrectionary movements sufficiently serious in the Turkish Provinces contiguous to Greece, I am persuaded it would be a signal for the general movement.[35]

The Greek embassy in London also reported the apprehensions of the Foreign Office concerning Russian involvement in Greece,[36] but until February 9 there was no implication by the British government that the insurrectionary movements in the provinces involved the Greek Court.[37]

Russian influence and anti-Turkish sentiments in Greece caused concern to all European representatives at Athens. Baron de Thile, the Prussian minister at Athens, visited the king on one occasion after an anti-Turkish demonstration by the university students and a number of Greek soldiers which took place in Athens. The Baron pointed out to the king the political danger of such demonstrations and expressed his disapproval of such events.[38] Finally, upon the suggestion of Wyse, the representatives of the four European Powers—England, France, Austria and Prussia—decided to send a collective note to the Greek government asking that it not get involved in the insurrection and that it remain in a position of neutrality. Paicos was warned that, "not only was the tranquility of the country endangered, but the King's liberty of action, his rights and person, and perhaps the dynasty."[39] This came as a shock to Otho, not so much because he and his throne were threatened as a result of this court's involvement in the insurrection, but because the Prussian and Austrian representatives signed the warning.

The four ministers who sent Paicos the warning about Greek government involvement in the insurrection advised Nechet Bey on diplomatic matters and gave him their full support. Upon the advice of Wyse, Nechet

Bey, wrote to Paicos to protest "against the incursions of armed men into Ottoman territory and accused Athens of not having done anything to stop these hostile activities."[40] Paicos replied that he was doing everything he could but the nation simply did not possess the necessary military force needed to intervene in the uprising taking place in the Turkish provinces.[41]

Nechet Bey felt that Paicos was not complying with the requests of the Porte so he went once again to Wyse and Rouen for advice. They suggested that another note of warning should be sent to Paicos signed by the four European representatives. Baron Leykam, representative of Austria, and Baron de Thile did not sign the note. As they explained, they did not have the proper authorization from their government to do so.[42] After the note was sent, Wyse and Paicos visited the king so they could get Otho's verbal commitment that Greece would follow a non-aggressive policy towards Turkey. The representatives took the opportunity to warn Otho that general war would have dangerous consequences for his throne.[43] In order to be on the safe side, Wyse, Stratford Canning and Sir Henry Ward, the Lord High Commissioner of the Ionian Islands, "thought it necessary to use part of the British Fleet stationed in the Mediterreanen," for any unexpected developments in Greece.[44] Instructions were also sent from London and Paris empowering the British and French ministers to order a blockade of the Greek capital, if they thought it necessary.[45]

Lord Clarendon took further steps to instruct Wyse to relay the British government's disappointment with Athens and with Paicos' refusal to conform to Nechet Bey's requests. Twenty-four hours before a final telegram was sent to Paicos with a list of demands by the Turkish charge d'affaires in Athens, Clarendon wrote the following letter to Wyse:

> You will inform Mr. Paicos that as friendly advice has not been wanting but has been disregarded as the connivance of the Greek Court and Government with the hostile movement against Turkey is now beyond question, and as Her Majesty's Government and that of the Emperor of the French are determined that their policy shall not be thus thwarted; the Greek Government must be prepared for the consequences of its own acts. If these consequences should be to endanger the throne and future welfare of Greece, the responsibility will rest upon the Greek ministers who have shown themselves to be ignorant or careless of the true interests of their own country.[46]

On March 7 Nechet Bey sent a telegram to Paicos with the following list
of demands: (1) The officers who took part in the uprising should be
punished after trial in a Greek court of law, (2) those officials who helped
to rouse the people against the neighboring state should be punished, (3)
those in the political circle (in government) should be penalized if they
contributed to the insurrection in any manner whatsoever, (4) *Aion* and
other government newspapers should be regulated so that they do not
excite the public mind with propaganda in favor of the revolution, and
finally:

> (5) to give assurances to the Sublime Porte that an investigation will
> be conducted to find the officer who opened the prisons of Chalcida
> and armed the criminals, and in conclusion, if after forty-eight
> hours until the setting of the sun of Tuesday 9 March, the Greek
> government has not granted a satisfactory answer to the demands
> of the Porte, he (Nechet Bey) is forced to ask for his passport as
> well as those of the entire personnel of the embassy.[47]

The time had come for the king to make a decision which would either
mean blockade and suffering of the consequences for the Greek people
or to take that daring step towards the realization of the *Megali Idea* and
ignore the Turkish demands.

In reality, at least in the reality as seen through the eyes of Pelikas, the
king wanted to fulfill his dream but at the same time he was afraid of the
numerous warnings from Western Europe. In his memoirs Pelikas writes:

> In the morning, the postponed Consular meeting took place before
> the King. The opinion not to hide a hint that the Greek government
> was at fault prevailed. The necessity to buy time because the oppor-
> tunity would be uncomparably better for us, when the Russian army
> had made advances, was clear . . . . With this spirit we examined one
> by one of Nechet Bey's demands and we thought, which one we
> should give an answer to. When we came to the resignation of the
> Professors, we said, that this sacrifice should be made for the good
> of the nation and the rest of the Ministers agreed. But the King with
> a certain emotion said: How! to start dismissing my personnel?
> Never! Paicos suggested, and we all approved, to present the answer
> tomorrow to the Parliament, as they do in all Constitutional States
> in order to gain support of the nation, and to appear to Turkey and
> to the Western Powers united and that of one will is the government
> and the nation . . . . The next day (after the secret meeting con-
> cerning the drafting of the answer to Nechet Bey) we returned.
> Paicos had worked with the King, who had kept the plans. We stayed

almost to midnight, but the plans were not sent to us, when we received an announcement from the four ministers bringing to the attention of the government, the announcement of Nechet Bey for its serious results. Because we announced during the day, that we rejected the requests of Nechet Bey, the ambassadors hurried them to make their announcement.[48]

On March 10 Nechet Bey announced the rupture of Greek-Turkish relations and left Athens. The Porte began to exile Greek residents of the Ottoman Empire as soon as relations broke off. All commercial relations were also broken between the two countries and the Sultan did not allow ships with the Greek flag to sail into Turkish ports and also ordered all the Greek diplomats in Turkey to leave.[49]

The four Powers were quick to express their displeasure as Pelikas pointed out above, to the Greek government's answer to Nechet Bey and naturally blamed the Greeks for the rupture of relations.[50] Wyse went so far as to say that:

Mr. Paicos' note to Nechet Bey which like so many other similar communications seem only to have in view to drive the Sublime Porte to a declaration of hostilities which would rescue this government from disgrace of any longer maintaining this ignoble hypocrisy, but which at the same time would give the signal of a national war, inviting every class and person, however, objecting to the present conduct of the government in the disastrous struggle.[51]

Even though Greece tried to defend its position in the recent interruption of relations with the Porte the fact remained that both the Greek Court and government were expecting such an outcome and many of them, perhaps most, were happy with the interruption of relations with a country which they never regarded as friendly. Pelikas wrote, that the morning after Nechet Bey left the Queen expressed her enthusiasm of the affair and that of her husband.[52]

The month of April brought a renewed tide of diplomatic opposition by the Western Powers against Greece. Baron de Thile visited the palace at the request of the king after the interruption of relations with the Porte. Instead of trying to cover up or blame the Turks for the recent events Otho and Amalia told the Prussian minister that the king of Greece was not at liberty to retreat. The reason for this as Wyse reported to the Foreign Office was that:

He [Otho] had received the divine mission to liberate the Christian races from the yoke of the Mohammedan and that mission he was bound to answer, and must at every venture fulfill. . . . The Baron de Thile considers all further effort fruitless and looks with dismay on the probable results to their Majesties personally and the Dynasty from the course now pursued.[53]

The Bavarian as well as the Austrian Court was very much displeased with the recent events in Greece and with the king's position in the entire affair.

Austria was especially concerned with the uprising in the Turkish provinces, perhaps as much as France and England for there was a real threat that the revolution could spread to Montenegro. Since the Greeks were an ethnic minority and were revolting in the name of nation and religion the rest of the Balkan people could sympathize with their struggle. Count Buol cooperated closely, therefore, with Clarendon and Drouyn de Lhuys. He sent a war vessel to Prevessa on April 21, and he was ready to cooperate militarily with the Turks in suppressing an unexpected uprising in Montenegro.[54] Britain and France were ready to take more radical steps against Greece. Five days before the Allied Powers warned Paicos that they were also considering interruption of relations with Greece, Clarendon instructed Wyse to inform the Greek government that he felt Nechet Bey's demands were fair and moderate. Further, the British government was greatly disappointed with Paicos' decision to reject the Turkish demands. The Greek government's answer to Nechet Bey was evasive and unsatisfactory. Clarendon went on to write:

That the so-called national movement to which their Majesties and the Greek Government affected to yield, has been created and stimulated by the Court and Government, that its subject was to excite the peaceable Christian subjects of the Porte to revolt, and that the Court and Government of Greece were therefore deliberately aiding the cause of the Emperor of Russia, with whom England and France are at war, and in injuring the Sultan, whose cause England and France are pledged to support, and that these being acts of direct hostility against two of the Protecting Powers, the King and Queeen of Greece must be prepared for the consequences.[55]

Matters appeared very critical for Greece. If Great Britain decided once again to blockade the ports of Greece she would have French military naval support and the moral support of the entire European community.

In 1850 Palmerston's blockade of Pireaus was opposed by every government in Europe and by most politicians in Europe including most British.[56]
The case, however, was not the same in 1854. No nation, including Russia
which was the only country which approved of the Greek uprising, would
come to the rescue of the young nation. The philhellinism of the Europeans
no longer existed at the level it had during the War of Independence, so
if the Allied Powers took measures against Greece they would have the
approval of European public opinion. The government in Athens knew
very well that its international position was weak and having no allies on
its side who were ready to support her, Greece had necessarily to conform
with the demands of the Western Powers.

Reports from the Greek embassy in London to Paicos indicated that it
was absolutely necessary for Greece to declare neutrality or suffer an
Allied occupation. Two days after Clarendon's dispatch of April 18 to
Wyse, Trikoupis informed Athens that a meeting took place in London
between Clarendon and the French minister there. They decided that
their governments should order their representatives in Constantinople
to prevent the Sublime Porte from declaring war against Greece, but for
the present "to seize the ports of Greece as a payment for the borrowed
loans to these (England and France)."[57] When Wyse visited Paicos on the
13 the latter knew of the intentions of the Allied Powers so he was prepared to answer to the warnings and threats of Wyse with excuses and
justifications for the present position of Greece. The Greek foreign minister did not attempt to conceal the role of the government in the uprising,
and even confirmed that Greece had indeed purchased the Russian ships
at Trieste for 120,000 florins.[58]

On April 11, Forth-Rouen and Wyse informed Paicos that any ships
flying the Greek flag would be searched for arms and munitions, and if
such are among the cargo of the ships they would be confiscated. Furthermore, the two representatives warned that the Russian ships purchased
by Greece for purposes of war would "be stopped and detained by the
English and French naval forces" if they were to be put to use against
Turkey.[59] Paicos realized that the worst was yet to come. He wrote to
Mavrokordatos in Paris and asked him to appeal to Drouyn de Lhuys
and Thouvenel in order to review the situation in Greece. The Prime
Minister felt that the threats from the French and English were unjustified since Greece, after all, did try to arrive at a compromise with the
demands of Nechet Bey but the latter chose to break relations with the

Greek government instead of working out the differences.[60]

But how could France compromise her Near Eastern interests for the sake of Greece? The compromise had to be made by Otho for he was in no position to do otherwise. Instead of softening his position, however, the king was more determined than ever to carry out his expansionist foreign policy. He was convinced that the revolution would be successful and that the Western Powers would then have to recognize that their interests were with a greater Greece and not with a weak Turkey. The Queen went ever further:

> What can the Western Powers do to us, the Queen added, they'll take over Athens? Let them come; See here, we leave them our palaces; we won't touch anything. If they wish to stay here we are moving to Thessaly. They"ll prevent our ships from sailing? See here, Divine Providence is helping us;. . . they'll take a few of our war ships and will not allow us to move toward the sea? . . . they will not tie our hands and feet and then say to the Turks: "Come and kill them." But they will burn a few of our cities or our ships? In the revolution of 1821 also they burned but Greece rebuilt, the damage is only material.[61]

The only experience Greece had of a blockade was that of 1850, and it was primarily the commercial class which suffered more than any other class. The economy in general was also effected, however, since the commercial class was one of the strongest economic sectors in Greece. The king only experienced humiliation of a political and moral nature not of the economic stress which did his people.

In the face of the threats and warnings of the Western Powers the Greek Ministerial Council was divided, some fully supporting the foreign policy of Otho, others too afraid to follow extreme measures which could lead to damaging results for the welfare of the nation. Two of the ministers, Pelikas and Provelgios, who were realistic enough to forsee the consequences of the *Megali Idea* policy asked Otho to accept their resignations as a means of protest and disapproval of the present course followed by Greece.[62] Not even protests from his own ministers, however, were sufficiently strong to change the king's plans.

The British and French ministers at Athens realized that if the pro-Russian ministry was dismissed by Otho and was substituted by "English" and "French" politicians, then possibly the king would be persuaded, if not forced, through the influence of the two Western Protecting Powers to give up his policy of expansionism. In a meeting with the representatives of Austria, Prussia and Bavaria, who tried to persuade the king to change the course of his actions, Otho flatly rejected the idea of change of ministry. All the ministers of the four Western Powers admitted that even if there was to be a change of government "it would be impossible . . . to find anyone in the present state of affairs, to accept such an arrangement, or if they did, there was no one, after former experience, who could trust His Majesty."[63] On April 21, Wyse informed the Foreign Office that the king of Greece ignored the advice not only of the Allied Powers but also of the Germanic Powers and "still insists on believing the Russian promises."[64] Otho was not so much sold on Russian promises, however, as he was on the *Megali Idea*. At one point after the Greek-Turkish break of relations he wanted to lead an expedition to Thessaly and to proceed on with an army to Constantinople. He was persuaded, however, not to carry out such a mission by his ministers, especially by Pelikas and Provelgios.[65] Under such leadership it was inevitable that an occupation was the next calamity that Greece would suffer.

C. The Occupation of Greece

On April 9, the four European Powers—England, France, Austria and Prussia—signed a protocol at Vienna laying down the measures to be taken concerning Greece.[66] There was disagreement between the French foreign minister and Clarendon as to how the occupation of Greece should be handled. Drouyn de Lhuys feared that a blockade at Piraeus such as that of 1850 would create panic and chaos in the mainland whereas a blockade in Thessaly and Epirus was more practical under the circumstances sicne there were the areas of trouble. Clarendon opposed this proposition because he feared that an Anglo-French blockade in Epirus and Thessaly would stimulate more uprisings which could possibly spread as far as Constantinople.[67]

The Germanic Powers on the other hand which were sympathetic to Otho and were deeply concerned about the effects an occupation would have on his throne voiced their opinions against both Clarendon's and Drouyn de Lhuys' plans of occupation. Franz Josef wrote to Maximilian:

> I will willingly give you the promise that, whatever results tue war might have, I would not permit any agreement which would be

against the continued existence of the kingdom of Greece under the Bavarian Dynasty. I would even enlist my good services with England and France so that these Powers could express their opinions and act accordingly. I would look upon it as a political advantage, if Greece were to find her supporters in the Germanic Powers.[68]

Otho was fortunate in that he still had some protection for this throne from the Germanic Powers. As he was aware of this he acted as the absolute monarch which he was from 1837 to 1843. On May 2, he ordered the chambers closed by royal ordinance. Pelikas immediately protested this act. Other politicians also protested for they felt that at times of crisis, as the one Greece was suffering, there was a need to maintain the Chambers in session.[69] The king argued that the government was in need of funds so he thought that by closing the chambers he would save money from the salaries of senators. The reason behind Otho's act however, was the fear that "the senate might take some hostile act leading to the fall of the Cabinet."[70]

The Allied Powers (France and England) decided to use the payments due by Greece to the Protecting Powers for the guaranteed loan as an excuse to justify legally their occupation of Greece. Wyse addressed a note to the Greek government on May 10 stating that:

Her Majesty's Government will no longer allow the revenues of Greece, the first proceeds of which should by Treaty be appropriated to the payment of the charges of the Greek loans, to be diverted from that object and applied to the promotion of schemes in the interest of a Power with which they are at war; and that if it persists in its present misguided policy the Greek Government must not surprised if measures are taken by England and France . . . to control the receipts and expenditures of the Greek ex-chequer, and to deprive the Greek Government of these pecuniary resources which are so wantonly misapplied.[71]

Rouen sent a similar note to Paicos stating the rights of French interference in Greek Affairs since Greece had not been capable of discharging her obligations to the French government.[72] Drouyn de Lhuys was even more severe with the Greek government than Clarendon. He warned Paicos that Greek war ships should not sail in the open sea, and if any of them violated this warning they would be subject to confiscation by French naval forces.[73]

On May 13, French and British war ships entered the port of Piraeus. The next day Wyse and Rouen sent an ultimatum to the Greek government. When Otho realized that his throne was at stake he gave up his current policy and publicly declared the neutrality of Greece in the conflict between the Allied Powers and Russia.[74] All the advice and warnings from the European leaders concerning a possible Anglo-French occupation in the event Greece antagonized Turkey were insufficient to persuade the king to change his policy. He was so blinded by the enthusiasm of the *Megali Idea* that only a foreign invasion could make him realize the stupidity of his foreign policy. As a result of the irresponsible conduct of the Greek monarch and of the British and French who were ready to occupy any country that would stand in the way of their political, economic and strategic interests, the people of "little Greece" suffered a three-year long invasion.

With the declaration of neutrality came the fall of the pro-Russian ministry as the Allied Powers had wished and Alexander Mavrokordatos was summoned by the king on May 16, to form a new ministry.[75] The new administration announced shortly after it took power the position of Greece in relation to the Western European Powers:

We feel the dreadful position of Greece in which the nation's matters are found. Commerce was eliminated from the hands of thousands of businessmen, navigation was condemned to idleness, and other dangers threatened the nation, abandoned to the disfavor of the Great Powers. . . . His Majesty our King, respecting in his fatherly concern these sufferings and dangers he consented to the two naval Powers, England and France, complete neutrality because from this the dangers are prevented and the benefits, we were being deprived of, are being recovered. We respect as no one else the kind sympathy of the Greeks for our brothers in whose fortune are concerned the Great Powers.[76]

The new cabinet was made up of members of the "English" and "French" parties who were against the policy of expansionsim and were not puppets of the crown as were previous ministers ever since Kolettes. As a result of the change of ministry, and of course the Anglo-French occupation, the king's power was substantially diminished. If it was not for the powerful influence of the Germanic Powers who had not yet committed themselves in the Crimean War,[77] the king of Greece would have been forced to abdicate.

Baron de Thile received instructions from his government to protect the king's rights against any possible abuses of the Occupying Powers.[78] The King of Prussia was very disappointed to hear of the Anglo-French occupation of Greece and was mostly worried about Otho's future when he wrote to Maximilian that the kingdom of Greece was dearly regarded by him. Otho's father, Ludwig, further wrote that he opposed the sinister plans of the Protecting Powers with regards to Greece and that their recent occupation was illegal and would never be recognized by his kingdom. He noted that:

> A state which has been brought into existence by Three should be devasted by Two, that the creation of the Three shall be accepted and represented in the European family of States. In the same way "we" will only recognize the disintegration of the state of Hellas by the general decision of all. European Monarchs: but we can guarantee immediately that we shall not recognize such a beginning. This is my proposal.[79]

Even though Otho still had the German support, the occupying forces made his position very difficult in the realm. He began retreating to the wishes of Wyse and Rouen on matters of policy and government personnel. One of the matters in which the two representatives of England and France came to sharp opposition with the king of Greece was about the appointment of General Kalergis as Minister of War. Kalergis was exiled[80] to England where he had met Napoleon III and had become a very close friend of his. When the occupation began Kalergis, as well as the other members of the Ministerial Council, was forced upon the king. At first Wyse objected to the Kalergis appointment because he feared that the General was a radical pro-"French" politician and could present problems to the British interests in Greece. Rouen, however, insisted that Kalergis be retained in the ministry and the French minister's wish prevailed.[81]

The removal of the king's pro-Russian advisors was another desired goal of Wyse and Rouen which was achieved with the occupation.[82]

> Before the ministry would accept office they required the retirement of General Spiro Millos, General Mamouris, General Gardiakotti Grivas and General Kolokotroni, Grand Marechal, from their post of aides de camp to His Majesty. This post is more than honorary in this country. It allows continual and easy access to the royal ear; these generals have been recently charged with the special task of

supporting the insurrection and generals, Spiro Millos, Mamouris and Kolokotronis, have been the zealous and unscrupulous abettors and chief leaders under Russian auspices of the whole intrigue.[83]

Kalergis was instrumental in many schemes to degrade Otho for reasons of revenge and for political reasons as well. As long as he had the French Legation's support, he was ready to display his powers with unlimited selfishness and disregard for the humiliation of Greece which the Occupying Powers were responsible for and he was an instrument of thier plans. "The conspicuous role," writes Donta, "which the French dramatized with Rouen as its leader, allowed Kalergis, since Mavrokordatos had not yet arrived from Paris, to become, in the protection of the French, all powerful."[84] The king and Greece itself were further humiliated by the continuous displays of French military strength which Admiral Tinan,[85] head of French occupation forces, was so anxious to parade in the streets of Athens and even in front of the gates of Otho's palace.[86]

Such abuses by the French and General Kalergis forced Otho to call quickly for Mavrokordatos' return to Athens. The new administration had been declared in the middle of May but the new prime minister was not in Greece to lead the government. After he received a letter from the king on May 27, requesting that he form and lead the new ministry,[87] Mavrokordatos responded that he preferred to serve as ambassador to Paris. The reason for the decline of the king's request by the minister was that he wanted to be certain that Otho understood clearly that there would be no pro-French favoritism played by Mavrokordatos, and he further wished to clarify the king's position toward the future government of Greece.[88] The king wrote to Mavrokordatos once again persuading him to return to Athens by the middle of July.[89]

The new Prime Minister was sworn-in on the moring of July 29, and took over the Ministry of Foreign Affairs, held by Argyropoulos who became Minister of Finance, since May 16. Otho assured the new prime minister of the cooperation of the court in both domestic and foreign affairs,[90] so there were no problems to be expected since no antagonism between court and government would exist. Otho, however, was used to being an absolute ruler and his sense of the word "cooperation" did not mean subordination to the Occupying Powers, as Rouen and Wyse thought.

Before Mavrokordatos was sworn-in he met with the representatives of the Allied Powers on July 23 to discuss what they thought "ought to

be the policy of the government before he formally accepted office."[91]
The king was informed by Mavrokordatos that it was his intention to
schedule such a meeting with Rouen and Wyse and Otho had approved,
but not without expressing his discontent with both representatives.
Rouen wrote to Drouyn de Lhuys that, "the king's insistence in forcing
the new ministers to protest against the Anglo-French occupation, had
produced a very bad impression on public opinion and he had given
reasons concerning the steady willingness of this Prince to keep his
promises opposite France and England."[92] Wyse also wrote to his government that Rouen denied that there were any grounds for the impressions
which had taken possession of the king. He also maintained that the
policy carried out by both the French and British Legations in Athens
was straight forward and could be summarized in two categories, (A)
the observence of Greek neutrality and (B) a radical political change
in system for the future. Wyse went on to write:

> With regard to the second object we held in view, a radical change
> of the whole system. . . . There was no one department of govern-
> ment which did not need the largest and most sweeping reforms.
> Each of these would in turn demand and receive his most careful
> attention. Elections were to be made free, finance rescued from
> ruin, corruption repressed, good faith and national credit restored.
> In seconding all these desirable ameliorations, our two governments
> had but one policy, as one purpose, the permanent happiness and
> security of Greece.[93]

If one reads beyond all the fine things Wyse and Rouen had in mind for
Greece, it is obvious that political and financial control were the objectives strived for by both France and England. The Occupying Powers
were promising freedom from the bonds of absolutism, the restoration
of the principles of the constitution and stability, economic and political,
for Greece while their naval forces occupied Greece thus denying her
independence. Futhermore, Wyse and Rouen, wished to eliminate the
powers of the king and give those powers not to the people of Greece
but to their respective countries. What is worse than the hypocrisy of
the Occupying Powers is the fact that the Greeks believed in the myth
that the Protecting Powers would really help their nation to achieve its
goals, whether they would be national expansion, as in the case of the
"Russian" party, internal reform as was the case with the "English"

party or both as the followers of the "French" party believed. The Greeks in any case were the ones deceived.

One of the immediate concerns of the Allied Powers was the restoration of Greek-Turkish relations and the end of all traces of the revolution in the provinces. In order to be successful in their task the complete co-operation of the court and government were essential. Monsieur Guerin, French consul at Syra, was selected by Rouen to represent France in Lamia where negotiations were to open in order to end hostilities and restore relations between Greece and the Sublime Porte. Merlin, vice consul at Athens, was the British representative and Colonel Pakenor represented the Greeks.[94] The Greek ministry and especially General Kalergis worked with the British and French representatives to insure the end of the insurrection and the end of brigandage so further hostil-ities with the Porte might be prevented. Most of the chiefs of the Greek insurrectionary bands were out of Turkish territory by the middle of June.[95] Rouen reported to the Quai d'Orsay on June 7, that:

> Theodore Grivas, Tsalellas, Ragos and a great number of officers returned to Greece already, in order to declare submission to the government. Epirus may regard such time as very peaceable. The defeat of the Greeks in Skoulikargia provoked the last blow in the revolution of that Province.[96]

Grivas, as well as other leaders of the insurrection promised to support the new ministry even though it was in fact a "ministry of occupation."[97] One of the immediate consequences of the Anglo-French occupation was the political division created among politicians as well as the public. There was a sharp division between those who supported the Anglo-French intervention in Greece and those who were Russian supporters. The division was even sharper when the king became the spokesman against the Anglo-French occupation and Kalergis the spokesman of the occupying forces. In June the Minister of War went so far as to defend the foreign troops to a group of Greek army officers who had been out-spoken about the abuses of the French in Piraeus and in Athens.[98]

Public opinion was an important concern of both Wyse and Rouen. In the beginning of the occupation Wyse believed that the people of Greece were thrilled to see foreign troops on their soil.[99] By the middle of August, however, he was very concerned about the rising of anti-French and anti-British attitudes among the Greeks. Wyse was convinced that the attacks of the Greek press against the foreign troops at Piraeus were in the interest of the Russians and the "Russian" party as well as the Camarilla. He wrote to Clarendon that there was little that he and Rouen could do to control the slanderous remarks of the press because it had the support of the entire government behind it. He went on to write that:

> The chief of these organs here are the *Aion* and the *Elpis*; the *Aion* the old supporter of Russian policy and proceedings and now of the Court; and the *Elpis* the newly stipended advocate of the same party, at times repeating in its columns the very language of the Palace, and even of the Queen.[100]

Wyse was correct in maintaining that the press shared the nationalism of the court and the "Russian" party but it also reflected the nationalist sentiments of the public which wished nothing more than the defeat of Turkey and her Western Allies who were occupying Greek soil.

Besides the blow to their independence shattered by the Powers who helped to create the nation of Greece, the occupied subjects fell victims to a physical disaster brought by the occupation forces. One of the worst cases of cholera ever to hit Greece was responsible for the lives of thousands in a very short period. A French ship carrying soldiers from the Crimea came to the port of Piraeus in early June. A number of men carrying the deadly disease were taken off the ship to be hospitalized in a temporary hospital set up by the occupying forces. This was the beginning of a disaster which claimed, it is estimated, seven thousand lives in Piraeus and thirty thousand in Athens.[101] A panic hit the country as people began leaving their property and loved ones to escape death. In Piraeus only sixty families were left after a few days of the spreading of the disease. Dragoumes who was fortunate to live through this catastrophe describes it in the following manner:

> After a short while the streets were converted to deserts, the working shops shut down, inside the houses all voices were morbid and the town from one end to the other became quiet from the infinite lack of people; only the sound of your own footsteps ascended to your spine and it roused your fright. Here and there you'd meet a man slow-walking alone with a face of wonder and lividness. . . . Laws, police, hospitals, doctors, everything and everyone had been paralyzed by fear and death.[102]

The disease spread as far as the islands when many people who carried it tried to escape the horror of Athens and Piraeus before they died.[103] Due to the cholera the occupying forces asked to be allowed to relocate at Patesia (an area outside Athens which was not contaminated), but their request was flatly denied by the Prime Minister who threatened to resign if the Anglo-French troops relocated.[104]

Mavrokordatos was only trying to prevent the disease from spreading any more than it already had, but apparently his denial to the forces' removal was received in bad faith by the French Admiral de Tinan. The Admiral chose to create a major incident and once again displayed his authority to the devastated Greek nation. When the Minister of Justice, P. Bargoles, recalled the alternate district attorneys of Patras and Nauplia and proceeded to promote the Justice of the Peace of Piraeus, Admiral de Tinan accused the minister of being a Russophile and even threatened him personally that action would be taken to have him removed from office. In view of such direct intervention by officials of the Occupying Powers in the affairs of the Greek state, Mavrokordatos could only vigorously protest to Wyse and Rouen and insist for an immediate settlement. Realizing the impact such an affair could have on the public mind and the European community after the press picked it up, the two representatives settled it immediately.[105] Direct and indirect intervention in Greek state affairs by the Allied Powers was what Greece could expect under the circumstances. It was the price that Greece had to pay for the foolishness of a nationalist-expanionist foreign policy pursued by an irresponsible monarch and a pro-Russian and royalist cabinet.

D. Restoration of Greek-Turkish Relations and the Treaty of Kalinja

The occupation of Greece by the two Western Protecting Powers was illegal for it violated the treaty of 1832 which guaranteed Greece its independence. Just as the British blockade of 1850 was illegal because France and Russia had not been informed of it until after it took place, similarly the 1854 Anglo-French occupation was illegal because Russia, the third Protecting Power, did not consent to the actions of the other two Powers.

For most Greeks as well as those sympathetic to Greece it was expected that the occupation like the blockade would be a temporary affair, but more than eight months had passed since the Anglo-French naval forces landed in Piraeus and there was no sign that they would be leaving. In an attempt to justify the continuing occupation of Greece, Wyse wrote the following dispatch to the Foreign Minister of Great Britain:

> The "occupation" was designed to secure Turkey from lawless aggression, and to establish good government in Greece. The Frontier is tranquil, but good government has only commenced. The most important organic laws, respecting Electoral and Municipal Reforms, the Regulation of the Press, the liberalizing of the tariff, the reorganization of Education, the reconstruction of the army, the ensuring the independence and purity of the bench, the revival of Commerce, the development of Industry, the re-establishment of friendly relations, based on commercial and extradition treaties, with Turkey, have all to pass. The purification of every Department of Administration from the corruption and incapacity in which the old system had flung them, has to be effected.[106]

If the facts supported these claims of the British minister perhaps the Greek historians would regard the period of the occupation as one of the greatest in Modern Greece. But how can any "occupation" of one nation by another, no matter what the good intentions of the Occupying Powers are, be beneficiary to the occupied people when it is a recognized fact by all those politically conscious that the first guiding principle of all nations is their own national self-interests. In spite of Wyse's theoretical jargon which was only intended, as was pointed out above, to justify an occupation of a helpless country, the issue of immediate concern to both ministers of the Allied Powers in Greece was the restoration of Greek-Turkish relations. The occupying forces would never leave Piraeus if relations between Greece and Turkey remained broken. In an interview which took place at St. Cloud between the Emperor Napoleon III and Mavrokordatos before the latter became prime minister, Napoleon expressed his determination to have Greece observe neutrality towards Turkey. He told Mavrokordatos that the king of Greece and the government must reestablish relations with the Porte otherwise, if the king intended to adopt another conduct, "he (Napoleon) should not only retain the force of 5,000 men now in Greece but if necessary increase it to 10,000 or even 20,000, until it was sufficient to accomplish this object."[107] The restoration of relations with Turkey was Mavrokordatos' goal who believed that Greek expansion was a dream for the present and a policy only for the future.

Early in August the Prime Minister took the first steps to open negotiations with the Sultan's government. He communicated with Lord Stratford de Redcliffe and proposed to send M. Barozzi, ex-consul at Adrianople, to represent Greece in Constantinople.[108] During this time Mavrokordatos also took measures to end brigandage on the Greek-Turkish frontiers realizing that the presence of this element in Greece presented a threat to the Ottoman Empire and could affect the Greek government's attempts to restore relations with Turkey. Furthermore, the new administration made efforts to restore Ottoman property plundered by the insurgents.[109]

In the first conference which was held at Constantinople between the representatives of England, France, Greece and Turkey, the Porte expressed its enthusiasm with the Mavrokordatos government and was pleased with his proposal of a commercial treaty between Greece and Turkey. Reshid Pasha, the Turkish representative at the conference, however, continued to press for "the recognition for the principle of indemnity," which meant that an already economically weak Greece would have to pay for damages it never committed directly since it never declared war on Turkey.[110] Stratford de Redcliffe, who was just as anxious as Napoleon and Mavrokordatos to have Greek-Turkish relations normalized again, was more concerned with the security of the Greek-Turkish frontiers than anythings else for he feared that the threat of a nationalist revolt could change the character of the Eastern Question. The Greeks on the other hand hoped to gain in commercial and navigation benefits from the Treaty. So the problem was to draw up such a compromise settlement which would satisfy all parties involved. Stratford wrote to Wyse on this matter that:

> It is essential to have the bases of the commercial treaty in a more intelligible and definite form. Turkey is securing to Greece the advantages desirable from commerce and navigation with the Imperial territories is entitled to have its tranquility guaranteed on the score of abuses in protection, and other matters of intercommunication between the two countries so delicately circumstanced towards each other.[111]

Stratford de Redcliffe accused Mavrokordatos of delaying the conclusion of the Treaty by not conforming to the stated wishes of the Porte, namely, the guarantees of security and the principle of indemnity.[112] By early December the Greek Prime Minister was persuaded by Rouen and Wyse to meet the demands of the Porte so that the treaty could be worked out.[113]

One of the major objections which the Greek government has concerning the procedures for the treaty negotiations before the substance of the treaty began to be negotiated was the demand of the Sublime Porte that Mavrokordatos should send to Constantinople an Envoy Extraordinary who was to beg pardon on behalf of the king of Greece, for what had happened in Epirus, Thessaly and Chalcidice. This seemed an outrageous demand to the Greek Court as well as to many supporters of Otho who felt that by fulfilling such a demand Greece would be admitting the king's involvement in the revolution. It was not only a humiliating act against the king but also against the honor of the Greek nation.

Immediately the Greek press attacked the Porte and its Allies for making such a demand on an occupied country. The following article was published in *Elpis* (Hope) in early January:

> That neither Mr. Mavrokordatos, nor any other minister of Greece will ever consent to such humiliation, is to us quite certain. We are only sorry to see that Mr. Mavrokordatos, who has sufficient perspicacity, did not long ago forsee that which we so long repeated; that as long as the war shall continue between the Western Powers and Russia, the reestablishment of our relations is an idle fancy. Since the Governments interested, in order to justify before the public opinion of Europe the measures taken against Greece, qualified the last struggle of the Christians in Turkey and the part which Greece took therein, as a Russian movement; . . . the hatred against Russia, inspired by Belligerent Powers, as well as those who remain neutral with the desire of humiliating her, and originated also the idea, that every Greek was a spy of Russia.[114]

Mavrokordatos' position was that of the middle man who was continuously pressured by Rouen and Wyse on the one hand and Otho on the other to carry out contradictory policies.

At the beginning of his appointment the Prime Minister seemed to please the king because he checked the power of Kalergis. Otho believed that Mavrokordatos would not be the sort of puppet to Wyse and Rouen that Kalergis was and, furthermore, the kng was convinced that the new Prime Minister would be devoted to the Crown. The good relationship that existed between the king and Mavrokordatos in July was replaced by antagonism in September. The reason for this, primarily, was the fact that the French and British representatives' pressure in Athens kept the new administration as far from the king's influence as possible. In a letter to Franz Josef, Otho complained that he had entrusted his Prime Minister the full cooperation of the Court but as he put it:

> Mavrokordatos was not able though until today to live up to my hopes, with which we supported him . . . . The foreign intervention in the internal affairs of the country which is based on the strength of the foreign forces stationed near the capital, prevent him in his actions . . . . I beg you then, as is the interest of the independence of Greece, that you take a stand and declare, that it is time to finally put an end to the occupation.[115]

Opposition to Mavrokordatos came not only from the king but from faithful ministers to the king whose devotion to Otho exceeded their devotion to their parties. Riga Palamides, Minister of the Interior, and Christides, Minister of Finance, were two of the most prominent political figures who turned against the prime minister, thereby, creating a schism within the administration. Consequently, the polarization of the two opposing forces, the Anglo-French on the one side and the royalists on the other, was becoming greater and the power of Mavrokordatos was diminishing.

On December 12, Riga Palamides wrote a letter to Fuad Pasha cautioning him and his government against the intentions of the Greek Prime Minister who happened to be a Phanariot.[116] He warned Fuad Pasha that Mavrokordatos should not be trusted in so far as the negotiations for the restoration of Greek-Turkish conflict were concerned.[117] When the British representative in Athens discovered that Palamides had warned Fuad Pasha about Mavrokordatos' intentions and that Christides in collaboration with the Minister of the Interior were waging war on the Prime Minister he felt that the entire affair was the scheme of the Crown. He wrote to Clarendon that:

> Mr. Christides' opinions are well known, and his late alliance with Riga Palamides and Gardiakotte Grivas is based on the hopes of giving them early effect. He would not venture on such a course, however, without the countenance of the Court, no more than the Court would show such countenance, unless they witnessed the

intimacy of M. Christides with the French Legation, and entertained the presumption, that no control had been exercised over
his designs, or such control had been in vain.[118]

The Mavrokordatos administration was made up of politicians affiliated
with both "French" and "English" parties and because the occupying
forces had one policy in the Near East it was assumed that these two
parties would hold the same. Even though this assumption holds true to
a large extent for the consensus on the foreign policy of the Mavrokordatos ministry, the same did not hold true for any other measure.
Furthermore, Mavrokordatos was a member of the "English" party
which those who belonged to the "French" had traditionally opposed.
But the feuds that were developing among the members of the ministry
were not due simply to party differences but to basic differences between
support of the Crown which to many meant support of Greece or support
of the Occupying Forces. And it was primarily the king who was behind
such a movement, for the obvious reasons, and not as much the French
Legation as Wyse emphasized.

Palamides and Christides charged that Mavrokordatos and the Allied
Powers were responsible for stalling the treaty with the Porte and by so
doing were responsible for the economic loss suffered by the Greek
commerce and navigation.[119] Barozze, however, gained the confidence
of the representatives of England, France and Turkey in Constantinople
and he made considerable progress in the negotiations.[120] By early May
the Greek Court and the two Western Powers agreed to a large extent
on the terms of the treaty between Greece and the Ottoman Empire.
Upon the advice of France and England, Andreas Koundouriotes was
appointed Minister to Constantinople and Riza-Halel Bey, Minister to
Athens. The treaty, which took almost a year to be worked out, was
signed at Kalinja on May 27, 1855, by Koundouriotes and Fuad Pasha.
The title of the treaty was "Treaty of Commerce and Navigation between
the Kingdom of Greece and the Ottoman Empire" and some of the key
articles in it are listed below:

Article I. "The subjects of His Majesty the King of Greece and thos of
His Imperial Majesty, the Sultan, can in each of the two States, exercise
reciprocally commerce by land and by sea, with total freedom and security."

Article II. "The subjects of each party in the contract will be exempt in the state of the other from all conscription and from all military service on land or sea, of whatever nature it may be."

Article IV. "The merchant ships, of the two High parties contracted, whether they are empty or carrying a cargo of merchandise or other articles of whatever type will navigate in complete freedom and security, under their own flag in the seas and waters of either country."

Article VIII. "The war vessels of each Power which meet ships belonging to the merchant marine of the other, will allow these to freely continue their route and even aid them in case of need."

Article XII. "The subjects of one and the other Power can freely buy and trade in any part of the two respective states merchandise bought from foreign countries without being subject to various dues. . . ."

Article XIX. "It is agreed that no war ships can provide and arm in the ports and the shores of either of the high contracted parties."[121]

This treaty which normalized commercial and navigational relations between the Porte and Greece lasted until 1897 when Greece made another attempt to bring the *Megali Idea* into reality,[122] and after the resolution of that conflict it was modified and it lasted until 1923.[123]

France and England, and especially Stratford, believed that they had achieved a major diplomatic victory by the negotiation of and success of this treaty and Stratford wrote to the Greek Prime Minister after the treaty was signed to express his satisfaction with its results.[124] Greece was also pleased with the establishment of the treaty. On June 8, the Chamber of Deputies and the Senate passed the treaty and issued it henceforth as a law of the nation.[125]

Wyse felt that the Treaty placed the relations of Greece "with Turkey, on a far surer and clearer foundation, than they were before and . . . it will much facilitate, it is to be hoped, for the future, the maintainance of peace and order between the two countries."[126] The people who benefited most were those in commerce for during the year of disrupted relations with Turkey they suffered greatly and as a result the Greek economy also deteriorated considerably. As Wyse remarked in a note appraising the Treaty:

> Its (the Treaty's) immediate results to the commercial interests of this country are incalculable. Mr. Consul Wilkinson states it to me, to be his conviction that had the state of interruption and exclusion, consequent on the breaking up of diplomatic relations between Greece and Turkey been allowed to continue, it necessarily would have been had not overtures for the present Treaty been made through this Legation and the Embassy in Constantinople, there is little doubt, that Greek commerce would have suffered a distrubance very little different from general bankruptch and ruin.[127]

In spite of the general approval and enthusiasm concerning the Treaty there was some opposition by the press under the control of Riga Palamides, C. Levides, Soutso and Christides, all well known royalists who were opposed to Mavrokordatos and the Anglo-French attempts to restore Greek-Turkish relations.[128] Otho and his followers did not care so much about the fact that the economy of Greece benefited from the Treaty as they could only see that the Treaty was the result of Anglo-French collaboration with Mavrokordatos, and the Sublime Porte representing the defeat of the court's foreign policy.

CHAPTER FIVE

THE PROLONGED OCCUPATION, 1854-1857

A. Otho's Expansionist Foreign Policy After the Declaration of Neutrality

One of the questions which scholars of modern Greek history and the Eastern Question are concerned with is the long and illegal Franco-British occupation of Greece. Why did the Anglo-French naval forces stay in Greece almost a year after the Treaty of Paris was signed? What was the purpose behind the prolonged occupation? It is clear why troops had to be sent to Greece in May 1854 but the question of why these troops stayed there for such a long period of time has not been dealt with in detail by historians. To answer these questions the factors of economic and political control of Greece by the Western Powers as well as the persistent expansionist, pro-Russian in many respects, foreign policy of Otho will be examined in this final chapter.[1]

Otho's foreign policy was responsible for the occupation of 1854 and its devastating economic, political and social consequences. Yet some of the most prominent Greek historians have vigorously defended that foreign policy. Kyriakides writes the following:

> The policy of Otho was the national policy, undoubtedly then it was the duty of the Greek people to observe this stand, which he observed; if it was not benefited, it it was harmful, this is irrelevant; its stand, its past, its history, this was the policy sketched and this was what King had to follow having in conscience his national mission.[2]

Another historian eulogizes the policy of the Greek Court in the following manner:

> This policy not rightfully, was characterized as exclusively dynastic policy. It was a policy which the people wanted. . . . As much as it looked Russian on the surface as from the facts that policy, the responsibility from which the Crown courageously resumed, was Greek policy.[3]

Another Greek historian who favored the policy of the Court characterized the Queen as brave and patriotic and sympathized with the difficult problems facing Otho and Amalia. According to Filaretos, the king and queen were determined "in the fulfillment of the country's duty."[4]

Undoubtedly nationalist and royalist favoritism has prevailed in the interpretations of these historians at the expense of historical objectivity. But for the sake of this so-called "historical objectivity"when such motives as nationalism and royalism are set aside, the policy of the Greek Court turns out to be very unrealistic and harmful, in the light of the deplorable condition of the Greek nation and also the Near Eastern policy of the Western Powers.

Otho and Amalia vainly pursued a dream of expansionism since the Kolettes administration reintroduced the *Megali Idea* to the Greek people. The king and queen sought the opportunity since the Mousouros Incident to antagonize the Ottoman Empire and to have an open conflict with the Turks in the hope of gaining the Turkish provinces north of the Greek frontier. During the Holy Places controversy the Greek Court prepared the people through its propaganda to be ready to face the Turkish enemy in war. And before the Menshikov Mission had finally been declared a failure Otho had started supporting the insurrection in the provinces of Thessaly and Epirus.

The foreign policy of the *Megali Idea* which began as a dream for Otho and Amalia during the Kolettes administration was on its way to becoming a reality in 1853, at least as far as many Greeks were concerned. It was clearly a deception, however, for the king and many government officials to believe that Greece could expand its frontiers when the Great Powers were all against such a measure. One wonders, therefore, if it was wise of Otho and Amalia to risk the destructive consequences of an Anglo-French occupation, which lasted from May 1854 to February 1857, for a dream that could never come true under the circumstances of 1854. It was a greater wonder, however, that the royal couple pursued the dream of expansion even after Greece was occupied by the foreign forces. Indeed, it was true that the Greek Court never changed the foreign policy which was handed to it by Kolettes, until the force of the Occupying Powers fell so great upon Greece as to make certain that the policy of expansionism would not be repeated.

A few days after the king announced the neutrality of Greece in the Crimean War the British Legation in Athens informed the Foreign Office of secret Court support to the insurgents. Wyse wrote to Clarendon concerning the king's covert attempts to continue the insurrection.

> At Athens cart loads of powder and other ammunition continued to be conveyed with secrecy, for the purpose of being formed into cartridges to the different stores. At the Piraeus, a considerable quantity of powder was transmitted to the government magazine store there by superior orders for the purpose, it would seem, of being embarked covertly...On the 25th inst. a body of 300 armed volunteers were collected together at Argos by the Deputy of that place, who had received 20,000 drachmas from Athens for the purpose, and a short time afterwards they started for the Frontier.[5]

This report of the British Legation in Athens indicated that the king and a great number of sympathizers of the insurrection were determined to continue the struggle against the Turks even after the king's official declaration of Greek neutrality. Otho never really made the transition from the expansionist policy to a course which called for internal development and economic growth. Rouen reported to his government after the occupation took place that the king had not accepted the full implications of his neutrality declaration and that Otho wished to present his position in the European community as a victim of the Occupying Powers.[6] Wyse also hinted the same thing to Clarendon when he wrote that if Otho had accepted the terms of neutrality he would not have objections to the changes of his Russophile advisors who were all connected with the developments of the insurrection.[7] Such an attitude of the king gave cause to the Allied Powers to suspect Otho of Russophilism and as long as such suspicions existed and the Crimean War continued there was no chance that the occupation of Piraeus would be ended.

Only two weeks after the declaration of neutrality, Otho wrote to his father:

> I would prefer undoubtedly instead of retreating in the supremacy of force, to attack Turkey and with bravity (*palikaria*) to bring through and to win the goal, which I designed. . . .I retreat with difficulty when the cession of a certain thing is attempted with impudence and with repression.[8]

The king meant every word he wrote. Incidents which revealed his support to the *Megali Idea* policy occurred almost as soon as the Allied Forces had landed on Piraeus.

On June 25, a senator and a doctor by the name of Tasseos left Piraeus with ammunition and money in order to renew the aggression in Pelio, a village in the province of Thessaly. Tasseos was captured by a French agent, however, before he reached his destination.[9] According to the intelligence information of the British Legation in Athens:

> This attempt has been got up at the instigation of the "Russian" and Court party here, that it has been aided by funds and ammunition supplied by them, that among the chief agents in the matter are not only persons directly connected with the late administration, but also persons at this moment in the immediate service of His Majesty and in constant communication with him, and that a portion of these funds was supplied by the Directors of the National Bank.[10]

After the Tasseos incident it was discovered that the queen of Greece was personally involved in a scheme concerning another insurrection to take place in Crete. Apparently, Amalia had received 140,000 roubles from Russia for the purpose of exciting an uprising in Crete. Various individuals in Greece who shared the dream of national expansion with the Court gave another 70,000 drachmas to the Queen. A group of three hundred Cretans then assembled outside of Athens ready to depart for Crete at about the same time that a new ministry was forming.[11] The insurrection never took place in Crete because General Kalergis who was supposedly sent to Paris in order to bring back arms for the Cretans did not return to the island with the ammunition. Even though nothing became of the queen's attempt to start a Cretan insurrection, it did not help the position of Greece at all because the Allied intelligence found out about the scheme.

The Occupying Powers' concern was not limited to the expansionist plans of Otho and Amalia but extended to the press propaganda, to the political groups which were pro-Russian and wanted to see a Greater Greece, and to the various Hetairias (secret organizations) whose goal was to free all the Greeks from the Ottoman Empire by raising money, arms and recruiting volunteers. Both Wyse and Rouen knew that the insurrection had public support and both representatives felt that their job was to prevent any further excitment among the public which could lead to renewed Greek-Turkish hostilities.

There were two means through which a great deal of propaganda against the Turks was carried out. The first was the press which continuously attacked the Allied Powers for illegally occupying Greece while at the same time it supported the king and the insurrection. The second was the local government officials who by virtue of their position had an enormous influence on the public mind. Most government officials throughout Greece were appointed before the Mavrokordatos ministry of 1854 and they were pro-Russian. So even though the central government had changed, the majority of government officials had remained the same and they continued to propagate war against Turkey even after May 1854.

The two papers which engaged in editorial attacks against the occupying powers and were both sympathetic to Russia and to Otho were the *Aion* and *Elpis*.[12] By the middle of August, after the cholera had broken out, these two papers were waging such a verbal war on the Occupying Powers that Rouen demanded that Mavrokordatos take positive action against the editors responsible. Mavrokordatos was not at liberty to carry out every demand the French and British representatives had to make for he had the force of the Crown checking his powers constantly.[13] As a result of the Prime Minister's failure to act upon the command of the French minister, a group of forty men were sent from Piraeus to Athens on September 21, by the order of Admiral Tinan to smash the printing presses of the *Aion*, close the office of *Elpis* and place under arrest the ˏeditors of the two newspapers, John Philimon and Constantine Levides.[14] Wyse maintained and, undoubtedly, so did Rouen that:

> The real object (of the press) was to establish such a state of opinion and feeling in the Provinces and especially in the frontier, as regarded both Russian and Western Powers, no matter by what means, as should render it practicable the first opportunity to resume the late system of excitement and aggression, and furnish them with minds and men as well as funds and ammunition, entirely for the invasion of the Turkish Provinces.[15]

There was a certain element of truth in this observation but it was no justification to destroy the property of the Greek newspapers and to illegally arrest the two editors. The violation of Greek independence first occurred in May by the Anglo-French invasion of Greece. Then private property violations in Greece by foreign troops and finally the violation of the citizen's freedom guaranteed by the constitution was executed all in the name of the national interests of the Occupying Powers.

The French and the British felt that by the destruction of the opposition press they could win over public opinion to their side but as in the case of the 1850 British blockade this did not happen. Instead, the people turned Russophile more than ever before[16] and this only increased Wyse's and Rouen's irritation. It seemed that the germ of Russophilism which began to spread ever since 1850 kept spreading beyond control and one of the reasons for this, besides the course of events and the press propaganda, was the influence on the public mind which the local government authorities exercised.

The government authorities and most people who sympathized with the insurgents believed that the Anglo-French occupation as well as the Mavrokordatos ministry, which was publicly known as the "Ministry of occupation," were only temporary. Many Greeks thought that since the blockade of 1850 did not last long by the same token the occupation of 1854 would be terminated quickly. As Wyse informed his government in early September:

> The authorities, mostly placed in their situation by a pro-Russian Ministry, are still nourished with the false hope that all present men and measures are temporary, that the incursions on Turkey are only suspended, that the German Powers will compell, at least by diplomacy the two Allied Powers to withdraw their troops from Greece, that the King thus free from further control, will once more resume his ancient Counsellors, with whom he has never ceased to communicate and that the "status quo ante" will be reestablished triumphantly and without difficulty.[17]

This line of thought was also shared by Rouen and both representatives of the Occupying Powers were pressing Mavrokordatos to adopt strict measures against Russophilism. The Prime Minister could not do so in the open and directly because to fight Russophilism would mean attacking the Court and the king himself. He came to the point where he could no longer be torn by the two forces of the Western Powers on the one side and the Court on the other, so he threatened to resign if he was not left alone to run the government his own way.[18]

In a personal visit to the Prime Minister by Wyse and Rouen, the two representatives listed a number of complaints, all tied to the issue of Russophilism and the government's failure to repress it. Mavrokordatos told the two ministers that:

> He was occupied in devising remedy to the evil, (spread of Russophilism) by a change in the Municipal Law itself, but until this could be brought to bear, he much feared he could not accomplish

what he felt, as well as we, (Rouen, Wyse), was every way so desirable. I admitted the reasoning of Mr. Mavrokordatos as far as it went, but I regretted it did not go further.[19]

The Prime Minister further indicated "that it was much easier to make or accept these suggestions, then to give them effect."[20] Besides the issue of Russophilism in the Court, in the press and in public offices, there was an even more serious matter which attracted the attention of the Allied Powers in Greece, namely, brigandage. This was an old problem which always worried the Turks for it presented a threat to their Christian occupied provinces. Brigandage was also Palmerston's concern from 1844 to 1851 and it received criticism from the French who like the British were determined to defend the integrity of the Ottoman Empire. After Otho declared Greek neutrality in May 1854, the Turkish authorities in the Greek-populated provinces of Thessaly, Epirus and Macedonia took advantage of their superior position, since they were aided by Anglo-French forces, and began mistreating and even murdering Christians in the provinces to avenge the acts of Greek insurgents.[21] As a result of the Turkish mistreatment of Christians and the intensive hunt for the Greek insurgents the latter were forced to become brigands in order to survive.[22] The problem of brigandage after the end of the Greek insurrection of 1854 was partially the result therefore of Turkish determination to mistreat and eliminate Greek insurgents in the provinces.

By November 1854, only a few months after the occupation, brigandage was steadily increasing not only in the Turkish provinces where the Greek revolts took place, but on the Greek-Turkish frontiers and throughout the entire country of Greece making life for the inhabitants as well as the government in Athens increasingly difficult. The European embassies informed the Greek government that they regarded brigandage in Greece as an obstacle to their Near Eastern policy and an advantage to the Russians.[23] Wyse who was the most severe critic of the rising brigandage went to the Greek Prime Minister and once again asked for his cooperation to repress this dangerous phenomenon. Mavrokordatos could do very little against the brigands for as Wyse noted in one of his dispatches to Clarendon, "there appears to be no Law in the Greek Code, sufficiently effective, to meet such a state of disorder. . . ."[24] Even if there was a law against brigandage

Mavrokordatos could not wage an open and total campaign to suppress the brigands because the pro-Russian elements in the country and many others who sympathized with the Court's *Megali Idea* policy would be against such a measure. Furthermore, the Prime Minister knew very well that Otho and his Court would greatly disapprove of brigand's repression since the king himself supported brigandage morally and in many cases financially and materially.

The Greek Court put the blame on Kalergis for the rise of brigandage even though the Minister of War did more than his share to cooperate with the Occupying Powers in suppressing it. As Wyse's report indicates Kalergis was eager to suppress brigandage:

> When General Kalergis mentioned to His Majesty a few days since that he was ready to take the most energetic course which could be desired to put down this growing calamity, the Queen opposed the difficulty which was to be expected from the Chambers and the Constitution, and on General Kalergis proposing an appeal to the country—"Never," was her answer, "as long as the occupation troops of the Allied Powers remained here."[25]

As far as the Western Powers were concerned brigandage was born and maintained as part of the Greek Court's policy. I mentioned above that under the Kolettes administration the government patronized brigand chieftains who were indeed considered as soldiers who would someday liberate all of the Greeks from the Turkish provinces. The king viewed brigands in the same respect since after all it was the contribution of the *Klefts* and *Armatoloi* who helped to liberate the Greeks in 1821. In so far as England and France were concerned Greek brigands were a Christian army when they crossed over to the Ottoman territory[26] and that presented a threat to the peaceful coexistence of the two neighboring states and more importantly brigandage served to the Russian advantage under the present circumstances.[27]

There was apprehension among the Allied Powers that the "Russian" party in collaboration with the Greek camarilla were planning renewed hostilities with Turkey so this explained their unwillingness to cooperate with Wyse and Rouen in suppressing brigandage. When the two representatives discovered that there were funds in the king's name at the National Bank of Greece which were to be used as the king wished, their suspicion about the king's intentions were confirmed. This prompted

Wyse to accuse Otho of still following the same policy currently as he had before the Allied occupation. He wrote to Clarendon:

> . . .such an attitude on the part of their Majesties and Court, as shall unmistakably discourage, in those who boast of their implicit obedience to their wishes, that continued hostility, sometimes open, sometimes concealed, against the government and the policy of the Western Powers which thwarts their effects, and proclaims to the country that the protection granted to Russia Partisanship is not extinct and that the opportunity is not perhaps distant when it may again be called, under royal auspices, and with hope of better issue, into action.[28]

The Greek government tried to do its best to convince the Foreign Office and the Quai d'Orsay that the effective measures had been adopted to deal with the problem of brigandage.[29] Britain and France were convinced otherwise. Walewski expressed his discontent with brigandage in Greece to M. Roque, Minister at Paris, after he had been informed of a certain case of brigandage in the village of Micali. Roque defended the Greek government as he reassured the French Foreign Minister that the authorities were doing their best of repress the existing menace.[30] It was useless to defend, however, acts which were taking place out in the open. By the spring of 1855 the problem was so severe that the Allies were forced to guard the roads between Athens and Piraeus in order to safeguard their own troops.[31]

Admittedly some of those engaged in bands of brigands were out to rob anyone but there was a number of ex-insurgents who were condemned by the Greek government for taking part in the revolution. According to British intelligence reports certain brigands in Boetia wanted full amnesty and they claimed that brigandage was the means they used to attain their goal.[32] In a letter to Boulgaris, President of the Council, the Boetia Brigands revealed their former plans of using brigandage as a means of creating the fall of the Mavrokordatos ministry so that they would be granted amnesty when a new ministry would come into power. They warned the Boulgaris administration, however, "that if the Ministers should persist in neglecting them, and not grant the amnesty in question they would act henceforth as real brigands. . ."[33]

The Western Allies would never have agreed with the Greek government to grant amnesty to the insurgents and of course the Porte would flatly reject any such measure in dealing with the rebels. The Turks, however, were anxious to put an end to this problem and Fuad Pasha met in a conference with the Greek prime minister at Constantinople and discussed a possible procedure for ending brigandage.[34]

The Sublime Porte was preoccupied with the war in the Crimea and had larger problems than the settlement of brigandage in Greece. It could not afford, however, to allow this menace to grow at the expense of more uprisings in its provinces. A quick settlement of this problem was sought, therefore, and in the first months of 1856 the real efforts to end brigandage began. On January 8, it was announced in the *Moniteur Grec* that the Minister of War, L. Smolenctz had drawn up several articles calling for the order of the Greek government to participate actively in the repression of brigandage in mainland Greece as well as in the Provinces. These articles were later to be adopted into law since no law existed against brigandage as was known in Greece.[35]

Two months after the *Moniteur Grec* announced the government's legal repression of brigandage, a treaty between Greece and the Porte was signed at Kalinja which called for the two countries' cooperation to suppress brigandage.[36] By the conclusion of this treaty it can be argued that technically Greece and Turkey were back on stable and friendly relations which were only to be disturbed again in the Cretan insurrection of 1866-1869.[37]

B. *The Fall of the Mavrokordatos Ministry*

Even since the "ministry of occupation" came to power, a political struggle began between the king and the Mavrokordatos administration. For the first time after a period of over twenty years of absolute rule the Bavarian dynasty in Greece was forced by France and England to share power with a ministry under their control.

At first Otho believed that Mavrokordatos would be able to check the abusive influence of the Occupying Powers in Greek internal and foreign affairs, and he also hoped that the prime minister would control the hostile acts of Kalergis, which the king thought were directed against him personally. As was pointed out in the last section, the Prime Minister had made it clear to Otho that he would have liked to rule constitutionally with as little foreign influence as possible. To run a "ministry of occupation" without the influence of the Occupying Powers, and to administer in a country which was ruled by an absolute monarch for as long as it had existed was an impossibility. Mavrokordatos was pulled by two opposing forces—the Monarchy and the Allied Powers—constantly until he got to a point where he was totally ineffective in so far as exercising his own will in matters of government. During the first few months of the "ministry of occupation" Mavrokordatos enjoyed the confidence of the king as well as that of Western Europe. The declaration of neutrality, the change of ministries and the new administration's attempts to restore relations with the Porte were all positive signs of good faith on the part of Greece toward the Allied Powers. Of course it took an armed force at Piraeus to win the good faith of Greece, but the important factor was that Greece won the confidence of both Clarendon and Drouyn de Lhuys. When Greece requested to resume possession of the three Russian frigates purchased by the Kriezes administration, but detained in Dalmatia,[38] both Clarendon and Drouyn de Lhuys consented to the Greek government's request.[39]

The Anglo-French Powers were also determined to maintain good relations with Otho and several months after the occupation even the king of Greece was optimistic about the friendly course of Greek foreign relations. "The Emperor of the French," he wrote to Ludwig, "expressed himself very friendly towards me and Greece, . . . Clarendon wrote confidentially a while ago the British ambassador here the following: 'I wish as Otho will allow us to be his friends, and he will never have the least cause to regret this.' You see from this that our foreign relations have improved."[40] On the surface it appeared that Greece was finally following a policy parallel to that of France and England but there was indeed a power struggle between the Greek Court and the Allied Powers for political domination in Greek internal and foreign affairs. As the Greek Legation in Paris informed Mavrokordatos, the main concern of France and England was the consolidation of Turkey and the reestablishment of equilibrium in Europe.[41] Greece, ever since the crisis of the Holy Places, had sided with Russia and its foreign policy was an obstacle to the plans and policy of Western Europe in the Near East. Even after the "ministry of occupation" had come in control, Clarendon could call Greece "a misgoverned country."[42] No matter how much effort went into trying to convince the Western Powers that Mavrokordatos had good intentions and that he was ready to cooperate willfully with them,[43] it was difficult to win their total confidence as long as they knew that the Bavarian dynasty in Greece was pro-Russian and would never give up their hopes of territorial expansion.

Otho wanted to rule by himself and he knew that somehow he had to remove the "ministry of occupation" and replace it with a Court ministry if he was to start drawing power away from the hands of Wyse and Rouen. Alone the king could not achieve such a political victory. He had to use diplomatic means and make use of his influence in the German courts. In September 1854 he wrote to Franz Jozef the following letter complaining about the intervention of the Occupying Powers in the state affairs of his kingdom:

> The condition of Greece, unfortunately, instead of improving, is continuously deteriorating. He (Mavrokordatos) feels it also but is unable to improve it. The foreign intervention in the internal affairs of the country, which is based on the strength of the foreign troops near the capital, prevent him, in his actions. You can understand with how much difficulty the prolongation of the occupation is connected. And I resort to your mediation for the removal of the occupation.[44]

The Austrian emperor answered that he would be glad to use his influence in the French Court on behalf of Greece but he felt that the possibility of renewed hostilities in the Turkish provinces by the Greeks was highly likely to reoccur so he thought that for the time being the occupation served a purpose.[45]

Otho was determined to have the influence of Wyse and Rouen diminished as much as possible and would not give up trying to fulfill this goal. As was mentioned in the previous section, the "ministry of occupation" was divided among extremists like Christides and Palamides, who were royalists and opposed actions Mavrokordatos had taken after the French and British Legations' consultation in Athens, and Kalergis with Rouen and Wyse behind him who went out of his way to please the Occupying Powers.[46] Kalergis was a personal friend of Napoleon III[47] and, apparently, the Emperor of the French was very pleased with the work and position of General Kalergis in the Greek government.[48]

The Minister of War took advantage of the fact that he had power-ful friends and became very obnoxious towards the king.[49] Otho waited for the opportunity to arrive so he could dismiss Kalgeris. This opportunity came in July 1855. There was a scandal involving the Minister of War and the wife of P. Pelygiannis, Minister for Foreign Affairs in 1849 during the Kriezes administration. This scandal re-ceived much publicity in the anti-Western press and was used by the queen to degrade Kalergis and diminish his power hopefully resulting in his downfall.[50] After the king requested the resignation of the Minister, Mavrokordatos promised on July 26 that in forty-eight hours he would have Kalergis' resignation at the palace. Instead of a resignation delivered by the Prime Minister, Otho received a visit from Mercier, the French representative who replaced Rouen, and Wyse who had come for an explanation of the king's actions.[51] The two ambassadors asked Otho not to take any affirmative action until they had time to contact their governments. On September 2, Otho was informed that both France and Britain were against the Kalergis dismissal for they did not know of anyone who could replace him as Minister of War.[52] The king declared, however, that all services between the Court and the Ministry of War were stopped and he would not sign any ordinances drawn by that ministry as long as Kalergis was in charge. All this chaos was devised by the Court to lead to only one thing, the fall of the "ministry of occupation" thus Otho's political triumph. In this respect Otho was successful for he had the help of the German Courts.

The Mavrokordatos administration would have fallen, however, even if a scandal involving one of his ministers had not occurred. First, there was factional division in the ministry, second, it was an administration set up in an emergency situation and under foreign force and finally, it represented the will of two opposing sides, the Crown and the Allied Powers. Mavrokordatos could not rule between such forces and had become very weak. As Wyse observed:

> If Mr. Mavrokordatos does not make up his mind to more ex-plicitness, determination and activity, he may as long find him-self placed in a position before the King on the one side and the public (he implies the Allied Powers) on the other which will leave him no choice between permanent acquiscence or a sudden retreat.[53]

The Prime Minister could not openly oppose the King's policy and obey orders given by the foreign invaders, but when the French and British asked for cooperation this is precisely what they had in mind. Both Mercier and Wyse felt that Mavrokordatos was becoming gradually weak and was unable to make government decisions.

In September the Greek Prime Minister went to see the British ambassador to discuss the difficulties of his administration. At the meeting Mavrokordatos stated that before he left Paris he was assured by Drouyn de Lhuys and Lord Cowley that there would be no change in the Greek dynasty or the removal of the king as long as the interests of the Allied Powers are not damaged by Greece. Further, he understood his position as that of a mediator between the king and the Powers.

> . . . in that sense he understood his mission, and was desirous to give effect to it legally and constitutionally. But he found here little either of Law or Constitution. He would conceive of two kinds of governments a constitution frankly carried out, or a despotism; but not a despotism under the forms of a constitution . . . . That is the present state of Greece and with that difficulty he has to contend. The government as it is now cannot act and cannot go on.[54]

Wyse of course placed all the blame for the weakness of the Mavrokordatos administration on the king but the Allied forces with their continuous demands on the prime minister, as Otho pointed out above, were also responsible for this phenomenon.

In the final analysis the Court was in many respects more desirous to end Mavrokordatos than the Allied Powers who merely regretted his weak position. The members of the Chamber, all appointed by the king, waged a war on the Mavrokordatos administration using as an excuse the Kalergis scandal. The press and public servants alike, all directed by the Court, also turned against the "ministry of occupation." In a dispatch from the British Legation in Athens Wyse summarized what he considered the main causes of Mavrokordatos' fall from power:

> All these circumstances combined leave no doubt of a common hostility, and concerted movement against M. Mavrokordatos. But his would be of little moment if M. Mavrokordatos were another man, or had long since, or would even now adopt another policy; the conspiracy might easily be defeated if he did not also

continue to conspire himself. Such, however, is, unfortunately, not the case. His first step was a mistake. He attempted to unite the character of a minister chosen deliberately by the king, with that of a minister selected by the Allied Powers. He has had his eye fixed on the chances of the future, instead of the necessities of the present; he had been consulting the stronger side and more permanent authority, whilst he should have acted without reference to either . . . . [55]

Under such strenous political circumstances it would have been difficult for any Prime Minister to retain the ncessary unity and strength of the administration to run the government efficiently and without encountering the sorts of problems which were responsible for the fall of the Mavrokordatos ministry. A much greater force had to intervene to bring about this fall, however, than merely the wish of the king of Greece. Franz Josef, finally, bent to the wishes of his cousin, Otho, and used his influence to have Britain and France discontinue their support of Mavrokordatos.[56] Otho had used well the only weapon left at his disposal, diplomacy, after the Anglo-French occupation. He knew that as long as the British and French needed the support of Austria and Prussian neutrality in the war against Russia, he could use his influence with the Germanic nations to pressure the Allied Powers to remove General Kalergis and of course along with him the entire "ministry of occupation." Wyse wrote concerning the near-fall of the "ministry of occupation":

> The first impression produced will be one of triumph in the Russian and German pro-Russian party here, and abroad; the assurance already given in the journals that the King, at the instance of Austria and Bavaria, has been restored to all his prerogatives and rights, and the Russian and anti-Western propagandims emanating from the Court, under the inspiration of the Russian Legation, and extending by the instrumentality by the German *Camarilla* and German Diplomacy to all parts of the country, and to West and East, will acquire for the moment fresh force.[57]

It had taken two months for the Germanic Powers (Prussia, Bavaria and Austria) to persuade Napoleon to withdraw his support from Kalergis but finally they succeeded.[58] After the "ministry of occupation" had fallen from power the French government still regarded the ousting of General Kalergis by Otho as "a victory of the Russian party over Western politics."[59] The emperor failed to view the situation as a struggle for power between the king of Greece and the continuous interference in Greek domestic affairs by the Western Powers. Both the British and French refused to accept Otho's schemes of Greek expanionism in isolation. As far as they were concerned there was a real connection between any Greek plans for expansion and Russian ambitions.

On September 27, Mavrokordatos handed in the resignation of the entire ministry to the king for to remain after the forced resignation of Kalergis would have created antagonisms with the French.[60] So the first victory of the Greek camarilla was achieved with the resignation of a ministry which was forced upon Greece by the British and French. For Mavrokordatos, September 27, was to be the last day of his long political career which was to a great extent damaged in 1844 as well as in 1855 by a petty Bavarian prince who believed himself to be more of a Greek nationalist than the Greeks themselves.

C. The Boulgaris Administration

The man who was chosen to replace Mavrokordatos was Demitris Boulgaris.[61] The new Prime Minister was born into a wealthy family on the island of Hydra and was known among the political circles in Athens for his despotic character. His father had worked for the Turkish armada and Boulgaris like Kolettes had come under the influence of Turkish customs.[62] One of the reasons that Otho selected him to serve as prime minister was because he had remained faithful to the monarchy in 1843 and had not participated in the revolution of the Constitutionalists.

Even though Greek historians have not dealt extensively with the Boulgaris administration and one historian even goes as far as to ascertain that the Boulgaris government did not face serious foreign difficulties,[63] it will be seen in this section that the problems of Greece with the Foreign Powers increased and tensions were not absent until the establishment of the Financial Commission of 1857.

The Greek Legation in Paris informed the government in Athens, that, "Monsieur Walewski at the news has reiterated the assurance that any hostile disposition did not exist on the part of France toward the King or against the new Cabinet. . . ."[64] The British were not as pleased as the French appeared to be about the change of ministries. Wyse speculated that:

> The object of this ministry, will be to detach the French from the English Legation, to divide the Ministers, and as they hope, the governments, and the means for this will be the distribution and displacements, without scruple, of office a malignant and treacherous press, in which, in France, as well as here, the most unbounded devotion to France and French Party and French interests will be professed. England, if not calumniated, will be kept in the background, and an intimate union attempted to be brought about between the French partisans so called, and the Russian, in this country to the exclusion always of England, so as at length to bring her to the isolated position in which they formally stood. In a word, it will be the system of M. Coletti on a larger and more vicious scale, and in more critical circumstances, agains succeeding to the fatal moderation of M. Mavrokordatos.[65]

Given this observation of the British ambassador in Athens, it can be seen why the British government was so apprehensive about ending the occupation. Every victory which the Crown scored the Allied Powers considered not as Greek but a Russian victory. Every time British policy and actions were attacked or intercepted in Greece, the Foreign Office considered it as a victory of the French or the Russians. Both England and France believed that the causes of the Greek insurrection against the Turks in 1854 were the product of Russian propaganda or Greek propaganda inspired by the Russians. They also maintained throughout the period of the Crimean War that any act by the Greeks against the Turks or their Allies was an act executed on behalf of Russia, or at least to her benefit against the interests of France and England.

On account of these assumptions entertained by the Allied Powers and, especially, Great Britain the removal of the foreign troops from Piraeus was a distant goal. In October Trikoupis, the representative in London, informed his government that the Western Powers were just as suspicious of Greek policy in the Near East a year and a half after the declaration of neutrality as they were during the months of the revolution. "The Allies," he wrote to Potles, "do not deny, that the neutrality is actually maintained, but they regard this as an act of necessary supervision, and that our Court is always pro-Russian."[66] After the "ministry of occupation" took power in May 1854, Otho had the opportunity to abandon the policy or irredentism and direct the country to a policy of peaceful coexistence with Turkey and emphasize internal growth and economic reform. Instead he continued to pursue a dream which Kolettes passed on to him and he prayed that the British and French would loose in the Crimean War so he could utilize his plans for expansion. As the British representative at Athens observed about the Greek royal plans for expansion:

> It is the state of "reverie" in which Her Majesty the Queen admits herself to be until soem success of Russia, some check of the Allies, some outbreak among the Christian races of the Ottoman Empire may present the opportunity to convert the "reverie" into project, and the project, if possible, into a "fait accompli." This is the great end of the existing policy. It may hold our hope to Greek vanity or Bavarian ambition, but it is not a state of confidence in us, nor of peace and good faith towards their Turkish neighbors.[67]

Wyse and Mercier began to attack the new administration as soon as it was formed and on October 1, in an interview at the Palace both representatives openly charged that the consititution in Greece was continuously violated and the country misgoverned.[68] Otho felt that it was not the place of Wyse or Mercier to criticize the administration and sovereignty of Greece, and he strongly considered such obnoxious criticisms as foreign intervention in Greek internal affairs. Furthermore, he believed that the Treaty of 1832, which guaranteed Greece its independence as a State to be ruled by one monarch, was violated by inconsiderate remarks of the French and British ministers.

When the ministry presented a draft to the king concerning the question of neutrality Otho requested that the paragraph referring to the advantages which Greek neutrality brought to the commercial and political stability of Greece should be modified.[69] The king would not admit to his country that his foreign policy in 1853-1854, before the occupation, was very costly to the nation, and this only irritated relations between Greece and Western Europe. But Otho did not stop infuriating the Allied Powers with this denial that he had embraced the

Megali Idea foreign policy. After the interview with Wyse and Mercier, the king decided to visit the Russian Church in Athens, an act which was intended to openly allow the world to know that he never regretted supporting the struggle against the Turks. The Greek press reported that the king's visit to the Russian Church was not planned but happened by chance. The Western Powers did not believe this story. The British intelligence in Greece informed the Foreign Office that:

> The King not only did not come to the Russian Church as pretended by chance, but the visit was arranged two days before, and communications were held between a member of the Russian Legation and a strong Russian partisan in communication with the Court. . . . The Russian clergy here, the singers, and the Russian Legation were all present, and the members of the Legation were in their evening dress, and the Charge d'Affairs of the Legation, M. Persiany, were the Grand Cordon of the Saviour. The prayers actually said were closed I understand with the Docology. . . which prayers in the Russian Church are followed, by prayers for the Imperial family nomination, and in time of war, with prayers for the success of their arms. At these prayers the King was present.[70]

The king could afford to display his apathy toward the Occupying Powers since he had the support of the Germanic Powers and his popularity in Greece had risen decisively as a result of the occupation. Many among the public viewed Otho as a hero, for he embraced the Greek national cause, and because of this, France and England humiliated him and the nation. As in 1850, the popularity of the Crown increased , and with the help of the German Courts, Otho was actually in a much stronger position than he appeared to his contemporaries.

After the first success of eliminating the influence of the Occupying Powers in Greece by causing the Mavrokordatos resignation, the king worked on another scheme which the Greek politicians had used before, namely, the dissolution of the Franco-British Legation coalition in Greece which antagonized the Court. The government press began a press war against England while it praised Napoleon III. Wyse interpreted the king's attempts to undermine British foreign policy in the following manner:

> Its real purpose is the propagation of Russian opinions and the maintainance of the present system of government under the

collar of German sympathy and protection, guided by the *Camarilla* and its diplomatic supporters here, and the means to be taken are flattery to France and hostility to England, if not between the Legations, at least between those who affect the designations of French and English partisans, and thus creating mistrust between the ministers, and if they can, between their governments, and allowing free scope to the King and his supporters for the exercise of their arbitrary power.[71]

Though the Greek Court's scheme was to divide the Franco-British coalition and to undermine British foreign policy in Greece by presenting the goals of the Foreign Office as contradictory and damaging to French interests in Greece, the king had always been much more favorable to France than to England. France and Russia had not shown as much interest in Greece since they became its Protectors as had the English. Even during the Kolettes administration when the French Legation exercised much influence in the government Great Britain, represented by Lord Edmond Lyons, in Athens, went to extremes in order to assume the protagonist role in Greek internal affairs. The result of Britain's struggles to become the dominant Protecting Power in Greece during the 1840's resulted in the blockade of 1850. Such measures were never adopted by France and Russia, although they were equal partners in the Protectorate. There was much more contempt, therefore, in the Greek Court as well as the nation for England than for either of the other two Protecting Powers.

In March 1855 when Otho wrote to his father to complain about the Occupying Powers in Athens, he stressed that the Emperor Napoleon and his Minister in Greece were much friendlier towards him and his Court than the British government.[72] In the effort of drawing France away from England and breaking their coalition Otho had help from Austria. The following dispatch clearly indicates that the Greek scheme to break the coalition was part of a larger plan worked out by the Germanic Powers:

. . . Baron Prokesch (Austrian minister in Athens) had informed the King, that he was enabled to assure him directly from His Majesty, the Emperor Napoleon, (for who he, Mr. Prokesch, had the greatest admiration) that he entertained for him, the King, the greatest sympathy; that the time was approaching when the two governments of France and England would be very probably obliged to relax or dissolve their union; that already France was drawing closer to Austria, and that Austria on her part becoming much more satisfied with France and proportionally dissatisfied with England; that the result of these new relations would be soon felt in Greece.[73]

Mercier, the French charge d'affaires in Athens upon hearing this news flately denied that the insinuations of Baron Prokesch were based on facts and praised the Anglo-French alliance.[74] The Austrians did not stop protecting the Bavarian Dynasty in Greece whether they had the support of France or not. Baron Prokesch after conferring with the king and queen announced that Otho had fallen victim to bursts of national feeling in Greece against Turkey so he could not be blamed for the events of the uprising of 1854. Furthermore, Prokesch communicated these observations to the Austrian government with the implication that the two Western Powers are unjustified in occupying Greece.[75]

The press played an important role in the scheme to shatter Anglo-French relations for the benefit of the Germanic Powers and the Bavarian Dynasty in Greece. *Elpis*, the newspaper edited and published by C. Levides, whom in the fall of 1854, the French troops had arrested, continued to publish articles with the intention of creating an Anglo-French rivalry in Greece such as the one which existed during the Kolettes administration.

> King Otho understood his mission in the East, not such as the convention of London considered it to be, when it formed a kingdom of a span's length, but such as Western Diplomacy should have considered it, had it looked upon the Greek Kingdom, as a political structure and not as a mite bestowed by Christian charity.

Concerning France the paper took a different attitude.

> The French Nation has generous sentiments, and does not measure politics with the mere yard of its manufactures: it became great by pursuing a generous policy and not a policy of "the yard."[76]

A number of other papers[77] also tried to do the same sort of thing as *Eplis*, and there was little doubt that behind them were the officers of the Greek Court and the "Russian" party.[78]

All the efforts, however, on the part of the king, the press and the Austrians, to flatter the government of France and to create some kind of friction between the French and British Legations in Athens did not help at all the situation of Greece at the Paris Peace Conference. The Greek government wished that it should have a representative at the Conference, if not for any other reason, than the termination of the occupation which had already lasted for two years. Alexander Rangabes,[79] the Minister of Foreign Affairs from February 1856 to February 1857, had made extraordinary efforts to have his country represented in Paris but the French and British governments argued that Greece did not participate in the Crimean War therefore could not be among the participants at the Conference.[80] Count Alexander Walewski, the French Foreign Minister, informed the Greek charge d'affaires in Paris that his country would not be represented in the Peace Conference and that she would not even be consulted concerning the privileges of the Christian subjects living under Ottoman rule.[81]

At the peace negotiations Baron Brunnow, who along with Count Orlov represented Russia, brought up the subject of the Franco-British occupation. The Allied Powers maintained that there was a need to keep the troops in Greece as the situation of brigandage had not been totally resolved and there were still incidents on the Greek-Turkish frontier caused by Greek radical nationalists who still hoped to liberate the provinces of Epirus, Thessaly and Macedonia from the Ottoman Empire.[82] Furthermore, the British and French representatives stated that there was still an excitement for war among the Greek people and under such conditions they argued the presence of Franco-British troops was necessary to insure tranquility in that country. The Germanic Powers, Austria, Bavaria and Prussia, revealed the same concern about the occupation of Greece as had the Tsar's representatives, but neither the French nor the British wished to go into any detailed discussion concerning the future status of Greece in relation to the Protecting Powers.

The failure of Greece to be admitted to negotiations was not only due to the fact that Greece was an insignificant state in the European community, but also because there was an ideological conflict between the irredentist policy of Otho and the guarantee of Ottoman integrity by the Western Powers at the Paris Peace Conference.[83] Furthermore, that Greece was a Protectorate of France, England and Russia placed her a step below the other European nations which were recognized as totally autonomous and independent from the other European Powes.

The Greek government intended to address a formal "protest to the different Courts of Europe, against the declaration respecting Greece at the Conference at Paris," but instead it "decided on presenting a Memorial or Note containing various propositions to the Legations of their Protecting Powers at Athens."[84] Seeing that there was no hope of gaining any concessions at the Conference, the Greek government decided to address a note to the Legations of the Occupying Powers in Athens in order to persuade them to reconsider removing their forces from Piraeus. Rangabes stated in the note that his govenment had friendly intentions toward the Ottoman State and the Western Powers and tried to reassure Wyse and Mercier that there would be no repetition of hostile actions towards Turkey on the part of the Greeks.[85] Neither respresentative trusted the words of the Greek Foreign Minister for they were convinced that the Greek government was not in the hands of the Consul but under the absolute control of the king. On this matter Wyse added the following report to the Foreign Office:

> We had deliberately and officially informed him that we should withdraw from all intervention either as to measures, or men in his administration, but that considering he had absorbed all the governing powers into his own hands, reduced the Constitution to a shadow, and was to all intents and effects an absolute monarch, we should be directed in our future relations towards him, by realities, and not by names, and placing the responsibility on him solely, and not his ministers or the Nation, for the future proceedings of his government.[86]

The French were similarly convinced that the king's intentions and policy could not be trusted as they maintained "that there was always in Greece much sympathy for Russia, much covetousness concealed in the Turkish Provinces."[87] The occupation would be retained therefore until both Britain and France decided that an administration was running the country which was trustworthy and reliable by the Western Powers. Wyse viewed with serious suspicion certain changes that had taken place in the Boulgaris ministry and this was the primary reason for the rejection by both Protecting Powers of lift the occupation.

"The truth is," Wyse wrote, "the whole object had in view for some time past, is to constitute a ministry partly, of daring partisans, partly of insignificant men, or whom the Court in case of need, can implicitly rely. This has now been nearly accomplished."[88] Unless some type of political influence could be exerted in the government in Athens by the Occupying Powers they would not consider leaving. The Germanic Powers were too weak to challenge the policy and actions of the two Powers in Greece and Russia had just finished a conflict with them over the Near Eastern Question and the new Russian Tsar, Alexander II, was not about to antagonize either France or England by opposing their occupation of Greece.[89]

The British and the French, to a certain degree, were more afraid of Russian influence in Greece than of new attacks by Greek insurgents against Turkey. The complaints of the Western Powers that Greece was misgoverned and that there was still a fear of renewed hostilities in the provinces were all used as justification to maintain their military and vanal forces in Piraeus. They would remain until a pro-British and pro-French government was in power in Athens. Before the Kolettes administration, Lyons, in a conversation with Prokesch had unfolded the British way of thinking about her Protectorate in the Near East—a view that later applied to the French as well:

A really independent Greece is an absurdity. Greece, is either Russian or English and, since she must not be Russian, she must be English. I cannot see that there is any doubt about that; no man in his senses would doubt it. England's role is outlined in these words—be sure that she will carry it out and she will smash every obstacle that he meets in her way. It is not a Tory or a Whig question; it is a national question. The King is not on our side, therefore he is Russian—but, mark you, we have not made a kingdom out of Greece in order to create a Russian Province.[90]

This attitude did not change in the course of fifteen years that had lapsed since Lyons had stated his country's position toward Greece. When in 1856 Britain and France proposed that Greece had to undergo reforms and improvements before the troops were ordered out of the country Russia could very well understand that such propositions were only intended to control Greek politics and finances. This is clearly revealed in a dispatch sent to Clarendon from Wyse:

As Russian Diplomacy seems to be much shocked at the present moment at the language held by the British and French Governments in referring to the state of Greece, and the pressing necessity which exists in the common interests of the three Powers, and of Europe, to provide means for its reform and improvement, your Lordship may perhaps not think it inopportune to recall to the recollection of its agents, who appear to have conveniently forgotten the fact, what was the language, (and it is to be pronounced the convictions of the Russian Government as to the state of this country, the conduct of the Sovereign and the duty imposed upon the Protecting Powers to such and obtain effective redress on former occasioms, but especially in 1843, previous to the establishment of the Constitution, a period which they are constantly impressing on us, (as a reason for the suppression of the Constitution) as one, compared to the present, of progress, order, purity and prosperity.[91]

The threat of Russophilism in Greece by the Court, the government and the people was indeed a much greater problem for the two Western Powers than was the threat of a nationalist uprising and not until some type of Franco-British control had been established in Greece to prevent a Russian influence in that country would the occupation be removed.

D. Economic Interests of England and France in Greece and the Ending of the Occupation

On 3 February 1853, Wyse sent a sixty-eight page dispatch to his government concerning: (A) the corrupt government of Greece, (B) the injustices practiced on all levels of government against the people, (C) the gross mismanagement of the finances of the country by the authorities. The passage below summarizes the major problems of the Greek government:

One of the crying evils of the Greek system is a machinery out of all proportion to the population and purpose . . . unhappily in a country like this with no manufacture, little agriculture, the professions crowded, and government employment the only resource , the task especially under the patronage of a *Camarilla*, is comparatively easy . . . . Ministers are too involved in the inequity themselves, too unprotected by public or parliamentary opinion, and too dependent on the caprices of the King or rather of those who rule him, to think seriously of check or correction of this abuse . . . .The presentation of a budget is an annual comedy; and Representative government itself rendered in the eyes of the country (in accomplishment of the long nourished desire to Court and *Camarilla*) an object of mistrust and contempt.[92]

Another comtemporary of Wyse, a French journalist, Edmond About, visited Greece and made the same observations about the political, economic and social condition of the country as Wyse. "Every minster," he wrote, "is ready to do anything in order to retain his post . . . .They think nothing else therefore but to retain their seat and to benefit as best their influence can be exerted from circumstances."[93] The system of government was indeed antiquated and there were no efforts made to improve the economic or political conditions in the country. Even some of the more conservative Greek historians who sympathize with the Crown admit the serious problems in the economy and the governmental system. Conditions in Greece seem even more deplorable when viewed by contemporaries such as Wyse or About who were exposed to the liberal political systems of France and England, or when viewed by modern historians or politicians who have been exposed to progressive movements of socialism and communism.[94]

One of the accounts concerning the political, economic and social conditions of Greece under the Bavarian Dynasty written by a contemporary, Professor S.I. Tzivanopoulos, shows that Greece had indeed made very slow progress since its establishment as an independent nation. The observations of Professor Tzivanlpoulos, who wrote under the dynasty of king George I (1863-1913), are very similar to those of Wyse and About. He criticized Otho for using the Guaranteed Loan of 60 million francs to surround himself and the Court with luxuries instead of using the money, as it was intended, "for public works, and relieving the distress."[95] Every aspect of Greek society was suffering from a disadvantage of one kind or another. The army was an institution greatly abused by the Bavarian Dynasty and the Greek politicians.

Under the pleas of preparing the means for the realization of the "Grande Idee" it was gradually increased to about 10,000 men, and swallowed 8,000,000 drachmas out of a budget estimated at

24,000,000. The organization and discipline did not increase in proportion to the numbers and expenditure, for this army was freely used not to maintain order, but to work the constitution and the result was an army of politicians.[96]

The municipal organization of the country was equally devastating.

We see that above 60,000,000 of drachmas of national produce have been wasted in the last 30 years, without any attempt being made to improve the internal condition of the country. The demarchs neglest all local business; and the people are power-less to do anything for themselves. No steps have been taken till now by the demarchs to make roads, to build a hospital, or establish a school; to open new markets for the improvement of agriculture, or to extend commercial enterprise. But the majority of them being obliged to act as subordinates to the Eparchs, and as agents of the central administration, became petty tyrants and offered a direct impediment to all material progress of the country.[97]

The businessman, the farmer, the worker, were all neglected by the Bavarian Dynasty in Greece and the only point of attention for Otho was the territories of Epirus, Thessaly and Macedonia. He wanted to expand for his own glory and rejected reform and development in a country which needed it the most.

Even though it is generally agreed among twentieth-century historians as it was agreed among contemporaries of the Othonian era that the Bavarian Dynasty in Greece made slow progress for the country, there are opposing views on this matter and one that deserves the attention of the historian is that of Alexander Rizo Rangabes. The ex-foreign minister, unlike Professor Tzivanopoulos, takes a different line of argument and holds that Greece actually started from point zero in 1832 when it joined the community of European nations and it made enormous progress in just a thirty year period under Otho. He con-cludes that the question for Greece is not internal development at all but territorial expansion. "It is not," he writes, "it will be agreed her example that European dipolmacy has a right to invoke, when denou-ncing that Christians of the East as incapable of self government, in order to evade the solution of the 'Eastern Question,' and to prolong the impossible existence of Turkey."[98] The work of Rangabes cannot be taken too seriously for it was written as a propaganda tool.[99] It

does, however, represent the nationalist point of view typical of those
who embrased the *Megali Idea* in the nineteenth as well as the twentieth
centuries. The two works, by Rangabes and Tzivanopoulos, outline
the dichotomy that existed in the Greek public mind; the approach
of Rangabes had its origin and derived its momentum for the Kolettes-
Otho dictatorship, whereas the Tzivanopoulos approach explains the
"English," and more specifically the Mavrokordatos plan for the
present and future condition of Greece.

This gap in opposing policies in Greece had to be filled as far as
France and England were concerned if they were to prevent Russia
from having the dominant role in Greece. Since it became impossible
to influence the politics in Greece through the ministry it became
necessary to find another means of control, namely, financial.

Throughout the Crimean War period up to the time of evacuation
in February 1857 the Occupying Powers were constantly pressing
Greece to meet its financial obligations towards them. In December
1854 the Greek government passed a law which gave it authorization
to raise 5,000,000 drachmas loan. Upon receiving this news the Foreign
Office objected on the grounds that Greece had first to pay the interest
on the 60 million francs loan before attempting to raise another loan.
Wyse had informed Paicos in January 1854, that although there was no
measure of opposition in Article 6 of the Treaty of 1832 prohibiting
the raising of any loan which the Greek government felt it needed, he
was surprised to find out that a loan was considered to be raised at a
time when there was attempt on the part of Greece to discharge its
former financial obligations towards the Protecting Powers. He went
on to state that:

> . . . when the King and Kingdom of Greece had bound themselves
> by that Treaty to see that the actual receipts of the Greek Treas-
> ury should "be devoted *first of all* to the payment of the interest
> and sinking fund for the repayment of the loan and that they
> should not be employed for any other purpose until those pay-
> ments should have been completely secured for the current
> year," and when not withstanding no such payments, withone
> slight exemption, from deficiency of funds or other causes had
> been made, I thought it singular and said so that a new engage-
> ment should be contemplated (this being the position of the old)
> or, at all events, without consulting with the Creditors or their
> representatives here.[100]

Since Greece was obligated by the Treaty to discharge its financial obligations to its Protectors first before trying to raise any other loans she found that the Great Powers could reject her proposals for new loans if they were not satisfied with the political establishment in Greece.[101] In 1854 the question of interest to be paid on the 60,-000,000 francs loan came up again, primarily for political reasons, even though the "ministry of occupation" was in control in Athens. In September Mavrokordatos informed the three Powers that the Greek government could not meet the payments on the interest of the 60 million francs loan. Persiany, the Russian charge d'affaires in Athens, responded mildly stating that he would inform his government on the matter.[102] The reply of the British representative was not nearly as sympathetic as that of Persiany or even Forth-Rouen.[103]

> The practical disregard shown by former Ministers of Finance to these undeniable claims, by not only not liquidating, but not even attempting to liquidate or even to notify the Protecting Powers, their inability to liquidate the samllest portion of these demands, was only equalled by the insolent indifference to official dùty and public opinion, by which through a puerile artifice, they annually paraded in the budget a certain sum, professedly destined for such an object, but of which, as no portion found its way into the Treasuries of the Protecting Powers, it is only charitable to suppose that it was never levied, or was diverted from its legitimate destination at least other state purposes. This with the clumsy annual mystification for the purpose of nominally swelling the return of receipts to some semblance of equality with Expenditures, . . .naturally produced in the whole government a disgraceful negligence of the public resources, and what was far worse, a fatal disregard to the most sacred public and private engagements.[104]

After the long lecture on economics by Wyse, the British government agreed, as had the other two Protecting Powers, "not to press the Greek government, at the present moment, for payment of the interest on the loan guaranteed by the Protecting Powers," but that Greece should make genuine efforts for regular payment of the interest.[105] As long as the "ministry of occupation" was in power the Western Powers would not pressure Greece as much to meet its financial obligations. Once Otho removed that ministry, however, the Occupying

Powers could no longer rely on political influence in Greece, so it became essential for them to start again asking for the delayed payments on the loan and ultimately to set up a system of financial control.

The Boulgaris administration unsuccessfully asked to be included in the Paris Peace Conference. Furthermore, the Allies did not desire to end the occupation. After Rangabes failed to gain any representation for his country in the Peace Conference, he began working toward the goal of removing the foreign troops from Piraeus. In an interview with Wyse and Mercier, the Greek foreign minister openly requested that the occupying forces be removed from Greece, but both representatives instantly rejected his request.[106] The reply of Wyse and Mercier was allowed by Rangabes to be published in the press in order to excite anti-western sentiment among the public. Part of the published reply is as follows:

> . . . that their governments did not see with satisfaction appointed into office men well known as professed enemies of Turkey; that brigandage continued to distress the country, and that the Greek government neglected to carry into operation such changes and reforms as were calculated to promote the internal welfare of the country; that the object of the occupation had not been to interfere with the internal government of the Kingdom. . . . But as the object of the occupation was to impede, on the part of Greece, the disturbances of the Ottoman Provinces on the frontier that the Powers, however, desirous they may be to remove their troops, still they cannot do so until sufficient guarantee shall be given by the Greek government, that Turkey shall remain unmolosted on the part of Greece.[107]

This publication naturally aroused great excitement among the Greeks who had been occupied for a period of two years but the reaction of the Western Powers to this article was also very bitter and immediately Wyse sent a dispatch to Rangabes complaining that secret diplomatic talks were allowed to be publicized in the press for the sole purpose of exciting the public mind.[108] Rangabes gained support from the public by exposing the Occupying Powers for their refusal to lift the troops from Piraeus, but neither France nor England would be persuaded by Greek public opinion in their policy towards Greece.

The concept of systematic financial control in Greece, which was implicit in the Treaty of 1832, appeared an inescapable resort for the Western Powers. Article 12, paragraph 6 of the Treaty gave the right to the Protecting Powers to collect their money first, before the department of Finance had fulfilled any other financial obligations. Wyse who was familiar with this article of the Treaty was the first to suggest that the three Protecting Powers of Greece should set up a Financial Commission which would provide them with the interest of the guaranteed loan.

> It seems, therefore to me, incontestable that the representatives of the Three Powers, in the exercise of their strict right, all in discharge of their duty, not only are authorized under international convention but are required by the position to which this question has arrived, to inquire why it is the Treasury is not in a position to meet this debt, . . . and what remedies are to be applied to check these causes, and to bring the pecuniary condition of this kingdom into such order, as will enable it to fulfill (even in part) its obligations. . . . The first step then starting from these premises, which I venture to submit to your Lordship, is a "Commission of Inquiry" into "the state of the Greek Finances."[109]

Wyse, as well as Britain and France, expressed the desire to collect their payments on the interest from Greece but also to improve and reform the financial state of the country.

In June 1856, the British Parliament brought to discussion once again the poor and corrupt financial administration of Greece and attempted to justify the prolonged occupation as a result of Greek unwillingness to cooperate with the Western Powers and thinking who had not followed the Constitution of 1843.

> If the Greek Government had properly managed its financial affairs there would have been ample means to meet all the charges upon it. It had failed to do so; the liability had fallen upon the Powers which guaranteed the loan, and representation innumerable had been made upon the subject to the Greek Government, but without effect.[110]

Restrictions on Greek financial affairs became more rigid during the Boulgaris administration. In the autumn of 1856 the Greek government proposed a set of Laws for the alienation of the National Lands. Both Britain and France strongly objected to the sale of the National Lands and advised Rangabes that his government had not right to take such action without first consulting with the Protecting Powers. The Foreign Office advised Wyse to send the following message to the Greek foreign minister:

> I have received instructions from Her Majesty's Government that in as much as the Protecting Powers have a right under the Treaty of 1832 to claim the whole revenues of Greece arising from every source, while the National Lands have been mortgaged to the British Landholders with whom the Greek Government contracted loans in England in 1824 and 1825, and in which no interest has been paid since 1827, the protest against any sale or Allienation of the National Lands.[111]

The Foreign Minister obviously objected to the interference of the Protecting Powers in Greek internal affairs. But Wyse replied on two different occasions that the Greek government took the proposed measures, concerning the National Lands issue, before th Chambers to be passed before consulting with the three Powers to which Greece still owed money.[112] When Rangabes charged that the Chambers passed the bill therefore it was a matter out of his control, Wyse simply placed all the responsibility with the foreign minister.[113] The British and French Legations in Athens were informed that Rangabes actually favored passage of the bill and this is why Wyse entirely blamed him for it. There were, however, political reasons for the Franco-British opposition to the bill besides the obvious economic ones which were stated above by the British representative. These political reasons were described to the Earl of Clarendon by Wyse as follows:

> Mr. Boulgaris has been outvoted in the ministry, by Mr. Koumoundouros (the ally of General Spiro-Milio, and others of his party) by Mr. Rizo Rangabe and Mr. Chrystopoulos. Out of doors, General Spiro-Milios, Mr. Chrestides, and Mr. Levides give, it is reported, their aid, and laugh at the idea that our protests can have the least weight in retarding these measures, "We have plenty of these notes." is their reply, "and what harm have they done? have they stopped a single proceeding?" With other observations still more contumelious. They act under the patronage of

the Court and of its partisans, and the proposed Laws are represented as emanating directly from Her Majesty.[114]

The king as well as the ministers of the Boulgaris administration
realized that France and Great Britain had lost the political battle
which they had fought since the fall of the Mavrokordatos administration. The two Powers which occupied Greece for three years
had failed to formulate a ministry consisting of pro-British and pro-
French members, and of courseanti-Othonianmembers. Otho succeeded
through his use of diplomacy with the Germanic Powers to prevent
the French and the British from securing a Greek administration
which would be loyal to the two Western Protecting Powers.

Since France and England failed to exert their influence in Greece
by the means of a pro-Franco-British ministry in Athens the two
Powers resorted to the measure of financial pressure. They were determined to curb the king's power whether they exerted their influence
through a ministry of their choice or whether they forced the government to meet its financial obligations towards the Protecting Powers.

In December 1856, the Boulgaris administration having no other
choice when confronted with the demands that Greece should discharge its financial obligations towards the three Protecting Powers
assured the three Powers that the eventual resources of the country
would be provided for the Guaranteed Loan.[115] In spite of this reassurance from Athens that Greece would do its best to clear its financial obligations towards France, Russia and Great Britain, Walewski
and Clarendon were not satisfied with such promises which the Greek
government had made before but had failed to keep. The following
dispatch from Claredon stated the official position of Great Britain
and France:

> . . . it is conformity with this principle that Her Majesty's Govern-
> ment have determined in concert that of France to propose to
> the Greek Government that the Representatives at Athens of
> the three guaranteeing Powers should form a permanent Com-
> mission empowered to receive and if necessary to call for all the
> information which may be required for enabling their respective
> governments to judge with regard to the due employment of the
> Public Funds. . . . In a word of duty of the Commissioners will
> be to keep the three governments regularly informed of what is
> going on, so that those governments may be enabled to form an

opinion of the manner in which the Greek Government deals
with the resources which are pledged for the payment of its
debts and if necessary retract the aspect given by them to the
proposals of the Cabinet of Athens. . . . if the Greek Government should acquire in the proposal without reserve, the two
governments would be disposed to look upon it as affording
a sufficient guarantee to admit of their withdrawing their troops
from Greece.[116]

The above dispatch makes it clear that unless the Greek government
agreed to the setting up of the Financial Commission the forces at
Piraeus would not be withdrawn. Britain and France wanted to lift
the occupation and replace it with a system of financial control. The
Political victory won by Otho in September 1855, when he replaced
the "ministry of occupation" with the Boulgaris administration, was
about to be countered with an Anglo-French economic victory in
Greece. This time the Germanic Powers could not come to Otho's
rescue as they had during the Crimean War, for the simple reason that
Austria was no longer needed by the Allies to over-power the force
of Russia in the Near East. Russia, the other country from which Otho
could expect help, consented to the setting up of a Financial Commission and the Treaty of 1832 made it legal for the Protecting Powers
to interfere in the domestic affairs of Greece.

The terms under which the Commission was to be set up made it
very easy for the Protecting Powers not only to check the Greek
finances but to control and operate them. This raised questions in
the British Parliament which felt that the occupying Powers were
replacing one means of force, the occupation, with another, the Financial Commission. "No doubt," said the Marquess of Clanvicarde, "we
ought to have some control over the finances of the country, as it was
our debtor, and we ought to take care of our debts; yet if such an
arrangement was carried too far, it would involve us in difficulties."[117]
To this objection the Earl of Clarendon responded that Greece had not
been responsible to the Protecting Powers in discharging its payments
and it became necessary therefore to resort to extreme measures. He
defended the idea of the Commission as one which would solve many
economic problems of Greece and would end political rivalry in that
country among the Protecting Powers.

He [the Earl of Clarendon] believed that the Protecting Powers were about to render essential service to Greece by the advice and assistance which the Commissioners would be able to render to her Government, and it was expected that the Greek Government might in this way have it in their power to effect certain administrative and financial reforms, . . .He believed the Commisison would be established in a few days and he hoped it would tend eventually to put an end to the contests for influence which had so often taken place between foreign Powers—contests which did no service to the Powers engaged and which only distracted and wounded the public feeling of the country which was so unfortunate as to be the subject of them.[118]

The people in Greek politics felt that no matter how one viewed the Commission, its purpose was financial control of Greece by the Protecting Powers. Rangabes immediately protested to the Powers against the establishment of the Commission but only Prince Alexander Gorchakov, who replaced Nesselrode in May 1856 as Minister of Foreign Affairs, showed any sympathy. The Russian diplomat maintained that the Emperor Alexander would not participate in such a Commission with such rigid measures taken against Greece by the Western Powers.[119] The Russian government's protest forced France and England to reconsider its harsh schemes of financial control and to adopt milder measures towards the Protectorate. When finally established, the Financial Commission was to have recommending and advisory powers only, a proposal which was readily accepted by the Greek Government and went into effect in February 1857.[120]

On February 19, the troops of England and France began the evacuation process and by the 27th of the same month they had all left Greek waters.[121] Greece was finally relieved of a three year occupation only to become burdened with the permanent establishment of a Financial Commission.

CONCLUSION

In the years which have passed since the Greek insurrection of 1854 there have been numerous attempts to interpret the role of Greece in the Eastern Question. The predominate view among Greek historians concerning the 1854 insurrection and the role of Greece in the Crimean War can be summarized by the following passage from a modern account of the insurrection:

> The revolution in Epiros-Thessaly and Macedonia to shake off the Ottoman yoke, which was instigated by Greece by dispatching volunteer corps and which erupted as a result of the Crimean War, was a continuation of the 1821 struggle as a first endeavor to complete the ideological potential of the nation and the disposition of the Great Powers in respect to Hellenism.[1]

This conclusion is deduced from a close study of the insurrection in Thessaly in 1854. It reflects the typical Greek nationalist point of view held during the Crimean War period as well as today. The role of Greece in the Eastern Question for the Greek nationalist was the same in 1821 as in 1854, 1866-1869, 1897, and 1921.[2] The struggle for Greece to become an independent nation began in 1821 and ended—for most Greeks—in 1921. Therefore, the focus of this particular point of view is directed at only one objective, namely territorial expansion. The insurrection of 1854 and the insurrection which followed later were all continuations of the War of Independence.

Among the factors which are not considered under this line of thought adopted by Greek nationalists are the role of domestic politics in the events of the nation's history, the influence of international politics in the foreign and domestic policies of the state and finally, the importance of the various socio-economic factors which exercise a great deal of control in society. During the War of Independence there was no nation of Greece, only Greeks who fought with the aid of the Great Powers to achieve their independence. In 1854 there was a nation of Greece and it was the king who actually organized and supported the insurrection against Turkey, therefore the role of Greece in the Eastern Question was totally different in 1854 than it was during the War of Independence.

In the process of change and early development, Greece formed a number of classes, namely, the merchant, the professional, the working class and the peasantry. Political parties were also developed to such a degree that by 1843 there was a successful constitutional revolution by those progressively minded in politics. Finally, the most important factor in the history of the nineteenth century was the constant foreign intervention in the internal affairs of the country. The second phase of the role of Greece in the Eastern Question has, therefore, these elements which are unique and for this reason the occurrences of 1854 cannot be explained by the circumstances of 1821 or 1897 but only by 1854 alone without, of course, loosing focus of the country's history since the War of Independence.

The socio-Economic factor in the insurrection must be viewed historically as it was effected by three important events in Greece: First, a constitutional revolution and its failure to materialize as a result of the Kolettes triumph in 1844, second, the British blockade of Greece in 1850, and third, the uprising of the Greeks in the Turkish provinces and the occupation of Piraeus. The failure of the constitution and the triumph of Kolettes resulted in thp failure of the merchant and professional classes to exert its influence in society and win economic and political predominance. Kolettes, unlike Mavrokordatos who favored economic development, internal growth and reform carved out an expansionist foreign policy which would only damage the interests of the business world in Greece. The merchant class had nothing to gain from such a policy and everything to loose since its trade with Turkey and the Great Powers would be damaged in case of a Greek-Turkish conflict. The administration of Kolettes, therefore, indirectly antagonized by its policy the middle class of Greece which was the backbone of the Greek economy. There was a class schism created as a result of the triumphant exaltation of the *Megali Idea*; the lower classes, especially the peasants support nationalist expansion while the middle class opposses it. The third group of people which formulated the strength of the expansionist group was the chieftains and brigands and the wealthy Greeks of Europe who entertained nationalist dreams.

The blockade of 1850 tended to widen the schism between the middle class and lower class allowing room also for exceptions such as military personnel, brigands, and wealthy adventurers. For the economy of the country the blockade was simply disastrous. The class which suffered the most was the middle class so this experience was the last thing desired to reoccur by merchants and businessmen. Those who were already burning with nationalism became even more radical as a result of the blockade and the rise of Russophilism in the early years of the 1850's is a good indication of that phenomenon.

Finally, the events of 1854 completed the schism. The lower class led by the Court politicians and by brigands fully accepted the idea of a regenerated Byzantine Empire and morally as well as materially supported the insurrection. On the other hand the middle class as well as the large part of the working class involved in navigation and commerce resented the insurrection fearing another blockade and perhaps worse consequences. The finest hour for the king and those who supported his cause came in March and April 1854, but it was followed by the sad disappointment of an occupation in May. The triumph of the middle class was April 1855 when the Treaty of Commerce and Navigation was signed at Kalinja. The economy suffered greatly as a result of the *Megali Idea* policy from 1844 to 1855 and the irony is that the governing class with its broad mass support was engaged in a foreign policy that contradicted the economic interests of the nation, that is, those of the merchant and business classes. In the world of nineteenth century Europe which had seen the rise of the middle class, Greece in its desperate efforts of national expansion jeopardized the very existence of this class.

Aside from the socio-economic factors which were unique to the developments of 1854, the importance of political factors were also unique to the role of Greece in the Crimean War phase of the Eastern Question. If Mavrokordatos had not been forced to resign in 1844 and had remained in power, the 1854 revolution could have been avoided. Kolettes' victory marked the beginning of a new domestic and foreign policy which led to the insurrection and its consequences. He destroyed the work of the constitutional revolution only to replace it with arbitrary government and handed down to Otho a foreign policy which could only lead Greece to disaster. Parliamentary government did not succeed and internal reform and development were disregarded by the

King. The British blockade did not teach Otho a lesson in discipline to the Great Powers and the occupation of Piraeus only excited his dreams of expansion to an even greater level. Pointing out the absurdity of the *Megali Idea* policy of the Greek Court Dr. Nomikos writes, in 1854 under the leadership of Otho, this nation of one million people living on 47,000 square kilometers rose to measure itself up against the combined might of the Ottoman Empire and the major European Powers."[3] The character of politics cannot be disregarded in the direct influence it exercised over the events of the insurrection of the Christians in the Turkish provinces. The absence of such politics during the War of Independence is one more factor which accounts for the differentiation of first Greek rebellion against the Turks from the second.

Finally, the role of international politics in Greece contributed to the uniqueness of the 1854 experience. During the Othonian era there was a constant rivalry among the Protecting Powers for political control in Greece. The Anglo-French rivalry in 1844 replaced the Anglo-Russian rivalry and the rivalry between Russia and the combined efforts of France and England replaced the Franco-British rivalry after 1850. Kolettes was responsible to a great extent for the Anglo-French rivalry but in spite of this charismatic dictator who enjoyed antagonizing England, there would have been a rivalry among the Powers for control of policies in Greece since this country was important to control for strategic and commercial reasons.

Great Britain proved in the decade before the occupation that no risk was too great for the political domination of Greece. In 1850 Palmerston blockaded the country's ports because he could not get satisfaction from the Greek government for his political demands. In 1854 both France and England occupied the country for it had decided not to accept their Near Eastern Policy. They retained the occupation for three long years, a year even after the Paris Peace Treaty was signed because they wanted to gain political control. When their efforts failed, they decided the next best thing to political control was financial control so they set up the Financial Commission and then removed the occupying forces.

The Germanic Powers and Russia, to a lesser extent, were the balance of power in Greece during the Crimean War period and in many respects during the entire period of the reign of King Otho. Austria, Prussia and Bavaria were the protectors of the crown against any possible abuses which could be inflicted upon it by the Protecting Powers. In 1850 the Germanic Powers joined the rest of Europe in defending Greece against Palmerstonian aggressive diplomacy in that nation. In 1854 and throughout the Crimean War Austria and the other two Germanic states gave Otho their full support when his throne and power was endangered by the Occupying Powers.

Russia during the six year period of 1844-1850 had become, to a large extent, aloof from Greek affairs but in 1850 the Tsar came out very strong in support of the king against Britain. During the Holy Places question Russia took the role of the protector and defender of the Orthodox Christians of the Ottoman Empire and flirted with Greece during the entire affair. In 1854 Nesselrode announced that his country approved of the Greek insurrection and in that same year the Tsar made it known to the world that his struggle against Turkey was in defence of the Christians of the Near East. At the Conference in Paris Russia tried to eliminate Anglo-French influence in Greece and asked what were these Powers intending to do about the occupation. Finally, Russia defended Greece before the Financial Commission was established by protesting to the harsh measures of the Commission.

The foreign policies of the Powers in Greece, the politics of the court, and the socio-economic factors which existed in 1854 were absent during the War of Independence. Greece discovered after the Crimean War that its role in the Eastern Question had undergone radical transformation so the same goals which were sought for in 1821 could not be hoped to be realized thirty years later under the same circumstances as took place during the War of Independence. One indication of the realization process that took place was the abolition of the "foreign" parties that is "English," "French" and "Russian." The end of the Crimean War marked the end of these parties as Greeks realized that their interests could not be identical with those of any other country than their own.

APPENDIX

British interests in Greece were not strategic and political only but economic as well. The British currant traders of Patras had established an economic stronghold in Greece and exercised a great deal of influence in the economic policy of the Greek government. In the early months of 1853 the British currant traders urged Thomas Wood, British Consul at Patras, to stop a fixed duty on currants introduced by Christides, minister of Finance.[1]

When losses were suffered in the currant trade as a result of a blight the British Legation in Athens demanded that the Greek government should be held responsible for reimbursing the British merchants since the merchants paid a fixed duty on a bad crop of export.[2]

By December 1853, the British currant merchants in Patras and the Ionian Isles demanded a reduction of duty in England for their products. Wyse was able to persuade the new minister of finance, Provelgios, to comply with the demands of the British Legation concerning the economic benefits of the British merchants. The British representative in Athens felt that a reduction of duty on currants would benefit the Greek economy as well as the British merchants of Greece. He felt therefore, that "if the Greek Government are to receive concessions, it ought not to refuse at least its cooperation, to render them available, and reduction of duty in England ought to suggest and be accompanied by a sweeping away of all unnecessary and vixatious interference, and a security of a judicious and steady commercial policy in Greece for the future."[3] The beneficiary of the lower duty on currants from Greece would clearly have been the British merchants of Patras and thus Great Britain. Greece had little to benefit since it would be forced to grant more concessions to the British.

Under the administration of Mavrokordatos fixed duties went into effect[4] much to the satisfaction of the British Legation and merchants of Patras. Under the administration of Boulgaris the ministry of finance thought it profitable to do away with the fixed duty and reintroduce the "old system of Protocols." Upon this news Wyse filed the following report at the Foreign Office. "Currants form a very large item in the annual list of her (Greece) exports, and the more or less extension of the market and production, is to her a matter of vital moment. We are the chief cconsumers, but not dependent for the article on her. If we were to recur to force instead of reason, we have at any time the remedy in our hands."[5] Wyse was successful—at least—in persuading the minister of finance not to change the existing law on currant trade.[6] Obviously the presence of the Anglo-French troops persuaded the Boulgaris government to comply with British demands.

NOTES

Notes to Introduction

1. The Greeks of the nineteenth century had the Byzantine Empire in mind when they characterized the nation as "little Greece."
2. E. About, *E Hellada tou Othonos* (E Synchrone Hellada, 1854), translated by A. Spelios, La Grece Contemporaine (Athens), 52, who was writing before 1854 recorded that the population of Greece was 950,000. A.R. Rangabes, *Greece: Her Present Progress and Position* (New York, 1867), 22, maintains that the population of Greece in 1853 was 1,042,529. E. Nomikos, "The International Position of Greece During the Crimean War" (Ph.D. dissertation, Stanford University Press, 1962), 290, has it at 1,000,000 for 1854 and it is safe to say that this is the correct figure.
3. Nomikos, "International Position of Greece," 290.
4. For the text of the Treaty of May 7, see *British and Foreign State Papers*, XIX, 33-41. Also see G.F. Martens, *et al.*, eds., *Recueil des Traités d.alliance, de paix, de trêve et plusieurs autres actes servant à la connaissance des relations étrangères des puissances et états de l.Europe depuis 1761 jusqu.a present*, X, 550-64. Gottinque, 1819-1944 (title changes to *Nouveau recueil général des traites '* . . from IX on).
5. Armansperg was appointed president during the first Regency in Greece by a decree of 5 October 1832 of Ludwig, King of Bavaria. Armansperg was known for his liberal tendencies and this is the reason he was favored for the Regency in Greece which he shared with the first regency headed by Professor Ludwig von Maurer and Major-General Karl Wilhelm von Herdeck. See J.A. Petropoulos, *Politics and Statecraft in the Kingdom of Greece, 1833-1843* (Princeton, 1968), 155, for the period of the first Regency see 153-217.
6. S.I. Tzivanopoulos, *Katastasis tes Hellados epi Othonos kai Proskokiai Aftis Ypo ten Aftou Megalioteta Georgious A Basilea Hellinon* (The Condition of Greece under Otho and Her Expectations under His Majesty George I, King of the Greeks) (Athens, 1864), 4-5.
7. See Petropoulos, *Kingdom of Greece*, 434-52.
8. For the full text of the Constitution see G. Aspreas, *Politike Historia tes Neoteras Hellados* (Political History of Modern Greece) (Athens), I, 175-84.

9. All transliterations and translations in this work are those of the author unless otherwise indicated.

10. See Petropoulos, *Kingdom of Greece*, 96-106, for the origin of the parties.

11. K. Strupp, ed., *La situation internationale de la Grece (1821-1917); Recueil de documents choisis et édités avec une introduction historique et dogmatique* (Zurich, 1918), 136-39.

12. J.A. Levandis, *The Greek Foreign Debt and the Great Powers, 1821-1898* (New York, 1944), 36.

13. Petropoulos, *Kingdom of Greece*, 291-320.

14. *Ibid.*, 137-41.

15. F.O. 32/205 (No. 33) *Confidential*, Wyse to Clarendon, Athens, March 23, 1853.

Notes to Chapter One

1. D. Fotiades, *Othonas: E Exosis* (Otho: The Exile) (Athens, 1975), 26.

2. For details on the resignation of Mavrokordatos and the summoning of Kolettes see Aspreas, *Modern Greece*, I 188-92, also P. Karolides, *Synchronos Historia ton Hellinon kai ton Loinon Laon tes Anatoles, 1821 mechri 1921* (Contemporary History of the Greeks and the Rest of the People of the East 1821 until 1921) (Athens, 1922), III, 138-70. For details on the revolution of 1843 see D. Fotiades, *Othonas: E Monarchia* (Otho: The Monarchy) (Athens, 1963), 281-369, see also B. Jelavich, *Russia and the Greek Revolution of 1843* (Munich, 1966). For details on the origin, nature and purpose of the Greek political parties see A. Skandames, *Selides Politikes Historias kai Kritikes, E Triakontaetia tes Basileias tou Othonos, 1832-1862* (Pages of Political History and Criticism, The Thirty-year Kingdom of Otho, 1832-1862) (Athens, 1961), 596-660, also Petropoulos, *Kingdom of Greece*, 53-106.

3. Karolides, *History of the Greeks*, III, 145-46.

4. Fotiades, *Otho: The Exile*, 29, also see Nikos A. Antonakeas, *Favlokratia, 1821-1950* (Government by Villains, 1821-1950) (Athens, 1950), I, 32.

5. N. Dragoumes, *Historikai Anamneseis* (Historical Recollections) (Athens, 1925), II, 124-126.

6. "Revue de Deux Mondes" quoted in Dragoumes, *Recollections*, II, 127.

7. G. Kordatos, *Historia tes Neoteras Helladas* (History of Modern Greece) (Athens, 1957-1958), III, 367-76.

8. Douglas Dakin, *The Unification of Greece*, 1770-1923 (London, 1972), 80-82.

9. Aspreas, *Modern Greece*, I, 206-210.

10. L. Bower and G. Belitho, *Otho I: King of Greece: A Biography* (London, 1939), 137.

11. Mavrokordatos had 53 Deputies while the Kolettes-Metaxas coalition had 67. See Fotiades, *The Exile*, 31.

12. Aspreas, *Modern Greece*, I, 196.

13. Cited in Karolides, *History of the Greeks*, III, 205-206.

14. The apparent cause for the withdrawal of Metaxas from the Kolettes Government was that the Napists-"Russian" party—wanted to control Church affairs. Metaxas had asked for the Ministry of Ecclesiastical Affairs but was denied by the Prime Minister since two of his men, (R. Palamides and D. Kalifronas), also had a strong claim to it. See Karolides, *History of the Greeks*, III, 523-24.

15. *Aion*, September 2, 1845.

16. G. Makrygiannes, *Makrygianne Apomnemoneumata* (Makrygianne Memoirs) (Athens, 1972), 290-291.

17. Otho to Metternich, Athens, April 27, 1846, quoted in Skandames, *Political History*, 942.

18. E. Kyriakides, *E Historia tou Synchronou Hellinismou apo tes Idryseos tou Basileiou tes Hellados 1832-1892* (History of Contemporary Greeks from the Founding of the Kingdom of Greece, 1832-1892) (Athens, 1972), I, 523-24.

19. Karolides, *History of the Greeks*, III, 337-40. The translation used here is in Petropoulos, *Kingdom of Greece*, 509-10.

20. G.N. Philaretos, *Xenokratia kai Basileia en Helladi, 1821-1897* (Foreign Rule and Royalty in Greece, 1821-1897) (Athens, 1897), 82.

21. T. Tatsios, "The *Megali Idea* and the Greek-Turkish War of 1897: The Impact of the Cretan Problem on Greek Irredentism, 1866-1897" (Ph.D. dissertation, Columbia University, 1973), 26.

22. During the Kolettes Administration the Great Powers Near Eastern Policy was the maintenance of the status quo. See M.S. Anderson, *The Eastern Question*, 1774-1923 (New York, 1968), 112-113.

23. Cited in Fotiades, *The Exile*, 43.

24. Petropoulos, *Kingdom of Greece*, 509.

25. In the correspondence between Princess Lieven and Lord Aberdeen there is a desire expressed on the part of both France and England not to

have a confrontation over Greek affairs, Jones E. Parry, *The Correspondence of Lord Aberdeen and Princess Lieven, 1832-1854* (London, 1938-39), I, 216-17, 225.

26. Cited in Karolides, *History of the Greeks*, III, 192-193.

27. Cited in *Ibid.*, 194.

28. Dragoumes, *Recollections*, II, 135.

29. Aspreas, *Modern Greece*, I, 203.

30. Kyriakides, *Contemporary Greeks*, I, 527.

31. Palmerston was chiefly responsible for the deeper British involvement in Turkey and the Near East for economic, strategic and political reasons. See G.D. Clayton, *Britain and the Eastern Question: Messolonghi to Gallipoli* (London, 1971), 73-79.

32. Brigandage was a phenomenon that had been in existence for as long as Greece was under the domination of the Porte. Brigands became the heroes of the country during the War of Independence as they took the name of *klefts* (thieves) and *armatoloi* (guerrilla warriors). Brigandage continued after the War of Independence as many hoped to free all of the Greek territories.

33. Sessions of May 22, 1845, Hansard, 3rd Series. LXXX, 756.

34. George Finlay, *A History of Greece from its Conquest by the Romans to the Present Time, B.C. 146 to A.D. 1864*, VII, (Oxford, 1877), 200.

35. *Ibid.*, 200-1, also L. Sergeant, *Greece in the Nineteenth Century: A Record of Hellenic Emancipation and Progress, 1821-1897* (London, 1897), 236-7.

36. Douglas Johnson, *Guizot: Aspects of French History* London, (Routledge & Kegan, Paul, 1963), 312-13.

37. Anderson, *Eastern Question*, 108.

38. Kyriakides, *Contemporary Greeks*, I, 525-6.

39. Sessions of July 31, 1845, Hansard, 3rd series, LXXXII, 1279.

40. Russia approved of the Kolettes government even though she did not support it. Nesselrode to Meyendorff, St. Petersburg, December 5, 1844, Nesselrode, compte de *Lettres et Papiers du Chancelier Compte de Nesselrode 1770-1856*, VIII, 261.

41. Anderson, *Eastern Question*, 112.

42. W. Miller, *The Ottoman Empire and its Successors, 1801-1927* (Cambridge, 1936), 177.

43. Karolides, *History of the Greeks*, III, 252.

44. Karatasos was an aid de camp of Otho, Fotiades, *The Exile*, 48. Also see Athanasios Angelopoulos, *Dimitrios Tsamis Karatasos* (Balkan Studies, XVII, 1976).

45. Aspreas, *Modern Greece*, I, 204.

46. Karolides, *History of the Greeks*, III, 256-57.

47. Mousouros was a Greek Phanariot (Constantinople) who was loyaly serving the Sublime Porte.

48. Kyriadkides, *Contemporary Greeks*, I, 557.

49. Aspreas, *Modern Greece*, I, 205, claims that the British embassy in Constantinople was also giving instructions to the Turkish embassy in Athens, Lyons and Kolettes were on very hostile terms, (see Bower, *Otho 136)* so the former had personal as well as political reasons to blame Kolettes for the occurrence at the palace dance.

50. The Sultan was Metzid a peace loving ruler Grand Vizier was Reshid Pasha, and foreign minister Aali. Both Aali and Reshid were "European-minded" politicians.

51. See Petropoulos, *Kingdom of Greece*, for the period before 1844 for Anglo-French rivalry in Greece.

52. Evelyn Ashely, *The Life of Henry John Temple, Viscount Palmerston, 1846-1865* (London, 1876), 181-82.

53. Robert Bullen, *Palmerston, Guizot and the Collapse of the Entent Cordiale* (London, 1974), 75-78, see also Guizot to Aberdeen, October 28, 1844, quoted in E. Driault and M. Lheritier, *Histoire Diplomatique de la Grece de 1821 a nos jours* (Paris, 1925-6), II, 268-69.

54. Skandames, *Political History*, 940, also see Bower and Bolitho, *Otho I*, 139.

55. Aspreas, *Modern Greece*, I. 202.

56. Bullen, *Entente Cordiale*, 75.

57. The following letter from Guizot to Kolettes which was sent 17 April 1845 reveals the entuhusiasm of the French Government toward the Kolettes administration. ::mon cher et honorable ami, pardonner moi, mon long silence, j'ai tort, mais je suis pardonable . . .vous avez trés bien conduit les affairs de la Grèce' Elle enfin un gouvernement, un gouvernement Grec' Durez, durez et continuant' C'est ce que je vous demande' C'est le premier interet de votre pays comme le premier desir de vos amis en Europe . . . ." cited in Kyriakides, *Contemporary Greeks*, I, 534.

58. *Ibid.*, 535.

59. V.J. Puryear, *International Economics and Diplomacy in the Near East, 1834-1853* (Stanford, 1935), 117.

60. Cited in Karolides, *History of the Greeks*, III, 364.

61. S.B. Markezines, *Politike Historia tes Neoteras Hellados* (Political History of Modern Greece) (Athens, 1966).

62. This loan of 60 million francs was guaranteed to Greece by the Protecting Powers by the Treaty of 7 May 1832. See Martens, *Recueil des*

Traites, X, 550-64, also Strupp, *La situation internationale de la Grece*, 125, and Levandis.

63. Hansard, 3rd series, LXXVIII, 902-903.

64. Session of July 31, 1845, *Ibid.*, 3rd series, LXXXII, 1280.

65. Aberdeen to Lyons, Foreign Office, October 2, 1845, British and Foreign State Papers, XLV.

66. George Finlay, *History of Greece*, VII, is one of the historians partial to the British Government. Also Lewis Sergeant, *Greece*, shares similar views though not as notoriously British as those of Finlay.

67. Cited in Bower & Bolitho, *Otho I*, 155-65.

68. Sessions of February 23, 1846, Hansard, 3rd series, LXXXIII, 1389-90.

69. D. Petrakakos, *Koinobouleutike Historia Hellados* (Parliamentary History of Greece) (Athens, 1935-1946), 137-38.

70. Makrygiannes, *Memoirs*, 198-199.

71. Cited in Kordatos, *Modern Greece*, III, 421-42.

Notes to Chapter Two

1. For political development during the period 1847 to 1853, see Aspreas, *Modern Greece*, I, 210-220, also Petrakakos, *History of Greece*, 137-153.

2. Fotiades, *The Exile*, 74, also Makrygiannes, *Memoirs*, 300-301.

3. The Greek Senate (Gerousia) or Council of Elders, began openly to oppose the unconstitutional practices of the monarchy and asked that the king uphold the principles of the Constitution. This attack on the monarchy by the Senate came as a shock to Otho for senators were appointed by the Crown. See Petrakakos, *History of Greece*, 140.

4. For the Makrygiannes rising see Kordatos, *Modern Greece*, III, 238-239.

5. Skandames, *Kingdom of Otho*, 451, also Bower-Bolitho, *Otho I*, 168.

6. Fotiades, *The Exile*, 77.

7. Cited in Karolides, *History of the Greeks*, III, 396.

8. For the letter of Glarakes to Palmerston see *Ibid.*, 410-411.

9. Mr. B. Cochrane declared in the House of Commons that, "I am pledading for a country from which we, in common with all Europe . . . derive all that softens and refines the heart, and all that gives life and animation to our debates. It is the cause not of Greece and her isles . . . but the cause of constitutional liberty in all parts of the world." And Palmerston added to this that the Greek "sovereign should give to the

Greek nation a constitutional system of government." Session of March 2, 1848, Hansard, 3rd series, *Commons*, XCVII, 137-38.

10. For the memorandum see Kordatos, *Modern Greece*, III, 453.

11. Petrakakos, *History of Greece*, 141-45.

12. The letter of Nicholas to Otho is cited in Skandames, *Kingdom of Otho*, 958-60.

13. Russia was opposed to the enlargement and the strengthening of Greece. It was also committed to act in cooperation with Great Britain in deciding the fate of the Ottoman Empire. See Anderson, *Eastern Question*, 111-12.

14. Mousouros was shot and wounded by a Greek radical on 28 April 1848. After this incident he was transferred to the London Embassy. The Porte took no hostile action against the government of Greece for the shooting of its ambassador. For details on the solution of the Mousouros incident see Kyriakides, *Contemporary Greeks*, I, 569-97.

15. See Chapter III section A.

16. The authoritative work on the 1848 Greek revolts is Tasos Bournas, *To Helliniko 1848* (The Greek 1848) (Athens, 1952).

17. See Aspreas, *Modern Greece,* I, 212-13, for details.

18. Philaretos, *Foreign Rule*, 86-7.

19. When the government of Louis-Philippe fell from power in 1848 "the prestige of France in Greece fell so low that the French charge d' affaires found it difficult to change francs imto drachmas." See Bower-Bolitho, *Otho I*, 171.

20. For details on the dispute see Karolides, *History of the Greeks*, III, 434-37.

21. Cited in Kordatos, *Modern Greece*, III, 462.

22. Robert Seton-Watson, *Britain in Europe, 1789-1914*, (Cambridge, 1933), 235.

23. Kordatos, *Modern Greece*, III, 462-63.

24. For the life and career of Stratford Canning see L. Lane-Poole, *The Life of the Right Honourable Stratford Canning, Viscount Stratford de Redcliffe from His Memoirs and Private and Official Papers*, (London, 1888).

25. Canning quarrelled with both Lyons and Sir Richard Church within two days of his arrival at Athens and stated publicly that they— Church and Lyons—were personal enemies of the King. This made the position of Lyons in Athens very difficult after this affair even though he still had the support of Palmerston. See Bower-Bolitho, *Otho I,* 173-75.

26. *Camerilla* was the label given to the Greek Court as it was often compared with the Spanish Court.

27. For the full text of questions and answers see Dragoumes, *Recollections*, 137-50.

28. Kordatos, *Modern Greece*, III, 545.

29. Dragoumes, *Recollections*, 134-35.

30. The period 1844 to 1850 in British relations with Greece has been labeled accurately as "cold" see *The Cambridge History of British Foreign Policy*, edited by A.W. Ward and G.P. Gooch, II (New York, 1815-66), 594-96.

31. In 1839 the Governor of the Ionian Islands wrote to Lyons that the two disputed islands belonged rightfully to the Ionian Islands. In 1849, Wyse, who had replaced Lyons, wrote to Glarakes that Elaphonese and Sapientza were under the jurisdiction of the Ionian Islands, so Greek authorities had no legal right to these islands. The Greek government considered the two islands part of Peloponnese and chose to ignore the claims of the British authorities. Great Britain had a legal claim to Elaphonese and Sapientza according to the Treaty of Paris (5 November, 1815), the second article of which read "all islands, small and large and those uninhabited lying between the coasts of Peloponnese and Albania" should be considered dependant to the Ionian government. For details on this subject see Fotiades, *The Exile*, 126-28, also Kyriakides, *Contemporary Greeks*, I, 585-87.

32. For documentation on this subject see *British and Foreign State Papers 1849-1850*, XXXIX under Greece: Correspondence with Great Britain. "Plunder of Six Ionian Boats at Salcina 1846-1847," 315-32.

33. On the day of Good Friday a mob in Athens raided his house—for he was a Jew and identified with Judas—and burned and destroyed several of his valuables. Instead of going to the Greek authorities and trying to settle the matter in court Mr. Pacifico went to the British embassy making it thus an international incident. See Kyriakides, *Contemporary Greeks*, I, 588-89, also Driault, *Histoier Diplomatique*, 328-33.

34. For Pacifico's claim see *British and Foreign State Papers, 1850-51*, XL, 619-26.

35. A. Thomaidou, *Historia Othonos*, (History of Otho). (Athens, Kostichairopoulos).

36. There were two grievances against Greece by the British government which are of some significance. 1. The ill-treatment of British officers of a ship, "Fantome" by Greek authorities at Patras. See *British and Foreign State Papers, 1849-50*, XXXIX, (Correspondence between

Great Britain and Greece, respecting an outrage committed upon a Boat's Crew of Her Britanic Majesty's ship "Fantome" at Patras 1848), 216-53. 2. Correspondence between Great Britain and Greece respecting the ill-treatment of Ionians at Patras and Pyrgos, 1846-47, 254-313.

37. Finlay to Aberdeen, London, October 18, 1842. *British and Foreign State Papers*, XXXIX, 410-12.

38. Lyons to Coletti, Athens, June 17, 1846, *British and Foreign State Papers*, XXXIX, 430-31.

39. Colokotronis to Lyons, Athens, November 9, 1848, *British and Foreign State Papers*, XXXIX, 480-81.

40. Kyriakides, *Contemporary Greeks*, I, 592-95.

41. Kordatos, *Modern Greece*, III, 553.

42. Cited in A.J.P. Taylor, *The Struggle for Mastery in Europe*, 1848-1918 (Oxford, 1971), 35.

43. Palmerston to the Lords Commissioners of the Admiralty, Foreign Office, November 30, 1848, *British and Foreign State Papers*, XXXIX.

44. Karolides, *History of the Greeks*, III, 465-66.

45. Kyriakides, *Contemporary Greeks*, I, 596-97.

46. Cited in Driault, *Histoire Diplomatique*, II, 342-43.

47. Thouvenel to Wyse, Athens, January 5, 1850, and Persiany to Wyse, Athens, January 5, 1850, *British and Foreign State Papers*, XXXIX. Also see for the Greek translation of these dispatches Kordatos, *Modern Greece*, III, 555-57.

48. Cited in Bower&Bolitho, *Otho*, 184, also in Petrakakos, *History of Greece*, 147-49.

49. Karolides, *History of the Greeks*, III, 496.

50. Kordatos, *Modern Greece*, III, 559-60.

51. Cited, *ibid.*, 500.

52. Karolides, *History of the Greeks*, III, 502-504.

53. See Taylor, *Mastery in Europe*, 34-35.

54. Drouyn de Lhuys to Palmerston, London, February 7, 1850, *British and Foreign State Papers*, XXXIX.

55. Palmerston to Drouyn de Lhuys, Foreign Office, February 12, 1850, *British and Foreign State Papers*, XXXIX.

56. Sessions of February 4, Hansard, 3rd series, *House of Lords*, CVIII, 258.

57. Sessions of March 11, *Ibid.*, 3rd series, CIX, 645-47.

58. Charles C.F. Greville, *The Greville Memoirs: A Journal of the Reign Queen Victoria from 1837-1852*, II (New York, 1885), 425-26.

59. Driault, *Histoire Diplomatique* II, 448-50, see also Palmerston to Bloomfield, March 27, 1850, cited in Ashley, *Palmerston*, 196-97.

60. For the negotiations of Drouyn de Lhuys in London and the rupture of Franco-British relations over the failure to reach an agreement in the Greek crisis, see Kyriakides, *Contemporary Greeks*, I, 604-07, see also Karolides, *History of the Greeks*, III, 520-25, also Driault, *ibid.*, 352-61.

61. Palmerston to Normandy, Foreign Office, May 17, 1850, cited in Ashley, *Palmerston*, 201-02.

62. Session of May 17, Hansard, 3rd series, *House of Lords*, III, 159-61.

63. Londos, Greek Foreign Minister, agreed to British demands on April 15th but this settlement which was reached without the French mediation resulted in a total British diplomatic victory. This was the reason negotiations in London were discontinued.

64. Karolides, *History of the Greeks*, III, 520.

65. The English government thought that the blockade would cause political turmoil in the country bringing the Court government down from power and making Otho unpopular. Furthermore it hoped that the "English" party would benefit from all of this and would rise as the popular party. None of this occurred however. On the contrary the Greek people stood firmly behind the king. See Aspreas, *Modern Greece*, 182.

66. Fotiades, *Exosis*, 141.

67. Karolides, *History of the Greeks*, III, 525-34, also L. Th. Kaskaris, *Diplomatike Historia tes Hellados*, 1821-1914 (Diplomatic History of Greece, 1821-1914)) (Athens, 1947), 69-70.

68. Cited in Driault, *Histoire Diplomatique*, II, 362.

69. *Ibid.*, 362-65, for details on the British concern on brigandage in Greece.

70. See Laskaris, *History of Greece*, 53-4.

71. Kordatos, *Modern Greece*, III, 566-67.

72. Charles E. Frazee, *The Orthodox Church and the Independent Greece*, 1821-1852 (Cambridge, 1969), 173.

73. The reason that the Tsar and the "Russian" party were against the autocephalour church in Greece in 1833 was because they wished to exert political influence through the Patriarchy in Constantinople. See About, *Grece*, 178.

74. Russia did not favor Kolettes, even though the "Russian" party did, for the Tsar felt that Kolettes was devoted to the king and therefore to an autonomous Greek Orthodox Church. See Frazee, *The Orthodox Church*, 166.

75. The first to normalize relations between the Greek Orthodox Chruch and the Patriarchate was made by Patriarch Anthimos IV in December 1849 when he attended the funeral of the devoted servant to Otho in Constantinople (Rizo-Neroulos, Minister to the Porte). *Ibid.* 171-74

76. Kordatos, *Modern Greece*, III, 567.
77. Frazee, *The Orthodox Church*, 175.
78. Cited in Petrakakos, *History of the Greeks*, 151-52.
79. Kordatos, *Modern Greece*, III, 568.
80. Cited in Frazee, *The Orthodox Church*, 179-180.
81. General Aupick, French Ambassador at Constantinople, made the first demand in 1850. H.W.V. Temperley, *England and the Near East, The Crimea* (London, 1939), 287.
82. *Ibid.*, 287-88.
83. Ann Pottinger Saab, *The Origins of the Crimean Alliance* (Charlottsville, 1977), 5-6.
84. Miller, *The Ottoman Empire*, 200.
85. Professor Stavrou maintains that the Holy Places had become a Russian interest center during the decase of the 40's of the nineteenth century. At the same time French interest also began increasing in that part of the world so "this produced a religious and diplomatic debate involving directly Russia and France." The confrontation therefore which broke out into a major diplomatic war in the early 1850's had its origins a decade earlier. See G.T. Stavrou, "Russian Interest in the Levant 1843-1848" *Middle East Journal*, 17 (1963): 91-103.
86. Saab, *Crimean Alliance*, 10.
87. *Ibid.*, 11. See also Hugh Seton-Watson, *The Russian Empire*, 1801-1917 (Oxford, 1967), 864.
88. V.J. Puryear, *England, Russia and the Straits Question*, 1844-1856 (Berkeley, 1931), 197.
89. Saab, *Crimean Alliance*, 19, also see for details on the rising of Montenegro Temperley, *The Crimea*, also F.L. Stevenson, *A History of Montenegro* (London, 1912), 183-84.
90. Cited in Frazee, *The Orthodox Church*, 184.
91. Chrisoforos Papoulakos was a monk who apparently went mad—had a vision—and went around the country preaching that all evils in Greece were due to the Catholic king, Otho. The "Orthodox" party decided to capitalize on this situation of the mad-man in order to revenge the king who was responsible for throwing out of the government the prominent Russophile Kolokotrones, and also for becoming the ceremonial head of the Greek Orthodox Church while he remained a Catholic and refused to convert to the religion of the Greek people. For details see Fotiades, *The Exile*, 167-78, also Kordatos, *Modern Greece*, III, 582-88.
92. Frazee, *The Orthodox Church*, 185-86.
93. Cited in Temperley, *The Crimea*, 303.
94. M.S. Anderson, *The Great Powers and the Near East*, 1774-1923 (Documents of Modern History) (London, 1970), 70.

95. Puryear, *The Straits Question*, 261.

96. F.O 32/205, Wyse to Clarendon, Athens, March 17, 1853.

97. Grece 61 (Files 196-201) Rouen to Drouyn de Lhuys, Athens, March 27, 1853.

98. F.O. 32/205, *Confidential*, Wyse to Clarendon, Athens, March 23, 1853. The same observation are made by Rouen, see Grece 61 (No. 25) Rouen to Drouyn de Lhuys, Athens, March 27, 1853.

99. Theodore Martin maintains that the Tsar had told Seymour that he opposed an extension of the Greek state, but a few months later Russian agents were preparing the Greeks for a war against Turkey on the frontier. He further claims that Russia helped in organizing troops for the insurrection and that on March 2, 1854 Count Nesselrode sent a note to all Russian representatives abroad "in which active support of Russia to the movement was promised. . . ." It is highly doubtful that Russia gave any support to the Greek insurrection of 1854 other than moral support. The insurrection as it will become clear in the following pages was the work of the Greeks and the Greek government. Theodore Martin, *The Life of His Royal Highness the Prince Consort*, III, (London, 1877), 53-4.

100. D. Donta, *E Hellas kai ai Dynameis kata ton Krimaikon Polemon* (Greece and the Powers During the Crimean War) (Thessalonike, 1973), 23.

101. *Ibid.*, 23, also see M.S. Anderson, *Near East*, 69. "(d) Reestablishment of the Byzantine Empire, (e) Reunion with Greece, (f) Impossibility of both."

102. Grece 61 (no. 27) Fort-Rouen to Drouyn de Lhuys, Athens, April 7, 1853.

103. F.O. 32/205, *Confidential*, Wyse to Clarendon, Athens, March 23, 1853.

104. The government at the opening stages of the Greek-Turkish hostilities was made up of individuals loyal to the Crown! The Minister of Foreign Affairs was A. Paicos, the Minister of Worship and Education was S. Vlahos, the Minister of War, Spiromelios, all affiliated members of the "Russian" party. The Prime Minister Admiral Kriezes, Minister of the Interior, Riga Palmides, and Minister of Justice Sp. Pelikas all were affiliated with the "French" party. Of all the ministers only Pelikas showed any definte signs of opposition to inviting hostilities between Greece and Turkey.

105. Commercial class included primarily Greeks involved in navigation and trading. For details on the commercial families in Greece and their growth see Petropoulos, *Kingdom of Greece*, 56-7.

106. Donta, *The Crimean War*, 24.

Notes to Chapter Three

1. E. Grasset to General Lafitte, Salonique, tom. 24 (1850-1858), 82-107, Thessalonike, 24-12-1850, cited in Elias Pangiotes Georgiou, "Gallikou Schediou Aposbeseos tes Thessalikes Epanastaseos tou 1854" (French Plans to Extinguish the Revolt of Thessaly in 1854) *Thessalika Chronika*, (Athens, 1965), 746. Nomilos, "International Position of Greece" has the Thessaly population at 250,000 of whom four fifths were moslem. The source for these figures is questionable this is why I have chosen to use the figures derived from French documentations.

2. Nomikos, "International Position of Greece," 83.

3. Greek brigands of Asia Minor influenced by anti-Turkish propaganda were transported on Greek ships to the Aegean Islands with a final destination of Thessaly. Donata, *The Crimean War*, 25.

4. D.G. Koutroumbas, *E Epanastasis tou 1854 kai ai en Thessalia, Idia Epicheireseis* (The Revolution of 1854 and the Thessaly Undertaking) (Athens, 1976).

5. A.Y.E. 1853 4/1a (no. 330), Metaxas to Paicos, Constantinople, March 2, 1853.

6. The real concern of the Greek government was over the 3,000 armed Turkish troops concentrated on the Thessaly-Epirus frontier. Donata, *The Crimean War*, 26-7.

7. A.Y.E. 1853 4/1a (No. 54), Copy (Dispatch of the Turkish Foreign Minister).

8. A.Y.E. 1853 4/1a (No. 1393), Paicos to Metaxas, Athens, March 19, 1853.

9. Donata, *The Crimean War*, 28.

10. F.O. 32/205, *Confidential*, Wyse to Clarendon, Athens, March 23, 1853.

11. *Ibid.*

12. Grece 61 (No. 33), Rouen to Drouyn de Lhuys, Athens, April 1, 1853.

13. Paicos, Foreign Minister, Vlachos, Minister of Education and Religion and Sp. Melios, Minister of War, were all members of the "Russian" party and were supported by Queen Amalia. A Krieze, Prime Minister and Minister of the Navy, R. Palamedes, Minister of the Interior, and S. Pelikas, Minister of Justice, were moderate pro-French politicians who would support the Crown and the "Russian" party.

14. Grece 61 (No. 33), Rouen to Drouyn de Lhuys, Athens, April 1, 1853, also F.O. 32/206, Wyse to Clarendon, Athens, April 7, 1853.

15. Grece 61 (No. 33), Rouen to Drouyn de Lhuys, Athens, April 1, 1853, also F.O. 32/206, Wyse to Clarendon, Athens, April 7, 1853.

16. Cited in Driault, *Histoire Diplomatique*, II, 376.

17. F.O. 32/206 (copie), Paicos to Neshid Bey, Athens, April 5, 1853.

18. Kordatos, *Modern Greece*, III, 600.

19. Donata, *The Crimean War*, 31-2.

20. *Ibid.*, 32-3.

21. F.O. 32/206, Wyse to Clarendon, Athens, April 26, 1853.

22. F.O. 32/206, Wyse to Clarendon, Athens, April 29, 1853.

23. F.O. 32/206, Wyse to Clarendon, Athens, May 1, 1853, also see Grece 61 (No. 32), Rouen to Drouyn de Lhuys, Athens, April 22, 1853.

24. See Temperley, *The Crimea*, 324-29.

25. Bower & Bolitho, *Otho I*, 190-91.

26. A.Y.E. 1853, Wyse to Paicos (copy) Athens, May 7, 1853.

27. Kordatos, *Modern Greece*, III, 599-600.

28. F.O. 32/206, Wyse to Clarendon, Athens, June 2, 1853.

29. A.Y.E. 1853 (copie), Paicos to Wyse, Athens, May 13, 1853, also A.Y.E. 1853 (copie) Paicos to Wyse, Athens, May 26, 1853.

30. A.Y.E. 1853 4/1c, Wyse to Paicos, Athens, June 4, 1853, also, F.O. 32/206, Wyse to Paicos, Athens, June 4, 1853.

31. Dr. Donata argues that there was no call for such harsh warning by Clarendon to Greece, since it could do little good and even perhaps cause the Greek government and the people to become more attached to Russia. It remains, however, that the Greek government had done nothing to show that the troops in the frontiers would be removed and furthermore brigandage continued to grow. Given that the Greek court government and the majority of the people were turning pro-Russian and anti-Turkish there was very little else Clarendon could do under such circumstances. For Donata's argument see *The Crimean War*, 44-5.

32. F.O. 32/207, Wyse to Clarendon, Athens, July 17, 1853.

33. See Grece 62 (No. 47), Rouen to Drouyn de Lhuys, June 7, 1853. France was also concerned over the fact that Menshikov had frequently visited the Greek charge d'affaires while in Constantinople. See Grece 62 (No. 49), Rouen to Drouyn de Lhuys, June 10, 1853.

34. A.Y.E. 1853, Paicos to Nechet Bey, Athens, July 7, 1853.

35. For more on this see A.Y.E. 1853 4/1b, Peri ktematon kata ta Methoria Proxenike Allelographia (Concerning the Embassy Correspondence of the Lands on the Frontier). (No. 8508), jesty the King, also (No. 142) Gregoriades (agent at Arta) to the Epirus and Albania Embassy of Greece.

36. The Ottoman regular troops were pulled out of the Provinces in June and reports from the Greek embassies in the Provinces complained about Albanian irregular troop abuses.

37. Donata, *Crimean War*, 47.

38. The movement for a Greek-Turkish war was pushed behind the scenes by such extremist nationalists as Spiro-milio and Scarlato Soutzo who were instrumental in having their influence exerted in the Greek Court, see Grece 63 (No. 69), Rouen to Drouyn de Lhuys, Athens, July 29, 1853. Also Grece 63 (No. 74), Rouen to Drouyn de Lhuys, Athens, August 17, 1853. It cannot be deduced from this that the king was really pushed into a conflict he did not ask for. Because as the next section will reveal the role of the king in the preparations for war was very much of his own will.

39. See *Ibid.*, 48-9.

40. Hetaerias were the various nationalist liberation organizations which provided money and supplies for the cause of freeing the Greeks from Turkey and reestablishing a "Greater Greek" nation.

41. A.Y.E. 1853, Wyse to Paicos, Athens, September 19, 1853.

42. See Donata, *Crimean War*, 49-50.

43. Aspreas who is a royalist argues in this manner, see *Modern Greece*, I, 224-30.

44. Philaretos, *Foreign Rule*, 98.

45. Kordatos, *Modern Greece*, III, 605.

46. Otho to Ludwig, Athens, June 7, 1853, cited in Skandames, *Kingdom of Otho*, 970.

47. *Ibid.*, 971.

48. The Constitution had not really been enforced in Greece since Kolettes became Prime Minister in 1844 (see Chapter I). Otho had nothing to fear from opposition since he had done away with the Constitutionalists of 1843. Metaxas was sent to Constantinople as ambassador, Mavrokordatos to Paris and Trikoupis to London. So the leading politicians who could get elected were not even in Greece. For details of the 1853 elections see Petrakakos, *History of Greece*, 153-55, also Kordatos, *Modern Greece*, III, 576-81.

49. F.O. 32/207, *Confidential*, Wyse to Clarendon, Athens, September 27, 1853.

50. *Ibid.*

51. The F.O. series for the years 1853-1857 contains numerous reports concerning British economic interests in Peloponnese, and especially in Corinth. In many of these dispatches the Consul at Patras ask Wyse to use his influence with the Greek government to favor the interests of the British commerce. See *Appendix*.

52. The last dispatch in A.Y.E. 1853, Wyse to Paicos, Athens, September 14, 1853.

53. Koutroumbas, *The Revolution of 1854*, 29-30.

54. F.O. 32/208, Wyse to Clarendon, Athens, October 7, 1853.

55. *Ibid.*

56. About, Grece, 231-35. Certain brigands were used as defenders of the regime. They exercised police functions and were used as the private army of the kings.

57. F.O. 32/208, Wyse to Clarendon, Athens, October 26, 1853.

58. Otho to Ludwig, Athens, November 27, 1853, cited in Skandames, *Kingdom of Otho*, 972-73.

59. Cited in Bower & Bolitho, *Otho I*, 191-92.

60. Translation used here is from Bower & Bolitho, *Otho I*, 193-95. For the French and Greek texts see Petrakakos, *History of Greece*, 155-57.

61. *Ibid.*, Petrakakos, 157-60.

62. Donata, *Crimean War*, 80, has put forward this argument.

63. S. Pelikas, *Apomnemoneumata tes Ypourgeias Spiridonos Pelika* (Memoirs of the Ministry of Spiridon Pelika) (Athens, 1893).

64. *Ibid.*, 140.

65. Petrakakos, *History of Greece*, 160-62.

66. See F.O. 32/208, Wyse to Clarendon, Athens, October 27, 1853, For the French translation of the *Aion* article see F.O. 32/208, X/Lo6972, 82-86.

67. Paicos took action against Professor Bambas but the article was not censored to the satisfaction of the Turkish charge d'affaires or Wyse. See *Ibid.*

68. A.Y.E. 1853, Nechet Bey to Paicos, Athens, December 3, 1853.

69. Donata, *Crimean War*, 62-63.

70. The Ziakas movement gave rise to revolutionary societies in Thessaly, see Koutroumbas, *The Revolution of 1854*, 69, 70-2, also Donata, *Crimean War*, 63-4.

71. F.O. 32/208, *Confidential*, Wyse to Clarendon, Athens, November 17, 1853.

72. A.Y.E. 1853, *Confidential*, Paicos to Trikoupes, November 15, 1853.

73. In December 1853 Otho chose to send ambassadors and other agents to foreign countries "without requiring the sanction of the Greek Chambers." This caused a good deal of concern in the Foreign Office and Clarendon instructed Wyse to inform Paicos of Her Majesty's government dissatisfaction with the king's abuse of his powers. The concern of Clarendon was not so much the abuse of power by the king, as the overspending for civil and military maintenance. . . . "at a time, when the

establishment both civil and military is kept up in Greece, is far to great for its revenue, any measures which entail unnecessary expense, can only be considered as exhibiting an absence of good faith towards their governments, who are still burdened with the debt of Greece." See A.Y.E. 1853, Wyse to Paicos, Athens, December 15, 1853.

74. F.O. 32/208, Wyse to Clarendon, Athens, December 17, 1853.

75. Koutroumbas, *The Revolution of 1854*, 24-5.

76. *Ibid.*

77. The General Derven Aga Suleiman Bey Frasare was pressuirng the villagers of Radovichi to provide the necessary funds for the salaries of 2,500 of his men. Zeine, an Albanian Turkish agent at Arta went to the villagers of Peta demanding money and food supplies. These abuses of the Turks could not be tolerated by the Greeks who knew that they had the mother country to rely in case they took arms against the Turks. See Kyriakides, *Contemporary Greeks*, 639-40, also see for the Radovichi uprising A.Y.E. 1854 (4/1) No. 18, Papakopoulos to the Province of Valtos, January 16, 1854, also A.Y.E. 1854 (4/1) No. 54, Skylodemos to the Earch of Valtos, January 19, 1854, also A.Y.E. 1854 (4/1) No. 557, A. Deoulas to the Ministry of the Interior, January 17, 1854.

78. See Pelikas, *Memoirs*, 140-44.

79. Takis Lappas, "Agnosta Hartia gia ten Epanastase tou 1854" (Unknown Papers for the Revolution of 1854) *Thessalika Chronica*, Athens, 1965.

80. *Ibid.*, 643.

81. Pelikas, *Memoirs*, 141.

82. "It is apprehended that in the event of movements in Servia, Macedonia or Epirus, England and France may be induced to take coercive or precautionary measures by occupation or otherwise." See F.O. 32/208, Wyse to Clarendon, Athens, November 1853.

83. Pelikas, *Memoirs*, 141.

84. Karaiskakes with 2,500 men seized the town of Arta and Grivas with 300 men took over Pente Pegadia and Peta of Epirus. At the same time that Karaiskakes and Grivas were making advances other revolutionaries (Kitsos Tsavelas, Giannes Bagos, Giannes and Nicholas Stratos, Andreas and Demitri Iskos and George Barnakokes, all volunteers) entered into Turkish soil and began attacking Turkish villages. See Kordatos, *Modern Greece*, III, 610-11, also Kyriakides, *Contemporary Greeks*, 640-43, also Koutroumbas, *Revolution in 1854*, 68.

85. Cited in Kordatos, *Modern Greece*, III, 611.

86. Finlay, *History of Greece*, 222.

87. The wealthy Greeks did not join the revolution for it would mean risking their property for an ideal called "Greece." *Ibid.*, 634.

88. See below, page 132.

89. Cited in Koutroumbas, *Revolution of 1854*, 85.

90. Saab, *Crimean Alliance*, 140.

91. Frank Edgar Bailey, *British Policy and the Turkish Reform Movement: A Study in Anglo-Turkish Relations, 1826-1853* (New York, 1970), 228, maintains that the Tanzimat was only "a step away from the old autocratic feudal order."

92. Sessions of March 13, 1854, Hansard, 3rd series, CXXXI, 706.

93. *Ibid.*, 707.

94. Saab, *Crimean Alliance*, 141.

Notes to Chapter Four

1. Koutroumbas, *Revolution of 1854*, 75-7, also see Pelikas, *Memoirs*, 151.

2. F.O. 32/215, Wyse to Clarendon, Athens, February 13, 1854, also see Nomikos, *International Position of Greece*, 151-53.

3. *Ibid.*, Nomikos, 153.

4. These Turks were carrying supplies and were captured by Nico Kaskares and his band. See Kyriakodes, *Contemporary Greeks*, 644.

5. Wyse reports on March 5 that Grivas had increased his forces from three hundred to four hundred. F.O. 32/215, Wyse to Clarendon, Athens, March 15, 1854.

6. Father Basilios Sioufas, *E Epanastasis tou 1854 kai e Katastrophe tes Gralistes* (The Revolution of 1854 and the Catastrophe of Cralistes) *Thessalika Chronika* (Athens, 1965), 464.

7. Koutroumbas, *Revolution of 1854*, 68, 82, also see Kyriakides, *Contemporary Greeks*, 645, also Nomikos, *International Position of Greece*, 156-57.

8. Nomikos, *International Position of Greece*, 158.

9. F.O. 32/215, Wyse to Clarendon, Athens, February 13, 1854.

10. Otho to Ludwig, Athens, January 29, 1854, cited in Skandames, *Kingdom of Otho*, 973-74.

11. Koutroumbas, *Revolution of 1854*, 82.

12. Nomikos, *International Position of Greece*, 159.

13. Kordatos, *Modern Greece*, III, 614.

14. *Ibid.* Koutroumbas, 83.

15. Nomikos, *International Position of Greece*, 162.

16. F.O. 32/215, Wyse to Paicos, Athens, March 17, 1854.

17. Koutroumbas, *Revolution of 1854*, 85.

18. See Athanasios A. Angelopoulos, *Dimitrios Tsamis Karatasos*, XVII, *Balkan Studies*, 49-51.

19. F.O. 32/215, Wyse to Clarendon, Athens, March 17, 1854.

20. Kordatos, *Modern Greece*, III, 615-16.

21. Osman Pasha launched the attack on Peta on April 26. See Nomikos, *International Position of Greece*, 175-77.

22. F.O. 32/216, Wyse to Clarendon, Athens, April 27, 1854.

23. For the Platanon Battle see Koutroumbas, *Revolution of 1854*, 94-99.

24. *Ibid.*, 99-101.

25. Pelikas refused to pardon the prisoners as the other ministers wished. See Pelikas, *Memoirs*, 147-49.

26. For details see Koutroumbas, *Revolution of 1854*, 145-52.

27. Kordatos, *Modern Greece*, III, 227.

28. Koutroumbas, *Revolution of 1854*, 101-03, also Kordatos, *Ibid.*, 621-42, uses many sources to cover the Macedonian revolt.

29. F.O. 32/216, Wyse to Clarendon, Athens, April 7, 1854.

30. Koutroumbas, *Revolution of 1854*, 100.

31. F.O. 32/216, Wyse to Clarendon, Athens, April 14, 1854. Rouen and Wyse addressed a note to Paicos on April 11 warning him that the Naval Forces of France and England were instructed to visit Greek ships even on Greek waters, which were suspected to carrying arms and munition. See F.O. 32/216, Wyse to Clarendon, Athens, April 26, 1854.

32. F.O. 32/217, Grivas to Georgandas, *Agrapha*, April 2, 1854, see also *Moniteur Universel* (No. 132), May 12, 1854.

33. See T.E. Evagelidos, *Historia tou Othonos Basileos tes Hellados 1832-1862* (History of Otho King of Greece, 1832-1862) (Athens, 1893), 549-50.

34. See F.O. 32/215, Wyse to Clarendon, Athens, January 17, 1854, also F.O. 32/215, Wyse to Clarendon, Athens, January 27, 1854.

35. F.O. 32/215, Wyse to Clarendon, Athens, February 7, 1854.

36. A.Y.E. 1854 (no. 3), Trikoupis to Paicos, London, January 19, 1854, also (No. 5), Trikoupis to Paicos, London, February 6, 1854.

37. A.Y.E. 1854 (No. 9), Trikoupis to Paicos, London, February 9, 1854.

38. F.O. 32/215, Wyse to Clarendon, Athens, February 10, 1854.

39. F.O. 32/215, Wyse to Clarendon, Athens, February 13, 1854.

40. Nomikos, *International Position of Greece*, 230.

41. F.O. 32/215, Wyse to Clarendon, Athens, February 16, 1854.

42. F.O. 32/215, Wyse to Clarendon, Athens, February 16, 1854.

43. Donata, *Crimean War*, 90-91.
44. Nomikos, *International Position of Greece*, 232-34.
45. *Ibid.*, 242.
46. Mavrokordatos Archive 008,873, Clarendon to Wyse, Foreign Office, March 6, 1854.
47. Evagelides, *Otho*, 550.
48. Pelikas, *Memoirs*, 157-60.
49. A.Y.E. 1854, (4/1d) see file labeled as Diakopai Sheseon Hellados-Turkias (Interruption of Greek-Turkish Relations), also A.Y.E. 1854 (4/1) Fuad Pasha.
50. Nomikos, *International Position of Greece*, 256.
51. F.O. 32/215, Wyse to Clarendon, Athens, March 17, 1854.
52. Pelikas, *Memoirs*, 162-63.
53. F.O. 32/216, Wyse to Clarendon, Athens, April 1, 1854.
54. Nomikos, *International Position of Greece*, 259-60.
55. Mavrokordatos Archive, 008,888, No. 39, Clarendon to Wyse, Foreign Office, April 8, 1854.
56. Parliamentary opinion was against the blockade of 1850. In 1854 the Greek insurrection, however, was severely criticized. See sessions of March 13, 1854, Hansard, 3rd series, CXXXI, 704-52.
57. A.Y.E. 1854 (18/3), Trikoupis to Paicos, London, April 10, 1854.
58. F.O. 32/216, Wyse to Clarendon, Athens, April 14, 1854.
59. F.O. 32/216, Wyse to Clarendon, Athens, April 26, 1854.
60. Mavrokordatos Archive, 008-897, Paicos to Mavrokordatos, Athens, April 30, 1854.
61. Pelikas, *Memoirs*, 166.
62. Kyriakides, *Contemporary Greeks*, 663-64.
63. F.O. 32/216, *Confidential*, Wyse to Clarendon, Athens, April 21, 1854.
64. *Ibid.*
65. Kordatos, *Modern Greece*, III, 646.
66. Donata, *Crimean War*, 122-23.
67. A.Y.E. 1854 (18/3), Trikoupis to Paicos, London, April 10, 1854.
68. Cited in Bower & Bolitho, *Otho I*, 198-99.
69. Pelikas, *Memoirs*, 199-201.
70. Nomikos, *International Position of Greece*, 273.
71. Cited in Levandis, *Greek Foreign Debt*, 50.
72. *Le Moniteur Universal* (No. 134), May 14, 1854.
73. Donata, *Crimean War*, 127-28.
74. F.O. 32/217, Wyse to Clarendon, Athens, May 27, 1854.
75. A. Mavrokordatos, President of the Council and Minister of

Finance, Riga Palamides, Minister of the Interior, Admiral Canaris, Minister of Marine, P. Argyropoulos, Minister of Foreign Affairs, General Kalergis, Minister of War, Calligas, Minister of Justice, and Psylas, Minister of Religion and Public Instruction.

76. Cited in Kordatos, *Modern Greece*, III, 648.

77. For the ambivalant attitude of the Habsburg Empire in the Crimean War, see B. Jelavich, *The Habsburg Empire in European Affairs, 1814-1918* (Chicago, 1969), 69-79. Also see Paul W. Schroedor, *Austria, Great Britain and the Crimean War* (Cornell University, 1972), 143-231.

78. Donata, *Crimean War*, 134-35.

79. Cited in Bower & Bolitho, *Otho I*, 200, see also Skandames, *Kingdom of Otho*, 978-79.

80. Kalergis took part in the September Revolution of 1843 ans was one of the most hated enemies of Otho.

81. Donta, *Crimean War*, 135-36. Kalergis wanted to replace Otho with a French prince and this presented a direct threat to Otho but also an indirect threat to Great Britain, see Kordatos, *Modern Greece*, III, 650.

82. Donta, *Crimean War*, 137-38.

83. F.O. 32/217, *Confidential*, Wyse to Clarendon, Athens, June 12, 1854.

84. Donta, *Crimean War*, 139.

85. In March 1854 Admiral Tinal warned the Greeks of Thessaly that France was committed to help defend the Turkish soil and that they, the Thessaloi, should not aid the revolutionaries. See Georghiou, "Thessaly Insurrection of 1854," 740.

86. Dragoumes, *Recollections, 192.*

87. *Mavrokordatos Archives 008-909, Otho to Mavrokordatos, Athens, May 27, 1854.*

88. *Donta, Crimean War*, 141. Otho had sent an official dispatch to Mavrokordatos on May 16 ordering him to become prime minister, see Mavrokordatos Archives 008-911, Otho to Mavrokordatos, Athens, May 16, 1854.

89. Mavrokordatos owed the sum of 50,000 drachmas in debts to French lenders which had to be paid by the Greek government if he wished to be allowed to leave Paris. This delayed his return to Greece. See Petrakakos, *History of Greece*, 163, also Koutroumbas, *Revolution of 1854*, 158-59.

90. F.O. 32/219, Wyse to Clarendon, Athens, July 31, 1854.

91. F.O. 32/219, Wyse to Clarendon, Athens, July 27, 1854.

92. Grece 68 (No. 87), Rouen to Drouyn de Lhuys, Athens, June 7, 1854.

93. F.O. 32/219 (No. 192) Wyse to Clarendon, July 27, 1854.

94. Professor Georgiou, *Thessaly Insurrection of 1854*, maintains that the Thessaly undertaking was terminated primarily due to the intervention of the Allied Powers and especially France when M. Guerin was sent to Lamia in June. See Georgiou, 740-45. Colonel Pakonor was sent to disband the large force which Hadji-Petros commanded in Thessaly. According to Wyse 10,000 men were led by Hadji-Petros who fought his last battle against the Turks on June 6. See F.O. 32/217, Wyse to Clarendon, Athens, June 7, 1854. Also see Koutroumbas, *Revolution of 1854*, 166-68.

95. F.O. 32/218, Wyse to Clarendon, Athens, June 17, 1854.

96. Grece 68 (No. 87), Rouen to Drouyn de Lhuys, Athens, June 7, 1854.

97. Grivas was considerd suspicious by the new administration and was not trusted by the ministers. See Koutroumbas, *Revolution of 1854*, 178. For the retreat of the chiefs see F.O. 32/218, Wyse to Clarendon, Athens, June 17, 1854, also Mavrokordatos Archive 008, 916, Grivas to Louka, May 26, 1854.

98. F.O. 32/218, Wyse to Clarendon, Athens, June 27, 1854.

99. F.O. 32/218, Wyse to Clarendon, Athens, July 7, 1854.

100. F.O. 32/220, *Confidential*, Wyse to Clarendon, Athens, August 22, 1854.

101. Fotiades, *The Exile*, 227.

102. Dragoumes, *Recollections*, II, 197-98.

103. Fotiades, *The Exile*, 297-98.

104. Evagelides, *Otho*, 572-79, also Kyriakides, *Contemporary Greeks*, 672-673.

105. Evangelides, *Ibid.*, 579-81.

106. F.O. 32/227 (No. 7), Wyse to Clarendon, Athens, January 17, 1855.

107. F.O. 32/218, Wyse to Clarendon, Athens, July 8, 1853.

108. F.O. 32/219, Wyse to Clarendon, Athens, August 11, 1854.

109. F.O. 32/220, Wyse to Clarendon, Athens, September 11, 1854, also F.O. 32/220, Wyse to Clarendon, Athens, September 7, 1854.

110. Mavrokordatos Archive 008-971, Barozze to Mavrokordatos, Constantinople, September 28, 1854, also F.O. 32/221, Wyse to Clarendon, Athens, September 27, 1854.

111. F.O. 32/222, *Private*, Stratford de Redcliffe to Wyse, Constantinople, November 29, 1854.

112. Barozze informed Mavrokordatos that Stratford de Redcliffe was a philhellene and "hoped for a great future for our country" but that he wanted things his way. Mavrokordatos Archive 008-971, Barozze to Mavrokordatos, Constantinople, September 28, 1854.

113. F.O. 32/222, Wyse to Clarendon, Athens, December 7, 1854.

114. *ELPIS* (No. 788), Athens, January 1, 1854.

115. Otho to Francis Josef, Athens, September 1, 1854. Cited in Skandames, *Kingdom of Otho*, 980-81.

116. Phanariotes came from a section in Constantinople and many of them worked in the Greek or Turkish government. They were well off and many took part in the War of Independence. The Turks viewed them with suspiciion.

117. Mavrokordatos Achive 009,043, Secret and Confidential, Barozze to Mavrokordatos, Constantinople, January 3, 1855.

118. F.O. 32/227, *Confidential*, Wyse to Clarendon, Athens, January 24, 1855.

119. F.O. 32/227, Wyse to Clarendon, Athens, February 14, 1855.

120. Mavrokordatos Archive 009,051, Barozze to Mavrokordatos, Constantinople, January 27, 1855. It was fortunate for Mavrokordatos that the Porte did not take the propaganda letter of R. Palamides seriously and continued the negotiations in good faith, see Mavrokordatos Archive 009,048, Barozze to Mavrokordatos, Constantinople, January 20, 1855. After Koundouriotes was appointed Minister at Constantinople Fuad Pasha expressed his governments full confidence in Mavrokordatos, see A.Y.E. 1855, 19/1 (No. 71), Koundouriotes to Mavrokordatos, Constantinople, April 24, 1855.

121. For the full text in Turkish, Greek and French see A.Y.E. 1855 a.a.k.H. This treaty is also in *British and Foreign State Papers*, LVI, 1381-89, also in G. Moradounghian, ed., *Recueil d'actes internationaux de l'empire Ottoman*, II (Paris, 1897-1903), 437-44.

122. See F. Tatsios, "The *Megali Idea* and the Greek-Turkish War of 1897: The Impact of the Cretan Problem on Greek Irredentism; 1866-1897," Ph.D. dissertation, University of Columbia, 1973.

123. Donta, *Crimean War*, 144.

124. Mavrokordatos Archive 009, 088, Stratford de Redcliffe to Mavrokordatos, Constantinople, June 9, 1855.

125. Mavrokordatos Archive 009, 087, The Treaty and the Resolution of the Chambers and Senate are included.

126. F.O. 32/230, Wyse to Clarendon, Athens, July 17, 1855.

127. *Ibid.*

128. F.O. 32/230, Wyse to Clarendon, Athens, July 17, 1855.

Notes to Chapter Five

1. There is only one work which deals with the role of Greece in the Crimean War, that of Domna Donta, *Crimean War*. This study focuses on

the years 1853-1854, from the beginning of the Menshikov Mission to the beginning of the Mavrokordatos administration. It does not cover the entire history of the occupation and its consequences. Another recent study on the Greek-Turkish war of 1854 is that of Dimitri Koutroumbas, *Revolution of 1854*. This is a study focusing mostly on the Thessaly revolt of 1854 and does not go beyond that year. Otho works on the Othonian period such as Skandames, *Kingdom of Otho*, Trifonas Evagelides, *Otho*, and other works mentioned throughout this study have not dealt with the diplomatic aspects of the period 1854 to 1857 nor have they covered the consequences of the occupation. Driault's *Histoire Diplomatique* is the only work which briefly covers the diplomatic relations of Greece and the Great Powers beyond 1854 but it fails to tie in the domestic political scene.

2. Kyriakides, *Contemporary Greeks*, I, 674.

3. Aspreas, *Modern Greece*, I, 224-25.

4. Philaretos, *Foreign Rule*, 103-04.

5. F.O. 32/217, Wyse to Clarendon, Athens, May 31, 1854.

6. Grece 68 (No. 90), Rouen to Drouyn de Lhuys, Athens, June 17, 1854.

7. F.O. 32/217, *Confidential*, Wyse to Clarendon, Athens, June 12, 1854.

8. Otho to Ludwig, Athens, June 3, 1854. Cited in Skandames, *Kingdom of Otho*, 977.

9. Koutroumbas, *Revolution of 1854*, 162.

10. F.O. 32/219, Wyse to Clarendon, Athens, July 17, 1854.

11. F.O. 32/219, *Confidential*, Wyse to Clarendon, Athens, July 22, 1854.

12. There were other papers which were against the Allied Powers. Panhellenism ran an article after the occupation questioning its legality. See *Moniteur Universal*, June 19, 1854.

13. F.O. 32/220, *Confidential*, Wyse to Clarendon, Athens, September, 13, 1854.

14. Kyriakides, *Contemporary Greeks*, I, 672, Kordatos, *Modern Greece*, III, 653, also see F.O. 32/220, Wyse to Clarendon, Athens, September 22, 1854.

15. F.O. 32/220, Wyse to Clarendon, Athens, September 27, 1854.

16. Kordatos, *Modern Greece*, III, 554.

17. F.O. 32/220, Wyse to Clarendon, Athens, September 7, 1854.

18. Aspreas, *Modern Greece*, I, 233.

19. F.O. 32/221, *Confidential*, Wyse to Clarendon, Athens, November 12, 1854.

20. *Ibid.*

21. Koutroumbas, *Revolution of 1854*, 176-80.

22. There were 8,000 Epirotes, 6,000 Thessaloi, 2,000 Cretans, Hydraens, Maniates and others, see *Ibid.*, 178.

23. A.Y.E. 1855 (a.a.k./1), *Confidential*, Potles to Trikoupis, Athens, September 22, 1855.

24. F.O. 32/222, Wyse to Clarendon, Athens, November 27, 1854.

25. F.O. 32/228, Wyse to Clarendon, Athens, April 4, 1855.

26.

27. A.Y.E. 1855 (a.a.k./A), No. 129, Note Verbal, Athens, August 12, 1855.

28. F.O. 32/229, Wyse to Clarendon, Athens, June 5, 1855.

29. A.Y.E. 1855 (a.a.k./A), No. 203, Potles to Trikoupes, Athens, October 15, 1855. (Potles was foreign minister under the Boulgaris administration, see below section C.)

30. A.Y.E. 1855 (18/2), No. 259, *Confidential*, Roques to Potles, Paris, October 14, 1855.

31. Bower & Bolitho, *Otho I*, 203.

32. F.O. 32/233, *Confidential*, Wyse to Clarendon, Athens, November 20, 1855. In the same report Wyse wrote that a group of brigands was caught and held for the abduction of the French Captain Bertrand at Piraeus.

33. *Ibid.*

34. A.Y.E. 1855 (19/1), Np. 35, *Confidential*, Koundouriotes to Sylvergos, Constantinople, October 10, 1855.

35. *Moniteur Grec*, Athens, January 8, 1856, No. 30382, in F.O. 32/239.

36. The Treaty was ratified 3 June 1856, signed 8 April, 1856. See Noradoughian, *Recueil d'actes interna tionaux*, II, 90, 93, also see *British and Foreign State Papers*, LVI, 1389-1391.

37. See D. Donta, *Greece and the Great Powers, 1863-1875* (Thessalonike, 1966).

38. A.Y.E. 1855 (99/1), No. 107, Trikoupis to Argyropoulos, London, June 25, 1854.

39. Greece was also allowed to regain possession arms and ammunition detained at Malta and Corfu. See A.Y.E. 1855 (99/1), Clarendon to Trikoupis, Foreign Office, July 5, 1854, also A.Y.E. 1855 (99/1), No. 145, Trikoupis to Mavrokordatos, London, September 9, 1854.

40. Otho to Ludwig, Athens, February 4, 1855. Cited in Skandames, *Kingdom of Otho*, 986-87.

41. A.Y.E. 1855 (18/2), No. 776, Roque to Mavrokordatos, Paris, August 2, 1854.

42. *Ibid.*

43. A.Y.E. 1855 (a.a.k./A), *Confidential*, Argyropoulos to Roques, Athens, July 9, 1855.

44. Otho to Francis Josef, Athens, September 1, 1854. Cited in Skandames, *Kingdom of Otho*, 980-81.

45. *Ibid.*

46. On June 10 Kalergis treated the troops and other British and French officials to a dinner at the Parthenon which was converted into a restaurant to accomodate the invading forces. Fotiades, *The Exile*, 224.

47. See Karolides, *History of the Greeks*, IV, 530-31.

48. Petrakakos, *History of Greece*, 164.

49. He would go to the palace to get the king's signature and he would ask that the orders be signed without delay, Kordatos, *Modern Greece*, III, 656.

50. Fotiades, *The Exile*, 238-40.

51. Kordatos, *Modern Greece*, III, 658.

52. Petrakakos, *History of Greece*, 169.

53. F.O. 32/229, Wyse to Clarendon, Athens, June 5, 1855.

54. F.O. 32/231, *Most Confidential*, Wyse to Clarendon, Athens, jSeptember 4, 1855.   64

55. F.O. 32/231, *Confidential*, Wyse to Clarendon, Athens, September 8, 1855.

56. Kordatos, *Modern Greece*, III, 658.

57. F.O. 32/231, *Confidential*, Wyse to Clarendon, Athens, September 29, 1855.

58. Fotiades, *The Exile*, 239-240.

59. A.Y.E. 1855 (18/2), No. 259, *Confidential*, Roques to Potles, Paris, October 14, 1855.

60. See Skandames, *Kingdom of Otho*, 990-91, also A.R. Rangabes, *Apomnemoneumata* (Memoirs), III, (Athens, 1894), 319.

61. The new ministry was sworn in on October 4, 1855 with Trikoupis as President of the Council and Minister of Foreign Affairs, however, he did not accept the position and Boulgaris who was originally chosen for the position of Minister of the Interior became Prime Minister.

62. Fotiades, *The Exile*, 240-41, Also see Kordatos, *Modern Greece*, III, 658-59.

63. Aspreas, *Modern Greece*, I, 235.

64. A.Y.E. 1855 (18/2), No. 254, Roque to Sylvergos, Paris, October 11, 1855.

65. F.O. 32/231, *Confidenial*, Wyse to Clarendon, Athens, September 29, 1855.

66. A.Y.E. 1855, (18/1), *Private and Confidential*, Trikoupis to Potles, London, October 21, 1855.

67. F.O. 32/232, Wyse to Clarendon, Athens, October 6, 1855.

68. Bower & Bolitho, *Otho I*, 206-07.

69. F.O. 32/232, *Confidential*, Wyse to Clarendon, Athens, November 13, 1855.

70. F.O. 32/233, Wyse to Clarendon, Athens, December 4, 1855.

71. F.O. 32/233, Wyse to Clarendon, Athens, December 4, 1855.

72. Otho to Ludwig, Athens, March 16, 1855. Cited in Skandames, *Kingdom of Otho*, 991-92.

73. F.O. 32/233, *Confidential*, Wyse to Clarendon, Athens, December 19, 1855.

74. *Ibid.*

75. F.O. 32/239, Wyse to Clarendon, Athens, February 26, 1856.

76. *Elpis*, No. 833, December 21, 1855.

77. F.O. 32/239, Wyse to Clarendon, Athens, February 6, 1856, also F.O. 32/239, Wyse to Clarendon, Athens, January 8, 1856.

78. *Anexartetos*, No. 253, Athens, January 14, 1856, (a court paper) published an article pointing out the dilemma facing the Western Powers in regards to the Eastern Question. The conclusion arrived in the article was that the Christians of the Ottoman Empire would eventually win their cause for Turkey is getting weaker and Christians and Muslims cannot coexist equally in the same state. The Crimean War only helped the Christian subjects of Turkey but weaken the Ottoman State which was wrongly supported by the Western Powers.

79. When Alexander Rangabes was notified by the Prime Minister that the king chose him as the new minister for Foreign Affairs he went to Otho and explained that he could not accept the position for he and Wyse had "bad relationship." The king and queen insisted, however, that Rangabes should accept the ministry so the former yielded to the wishes of the Crown. See Rangabes, *Memoirs*, III, 325-29.

80. Laskaris, *History of Greece*, 411. Trikoupis reported to the Greek government that Greece was excluded from the Conference before Rangabes became Foreign Minister. See A.Y.E. 1856, No. 33, *Confidential*, Trikoupis to Potles, London, February 21, 1856.

81. Driault, *Histoire Diplomatique*, II, 411.

82. A.Y.E. 1856 (18/1), No. 70, Trikoupis to Rangabes, London, April 20, 1856.

83. Markezines, *Political History*, I, 234-36.

84. F.O. 32/241, *Confidential*, Wyse to Clarendon, Athens, May 28, 1856.

85. F.O. 32/242, Rangabes to Mercier, Athens, May 21, 1856.

86. F.O. 32/242, Wyse to Clarendon, Athens, June 18, 1856.

87. Driault, *Histoire Diplomatique*, II, 412-13.

88. F.O. 32/243, Wyse to Clarendon, Athens, July 22, 1856.

89. Russia would only go as far as to commit herself verbally to aid Greece as one of the Protecting Powers. "Baron Brunnow assured those present (at the Conference) that Russia would associate itself in improving the state of affairs in Greece." Nomikos, *International Position of Greece*, 286.

90. Cited in Bower & Bolitho, *Otho I*, 106-07.

91. F.O. 32/244, Wyse to Clarendon, Athens, August 12, 1856.

92. F.O. 32/205, No. 10, Wyse to Clarendon, Athens, February 3, 1853.

93. About, *Grece*, 153.

94. Kordatos, *Modern Greece*, III, Fotiades, *The Exile*, T. Bournas, *Historia tes Neoteras Helladas* (History of Modern Greece) (Athens, 1974), G. Zevgos, *Syntome Melete tes Neoellinikes Historias* (A Short Study of Modern Greek History) (Athens), N.G. Svoronos, *Episkopesi tes Neoellinikes Historias* (A Survey of Modern Greek History) (Athens, 1976), all look to the Othonian period as an era of absolutism guided by the principles of corruption and adventurous imperialism.

95. Tzivanopoulos, *Condition of Greece*, 4.

96. *Ibid.*, 26.

97. *Ibid.*, 30.

98. Rangabes, *Greece*, 102.

99. The work was first published in France under the title *Ca Turkie ou La Grece*. When it was published in English, Rangabes was serving as representative of Greece in Washington, D.C. in 1867.

100. A.Y.E. 1853, (8/1), Wyse to Paicos, Athens, January 5, 1854.

101. A.Y.E. 1853, 8/1, Wyse to Paicos, Athens, January 5, 1854.

102. A.Y.E. 1854, 8/1, Persiany to Mavrokordatos, Athens, September 11, 1854.

103. A.Y.E. 1854 8/1, Forth-Rouen to Mavrokordatos, Athens, September 15, 1854.

104. A.Y.E. 1854, 8/1, Wyse to Mavrokordatos, Athens, October 28, 1854.

105. A.Y.E. 1854, 8/1, Clarendon to Wyse, Foreign Office, October 9, 1854.

106. F.O. 32/243, Wyse to Clarendon, Athens, July 9, 1856.

107. *Elpis*, No. 858, Athens, June 23, 1856.

108. F.O. 32/243, Wyse to Rangabes, Athens, July 9, 1856.

109. F.O. 32/243, Wyse to Clarendon, Athens, July 12, 1856.

110. Session of June 2, 1856, Hansard, 3rd series, CXII, 852-54.

111. A.Y.E. 1856, 8/1, Wyse to Rangabes, Athens, September 25, 1856, also see F.O. 32/245, Wyse to Rangabes, Athens, September 28, 1856, also F.O. 32/245, Confidential, Wyse to Clarendon, Athens, October 7, 1856.

112. A.Y.E. 1856, 8/1, Wyse to Rangabes, Athens, October 14, 1856.

113. F.O. 32/245, Wyse to Rangabes, Athens, October 27, 1856.

114. F.O. 32/245, *Confidential*, Wyse to Clarendon, Athens, October 7, 1856.

115. A.Y.E. 1856, 8/1, No. 35, Communication francais a M. Mercier, Paris, December 6, 1856.

116. A.Y.E. 1856, 8/1, Clarendon to Wyse, Foreign Office, December 12, 1856.

117. Sessions of February 12, 1857, Hansard, 3rd series, CXLIV, 510.

118. *Ibid.*, 511-12.

119. Levandis, *Greek Foreign Debt*, 51.

120. F.O. 32/252, Wyse to Clarendon, Athens, March 3, 1857. Wyse reported on March 3 that the evacuation was completed as two meetings of the Financial Commission had taken place. The first meeting was on February 18, the socond on February 25. The representatives were Wyse, de Montherot, Ogeroff.

121. In the spring of 1857 Wyse returned to England. "On March 27, 1857, it had been announced that the Queen intended to confer on him a knight-Commandership of the Order of the Bath, and on his arrival in England he was received by Her Majesty and by his old friend the Prince Consort, both of whom congratulated him heartily on his services throughout the difficult war years." James Johnston Auchmuty, *Sir Thomas Wyse, 1791-1862* (London, 1939).

Notes to Conclusion

1. Koutroumbas, *Revolution of 1854*, 217.

2. These dates indicate the struggle of the Greeks who tried to carve out a nation for themselves from the Ottoman Empire.

3. Nomikos, *International Position of Greece*, 290.

Notes to Appendix

1.   F.O. 32/207, C.C. Ignate and Co. to T. Wood, Patras, April 26, 1853.
2.   F.O. 1/207, Wyse to Paicos, Athens, June 30, 1853.
3.   F.O. 32/208, Wyse to Clarendon, Athens, December 27, 1853.
4.   F.O. 32/222, British and Ionian Merchants to T. Wood, Patras, October 10, 1854.
5.   F.O. 32/240, Wyse to Clarendon, Athens, April 15, 1856.
6.   F.O. 32/241, Wood to Wyse, Patras, April 28, 1856.

BIBLIOGRAPHY

ARCHIVES

1. The Historical Archives of the Greek Ministry of Foreign Affairs—
Athens

1853
(I)   Peri ton ypo tes Othomanikes Pelys Diekdikoumenon paramet-
horion chorion (Concerning the Ottoman Porte's Claims on
Boundary Territories).
(II) Peri tes Apostoles Ellenikon Strateumaton eis ta Methoria (Con-
cerning the Greek Military Mission to the Frontier).
(III) Peri daneiou 5 ekkatomeriou drachmon (Concerning a 5 Million
Drachmas Loan).
(IV) Presbeia Ellades en Londino (Greek Embassy in London).

1854
(I)   Peri Othomanikon Methorion (Concerning Othoman Boundaries).
(II) Diakopai scheseon Elladon-Turkias (Interruption of Greco-
Turkish Relations).
(III) Peri Ellinikon daneion 60 ekkatoemerion drachmon (Concerning
Greek Loans 60 Million Drachmas).
(IV) Peri Daneiou 5 ekkatomiriou drachmon (Concerning a 5 Million
Drachmas Loan).
(V)   Presbeia Ellados en Londino—Spiridon Trikoupis (Greek Embassy
in London—Spiridon Trikoupis).
(VI) Presbeia en Londino (Embassy in London).

1855
(I)   Presbeia Ellados en Londino (Greek Embassy in London).
(II) Syntheke Emporiou kainautelias metaxe Ellados ke Othomakikes
Autokratorias (Commercial and Navigation Treaty Between the
Kingdom of Greece and the Ottoman Empire).
(III) Presbeia Ellados en Londino (Greek Embassy in London).
(IV) Presbeia Ellados in Parisi (Greek Embassy in Paris).

(V)   Presbeia Ellados en Konstantinoupole (Greek Embassy in Con-
       stantinople).
(VI)   Peri Aglo-Galicon Strateumaton kaieidesispresbeion ke proxeneion
       (Concerning Anglo-Feench Troops and Intelligence from Con-
       sulates and Embassies).

1856
(I)   Allelographia meta paraproxenikon archon (Correspondence
       of Consulates).
(II)   Presbeia en Londino (Greek Embassy in London).
(III) Presbeia en Parisi (Greek Embassy in Paris).
(V)   Presbeia en Londino (Greek Embassy in London).
General State Archives Athens.
Alexandros Mavrokordatos Archive.

2. Public Record Office.
                              London
   Foreign Office
   Greece: General Correspondence
   F.O. 32/205-208-1853
   F.O.32/215-222-1854
   F.O. 32/227-233-1855
   F.O. 32/239-246-1856
   F.O. 252-252-1857

3. Archive du Ministere des Affaires Etrangeres, Quai d'Orsay,
                              Paris
   Correspondence Politique, Grece, [vols. 61, 62, 68].

PUBLISHED SOURCES

1. Printed Documents
   British and Foreign State Papers
   Vol. XXXIX, 1849-1850, London, 1863.
   Vol. XL, 1850-1851, London, 1863.
   Vol. XLV, 1854-1855, London, 1865.
   Vol. XLVI, 1855-1856, London, 1865.
   Hansard's Parliamentary Debates, Third Series
   Vol. LXXX (1845)
   Vol. LXXXII (1845)
   Vol. LXXXIII (1846)

Vol. XCVII (1848)
Vol. CVIII (1850)
Vol. CXI (1850)
Vol. CXXXI (1854)

2. Newspapers
   Le Moniteur universel; journal officiel de l'empire francis, Paris.
   Elpis (Hope), Athens.

3. Collected Works
   Anderson, M.S. *The Great Powers and the Near East, 1774-1923* (Documents of Modern History). London, 1970.
   Martens, G.F. von, *et al.*, eds. *Recueil des Traités d'alliance, de paix, de tréye et plusieurs autres actes servant à la connaissance des relations étrangeres des puissances et etats de l'Europe depuis 1761 jusqu' à present*. 134 vols. Gottingue, 1819-1944 (title changes to *Nouveau recueill général des traités. . . . from Vol. IX on)*.
   Noradounghian, G., ed. *Recueil d'actes insternationaux de l'empire ottoman*. 4 vols. Paris: 1897-1903.
   Strupp, K., ed. *La situation internationale de la Grç ce (1821-1917); Recueil de documents choisis et édit[s avec une introduction historique et dogmatique*. Zurich; 1918.

4. Memoirs, Biographies, and Contemporary Accounts
   About, E. *E Hellada tou Othonos* (E Synchrone Hellada, 1854). Translated by A. Spelios, *La Grece Contemporaine*. Athens: Tolides Bros.
   Bower, L. & Bolitho, G. *Otho I: King of Greece A Biography*. London 1939.
   Dragoumes, N. *Historikai Anemneseis* (Historical Recollections), 3rd ed., 2 vols. Athens: Stochaste, 1925.
   Evagelides, T.E. *Historia Tou Othonos Basileos tes Hellados, 1832-1862* (History of Otho King of Greece, 1832-1862). Athens: Aristides G. Galanos, 1893.
   Fotiades, D. *Othonas: E Exosis* (Otho: The Exile). Athens: Dorikos, 1975.
   Greville, C.C.F. *The Greville Memoirs. A Journal of the Reign of Queen Victoria from 1837 to 1852*. Edited by Henry Reeve, b vols. New York: D. Appleton & Co., 1885.

Lane-Poole, S. *The Life of the Right Honourable Stratford Canning. Viscount Stratford de Redcliffe from his Memoirs and Private and Official Papers*. London: 1888.

Makrygiannes, G. *Makrygianne Apomemoueumata* (Makrygiannes Memoirs). Athens: Tolides, 1972.

Martin, Theodore. *The Life of His Royal Highness the Prince Consort*. 4 vols. London: 1877.

Pelikas, S. *Apomnemoneumata tes Ypourgeias Spiridonos Pelika* (Memoirs of the Ministry of Spiridon Pelika). Athens: 1893.

Rangabes, A.R. *Apomemoneumata* (Memoirs). 4 vols. Athens: The Estia Press, 1894.

Thomaidou, A. *Historia Othonos* (History of Otho). Athens: Kosti Chairopoulos.

Tzivanopoulos, S.I. *Katastasis tes Hellados epi Othonos kai Prosdokiai Aftis Ypo ten Aftou Megalioteta Georgiou A. Basilea Hellinon* (The Condition of Greece under Otho and Her Expectations under His Majesty George I, King of the Greeks). Athens: K.N.B. Nake, 1864.

5. Monographs and General Accounts

Anderson, M.S. *The Eastern Question, 1774-1923*. New York: MacMillan, 1968.

Angelopoulos, Athanasios. *Dimitrios Tsamis Karatasos*. Balkan Studies, XVII, 1976.

Antonakeas, Nikos A. *Favlokratia, 1821-1950* (Government by Villains). 2 vols. Athens: 1950.

Ashley, Evelyn. *The Life of Henry John Temple Viscount Palmerston, 1846-1865*. 2 vols. London: 1876.

Aspreas, G. *Politike Historia tes Neoteras Hellados* (Politica History of Modern Greece). 2 vols. Athens: Chrisima Biblia.

Auchmuty, James Johnson. *Sir Thomas Wyse, 1791-1862*. London: 1939.

Bailey, Frank Edgar. *British Policy and the Turkish Reform Movement: A Study in Anglo-Turkish Relations, 1826-1853*. New York, 1970.

Bournas, T. *To Helliniko 1848*. (The Greek 1848). Athens: 1952.

Bournas, T. *Historia tes Neoteras Helladas* (History of Modern Greece). Athens: Tolides Bros., 1974.

Bullen, R. *Palmerston, Guizot and the Collapse of the Entente Cordiale*. London: University of London, 1974.

Clayton, G.D. *Britain and the Eastern Question: Messolonghi to Gallipoli*. London: University of London Press, 1971.

Dankin, Douglas. *The Unification of Greece, 1770-1923*. London: Ernest Benn, Ltd. 1972.

Donta, Domna N. *Greece and the Great Powers, 1863-1875*. Thessaloniki: Institute for Balkan Studies, 1966.

Driault, Edouard and Lheritier, Michel. *Histoire Diplomatique de la Grece de 1821 a nos jours*. 5 vols. Paris: Les Presses Universitaries de France, 1925-1926.

Finlay, George. *A History of Greece from its Conquest by the Romans to the Present Time, B.C. 146 to A.D. 1864*. Oxford: Clarendon Press, 1877.

Frazee, Charles E. *The Orthodox Church and Independent Greece, 1821-1852*. Cambridge: 1969.

Georgiou, E.P. *Gallikon Schedion Aposbeseos tes Thessalikes Epanastaseos tou 1854* (French Plans to Obliterate the Thessaly Insurrection of 1854). Thessalika Chronika, 1965.

Jelavich, B. *The Habsburg Empire in European Affairs, 1814-1918*. Chicago: Rand McNally and Co., 1969.

Jelavich, B. *Russia and the Greek Revolution of 1843*. Munich: 1966.

Johnson, Douglas. *Guizot: Aspects of French History*. Routledge & Kegan Paul, 1963.

Karolides, P. *Synchronos Historia ton Hellinon kai ton Koinon Laon tes Anatoles, 1821 mechri 1921* (Contemporary History of the Greeks and the Rest of the People of the East, 1821 until 1921). 7 vols. Athens: Panel. Leukomatos, 1922.

Kordatos, G. *Historia tes Neoteres Helladas* (History of Modern Greece). 5 vols. Athens: 1957-1958.

Koutroumbas, D.G. *E Epanastasis tou 1854 kai ai en Thessalia, Idia, Epicheireseis* (The Revolution of 1854 and the Thessaly Undertaking). Athens: 1976.

Kyriakides, E. *Historia tou Synchronou Hellinismou apo tes Idryseos tou Basileiou tes Hellados, 1832-1892* (History of Contemporary Greeks from the Founding of the Kingdom of Greece, 1832-1892). 2 vols. Athens: B.N. Georgiades, 1972.

Lappas, Takis, *Agnosta Hartia gia ten Epanastase tou 1854* (Unkown Papers for the Revolution of 1854). Athens: Thessalika Chronika, 1965.

Laskaris, L. Th. *Diplomatike Historia tes Hellados, 1821-1914* (Diplomatic History of Greece, 1821-1914). Athens: 1947.

Levandis, J.A. *The Greek Foreign Debt and the Great Powers, 1821-1898*. New York: Columbia University, 1944.

Markezines, S.B. *Politike Historia tes Neoteras Hellados* (Political History of Modern Greece). 4 vols. Athens: Papyros, 1966.

Miller, W. *The Ottoman Empire and its Successors, 1801-1927*. Cambridge, England: The University Press, 1936.

Nesselrode, Compte de. *Lettres et Papiers du Chancelier Compte de Nesselrode, 1760-1856*. 11 vols. Paris: 1904-1912.

Nomikos, E. "The International Position of Greece During the Crimean War." Dissertation, Stanford University Press, 1962.

Parry, Jones E. *The Correspondence of Lord Aberdeen and Princess Lieven, 1832-1854*. London: 1938-39.

Petrakakos, D. *Koinobouleutike Historia Hellados* (Parliamentary History of Greece). Athens: 1935-1946.

Petropoulos, J.A. *Politics and Statecraft in the Kingdom of Greece, 1833-1843*. Princeton, N.J.: Princeton University Press, 1968.

Philaretos, G.N. *Xenokratia kai Basileia en Helladi, 1821-1897* (Foreign Rule and Royalty in Greece, 1821-1897). Athens: Kousoulinou, 1897.

Puryear, V.J. *International Economic and Diplomacy in the Near East, 1834-1853*. Stanford, 1935.

Puryear, V.J. *England, Russia and the Straits Question, 1844-1856*. Berkeley, 1931.

Saab, Ann Pottinger. *The Origins of the Crimean Alliance*. Charlottesville: University Press of Virginia, 1977.

Schroeder, Paul W. *Austria, Great Britain and the Crimean War*. Cornell University, 1972.

Sergeant, Lewis. *Greece in the Nineteenth Century: A Record of Hellenic Emancipation and Progress, 1821-1897*. London: T.F. Unwin, 1897.

Seton-Watson, Robert. *Britain in Europe, 1789-1914*. Cambridge: 1933.

Seton-Watson, Hugh. *The Russian Empire, 1801-1917*. Oxford: 1967.

Siofas, Father Basilios. *E Epanastasis tou 1854 kai E Katastrophe tes Gralistes* (The Revolution of 1854 and the Catastrophe of Gralistes). Athens: Thessalika Chronica, 1965.

Skandames, A. *Selides Politikes Historias kai Kritikes, E Triakontaetia tes Basileias tou Othonos, 1832-1862* (Pages of Political History and Criticism, The Thirty-year Kingdom of Otho (1832-1862). Athens: 1961.

Stavrou, G.T. "Russian Interests in the Levant, 1843-1848." *Middle East Journal* 17 (1963).

Stevenson, F.L. *A History of Montenegro*. London: 1912.

Svoronos, N. G. *Episkopesi tes Neoellinikes Historias* (A Survey of Modern Greek History). Translated by A. Asdpacha. Athens: Themelio, 1976.

Tatsios, T. "The Megali Idea and the Greek-Turkish War of 1897; The Impact of the Cretan Problem on Greek Irredentism, 1866-1897." Ph.D. dissertation, University of Columbia, 1973.

Taylor, A.J.P. *The Struggle for Mastery in Europe, 1848-1918.* Oxford University Press, 1971.

Temperley, H.W.V. *England and the Near East, The Crimea.* London: 1939.

The Cambridge History of British Foreign Policy. Vol. II, 1815-1866. Edited by A.W. Ward and G.P. Gooch. New York: Octagon Books, 1970.

Thomaidou, A. *Istoria Othonos* (History of Otho). Athens: Koste Hairopoulos, (no date).

INDEX

EAST EUROPEAN MONOGRAPHS

41. *Boleslaw Limanowski (1835-1935): A Study in Socialism and Nationalism*. By Kazimiera Janina Cottam. 1978.
42. *The Lingering Shadow of Nazism: The Austrian Independent Party Movement Since 1945*. By Max E. Riedlsperger. 1978.
43. *The Catholic Church, Dissent and Nationality in Soviet Lithuania*. By V. Stanley Vardys. 1978.
44. *The Development of Parliamentary Government in Serbia*. By Alex N. Dragnich. 1978.
45. *Divide and Conquer: German Efforts to Conclude a Separate Peace, 1914-1918*. By L. L. Farrar, Jr. 1978.
46. *The Prague Slav Congress of 1848*. By Lawrence D. Orton. 1978.
47. *The Nobility and the Making of the Hussite Revolution*. By John M. Klassen. 1978.
48. *The Cultural Limits of Revolutionary Politics: Change and Continuity in socialist Czecholslovakia*.
48. *The Cultural Limits of Revolutionary Politics: Change and Continuity in Socialist Czecholslovakia*, By David W. Paul. 1979.
49. *On the Border of War and Peace: Polish Intelligence and Diplomacy in 1937-1939 and the Origins of the Ultra Secret*. By Richard A. Woytak. 1979.
50. *Bear and Foxes: The International Relations of the East European States 1965-1969*. By Ronald Haly Linden. 1979.
51. *Czechoslovakia: The Heritage of Ages Paşt*. Edited by Ivan Volgye and Hans Brisch. 1979.
52. *Prime Minister Gyula Andrássy's Influence on Habsburg Foreign Policy*. By János Decsy. 1979.
53. *Citizens for the Fatherland: Education, Educators, and Pedagogical Ideals in Eighteenth Century Russia*. By J. L. Black. 1979.
54. *A History of the "Proletariat": The Emergence of Marxism in the Kingdom of Poland, 1870-1887*. By Norman M. Naimark. 1979.
55. *The Slovak Autonomy Movement, 1935-1939: A Study in Unrelenting Nationalism*. By Dorothea H. El Mallakh. 1979.
56. *Diplomat in Exile: Francis Pulszky's Political Activities in England, 1848-1840*. By Thomas Kabdebo. 1979.
57. *The German Struggle Against the Yugoslav Guerrillas in World War II: German Counter-Insurgency in Yugoslavia, 1941-1943*. By Paul N. Hehn. 1979.
58. *The Emergence of the Romanian National State*. By Gerald J. Bobango. 1979.
59. *Stewards of the Land: The American Farm School and Modern Greece*. By Brenda L. Marder. 1979.
60. *Roman Dmowski: Party, Tactics, Ideology, 1895-1907*. By Alvin M. Fountain II. 1980.
61. *International and Domestic Politics in Greece During the Crimean War*. By Jon V. Kofas. 1980.

DATE DUE

The Joint Free Public Library
of
Morristown and Morris Township
1 Miller Road
Morristown, New Jersey 07960

Campaign
The Road to Trenton

Gregory T. Edgar

D1524583

Heritage Books, Inc.

Published 1995

HERITAGE BOOKS, INC.
1540E Pointer Ridge Place, Bowie, Md. 20716
(301) 390-7709

ISBN 0-7884-0185-8

A Complete Catalog Listing Hundreds of Titles
On History, Genealogy, and Americana
Available Free Upon Request

ACKNOWLEDGEMENTS

The author extends his grateful appreciation to Donald Walcott for reading the early drafts, and to the following:

The Connecticut State Library, for excerpts from two unpublished letters in the Connecticut State Archives collection, written by Isaac Gallup (973.3D33) and Noyes Palmer, Jr. (973.3D5212P).

Rutgers University Press, for excerpts from *Revolution in America: Confidential Letters and Journals 1776-1784 of Adjutant General Major Bauermeister of the Hessian Forces*, by Carl Leopold Bauermeister, edited by Bernhard A. Uhlendorf, copyright 1957 by Rutgers, The State University.

Yale University Press, for excerpts from *Diary of the American War: A Hessian Journal*, by Captain Johann Ewald, translated and edited by Joseph P. Tustin, copyright 1979 by Yale University Press.

Harvard University Press, for excerpts from *Diary of Frederick Mackenzie: Giving a Daily Narrative of his Military Service as an Officer of the Regiment of Royal Welsh Fusiliers During the Years 1775-1781 in Massachusetts, Rhode Island and New York*, by Frederick Mackenzie, Harvard University Press, copyright 1930, 1958 by the President and Fellows of Harvard University.

Excerpts of Joseph Plumb Martin's reminiscences are from *Private Yankee Doodle*, George F. Scheer, ed., Little, Brown, 1962.

Excerpts of Friedrich Ernst von Muenchhausen's journal are from *At Howe's Side 1776-1778*, Ernst Kipping and Samuel Smith, ed., Philip Freneau Press, 1974.

The Jeremiah Wynkoop anecdote is from *The Spirit of '76 and Other Essays*, by Carl Becker, Augustus M. Kelley Pubs., 1966.

Excerpts of John Greenwood are from *The Revolutionary Services of John Greenwood of Boston & New York 1775-1783*, Isaac Greenwood, ed., DeVinne Press, 1922.

ALSO BY GREGORY T. EDGAR

Available from Heritage Books:

"Liberty or Death!" The Northern Campaigns in the American Revolutionary War. Nominated for the 1995 Cincinnati Award.

Available directly from Gregory T. Edgar, at 131 Pinnacle Road, Ellington, CT 06029:

"Are the Yankees Cowards Now?" A Story of Bunker Hill. Nominated for the 1996 Fraunces Tavern Museum Book Award.

Gone to Meet the British, A Novel of the American Revolution.

CONTENTS

INTRODUCTION

During the first year of the American Revolutionary War - roughly April of 1775 to February of 1776 - most Americans still considered themselves faithful English subjects. This was true of both the Whigs (patriots) and the Tories (loyalists). They were strongly loyal to their sovereign, King George III. They thought it was his extremist ministers and the hard-liners in Parliament who were to blame for the conflict. Even George Washington, as late as January 1776, still offered toasts of good health to King George III, and referred to his enemy in the field as the "ministerial army," saying he could not bring himself to think of them as the King's army.

All this started to change in January of 1776. Americans read in their newspapers of harsh new measures passed by Parliament, and of their King's refusal to even read the Continental Congress's petition asking His Majesty to intercede between the colonies and Parliament. More shocking was the news about the King himself: he had hired German mercenaries to help the British Army fight his American subjects. And he had given a public speech to Parliament, denouncing the Americans and making it clear that he would insist on subjugation rather than reconciliation with the colonies.

For years, since the political crisis that led to the war began in 1763, American propagandists had painted the Parliament and the King's cabinet ministers - but not the King - as their persecutor. The King's personal views had not been known, until copies of his speech to Parliament reached America. Now Americans could start "opening up" to arguments in favor of independence. At this opportune time, a political pamphlet titled *Common Sense* was published, written by Thomas Paine, a former Londoner now living in Philadelphia. Paine used the language of the common man to argue that Americans must give up their reluctance to consider independence; they could not put it off any longer.

An instant sensation, the little book was snapped up as fast as the presses could print it. In a country with only 600,000 white families, it

sold an astounding 300,000 copies. Paine's arguments in favor of severing all ties with England were hotly debated in taverns and newspapers from Maine to Georgia.

By the spring, individual colonial legislatures were calling for constitutional conventions to establish themselves as independent states. A divided Continental Congress put off debating a resolution on independence until July. Those in favor of independence wanted to put off the vote until unanimity could be reached. By the end of the second of July, after two dramatic days of debates and votes, Congress voted twelve to none, with one abstention, in favor of independence. John Adams the next day wrote home to his wife, Abigail, predicting that future generations would celebrate the second of July as the great anniversary of the nation's birth.

The next two days, July 3 and 4, were spent picking apart Thomas Jefferson's draft, word by word, until it was finally approved. The document was thought at the time to be a formality, a written explanation why the Congress had voted for independence. However, the Declaration of Independence soon began taking on a stature of its own. For a while, no new member of Congress was allowed to take his seat until he first signed the original copy of the Declaration - which means some of the signatures we see on it today are of people who had nothing to do with its passage. This policy was discontinued after four months.

Declaring independence was one thing; proving it on the battlefield would be more difficult. Though George Washington had forced the British from Boston in March, 1776, they returned in greater force in July, this time at New York. The British achieved a stunning series of victories over the "rabble in arms" that called itself a Continental Army. Washington lost New York and a good portion of his army, and was chased all over Westchester County and across the Hudson into New Jersey. He could not stop his army's flight until he crossed over the Delaware into Pennsylvania, putting a river between himself and his enemy.

By now it was December, so the British generals gave up the chase

and returned to New York, leaving several cantonments of troops at different locations in New Jersey to pacify the country and make it safe for loyalists to reassert control of local government. With the end of the year fast approaching and enlistments about to expire, and perhaps with them the Revolution itself, Washington concluded that "desperate times require desperate solutions." He led his remnant of an army back across the Delaware on Christmas night, and marched through a blizzard to surprise the enemy at Trenton, New Jersey.

Encouraged by their success, many of the troops responded favorably to Washington's personal plea for them to re-enlist. The result was another victory a week later, at nearby Princeton. New recruits in the spring would bring the army back up to fighting strength again. The darkest hour had passed, and the Revolution would continue after all.

LIST OF MAPS

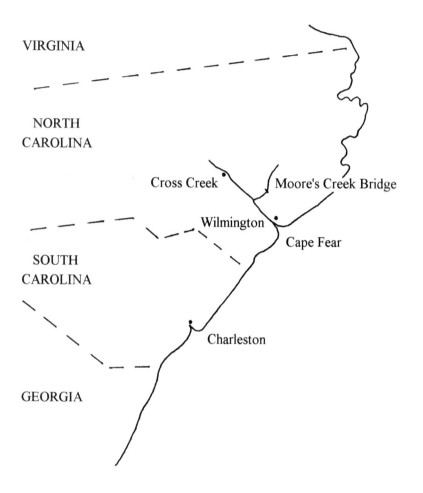

MOORE'S CREEK AREA

VIRGINIA

NORTH
CAROLINA

Cross Creek

Moore's Creek Bridge

Wilmington

Cape Fear

SOUTH
CAROLINA

Charleston

GEORGIA

x

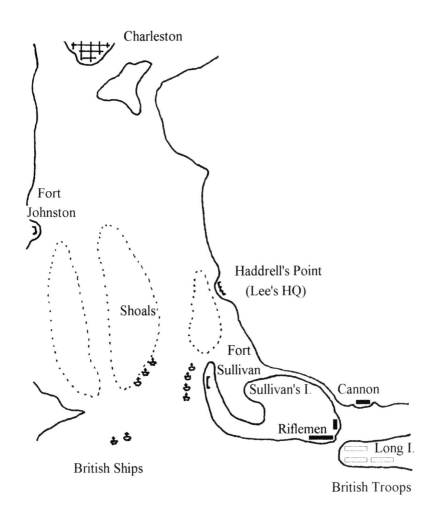

BATTLE OF CHARLESTON
June 28, 1776

Charleston

Fort Johnston

Haddrell's Point
(Lee's HQ)

Shoals

Fort Sullivan

Sullivan's I.

Cannon

Riflemen

Long I.

British Ships

British Troops

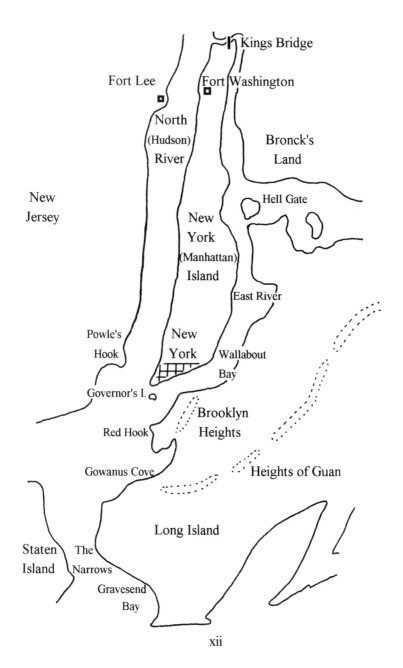

NEW YORK AND ITS ENVIRONS

Kings Bridge

Fort Lee

Fort Washington

North

(Hudson)

River

Bronck's

Land

New

Jersey

Hell Gate

New

York

(Manhattan)

Island

East River

Powle's

Hook

New

York

Wallabout

Bay

Governor's I.

Brooklyn

Red Hook

Heights

Gowanus Cove

Heights of Guan

Long Island

Staten

Island

The

Narrows

Gravesend

Bay

xii

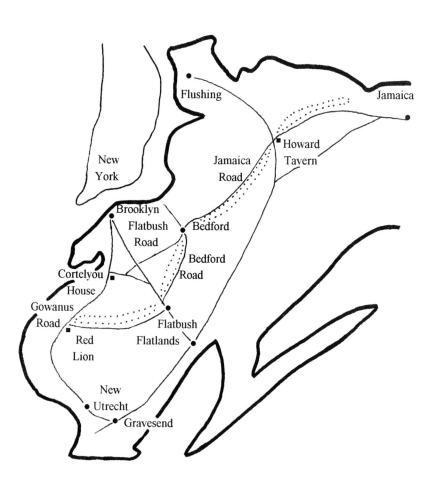

LONG ISLAND ROADS AND VILLAGES

Flushing

Jamaica

New
York

Jamaica
Road

Howard
Tavern

Brooklyn
Flatbush
Road

Bedford

Bedford
Road

Cortelyou
House

Gowanus
Road

Flatbush

Red
Lion

Flatlands

New
Utrecht

Gravesend

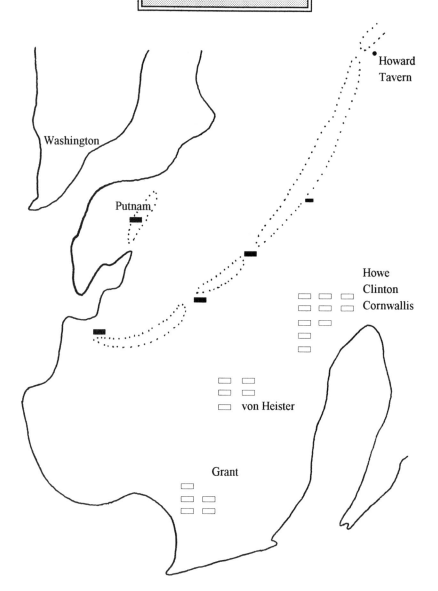

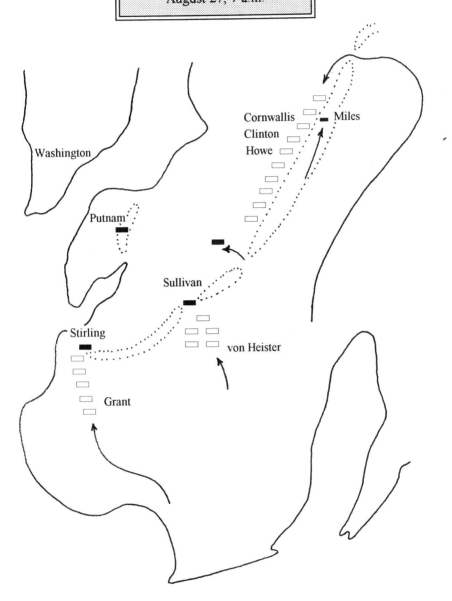

BATTLE OF LONG ISLAND
August 27, 7 a.m.

Washington

Putnam

Cornwallis   Miles
Clinton
Howe

Sullivan

Stirling

von Heister

Grant

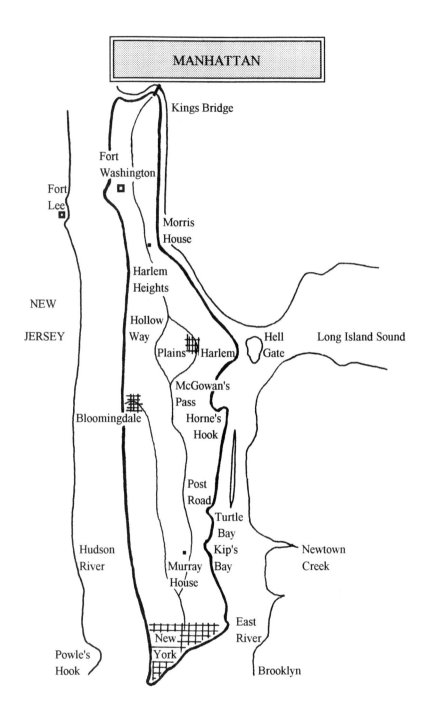

MANHATTAN

Kings Bridge

Fort
Washington

Fort
Lee

Morris
House

NEW

JERSEY

Harlem
Heights

Hollow
Way

Plains

Harlem

Hell
Gate

Long Island Sound

McGowan's
Pass

Bloomingdale

Horne's
Hook

Post
Road

Turtle
Bay

Newtown
Creek

Hudson
River

Murray
House

Kip's
Bay

East
River

Powle's
Hook

New
York

Brooklyn

xvi

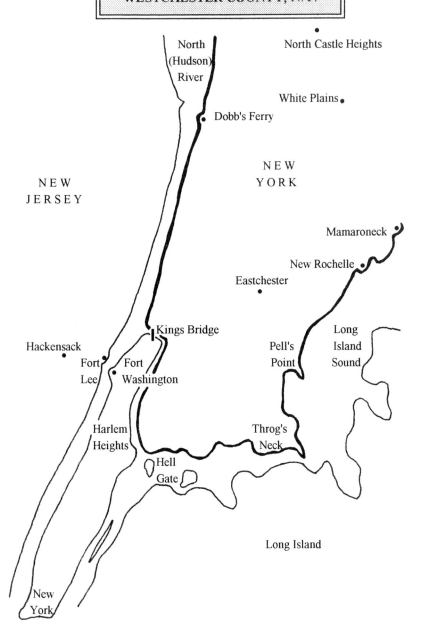

WESTCHESTER COUNTY, N.Y.

North Castle Heights

North
(Hudson)
River

White Plains

Dobb's Ferry

NEW
YORK

NEW
JERSEY

Mamaroneck

New Rochelle

Eastchester

Kings Bridge

Long
Island
Sound

Hackensack

Pell's
Point

Fort
Lee

Fort
Washington

Harlem
Heights

Throg's
Neck

Hell
Gate

Long Island

New
York

xvii

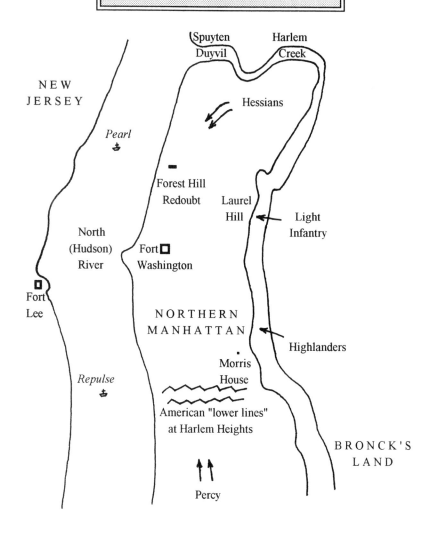

BATTLE OF FORT WASHINGTON
November 16, 1776

Spuyten Duyvil

Harlem Creek

NEW JERSEY

Hessians

Pearl

Forest Hill Redoubt

Laurel Hill

Light Infantry

North (Hudson) River

Fort Washington

Fort Lee

NORTHERN MANHATTAN

Highlanders

Morris House

Repulse

American "lower lines" at Harlem Heights

BRONCK'S LAND

Percy

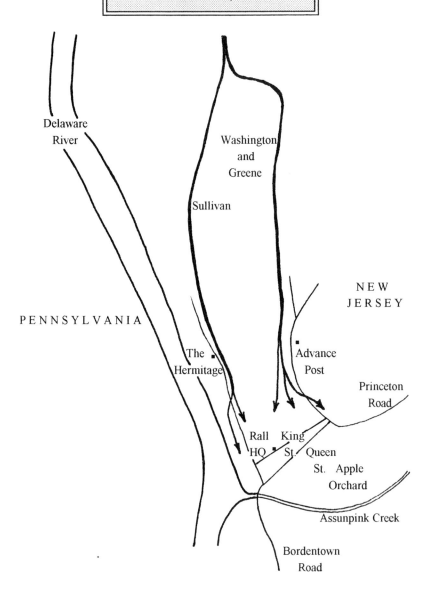

BATTLE OF TRENTON
December 26, 1776

Delaware River

Washington and Greene

Sullivan

NEW JERSEY

PENNSYLVANIA

The Hermitage

Advance Post

Princeton Road

Rall HQ

King St.

Queen St.

Apple Orchard

Assunpink Creek

Bordentown Road

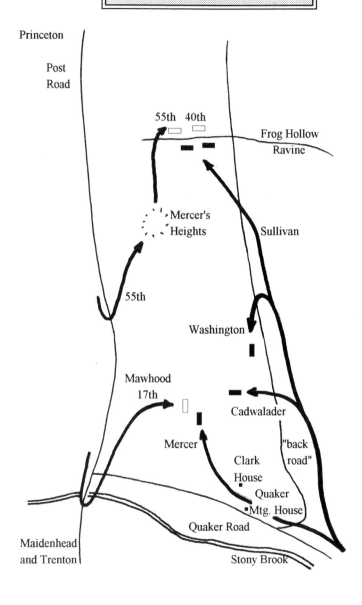

BATTLE OF PRINCETON
January 3, 1777

Princeton

Post
Road

55th   40th

Frog Hollow
Ravine

Mercer's
Heights

Sullivan

55th

Washington

Mawhood
17th

Cadwalader

Mercer

"back
road"

Clark
House

Quaker
Mtg. House

Quaker Road

Maidenhead
and Trenton

Stony Brook

CHAPTER ONE
WASHINGTON FORCES
THE BRITISH FROM BOSTON
JULY 1775 - MARCH 1776

"The bay is open - everything thaws here except Old Put. He is still as hard as ever, crying out for powder, powder, ye gods, give us powder!"

> *- An American colonel, describing General Israel Putnam's eagerness for battle, in the winter of 1776.*

To the colonial patriots, or "rebels" as the loyalists and the British called them, it was the British Army - the "redcoats" - that had started this war. Back in April, they had boldly marched out of Boston into the countryside. Their disastrous expedition - to arrest John Hancock and Samuel Adams at Lexington, then continue on and destroy rebel munitions at Concord - had accomplished none of its objectives. The exhausted soldiers marched the eighteen miles back to Boston through a gauntlet of angry farmers shooting from behind trees and stone walls. The professionally trained British Regulars had been humiliated by a mob of untrained irregulars.

The Regulars were eager for revenge, and they soon had their chance. In June, the rebels had the audacity to throw up an earthwork fort on Breed's Hill, above Charlestown, less than a mile from British occupied Boston. In the misnamed Battle of Bunker Hill, the British charged up Breed's Hill three times, suffering terrible casualties, before finally chasing the rebels from the hill.

After the battle, the rebels were more determined than ever to force

the British from Boston. They continued digging in, surrounding Boston and its 6,000 man British Army with endless earthworks, manned by nearly 20,000 New England militia, or "Yankees."

At this point in the war, the Americans were not yet interested in independence from Britain, just a redress of their grievances with Parliament. But the British government was not looking for a peaceful settlement to the conflict. A majority in Parliament agreed with the following private sentiments of King George III:

> No consideration could bring me to swerve from the present path which I think myself duty bound to follow. Once these rebels have felt a smart blow, they will submit; and no situation can ever change my fixed resolution, either to bring the colonies to a due obedience to the legislature of the mother country, or to cast them off!

Most of the action of any consequence was out at sea. American "privateers" (privately owned former merchant ships, refitted for combat) were capturing British ships trying to bring food, clothing, coal and other supplies to the army at Boston. William Bartlett, after capturing a ship from the Carribbean, sent its cargo to American headquarters at Cambridge, with a note to General Washington: "The oranges, being directed to his Excellency General Gage, hope they will be the more acceptable to his Excellency General Washington."

After June's Bunker Hill battle, the remainder of 1775 saw very little action around Boston, other than an occasional skirmish between scouting or foraging parties. The British waited for reinforcements that would not arrive until the spring of 1776. In the meantime, they kept up their artillery bombardment of the American lines. Despite an occasional casualty from the shelling, the Yankees "became so accustomed" to it that "for half a pint of aniseed water one soldier who was a little timid could get another to stand for him as sentry in the most perilous place."

At least one British officer became disillusioned about the service that he was sent to America to perform, as he relates in the following letter he wrote home:

> I am clearly of opinion that nothing further will be attempted by us till we have received a considerable reinforcement. When they arrive here, tis said the fate of America will be decided, and that troops will be perpetually quartered in every town on the continent, to enforce submission, and promote the designs of administration.
>
> Till my arrival here, I acknowledge I was ignorant enough to imagine that the Colonists had renounced their Sovereign and were actually contending for absolute independence; but I am now convinced that they desire nothing more than peace, liberty and safety, the same situation as they were in at the close of the last war.
>
> For my part, I always said and thought that violent measures would do no good here; and we now find that they have done a great deal of mischief, for the Colonies are so firmly united by them and become so desperate that they court death to avoid slavery. And the soldiery are [so] fully convinced of the truth of it, from what they saw at Bunker's-hill, that they will expect to a man to lay their execrated bones in this country.
>
> But should the scurvy, the bloody flux, and the yellow fever continue to rage in our camp, as it has done for some time past, there will be no occasion for fighting to destroy us; death will make a sufficient and terrible carnage without it. I am determined to resign my commission, and return to my native country.

Epidemics of smallpox, scurvy and other diseases plagued the city, and "ten to thirty" burial parties daily filled the streets on their way to

the cemeteries. One British official wrote, "You meet as many dead folks as live ones in Boston streets."

In the American camp, General Washington was preoccupied with organizing his "rabble in arms" into an army. The need for some method of distinguishing rank became apparent to him one day when a determined sentry, not knowing what the Commander-in-Chief looked like, barred him from entering his own headquarters. The next day, the general bought a blue silk ribbon to wear across his chest, between his blue and buff great-coat and his white waistcoat. From then on, all officers of the various ranks would wear color-coded ribbons, or "cockades," in their three-cornered hats.

Almost no one owned a uniform, except for officers who paid seam-stresses to make them one. Most of the Yankees wore a round, wide-brimmed farmer's hat, homespun shirt and trousers, a long frock, and cowhide shoes rather than boots.

Having spent much time in the wilderness during the late French War, Washington appreciated the comfort and practicality of the long hunting shirt worn by the Virginia riflemen. It had the added benefit of being "a dress justly supposed to carry no small terror to the enemy, who think every such person a complete marksman." As early as July 10, he suggested Congress make the hunting shirt the standard uniform of the army. "I know of nothing which, if put in practice, would have a happier tendency to unite the men, and abolish these provincial distinctions that lead to jealousy and dissatisfaction." Silas Deane de-scribed the garment:

> They take a piece of tow cloth that is stout, and put it in a tan-vat until it has the shade of a dry or fading leaf; then make a kind of frock of it, reaching down below the knee, open before, with a large cape. They wrap it round them tight, on a march, and tie it with their belt.

Having no luck with Congress, Washington wrote to the New Eng-land governors about his proposal to adopt the hunting shirt as a

standard. But, again, his efforts met with no success. Rhode Island's Governor Cooke replied that there was no tow cloth available to be purchased. It is romantic to think of our revolutionary soldiers in handsome uniforms. Indeed, the colonies, sometimes individual regiments or even companies, had unique styles and colors for their official uniform. But, in most cases, these uniforms never progressed past designs on paper.

The enlistments of the original New England army were due to expire in December. Congress had approved Washington's plan for its reorganization into a truly Continental Army with twenty-eight regiments of 728 men each. This required the dissolution of all the existing regiments, since the army had been composed of forty regiments of various sizes. Thus, with twelve fewer regiments, many an officer would have to lose his command.

When Washington called for the names of those officers who intended on remaining in the service, most of the officers, at first, did not respond. They hesitated, not knowing what their new rank would be. So Washington and his generals compiled an officers roster for the new army. Most of the officers whose rank had been lowered lost no time in petitioning their colonial assembly to persuade Washington to change his mind. Many simply refused to remain and be insulted by a demotion. They went home, and in many cases their men went with them. Exasperated, Washington wrote to his friend, Joseph Reed, in Philadelphia:

> Such a dearth of public spirit and such want of virtue, such stockjobbing, and fertility in all the low arts to obtain advantages of one kind or another, in this great change of military arrangement, I never saw before, and pray God's mercy I may never be witness to again. Could I have forseen [it] ..., no consideration upon earth should have induced me to accept the command. A regiment or any subordinate department would have been accompanied with ten times the satisfaction, per-

haps the honor.

Enlistment results for the new army were disappointing. Most of the soldiers would not re-enlist "until they knew their colonel, lieutenant-colonel, major and captain." The men objected to the idea of serving under officers from a different colony. The men in Simeon Lyman's company declared that they would go home to Connecticut when their enlistments expired on December 10, 1775. A week before, Virginia's General Lee had attempted to persuade them to stay just until the fourteenth, when replacement militia from Connecticut were due to arrive. The men were not receptive to the idea, or to the former Englishman's arrogance.

> General Lee came in and the first words was, "Men, I do not know what to call you, you are the worst of all creatures," and flung and curst and swore at us, and said if we would not stay he would order us to go on Bunker Hill, and if we would not go he would order the riflemen to fire at us. There was one that was a mind to have one of his mates turn out with him. The general see him, and he catched his gun out of his hands and struck him on the head, and ordered him to be put under guard.

A few days later, General Lee wrote to a congressman about his unsuccessful effort:

> Some of the Connecticutians who were homesick could not be prevailed on to tarry, which means in the New England dialect to serve any longer. They accordingly marched off. In passing through the lines of other regiments, they were horribly hissed, groaned at, and pelted.

General Lee sent a notice to innkeepers along the road to Connecti-

cut, warning them not to feed or lodge the homeward-bound men. Lee also posted a copy of the notice on his own door. But, Simeon Lyman wrote, "the paper was took down as soon as it was dark, and another put up that General Lee was a fool and if he had not come here we should not know it."

Like the men of Connecticut, many of the Rhode Island troops also could not be persuaded to stay. Rhode Island's General Nathanael Greene tried to explain their actions:

> I was in hopes that ours would not have deserted the cause of their Country. But they seem to be so sick of this way of life, and so home sick, that I fear the greater part and the best part of the troops from our Colony will go home. The regiment raised in the Colony of Rhode Island [for home service] has hurt our recruiting amazingly; they are fond of serving in the army at home, and each feels a desire to protect his own family.

In a similar letter to General Washington, Connecticut's Governor Trumbull explained the departure of some of the Connecticut troops:

> The pulse of a New England man beats high for liberty. His engagement in the service he thinks purely voluntary; therefore, in his estimation when the time of inlistment is out he thinks himself not holden without further engagement. This was the case in the last war.

This tendency to depart when enlistments expired was so widely practiced and commonly understood that almost no letters or diaries during the war argued against it. And it was not limited to the New Englanders, as witnessed by William Thompson, a rifleman colonel from Pennsylvania. When a junior officer was considered for promotion above him, Thompson threatened to go home and "fix my tent on the rocks of Cannegoquinet, and in good whiskey toddy drink General

Washington, Lee and one or two more, and pray that success may attend the American arms, and in sure and certain hope that our liberties will be secured, lay me down and rest."

These traditional practices and attitudes toward military service would, throughout the war, hamper the efforts of Washington and the Congress to build and maintain a Continental Army large enough to be effective. Relatively few Americans spent more than one consecutive term of enlistment in the army. Most preferred to wait until the enemy ventured near their home, then answer the call for "levies" (short term state troops) to reinforce the army in the emergency.

Washington preferred men willing to enlist as "regulars" in the Continental Army. He spent many hours corresponding with the governors, requesting faithful adherence to Congress's quotas. Sometimes he had to dispatch officers to recruit men for the army. Captain Alexander Graydon, a Pennsylvanian, described such an assignment:

> My recruiting party was sent out in various directions; and each of my officers, as well as myself, exerted himself in the business. A number of fellows at a tavern, at which my party rendezvoused, indicated a desire to enlist, but although they drank freely of our liquor, they still held off. I soon perceived that the object was to amuse themselves at our expense, and that if there might be one or two among them really disposed to engage, the others would prevent them.
>
> One fellow in particular, who had made the greatest shew of taking the bounty, presuming on the weakness of our party - consisting only of a drummer, corporal, my second lieutenant and myself - began to grow insolent, and manifested an intention to begin a quarrel. He no doubt calculated on giving us a drubbing. I resolved, that if a scuffle should be unavoidable, it should, at least, be as serious as the hangers [short swords] which my

lieutenant and myself carried by our sides could make it. Our endeavor, however, was to guard against a contest; but the moderation we testified was attributed to fear.

At length, the arrogance of the principal ruffian rose to such a height that he squared himself for battle and advanced towards me in an attitude of defiance. Taking excellent aim, I struck him with the utmost force between the eyes and sent him staggering to the other end of the room. Then instantly drawing our hangers, and receiving the manful co-operation of the corporal and drummer, we were fortunate enough to put a stop to any further hostilities.

It was some time before the fellow I had struck recovered from the blow, but when he did, he was quite an altered man. He was as submissive as could be wished, begging my pardon for what he had done, and although he would not enlist, he hired himself to me [to help with recruiting] ... as a fifer, in which capacity he had acted in the militia. During the time he was in this employ he bore about the effects of his insolence, in a pair of black eyes. This incident would be little worthy of relating, did it not serve in some degree to correct the error of those who seem to conceive the year 1776 to have been a season of almost universal patriotic enthusiasm.

The disappointing results of his reorganization of the army, coupled with anxiety over whether the new British commander, General Howe, would take advantage of the situation, caused Washington many sleepless nights. In early January, 1776, he wrote to a trusted confidant back home:

Search the vast volumes of history through, and I much question whether a case similar to ours is to be found; to wit, to maintain a post against the flower of

9

the British troops for six months together without [powder] ... and to have one army disbanded and another to raise, within [sight of the] ... enemy. It is too much to attempt.

The reflection on my situation and that of this army produces many an unhappy hour when all around me are wrapped in sleep. I have often thought how much happier I should have been if, instead of accepting the command under such circumstances, I had taken my musket on my shoulder and entered the ranks; or, if I could have justified the measure to posterity and my own conscience, I had retired to the back country and lived in a wigwam.

Fortunately, Howe did not take advantage of the weakness of the Continental Army during the transition period. After Bunker Hill, Howe had no desire to repeat the mistake of sending his infantry against Yankee marksmen standing behind breastworks.

On January 1, 1776, General William Heath, of Massachusetts, noted in his journal the great changes in the army. "The officers and men of the new regiments were joining their respective corps; those of the old regiments were going home by hundreds and thousands." That very same day, Washington, in an attempt to bring a sense of unity to the "mixed assemblage" that composed his army, hoisted a new flag "in compliment to the United Colonies." It had thirteen red and white stripes, and the crosses of England and Scotland in the top left corner. The British, on seeing it, thought it was a flag of surrender. Washington learned this, a few days later, from "a person out of Boston," and remarked, "By this time I presume they begin to think it strange that we have not made a formal surrender."

So, with the army's new structure in place, and the enemy content to sit in Boston until spring, Washington had only to wait, in hope, for the return of Henry Knox. The day after Lexington and Concord, Knox, a young, stocky bookseller, had abandoned his books (all ex-

cept a few on artillery and the art of military engineering), and escaped from Boston. His wife, Lucy, had smuggled out his sword under her petticoats. Since then, Knox had put his book knowledge to practical use building fortifications.

In late November, 1775, Washington had sent Henry Knox to Fort Ticonderoga on Lake Champlain's New York shore. Knox's mission: transport several dozen cannon overland 300 miles to the patriot army outside Boston. Washington gave Knox a draft for $1,000 to rent oxen, build sleds, and hire teamsters. According to General Washington, the cannon absolutely must be brought to camp, "the want of them is so great that no trouble or expense must be spared to obtain them." This $1,000 was all the war chest could provide, and Knox personally furnished the remaining $2,500 he ultimately needed for the trip. It would be several years before Congress would reimburse him. By then, "civilian volunteer" Knox would be Major-General Knox.

Accompanied by his young brother and a servant, Knox reached Ticonderoga, New York, on December 5th. He selected 43 cannon, 16 mortars, 23 boxes of lead, and a barrel filled with 30,000 flints (an item Washington had insisted Knox not forget). The total weight of the stores to be transported amounted to sixty tons. On December 17th, he wrote to Washington from Fort George, south of Ticonderoga: "I have made forty-two exceeding strong sleds and have provided eighty yokes of oxen to draw them as far as Springfield, where I shall get fresh cattle to carry them to camp. I hope in sixteen or seventeen days time to present to your Excellency a noble train of artillery." It would take more than twice that long, but he would make it.

While Knox's men were suffering from exhaustion and frostbite in the Berkshires, the British were relieving their boredom by converting Faneuil Hall into a house for dramatic productions (a form of entertainment, until then, banned in Boston). General Burgoyne, an accomplished playwright, wrote a farce for the soldiers to perform. A Boston paper reported, in December, "We are informed that there is now getting up at the theatre, and will be performed in the course of a fortnight, a new farce, called the Blockade of Boston." The printer of

another newspaper, outside Boston, reprinting this news, added his own opinion that, "It is more probable, before that time, the poor wretches will be presented with a tragedy called the Bombardment of Boston."

A cordial invitation was sent to "George Washington, Esq.," with a copy of the playbill. Although fond of theater, Washington did not attend. However, he added his own bit of drama to opening night by sending Captain Thomas Knowlton and 200 Connecticut troops to raid Charlestown the night of the play. As the British soldiers were busy dressing as women, Negroes, rebel leaders, etc., Knowlton led his men single file across the narrow causeway separating the mill pond from the Charles River, thus bypassing the British outpost on Charlestown Neck. Knowlton's force was on its way to burning the few houses still standing in Charlestown after the fire of June 17th. Just above them, on Bunker Hill, British soldiers were in their fortifications. Private John Greenwood's parents were watching the play in Boston's Faneuil Hall, and later described the action to him:

> Just as the play was at its height, and as one of the actors was representing a Yankee sentinel, rigged out as a tailor, with his paper measures hanging over his shoulders and his large shears sticking out of his pocket, etc., resting or leaning upon his gun and conversing with a countryman who had a newspaper - just at that very time, the houses at Charlestown set on fire. This produced such an alarm in Boston that a sergeant rushed upon the stage and cried out as loud as he could: "To arms! to arms! gentlemen, the rebels are upon us!" The audience thought he was acting part of the play and clapped him stoutly because he did so well, and it was some time before he could make them understand it was no sham. When they did, however, they tumbled downstairs, over one another as fast as they could.

A British officer there that night also noted the reaction to the alarm:

> The audience clapped prodigiously. But soon finding their mistake, a general scene of confusion ensued. They immediately hurried out of the house to their alarm posts, some skipping over the orchestra, trampling on the fiddles, and everyone making his most speedy retreat. The actors, who were all officers, calling out for water to wash the smut and paint from their faces; women fainting; and, in short, the whole house was nothing but one scene of confusion, terror and tumult.

With Henry Knox and the big guns from Ticonderoga nearing arrival, Washington desired the troops to steel themselves, mentally, for an imminent battle. His general orders of the day, for February 26th, included an admonishment:

> All officers, non-commissioned officers, and soldiers are positively forbid playing at cards and other games of chance. At this time of public distress, men may find enough to do in the service of their God and their country without abandoning themselves to vice and immorality. As the season is now fast approaching when every man must expect to be drawn into the field of action, it is highly important that he should prepare his mind for it. It is a noble cause we are engaged in. Our posterity depends upon the vigor of our exertions; in short, freedom or slavery must be the result of our conduct. If any man in action shall presume to skulk, hide himself, or retreat from the enemy without the orders of his commanding officer, he will be instantly shot down as an example of cowardice; cowards having too frequently disconcerted the best formed troops by their

dastardly behavior.

Reports that the rebels were assembling materials for the construction of earthworks stirred General Howe to action. On February 13th, he had a party of cavalry rowed southward, across Boston Harbor to Dorchester. They drove off a party of rebels there, capturing two of them, but found no evidence of fortifications started or planned. After burning a few vacant houses, they returned to put Howe's mind at ease. He felt reassured now that Washington had no intention of attacking him, or of fortifying the ominously close Dorchester hills. Howe wrote to Lord Dartmouth, "We are not under the least apprehension of an attack upon this place from the rebels, by surprise or otherwise." He then added his personal wish "that they would attempt so rash a step." Howe, by now tired of Boston, patiently waited for the arrival of more transports and provisions, so he could move his army to New York.

Two days after Howe wrote that letter, severe weather provided "some pretty strong ice," on which the Americans could cross to Boston. Washington again put his proposition to his top generals. There were now 9,000 Continentals and 7,000 militia in camp, compared to perhaps 5,000 British effectives in Boston. He felt that a surprise "stroke well aimed might put a final end to the war." However, the consensus of his council of war was that an attack would be too risky without sufficient powder for a strong supporting cannonade. Disappointed, the commander wrote to his friend, Joseph Reed, "Behold, though we had been waiting all the year for this favorable event, the enterprise was thought too dangerous. Perhaps it was; perhaps the irksomeness of my situation led me to undertake more than could be warranted by prudence."

But powder was trickling in, some from European merchants, some from British ships captured at sea, as well as some manufactured from saltpetre in the colonies. New York, though blockaded by British men-of-war, was a prime smuggling point. In an agreement with the city, the British admiral there allowed shipping to go in and out of the

port as long as the men-of-war were provided with firewood and food-stuffs from loyalists willing to sell to them. More often than not, the American merchant vessels carried munitions hidden amongst their cargoes, destined for the rebel army in Massachusetts.

With the powder supply increasing, and cannon to make use of it now available, Washington could take action to force Howe to either come out and fight or sail away. On February 26th, Washington made plans "to take post on Dorchester Heights, to try if the enemy will be so kind as to come out to us." He wrote to John Hancock, "I should think, if anything will induce them to hazard an engagement, it will be our attempting to fortify these heights, as, on that event's taking place, we shall be able to fire upon a great part of the town, and almost the whole harbor."

The problem would be how to build earthworks when the ground was frozen. They had already discovered what intrenching in winter was like. Lieutenant-Colonel Jeduthan Baldwin, of Massachusetts, writing in his diary back on January 19th, described the work at Lech-mere's Point in Cambridge: "the ground has frosen 22 inches deep as hard as a rock, & in one night it frose in the trenches 8 inches deep so that we pryed up cakes of frosen earth 9 feet long & 3 feet broad." The earthworks at Lechmere's Point took from November to late Feb-ruary to complete. How could they expect to accomplish a similar feat in one night atop Dorchester's hills? Colonel Rufus Putnam, of Mas-sachusetts, supplied the answer - the breastworks could be made of "fascines" (bundles of sticks and brush) held in place by "chandeliers" (wooden frames). This had been a successful intrenching method used in the recent war against the French, and in other wars as far back as the Roman Empire.

Washington prepared for battle. He advertised for nurses, and or-dered 2,000 bandages. He also ordered a light wagon for himself, equipped with two folding tables, eighteen camp stools, and a tent. He set March 4th as the date for occupying Dorchester Heights, so the provoked British Army would attack on March 5th, the sixth anniver-sary of the "Boston Massacre." To lend a hand, the nearby towns

were requested to send their militia to enlist for three days, starting March 4th.

On the evening of March 2nd, Knox's big guns, now in place at Lechmere's Point and at Roxbury, near Boston Neck, began a three night bombardment of Boston. This was to distract Howe from the work to be done on the third night atop Dorchester Heights. Although only thirteen balls were fired on the first night, at least one of them took effect. John Greenwood, whose parents were still in Boston, later learned from them that "while our troops were firing into Boston over Roxbury Neck, a ball from a 9-pounder struck into the British guard-house and carried off the legs of ten men as they were sitting on a bench together." This was corroborated by British Colonel Charles Stuart, who wrote, "Their shells took effect near the centre of the town and tore several houses to pieces. One shot killed 8 men of the 22nd Regt." Another letter, dated March 4th: "The rebel artillery officers are at least equal to our own. In the number of shells that they flung last night not above three failed. This morning we flung four, and three of them burst in the air."

The evening of March 4th, Brigadier-General John Thomas led two thousand Yankees up Dorchester's hills, shielded from British sight by a long screen of hay shocks tied together to hide the passing ox-carts and men. Directed by Colonels Gridley and Putnam, they worked feverishly from 7 p.m. to 3 a.m., when they were relieved by another two thousand.

The meager American bombardment at Lechmere and Roxbury sparked a larger, louder return fire from Boston. The noise and smoke helped conceal the construction from British ears and eyes. The weather was also cooperating, as the Reverend David Gordon, digging on Dorchester Heights that night, later recalled:

> The wind lay so as to carry away what noise could not
> be avoided, driving the stakes and picks against the fro-
> zen ground. It was hazy below so that our people could
> not be seen, tho' it was a bright moonlight night on the

hills.

As early as 10 o'clock that night, a British sentry came to Brigadier-General Francis Smith with word that the Americans "were at work on Dorchester Heights." Smith promptly went to Province House and called the Commander-in-Chief away from the gambling table. The scene was reminiscent of the night before the Battle of Bunker Hill, when Generals Gage and Howe had been informed of rebel activity on Charlestown's hills. As Gage had done back then, Howe quickly decided he would deal with the situation in the morning. He returned to his mistress at the faro table. It began to appear as though June 17 was going to repeat itself.

Atop Dorchester Heights, the construction went on through the night, as described by General Heath:

> The Americans took possession of Dorchester Heights and nearly completed their works on both hills by morning. Perhaps there never was so much work done in so short a space of time. The adjoining orchards were cut down to make the abatis, and in a very curious and novel mode of defense was added to these works.
>
> The hills on which they were erected were steep and clear of trees and bushes. Rows of barrels, filled with earth, were placed round the works. They presented only the appearance of strengthening the works, but the real design was, in case the enemy made an attack, to have rolled them down the hill. They would have descended with much increasing velocity, as must have thrown the assailants into the utmost confusion, and have killed and wounded great numbers. This project was suggested by a merchant of Boston. We waited with impatience for the attack, when we meant to emulate and hoped to eclipse the glories of Bunker's Hill.

Washington sent 800 riflemen to the Dorchester shore to cover the workers, and "to gald the enemy sorely in their march from their boats and in landing." At the same time, General Putnam was standing by with 4,000 men, ready to cross the Charles River, under the protective cover of floating batteries, to attack Boston once Howe weakened it by sending assault troops away to Dorchester. These troops under Putnam would work their way through the city to the Neck, and there force the gates open to allow entry of more troops from Roxbury. Putnam eagerly awaited his assignment. Colonel Moylan wrote, "The bay is open - everything thaws here except Old Put. He is still as hard as ever, crying out for powder, powder, ye gods, give us powder!" Joseph Reed, hearing that Putnam was selected, replied in a return letter to Washington, "I supposed Old Put was to command the detachment intended for Boston ... I do not know any officer but himself who could have been depended on for so hazardous a service."

At dawn, sunlight revealed two forts, one each on two close hills, with a long breastwork connecting them. Howe, though forewarned, was astonished at what he saw through his spyglass. "The rebels," he declared, "have done more in one night than my whole army would have done in a month." He wrote to Lord Dartmouth, "It must have been the employment of at least twelve thousand men." One of his officers wrote, "They were raised with an expedition equal to that of the Genii belonging to Aladdin's Wonderful Lamp."

Howe was not the only astonished British commander. "The admiral told the general that the place must be attacked immediately or he could not remain with his ships in the harbor." However, try as they might, the British cannon could not be elevated enough to reach the forts on Dorchester Heights.

Inside one of the forts, Dr. Thacher recorded the confident mood of the Americans:

> The enemy, having discovered our works, commenced
> a tremendous cannonade from the forts in Boston and
> from their shipping in the harbor. Cannon shot are con-

tinually rolling and rebounding over the hill; and it is astonishing to observe how little our soldiers are terrified by them.

During the forenoon we were in momentary expectation of witnessing an awful scene. Nothing less than the carnage of Breed's Hill battle was expected. The hills and elevations in this vicinity are covered with spectators to witness deeds of horror in the expected conflict. His Excellency General Washington is present, animating and encouraging the soldiers, and they in return manifest their joy and express a warm desire for the approach of the enemy.

The Virginian spoke to the men, saying, "Remember it is the 5th of March, and avenge the death of your brethren." Meanwhile, in Boston, Howe formulated his plan of attack.

I determined upon an immediate attack, with all the force I could transport. Regiments were expeditiously embarked on board transports to fall down the harbor, and flat-boats were to receive other troops, making the whole two thousand four hundred men. The descent was to be made the night of the 5th.

Departure from Boston was planned for high tide, at 7 o'clock the evening of March 5th. By the next morning, the 2,400 Regulars were expected to be in place on the southeastern tip of Dorchester peninsula. From there, they would climb the more easterly of the two hills and attack that fort, protected by it from the guns of the other fort behind it. This choice of direction for the assault showed that Howe had learned from his mistakes the previous June. The walls, and the twenty cannon on platforms atop Dorchester Heights all faced north - toward Boston. By approaching only one of the forts, and its southeast end, Howe would disappoint Washington, who hoped Howe

would again rush into a frontal assault.

The British troops were given strict orders not to load their muskets, forcing them to rely on their bayonets. Howe wanted to make sure another costly mistake of the earlier battle would not be repeated - the Regulars stopping their charge to return musket fire.

On the afternoon of March 5th, a Bostonian watching the troops lined up on Boston's south shore, waiting to embark, noticed "they looked, in general, pale and dejected, and said to one another that it would be another Bunkers Hill affair or worse." A British officer wrote home:

> This is, I believe, likely to prove as important a day to the British Empire as any in our annals. We underwent last night a very severe cannonade, which damaged a number of houses, and killed some men. This morning at day-break we discovered two redoubts on the hills of Dorchester. We must drive them from their post, or desert the place. Adieu balls, masquerades, &c. for this may be looked upon as the opening of the campaign.
>
> It is worth while to remark, with what judgement the leaders of the rebels take advantage of the prejudices, and work upon the passions of the mob. This 5th of March is the anniversary of what they call the bloody massacre. If ever they dare stand against us it will be today; but I hope tomorrow to be able to give you an account of their defeat.

But there arose "a hurrycane, or terrible storm" that evening. "Many windows were forced in, sheds and fences blown down and some vessels blown on shore." Connecticut's Samuel Webb recorded in his journal the next day, March 6th, "the heavy gale from S.E. last night blew two of the transports on the shore of the harbour at Boston." The attack was postponed. Washington viewed the storm as "a most fortunate circumstance for them and unfortunate for us, as we

had everything so well prepared for their reception that I am confident we should have given a very good account of them."

Although it deprived him of the battle he had waited eight months for, the "finger of Providence" allowed Washington enough time to take further measures to strengthen his defenses. The forts were completed and furnished with more of Knox's guns, and breastworks were built to protect against an assault from the south. Howe reported to his superior in London:

> The weather, continuing boisterous the next day and night, gave the enemy time to improve their works, to bring up their cannon and to put themselves into such a state of defence that I could promise myself little success by attacking them under all the disadvantages I had to encounter.

It must have been a relief for Howe. His young engineer, Archibald Robertson, heard that at a council of war several of Howe's top officers "had advised the going off altogether" - quitting Boston. "The General said it was his own sentiments from the first, but thought the honour of the Troops was concerned." Fortunately for Howe's men, the storm allowed him to save face in cancelling the assault.

Howe decided the time had come to make preparations to evacuate Boston. These were trying days for John Andrews and other "Whigs," or patriots, who had stayed in Boston after the war started the previous April, hoping to preserve their property. The departing British soldiers took this opportunity to plunder Boston's houses and shops before they left "this cursed place." Andrews wrote to a friend:

> I had care of six houses with their furniture and as many stores filled with effects for eleven months past, and at a time like this I underwent more fatigue and perplexity than I did through the whole siege; for I was obliged to take my rounds all day, without any cessation,

and scarce ever failed of finding depredations made upon some one or other of them. I was finally necessitated to procure men at the extravagant rate of two dollars a day to sleep in the several houses and stores for a fortnight before the military plunderers went off.

These plunderers were under the charge of a "Tory," or loyalist, named Crean Bush. On March 8, he was commissioned by General Howe to seize any "goods in the town of Boston which, if in possession of the rebels, would enable them to carry on war." Bush interpreted his charge liberally, and used the soldiers Howe provided to completely fill up the brigantine *Elizabeth*. Such authorized looting inspired bands of British soldiers and sailors, "carrying destruction wherever they went; what they could not carry away they destroyed." Later, while at sea, the *Elizabeth* was captured by American privateers, Crean Bush was arrested, and the stolen property returned.

Now that the British were about to quit Boston, those inhabitants not planning to go with them feared that Admiral Shuldham, whose ships had moved in to surround their city, might bombard it with "hot shot" (heated cannon balls). The June 17th burning of Charlestown, just across the river, was still a vivid memory. The town selectmen expressed their concern to one of General Howe's representatives. After learning Howe's reply, one of the selectmen, under a flag of truce, sent a letter to Washington:

> General Howe has assured he has no intention of destroying the town, unless the troops under his command are molested during their embarkation, or at their departure, by the armed force without. Our fears are quieted with regard to General Howe's intentions. We beg we may have some assurance that so dreadful a calamity may not be brought on by any measures without.

But Washington refused to reassure Boston's selectmen. Calling

Howe's reply to the selectmen "an unauthorized paper, without an address, and not obligatory upon General Howe," Washington told them he "would take no notice of it." The selectmen returned to Boston with their hopes dashed and their fears intact. The American commander was being cautious. Washington suspected this proposed agreement might be a ploy by Howe to have his enemy relax while he made offensive plans.

The Virginian kept his army at work strengthening the lines. And, at the cost of five lives, they built a third fort - this one on Nook's Hill, Dorchester's highest and closest to Boston. The construction of this last fortification hastened Howe's evacuation. When, on March 16, Howe's artillery could not force the strong detachment there to evacuate, he resolved to depart the city without further delay. Connecticut's Isaac Gallup was there that night. The next week he wrote home:

> On Saturday night the 16 instant we took possession of Dorchester Point. The enemy kept up a steady fire all night. In the morning when the enemy could see our works they began to hoist sail and push out of the harbour as fast as possible in the greatest confusion. Our regiments were paraded expecting they ware coming out to attack us. We ware kept under arms till about 12 oclock when the Select men of the town came out and gave information that they all had deserted the town. The enemy left a large quantity of wheat, about fifty morters, shots and shells, about 100 horses. The most of the cannon were plugged up fast. But have got the most of them drilled out since.

Approximately 9,000 soldiers, 1,100 loyalists, and 1,200 women and children of the soldiers quickly boarded and left that morning on about 125 ships, many of them fishing boats. The motley fleet lingered offshore for ten days before setting sail for Halifax, Nova Scotia. Abigail Adams thought their naked masts "looked like a forest." To

the loyalists, many of whom were aristocratic in nature, the exodus was humiliating. One wrote of being in a small cabin with 37 others, "obliged to pig together on the floor, there being no berths." Even one of the British officers wrote that the overcrowding "could not be more horrible." But another officer was not so gloomy, writing to a friend in England, "We have one consolation left. You know the proverbial expression, 'neither Hell, hull nor Halifax' can afford worse shelter than Boston."

The American troops quickly entered the former British lines and, in the process, found a few surprises. On Bunker's Hill, they found that the British had left some cannon in the fort, but also "two effigies, stuffed with straw, to stand sentry with guns upon their shoulders." One of them had a placard on its breast, reading "Welcome Brother Jonathan." Upon entering Boston, they found that one "earthwork" that had looked so imposing from the American lines was really a long pile of horse manure!

Just about the last British soldier to leave was Lieutenant Adair of the Marines, who had the task of dropping "crow's feet" (four-pointed irons, which always fall with one point facing up) on the ground, outside the gates on Boston Neck. Martin Hunter, a British officer, recorded what happened when Adair performed his task, just as the last of the soldiers were clambering into the longboats to be rowed out to the ships: "Being an Irishman, he began scattering the crow's feet about from the gates towards the enemy, and of course, had to walk over them on his return, which detained him so long that he was nearly taken prisoner."

As quickly as the British sailed away, Washington had his own army on the march for New York, which he expected was Howe's destination. Earlier that winter, Washington had sent General Lee and some of the southern regiments to that city to begin defensive preparations.

Only those soldiers who were enlisted for the duration of the year marched to New York; the remainder stayed in the Boston area. There, under the direction of General Artemas Ward, they destroyed the British works atop Bunker Hill, strengthened those in Boston and

Castle Island, and built an additional fort on Noddle Island.

But the British never returned to invade Boston. After spending two months at Halifax to stock up on provisions and leave off the refugee loyalists from Boston, Howe would sail to New York in June. By then, enough reinforcements having arrived from England, he would be ready to begin an offensive campaign on a much larger scale.

Not surprisingly, the pious New Englanders, who considered themselves God's chosen people, attributed Howe's exodus to God being on the patriots' side. Typical was the opinion of one Yankee, writing of the March 5th storm that had cancelled Howe's attack: "when I heard in the night how amazingly strong the wind blew, I concluded that the ships could not stir, and pleased myself with the reflection that the Lord might be working deliverance for us and preventing the effusion of blood." The Pennsylvania Evening Post concluded its account of the events of March 17, 1775 with the following note:

> This afternoon, a few hours after the British retreated, the Reverend Mr. Leonard preached at Cambridge an excellent sermon, in the audience of his Excellency the General, and others of distinction, well adapted to the interesting event of the day, from Exodus xiv. 25: "the Egyptians said, Let us flee from the face of Israel, for the Lord fighteth for them against the Egyptians."

"'Tis time to depart!"

> *- Thomas Paine, writing in his pamphlet, "Common Sense."*

2. We the Citizens of Mecklenburg County do hereby desolve the political bands which have connected us to the Mother Country & hereby absolve ourselves from all allegiance to the British crown ...

3. We do hereby declare ourselves a free & independent people ...

The above excerpts are taken from what came to be known as the "Mecklenburg Declaration of Independence." In the spring of 1775, Thomas Polk, the political and military leader of the backwoods North Carolina county of Mecklenburg, issued an order directing each of the county's militia companies "to elect 2 persons & delegate to them ample powers to devise ways & means to aid & assist their suffering brethren in Boston." The delegates, mostly farmers but also including four graduates of the College of New Jersey (Princeton), convened at the county seat on May 19, 1775.

Their intended business had suddenly become more complicated when, just two days earlier, "official news, by express, arrived of the battle of Lexington." The result of the meeting was a set of resolves, announced to a crowd outside the courthouse the next day, declaring

the county independent and setting up temporary measures of government. An express rider was dispatched to carry a copy of the resolves to North Carolina's congressmen in Philadelphia. A letter addressed to them requested that they "use all possible means to have said resolves sanctioned and approved by the general Congress." The three congressmen sent the express rider home, explaining to him that "it was deemed premature to lay them before the house" for debate.

Reconciliation, not independence, was the objective in mid-1775. The time was not yet right to debate independence, though the whole continent appeared to be in a military posture. After the British raid on Lexington and Concord, Boston's Dr. Joseph Warren, master propagandist, used the raid to the best possible advantage. Even some conservative leaders agreed with the radicals that the colonies must unite and fight for their liberties. Armed resistance was seen as a necessity, to force Britain to restore American rights.

Virtually everyone was confident of a quick peace and accomodation. Surely, after the news of Bunker Hill's 1,054 British casualties reached London, the King would intervene and make Parliament come to its senses. Thomas Jefferson, on August 25th, wrote that "another drubbing" like that one would end the conflict's military phase and begin the diplomatic phase. George Washington, on his way north to Massachusetts in June to take command of the army, wrote home that he would be back on the plantation by the fall. Benjamin Franklin expected to soon return to London as chief negotiator for the colonies.

Even the men who come readily to our minds when we think of independence were, like the rest, aiming for reconciliation with Britain. Jefferson, in the fall of 1775, wished for a restoration of just rights followed by re-union, since he would rather be "in dependence on Great Britain, properly limited, than on any other nation on earth, or than on no nation." John Adams, who felt that independence would mean mob rule, wrote to Mercy Otis Warren in January, 1776, that independence was "utterly against my inclinations." A fellow Virginian, after mentioning to George Washington that the outcome of the war

might be independence, noted that the general stated "with perfect sincerity that if ever I heard of his joining to any such measures I had his leave to set him down for everything wicked."

Why were Americans so much against the idea of a total break with Britain? There were several reasons. One was loyalty to their sovereign, King George III. Also, many political leaders were merchants and knew that, as part of the British Empire, Americans belonged to the greatest protected trading area in the world. They found it difficult to conceive of their ships crossing and recrossing the Atlantic without the British Navy to protect them. Another kind of opposition to independence stemmed from a realistic assessment of America's chances in a war against the greatest military power on earth.

Independence was also not likely to be achieved unless "The United Colonies" stopped feuding. In several places settlers from one colony were shooting at those of another: New Yorkers and residents of the New Hampshire Grants; Pennsylvanians and Virginians in the disputed Fort Pitt area; and Connecticut emigrants and local farmers in the Wyoming Valley of northeastern Pennsylvania. Virginia's Carter Braxton felt sure that if Congress declared independency "the continent would be torn to pieces by intestine wars and convulsions. Previous to independence all disputes must be healed and harmony prevail."

In North Carolina's western hills and along New York's Hudson River, the common people had in recent years made unsuccessful revolts against the aristocracy, and for it their leaders had suffered execution. Their enmity for the aristocrats, some of whom were now leading the fight against Britain, was even greater than it was against Parliament. It was the danger posed by these uprisings and the specter of more in all parts of the continent that explained the most prevalent sentiment against independence - fear of social revolution. New York's Gouverneur Morris predicted that if the conflict with Britain continued, "farewell aristocracy ... we shall be under the domination of a riotous mob." The solution, he said, was "re-union with the parent state." South Carolina's John Bull commented on the rise of the power of the people:

The men of property begin at length to see that the
people, who have hitherto been obediently made use of
by their numbers and occasional riots to support the
claims set up in America, have discovered their own
strength and importance, and are not now so easily governed by their former leaders.

In South Carolina, a clergyman denounced "every silly clown, and
illiterate mechanic" who undertook to censure his governor, and he
declared they should keep to their own rank. The outraged mechanics
demanded that the minister be fired, and he was. The tale was soon
printed and spread by word of mouth throughout the colonies.

Ever since the fall of 1774, the rural counties of western Massachusetts had been clamoring for a political revolution within that colony.
They wanted to resurrect the former charter of 1629, which would
allow them to elect their own officials and govern themselves, not be
ruled by appointees of the governor or his council. The current charter of 1691 made it too difficult for the will of the people to be put
into practice, because under it "a party is so easily made of the most
powerful men in every county, and even town, against the common
people." The eastern leaders appealed to the Continental Congress for
advice in the controversy. The answer that came advised the Provincial Congress that if they could not maintain a secure government
under the charter of 1691 they should live without government. The
Congress could not advise them to set up a new government under the
old charter, since that would be an implicit declaration of independence.

So, throughout the colonies, there was evidence of an increasing
desire by the common people for more political power. The political
leaders, fearing social revolution, worked to prevent this. One way
was to make sure the Continental Congress did not pass any radical
measures. In Pennsylvania, John Dickinson led the conservatives in
having the legislature vote on what its delegates' instructions should

be, in case a resolution on independence should come to a vote in Congress. By the end of 1775, Pennsylvania, New Jersey, Delaware, Maryland and North Carolina had all issued similar instructions, forbidding their delegates from voting for any resolutions "that may cause or lead to a separation from our mother country, or a change of the form of this government." Delaware added that its delegates should "studiously avoid everything disrespectful or offensive to our most gracious sovereign," King George III.

The self-assurance of the conservatives and moderates began to slowly be deflated on the first of November. That morning, as on every morning, Congress convened at nine o'clock and its secretary, Charles Thomson, read aloud letters from generals, governors and others corresponding with Congress. This day's mail included some letters smuggled across the Atlantic from Arthur Lee, a Virginian then residing in London. He wrote of rumors that King George III was seeking thousands of foreign mercenaries to supplement his already beefed up army. Lee also sent a copy of the King's royal proclamation of August 23rd, declaring that the colonies were "engaged in open and avowed rebellion," and that anyone in England caught corresponding with Americans would be brought to "condign punishment."

The worst news was that the King had refused to receive their Olive Branch Petition, in which the Congress had professed their loyalty to King George III and asked him to intercede in the colonies' dispute with Parliament. In the words of Lord Suffolk, "The King and his Cabinet are determined to listen to nothing from the illegal congress, to treat with the colonies one by one, and in no event to recognize them in any form of association." The conservatives and moderates began to despair. North Carolina's Joseph Hewes commented, "we have scarcely a dawn of hope" for reconciliation. Though their faith in the King may have been shaken, "the fondest hopes and dreams" of most of the delegates was still for a peaceful accomodation and reunion with Britain on constitutional principles guaranteeing American liberties.

This news that the King was aggressively pushing the war, to en-

force Parliament's harsh new laws, was a shock to the patriots. For, while rebelling against Parliament, they had been firmly loyal to the King. Even as late as January, 1776, nine months after war broke out, Washington's officers still toasted the King at their mess. John Adams, years after the Revolution, wrote:

> There is great ambiguity in the expression, there existed in the colonies a desire for independence. It is true there always existed in the colonies a desire of independence of Parliament in the articles of internal taxation, and internal policy, but there never existed a desire of independence of the Crown.

Loyalty to the King allowed the patriots to believe that their actions were not those of rebels and traitors, but of true Englishmen resisting the tyranny of a government gone mad. It was not common practice, under Britain's system of government, for the King to publicly reveal his opinions and desires. So, not knowing the King's feelings, the colonists incorrectly assumed he disagreed with the hard-line policies of his ministers and the majority of Parliament. But, in fact, the King had instructed his ministers to devise those policies. George Washington wrote that he could not bring himself to think of Howe's army "as the King's troops," so he referred to them as "the ministerial army."

For the colonists to give up their hopes for reconciliation and to seriously consider independence would require a change of attitude regarding their allegiance and reverence for the King. This could not even be attempted by American propagandists, since they had spent the last dozen years convincing the public that it was the King's ministers who were the villains. There had been no evidence that the King had been a co-conspirator. But now, with his August 23 proclamation and his refusal to read Congress's second petition, he was beginning to publicly reveal his position. New York's John Jay, years later, recalled that he had never "until after the second Petition of Congress" heard any American "express a wish for the independence of the colonies."

32

Jeremy Belknap, a chaplain with the army outside Boston, observed that by January independence was becoming "a favorite point" with the troops, who now found prayers and toasts for King George III offensive. In Virginia, Thomas Jefferson wrote John Randolph that the colonists' will to take the one remaining step - "declare and assert a separation" - is growing "under the fostering hand of our King."

But Samuel Adams knew that Congress, like the majority of the American people, was not yet ripe for independence. So he kept quiet about the subject on the floor of the Congress, while he slowly worked behind the scenes, ripening one congressman's mind at a time around a tavern table. As he had once told Boston's hot-headed Dr. Thomas Young, "Patience is characteristic of the patriot. It requires time to bring honest men to think and determine alike." The other prominent independence men, Richard Henry Lee and Benjamin Franklin, followed Sam Adams's policy of waiting:

> We cannot make events. Our business is wisely to improve them. Mankind are governed more by their feelings than by reason. Events which excite those feelings will produce wonderful effects.

Two such "events" were the aggressive efforts of the royal governors of Virginia and North Carolina to win back those colonies. On New Year's Day, 1776, Virginia's governor burned Norfolk, thus giving the radicals a powerful boost in their efforts to convince Southern moderates that reconciliation was impossible. The following month, North Carolina's governor attempted to rally loyalists, only to be defeated at Moore's Creek by the patriot-controlled militia. Sam Adams hoped that British troops would soon arrive in the South, for "one battle would do more towards a declaration of independency than a long chain of conclusive arguments in a provincial convention or the Continental Congress."

However, the spark which Adams was waiting for had already been struck, and not by the guns of British soldiers. Instead, it was the

King's state-of-the-empire speech given on October 26, 1775, the first day of a new session of Parliament. George III was preparing Parliament for the primary work before that session: suppressing the rebellion, forcing the colonists to submit to Parliamentary supremacy. From the King's speech:

> ... [The colonists] meant only to amuse, by vague expressions of attachment to the parent state, and the strongest protestations of loyalty to me, whilst they were preparing a general revolt. ...
>
> The rebellious war now levied is become more general, and is manifestly carried on for the purpose of establishing an independent empire.
>
> It is now to put a speedy end to these disorders by the most decisive exertions. For this purpose I have increased my naval establishment and greatly augmented my land forces ...
>
> I have also received the most friendly offers of foreign assitance. When the unhappy and deluded multitude, against whom this force will be directed, shall become sensible of their error, I shall be ready to receive the misled with tenderness and mercy.

Copies of the King's speech first arrived in Boston as 1775 came to a close. The British commander, General William Howe, was instructed to make sure copies made their way into rebel hands. The King's speech was expected to awe the Yankee rabble into giving up the fight, but it had the opposite effect. It excited the soldiers to a greater zeal and provided them with a justification for continuing what they were doing - waging war against the King's army.

General Washington, himself, was now leaving the reconciliation camp and joining the radical camp of Sam Adams and the Virginians, Richard Henry Lee, General Charles Lee and General Horatio Gates. In January, Washington wrote:

With respect for myself, I have never entertained an idea of an accomodation, since I heard of the measures which were adopted in consequence of the Bunker Hill fight. The King's speech has confirmed the sentiments I entertained upon news of that affair; and if every man was of my mind, the ministers of Great Britain would know, in a few words, upon what issue the cause should be put. I would tell them that we had done everything that could be expected from the best of subjects, and that if nothing else would satisfy a tyrant and his diabolical ministry, we are determined to shake off all connections with a state so unjust.

Despite the change in his feelings, Washington did not urge Congress to declare independence, as his subordinate generals, Lee, Gates and Greene, did. The King's speech reached Congress on January 8, and its arrival appeared, to Sam Adams, as the signal to finally openly discuss the subject. On the floor of the Congress, where he rarely spoke, Adams denounced the speech and the King, and said he hoped Americans would now "act the part which the great Law of Nature points out."

But the opinions of fifty-six men from diverse backgrounds and constituencies could not be changed so quickly. The next day, January 9, Pennsylvania's James Wilson - who opposed independence, and knew that a majority in Congress did, too - moved that "the Congress expressly declare to their constituents and the world their present intentions respecting an independency, observing that the King's speech directly charged us with that design." A committee of five, all opponents of independence, was appointed to draft an address to the people. Wilson presented the draft on February 13th, but by then a few newly-elected delegates favoring independence had replaced some opposing it, and by a slim margin Congress voted to table the address.

On February 26th, Secretary Thomson read aloud smuggled letters

from England reporting that an army of 25,000 British and Germans was soon to be on its way to America. Propagandists jumped on this news and exploited the popular feeling that the Germans, being foreign mercenaries and not Englishmen, would be as barbaric as the Indians on the frontier.

Along with these letters came a copy of the newly-enacted American Prohibitory Act, which ordered the British Navy to seize and confiscate all American merchant vessels and cargoes, "as if the same were the ships and effects of open enemies." Some of the radicals claimed that, by removing the colonies from "under the King's protection," this "declaration of war" abrogated any allegiance due him, and thus made the colonies independent states. John Adams, by now in the pro-independence group, was glad this "act of independency" had come from Parliament and not Congress. He thought it "very odd that Americans should hesitate at accepting such a gift." Richard Henry Lee commented that it was "curious to observe that whilst people here are disputing and hesitating about independency, the court, by one bold act of Parliament, have already put the two countries asunder."

Maryland's Robert Alexander, like other moderates who hoped for reconciliation, was stunned by this new act. Alexander wrote that he did not know what Congress would do, but

> with me every idea of reconciliation is precluded by the conduct of Great Britain. Independency I have often reprobated both in public and private, but am now almost convinced the measure is right and can be justified by necessity.

But the conservatives still held out against the idea, hoping to forestall any vote on independence until the King's commissioners, mentioned in the Prohibitory Act, might arrive in Philadelphia. In April, 1776, as pro-independence feeling in Congress and the country grew, an anxious Robert Morris cried out, "where the plague are these commmissioners, if they are to come; what is it that detains them?"

Those favoring independence were also anxious. Joseph Reed wrote to Washington that he was infinitely more afraid of British commissioners than he was of their generals and armies, for "if their propositions are plausible, and behavior artful, I am apprehensive they will divide us."

* * * * *

The mood of the people of America shifted toward independence faster than did the minds of Congress. From Maine to Georgia, newspapers and taverns were the places for hot debates on the belligerent acts of the royal governors in North Carolina and Virginia, as well as the King's speech, the Prohibitory Act, and the hiring of German mercenaries to kill English subjects in America. But the pen of an obscure erstwhile corsetmaker did by far the most to dispel "the prejudice of the mind against the doctrine of independence."

Thomas Paine was a citizen of London who came to America in 1774. In London, he had failed at every occupation he had tried since, as a fifteen-year-old, he had run away from his harsh, narrowminded Quaker father. When he came to Philadelphia he was penniless and carried only a letter of recommendation from Benjamin Franklin. It was enough to land him a job as assistant editor of the <u>Pennsylvania Magazine</u>. His forceful and controversial articles soon created a growing subscription list for the little magazine. Having experienced years of oppression in England, Paine was convinced that the colonies should reject all connections with that corrupt society. He boldly wrote his convictions on this and other issues, such as slavery, equal rights for women, and the use of organized religion to oppress the poor. Finally, he was fired for expressing too many radical ideas.

Paine continued to write articles on social issues and America's crisis with England, though he had difficulty finding printers willing to publish his inflammatory essays. Fortunately, he was sought out and encouraged by scientist David Rittenhouse, as well as college president John Witherspoon and physician Benjamin Rush. All three were mem-

bers of Dr. Franklin's American Philosophical Society. According to Rush's memoirs, he gave Paine the idea of writing a pamphlet arguing the need for independency (a project Rush says he originally intended to do himself, until he discovered Paine's talent).

On January 9, 1776, Paine's fifty-five page pamphlet, *Common Sense*, was published anonymously. Paine insisted on the anonymity as well as the dispensation of his royalties, every cent of which would be spent on mittens for the American army in Canada. The authorized edition sold 120,000 copies in the first three months. Numerous pirate editions accounted for twice that amount, making the total number of copies sold perhaps 300,000 - in a country of only 600,000 white families! It far outsold Franklin's *Poor Richard's Almanack* and everything else that had ever been printed in America except the Holy Bible.

For the most part, the ideas in *Common Sense* were not new, having appeared in newspapers and political pamphlets during the previous twelve years. What set *Common Sense* apart was its stirring prose, so unlike the stiff political writings of the time. It was written in language that the common man could understand and which kept the reader's attention - or the listener's, for Paine's rhetoric and persuasive style had a more powerful impact when read aloud in countless homes and taverns.

The treatise built up slowly to a logical conclusion and a recommended plan of action for America. It started with a discussion on the origin and types of government, using ideas from the writings of James Otis, John Adams, Thomas Jefferson and others. Then, in the second part, came something other political writers had not yet dared do - a careful scrutiny and rejection of monarchy, especially that of England.

> England since the conquest had known some few good monarchs, but groaned beneath a much larger number of bad ones; yet no man in his senses can say that their claim under William the Conqueror is a very honorable one. A French bastard landing with an armed banditti and establishing himself King of England against

the consent of the natives, is in plain terms a very paltry rascally original. It certainly hath no divinity in it. ...

In England a king hath little more to do than to make war and give away places; which, in plain terms, is to empoverish the nation and set it together by the ears. A pretty business indeed for a man to be allowed eight hundred thousand sterling a year for, and worshipped into the bargain! Of more worth is one honest man to society, and in the sight of God, than all the crowned ruffians that ever lived.

This was followed by the third part - "Thoughts on the Present State of Affairs in America" - in which Paine argued that reconciliation was not only impossible but thoroughly undesirable. He pointed out the absurdity of a continent being ruled by an island 3,000 miles away, and reminded the reader that England's "own interest leads her to suppress the growth" of the American economy. One by one, the major arguments for reconciliation were knocked down, including loyalty to the mother country, and the supposed economic advantages of continued membership in the British Empire.

But Britain is the parent country, say some. Then the more shame upon her conduct. Even brutes do not devour their young, nor savages make war upon their families ... Europe, and not England, is the parent country of America. This new world hath been the asylum for the persecuted lovers of civil and religious liberty from every part of Europe. Hither have they fled, not from the tender embraces of the mother, but from the cruelty of the monster; and it is so far true of England, that the same tyranny which drove the first emigrants from home pursues their descendants still.

I challenge the warmest advocate for reconciliation to show a simple advantage that this continent can reap, by

being connected with Great Britain. ... Our corn will fetch its price in any market in Europe ... any submission to, or dependence on, Great Britain tends directly to involve this continent in European wars and quarrels, and sets us at variance with nations who would otherwise seek our friendship, and against whom we have neither anger nor complaint. As Europe is our market for trade, we ought to form no partial connection with any part of it. ...

Europe is too thickly planted with kingdoms to be long at peace, and whenever a war breaks out between England and any foreign power, the trade of America goes to ruin, <u>because of her connection with Britain</u>. ...

Everything that is right or reasonable pleads for separation. The blood of the slain, the weeping voice of nature cries, <u>'Tis time to part</u>.

Just as Paine broke new ground by ridiculing Americans' loyalty to the King, he also was the first to express America's destiny as that of the oppressed peoples of the entire world, labeling it "the cause of all mankind" and declaring that the "sun never shined on a cause of greater worth."

O ye that love mankind! Ye that dare oppose not only the tyranny but the tyrant, stand forth! Every spot of the old world is overrun with oppression. Freedom hath been hunted round the globe. Asia and Africa have long expelled her. Europe regards her like a stranger, and England hath given her warning to depart. O receive the fugitive, and prepare in time an asylum for mankind.

Paine then presented the advantages of a confederation, and he argued that the colonies could stand on their own feet militarily and economically. Predictably, he ended the pamphlet by recommending

Congress adopt a declaration of independence, to enable America to purchase desperately needed munitions, without which the war could not continue and America would have to submit to Parliament. The munitions would have to come from other countries, such as France and Spain.

But, Paine argued, those countries would <u>not</u> help the colonies without such a declaration, for two reasons: 1) If reconciliation was achieved, the British Empire would remain strong, and any nation that helped the rebels would then receive her wrath. 2) "While we profess ourselves the subjects of Britain, we must in the eyes of foreign nations [monarchs], be considered rebels. The precedent is somewhat dangerous to <u>their peace</u>" to assist a people rebelling against monarchy. A declaration to the world "setting forth the miseries we have endured and the peaceful methods which we have ineffectually used for redress" would prove "we have been driven to the necessity of breaking off all connections with her." Thus, independency would appear legitimate to the European kings who could then offer assitance without moral reservations.

Paine concluded by stating that until independence is declared, America "will feel itself like a man who continues putting off some unpleasant business from day to day, yet knows it must be done, hates to set about it, wishes it over, and is continually haunted with the thoughts of its necessity."

Publication of *Common Sense* could not have been better timed, coming as it did soon after news of the King's speech, his contracting with German princes, and the Prohibitory Act. With emotions aroused, Americans were handed the message they wanted to hear, read and discuss. The tone of Paine's masterpiece was that of an angry, indignant man who had reached the end of his patience with his oppressor. Suddenly, the taboo topic was out in the open, and it quickly dominated the written and spoken word throughout the colonies.

Rebuttals were soon in print, too. A Philadelphian wrote to a relation in England:

Quaker Tories have published what they call an answer to it. It is called *Plain Truth*. It is not a contemptible performance, but very inferior to *Common Sense*. Our news-papers are replete with essays on the subject; and the general tenor of them is independency. *Common Sense* has made innumerable converts to that side. It is said to be the work of Dr. Franklin, and Messrs. Dickinson and Adams.

One Marylander wrote, "If anyone knows the author of *Common Sense*, tell him he has done wonders and worked miracles - made Tories Whigs." From Massachusetts, George Washington wrote:

My countrymen, I know, from their form of government and steady attachment heretofore to royalty, will come reluctantly into the idea of Independence. But time and persecution bring many wonderful things to pass; and by private letters which I have lately received from Virginia, I find *Common Sense* is working a powerful change there in the minds of men.

Christopher Gadsden, Congressman from South Carolina and by far that colony's most radical leader, was greatly inspired by the little book. With the British reportedly making plans to attack Charleston, he was recalled by the South Carolina Provincial Congress to serve in his capacity as colonel of a militia regiment. Prior to sailing from Philadelphia, he purchased three copies of *Common Sense*, just published that week: one copy for himself, one for the South Carolina Provincial Congress, and the third to send to Savannah as an antidote to the loyalism that still gripped Georgia.

During the voyage, he read the book again, this time underlining the passages he planned to use in a speech before South Carolina's Provincial Congress. Before reaching South Carolina's shores, however, two British warships sighted and bore down upon the small merchant ves-

sel. What a prize for the lucky British sea captain the infamous Christopher Gadsden would make, complete with an underlined seditious tract, and his private annotated journal of the proceedings of the rebel Congress. But Gadsden avoided capture. His vessel quickly entered a North Carolina inlet, and Gadsden made the rest of the way home by land.

After nearly three weeks, much of it through Tory-infested territory, Gadsden finally arrived in Charleston. His speech stunned the Provincial Congress by its open advocacy of independence. The speech fell upon the members "like an explosion of thunder." They were horrified by the harsh denunciation of their King and frightened by the specter of the colony being linked in a permanent union with the northern colonies. They feared domination by the more populous lower classes, and perhaps mob rule. The Provincial Congress met the next day in a special session to oust the dangerous Gadsden by making him a judge.

The little book was also making a splash in Europe, where pirate editions were printed in Paris, Rotterdam, London and other cities. There, as in America, the anonymous author was suspected to be either Benjamin Franklin or Samuel Adams. A newspaper in London reported, the young "Prince of Wales has been discovered by the Queen Mother, reading a copy of Doctor Franklin's dreadful pamphlet, *Common Sense*, and in response to the Queen's searching questions, refused to confess how he got the copy."

* * * * *

Congress gradually moved toward a complete break with Britain during the first four months of 1776. It sent Silas Deane to France to secretly purchase supplies for the army. It responded favorably to South Carolina's request for advice on whether that colony should adopt a new constitution. After news of the Prohibitory Act reached Philadelphia, Congress declared all American ports open to trade with all non-British nations. Only two items could not be imported - slaves and East India tea.

But the individual colonies appeared to be moving faster than Congress. On March 7th, an attempt by Georgia's royal governor to seize Savannah by naval power was put down by patriot militia, and at last that colony came under patriot control. Four weeks later, Georgia's Assembly sent new delegates to Congress, with no restrictions regarding how they should vote on independence measures. South Carolina adopted a new constitution, and Patrick Henry was called home to help draft one for Virginia. In North Carolina, on April 12th - shortly after the governor's military venture was crushed by patriot militia at Moore's Creek - the Provincial Congress reversed its earlier instructions and resolved that their delegates should "concur with the Delegates of the other Colonies in declaring Independency." On May 4th, the Rhode Island General Assembly gave its delegates a free reign to vote as they wished, and it declared that henceforth all legal documents which had in the past been issued in the name of the King should instead be issued in the name of the governor and the colony.

From western Massachusetts, the patriot leader Joseph Hawley, writing to Sam Adams, predicted that if Congress waited any longer to declare independence, "a great mob" would march to Philadelphia, disperse Congress, and appoint others in their place who were more assertive. "The people are ahead of you," he advised, "strike while the iron is hot." Robert Morris received the same kind of warning from a Virginian:

> For God's sake why does your Congress continue in this horrible, nonsensical manner? Why not at once take the step you must take soon? ... [Otherwise] you will force at last the people to attempt it without you - which must produce a noble anarchy.

But the radicals in Congress suspected a declaration of independence would do more harm than good if it were not unanimous. Although by April a majority of Congress was in favor of it, their hands were tied by the fact that several delegations were under orders

from their legislatures to vote against independence. Richard Henry Lee, the Adamses and others were busy writing to, and in some cases meeting with, patriot leaders in those recalcitrant colonies, urging them to have their legislatures rescind those instructions, as had already been done in North Carolina. This strategy worked in several of the colonies.

The hardest nut to crack was Pennsylvania. For decades, the voting districts had been unfairly drawn in favor of Philadelphia, where the conservative Quakers dominated the politics. In the spring of 1776, hundreds of riflemen from the frontier and the more recently settled towns were in Philadelphia, trying to intimidate the Pennsylvania Assembly into correcting this inequity, as well as reversing their instructions against independence. The patriot leaders of Philadelphia called for a public meeting outside the statehouse on May 20th. About 7,000 people attended, and listened to the reading of a resolve that Congress had just passed, calling for the colonies to establish new governments. The mass meeting then voted that the Assembly's instructions against its delegates voting for independence should be rescinded, that the present Assembly had no authority to form a new government, and that a convention of members popularly elected should be called to develop a new constitution. Finally, on June 14th, the Assembly voted to rescind the instructions. The Assembly then adjourned, never to meet again.

A convention was held that summer, resulting in a new Pennsylvania Constitution that included democratic reforms. The convention also issued instructions to the colony's delegates, urging them to concur with the rest of Congress in voting for independence. The radicals had won out over the men in power. They had used what by now had become classic revolutionary tactics: hold a carefully controlled "public meeting" to intimidate those in power and spread revolutionary ideas, then call for a "convention" of democratically chosen delegates to form a new government.

John Adams commented on the downfall of the Quakers: "The timid politics of some men of large property here have almost done

their business for them. They have lost their influence and grown obnoxious." They had lost power by blindly resisting the popular feelings toward independence and political change. In most other colonies, enough established leaders and men of large property had the wisdom to remain a part of the popular movement, however much they abhorred its ideas, so as to exercise a measure of influence in shaping the political future. New York's aristocratic Robert Livingston, who was wisely "swimming with a stream which it is impossible to stem," had advised Pennsylvania's conservative leaders "that they should yield to the torrent if they hoped to direct its course." But they had not taken his advice. Never again would the Quakers be a dominating political force.

While efforts were being made to bring South Carolina, Maryland, Delaware, Pennsylvania and New York over to the side favoring independence, John Adams and Richard Henry Lee were each writing letters, urging patriot leaders back home to have their colony be the first to instruct its delegates to propose independence in Congress. Since Congress had no real power and relied solely on the willingness of the thirteen colonial legislatures to abide by and enforce its wishes, Adams felt that any proposal of such magnitude as independence must originate in one of those legislatures. John Adams received the disappointing answer that the Massachusetts Assembly would solicit its individual towns concerning how the Assembly should instruct the colony's delegates.

Richard Henry Lee wrote home to Patrick Henry, stressing that Virginia had led in the past and should act now to arouse America from "the fatal lethargy" into which she had been thrown by the middle colonies. Repeating one of Paine's arguments from *Common Sense*, Lee urged that America would need foreign alliances, but no foreign power would help us "until we take rank as an independent people." On May 15th, the Virginia Convention resolved, by a vote of 111 to 1, that its delegates in Philadelphia "be instructed to propose to that respectable body to declare the United Colonies free and independent states." So, on June 7th, following these orders, Richard Henry Lee

proposed three resolutions in Congress:

> Resolved, That these United Colonies are, and of right ought to be, free and independent States.
>
> That it is expedient forthwith to take the most effectual measures for forming foreign alliances.
>
> That a plan of confederation be prepared and transmitted to the respective Colonies for their consideration and approbation.

These proposals were stated on Friday, June 7th. Since it was the custom of Congress to not debate any motion until everyone had a chance to sleep on it, the issue was taken up Saturday, the 8th, and again on Monday, the 10th. Six colonies were in favor; seven were opposed, including the closely split North Carolina delegation. The deciding fence-rider there, Joseph Hewes, was being targeted for conversion by John Adams. Late in the day on Monday, Adams was reading aloud several letters and reports he had obtained from North Carolina, describing the proceedings there in favor of independence. At last, Hewes stood up, raised his hands above his head, and cried out, "It is done, it is done, and I will abide by it!" His vote would now make 7 colonies to 6 in favor of Lee's resolution. Adams later remarked, "I would give more for a perfect painting of the terror and horror upon the faces of the old majority at that moment than for the best piece of Raphael!" However, before a vote could be taken, South Carolina's Edward Rutledge stood up and loudly moved that the decision be postponed until the first of July. The motion was carried.

According to Thomas Jefferson, "the colonies of New York, New Jersey, Pennsylvania, Delaware, Maryland and South Carolina were not yet matured for falling off the parent stem." The postponement of debate on Lee's resolutions was due mainly to the fear "That if such a declaration should now be agreed to, these delegates must retire & possibly their colonies might secede from the Union."

Three committees were formed, to avoid any delay come July, in

case Lee's three resolutions should be adopted. One committee was charged with drafting a treaty for foreign alliances. Another committee, chaired by John Dickinson, would draft articles of confederation. (Evidently, Franklin's unsolicited articles of confederation of the year before were ignored.) And the last committee, consisting of Jefferson, Franklin, John Adams, Roger Sherman and Robert Livingston, was "to prepare a declaration of independence." John Adams confidently predicted that, in the first week of July, "the last finishing strokes will be given to the politics of this revolution. Nothing after that will remain but war."

It is much, much easier for one person to write something than for five. Many years later, John Adams recalled how it was settled that the young Jefferson should write the draft:

> I think he had one more vote than any other, and that placed him at the head of the committee. I had the next highest number, and that placed me the second. The committee met, discussed the subject, and then appointed Mr. Jefferson and me to make the draught, I suppose because we were the two first on the list.
> The sub-committee [Jefferson and Adams] met. Jefferson proposed to me to make the draught.
> I said, "I will not."
> "You should do it."
> "Oh! no."
> "Why will you not? You ought to do it."
> "I will not."
> "Why?"
> "Reason enough."
> "What can be your reasons?"
> "Reason first - You are a Virginian, and a Virginian ought to appear at the head of this business. Reason second - I am obnoxious, suspected and unpopular. You are very much otherwise. Reason third - You can

48

write ten times better than I can."

"Well," said Jefferson, "if you are decided, I will do as well as I can."

"Very well, when you have drawn it up, we will have a meeting."

Jefferson's own account of his selection states merely that, "The committee for drawing the declaration desired me to do it." He denied Adams's claim that he asked the Bostonian to write it. Judging from the skilled political writings of John Adams and the vanity he revealed in his diary and private correspondence, it is also unlikely that he would have told Jefferson, "You can write ten times better than I can." What probably happened was that Adams deferred to Jefferson because he was a Virginian - the resolution was introduced by a Virginian, and it had been the New England delegates' strategy ever since the beginning of the first Congress to have Virginia take the lead, in order to influence the South and provide cement for the shaky union.

Thomas Jefferson would have preferred being at home, helping draft Virginia's constitution, a document he felt was vastly more important than this declaration. But the House of Burgesses had turned down his request to be excused from his duties in Philadelphia so he could return to Williamsburg. The declaration was expected to be simply a rehash of the past dozen years' grievances, followed by a statement declaring the end of allegiance to King and Parliament. Had John Adams suspected that the declaration would become the most prized and honored document of the entire revolutionary period, he probably would have insisted on at least co-authorship. But then, knowing the legalistic and scholarly style of his political writings, it probably would have been a wordy, dry exposition with few if any memorable phrases or ideas.

Why was the task not assigned to Benjamin Franklin, the most distinguished and experienced man on the committee (in fact, in all of America)? The famous author, diplomat and scientist was now

seventy years old and suffering from gout. He had to be carried to the state house each morning, seated in a chair sedan suspended between two poles shouldered by husky parolees from the City Jail. Franklin had just returned from an exhausting trip to Montreal, an unsuccessful attempt by Congress to persuade the Canadians to join "the common cause." Franklin also had what seemed to be an unbreakable habit of interjecting levity into the most serious of speeches and essays. It was said at the time that if he had written the declaration it would have contained a joke or two. Besides, Franklin hated to write anything that would be subject to analysis and revision by a committee, let alone the whole Congress.

As for the other members of the committee: Roger Sherman, a former cobbler and apothecary, only recently a lawyer, was no writer; Robert Livingston, though he felt independence was "inevitable and necessary," was against it "at this time." He returned to New York, to avoid having anything to do with it.

Jefferson was not content to simply list grievances and flatly state America's final break with Britain. Though his Declaration included a list and a final statement of separation, they were preceded by two opening paragraphs that made the Declaration a moving symbol of America's mission to the freedom-seeking peoples of the world. With compactness and simplicity, these few sentences express the philosophy that became the foundation of American democracy.

In composing the Declaration, Jefferson drew upon the doctrines of natural rights and the social contract of government expressed by John Locke and other European philosophers of the Enlightenment then so popular in America. According to these doctrines, all men are born with the rights to their life, liberty and property. To protect these rights, men form governments, under which an unwritten contract exists between the ruler and his subjects. They owe him allegiance in return for his protection of their rights. This theory contrasted with the earlier doctrine of absolute monarchy, in which the monarch's rule was absolute and unquestioned, since it was thought to be by divine right. Under the new social contract and natural rights philosophy, if

the ruler ceases to protect his subjects' rights, it is their duty to rebel and overthrow his rule. This Jefferson explained in the second paragraph of his draft:

> We hold these truths to be sacred & undeniable; that all men are created equal & independent; that from that equal creation they derive rights inherent & inalienable, among which are the preservation of life, & liberty, & the pursuit of happiness; that to secure these ends, governments are instituted among men, deriving their just powers from the consent of the governed; that whenever any form of government shall become destructive of these ends, it is the right of the people to alter or to abolish it.

These ideas had been expressed by European philosophers and American pamphleteers for many years. Jefferson's adaptation of them caused many, including Richard Henry Lee and John Adams, perhaps out of jealousy, to accuse him of plagiarism. Jefferson's reply was that the Declaration was not intended to be "new principles, or new arguments, never before thought of ... it was intended to be an expression of the American mind."

Although the ideas were familiar, the way Jefferson presented them was not. He did not refer to Parliament or to the rights of Americans as British subjects. In these respects the document differed markedly from earlier political works of the period. Two years before, in his *Summary Views of the Rights of British Americans*, Jefferson expressed the idea that the colonists left the jurisdiction of Parliament and were in a "state of nature" (without government) when they first landed in North America. But, they voluntarily chose to submit to the British King, "who was thereby made the central link connecting the several parts of the empire." Under this theory, which implied throughout the Declaration, the actions of Parliament and the rights of Americans as British subjects were irrelevant to the matter at hand -

justifying independence. The only relationship that mattered was that between the British King and the Americans.

Therefore, the bulk of the rest of the Declaration is a list of twenty-seven charges against the King, proving that he deliberately chose to deprive Americans of their natural rights, which he, as their King, should have been working to protect, not destroy. Many of these twenty-seven charges might have more fairly been assessed against Parliament, but it was necessary to portray British policy as being centered in the King, both as a symbol and a person. Thus, Jefferson concludes the charges by labelling King George III a tyrant, something John Adams and many others considered offensive and going too far.

So, by the summer of 1776, thanks to Paine and now Jefferson, the King had joined, if not supplanted, Parliament as the villain and prime motivator for thousands of Americans suffering the hardships of war. It also solved the dilemna that "loyal" patriots were struggling with, as explained by Joseph Barton, of Delaware, after reading the Declaration: "I could hardly own the King and fight against him at the same time, but now these matters are cleared up. Heart and hand shall move together."

The draft was reviewed by Adams and Franklin, who each offered only one minor adjustment, and Sherman, who offered none. Then Jefferson "reported it to the house on Friday the 28th of June, when it was read and ordered to lie on the table" until the agreed upon date to re-address Lee's resolutions - July first.

CHAPTER THREE
FOUR DAYS IN JULY

"The second day of July, 1776, will be the most memorable epocha in the history of America. I am apt to believe that it will be celebrated, by succeeding generations, as the great anniversary festival."

- John Adams, writing to his
wife, Abigail, on July 3, 1776.

When Congress convened at 9 a.m. on July first, it was already 81 degrees and very humid. Outside, dark rainclouds were approaching and distant thunder could be heard booming ominously, as if an omen for the business about to be transacted. Big green-black horseflies flew in the windows from the livery stables across the street. They buzzed about hungrily, settling, unnoticed, on the legs of the delegates to bite sharply through their silk stockings. The doors and windows soon had to be closed to keep them out.

As usual, the first order of the day was for the secretary, Charles Thomson, to read the day's mail. Among the letters was one from General Washington, reporting that what appeared to be General Howe's fleet was approaching New York's harbor. Thoughts of war now occupied the minds of many delegates, though some were preoccupied with glancing about the room, looking for key members missing from some of the delegations.

Two of Delaware's three delegates, Thomas McKean and Caesar Rodney, were for independence, while the third was opposed. But Rodney, a brigadier-general in Delaware's militia, had been called home to quell a Tory uprising. This left a split delegation, and thus a

cancellation of Delaware's vote. McKean, on June 30th, had sent an express rider to bring Rodney back to Philadelphia. Now Congress was about to consider and probably vote on Richard Henry Lee's resolutions, and Rodney had not yet appeared. McKean's request for postponement was denied.

When Robert Livingston returned to New York, he told the Provincial Congress there that, unless they rescinded their 1775 instructions to their delegates, New York might be the only colony not voting for independence. So far, New York stood firmly by those instructions.

Pennsylvania's Assembly two weeks ago had, under pressure, rescinded its earlier instructions, and the new Convention had issued instructions in favor of independence. However, six of Pennsylvania's seven delegates were still opposed, and might vote contrary to the "will of the people." The seventh member, Benjamin Franklin, was working day and night trying to persuade a few of the six whom he felt were sitting on the fence and might be won over to the independence side.

John Jay had recently returned to New Jersey to urge that Provincial Congress to issue new instructions. Instead, it sent new delegates, who had not yet arrived. It was not known what instructions or inclinations they would bring with them.

South Carolina was busy preparing a state constitution, something that required its best minds. So its delegates had been called home, and replaced by new ones. The originals, except for the radical Christopher Gadsden, had been outspoken against independence. The new arrivals said they were unsure how they would vote on Lee's resolutions. They, like many colonists, felt that "provincial and local independence" was the issue; a union with other colonies, as proposed in Lee's third resolution, was something they were not prepared for. These five aristocratic plantation owners would have serious reservations about a confederacy with Yankees. Outside of New England, New Englanders were looked down on for their social levelling. Edward Rutledge, leader of the South Carolina delegation, was determined "to vest the Congress with no more power than is absolutely

necessary."

After the noon recess, discussion of the Lee resolutions was at last taken up, Congress having tabled it back on June 10th. But first, a delegate from Maryland rose to read aloud a resolution just arrived by an express rider. Samuel Chase had left Congress in late June to try to convince the Maryland Convention to rescind its earlier instructions prohibiting Maryland's delegates from voting for Lee's resolutions. Now, as the new instructions - authorizing a vote for independence - were read aloud, a joyful shout went up from the Massachusetts and Virginia delegations.

Next, Lee's first resolution was read, to refresh everyone's memory so debate could commence. Despite the mid-day hour, candles had to be lit, as storm clouds darkened the sky, broken only by occasional flashes of lightning. Franklin sat secure in the knowledge that one of his inventions, the lightning rod, was atop the statehouse. The windows had to be secured more tightly to keep out the howling wind, which was making the candle flames flicker.

A few delegates took this opportunity to whisper to each other their wish that they could dispense with lengthy debate, since the arguments had all been heard many times during the last few months, and it was unlikely that debate would change any minds now. But such hopes were dashed when John Dickinson rose to give a lengthy speech advocating the postponement of independence.

> My conduct this day may give the finishing blow to my once too great and now too diminished popularity. Though I should lose the affections of my country, though I should lose life itself, I must speak out and speak the truth as I see it. ...
>
> If we, by our declaration of independence, have bound ourselves to a war with Britain, what does France have to do but sit back? Sit back and intimidate Britain until Canada is put back into her hands. Then she can sit back and intimidate us. I say the time is not yet ripe for

proclaiming it. Instead of help from foreign powers it will bring us disaster. ...

I say we should keep Great Britain believing that we mean reconciliation. The whole nation is armed against us; the wealth of the empire is poured into her treasury; we shall weep at our folly!

John Adams later recalled Dickinson's speech as one of "great length, and eloquence." The New Jersey delegation had not yet arrived; neither had Caesar Rodney from Delaware; and now a few of the fence-sitters could be seen nodding their heads in agreement with Dickinson's appealing arguments. Sam Adams, with a troubled look on his face, leaned over and whispered to his cousin John, "It won't go through. Dickinson will have his way."

Dickinson finally finished and sat down. There was a long pause, as "no member rose to answer him." The flaming oratory of a Christopher Gadsden or a Patrick Henry was needed now, but the former was at home, leading a regiment of militia, and the latter was also at home, helping draft Virginia's constitution. As for Franklin, Jefferson and Sam Adams, they all had an aversion to speaking out on the floor of Congress. The rebuttal fell to John Adams, who was not as eloquent as Dickinson, but could be just as long-winded. Adams bluntly put forth the arguments, though they had "all been hackneyed back and forth a hundred times before."

After Adams finished speaking, it appeared that the vote could finally be taken. That is, until there was a knock at the door. Adams relates:

Before the final question was put, the new delegates from New Jersey came in, and expressed a great desire to hear the arguments. All was silence; no one would speak; all eyes were turned upon me.

Mr. Edward Rutledge came to me and said, laughing, "Nobody will speak but you upon this subject. You

have all the topics so ready that you must satisfy the gentlemen from New Jersey."

I answered him, laughing, that it had so much the air of exhibiting like an actor or gladiator, for the entertainment of the audience, that I was ashamed to repeat what I had said twenty times before, and I thought nothing new could be advanced by me. The New Jersey gentlemen, however, still insisting on hearing at least a recapitulation of the arguments, and no other gentleman being willing to speak, I summed up.

Adams concluded his speech: "For me, the die is cast. Sink or swim, live or die, to survive or perish with my country, that is my unalterable resolution!" He then sat down, and the men from New Jersey quickly whispered to each other. Then Reverend John Witherspoon, president of the College of New Jersey, rose to proclaim, "New Jersey is plump for independence." Mr. Alsop of New York then remarked, "The oratory is fine, but the hard facts show we're not ripe for it." "We're more than ripe for it!" retorted the clergyman from Princeton. "And some are in danger of rotting for want of it!" "Hear, hear," seconded Sam Adams, and suddenly the room was astir with a flurry of angry voices. When order was restored, Roger Sherman moved that the vote be taken.

Since Congress was at the moment sitting as the "Committee of the Whole," a vote could be taken without it being binding or recorded in the official Journal of the Congress. After the vote, the Committee of the Whole could revert back to a general session and take a binding vote. Secretary Thomson polled the thirteen delegations for an unofficial vote. The results: only nine were for the "resolution respecting independency." Jefferson's notes explain the actions of the other four colonies:

South Carolina and Pennsylvania voted against it. Delaware having but two members present, they were

divided. The delegates from New York declared they were for it themselves, & were assured their constituents were for it, but that their instructions having been drawn near a twelvemonth before, when reconciliation was still the general object, they ... thought themselves not justified in voting on either side ...

Mr. Rutledge of South Carolina then requested the determination might be put off to the next day.

Congress adjourned without a formal vote being taken. Prior to adjourning, more letters had to be read aloud, including another just received from Washington, reporting that so far forty-five British transports and warships had arrived in New York harbor, with more on the horizon. The news struck a somber note as the meeting broke up. The rain and windstorm finally, and suddenly, pounded Philadelphia and its weary Congressmen hurriedly making their way from the statehouse.

Franklin, Adams and others worked "out of doors" (privately) trying to convince the Pennsylvania and South Carolina delegates that the vote must be unanimous. If even a single colony voted against independence, the British could establish a post there, from which they might persuade others. Edward Rutledge, South Carolina's opposition leader, agreed that he would switch his pivotal vote if Delaware and Pennsylvania both decided in favor of independence.

If Pennsylvania could be brought into the fold, it would truly earn its nickname as "the keystone colony." An exasperated Francis Lightfoot Lee, of Virginia, remarked as he left the state house, "The Pennsylvania delegates indulge their own wishes, tho' they acknowledge what indeed everyone knows, that they vote contrary to the earnest desires of the people."

It rained heavily, off and on, all that night. Somewhere out in that rain, without the benefit of moonlight, Caesar Rodney was blindly urging his horse on. There were more than eighty miles of muddy roads between Dover and Philadelphia. Over Rodney's left cheek was a

patch covering a large cancerous sore that would eventually take his life. He had been advised by his doctors to travel to England and seek out the best medical and surgical doctors available. He had been considering this, but would certainly not be able to do it if he reached Philadelphia in time to cast Delaware's deciding vote for independence.

The next morning, July second, amidst squall showers and beneath a dark and thundering sky, the delegates again gathered in the state house. These were serious-minded men, fully aware of the momentous decision they probably would be making before the day was over. Delaware's Caesar Rodney had still not arrived. But, more importantly, Pennsylvania's two strongest opponents of independence, John Dickinson and Robert Morris, were conspicuously absent. Hancock waited half an hour before calling for the day's session to begin. Several delegates rose to voice their opinion that the Congress should wait a while longer for Dickinson and Morris. Hancock responded by declaring that the Congress would not "take into farther consideration the resolution respecting independency" until Secretary Thomson read aloud the day's mail.

There were letters from Generals Benedict Arnold at Ticonderoga, New York, and Charles Lee at Charleston, South Carolina. Both pleaded for food, war supplies and fresh, healthy reinforcements. Arnold's smallpox-ridden, almost naked, and half-starved remnant of the northern army was trying to halt the southward advance of a much larger British army from Canada. Lee was coordinating Charleston's defense against a combined British army-navy operation. Secretary Thomson read Lee's letter, forwarded to the Congress by Washington: "I have never experienced a hotter fire in all my life. Twelve hours without inter- mission! For God's sake, my dear General, urge Congress to furnish me with a thousand cavalry without delay!" And, again, there was a letter from General Washington. This time he reported that, with the count of British ships at 110 and climbing, Howe's forces appeared to be much larger than when he had left Boston four months before. An attack was imminent, and Washington thought his own resources inadequate.

The Congress returned from the noon recess at one o'clock, only to find Dickinson, Morris, and Rodney all still absent. Hancock continued his delaying tactics by having the debate start with Lee's third resolution - to draw up articles of confederation. It was obvious that Congress was more divided on that issue than on independence. Agreement on articles of confederation would take months, perhaps years. Finally, Hancock, looking at the clock, concluded that he could not delay any longer. The matter must be put to a vote. Since no message had been received from Dickinson or Morris, they must be deliberately staying away, so as not to be responsible for possibly making Pennsylvania the only colony to vote against the measure, which even they realized must be unanimous to be effective. Morris later explained why he sat out: in "the service of his country, a good man will follow if he can not lead."

Virginia's Benjamin Harrison, who presided instead of Hancock whenever Congress resolved itself into the Committee of the Whole, asked that the three Lee resolutions be voted on together, to be accepted or rejected by a "yea" or "nay" from each delegate.

As they prepared to vote, the pounding of the rain lessened and the thunder became more distant, allowing Delaware's Thomas McKean to hear hoofbeats coming down Chestnut Street. After raising a window to look, he opened the front door and went outside. There he met an exhausted, soaked and mud-splattered Caesar Rodney, just then reining in his horse.

> Caesar Rodney I met at the State House door, in his boots and spurs ... After a friendly salutation (without a word on the business), we went into the Hall of Congress together ... after a few minutes the great question was put. When the vote for Delaware was called ... [Rodney] arose and said, "As I believe the voice of my constituents, and of all sensible and honest men is in favor of Independence, and my own judgment concurs with them, I vote for Independence."

All the New England delegates, to no one's surprise, voted "aye," as did those from Georgia, North Carolina, Virginia, and the recent convert, New Jersey. Maryland, thanks to Chase, also went in the affirmative; as did Delaware, 2 votes to 1, thanks to Caesar Rodney. Pennsylvania voted 3 to 2 for independence, because of the last minute conversion of Wilson and Morton, and the absence of Dickinson and Morris. South Carolina reversed its decision of the day before, and voted for independence, "for the sake of unanimity." Overnight, three colonies had been won over. The result: twelve ayes, and one abstention. New York, regretfully, abstained. Within two weeks, though, the New York delegation would receive new instructions, making it unanimous.

The Committee of the Whole reported the vote on Lee's resolutions to the Congress, which accepted it as official and binding, then adjourned.

Weather records for that day state that the squalls stopped about 2:00 that afternoon, the sky cleared up, and by 11:00 that night there was "fine moonlight." The storm had come and passed both in and outside the state house. The next morning, John Adams wrote home to his wife, Abigail:

> The second day of July, 1776, will be the most memorable epocha in the history of America. I am apt to believe that it will be celebrated, by succeeding generations, as the great anniversary festival. It ought to be commemorated, as the day of deliverance, by solemn acts of devotion to God Almighty. It ought to be solemnized with pomp and parade and shews, games, sports, guns, bells, bonfires and illuminations from one end of the continent to the other from this time forward forever more.
>
> You will think me transported with enthusiasm but I am not. I am well aware of the toil and blood and treas-

ure that it will cost us to maintain this Declaration and support and defend these states.

Yet through all the gloom I can see the rays of ravishing light and glory. I can see that the end is more than worth the means. And that posterity will tryumph in that days transactions.

Shortly before 9 a.m. on July third, Secretary Thomson discovered an anonymous note. Because President Hancock had not yet arrived, Thomson gave the note to Benjamin Harrison. He read it aloud to those members who had already arrived and those who were filtering in. "You have gone too far," the note read. "Take care. A plot is framed for your destruction and all of you shall be destroyed!" Thomson considered it a practical joke, but Harrison and several others thought otherwise. Philadelphia was full of Tories, a few of whom had recently been tarred and feathered for drinking the King's health and other "crimes." Perhaps Congress's transactions of the preceding day had leaked out, in violation of the vow of secrecy all delegates had taken.

This brought to mind the plot to assassinate General Washington, uncovered just the week before. The mayor of New York had been implicated, along with a member of Washington's bodyguard and others. Rumors held that the plot originated with the exiled Governor Tryon, then living on a British warship near New York. Tryon had also printed huge quantities of counterfeit Continental dollars, deflating the value of Congress's paper currency so the public would refuse to honor it.

Elbridge Gerry, of Massachusetts, called for a few members to go down into the state house cellar and search for a bomb. Hancock came in and, upon taking his seat, found the note. He tossed it aside and picked up the gavel, ready to open the day's session. Gerry repeated, "I think we ought to search the cellar." Old Stephen Hopkins, of Rhode Island, banged his cane against the leg of his chair, and yelled, "Let's get on with the meeting!" The crusty old Yankee's out-

burst, as usual, brought an indignant glare from some of the more refined aristocrats, who did not approve of such crude, "Yankee" behavior. Then North Carolina's Joseph Hewes stood and addressed the chair:

> I am against wasting time examining any cellars. I move that we treat this threatening note with the contempt it deserves and take no further notice of it. Myself, I'd as soon be blown to bits as proclaim to the world I was scared to death by a silly note!

Hancock agreed, and nodded to Thomson to start reading the day's correspondence. This day, there was no letter from General Washington. Much time was spent speculating why. An order was sent to Washington to move the "Flying Camp" of 10,000 militia from their present location at Amboy to Brunswick, New Jersey. From there, they would be able to move more quickly to either New York or Philadelphia, whichever city General Howe should choose to attack.

Finally, correspondence and other matters were dispensed with, and Jefferson's draft of a declaration proclaiming and justifying independence was read aloud from start to finish by Secretary Thomson. He was then directed to read it again, stopping after each paragraph, so the individual members could voice objections and suggest improvements. However, he found that he had to stop after every sentence, there were so many opinions to be aired and debated on almost every phrase. Perhaps sensing the historical importance that the document would have, almost everyone wanted to have a personal hand in its writing. "His Majesty" became "the King of England." "Deluge us in blood" was changed to "destroy us," and "neglected utterly" to "utterly neglected." The beginning of Jefferson's famous second paragraph, like so many other passages, was a marked improvement over the version in Jefferson's draft.

[Draft] We hold these truths to be sacred & undeni-

able; that all men are created equal & independent; that from that equal creation they derive rights inherent & inalienable, among which are the preservation of life, & liberty, & the pursuit of happiness.

[Revision] We hold these truths to be self-evident; that all men are created equal, that they are endowed by their Creator with certain unalienable rights, that among these are life, liberty, and the pursuit of happiness.

Jefferson sat in the back of the room, outwardly silent, but inwardly seething. On his lap, he held the portable desk on which he had written the draft. Now he used it to painfully scratch in the numerous deletions and changes. Years later, he recalled the scene:

> I was sitting by Dr. Franklin, who perceived that I was not insensible to these mutilations. "I have made it a rule," said he, "whenever in my power, to avoid becoming the draughtsman of papers to be reviewed by a public body."

To console Jefferson, Franklin also whispered to him the story of a hatter named John Thompson, who made a sign to hang above his shop entrance. It read, "John Thompson, Hatter, Makes and Sells Hats for Ready Money." To emphasize it, the figure of a hat was also painted on the sign. A friend studied the sign, and said the word "Hatter" was superfluous, since the sign already stated "Sells Hats." So Thompson thanked his friend for the advice, and made the sign over, without the word "Hatter." Another friend, observing the new sign, thought the word "Makes" unnecessary, since a man buying a hat does not really care who made it. Besides, it was a shop for selling hats, not a factory for making them, that Thompson intended the sign to advertise. So he again constructed a new sign. A third friend, seeing this new version, wondered why the sign referred to "Ready Money." Surely no one expected to buy a hat on credit. Again, the

sign was taken down and a new one made. This left only "John Thompson Sells Hats," and the figure of a hat. A regular customer, respected by Thompson for his patronage if not his opinion, read it aloud, "John Thompson Sells Hats," and remarked, "Ridiculous. John Thompson wouldn't give them away, would he?" The exasperated hatter succombed once again and made the final version, having only his name and the picture.

Jefferson, touched by his old friend's concern for his sensitivity, swallowed his pride and anger, and reconciled himself to the fact that the document, after all, was not his alone, but a Declaration from the entire Congress. He was particularly peeved about two deletions, though, as he related in his account of the deliberations:

> The pusillanimous idea that we had friends in England worth keeping terms with still haunted the minds of many. For this reason those passages which conveyed censures on the people of England [references to the Scotch troops as foreign mercenaries] were struck out, lest they should give them offense. The clause, too, reprobating the enslaving the inhabitants of Africa was struck out in complaisance to South Carolina and Georgia, who [unlike Virginia] had never attempted to restrain the importation of slaves and who on the contrary still wished to continue it. Our Northern brethren also I believe felt a little tender under those censures; for tho' their people have very few slaves themselves yet they had been pretty considerable carriers of them to others.

Congress adjourned, leaving the last half of Jefferson's twenty-seven charges against the King, and his closing paragraph on the final separation, for the next day, July 4th. That day, like the 3rd had been, was clear and slightly cooler than the turbulent 1st and 2nd of July, with temperatures now only reaching the mid-seventies. By 9 a.m. on the

4th, all fifty-six members were present. Hancock, sensing the mood of the Congress, asked if it wanted to consider the day's letters first. He was answered by a resounding "No!" There was a letter from General Washington, but it could wait. Overnight, a copy of Jefferson's uncorrected draft had been printed for each delegation, and now they were eager to finish altering it and have it printed. With copies in hand, there would be less re-reading aloud, so the revision process would go faster than the day before.

Altogether, by the time Congress finished that afternoon, it had made eighty-six changes to Jefferson's draft, reducing it from 1,730 words to 1,333. Among the deletions was the most poignant passage in the entire document. "We might have been a free & great people together; but a community of grandeur & of freedom it seems is below their dignity." If left in, this passage would have touched the hearts of thousands of Americans reading it that summer, as they reluctantly reconciled themselves to the final break with Britain.

When the last of the changes was made, the dinner hour was approaching. The Committee of the Whole reverted back to the Congress. Benjamin Harrison left the presiding officer's chair and gave it back to John Hancock, who quickly ordered Secretary Thomson to call the roll from north to south. The vote was the same as for Lee's resolutions, two days before: twelve "ayes" and one abstention - New York, still waiting. The document was accepted as revised.

Before adjourning, Hancock announced that, once the document was rewritten to include all the alterations agreed upon, he would sign it, as would Secretary Thomson as witness, and have it printed. The copies would then "be sent to the several assemblies, conventions and committees or councils of safety, and to the several commanding officers of the continental troops; that it be proclaimed in each of the United States, and at the head of the army."

Perhaps Hancock was trying to save the members from the hangman's rope, when he assured the Congress that his signature and Thomson's would suffice. However, within a few days, many of the

66

members were suggesting that everyone's signature be on the document.

On July 15th, Congress received New York's aye vote, making it unanimous. Hancock was so pleased that, on the 19th, he asked Congress if the Declaration could be recopied, changing the title to "The Unanimous Declaration ..." Also, it should be written on parchment this time, which would make it look more stately and dignified. Permission was granted, and the parchment work was contracted out, to be completed by the end of July. August 2nd was set as the date for signing the parchment copy. It was probably at this July 19th session that the resolution was passed requiring everyone to sign the parchment copy.

Thus, it was August 2, 1776, not July 4th, that the signatures were affixed. A few delegates, not present on August 2nd, signed later, as did several newly elected members during the next four months. New members could not take their seats in Congress until they signed the Declaration. This requirement was established "to prevent traitors or spies from worming themselves amongst us." Thus, some of the signatures are those of men who had nothing to do with the Declaration's passage.

According to John Adams, "there were several who signed with regret and several others with many doubts." Not so for John Morton, the last minute convert whose critical vote carried Pennsylvania (and with it South Carolina) for independence. Morton had struggled with his conscience for months; his mental anguish had affected his health. But, once he finally determined his course, he became more and more convinced he made the right decision. In the spring of 1777, Morton died. His family and friends had blamed him harshly for his vote. Reportedly, on his deathbed his last words were, "Tell them that they will live to see the hour when they shall acknowledge it to be the most glorious service I ever rendered my country."

Four members refused to sign, and had to resign from the Congress. Among them was John Dickinson. His *Letters From A Pennsylvania Farmer* and other works had helped bring on the revolution, but in the

end he could not turn against his sovereign, King George III.

Dickinson accepted a colonelcy in the Philadelphia militia, and was soon leading his regiment to the relief of New York. Though Dickinson would fight for his country, he considered it a senseless war. "I grieve for the fate of a brave and generous nation," he wrote, "plunged by a few profligate men into scenes of unmerited and inglorious distress. Why should nations meet with hostile eyes because villains and idiots have acted like villains and idiots?" Dickinson's action in battle would resurrect his reputation, and he would become President of Pennsylvania's Supreme Executive Council, and in 1781 Governor of Delaware. During the war, his lavish estate, Philadelphia's finest, would be burned to the ground by the British, and his family would become refugees.

On August 2nd, Hancock signed his name in huge letters, then held it up and exclaimed, "His Majesty can now read my name without spectacles, and may double his reward of 500 pounds on my head." Each delegation came forward and signed as a group. Probably thoughts of a noose came to the minds of some of the signers. Four days after the signing, Abraham Clark, delegate from New Jersey, sent a copy of the Declaration to a friend in the northern army on Lake Champlain, and wrote "Perhaps our Congress will be exalted on a high gallows."

In June, Elbridge Gerry, a small and slender man at barely 100 pounds, had asked whether every member would have to sign it, or just Hancock and Thomson. Contrary to the assurance given then, the decision for all to sign had since been made, and now they were each putting their name to the treasonous document. After signing his own name, the rotund Benjamin Harrison, heaviest man in Congress, turned and saw Gerry looking anxious as he awaited his turn with the pen. Harrison, in his deep, booming voice, jovially told Gerry, "When the hanging scene comes to be exhibited, my friend, I shall have all the advantage over you. With me it will be over in a minute. But you, you'll be dancing on air an hour after I'm gone."

Still another anecdote of the signing had Hancock stressing the need

for a united front: "We must be unanimous. There must be no pulling different ways. We must all hang together." To which Dr. Franklin quickly added, "Yes, we must indeed all hang together, or most assuredly we shall all hang separately."

Copies of the July 4th version, with only the signatures of Hancock and Thomson, had been quickly printed and distributed. Not until 1777 were copies of the August 2nd version published, showing all the signatures.

From one end of the new country to the other, the Declaration was read aloud at spontaneous public gatherings. It was greeted with demonstrations of delight, usually in the form of bonfires and discharges of muskets or thirteen cannon, despite the ban on unnecessary expenditure of gunpowder. In Charleston, an effigy of the King was ceremoniously buried beneath the Liberty Tree. In Huntington, Long Island, almost within sight of the British fleet, a similar effigy of the King, stuffed with gunpowder, was hung from the Liberty Tree, then lit as the people watched it explode with a great bang. In New York, General Washington included the following in his general orders of the day for July 9th:

> The several brigades are to be drawn up this evening on their respective parades, at six oclock, when the declaration of Congress is to be read with an audible voice.
>
> The General hopes this important event will serve as a fresh incentive to every officer, and soldier, to act with fidelity and courage, as knowing that now the peace and safety of his country depends, under God, solely on the success of our arms. And that he is now in the service of a State possessed of sufficient power to reward his merit, and advance him to the highest honors of a free country.

A company of militia was drawn up at the foot of Broad Way at 6 p.m. listening to the reading, as was a gang of local toughs. As the

document was read, the soldiers cheered. The hoodlums rang out loud huzzas after each charge against the King. When the reading was over, some of the militia joined these young toughs as they searched for and found a dozen ropes, then proceeded to the Bowling Green, the site of a statue of King George III mounted on a horse. After much tugging at the ropes, the statue "was pulled down by the populace."

Lieutenant Isaac Bangs the next day recorded plans to melt the lead statue down into musket balls. He expressed his hope that the "musket balls from the leaden George will make as deep impressions in the bodies of some of his redcoated and Tory subjects as the folly and pretended goodness of the real George have made upon their minds." The pieces were hauled in wagons to Litchfield, Connecticut, where local Daughters of Liberty molded 42,088 bullets from the statue. In Ebenezer Hazard's words, now "the bloody-backs could have melted Majesty fired into them." But the King's head was saved. It was fixed atop a flagstaff outside Fort Washington in upper Manhattan, until a loyalist officer hired two spies to steal it. It was then sent to Lord Townshend, "to convince them at home of the infamous disposition of this ungrateful people."

Public readings of the Declaration made for good business for local tavernkeepers. The rum was kept flowing in order to keep up with the countless toasts for the new nation, the Congress, etc., and against the King, his ministers, Parliament, and the British Army. One list of toasts included this one: "Perpetual itching without the benefit of scratching to the enemies of America."

Those who were ready for independence accepted it and rejoiced. The loyalists, and many of the moderates favoring reconciliation, scorned it privately - publicly if they dared. They could take some satisfaction in knowing that Hancock, by signing his name, had put his neck in a noose. Captain Alexander Graydon expressed the opinion of many moderates who had hoped for reconciliation and were now apprehensive about independence.

I acquiesce in the measure as it becomes daily more necessary, altho' I am of opinion that delaying it awhile longer would have had no bad tendency. On the contrary, it would still keep the door open for reconciliation, convince the world of our reluctance to embrace it, and increase our friends on t'other side of the water. But the greatest danger is that subtle, designing knaves, or weak, insignificant block heads may take the lead in public affairs. This they have already done, and much I fear, that such will be our rulers.

For an illustration of the moderate and loyalist perspectives, we turn to a memoir about Mr. Wynkoop, moderate member of New York's Provincial Congress. This conversation took place in June, between Wynkoop and his conservative father-in-law, Nicholas.

"I asked you to come," old Nicholas said after greeting us a little stiffly, "because I must know what you purpose to do. General Howe is about to take New York. The Philadelphia Congress is about to declare a separation from Great Britain. The so-called Provincial Congress of New York will hesitate, but it will probably support the measure. Am I to understand that you will burn your bridges and side with the rebels?"

With great seriousness and gravity, Mr. Wynkoop replied: "I wish you to believe, sir, that I have given the matter every consideration in my power and it seems to me that I can't do other than go with America. America is my country, and yours too, sir."

"America is my country." The voice of old Nicholas was shrill. "I have no great love for Britishers, as you know. Damn them all, I say! But I am too old to meddle with treason. Especially when it can't come to any good. Either we shall be crushed ... or we shall succeed,

in which case we shall be ruled by the mob. Which is better, God knows. What I can't see is why you have allowed the fanatics to run away with the cart. Fight if you must, but why close the door to reconciliation by declaring an independency?"

"We can't fight without it, sir. That's the whole truth of the matter. I was much against it, and so were most. But the necessity is clear. First we refused to trade, hoping that Britain would make terms as she had formerly done. Instead of making terms, Britain closed our ports and prepared to make war. To fight we must have supplies and munitions. We must have money. We can get none of these things without reviving trade; and to revive trade we must have allies, we must have the support of France. But will France aid us, so long as we profess our loyalty to Britain? France will give money and troops to disrupt the British Empire, but none to consolidate it. The act of separation will be the price of a French alliance."

For a long moment old Nicholas stood stiff and silent. Suddenly extending his hand, but turning his face away, he said, "Well, good by. Our ways part then."

"Don't say that, sir."

"I must say it. I must remain as I began - a loyal British subject. You have ceased to be one. I am sorry to have seen this day. But I must submit to necessity, and you must too."

Slowly old Nicholas ascended the stairs, tapping each tread with his cane. Half way up, he cried out, as if in anger, "Good bye, I say!"

"God keep you, sir," was all Mr. Wynkoop could find to reply.

In England, as in America, the Declaration received mixed reactions.

Some of the Whigs in Parliament boldly spoke out against the King's ministers, saying, "They drove the Americans into their present state of independency." While in East Windsor, Connecticut, a newborn baby was baptized Independence, in London a lady delivered triplets and named them Hancock, Adams and Washington.

Two pamphlets, published in London, detailed rebuttals of the Declaration's attempt to justify independence. One was written by former Massachusetts Governor Thomas Hutchinson. Like many an English writer, Hutchinson questioned whether Americans could call liberty an inalienable right of man, while "depriving Africans of their rights to liberty." The other pamphlet, written by John Lind, concentrated on logically disproving each of the charges against the King, while almost ignoring the opening paragraphs' philosophy of government. Lind wrote, "Of the preamble, I have taken little or no notice. The truth is, little or none does it deserve. The opinions of the modern Americans on government, like those of their good ancestors on witchcraft, would be too ridiculous to deserve any notice, if they had not led to the most serious evils."

If the Congress expected their proclamation of independence to have the immediate effect of obtaining a French alliance, they were mistaken. France did not formally recognize the new nation. King Louis XVI could not be expected to endorse a document which proclaimed that governments derive their powers from the consent of the people. Silas Deane, sent by Congress to purchase munitions in Paris, was told by Foreign Minister de Vergennes that to acknowledge the United States's existence would be construed by Britain as a declaration of war, something King Louis XVI was not yet prepared for. Time, and a few American victories on the battlefield, would change his mind.

Independence had come at last, but not through the efforts only of fifty-six men in Philadelphia. It had come from the clamor of thousands of common people from the granite hills of New Hampshire to the swamps of Georgia. Americans were angered by the actions of their beloved King George III, who had scorned their petitions and de-

clared war on his colonies as if they were a foreign nation. The voice of the people was heard and, one by one, their legislatures either went with this voice or, as in Pennsylvania's case, were replaced by new political bodies. The people had been slow to awake to their destiny, their legislatures even slower; but, by the spring of 1776, a reluctant America knew that the time had come when it must make that final break with Britain.

CHAPTER FOUR
SCOTTISH BROADSWORDS AND SIR PETER
PARKER'S BRITCHES: WAR IN THE SOUTH
FEBRUARY - JUNE 1776

"Fight on, my brave boys, don't let liberty expire with me today!"

> *- Sergeant McDaniel, dying of his wounds during the Battle of Charleston, June 28, 1776.*

Declaring independence was easy; proving it would be difficult. It would take several years of bloody fighting and terrible hardships before a peaceful independence would become a reality. During those first few weeks of summer, while Congress was preoccupied with the independence question, three separate British armies were confronting the Continental forces. One was in Canada, where Governor-General Carleton had been reinforced with 10,000 British and German soldiers, and would eventually oppose Benedict Arnold on Lake Champlain.

The second British army was in New York's harbor, General Howe having just arrived from Halifax. He now combined his original 6,000 man Boston army with an additional 25,000 British and German reinforcements. This was the King's big push to annihilate Washington's army, which was hastily throwing up defensive lines in New York and across the East River in Brooklyn.

The third British army was off the South Carolina coast, approaching Charleston. Their aim was to put the South under loyalist control, and break its shaky union with the middle and northern colonies. In the present chapter, we will examine this southern campaign. First, let us step back a few months and see what prompted the British govern-

ment in London to send part of their army, accompanied by a naval fleet, to the South.

The southern campaign of 1776 came about partly from solicitations made to the Secretary of State by the exiled royal governor of North Carolina, Josiah Martin. Martin had been appointed Governor of North Carolina in 1771. He inherited a colony that had just seen a potential civil war nipped in the bud by the previous governor.

For well over a decade, the more than 40,000 Scots, Irish and German settlers in the mountains of western North Carolina had tried to have their grievances redressed by that colony's legislature. However, North Carolina's legislature was dominated by the eastern, tidewater districts. This meant the mountain folk were grossly under-represented and overtaxed, compared to the easterners, who looked down their noses at these crude, "foreign" backwoods people.

Despairing of their futile efforts for justice, the backwoods people took over local courts, beat up and drove out tax collectors, and started to "regulate" taxes and fees on a fair basis. The governor took control of the situation by leading the militia into the mountains, and routing the "Regulators" at the Battle of Alamance in 1771. Then he hanged six of their leaders, ending the uprising. Now, five years later, the colonial government was dominated by patriot leaders, most of them from the same tidewater gentry whose earlier oppression had given rise to the Regulator movement.

Thousands of additional Scots had emigrated from Scotland to North Carolina during the five years since the Battle of Alamance. Among them was Flora McDonald, who had been one of the heroes of Scotland's failed uprising against England in 1745. When the Scots were crushed that year, Flora hid the Young Pretender, Bonnie Prince Charlie, from the victorious British Army's search parties. She guided him to the coast of Scotland, where a ship carried him off to the safety of France. Flora was caught, and served time in the Tower of London until it appeared that the spirit of Scotland was crushed. She was then released and went home to Scotland to find that songs and poems had been written praising her.

In 1775, North Carolina's Governor Josiah Martin was living on a British warship in Cape Fear, near Wilmington. He managed to persuade Flora McDonald, still much revered by the Scots in the Carolina hills, to support his attempt to win back the colony for the Crown. Martin had written to his superiors in London, promising that 20,000 armed loyalists would rise up and assist any British force sent to North Carolina. "The people are in general well affected," he wrote, "and much attached to me." Although a good many of the 20,000 Martin counted on had come to the colony after the Battle of Alamance and had not built up animosity against the tidewater patriots like the former Regulators had, Martin still had reason to be confident they would rise to his call to arms. During the large migrations of 1773 and 1774 from the Scottish Highlands, Governor Martin had granted the new arrivals free land, in return for taking an oath of allegiance to the King. He warned them now that he would take back the land of anyone who broke the oath.

King George III and his cabinet believed Martin's predictions, and similar ones from the other royal governors in exile. Civilian advisors like Richard Oswald, a Briton who had spent six years in Virginia, also predicted massive loyalist uprisings against the rebels, as soon as the British troops arrived. In February, 1775, Oswald had told Lord Dartmouth, Secretary of State for the Colonies, that the needs of the South were different from those of the North, due to its slave-labor economy and an influential "aristocracy" with "great family connexions."

If these families could be convinced that their interests were not the same as those of the "mob of northern yeomen," that "despicable rabble of rioters," that "confederacy of smugglers" in New England, then Virginia would withdraw from the rebellion. And Virginia would quickly be followed by the other southern colonies, who looked to her for leadership. Economic self-interest would convince the South to depart from the infatuated and distrusted Yankees.

Plans for a southern campaign were started by Secretary of State Lord Dartmouth, and carried through by his successor, Lord George Germain. Cape Fear, North Carolina, with its sheltered deep water,

would be a perfect base for a British fleet. This is why the King made sure Parliament exempted North Carolina when it passed the Prohibitory Act in late 1775, prohibiting the other twelve colonies from trading with Great Britain or the British West Indies.

Early in January, 1776, Martin received an answer from London: 2,000 Regulars, commanded by General Lord Cornwallis, were scheduled to sail from Cork, Ireland, in late November, and should arrive at Cape Fear by February. The fleet transporting them would include nine warships and be commanded by Admiral Sir Peter Parker. And General Sir Henry Clinton was heading south from Boston with an additional 200 troops. During a winter campaign, Clinton and Parker would put the South securely in loyalist hands, then sail north in time to join General Howe's summer campaign at New York.

The ecstatic Governor Martin, unwilling to wait for the Regulars to arrive, immediately sent word to Flora and others in the upcountry to gather their forces and, in early February, march to Cape Fear. Martin, anticipating the need for Gaelic-speaking recruiters, had earlier requested General Gage to send him two such British officers from Boston. Lieutenant-Colonel Donald MacDonald and Captain Donald McLeod, both wounded at Bunker Hill, arrived and were promptly interrogated by a patriot Committee of Safety. They were released when they told the committee they had simply retired and come to North Carolina to live the rest of their days in peace among their own people. Governor Martin secretly commissioned them as a brigadier-general and lieutenant-colonel.

Despite their best recruiting efforts, they soon realized that the governor grossly over-estimated the number of backwoodsmen willing to risk their lives against the patriot militia. Instead of the 20,000 Martin had predicted, only 1,750 set out from Cross Creek (present day Fayetteville, North Carolina) to march toward the sea. Almost all of them were Scots. Bagpipes skirled as they marched, their kilts displaying the plaids of the clans represented in this loyalist army: Stewarts, Campbells, MacLeods, McLeans, MacArthurs and others. One of the recruits was 14-year-old Hugh McDonald, who provides

this account:

> I well remember, that John Martin, who called himself
> a Captain in the contemplated regiment, came to the
> house of my father, who then lived near Cross Hill
> [present day Carthage, North Carolina] ... and after
> causing him to enlist, told him he must take me along
> with him. My father said I would be of no use to the
> army as a soldier, and as his wife was a sickly woman,
> and the children all weakly, I would be useful at home to
> the family.
> "Never mind your family!" was the reply. "He will
> count one to procure me a commission, and he will draw
> you a soldier's pay."
> My father told him that would be unjust.
> "If you do not take him with you, I will see you
> hanged," was Martin's reply to that; and my father was
> afraid of their threats.

Only 520 of the recruits had muskets, though they managed to confiscate an additional 130 guns from rebel farmers during the march.
Many of the remainder carried the double-edged, heavy broadswords
that had almost spelled defeat for the British Army at Culloden back in
1745. More recently, Highlander regiments in the British Army had
become famed for their courage in battles against the French. Considering this, the Continental Congress decided it would be prudent to
send emissaries to the Carolina hills, to ascertain the political views of
the Scots there. But the emissaries returned to Philadelphia without an
answer, not being able to speak Gaelic.

While the Scots marched, the British were supposed to be waiting
for them at the Cape Fear rendezvous. But the fleet of nine warships
and thirty transports, bringing fort-busting cannon and 2,000 Regulars,
was still at Cork in early February, the time of their expected arrival at
Cape Fear. Even after they finally left Ireland on February 13, they

would be so delayed by storms and contrary winds that the last ship would not arrive at Cape Fear until May 31.

So Governor Martin's loyalist army found not a welcoming army of British Regulars, but 1,100 armed North Carolina Continentals blocking their path along the west branch of the Cape Fear River. As soon as the enemy was sighted, two companies from the loyalist army turned around and went home to the hills, taking their badly needed guns with them. The loyalist army had dwindled now to 1,400. Trying to bluff the patriot Colonel James Moore into surrendering, MacDonald sent him a note ordering him to lay down his arms, or else "suffer the fate of an enemy of the Crown." Moore, his confidence bolstered by five light cannon, stood his ground and sent the messenger back with a note demanding MacDonald and his entire force take the Committee of Safety's Test Oath "to support the Continental Congress" or else be treated as "enemies of the constitutional liberties of America."

Not wanting to attempt battle without the British, MacDonald ferried his men across the Cape Fear River. He then sank his boats, and tried to dash down the opposite (east) bank to Wilmington. However, Moore was joined by 150 minutemen, under Colonel Richard Caswell, and several hundred patriot Rangers. When a messenger brought word that yet another 850 men, under Colonel Alexander Lillington, were approaching from the eastern counties, Moore gave Caswell two "field pieces" (light cannon) and sent him to join Lillington in blocking the loyalists' march. Meanwhile, Moore circled wide to come upon them from the rear.

After five days of marching and countermarching, MacDonald found his last route to the sea blocked. It was a stream called Widow Moore's Creek, which fed into the Cape Fear (Black) River from the northeast.

Caswell's men hastily constructed fortifications on the same (northern) side of the creek that the Scots were on, in order to prevent them from reaching the creek. Next they crossed over the bridge to the southern side, removing the wooden planks and smearing the un-

derlying wooden stringers with soap and bear's grease. Once on the southern side, they hid themselves and their two field pieces (affectionately named "Old Mother Covington and her daughter") behind breastworks they had built on that side.

MacDonald, in his sixties and still suffering from his Bunker Hill wound, was by now exhausted and desperate. His army was down to less than two barrels of flour. He took to a bed in a nearby farmhouse. His council of war that night, February 25, 1776, considered the situation. A night scouting party did not notice that the bridge had been tampered with. But they did come upon the "abandoned [north bank] camp & found there some horses and provisions," apparently left behind when the militia crossed to the other side of Widow Moore's Creek. The council of war read this as a good sign and "unanimously agreed that the enemy's camp should directly be attacked" before dawn.

The older officers, trained in the British Army, suggested they wait until full light, to be sure the intrenchments on the southern bank were also deserted. But the young men, eager for glory, carried the debate. Alexander McLeod, who had been on the altar about to wed Flora's daughter when the call to arms took him away, now offered to lead the charge, as did another young hothead, John Campbell. Though poorly armed, the loyalists would have the advantage in numbers over the rebels, about 1,400 to 1,000.

A member of the loyalist army describes what happened after "we found their fires [at the abandoned north shore camp] beginning to turn weak & concluded that the enemy were marched:"

> Mr. McLean [McLeod], with a party of about 40 men, was challenged by the enemies centinels [on the other side of the river], they observing him sooner than he observed them. He answered that he was a friend. They asked to whom. He replyed to the King. Upon his making this reply, they squatted down upon their faces to the ground. Mr. McLean uncertain but they might be

some of our own people that had crossed the bridge, challenged them in Gallic to which they made no answer, upon which he fired his own piece & ordered his party to fire, upon which the firings turned more general.

Another participant later recalled what followed in the dim light just before dawn: "Drums beat, bagpipes skirled," and eighty Highlanders, fiercely wielding two-edged broadswords overhead while shouting "King George and Broadswords!" charged out of the forest toward the enemy fortifications across the bridge. Right behind them, in three columns, came the rest of the loyalist army, with and without muskets. Perhaps it was good for Caswell's inexperienced militia that he had retreated to the other side of the creek. Young McLeod and Campbell led the charge across the bridge, some of the men slipping and falling into the creek, others making their way over the greased supports. When McLeod and several of the foremost men had crossed the bridge, Caswell's militia opened up. An account, titled the "Battle of Moore's Creek," was published in Pennsylvania and New York newspapers.

They were received with a very heavy fire, which did great execution. Captains McCloud [McLeod] and Campbell were instantly killed, the former having nine bullets and twenty-four swan shot through and into his body. The insurgents retreated with the greatest precipitation, leaving behind them some of their wagons, &c. They cut their horses out of their wagons and mounted three upon a horse. Many of them fell into the creek and were drowned. ... The battle lasted three minutes.

The loyalists, or "Tories," suffered seventy casualties, while their enemy had only one dead and one wounded. The militia brought forward the wooden planks, laid them down, crossed the bridge, and chased after the retreating Scots. The patriots, or "Whigs," not only

captured most of the routed army, but also took the opportunity to loot Tory houses in the area. Altogether, Colonel Caswell reported that his men captured or confiscated "fifteen hundred rifle-guns, all of them excellent pieces." Also taken was the 1,500 pounds sterling that Governor Martin had authorized for the campaign's recruiting and provision expenses.

But the "850 common soldiers taken prisoner" were soon "disarmed and discharged." In a proclamation translated into Gaelic, the North Carolina Provincial Congress apologized for the necessity of sending MacDonald and a few other leaders to Pennsylvania for safekeeping. And they promised that "no wanton acts of cruelty, no severity, shall be exercised to the prisoners; no restraints shall be imposed upon them, but what shall be necessary to prevent their using their liberty to the injury of the friends of America." The Provincial Congress also provided funds for the destitute families of these prisoners.

Such humane treatment, coupled with the memory of the defeat at Widow Moore's Creek, kept many others neutral. Fourteen-year-old Hugh McDonald was among those who were given "passports and permitted to return home ... [where] we were justly hissed at for our incredulity. But, notwithstanding this scouring and the just contempt of our fellow citizens, we remained at heart as stiff Tories as ever."

As a result of this signal victory, the warrior spirit soared among North Carolina patriots, one man describing it as a "universal ardor for fighting." Another wrote to a friend in the north, "You never knew the like in your life for pure patriotism." Five weeks after the battle, the Provincial Congress of North Carolina convened, and within three days it resolved "that the delegates for this colony in the Continental Congress be empowered to concur with the delegates of the other colonies in declaring independency."

* * * * *

When Washington observed Clinton leave Boston, he figured the

83

British general's destination was New York, and he expected Howe to soon follow with the rest of the army. So the American commander dispatched his best military tactician and engineer, Major-General Charles Lee, to march to New York and prepare the city's defenses. Lee was eccentric and obnoxious, but he was much respected as an experienced professional.

Charles Lee brought the vital military skills so lacking in American officers: engineering, tactics and, perhaps most important, organization. Generals like Israel Putnam had the courage that could inspire men to risk their lives in battle. But generalship also required skillful planning, both for battles and for maintaining a disciplined army. Once Lee began directing defensive preparations he was an inspiration, building confidence in the Americans' ability to resist the mightiest military machine on earth.

On his way from Ireland to North Carolina, General Sir Henry Clinton stopped in New York to investigate Governor Tryon's situation there (a refugee aboard a man-of-war). Tryon told Clinton that his old friend, Charles Lee, was now serving as a major-general in the rebel army and, in fact, was in the city now, preparing its defenses. Years before, when Lee had left the British Army to sell his services to the highest bidder in Europe, Clinton had given him several letters of introduction to important European political contacts.

Now, relying on his old friendship, Lee sent a message to the visiting general, asking if he planned to assault the city. Clinton returned a note, telling Lee why he was in New York, that he had only two companies of light infantry with him, and that he had no intention of harming the city, for he was on his way to North Carolina to pacify the South in conjunction with five regiments being sent from Ireland. Lee, dumbfounded by such candor, chose not to believe Clinton. He wrote to Washington: "This is certainly a droll way of proceeding. To communicate his full plan to the enemy is too novel to be credited." Apparently, Clinton did not believe that Lee would remain in the employ of the rebel Congress for long, and was trying to entice him to come along to Carolina. It didn't work.

In February, without consulting General Washington, the Continental Congress ordered Lee to take charge of the northern army in Canada. Reluctant to go to a freezing and smallpox-ridden army, Lee lingered in New York City just long enough, for within two weeks Congress changed its mind. The New York delegates had voiced their support for their own General Schuyler, and rumors had arrived in Philadelphia about a planned British southern expedition. So Congress decided Lee should head up a Southern Department of the Continental Army. New York breathed a sigh of relief when the obnoxious general finally left the city. During his stay, he had alienated all the city leaders, Whig and Tory alike.

While passing through Maryland, Lee was shown an intercepted letter from Secretary of State George Germain to Governor Eden. In the letter, Germain thanked Eden for his helpful reports, and informed him of the southern expedition to be headed jointly by General Clinton and Admiral Parker. Lee chastised Maryland's Provincial Congress and Council of Safety for not arresting Governor Eden for his "traitorous" correspondence with Germain. The Provincial Congress responded by admonishing General Lee for forgetting that, in America, military authority was subordinate to civil authority.

Lee soon moved on to Virginia and took up residence in the evacuated Governor's Palace in Williamsburg, an action frowned on by his fellow Virginians. Lee was dissatisfied with Virginians, too. In a letter to his friend, Richard Henry Lee, Charles Lee denounced the "namby-pambies of the senatorial part of the Continent" for growing "timid and hysterical." He judged the Virginia Committee of Safety "as desperately and incurably infected with this epidemical malady [namby-pambyism] as the Provincial Congress of Maryland." He criticized their placement of Virginia's troops, spreading them throughout the colony: "I wonder they did not carry it further and post one or two men by way of general security in every individual gentleman's house." To save money, the Committee supplied "no blankets for our men, who are, from want of this essential, dying by the dozens."

General Lee soon took charge, and concentrated the colony's nine

regiments in and around Williamsburg. Advancing to Norfolk, he fought a brief skirmish with Governor Dunmore's loyalists, forcing the exiled governor and his refugee ships to move further offshore. Lee then ordered the arrest of anyone suspected of supplying the governor with food or information. Houses were burned, livestock confiscated, and the entire population of Norfolk and Princess Anne Counties ordered to move inland, an order that was only halfheartedly enforced.

General Clinton and the army from Ireland assembled at the Cape Fear rendezvous in the spring, and learned they had arrived too late to avert the loyalist disaster at Widow Moore's Creek. With the original plan to join a loyalist force no longer operable, General Clinton and Admiral Parker had several heated arguments before they agreed on a new plan. The original instructions had stipulated that, should the commanders find Governor Martin's prediction of strong loyalist support not true, they should gain possession "of some respectable post to the southward" from which "the rebels might be annoyed by sudden and unexpected attacks of their towns upon the sea-coast during open winter." Clinton and Parker needed to accomplish something in this winter campaign (which was turning out to be a June campaign), before they must sail north to join Howe's summer campaign at New York.

Clinton wanted to go north to Maryland's Chesapeake Bay, which he considered an excellent base of operations and potential loyalist stronghold. But Parker thought the rich city of Charleston more attractive, his scouting ships having returned with word that the harbor was poorly defended by a partially built fort.

Admiral Parker prevailed over Clinton, and the fleet left Cape Fear, arriving off Charleston Bar on June seventh. South Carolina's President Rutledge had seen the scouting ships earlier, and had dispatched a frantic message by express rider to Lee, at that time still in Virginia's governor's palace: "For God's sake, lose not a moment."

Probably much to the relief of the Virginians, Lee quickly headed south again. His gout having improved in the warm weather, he was now able to ride a horse. He left his foot soldiers to follow as he gal-

oped off, hoping to reach Charleston before Clinton and Parker launched their assault. Following him marched a regiment of Virginians, to be joined on the way by a regiment of North Carolinians.

General Lee arrived at Charleston on June 4th, three days ahead of the British. A week later, his 1,900 foot soldiers arrived. He quickly took command of the defenses and set the city astir with patriotic fervor. Nearly every able-bodied citizen in town was coaxed into joining the effort. Barricades were thrown up at every likely landing place. Negroes (who outnumbered whites seven to one, in and around the city) were organized into fire-fighting corps and assigned city blocks, in case the British ships should attempt to set the city afire with hot shot. The women organized themselves, too. Lead sashes were "taken from the windows of the churches and dwelling houses, to cast into musket balls." General Lee also ordered several warehouses along the waterfront torn down, to eliminate them as targets and give patriot artillery batteries in the city a better chance of hitting the British ships.

Charleston harbor was exceedingly treacherous, with hidden shoals that made much of it impassable at low tide. The safest way for ships to move up the long harbor to the city was to hug its northern edge, close by sandy, swampy Sullivan's Island. This was precisely the spot the South Carolinians had selected for the new fort. With Colonel Christopher Gadsden, of the first militia regiment, away in Philadelphia for long periods of time, the task of constructing the fort had fallen to Colonel William Moultrie, of the second regiment.

Moultrie began building Fort Sullivan in January, but had not made much progress by early June. Under Lee's prodding, and the approach of battle, Moultrie stepped up the work, but not enough to satisfy Lee. According to Moultrie, the former Englishman had no conception of the effect the humidity and heat of coastal South Carolina had on men struggling with the tasks of constructing a fort. Moultrie had the easy-going ways and fiery personal courage of an Israel Putnam. But, like Putnam, he also lacked military knowledge and the prudence to plan a retreat route, should one become necessary. This would lead to

much friction between Lee and Moultrie.

Past the tip of Sullivan's Island, at Haddrell's Point, Lee established his headquarters and posted the Continentals he had brought south with him. Here he built breastworks to defend what he considered the best landing place for an assault on Charleston. Being doubtful that Colonel Moultrie's "good temper and easy nature" would allow him to maintain proper discipline on Sullivan's Island, Lee gave Moultrie and the other officers ample unsolicited advice. A few examples:

> Soldiers running at random whenever their folly directs is an abomination not to be tolerated. When you issue any orders, do not suffer them to be trifled with. Let your orders be as few as possible; but let them be punctually obeyed. Never fire without a moral certainty of hitting. One hundred and fifty yards is the maximum for muskets, and four hundred for cannon. Distant firing encourages the enemy, and adds to the pernicious persuasion of the American soldiers that they are no match for their antagonist at close fighting. It makes them cowards, is childish, vicious, and scandalous.

Years later, Colonel Moultrie recalled Lee's influence that June:

> General Lee arrived from the northward and took the command of the troops. His presence gave us great spirits, as he was known to be an able, brave and experienced officer, though hasty and rough in his manners, which the officers could not reconcile themselves to at first. It was thought by many that his coming among us was equal to a reinforcement of 1000 men, and I believe it was, because he taught us to think lightly of the enemy, and gave a spur to all our actions.
>
> After General Lee had waited upon the President and talked with him upon his plan of defence, he hurried

about to view the different works and give orders for such things to be done as he thought necessary. He was every day and every hour of the day on horse back, or in boats viewing our situation and directing small works to be thrown up at different places.

The British General Clinton consulted with some Negroes who, enticed by a promise of freedom, joined his army. They told him that the channel between Sullivan's Island and Long Island to its north was only 18 inches deep at low tide. Clinton therefore landed his entire force on Long Island on June 15th. He planned to have them wade across the channel, then march the three mile length of Sullivan's Island and attack the fort at its weakest point, the rear, while Parker's ships bombarded its front. Parker and Clinton spent several days exchanging messages, each suggesting battle plans to the other. Twice the scheduled day for the joint attack arrived, but was delayed by winds that went "flying suddenly round to the northward."

The delays allowed Colonel Moultrie to detach some of his South Carolinian forces from the fort. They marched to the northern tip of Sullivan's Island, where they set up field pieces. They went to work with picks and shovels and were soon intrenched "up to their necks." These 780 men waited, ready to make Clinton's crossing of the channel very interesting. Even after taking this precaution, however, General Lee felt that Moultrie's position would be untenable should he have to retreat. So he ordered Moultrie to abandon the fort and bring his men over to the mainland.

Moultrie, backed by President Rutledge, refused to abandon the fort. Rutledge reminded General Lee that the South Carolina government had not yet placed its armed forces under the authority of the Continental Congress. Therefore, technically, Lee could not force Moultrie to obey any of his orders. (Lee disagreed, but did not press the matter.)

Colonel Moultrie described Lee's concerns about Sullivan's Island:

When he [Lee] came to Sullivan's Island, he did not like that position at all; he said there was no way to retreat, that the garrison would be sacrificed; nay, he called it a "slaughter pen," and wished to withdraw the garrison and give up the post, but President Rutledge insisted that it should not be given up. Then General Lee said it was "absolutely necessary to have a bridge of boats for a retreat"; but boats enough could not be had, the distance over being at least a mile. Then a bridge was constructed of empty hogsheads buoyed at certain distances, and two planks from hogshead to hogshead; but this would not answer, because when Colonel Clark was coming over from Haddrell's with a detachment of 200 men, before they were half on, it sunk so low that they were obliged to return.

General Lee one day on a visit to the fort, took me aside and said, "Colonel Moultrie, do you think you can maintain this post?"

I answered him, "Yes, I think I can."

That was all that passed on the subject between us.

Another time Capt. Lamperer, a brave and experienced seaman, who had been master of a man-of-war and captain of a very respectable privateer many years ago, visited me at the fort after the British ships came over our bar; while we were walking on the platform looking at the fleet, he said to me: "Well, Colonel, what do you think of it now?"

I replied that "we should beat them."

"Sir," said he, "when those ships" (pointing to the men-of-war) "come to lay along side of your fort, they will knock it down in half an hour," (and that was the opinion of the sailors).

"Then," I said, "we will lay behind the ruins and prevent their men from landing."

Fort Sullivan was intended to be four-sided with a bastion at each corner, but only the front side and its two corner bastions, facing the harbor, were finished by the end of June. These consisted of a series of stacks of palmetto logs piled twelve feet high and dove-tailed together. Palmetto is a soft, spongy wood, native to the coast of South Carolina. Sand filled the spaces between these stacked logs, making the front wall's depth sixteen feet. In contrast to the front wall's 12-foot height, the west wall, facing Haddrell's Point, was only seven feet high, while the east and north (rear) walls existed only on the paper plan of the fort.

An assortment of 9-, 12-, 18- and 26-pounders stuck their barrels out embrasures to face the harbor. As many as 21 cannon could be manned at one time. The powder supply was only enough for thirty rounds, pitifully small compared to Admiral Parker's warships, which boasted 270 well-supplied guns. The inside of the fort was sand, hopefully loose and deep enough to swallow up the British bombs which would fly over the walls.

Lee had ordered Moultrie: 1) to construct a high screen to protect his men from "enfilade" (flank) fire coming over the low west wall, should Parker position any ships on that side; and 2) to dig a trench for protection against a land assault from the rear, should Clinton break through the defenses at the north end of the island. Moultrie ignored both orders, because of the oppressive heat and the fact that he considered such measures unnecessary.

Finally, the day for battle arrived. In the early morning of June 28th, Moultrie was on horseback inspecting Colonel Thompson's breastworks facing Long Island, when he observed Clinton's troops preparing to cross the channel. Moultrie turned around and galloped off toward the fort where his lieutenants, Francis Marion (later famed as the "Swamp Fox") and Isaac Motte, anxiously awaited his return. They had just sighted Parker's warships heading straight for the fort. Admiral Parker had already sent the flag signals agreed upon, telling Clinton to start his crossing of the channel.

In retrospect, Moultrie was fortunate that the battle began that morning, for just the night before Lee had sent a message to another colonel to report to headquarters in the morning to take over Moultrie's command. Apparently, despite what President Rutledge might say, Lee had finally decided that he could no longer tolerate Moultrie's continuing disobedience.

Sir Peter Parker had drilled his marines and seamen in techniques of climbing a fort's parapet and entering through its embrasures. The admiral was confident that just two rounds of fire from his 32-pounders would prepare the way for the landing of his men. Thus, when Parker received word from Clinton that no passage could be located shallow enough to wade across to the northern tip of Sullivan's Island, Parker returned a casual note assuring the general that he "thought himself fully equal to the attempt with the ships alone, and only expected from [Clinton's] troops the best cooperation in their power when he made it."

By ten o'clock the warships were in position. They dropped their anchors, on spring cables for the recoil effect of the firing. Closest to the fort's front wall were two 28-gun frigates, and two 50-gun men-of-war: the *Experiment* and the admiral's flagship, the *Bristol*. Also aboard the *Bristol* were the governors-in-exile of Georgia and both Carolinas, excitedly anticipating commencement of the campaign they had long dreamed of. Farther back (really, too far back) was the bomb throwing ship, *Thunder*. Between it and the four ships facing the fort was a second squadron, composed of three frigates carrying an additional 20, 28 and 28 guns. Their orders were to sail past the first squadron once the fighting started, and send enfilade fire into the fort from its western side, to force Moultrie's men away from their guns.

Although the *Thunder* commenced shelling somewhat earlier, it was nearly eleven o'clock before the first squadron opened fire. Moultrie ordered his men to concentrate their fire on the two fifty-gun ships directly in front of the fort, and to ignore the two frigates flanking them. Already by the time the fort had fired three rounds, a British officer noted they had knocked out "2 guns, & killed 7 men on board the

Bristol." A British surgeon described how the defenders effectively employed their limited ammunition:

> The Provincials reserved their fire until the shipping were advanced within point-blank shot; their artillery was surprisingly well served. It was slow, but decisive indeed; they were very cool, and took great care not to fire except [after] their guns were exceedingly well directed.

The surgeon also explained how the *Thunder* bomb-ship put itself out of action early, and the terrible damage suffered by the two men-of-war:

> Unfortunately the bomb was placed at such a distance that she was not of the least service. This, Colonel James, the principal engineer, immediately perceived; to remedy which, an additional quantity of powder was added to each mortar. The consequences were breaking down the beds and totally disabling her for the rest of the day.
>
> The *Bristol* and *Experiment* have suffered most incredibly: the former very early had the spring of her cable shot away ... [making her] lay end on to the battery and was raked fore and aft; she lost upwards of one hundred men killed and wounded. Captain Morris, who commanded her, lost his arm; the worthy man, however, died a week after. Twice the quarter-deck was cleared of every person except Sir Peter, and he was slightly wounded.

Admiral Parker's wound was to his buttocks, the result of a rebel cannon ball whizzing so close to his body that its force of wind took Parker's breeches off. This was acknowledged by five deserters who

came over to the Americans after the battle and stated that "the commodore had his breeches tore off, his backside laid bare."

Colonel Moultrie later recalled the battle:

> The *Thunder*, bomb, had the beds of her mortar soon disabled; she threw her shells in a very good direction; most of them fell within the fort, but we had a morass in the middle that swallowed them up instantly, and those that fell in the sand and in and about the fort were immediately buried so that very few of them bursted amongst us. At one time the Commodore's ship swung round with her stern to the fort, which drew the fire of all the guns that could bear upon her: we supposed she had had the springs of her cable cut away. The words that passed along the platform by officers and men were: "Mind the Commodore! Mind the two fifty-gun ships!" ... the Commodore, I dare say, was not at all obliged to us for our particular attention to him ...

> During the action Gen. Lee paid us a visit through a heavy line of fire and pointed two or three guns himself; then said to me, "Colonel, I see you are doing very well here. You have no occasion for me. I will go up to town again," and left us.

> When I received information of Gen. Lee's approach to the fort, I sent Lieut. Marion from off the platform, with 8 or 10 men, to unbar the gateway. Our gate not being finished, the gateway was barricaded with pieces of timber 8 or 10 inches square, which required 3 or 4 men to remove each piece. The men in the ships' tops seeing those men run from the platform concluded "we were quitting the fort," as some author mentions.

> Another says, "We hung up a man in the fort at the time of the action." That was taken from this circumstance: when the action begun (it being a warm day),

some of the men took off their coats and threw them upon the top merlons. I saw a shot take one of them and throw it into a small tree behind the platform. It was noticed by our men and they cried out, "Look at the coat!"

Never did men fight more bravely, and never were men more cool; their only distress was the want of powder ...

There cannot be a doubt but that, if we had had as much powder as we could have expended in the time, the men-of-war must have struck their colors or they would certainly have been sunk, because they could not retreat, as the wind and tide were against them ... They could not make any impression on our fort, built of palmetto logs and filled in with earth. Our merlons were 16 feet thick and high enough to cover the men from the fire of the tops. The men that we had killed and wounded received their shots mostly through the embrasures.

During the heat of the battle, Lee sent a messenger to the fort, with a note ordering Moultrie, once he ran out of ammunition, to "spike your guns, and retreat with all the order possible" to the mainland. Moultrie was not about to obey that order, so he decided to make his ammunition last as long as possible. He ordered his gunners to slacken their firing pace to one round every ten minutes. At one point in the afternoon, the fort's guns were silent for almost an hour. Admiral Sir Peter Parker thought the long silence meant that the rebel fort had been abandoned, but he had already changed his mind about landing a marine assault force. Moultrie explained the long period of silence:

The guns being so long silent was owing to the scarcity of powder which we had in the fort, and to a report that was brought to me "that the English troops were

landed between the advance-guard and the fort." It was upon this information that I ordered the guns to cease firing. We should reserve our powder for the musketry to defend ourselves against the land forces, there being a scarcity of powder at this time.

During this quiet spell, President Rutledge sent Moultrie some barrels, with a note:

> DEAR SIR,
> I send you 500 pounds of powder. You know our collection is not very great. I should think you may be supplied from Haddrells Point. HONOR and VICTORY, my good sir, to you, and our worthy countrymen with you.
>
> Yours,
J. RUTLEDGE
>
> P.S. Do not make too free with your cannon. Cool and do mischief.

Rutledge was incorrect in assuming that Lee, at Haddrell's Point, would replenish the fort's supply of gunpowder. He sent none. In fact, a few days before the battle, he took several barrels from the fort and distributed them to other defense posts.

By late afternoon, the firing from three miles north of the fort (where Clinton had tried to cross the channel separating Long Island from Sullivan's Island) had ceased. In his memoirs, Clinton recalled his field pieces on Long Island making "every demonstration, every diversion by cannonade while I ordered small arm'd vessels [flatboats] to proceed towards the shore, but they all got aground." One of his officers, Lord Rawdon, saw some of his troops find what might have been a passageway deep enough for the flatboats, but it was "so narrow as only to admit one boat abreast, exposed to the fire of a three gun battery which directly confronted them." Clinton was now

regretting that he had taken the word of local runaway slaves, and had not bothered to have soundings taken in the channel during the two weeks he had been on the island.

Now, when his 2,100 Regulars and 700 seamen tried to get out of the flatboats and wade across, they found, to Clinton's "unspeakable mortification," that it was rife with potholes up to seven feet deep. Again and again, they tried to find a favorable path, while being exposed to fire from Thompson's riflemen and his field pieces. Regretfully, Clinton finally called off the crossing and returned his men to Long Island. As one of his men explained later, even if they had found a passage, the Americans "would have killed half of us before we could have made our landing good."

Clinton next sent a hasty note to Admiral Parker suggesting that the Regulars could board transports, sail around past the fort, and land at Haddrell's Point, if Parker would provide a covering fire. The admiral, however, ignored the suggestion. So Clinton and his 2,800 fighting men took no active part in the battle, and were soon to be ridiculed in a popular song, *The Commodore Reports to the Lords of the Admiralty*:

> Bold Clinton by land
> Did quietly stand
> While I made a thundering clatter.
> But the channel was deep
> So he could only peep
> And not venture over the water.

One reason the admiral ignored Clinton's suggestion was that the ships to provide the covering fire were unavailable. These were the three frigates of the second squadron. Moultrie's memoir explains how they literally ran into some trouble trying to maneuver around to the west side of the fort:

> During the action three of the men-of-war, in going

round to our west curtain, got entangled together, by which the *Acteon* frigate went on shore on the middle ground [shoals]; the *Sphinx* lost her bow-sprit; and the *Syren* cleared herself without any damage. Had these three ships effected their purpose, they would have enfiladed us in such a manner as to have driven us from our guns.

It being a very hot day, we were served along the platform with grog in fire-buckets, which we partook of very heartily: I never had a more agreeable draught than that which I took out of one of those buckets at the time. It may be very easily conceived what heat and thirst a man must feel in this climate, to be upon a platform on the 28th June, amidst 20 or 30 heavy pieces of cannon in one continual blaze and roar, and clouds of smoke curling over his head for hours together; it was a very honourable situation, but a very unpleasant one.

During the action, thousands of our fellow-citizens were looking on with anxious hopes and fears, some of whom had their fathers, brothers and husbands in the battle; whose hearts must have been pierced at every broadside. After some time our flag was shot away; their hopes were then gone, and they gave up all for lost, supposing that we had struck our flag, and had given up the fort! Sergeant Jasper, perceiving that the flag was shot away and had fallen without the fort, jumped from one of the embrasures and brought it up through a heavy fire, fixed it upon a spunge-staff, and planted it upon the ramparts again. Our flag once more waving in the air revived the drooping spirits of our friends; and they continued looking on till night hid us from their view.

One of the men inside the fort, Major Barnard Elliot, the next day wrote to his wife:

The expression of a Sergeant McDaniel, after a cannon ball had taken off his shoulder and scouped out his stomach, is worth recording in the annals of America: "Fight on, my brave boys, don't let liberty expire with me today!"

Young, the barber, an old artillery man, who lately enlisted as sergeant, has lost a leg. Several arms are shot away. Not an officer is wounded.

My old grenadier, Serjeant Jasper, upon the shot carrying away the flagstaff, called out to Col. Moultrie: "Colonel, don't let us fight without our flag!"

"What can you do?" replied the Colonel. "The staff is broke."

"Then, sir," said he, "I'll fix it to a halbert and place it on the merlon of the bastion next to the enemy," which he did, through the thickest fire.

Colonel Moultrie finishes his account of the battle:

At night when we came to our slow firing we could here the shot very distinctly strike the ships.

At length the British gave up the conflict. The ships slipt their cables and dropped down with the tide, and out of reach of our guns. When the firing had ceased, our friends [in Charleston] for a time were again in an unhappy suspense, not knowing our fare till they received an account by a dispatch boat, which I sent up to town to acquaint them that the British ships had retired and that we were victorious.

Early the next morning was presented to our view the *Acteon* frigate hard and fast aground at about 400 yards distance. We gave her a few shot, which she returned, but they soon set fire to her and quitted her. Capt.

Jacob Milligan and others went in some of our boats, boarded her while she was on fire, and pointed 2 or 3 guns at the Commodore and fired them; then brought off the ship's bell and other articles, and had scarcely left her when she blew up, and from the explosion issued a grand pillar of smoke, which soon expanded itself at the top and, to appearance, formed the figure of a palmetto tree. The ship immediately burst into a great blaze that continued till she burnt to the water's edge.

Ultimately, this battle proved to be one of the most one-sided American victories of the entire war, the American casualties being only 12 men killed and 20 wounded. The British, by contrast, suffered one frigate destroyed and two men-of-war severely damaged. Their army and navy, combined, had nearly 100 killed and 300 wounded. One naval officer from the *Bristol* wrote home, describing the scene on its decks: "During the action no slaughter-house could present so bad a sight, with blood and entrails lying about, as our ship!"

Despite an expenditure of countless cannon balls and shells, propelled by an estimated 34,000 pounds of powder (compared to the Americans' 4,766 pounds), the British ships could not demolish the fort. A British officer blamed the failure on the fort's being "made of palmito trees of a stringy, tough substance, so that not a single shott could do any mischief but what went through the embrazures."

On July fourth, President Rutledge showed his gratitude by changing Fort Sullivan's name to Fort Moultrie, and by presenting his sword to Sergeant Jasper. The illiterate Jasper declined a commission, saying he was "not fit to keep officers' company." Three years later, he would be killed, attempting again to raise a fallen flag while under enemy fire.

General Lee was quick to praise the colonel he had sought to dismiss. In his report to Washington, Lee confessed he was "astonished" by the behavior of Moultrie's men and had "no idea that so much coolness and intrepidity could be displayed by a collection of

raw recruits."

The American press and Congress assumed that, as the top officer in charge of the city's defense, General Lee was responsible for the stunning victory, and thus gave him the credit. Congress, worried over the recently uncovered plot in New York to assasinate Washington, ordered Lee back to that city, where his talents would be needed and he would be readily available, should anything happen to the Commander-in-Chief.

Within a few days, five deserters went over to the Americans and told them the ships' carpenters were "all hard at work, and that we need not expect another visit from them at present." Clinton's troops lingered on Long Island until July 21 among the "millions of mosquitoes," while sleeping "upon the sea-shore, nothing to shelter us from the violent rains but our coats and miserable paltry blankets."

They finally sailed north on the transports, arriving at Staten Island on the first of August, to reinforce the Howe brothers for the attack on Washington's army at New York. En route, Captain Murray wrote to his sister in England, summing up the southern expedition as "one of the most singular events that has yet conspired to degrade the name of the British nation."

After five weeks spent in repairing the damaged fleet, Parker set sail for New York on August 2nd, the same day that news of the Declaration of Independence's passage reached Charleston. Together, Admiral Parker and General Clinton had achieved none of the southern expedition's objectives. The battle for Charleston, and perhaps the South, had a most surprising outcome, according to the reflections of one British officer. He wrote, "The invincible British Navy defeated by a battery which it was supposed would not have stood one broadside. This will scarcely be believ'd in England."

CHAPTER FIVE
NEW YORK PREPARES FOR WAR
JANUARY - JULY 1776

"The fate of unborn millions will now depend, under God, on the courage and conduct of this army. Our cruel and unrelenting enemy leaves us no choice but a brave resistance, or the most abject submission. This is all we can expect. We have therefore to resolve to conquer or die."'

- General George Washington,
addressing his army.

Back in 1775, when New York's inhabitants learned about Lexington and Concord, the city's more radical patriot faction, led by Isaac "King" Sears, had quickly seized political and military control of the city. Sears was an extremist, a mob leader equally disliked by loyalists and moderate patriots. However, he was a popular leader on the waterfront. Seamen and dock workers, long out of work because of the crisis with England, were easily persuaded by Sears to become Sons of Liberty. As such, they could use "the cause" to justify rioting against loyalists, most of them members of the hated upper class. Sears and the radicals ruled the city for several months, but eventually fell out of favor and were replaced by moderate patriots led by John Jay and Robert Livingston. So Sears moved to Greenwich, Connecticut, where he soon went to sea as a privateer. At the end of the war he would return to New York fabulously wealthy.

In January, 1776, Washington dispatched General Charles Lee to prepare New York's defense against a possible relocation there by the British Army. Washington had some misgivings about sending part of

his army to New York. He consulted John Adams, who replied that, as Congress's appointed Commander-in-Chief, he had full authority to place the city under military rule. To John Hancock, Washington wrote:

> I hope the Congress will approve of my conduct in sending General Lee upon this expedition. I am sure I mean it well, as experience [Boston] teaches us that it is much easier to prevent an enemy from posting themselves than it is to dislodge them after they have got possession.

As Lee travelled from Cambridge, carried on a litter, with his gouty leg propped up on pillows, he picked up 1,200 "Connecticutians" promised by Governor Trumbull. Isaac Sears met Lee on the way and told the general that New York was "a den of Toryism," more than half the populace favoring the British cause. Lee made Sears his adjutant-general and continued his march down the Post Road, determined to cleanse the backward city and at the same time safeguard it against British attack.

He was passed by hundreds of frightened refugees: men, women and children with their belongings piled on wagons or two-wheel carts, all heading north toward Kings Bridge and the mainland. They had heard that the army was coming. These New Yorkers did not trust the Yankee mob that called itself an army, nor the man they had heard was Lee's adjutant, "King" Sears. Mere mention of his name conjured up visions of riot and anarchy.

Upon arriving in New York at last, the Yankee soldiers promptly broke open and occupied the abandoned Tory mansions on lower Broad Way and neighboring avenues. They chopped down orchards and tore apart mahogany balustrades for firewood. "Oh, the houses of New York," a resident mourned, "if you could but see the insides of them occupied by the dirtiest people on the continent. If the owners ever get possession of them again, I am sure they must be years in

cleaning them."

By late spring, a discovery was made: loyalists had been providing the British with information, including a detailed report titled "State of the Fortifications of New York." The vengeful Sons of Liberty, led by Sears and Hercules Mulligan, made night raids on the houses of suspected citizens. Suspects were pulled from their beds and stripped, then tarred and feathered. If the victim was fortunate, he only had to ride through town in a cart while holding aloft a lantern. If not so fortunate, he was carried on a sharp rail between his naked legs - naked, that is, except for the tar and feathers. One soldier enthusiastically wrote home to Connecticut, "We had some grand Tory rides in this city this week; several of them handled very roughly. There is hardly a Tory face to be seen this morning."

Within the army's ranks, the old animosities between Yankees and Yorkers erupted into violent brawls. By the time Washington arrived in April, charges of "Tory turncoat" and "loyalist pimp" had precipitated so many injuries and hard feelings that he frequently had to use his general orders of the day to admonish his men, telling them, they can in "no way assist our cruel enemies more effectually, than [by] making divisions among ourselves."

After General Lee headed south in March, New York's defense was placed in the hands of Lord Stirling, a brigadier-general from New Jersey. His real name was William Alexander, but in America he was accepted as Lord Stirling, a title based on his distant relationship with Scotland's original Earl of Stirling. (Parliament's House of Lords refused to recognize this claim, because of his father's part in a Scottish uprising.) In 1776, the burly, fifty-year-old General Lord Stirling was a hard-drinking, hard-fighting man soon to be noted for his personal bravery in action. After the Battle of Long Island in the coming August, his officers would label Stirling "as brave a man as ever lived." Washington had written to Stirling from Cambridge, to impress upon him the paramount military importance of the city of New York:

It is the place that we must use every endeavour to

keep from them. For should they get that town, and the command of the North River, they can stop the intercourse between the northern and southern Colonies, upon which depends the safety of America.

In 1776, the city occupied only one square mile at the southern tip of Manhattan, also known as New York Island. It faced a wide, deep harbor, and was bounded on the east and west by the East and North (Hudson) Rivers. Thirteen miles to the north, the island was joined to the mainland by Kings Bridge. In Lee's opinion, the island city could not be defended indefinitely against the awesome naval power of the British Navy. "It is so encircled with deep navigable waters, that whoever commands the sea must command the town." The American force assigned to defend the city possessed not a single warship or transport.

But Washington had instructed General Stirling to carry "into execution with spirit and industry" General Lee's "very judicious plan of defense." So Stirling that spring proceeded with the elaborate plans Lee had left behind, when he had rode off to the south. Stirling went to the New York City Committee of Safety for help, and they cooperated zealously. At his request, they voted to call out all the citizens capable of "fatigue duty," to work on the proposed fortifications; blacks to work every day, whites every other day. The combined efforts of citizens and soldiers produced a prodigious amount of earthworks in and around the city.

A redoubt was built at Kings Bridge, to protect against the British Army landing north of Manhattan and trying to cross over to it by land. Toward the northern end of Manhattan the Hudson could boast a fort on each shore, facing each other and placed so as to stop British ships from sailing upriver. In addition, when General Israel Putnam arrived, he devised a booby-trapping operation, sinking old ships in the Hudson River between the two forts. Their submerged masts would form a barrier to stop the British ships. Only a narrow passage was left, whose location was told to trusted patriot pilots.

At the mouth of the Hudson, just west of the city, a battery was placed at Powle's Hook, New Jersey. There were also thirteen forts, redoubts or batteries along the city's waterfront. Every street leading from the shore was barricaded, as well as a dozen other streets, with the purpose of making the city "a disputable field of battle" should the British gain a foothold. These works resembled reclining porcupines, as wooden poles with sharpened ends extended out from earthen walls. North of the city, more intrenchments and redoubts were constructed, should the British Army land north of the city and, in conjunction with the Navy, attempt to place the city "between two fires." East of the city, entrance to the East River was controlled by strong batteries on Governor's Island and at Red Hook near Brooklyn.

Back in 1664, the British Navy had seized control of Nieu Amsterdam from the Dutch and renamed it New York. At that time, the village facing it on Nassau (Long) Island was called Breukelen, meaning "marshland." Over time, Breukelen became Breucklyn, Broucklyn, Breuckland, Brookland, Brookline, and finally Brooklyn. Now, in the summer of 1776, above the village of Brooklyn, a series of 100-foot hills known as Brooklyn Heights were being very strongly fortified all the way from Wallabout Bay to Gowaus Cove. Washington realized that, should British cannon and mortars be located atop them, these hills would play the same role that Dorchester Heights played when Howe had been forced to evacuate Boston in March.

Three forts and two redoubts were constructed on this stretch of just over a mile, with trenches connecting them. By July 22nd, General Nathanael Greene, in charge of Long Island's defenses, was confidently expecting another Bunker Hill. "We are," Greene wrote, "strongly fortified here, everything in readiness and the troops in good spirits. I have not the most distant apprehensions for this army."

Three thousand men were placed on Brooklyn Heights. The remainder of Washington's army was located at the other posts in and around New York. Thus, Washington was violating a cardinal rule of warfare by dividing his forces over sixteen miles of posts. Should the British warships silence the batteries protecting the mouth of the East

River, the 3,000 men on Long Island would be isolated.

As if preparations to defend the city were not enough to occupy George Washington's mind, he learned that Isaac Sears had been right about New York being "a den of Toryism." In late June, came the discovery of a plot to assasinate the Commander-in-Chief. The plot was believed to have been the creation of the exiled Governor Tryon. An army surgeon, William Eustis, wrote home to Boston about the scandal:

> The mayor of York, with a number of villains, would have given the enemy possession of the city with little loss. Their design was, upon the first engagement which took place, to have murdered (with trembling I say it) the best man on earth: Genl Washington. Our magazines [of gunpowder] were to have been blown up. Every General Officer who was active in serving his country in the field was to have been assassinated. Our cannon were to be spiked up.
>
> I have just now returned from the execution of one of the Generals Guard, hung in presence of the whole army. He is a Regular deserter. He appeared unaffected and obstinate to the last, except that when the chaplains took him by the hand under the gallows and bad him adieu, a torrent of tears flowed over his face. But with an indignant scornful air he wiped em with his hand from his face, and assumed the confident look. You remember General Greene commands at Long Island; with his last breath the fellow told the spectators, that unless Genl Greene was very cautious, the design would as yet be executed on him.

As it became apparent that New York would be one of the British objectives for the 1776 campaign, the Continental Congress, on June 4th, appealed to the governors and constitutional conventions of the

colonies to provide "levies" (troops enlisted for a short term) to assist the Continental Army. "Our affairs," Hancock wrote to the governors, "are hastening fast to a crisis; and the approaching campaign will, in all probability, determine forever the fate of America." The men of America were "called upon to say whether they will live slaves or die freemen." One of the new levies was a young Connecticut man named Joseph Plumb Martin:

> In the month of June orders came out for enlisting men for six months to go to New York. And notwithstanding I was told that the British army at that place was reinforced by fifteen thousand men, it made no alteration in my mind; I did not care if there had been fifteen times fifteen thousand. I never spent a thought about numbers; the Americans were invincible in my opinion. If anything affected me, it was a stronger desire to see them.

At Washington's request, Congress requested 23,800 levies be enlisted from Maryland to Massachusetts, the seven colonies closest to the city. Not actually a part of the Continental Army, these new regiments were state troops on loan to Congress. Only about one third of the projected 23,800 levies signed up, but also arriving to swell the army's ranks were several militia regiments. So the army, on this occasion and many others throughout the war as crises arose, was composed temporarily of three types of soldiers: "regular" troops (enlisted Continentals), state levies, and militia.

The army grew and shrunk, and grew some more, as men drifted in and out during July and August. Estimates of the army's paper strength peaked in late August at 28,400, though the number of "effectives" (men present and healthy enough to fight) was never much more than 19,000.

One reason for this great discrepancy was a "camp distemper," mentioned in almost every letter or journal written by the soldiers in New

York or any other prolonged campsite during the war. Though the medical term was dysentery, it was most commonly called "the bloody flux," and was caused by the unhealthy water from the city wells. New Yorkers who could afford it had always purchased drinking water carted in from outside the city. At any given time during the summer of 1776, about 20 percent of the army was suffering from the bloody flux.

Another reason for illness in the army was the temptation to spend off-duty hours in several houses of prostitution. These houses were known collectively as "the Holy Ground" because the real estate, ironically, was owned by Trinity Church. Again and again, the officer of the day and his guard were summoned to break up riots there, "knots of men and women fighting, swearing, crying 'Murder!' etc." Indeed, two soldiers were murdered in these houses, and another "castrated in a barbarous manner," prompting enraged soldiers to burn two of the houses to the ground. Harvard-educated Isaac Bangs wrote to his wife, telling her that he visited the Holy Ground several times "out of curiosity" but did not venture inside any of the houses. He found it "Strange that any man can so divest himself of manhood as to desire an intimate connexion with these worse than brutal creatures. Yet many of our officers & soldiers have, till the Fatal Disorder seized them & convinced them of their error."

Washington and his generals struggled to maintain a proper discipline among the citizen soldiers, not used to the restrictions of military life. A few glimpses from the general orders of the day (of General Greene and his successor, General Sullivan) on Long Island will give an idea of the headaches of training such an "army."

> May 29 [Gen. Greene] ... All officers are desired to be more careful of discovering the countersign to persons that have no right to know it. Any soldier on guard that discovers the countersign to any of his fellow soldiers that are not on guard is to be immediately confined. Every one that gives the countersign is to give it

as softly as possible so that if any person is listening he may not hear it. The sentries are not to suffer any person to stand near them, while they are on their posts.

July 28 ... The general is pained to discover inattention to the digging and filling vaults for the regts & to the burial of filth and putrid matter. The general directs ... to dig new vaults, and fill up old ones every 3 days, & that fresh dirt be thrown in every day to the vaults, & that all filth in and about the camp be daily buried.

Complaints are made of the troops stealing water mellons. Such practices must be punished. A few undisciplined rascals may ruin the reputation of a whole corps of virtuous men.

August 16 ... The gin shops and houses selling liquor [are] strictly forbidden to sell to soldiers. The general is determined to have any soldiers punished that may be found disguised with liquor.

Aug. 25 [Gen. Sullivan] The Gen is surprised to find the soldiers strolling about, notwithstanding repeated orders, miles distant from the lines, at a time when the enemy are hourly expected to make an attack.

It is a very scandalous practice, unbecoming soldiers whose duty it is to defend the liberty and prosperity of the inhabitants of the country, to make free with and rob them of that property; it is therefore ordered that no person take or make use of any corn, poultry or provision or anything else without the consent of the owners nor without paying the common price for them; and any breach of this order will be severely punished.

Though by late August there were at least 19,000 effectives ready to fight the British, more than half of them were almost totally lacking in discipline, training and experience. Several thousand also lacked mus-

kets. Colonel Henry Knox's artillery regiment (the only one in the army) was a mere 580 men, manning 120 cannon spread over sixteen miles of batteries. With this makeshift army, and no navy, Washington had ample reason to be anxious when he saw the size of the army and navy sent against him - the largest British force ever sent to America.

Between early July and mid-August, 25,000 British and nearly 8,000 German soldiers arrived. The fleets that brought them combined for a total of thirty warships (1,200 guns) and over four hundred transports and provision ships. General William Howe, ably assisted by his brother, Admiral Lord Richard Howe, had finally been provided with the resources to destroy Washington's army and end the rebellion. If all went well, after taking New York, General Howe would be met on the Hudson by a 10,000 man army, which was said to be on its way southward on Lake Champlain, having already kicked the American northern army out of Canada. This union would prevent land commu- nication between New England and the other colonies. The less rebellious middle and southern colonies would quickly come to their senses and abandon the New Englanders, and the rebellion would fall apart.

While General Howe formulated his battle plans, he camped his army of British Regulars and their German (or "Hessian" as they were usually called) allies on Staten Island. Many loyalists soon moved to Staten Island also, to be under the protection of the King's soldiers. But some of the loyalist refugees found life could also be hazardous living under the protection of the King's army. Lord Rawdon, an offi- cer under Clinton, wrote home to his father from Staten Island:

> The fair nymphs of this isle are in wonderful tribula-
> tion, as the fresh meat our men have got here has made
> them as riotous as satyrs. A girl cannot step into the
> bushes to pluck a rose without running the most immi-
> nent risk of being ravished. They are so little
> accustomed to these vigorous methods that they don't
> bear them with the proper resignation, and of conse-

quence we have most entertaining courts-martial every day.

Several transports with Highlanders have been taken by the rebel privateers; the rest are all arrived, and are so enraged against the Yankees for some insults offered to their captive comrades that I think the first corps of psalm-singers who come in the way of their broad-swords will be in a very awkward situation. The Hessians sing hymns as loud as the Yankees, though it must be owned they have not the godly twang through the nose which distinguishes the faithful.

Because New York and its environs had an abundance of Americans secretly or openly opposed to the rebellion, the British command was amply supplied with information detailing the location and strength of every rebel position. On July 12th, two frigates sailed up the Hudson, past the New York and Powle's Hook batteries and through the narrow "secret" passage between the sunken ships further upriver. The patriots on shore watching the ships sail past the submerged barricade were at first surprised, then enraged, as they quickly realized that someone must have informed the enemy. The ships continued on their way north, taking advantage of a southerly breeze to boldly sail past Forts Washington and Lee, exchanging fire as they sailed by. Barely scratched, the frigates anchored forty miles upriver at Tappan Bay. There they armed local loyalists, learned news of the British expedition on Lake Champlain, and temporarily stopped movement of provisions downriver to the rebel army. Reverend Shewkirk, of New York's Moravian Church, recorded the passage of the British frigates in his journal that day:

> [The Americans] fired from all the batteries, but did little execution. The wind and tide being in their favor, the ships sailed fast up the North River, and soon were out of sight. When they came this side of Trinity

Church, they began to fire smartly. The balls and bullets went through several houses. Six men were killed, either some or all by ill-managing the cannons, though it is said that a couple were killed by the ship's firing; one man's leg was broke, etc. The six were put this evening into one grave on the Bowling Green. The smoke of the firing drew over our street like a cloud, and the air was filled with the smell of the powder.

Washington's general orders the next morning indicate that Reverend Shewkirk was not the only man watching the two British frigates.

The General was sorry to observe yesterday that many of the officers and a number of the men, instead of attending to their duty at the beat of the drum, continued along the banks of the North River, gazing at the ships. Such unsoldierly conduct must grieve every good officer, and give the enemy a <u>mean</u> opinion of the army, as nothing shows the brave and good soldier more than in the case of alarms, coolly and calmly repairing to his post and there waiting his orders, whereas a weak curiosity at such a time makes a man look mean and contemptible.

Six days later, the British ships returned, successfully running the same gauntlet. It appeared that, despite the well-placed American batteries, the British Navy might be able to land the huge army above the city and trap the Americans, while using their other ships to prevent the 3,000 men on Brooklyn Heights from coming across the East River to Washington's assistance. Some of Washington's subordinates began urging him to abandon the city and move his forces to the mainland. Among them was his personal friend, Adjutant-General Joseph Reed. "I confess," Reed argued, "I do not see the propriety of risking the fate of America, to defend a city the greater part of whose inhabi-

tants are plotting our destruction."

Just where Howe would strike puzzled Washington during the hot, tense days of July and August. He wrote to Congress, "It might be on Long Island, on Bergen [New Jersey], or directly on the city." Though decidedly on the defensive, Washington felt frustrated that he could not at least harass the enemy by sending out raiding parties. The awesome British naval forces inhibited such attempts. In a letter to his brother, Washington confided his frustration "to have them so near, without being able to give them any disturbance."

On July second, the Virginian presented the kind of inspirational speech to his army that Congress hoped could replace gunpowder and other necessities of war for its poorly-equipped army:

> The fate of unborn millions will now depend, under God, on the courage and conduct of this army. Our cruel and unrelenting enemy leaves us no choice but a brave resistance or the most abject submission. This is all we can expect. We have therefore to resolve to conquer or die. Our own country's honor, all call upon us for a vigorous and manly exertion, and if we now shamefully fail we shall become infamous to the whole world.
>
> Let us therefore rely upon the goodness of the cause and the aid of the Supreme Being, in whose hands victory is, to animate and encourage us to great and noble actions.
>
> The eyes of all our country are now upon us, and we shall have their blessings and praises if happily we are the instruments of saving them from the tyranny meditated against them. Let us therefore animate and encourage each other, and show the whole world, that a free man contending for liberty on his own ground is superior to any slavish mercenary on earth.

But the cautious General William Howe did not hurry to attack Washington. The maneuvering of a large army, with the myriad of details it required, was not something to rush. In June, upon first arriving at Staten Island from Halifax, Howe had desired to annihilate Washington's army as soon as possible, before the rebels had a chance to organize a stout defense. But he received a letter from Germain, cautioning him to wait for the reinforcements expected soon from the southern expedition, England, and Germany, so "that your forces may be so increased as to render your success more certain."

Howe could not be sure, anyway, just how many men Washington had in arms to oppose him. Some informers claimed 15,000, others 35,000. A private in the rebel army wrote:

> Militia troops were flocking in from all parts of the country, and to quench the ardor of the British army and in some measure keep them at bay, all the commissaries and the stewards in the army were proclaiming almost continually that they issued more than one hundred thousand rations a day.

* * * * *

While General Howe was making his plans for the one "decisive action" which would be "the most effectual means to terminate this expensive war," his brother, Admiral Lord Richard Howe, arrived on July 12th with reinforcements from England and Germany. At 48, two years older than William, Richard "Black Dick" Howe (named for his swarthy complexion) had the medium height and stocky build that was characteristic of all the Howe brothers. Admiral Howe was known throughout the British Navy for his compassion and humane treatment of his men. Now he was coming to America as peace commissioner, appointed to negotiate a settlement with the rebellious colonies.

Before accepting that role, which he had privately sought for two years, he insisted that he be given command of all British vessels in

American waters, and that his brother William be the other commissioner. Thus, the top army and navy commanders were given the dual role of conquering the rebels and making peace with them. This apparent incongruity would be an important factor in their conduct of the war.

Since the fall of 1774, Prime Minister North and Secretary of State Dartmouth (replaced by Germain in late 1775) had sought the establishment of a peace commission. But the King, most of his cabinet, and a majority in Parliament were too much in favor of a military solution to allow any peace initiatives much of a chance. So North slyly tacked the peace commission onto the reactionary Prohibitory Bill.

It was with difficulty that Lord Howe's appointment was approved, since he was widely suspected of being too soft on the rebellious Americans. As the eldest remaining Howe, Richard had overseen the erection of a statue in London of his brother, George Augustus Howe, who had died valiantly in a joint American-British effort to take Ticonderoga away from the French in 1758. George Howe had had a close affection for Israel Putnam and other New Englanders he had fought alongside, and had even adopted their clothes as best-suited for North American combat. Reflective of this Anglo-American intimacy, the statue in London honoring George Howe had been funded with 2,500 pounds voted by the Massachusetts Assembly.

Admiral Howe wanted to make peace with the rebellious Americans, many of whom he regarded as personal friends. In 1774, he had asked his beautiful sister to query Benjamin Franklin across a chessboard about joining with him in an attempt to negotiate a peaceful solution to the crisis and avert war. Nothing had come of that attempt. Now, in 1776, sent to America as conqueror first and peace commissioner second, Howe was in a dilemma. He feared that conquering the colonies would make Americans sullen, difficult to govern, and prone to future uprisings. He did not want America to become another Ireland or Scotland. Sentiment and common sense thus dictated that he work toward a negotiated settlement.

After a nine week voyage from England, Admiral Howe's flagship entered "the Narrows," sailing past Staten Island on the left and Long Island on the right. He was saluted by the firing of cannon on "all the ships of war in the harbour, by the cheers of the sailors all along the ships, and by those of the soldiers on the shore" of Staten Island. The observer was Ambrose Serle, Lord Howe's secretary. Serle continued his notes for that day, July 12th:

> As soon as we came to anchor, Admiral Shuldham came on board, and soon after Genl Howe, with several officers of their respective departments. By them we learnt the deplorable situation of His Majestys faithful subjects; that they were hunted after and shot at in the woods and swamps, to which they had fled for these four months to avoid the savage fury of the Rebels ... Deserters and others flocked to the Kings army continually. We also heard that Congress had now announced the Colonies to be INDEPENDENT STATES, with several other articles of intelligence that proclaim the villainy and the madness of these deluded people.

Lord Howe was greatly disappointed to hear of the Declaration of Independence, whose passage meant that the rebels probably would not consider reconciliation until either: 1) Parliament recognized their independence, or 2) the rebel army at New York was totally destroyed. Nevertheless, Admiral Howe sent messengers to New Jersey and Rhode Island with letters addressed to the Continental Congress announcing his arrival as peace commissioner, and a promise of amnesty to all rebels who would renounce the rebellion and return to their former allegiance to the King. Also included in these packets were letters to all the governors, asking for help in making peace, and numerous private letters to individuals, testifying to Howe's sincere desire for reconciliation. The letters were deliberately left unsealed, so that the curious could read them and spread Howe's message through

the countryside.

Next, the admiral drafted a letter to George Washington, proposing that they discuss an accommodation. The messenger was met on Governor's Island by Washington's adjutant-general, Joseph Reed, who wanted to know how the letter was addressed. When told, "To George Washington, Esquire, etc., etc., etc.," Reed replied, "There is no such person in the army. I cannot receive a letter for General Washington under such a direction." Howe's messenger answered, "But this letter is of a civil rather than a military nature. Lord Howe has great powers to affect a reconciliation and only regrets that he did not arrive sooner" (before Congress passed the Declaration).

"No matter," replied Reed. "If Lord Howe wishes to communicate with General Washington he must address him properly." Howe's secretary, Ambrose Serle, noted in his journal his own reaction to this outrage, describing Washington as a former "little paltry colonel of militia at the head of a banditti of rebels."

Actually, Lord Howe was so intent on achieving peace that he had over-stepped his authority. His instructions had been to vigorously pursue the war, punishing rebels all up and down the coast, burning towns, destroying American merchant ships, impressing suspected rebels into the British Navy, etc., until the war ended in American acceptance of complete submission to Parliament. Only then was he to propose the peace terms.

Within a week, the Howes sent an officer to ask if "General Washington" would confer with the adjutant-general of the British Army. The matter to be discussed was a letter Washington had written to General Howe, complaining of reports that Americans captured in Canada were being maltreated. The American commander agreed to discuss it, and the next day received General Howe's adjutant with great ceremony in New York.

After discussing the prisoners, the adjutant was about to leave when he brought up the matter of reconciliation, saying that the King's desire for peace was clear in the appointment of the Howes as peace commissioners - two men who it was well known had no love for the King's

ministry. Washington acknowledged that the King had appointed two men of high reputation, but made it clear that only Congress had authority to discuss an accommodation. As for the commissioners, Washington stated flatly, the Howes could only "grant pardons" and "those who had committed no fault wanted no pardon, for they were only defending ... [their] indisputable right."

When the Congress received Howe's package of letters and saw for themselves that he offered nothing more than the terms in the Prohibitory Act (pardon after submission to Parliamentary authority), they ordered Howe's letters published, so "that the good people of these United States may be informed of the terms ... [with which] the insidious court of Britain has endeavoured to amuse and disarm them."

Congress also authorized Benjamin Franklin to reply to Admiral Howe's personal letter to him, so that Franklin's response could be published in the newspapers. Franklin wrote to his friend of many years, Lord Howe, telling him that, since he could only offer pardon upon submission, he had come to America in vain. Franklin admonished Howe on the folly of fighting a war to retain commercial interests, saying Britain's best hope of retaining the benefits of American trade was in making peace with her former colonies as an independent nation. The time for proposing submission to Parliament had passed.

To his sorrow, on July 30th, Lord Howe read this rebuke of his mission. He would have much preferred the glory of a peacemaker to the glory won through civil war, and was saddened by the rejection of his peace initiatives. He also was struck by attacks upon his character, and that of his brother William, in the rebel newspapers. Alluding to the well known bond between his late brother George and New Englanders, Howe told a loyalist that he hoped America would "one day be convinced that, in our affection for that country, we also are Howes." With some regret, the Howes decided to proceed with their battle plans.

CHAPTER SIX
WASHINGTON DEFENDS NEW YORK
AUGUST 1776

"Most of our generals, on a high hill in the lines, viewed it with glasses as we were retreating, and saw the enemy we had to pass through, though we could not. Many thought we would surrender in a body without fighting. When we began to attack, General Washington wrung his hands and cried out, 'Good God! What brave fellows I must this day lose!'"

> *- Anonymous Pennsylvania rifleman, after the Battle of Long Island, August 27, 1776.*

General Howe, remembering his own experience at Bunker Hill and hearing from Admiral Parker about the recent disaster at Charleston, concluded that the rebels were more determined and more capable than anticipated. The war probably could not be won in one "decisive action." And, his brother insisted, it should not be. Rather than permanently alienate the colonists with one devastating offensive, let gradual pressure dissolve the resistance. A steady advance, pushing back Washington's army and securing more and more territory to loyalist control, would create the impression of British invincibility without causing widespread loss of lives and property. The secured areas would be governed with leniency, restoring Americans' faith in British rule. In this way, the rebellion would dissolve peaceably.

General Howe rejected the advice offered by his subordinate generals, who wanted to land on Manhattan above the city, then surround and attack the rebel army. Rather, he opted to use safe, time-tested

siege tactics to force the Americans from Brooklyn Heights. Then, with British cannon atop those hills, Washington would be forced to abandon the city, commencing the slow process of British territorial conquest and disillusionment of the rebels. Moreover, the New York area would be excellent winter quarters for the army and navy, providing shelter as well as plenty of "friends of government" eager to sell provisions.

General Howe waited for the late arrival of a transport carrying kettles and canteens. After its cargo was finally brought ashore Staten Island on August 15th, the general determined to cross over to Long Island on the first morning of calm water. Calm water was required because of the very low draft of the flatboats being built for the purpose.

During the evening of August 21st, a terrible thunderstorm struck. According to some New Yorkers it was the worst in that city in over two decades. Its lightning killed four Americans atop Brooklyn Heights. A New York newspaper reported that several soldiers on Manhattan were also "struck instantly dead. The points of their swords, for several inches, were melted, with a few silver dollars they had in their pockets."

At dawn the next morning, August 22nd, the waters were calm. Eighty-eight boats brought 15,000 British Regulars across The Narrows to Long Island's Gravesend Bay. The flatboats were very shallow. Each had a flat bow attached to the sides by hinges, so it could be let down and facilitate the unboarding of men and field pieces almost at the water's edge. The whole operation was accomplished "without a mishap or delay," to the credit of the Howes' careful planning. By noon, all 15,000 troops were ashore and at work setting up tents, digging latrines, establishing pickets, etc. Gravesend Bay was chosen as the landing site because its flat, almost treeless shore would provide no cover for rebel riflemen or artillery. The Americans wisely chose not to oppose the landing, as explained by one of their brigadier-generals, Samuel Parsons, of Connecticut:

The landing of the troops could not be prevented at
the distance of 6 or 7 miles from our lines; on a plain under the cannon of the ships, just in view of the shore.
Our unequal numbers would not admit attacking them
on the plain when landed.

General Parsons was assigned the area around Gowanus Cove, the
closest American position to the Gravesend Bay landing site. Parsons
dispatched Colonel Hand's Pennsylvania riflemen to march "alongside
of them, in the edge of the woods," but to avoid a fight against such
superior numbers. An officer under Hand described the reconnaisance
in a letter to his wife:

We marched our forces, about two hundred in number, to New Utrecht to watch the movements of the
enemy. When we came on the hill we discovered a party
of them advancing toward us. We prepared to give
them a warm reception, when an impudent fellow fired,
and they immediately halted and turned toward Flatbush.

After observing "the main body" of the British Army also head for
Flatbush, Hand fell back toward the American lines on the Heights of
Guan, killing cattle and burning grain "very cleverly" as he went.
Some of the local Dutch farmers also headed for the American lines,
while others remained to welcome the King's officers.

Three days later, on August 25th, five thousand Hessians under
General Philip von Heister, "a tough old soldier of the Seven Years
War," crossed over to join General Howe at Gravesend. When the
British Regulars had crossed over from Staten Island, they had sat in
the flatboats while the seamen rowed the oars. The Hessian officers,
however, made their men stand at attention during the crossing, "with
muskets sloped and in column of march, preserving the well considered pomp of German discipline." The British and Hessian troops
were in high spirits, according to Israel Putnam's aide, Aaron Burr,

who talked to a British deserter. "They hold us in the utmost contempt," Burr wrote. "Talk of forcing all our lines without firing a gun. The bayonet is their pride. They have forgot Bunker Hill."

Washington had been informed by a spy the night before the crossing that the British were upon "the point of striking the long-expected stroke." According to the spy, they would be embarking for Long Island as well as the North River. Although a joint venture up the Hudson would not materialize, Washington had no way of knowing it was misinformation. He sent word, early on the morning of the 22nd, to General Heath at Kings Bridge to pick out "eight hundred or a thousand light, active men, and good marksmen," ready to move wherever needed at a moment's notice. He promised to send Heath some artillery "if we have not other employment upon hand, which General Putnam, who is this instant come in, seems to think we assuredly shall, this day, as there is a considerable embarkation on board the enemy's boats."

The next day, Washington announced the enemy landing to the men of his own army, through the vehicle for such communications - his general orders of the day. He again reminded them of their awesome duty:

> Remember, officers and soldiers, that you are freemen, fighting for the blessings of liberty; that slavery will be your portion, and that of your posterity, if you do not acquit yourselves like men. Remember how your courage and spirit have been despised and traduced by your cruel invaders; though they have found by dear experience at Boston, Charleston, and other places what a few brave men, contending in their own land and in the best of causes, can do against base hirelings and mercenaries.

He urged them, too, to be cool under fire, to wait for word from their officers before firing, and that anyone attempting to lie down,

hide, or retreat without orders must be instantly shot down as an example.

The command on Long Island had been in the capable hands of Brigadier-General Nathanael Greene, of Rhode Island. By August, he had a thorough knowledge of the topography of western Long Island, including the Heights of Guan, located between the Americans at Brooklyn Heights and their enemy at Gravesend and Flatbush. But, back on August 15th, Greene, "confined to his bed with a raging fever," had sent word to Washington that "he hoped through the assistance of Providence to be able to ride before an attack should be made, but felt great anxiety as to the result." Washington selected as Greene's replacement New Hampshire's Major-General John Sullivan, who had recently arrived in New York with 2,000 men from the disastrous Canadian campaign.

Probably on Washington's orders, Sullivan sent 2,400 men from the lines atop Brooklyn Heights forward to the passes in the Heights of Guan, to retard the British advance. Sullivan was "wholly unacquainted with the ground or country" assigned to him. Washington soon found the reports he received from Sullivan to be almost totally lacking in useful information.

At the same time, Washington became aware that Connecticut's Major-General Israel Putnam was "quite miserable" to be left in charge of New York City while the action appeared to be about to begin over on Long Island. He requested reassignment to Long Island. With most of Long Island's defenders hailing from Connecticut, Washington, for morale purposes, granted Putnam's request. So, on August 24th, he made yet another change in command, replacing Sullivan with "Old Put." He also sent over another two thousand men from Manhattan. Among these were some Delaware and Maryland Continentals, and Jedediah Huntington's Connecticut regiment, which included Thomas Knowlton's Rangers who had distinguished themselves at Bunker Hill.

Instructed to "soothe and soften" Sullivan's hurt feelings, Putnam decided to not change any of Sullivan's troop dispositions. Like his

predecessor, Putnam was also unfamiliar with Long Island. On the 26th, Washington came over from New York to inspect the lines, and "to view the motions of the enemy at Flatbush." Before returning to New York that evening, Washington left Putnam a sharp letter admonishing him for the lack of discipline in his advance guard along the Heights of Guan. The Americans there were wasting powder taking potshots at the enemy. The troops were wandering in all directions as they pleased, burning and looting houses. "Send out scouting parties, by all means," wrote Washington, but "under proper regulations." Since they were defending "every thing that is dear and valuable," they should "take uncommon pains to conduct themselves with uncommon propriety and good order." Nothing had been done to form "a proper line of defense" in the passes. Washington instructed Putnam to have the breastworks - "trees felled across the road" - strengthened the very next day (August 27th), and have more abbatises constructed at the passes.

* * * * *

General Sir Henry Clinton had led the advance guard across Gravesend Bay on August 22nd. As soon as the British position had been secured, he rode off to do some personal reconnaissance. Clinton was still seething over the blemish the recent southern expedition had put on his reputation. It had been his very first independent command and he wanted to make it a stepping stone to advancement. Instead, he had been no help to Admiral Parker in the assault on Charleston. Clinton, trained in the German theater of the Seven Years War (known in America as the French and Indian War), looked down his nose at generals, such as Howe, who had seen action only in America. He wanted desperately to make his mark, and Long Island might offer the chance. So, alone, he set out on horseback to observe the American positions and the passes along the Heights of Guan.

The Heights of Guan extended northward from The Narrows to Long Island Sound in a long cuesta, or ridge, which rose sharply on

the east side to heights of between 100 and 150 feet, then sloped very gently toward Brooklyn and other villages to the west. The whole ridge was so heavily wooded and choked with brush that it was virtually impassable, except at four depressions, or "passes." So the American defenders were concentrated at these passes. But communication would be difficult, due to the distances between the four passes.

At the first one, Gowanus Pass, the Narrows Road (also called the Gowanus Road) ran north from Gravesend, hugging the shore, and passed by Gowanus Cove on its way to Brooklyn. Two and a half miles to the north, the Flatbush Road went from the village of Flatbush west through Flatbush Pass and on toward Brooklyn. One mile further north, the Bedford Road went through Bedford Pass, and then on to Bedford and Brooklyn. Three miles north of Bedford Pass, the Jamaica Road cut through Jamaica Pass, then ran south for several miles along the west slope of the ridge to Bedford.

When Clinton did his reconnaisance, the Americans had in place about 2,800 men at or near the first three passes - but none at the more distant fourth one, Jamaica Pass. The men that Greene had placed there earlier had been called back by Sullivan. Like Putnam, Sullivan believed in the Bunker Hill theory, as a British officer explained in a letter a few days later:

> They had imagined (which, to say the truth, our former method had given them some reason to suppose) that we should land directly in front of their works, march up and attack them without precaution in their strongest points. They had totally neglected the left flank. The possibility of our taking that route seems never to have entered their imaginations.

It may not have entered the minds of Putnam and Sullivan, but it had entered Washington's. During his visit to Long Island on August 26th, he had instructed Putnam to assign five hand-picked horsemen to patrol Jamaica Pass. These five mounted sentries would have to suffice,

because the army had no cavalry to patrol the area. A few weeks before, a contingent of mounted gentlemen volunteers calling themselves the "Connecticut Light Horse" had arrived on Manhattan and offered their services, but were sent home by Washington because of the severe lack of forage.

Clinton observed the first three passes, with their breastworks of felled trees. With a local farmer as his guide, he kept going north for several miles until he came to steep, narrow Jamaica Pass. The farmer told Clinton that a road went up this "gorge" and then along the west slope of the ridge to Bedford, and from there on to Brooklyn. The farmer also claimed there were no rebels guarding it. This was true - the five horsemen had not yet been sent there.

Clinton quickly recognized this as a chance to redeem himself for the Charleston fiasco, and reestablish his reputation. If Jamaica Pass could be taken, a flanking movement could bring a column of troops behind the rebels at the other passes. This column could attack the rebels from the rear, while the rest of the army attacked from the front. He wrote down his plan, and Howe's chief staff officer eagerly brought it to headquarters.

Clinton, who never met with Howe except when Howe requested his presence, went to his own quarters to anxiously await Howe's response. According to Clinton's memoirs, he found out that his plan "did not seem to be much relished" by Howe's other subordinates, chiefly Major-General James Grant, who dismissed it "as savouring too much of the German school." Grant favored marching right up to the Americans at whichever pass would most quickly lead to Brooklyn Heights. A vehement anti-American, Grant had declared in the House of Commons "that the Americans could not fight, and that he would undertake to march from one end of the continent to the other with five thousand men."

Howe was used to receiving irritating memorandums from Clinton, offering advice that was neither solicited nor appreciated. Clinton was a talented but humorless officer, overly sensitive, and a hard man to know. However, this time Howe was inclined to accept Clinton's pro-

posal. If it worked, it would greatly reduce the amount of blood to be shed on both sides, and start the series of routs and retreats that would lead the Americans to be disillusioned with the war.

There was definitely risk in Clinton's plan. A large detachment would have to march through unfamiliar territory, in the dark, then seize control of a steep, narrow gorge that could easily be defended. A successful ambush by the rebels could be devastating to the isolated flanking column. But Howe listened to Oliver DeLancey, Sr., a loyalist he trusted. DeLancey had escaped New York a few nights earlier by rowing a canoe down the Hudson. Now he assured General Howe that the route to Jamaica Pass was an easy night march, and he would have no difficulty finding local guides to lead them through the darkness.

On August 25th, Howe sent for Clinton. The Commander-in-Chief was not outwardly enthusiastic. Clinton later recalled the meeting: "In all the opinions he ever gave me, [Howe] did not expect any good from the move." The stone-faced commander told Clinton that he accepted the plan.

As second in command - traditionally, the officer to lead an attack - Clinton would be in charge of the column's "avant-garde." With this advance party, he should seize the pass, then wait for Generals Howe, Cornwallis and Percy to bring up the bulk of the flanking party of 10,000 British Regulars. Meanwhile, General Grant would lead 5,000 Regulars toward Gowanus Pass, and von Heister's 5,000 Hessians would likewise demonstrate in front of Flatbush Pass. When the flanking party was through Jamaica Pass and nearing Bedford, they would fire two cannon to signal Grant and von Heister to attack in earnest.

During the next day, the 26th of August, fully half of the 20,000 troops that had landed at Gravesend were repositioned to Flatlands, a village closer to Jamaica Pass. Would such a movement, visible to the rebels at Flatbush Pass, alert them that Howe might be considering turning the American left? Howe must have been uneasy, not knowing the answer.

Early that evening, 10,000 British Regulars paraded at Flatlands.

Among them was Clinton's avant-garde, consisting of two thousand foot soldiers (many of them light infantry trained for wooded hilly conditions), 14 field pieces, and nearly one thousand mounted dragoons. Dragoons were trained for the flexible warfare that would be common in this non-European theater. Armed with long sabers, pistols, and fusils (shortened muskets), they were taught to fire while riding, taking care not to place the barrel close to the horse's ears. Unlike the traditional heavy cavalry, the dragoons would dismount and fight on foot, if necessary, then mount and ride again to the next point of action. They were impressive on the parade ground, one thousand armed dragoons with their feathered black helmets, scarlet coats, and black boots reaching to mid-thigh.

At eight o'clock in the evening, Clinton gave the order to march. He ordered the 72nd regiment to form a screen between the marching column and the Americans, "for the purpose of drowning the noise of our cannon over the stones, masking our march, and preventing the enemy's patrols from discovering it." All the tents were left standing, for the Americans to see at first light the next morning and think the troops were still asleep.

Captain Oliver DeLancey, Jr., and his company of dragoons led the advance, guided by three Tory farmers. Just behind DeLancey's company and spread out on both sides of it was the light infantry company of 34-year-old Captain William Glanville Evelyn. These two young captains would spend the next several anxious hours peering into the darkness trying to spot rebel bushwackers. Evelyn's flankers walked softly, with bayonets fixed to the ends of their muskets. Their orders were to kill or capture, but at all cost silence every living thing they met.

As they headed north on the road to Flushing village, which lay beyond Jamaica Pass, Clinton's main source of anxiety was the noise the metal-rimmed cannon wheels made as they went "over the stones." Soon the long column left the main road in favor of a less conspicuous wagon track that ran roughly parallel to the road. After another mile or two, Clinton halted. Howe and Cornwallis sent messengers to the

front to find out why the column had stopped moving. They returned, saying the local guides were explaining to Clinton that directly ahead was a creek crossed by Schoonmaker Bridge. The bridge was so narrow that it had to be passed by the men in single file. Here, Clinton knew, was a perfect spot for a rebel ambush, in the event that any deserter, spy, or Whig farmer had gone ahead to warn the rebels.

Clinton ordered Evelyn's company to open a skirmish line and take the bridge by storm if necessary. Not a man was allowed to load his musket. The enemy must be silenced with the bayonet. Here was the chance for glory that Evelyn had thirsted for. He led his men as they quietly charged across the bridge, one in back of another, and dashed into the dark woods on the other side, straining their eyes for hidden rebel marksmen. Nothing. No one anywhere. The long column slowly marched across the bridge, while the cannon and dragoons splashed in the creek.

The column stopped once more. It was time to leave the northbound wagon track and head west, through a cornfield, and a vegetable garden that was trampled underfoot in the dark. Between two and three o'clock in the morning, DeLancey's dragoons and Evelyn's light infantry emerged onto the main road less than a quarter mile short of the pass. They were startled by the sound of hoofbeats on the road, coming from the east and heading for the pass. DeLancey challenged the riders, ordering them to identify themselves. His American voice proved helpful, as one of the riders responded, "Americans - friends!" DeLancey put his spurs to his horse's sides and lunged into the darkness, quickly followed by his dragoons. A moment later, five overwhelmed American lieutenants, barely out of their teens, found themselves surrounded by upraised sabers. They meekly surrendered and were escorted to Clinton.

Having been ordered to the pass just the evening before, the five zealous young patriots had found the pass empty. So they had decided to ride down the road a ways toward the British camp, hoping to be in position to hear any enemy column long before it approached the pass. This, they thought, would allow them enough time to make the long

ride back to Bedford to give warning. They never dreamed that the enemy would come up behind them instead of in front of them. Clinton's guide had been wise to leave the road and cut through the fields.

Like most low-ranking officers in Washington's army, the five young captives were wearing civilian clothes. Because of their lack of uniforms, Clinton accused them of being spies and threatened them with immediate hanging. The general demanded to know how many men were guarding the pass. "None." Clinton told them he did not believe them, and he went on threatening and asking how many defenders were at the pass. One of the captives finally admitted that the only people nearby were a tavernkeeper named Howard, and his family, asleep in their home at the base of the pass.

Having admitted this much, the young American then angrily objected to Clinton's continued threats, telling the general that "under other circumstances he would not dare insult them in that manner." Clinton snapped back, "You're an impudent rebel!" and warned them all to be careful, lest they find themselves swinging from the nearest tree. The rebel then declared that Washington would hang man for man in return, and as for himself, he would not give out any more information.

But he had already told the British general what he wanted to know. Clinton sent Captain Evelyn and his company of light infantry ahead to surround the Howard house and take the inhabitants captive. Questioning of Howard confirmed what the rebel had said: incredibly, the American command had left the pass undefended, except for the five young men, who imprudently left it to go trotting down the road in search of the enemy.

The exultant Clinton sent detachments of light infantry and dragoons to secure the pass. The guides being unfamiliar with the pass, it became necessary to awaken Howard again and force him at gunpoint to lead the way up Rockaway Path. The remainder of the avant-garde was ordered to lie down and rest, and open their haversacks to eat their cold breakfast. Clinton waited in the Howard house while a messenger rode back to tell General Howe to bring up the remainder of

the column.

Two hours later, a very nervous Howe arrived and okayed the advance up the narrow, winding pass, from whose wooded slopes a few hundred riflemen could easily have blocked, or at least stalled, the ten thousand British. Trees had to be felled to make the Rockaway Path wide enough for the passage of cannon. On Clinton's orders, saws brought for the purpose were used instead of axes, so the rebels further south on the ridge would not hear. Then the six-horse teams were driven hard, pulling the heavy field pieces up the steep, uneven path.

Soon Clinton was leading his less composed superior general and the 10,000 Regulars down the Jamaica Road toward the rear of the 2,400 Americans at the other passes. He could hear the booming of cannon in the distance, where von Heister was demonstrating in front of Flatbush Pass. Howe could not believe the magnitude of the rebels' negligence. He urged Clinton to form a line of battle. Surely there must be at least a few hundred Americans hiding, ready to strike at the column as it marched along the west slope of the ridge toward Bedford. Clinton, lacking Howe's caution, scoffed at the notion. The fight was as good as over.

At Bedford, several Americans on horseback were seen in the distance. After watching the advancing column for a few moments, they galloped off. Were they going to warn their generals, or just fleeing with no intention of warning anyone? The only obstacle en route, a single breastwork at Bedford, was deserted by the time the British reached it. With a hint of mockery in his words, Clinton wished Howe the "joy of future victory," then took charge of the light infantry again and went storming down the road. Howe ordered the two cannon fired, one after the other, signalling von Heister and Grant to stop demonstrating and begin their attacks in earnest.

* * * * *

Sullivan, at Flatbush Pass, observed von Heister's division demonstrating in front of him and suspected they were stalling for time until

Grant could reach his objective, Gowanus Pass. No message came from Bedford to tell Sullivan the real reason why von Heister was stalling.

Further to the southwest, General Grant, so eager to have at "the rebel dogs," had started his 5,000 British Regulars from Gravesend shortly before midnight. By dawn, his wide long column was approaching the Americans at Gowanus Pass. Two thousand marines came ashore to reinforce him. These could be seen from New York's rooftops, where people all over the city, many still in their nightshirts, had heard the thundering of cannon and rushed upstairs to observe the spectacle. Among them was Samuel DeForest, a private from Connecticut.

> British soldiers [marines] were landing at the foot of a road perhaps three-quarters of a mile south of Brooklyn Ferry. ... their burnished arms, which came in contact with the rays of a brilliant morning sun, gleamed like sheets of fire.
>
> About eleven o'clock, Colonel Lewis had orders to march his regiment along the dock opposite Brooklyn Ferry, and when there was an officer on horseback, we concluded he was one of the general's aides. He informed us that he was calling for volunteers to turn out and man every watercraft which lay along the dock. "All must know there was dreadful fighting, and if our men were driven to retreat we wish to be able to bring them over this side."
>
> One Wells Judson and myself turned out. A periauger [boat] was committed to our charge, and we landed at Brooklyn Ferry about one o'clock. The thunder of the British artillery, the roaring of the small arms of both armies, was tremendous.
>
> Judson and I walked up the ferry road and lay down under a shade, for it was very warm, and drank some

cold water. While we lay under the board fence perhaps an hour, ruminating on the terrors of the day, we heard the tramping of men just over the knoll, but we [had] hardly time to think before they hove in sight, and the road was filled with redcoat Regulars, and again we had hardly time for surprise before we saw they were prisoners, and they were hurried over the ferry and through the city and over the Hudson into Jerseys.

Washington belatedly sent several hundred reinforcements over from New York. But he still kept more than half his army on Manhattan, thinking the Howe brothers might be planning a double attack. Although two of Lord Howe's ships managed to sail up close enough to Red Hook to bombard it, Howe's attempt to send five warships to the East River to stop the crossing of reinforcements failed, because of a stiff north wind and an ebbing tide.

Among the reinforcements Washington sent was fifteen-year-old Joseph Plumb Martin, one of the recently arrived levies from Connecticut. Young Private Martin's excellent narrative provides us with a glimpse of the thoughts and actions of men and boys on the way to their first battle:

> I saw our sergeant major directing his course up Broadway, towards us, in rather an unusual step for him. He soon arrived and informed us the regiment was ordered to Long Island. This was not unexpected to me, yet it gave me rather a disagreeable feeling. I then went to the top of the house where I had a full view of that part of the Island. I distinctly saw the smoke of the field artillery, but the distance and the unfavorableness of the wind prevented my hearing their report, at least but faintly. The horrors of battle then presented themselves to my mind in all their hideousness; I must come to it now, thought I. Well, I will endeavor to do my duty as

135

well as I am able, and leave the event with Providence. We were soon ordered to our regimental parade, from which, as soon as the regiment was formed, we were marched off for the ferry.

At the lower end of the street were placed several casks of sea bread, nearly hard enough for musket flints; thethe casks were unheaded and each man was allowed to take as many as he could as he marched by. As my good luck would have it, there was a momentary halt made; I improved the opportunity thus offered me, as every good soldier should upon all important occasions, to get as many of the biscuit as I possibly could; no one said anything to me and I filled my bosom and took as many as I could hold in my hand, a dozen or more in all, and when we arrived at the ferry stairs I stowed them away in my knapsack. We quickly embarked on board the boats. As each boat started, three cheers were given by those on board, which was returned by the numerous spectators who thronged the wharves.

We soon landed at Brooklyn, marched up the ascent from the ferry to the plain. We now began to meet the wounded men, another sight I was unacquainted with, some with broken arms, some with broken legs, and some with broken heads. The sight of these a little daunted me, and made me think of home, but the sight and thought vanished together.

We marched a short distance, when we halted to refresh ourselves. Whether we had any other victuals besides the hard bread I do not remember, but I remember my gnawing at them; they were hard enough to break the teeth of a rat. One of the soldiers complaining of thirst to his officer - "Look at that man," said he [the officer], pointing to me; "he is not thirsty, I will warrant it." I felt a little elevated to be styled a man.

While resting here, which was not more than twenty minutes or half an hour, the Americans and British were warmly engaged within sight of us. What were the feelings of most or all the young soldiers at this time, I know not, but I saw a lieutenant who appeared to have feelings not very enviable. He ran round among the men of his company sniveling and blubbering, praying [asking] each one if he had aught against him, or if he had injured anyone that they would forgive him, declaring at the same time that he, from his heart, forgave them if they had offended him. Had he been at the gallows with a halter about his neck, he could not have shown more fear or penitence. A fine soldier you are, I thought, a fine officer, an exemplary man for young soldiers! I would have then suffered anything short of death rather than have made such an exhibition of myself; but as the poet says:

> "Fear does things so like a witch,
> 'Tis hard to distinguish which is which."

... While we were resting here, our lieutenant-colonel and major ... took their cockades from their hats; being asked the reason, the lieutenant colonel replied that he was willing to risk his life in the cause of his country, but unwilling to stand a particular mark for the enemy to fire at. He was a fine officer and a brave soldier.

We were soon called upon to fall in and proceed. We had not gone far, about half a mile, when I heard one ask another where his musket was. ... having left it where we last halted, he was inspecting his side as if undetermined whether he had it or not, he then fell out of the ranks to go in search of it. One of the company, who had brought it on (wishing to see how far he would go

137

before he missed it) gave it to him.

At the Long Island division's headquarters on Brooklyn Heights, Major-General Israel Putnam was awakened at 3 a.m. and told that the British were on the march toward Gowanus Pass. Acting on Washington's orders to hold the pass "at all hazards," Putnam hurried to Lord Stirling's tent, awakened him, and ordered him "to march with the two regiments nearest at hand" to meet the enemy. So Stirling went forward with two field pieces and the troops that Washington had sent over the day before - Haslet's Delawares and Smallwood's Marylanders. These 900 untried young "soldiers," most of them less than two weeks with the army, marched down the hill toward Gowanus Pass. General Stirling:

> We proceeded to within half a mile of the Red Lion, and there met Colonel Atlee, with his [Pennsylvania] regiment, who informed me that the enemy were in sight; indeed, I then saw their front between us and the Red Lion. I desired Colonel Atlee to place his regiment on the left of the road [Parsons' Connecticut was on the right side], and to wait their coming up, when I went to form the two regiments I had brought with me along a ridge from the road up to a piece of wood on top of the hill. This was done instantly, upon very advantageous ground.
> Our opponents advanced and were fired upon in the road by Atlee's, who, after two or three rounds, retreated to the wood on my left and there formed. By this time Kachline's [Pennsylvania] riflemen arrived; part of them I placed along a hedge under the front of the hill and the rest in the front of the wood.
> The troops opposed to me were two brigades of four regiments each, under the command of General Grant, who advanced their light troops to within one hundred

and fifty yards of our right front and took possession of an orchard there, and some hedges that extended towards our left; this brought on an exchange of fire between those troops and our riflemen, which continued for about two hours, and then ceased by those light troops retiring to their main body.

In the mean time, Captain Carpenter brought up two field-pieces, which were placed on the side of the hill, so as to command the road and the only approach for some hundred yards. On the part of General Grant there were two field-pieces: one howitzer three hundred yards [in] front of our right and ... [another, 600 yards in] front of our left on a rising ground. One of their brigades formed in two lines opposite to our right, and the other extended in one line to the top of the hills in front of our left.

In an orchard on the left side of the pass, Colonel Atlee's Pennsylvanians were standing in fixed formations. They repeatedly fought off British attempts to flank them. Grant was not yet fully committing all his troops to a determined assault, still waiting for evidence that Clinton had arrived behind the American positions at the other passes. But to the Americans defending Gowanus Pass, it was a deadly serious affair, even if Grant chose to only send his Regulars at them one regiment at a time. For four hours, the Americans defending the Gowanus Road were worn down physically and emotionally, every minute expecting that final massive advance by Grant's entire force. During that time, the fighting was fierce. At one point, General Parsons saw "sixty dead Regulars on the field, heaped in two piles." Colonel Atlee describes his resistance to Grant's flanking maneuvers:

I received a reinforcement of two companies of the Delawares, under Captain Stedman, with orders from Lord Stirling to file off further to the left and prevent, if

possible, a body of the enemy observed advancing to flank the brigade. ...

I espied at the distance of about three hundred yards a hill of clear ground, which I judged to be a proper situation to oppose the troops ordered to flank us, and which I determined, if possible, to gain before them. At the foot of this hill a few of Huntington's Connecticut Regiment, that had been upon the picket, joined me. In order to gain and secure the hill, I ordered the troops to wheel to the right and march up the hill abreast. When within about forty yards of the summit, we very unexpectedly received a very heavy fire from the enemy taken post there before us, notwithstanding the forced march I made.

Upon receiving the above heavy fire, which continued very warm and they secure behind the hill, a small halt was made, and the detachment fell back a few paces. Here Capt. Stedman, with all the Delawares except the Lieutenants Stewart and Harney with about sixteen privates, left me and drew after them some of my own. The remainder after recovering a little from this, their first shock, I ordered to advance, at the same time desiring them to preserve their fire and aim aright.

They immediately, with the resolution of veteran soldiers, obeyed the order. The enemy, finding their opponents fast advancing and determined to dispute the ground with them, fled with precipitation, leaving behind them twelve killed upon the spot and a lieutenant and four privates wounded. In this engagement I lost my worthy friend and Lieutenant-Colonel [Parry], shot through the head, who fell without a groan, fighting in defence of his much injured country. In the midst of the action I ordered four soldiers to carry him as speedily as possible within the lines at Brookline.

Prospects looked bleak for Atlee when his courageous men discovered their cartridge pouches were empty and those they had taken off the dead Regulars were nearly gone, too. But, just then, "very luckily" Huntington's ammunition cart arrived.

With the new addition of the Delaware and Maryland Continentals, Stirling now had almost 2,000 men to hold Gowanus Pass. The Delawares, in particular, were remarkable in their blue uniforms with red trim, resembling the Hessians, except for the "green bough or branch of a tree in their hats."

Grant's flanking maneuver not meeting with success, he brought up his artillery and attacked Stirling's right. There, Lord Stirling had Haslet's Delawares and Smallwood's Marylanders in a large exposed V formation. They stood their ground against the British, despite "heavy fire from their cannons and mortars." A Maryland rifleman describes the action:

> [Stirling] drew up in a line and offered them battle in the true English taste. The balls and shells flew very fast. Our men stood it amazingly well, not even one showed a disposition to shrink. Our orders were not to fire till the enemy came within 50 yards of us; but when they perceived we stood their fire so coolly and resolutely, they declined coming any nearer, though treble our number.

Grant's repeated attacks met with the same result - a standoff. Perhaps he had misjudged the rebels when he claimed in Parliament that he could march the length of the continent with only 5,000 Regulars. Reportedly, the morning of the battle, Stirling had referred to Grant's well-known remark when Stirling reached Gravesend Pass: "He may have 5,000 with him now. We are not so many. But I think we are enough to prevent his advancing further on his march over the continent than that [Gowanus] mill-pond."

* * * * *

While Stirling was holding off Grant, the action was starting one and a half miles to the north. There General von Heister's 5,000 Hessians were using their artillery to hold Sullivan's attention at Flatbush Pass. Bedford Pass, defended by Colonels Wyllys and Chester, was ignored by the enemy. Colonel Miles and his regiment of Pennsylvania riflemen were roving along the eastern slope, "towards Jamaica, to watch the motion of the enemy and give intelligence" about any movements in the direction of Jamaica Pass. For more than an hour, Miles and Clinton marched parallel to each other without one hearing the other because of the dense woods of the ridge separating them - Miles on the eastern slope heading north, Clinton on the western slope heading south toward Bedford. Miles explains how he discovered, too late, Clinton's long column marching on the Jamaica Road:

> After marching [north] nearly two miles, the whole distance through woods, I arrived within sight of the Jamaica road, and to my great mortification I saw the main body of the enemy in full march between me and our lines, and the baggage guard [at the rear of their column] just coming into the road.
>
> I took the adjutant with me and crept as near the road as I thought prudent, to try and ascertain the number of the baggage guard, and I saw a grenadier stepping into the woods. I got a tree between him and me until he came near, and I took him prisoner and examined him. I found that there was a whole brigade with the baggage, commanded by a general officer.
>
> I immediately returned to the battalion and called a council of the officers and laid three propositions before them: 1st, to attack the baggage guard and endeavor to cut our way through them and proceed to Hell Gate and

so cross the Sound; 2nd, to lay where we were until the whole had passed us and then proceed to Hell Gate; or, 3d, to endeavor to force our way through the enemy's flank guards into our line at Brooklyn. The first was thought a dangerous and useless attempt as the enemy was so superior in force. The 2nd I thought the most eligible, for it was evident that adopting either of the other propositions we must lose a number of men without affecting the enemy materially, as we had so small a force, not more than 230 men. This was, however, objected to, under the idea that we should be blamed for not fighting at all, and perhaps charged with cowardice, which would be worse than death itself.

The 3d proposition was therefore adopted, and we immediately began our march, but had not proceeded more than half a mile until we fell in with a body of 7 or 800 light infantry, which we attacked without any hesitation, but their superiority of numbers encouraged them to march up with their bayonets, which we could not withstand, having none ourselves. I therefore ordered the troops to push on towards our lines.

We had proceeded but a short distance before we were again engaged with a superior body of the enemy, and here we lost a number of men, but took Major Moncrieffe, their commanding officer, prisoner. But he was a Scotch prize, for Ensign Brodhead, who took him and had him in possession for some hours, was obliged to surrender himself.

Finding that the enemy had possession of the ground between us and our lines, and that it was impossible to cut our way through as a body, I directed our men to make the best of their way as well as they could; some few got in safe, but there were 159 taken prisoners. I myself was entirely cut off from our lines and therefore

endeavored to conceal myself, with a few men who would not leave me. I hoped to remain until night, when I intended to try to get to Hell Gate and cross the Sound; but about 3 o'clock in the afternoon was discovered by a party of Hessians and obliged to surrender.

At Bedford Pass, Colonels Wyllys and Chester, with their Connecticut levies, could hear Miles engaged with the enemy. They decided to retreat, although no enemy had yet come close to Bedford Pass. Leaving Miles to his fate, they were able to reach the Brooklyn lines with little loss.

A harsher fate awaited the Americans at Flatbush Pass. When Clinton reached Bedford, he divided his own large force in half, as planned. Cornwallis led the grenadiers on down the road toward Brooklyn, to trap Stirling between himself and Grant. Clinton took the light infantry and dragoons toward Flatbush Pass and Sullivan's men. Flankers fanned out into the woods on both sides of the road.

Sullivan was not even aware of Clinton's approach. He and his perhaps one thousand men defending Flatbush Pass were preoccupied with the steady advance of 5,000 blue-uniformed Hessians in front of them. They marched in three columns, muskets at their shoulders, bayonets reflecting the mid-morning sun. Keeping in their rigid parade ground formations, they reached the dense woods at the foot of Prospect Hill and continued up it, trying their best not to let the trees and bushes interfere with their tight lines.

One of their officers proudly recalled the troops halting at intervals to re-dress their lines, then advancing again "with colors flying [their flag was the golden lion of Hesse on a blue background] to the music of drums and hautboys [wooden oboes]. They did not fire a shot, but pressed steadily forward until they could employ their bayonets."

Ahead of them, to the left and right, von Donop's green-coated "jagers" (riflemen, also called "chausseurs") moved from tree to tree, firing with their rifles, forcing Sullivan's pickets to fall back. Mostly foresters and gameskeepers from the Bavarian Black Forest, they car-

ried short, heavy, large-bore rifles without bayonets. These guns were the models from which early Pennsylvania gunsmiths (mostly German immigrants) had developed the famed American long-barrelled, small-bore weapon. After the war, many of these Pennsylvania gunsmiths would move west, and their weapon would be known from then on as the Kentucky rifle.

Sullivan soon realized he could not hold off the Hessians, who outnumbered him five to one. He issued a command for an orderly retreat. But it was too late, Clinton's light infantry were closing in. A group of retreating men, dragging three light cannon, swung them around and fired grapeshot at the redcoats approaching through the trees. But this only momentarily halted the British advance.

Another American artillery crew took off, after seeing their lieutenant fall. A volunteer named John Callender stopped them and made them return to their gun. He led them in firing and held that position until overrun by the enemy, when the crew finally ignored Callender and ran away. Callender refused to run, and soon found a bayonet at his breast. A British officer, admiring his courage, stopped the soldier and took Callender prisoner. A former artillery officer from Massachusetts, John Callender had been stripped of rank by Washington's investigations into allegations of cowardice at Bunker Hill. He would finally be exonerated in 1777, after being exchanged for an imprisoned British officer.

Von Heister's three columns were now cresting the hill. Sullivan had some of Kachlein's Pennsylvania riflemen and Knowlton's Bunker Hill veterans to slow down the Hessian pursuit. To these men, thousands of bayonets coming over the hill toward them must have been an awesome sight. Some of them turned and ran to catch up with the rest of Sullivan's retreating forces. Others stood their ground and fired. But, not stopping to return fire, the Hessians came upon them before they could finish the time-consuming job of reloading their rifles. The butt end of a rifle is a weak weapon against several bayonets. Colonel von Heeringen reported, "The English soldiers did not give much quarter [mercy] and constantly urged our men to follow their example.

The greater part of their riflemen were pierced to the trees with bayonets." Clinton's dragoons arrived in time to cut off their retreat. Some of the British officers were shocked at the sight of their German allies unmercifully bayoneting to death Americans who had thrown down their weapons and put up their hands.

Not all the British officers disapproved of such conduct by their allies. Simon Fraser, of the Scotch Highlander Regiment, reported after the battle:

> It was a fine sight to see with what alacrity they dispatched the rebels with bayonets, after we had surrounded them so that they could not resist. We took care to tell the Hessians that the rebels had resolved to give no quarter to them in particular; which made them fight desperately, and put all to death who fell into their hands.

One Hessian, captured two months later at another battle, said the British were still at it then, telling the Hessians, "that Americans are savages and barbarians, and have their [captives'] bodies stuck full of pieces of dry wood and in that manner burned to death."

Some Americans, not trusting the mercenaries to give them quarter, tried deception: clubbing their muskets to the ground (a universal gesture of surrender), they waited for the relaxed Hessians to approach them, then quickly turned their guns right side up to fire point-blank at the Hessians. After seeing or hearing of such incidents, the enraged Hessian troops became more brutal than ever. Despite the slaughter, though, many prisoners were taken alive. Among them was General Sullivan himself, found hiding in a cornfield.

Between the wooded Heights of Guan and the Brooklyn lines was a broad stretch of open country, pastures and hayfields. It was here that the dragoons, astride their horses, waited in line, sabers drawn with the point resting on the shoulder. Sullivan's men broke ranks and ran from the woods onto the plain, every man for himself. Trumpets sounded.

Hundreds of dragoons spurred their horses, and swept down on the fleeing rebels.

Until Sullivan's men saw the dragoons, they had been confident they could safely outrun their enemies, who were on foot and weighted down by their equipment, and tired from their march. They did not count on being confronted by a mounted enemy. It was a massacre, as dozens of Americans felt the sharp steel of sword or bayonet. Desperately, they formed groups and tried to break their way through. Without bayonets they could only shoot, then use their muskets as clubs. One man who did not make it was Colonel Philip Johnston of New Jersey, who died that day, his 35th birthday.

Von Heister, seeing an easy rout developing, dispatched one of his three columns to march to Gowanus Pass and assist his British ally, General Grant. By now (about 11 a.m.) Cornwallis had reached the Gowanus Road and Grant's troops were making a determined push at the rebels. General Stirling had been forced to fall back, toward Gowanus milldam. Atlee, in front and to the left of Stirling, busy covering Stirling's flank, was not aware that Stirling had fallen back. We pick up Atlee's account again:

> I fully expected, as did most of my officers, that the strength of the British army was advancing in this quarter to our lines. But how greatly were we deceived when intelligence was received by some scattering soldiers that the right wing and centre of the army, amongst which were Hessians, were advancing to surround us. This we were soon convinced of by an exceeding heavy fire in our rear. I once more sent my adjutant to Lord Stirling, to acquaint him with the last success obtained by my party, and to request his further orders.

After waiting about forty-five minutes, "receiving no answer, the adjutant not returning," Colonel Atlee ordered his regiment to march to

the rear, where he hoped to find the rest of Stirling's brigade.

> How great was my surprise I leave any one to judge
> when, upon coming to the ground occupied by our
> troops, to find it evacuated and the troops gone off ...
>
> Finding no passage, we retired to an eminence about
> sixty perches from the road, to consult whether best to
> conceal ourselves in the adjacent swamps or divide into
> small parties, when we espied a party of Hessians who
> had discovered and were endeavouring to surround us.
> The opinion we had formed of these troops determined
> us to run any risk rather than fall into their hands; and
> finding after all our struggles no prospect of escaping,
> we determined to throw ourselves into the mercy of a
> battalion of Highlanders posted upon an eminence near
> the Flatbush road, not far from where we had last sat.
> This we did about five o'clock in the afternoon to the
> number of twenty-three, thereby escaping the party of
> Hessians who came to the Highlanders immediately after
> our surrender.

Stirling had not intentionally abandoned Atlee, but had been surprised and overwhelmed by the enemy coming into his rear. Around eleven o'clock, he had found himself attacked in the front by Grant's entire force and in the rear by the newly arrived grenadiers under Cornwallis, finally completing their march started fourteen hours before at Flatlands. Stirling's splendid Delaware and Maryland Continentals, the two largest and best equipped regiments in the army, gave ground very slowly, their ranks still nearly "full, their uniforms smart, their weapons the best that money could purchase, their courage high."

In fact, the Delawares were the fanciest (and almost the only) uniformed regiment in the army. In their blue uniforms with red trim, they were mistaken for Hessians by a British colonel who saw them

firing upon his grenadiers. The British colonel sent forward a Captain Wragg to tell them to stop firing on their allies. The unfortunate captain did not discover until within a few yards from them that they were Americans. Lieutenant Popham, of the Delaware regiment, still recalled the incident when he retold it many years later at the age of ninety-one:

> Captain Wragg and 18 men, supposing us to be Hessians by the similarity of our dress, approached too near. Before he discovered his mistake, my company attacked and took them prisoners. I was immediately ordered with a guard to convey them across the creek to the rear of our lines.
>
> On descending the high ground we reached [Gowanus milldam] ... the enemy brought a couple of pieces to bear upon us, which, when Wragg saw, he halted in hope of a rescue. But on my ordering him to march forward instantly, or I should fire on him, he moved on.
>
> We waded in up to our knees. An old canoe that had been split served to help those who wanted to cross a deep hole in the creek by pushing it across. [I] was so fatigued with anxiety and exercise that I sat down on the mud with the water up to my breast till my charge were all safely landed on the rear.

Their escape was very fortunate. Many Americans died in the Gowanus creek and milldam that day. Stirling decided to use some of his best troops for a rear-guard action to hold off the enemy long enough for most of his brigade to wade and swim across to the safety of the Brooklyn lines.

Stirling selected Major Mordecai Gist for this rear guard action. Major Gist was temporarily in command of Colonel Smallwood's Maryland regiment; the colonel just then was making his way over from New York, where he had been on court-martial duty. With Gist

and about 250 of his Marylanders, Stirling advanced up the Gowanus Road toward Brooklyn to meet the approaching enemy (Howe and Cornwallis).

The British officers were stunned by the audacity of these rebels boldly marching toward them in perfect V formations. For a minute, Cornwallis's troops did nothing but watch, and perhaps admire the courage of these heretofore contemptible rebels. Then they welcomed the Marylanders with hundreds of muskets and two field pieces firing grapeshot and canister. The Americans halted and fell back, only to advance again - five times. Major Gist, one of the few who survived, wrote that Stirling "encouraged and animated our young soldiers with almost invincible resolution." Stirling also survived to write of this desperate attempt:

> I found that General Howe, with the main body of the army, was between me and our lines, and saw that the only chance of escaping being all made prisoners was to pass the creek. In order to render this the more practicable, I found it absolutely necessary to attack a body of troops commanded by Lord Cornwallis, posted at the [Cortelyou] house near the upper mills. This I instantly did, with about half of Smallwood's, first ordering all the other troops to make the best of their way through the creek. We continued the attack a considerable time, the men having been rallied and the attack renewed five or six several times, and were on the point of driving Lord Cornwallis from his station, but large succors [reinforcements] arriving rendered it impossible.

At one point, Stirling's desperate men, decimated by flying lead, had rushed the Cortelyou House, and forced the British gunners to desert their cannon. General Cornwallis fled through the back door. But, just then, British reinforcements arrived, forcing Stirling to fall back again. General Stirling continues:

I [then] endeavored to get in between that house and Fort Box [on Brooklyn Heights], but on attempting it, I found a considerable body of troops in my front, and several in pursuit of me on the right and left, and a constant firing on me. I soon found it would be in vain to attempt to make my escape, and therefore went to surrender myself to General von Heister, commander in chief of the Hessians.

. The proud Scotsman sought out the German general rather than surrender to a Briton. Of the approximately 270 heroic men fighting this rear guard action, only ten managed to reach the Brooklyn lines. One was an anonymous rifleman:

We forced the advanced party which first attacked us to give way, through which opening we got a passage down to the wide of a marsh, waded over, and then swam a narrow river, all the while exposed to the enemy's fire. The whole right wing of our battalion, thinking it impossible to march through the marsh, attempted to force their way through the woods where they, almost to a man, were killed or taken. The Maryland battalion has lost 259 men, amongst whom are twelve officers.

Most of our generals, on a high hill in the lines, viewed it with glasses as we were retreating, and saw the enemy we had to pass through, though we could not. Many thought we would surrender in a body without fighting. When we began to attack, General Washington wrung his hands and cried out, "Good God! what brave fellows I must this day lose!"

All afternoon, American soldiers fortunate to have eluded the enemy

straggled into the lines on Brooklyn Heights to spread panic there. Precious cannon and hundreds of small arms had been left on the battlefield, making the men who reached the lines almost useless, should Howe press on to attack their fortifications there.

At 11 o'clock, while Stirling was courageously making his stand at Cortelyou House, von Donop's grenadiers raced across the plain toward the American forts and trenches atop Brooklyn Heights. Clinton had noticed that the Jamaica Road was undefended where it led to Fort Putnam, and he gave General Vaughn permission (despite Howe's prior orders against it) to assault the fort. Clinton later explained, "I had at that moment but little inclination to check the ardor of our troops when I saw the enemy flying in such a panic before them."

General Howe was watching from a hill, and quickly dispatched a staff officer at full gallop with orders to halt. General Vaughn and several other general officers sent Howe passionate pleas to be allowed to advance, insisting that the rebels were entirely within their power. "It required repeated orders," Howe wrote to Germain later, "to prevail upon them to desist from the attempt." It was hard for the victorious generals to stop their pursuit of "Mr. Washington and his dirty pack of New England long-faces, a vagabond army of ragamuffins." Howe called off the battle around noon, telling his generals, "That is enough fighting for one day."

General Howe had no way of knowing that the Brooklyn Heights fortifications at the time were manned by only 800 men, many of them without weapons. However, Howe did know that they were strongly built. And he could recall quite vividly experiencing "a moment that I never felt before" fourteen months earlier, when he stood in a hayfield at the base of Bunker Hill and saw countless soldiers and every staff officer around him shot down by intrenched Americans.

Three years later, Howe would be called before a Parliamentary committee to explain why he rejected his subordinates' pleas for an immediate attack on the rebel lines. Howe recalled that he chose not to "risk the loss that might have been sustained in the assault." And he reminded his interrogaters that, unlike the populous rebels, his de-

pleted forces could not be easily replenished.

> The most essential duty I had to observe was, not
> wantonly to commit His Majesty's troops where the ob-
> ject was inadequate. I well knew that any considerable
> loss sustained by the army could not speedily nor easily
> be repaired.

Howe's engineer, John Montresor, described the rebel lines to the
same committee as "cannon-proof with a chain of five redoubts, or
rather fortresses, with ditches, as had also the lines that formed the intervals, raised on the parapet and the counter-scarp, and the whole
surrounded with the most formidable abbatises." Montresor concluded that "they could not be taken by assault, but by approaches."

Howe opted for "regular approaches," the term for digging trenches
of your own under cover of darkness each night, gradually zigzagging
closer and closer to the enemy lines, until you can bring cannon close
enough to fire at point-blank range. Such siege tactics take time, but
result in the capture of the enemy lines at "a very cheap rate" in casualties, compared to an assault. Howe contended that no general ought
to expose his troops to avoidable dangers, particularly when the
objective could be gained without risk. "In this instance," he held,
"from the certainty of being in possession of the lines in a very few
days by breaking ground, to have permitted the attack in question
would have been inconsiderate and even criminal."

* * * * *

By the evening after the battle, Washington had sent over enough
reinforcements to bring the total on Brooklyn Heights to about 9,000.
The commander had arrived late in the morning, just in time to view
the slaughter at Gowanus Creek. He spent the rest of the day examin-
ing the lines, offering strong, hopeful words of encouragement to the
despondent men. That night he "made the rounds," travelling from

one end of the lines to the other, inspiring confidence and vigilance in the sentries. Washington was now anticipating the one climactic battle on his terms that he had been waiting for. Lieutenant Joseph Hodgkins wrote home to his wife in Massachusetts the next morning: "It seems the day is come, on which depends the salvation of this country. It is the determination to defend our lines to the last extremity."

But on August 28th, the day after the battle, the two armies, just one mile apart, stayed put. Through the rain that fell most of the day, they watched each other across the open ground. The only significant action occurred at the end of the day, outside Fort Putnam, which guarded the American left flank. Joseph Plumb Martin recorded the skirmish:

> A few of our men went over the creek upon business that usually employed us, that is, in search of something to eat. There was a field of Indian corn at a short distance from the creek, with several cocks of hay about halfway from the creek to the cornfield; the men purposed to get some of the corn, or anything else that was eatable.
>
> When they got up with the haycocks, they were fired upon by about an equal number of the British, from the cornfield; our people took to the hay, and the others to the fence, where they exchanged a number of shots at each other, neither side inclining to give back. A number, say forty or fifty more of our men, went over and drove the British from the fence; they were by this time reinforced in their turn, and drove us back.
>
> The two parties kept thus alternately reinforcing until we had the most of our regiment in the action. After the officers came to command, the English were soon routed from the place, but we dare not follow them for fear of falling into some snare, as the whole British army was in the vicinity of us.

With the British advance party apparently "routed," the American command pulled the pickets into the fort. This is exactly what General Howe had wanted the Americans to do. The next morning, as the early sun filtered through the gray drizzle, the defenders could see a long, muddy hump about 600 yards from the fort. It was a British redoubt and network of trenches, thrown up during the night. General Howe had begun his regular approaches.

Thomas Mifflin was an aristocratic Pennsylvanian who had rejected the pacifism and neutralism of his Quaker parents and become a violent independence man. Thirsting for action, he had resigned his job as quartermaster and become a brigadier-general. On the evening of the 28th, Mifflin offered to "make the rounds" while Washington and Putnam got some sleep. As he talked to the officers and soldiers on night guard duty, he became more and more alarmed by what he was told. A colonel along the vulnerable left flank told him that the militia there were discouraged and talking surrender. The men were soaked from the continuing rain, those in the trenches had to stand in water halfway up their legs, and "shaves" (rumors) were spreading that the British would attack in the morning, since the rain made gunpowder inoperable and the Americans were known to have virtually no bayonets.

By 4:30 a.m., Washington was awake and writing a report to Congress. After he finished, Mifflin came in and reported what he had heard on his rounds. Mifflin told Washington that within two days the entire force on Brooklyn Heights might surrender en masse. "You must either fight or retreat immediately. What is your strength?" "Nine thousand," answered Washington. "It is not sufficient," Mifflin declared, "we must retreat."

The words seemed to echo the thoughts running through the proud Virginian's mind the last day or so. A British deserter had informed him that everyone in the British camp expected Admiral Howe to place some warships between Brooklyn and New York, where they could shell the rebel intrenchments and seal off their escape. But so far, strangely, the admiral had failed to do so. The way was still clear for a

crossing back to Manhattan.

Washington told Mifflin that he would call a council of war. Would he be willing to propose a retreat at the meeting? Mifflin was appalled that the respected gentleman farmer turned Commander-in-Chief would not face up to proposing it himself. Mifflin kept his feelings to himself and agreed to do it, but he insisted on one provision, "lest his character should suffer." If the council of war voted for a retreat, he wanted to command the rear guard, which would cover the retreat if the enemy should discover it and attack. And, if the council voted for an attack, Mifflin wanted command of "the van," the leading edge of the attack force. Washington agreed. This meeting was the beginning of an alienation between the two men that would culminate in 1777, when Mifflin would be one of the plotters in a conspiracy to replace Washington as commander.

The council met that afternoon at Philip Livingston's Brooklyn summer cottage. They agreed unanimously to retreat. During the morning of the 29th, several hours before the council met, Washington had a secret verbal order delivered to the quartermaster-general at Kings Bridge to commandeer "every kind of water craft from Hell Gate on the Sound to Spuyten Devil Creek [west of Kings Bridge] that could be kept afloat and that had either sails or oars, and have them all in the east harbor of the City by dark." If asked, the officer carrying out this order should say the boats would be used to bring over "reinforcements from New York Island." Washington worked all day making plans for the crossing to take place that night.

The retreat would be kept secret from all but his council of war. The troops must not know, lest panic set in and all chance of an orderly, silent retreat vanish. This the British would easily observe and take advantage of with a quick attack. Washington issued an order for the evacuation of sick and wounded to New York. And he announced that "troops are expected this afternoon from the flying camp in Jersey." To make room for these newcomers, "a proportionate number of regiments" were to be relieved and others shifted. All regiments were ordered to be ready to move at 7 p.m.

We return now to the memoirs of Joseph Plumb Martin, to learn what effect this all had on the soldiers.

> Just at dusk, I, with one or two others of our company, went off to a barn, about half a mile distant, with intent to get some straw to lodge upon, the ground and leaves being drenched in water, and we as wet as they. While I was fumbling about the floor, [I] heard several others, as it appeared, speaking on the mow. Poor fellows, they had better have been at their posts than skulking in a barn on account of a little wet, for I have not the least doubt but that the British had possession of their mortal parts before the noon of the next day.
>
> I ... returned as fast as I could to the regiment, the men were all paraded to march. We were strictly enjoined not to speak, or even cough, when on the march. All orders were given from officer to officer, and communicated to the men in whispers. What such secrecy could mean we could not divine. We marched off in the same way that we had come on to the island, forming various conjectures among ourselves as to our destination. Some were of opinion that we were to endeavor to get on the flank, or in the rear of the enemy. Others, that we were going up the East River to attack them in that quarter; but none, it seems, knew the right of the matter. We marched on, however, until we arrived at the ferry, where we immediately embarked on board the batteaux and were conveyed safely to New York, where we were landed about three o'clock in the morning, nothing against our inclinations.

The crossing was accomplished thanks largely to the seamanship of the "Marblehead amphibians," fishermen in Colonel John Glover's Marblehead, Massachusetts, regiment. During the next few months,

they would prove to be one of Washington's most reliable regiments.

Washington was risking a lot: should either General or Admiral Howe discover what he was attempting, an immediate attack by land or sea would place him in a very vulnerable position. A single deserter could spell disaster. At least the weather appeared to favor Washington's bold move. Private Samuel DeForest describes the storm that occurred that night of August 29-30:

> A most wonderful thunderstorm took place. The thunder and the lightning was dreadful. The clouds run so low that they seemed to break over the houses, and the water run in rivers. The darkness was so great that the two armies could not see each other, although within one hundred rods of each other.

Mrs. John Rapalie, a Brooklyn Tory, heard the commotion and guessed what was going on. Three months earlier, she had obstinately ignored the warnings of local patriot committeemen to discontinue drinking British tea. They caught her again one day, contemptuously sipping tea at her regular tea hour. The committee's threats proved real indeed, as enraged militiamen fired a cannon at her house. The ball went through her glass window, past her sitting form at the table and lodged itself in the wall. Afterwards, she took great pleasure in pointing out the ball to her friends. Now, as the rebel general was attempting to make good the escape of his trapped army, she saw her chance for revenge. She sent her slave to sneak past the rebel lines and inform the British. The slave successfully made it to the King's forces, but the soldiers there were all Hessian. He could not speak a word of their language and they could not understand him, so they sent the troublesome slave back where he came from.

At first, the crossing was hampered by a northwest wind, making sails useless. Nothing but oars could be used. The Marblehead fishermen set to work wrapping the oars to muffle their splash. An officer sent word to Washington that they could never get all the men and

supplies, including heavy artillery, across before dawn. The messenger could not find the commander, so the embarkation continued uninterrupted. About 11 p.m., the northwest wind disappeared, replaced by a southeast zephyr - the best possible wind for boats crossing from Brooklyn to New York, or, for that matter, for the British fleet to sail up from The Narrows to stop the crossing. But Admiral Howe's frigates and sloops were staying put that night.

For the rear guard, Washington gave General Mifflin his best battle-tested troops - what was left of the Maryland and Delaware Continentals, and Colonel Hand's riflemen, all of whom had served well under fire. One soldier later recalled they "kept up fires" all night to deceive the enemy sentries. Among this rear guard was Benjamin Tallmadge, who explains how yet another blessing of nature - fog - assisted Washington in his attempt to sneak off an entire army from under the British noses:

> By 10 o'clock, the troops began to retire from the lines in such a manner that no chasm was made in the lines, but as one regiment left their station on guard, the remaining troops moved to the right and left and filled up the vacancies, while General Washington took his station at the ferry and superintended the embarkation of the troops.
>
> It was one of the most anxious, busy nights that I ever recollect, and being the third in which hardly any of us had closed our eyes in sleep, we were all greatly fatigued. As the dawn of the next day approached, those of us who remained in the trenches became very anxious for our own safety, and when the dawn appeared there were several regiments still on duty. At this time a very dense fog began to rise, and it seemed to settle in a peculiar manner over both encampments. I recollect this peculiar providential occurrence perfectly well; so very dense was the atmosphere that I could scarcely discern a

man at six yards' distance.

Howe had surprised Washington on the 27th, but now, three nights later, the Virginian was pulling off an even bigger surprise. However, the crossing was not entirely without incident. Colonel von Heeringen had during the night pushed his men forward to a rise that overlooked the rebel lines near Gowanus Creek. At dawn, he observed the evacuation and sent a lieutenant on horseback to Howe's headquarters. Howe ordered an immediate advance. The troops reached the water's edge just as the last boatload of Americans was in mid-stream. Noyes Palmer, Jr., wrote home to his parents in Connecticut that day, describing that last boat, occupied by Brooklyn citizens trying to follow the departing army:

> While the soldiers was a coming off last night there was a boat that was loaded with women and children. The Regulars fired a shot from our fort and from our cannon into the boat, which sunk her and all of them was drowned.

Though Washington had saved his army, it was a depleted one, having lost about 200 killed and 800 captured in the Battle of Long Island. Many of the captured Americans were marched off to Flatbush, where they would be held until more permanent quarters could be found. Three American officers and their British guards were stopped on the way there by some Tories trying to sell fish to the guards. One of the American officers offered to buy some, too. The fishmongers replied that they did not sell to "rebels," a term no patriot could stand being called. One witness reported, "This produced reproachful language on both sides, when the officers, laying hold of the fish, began to bandy them about the jaws of the ragamuffins that had insulted them."

The British found that some of these contemptible "mean spirited scoundrels" they had captured showed what they were made of as they

suffered with their wounds. One such American was Joseph Jewett, of Connecticut, a soldier since the day after Lexington. He took 36 hours to die of bayonet wounds to the chest and stomach. On the day after the battle, he "was sensible of being near his end, often repeating that it was hard work to die."

The Battle of Long Island marked a turning point in the public's love affair with the rifle. The terrible fate of Sullivan's riflemen at Flatbush Pass proved the folly of depending on rifle companies unprotected by artillery or musket companies. Without sufficient time to reload, riflemen were defenceless against enemy bayonets. No longer objects of terror, the fabled riflemen were now contemptible in the eyes of their enemies. "These frightful people," remarked a Hessian officer after the battle, "deserve pity rather than fear." Congress was soon requested to have its newly ordered muskets equipped with bayonets two inches longer than those used by the British, so American soldiers could have an advantage in bayonet fighting. The next year, Congress instructed the colonel of a newly recruited rifle regiment to stay home unless they could set out for the army equipped with muskets instead of rifles.

Though Washington's attempt to hold Long Island ended in a costly defeat, at least two hopeful signs came from the battle. First, the army had not dissolved or been destroyed in its first major test. And second, at least some of the troops showed that they could keep ranks and execute maneuvers while under heavy fire. Amidst the fear, anxiety and confusion, Stirling's Continentals displayed amazing presence of mind and discipline. With more such men as these, George Washington could build himself a real army.

Captain George Collier, commander of the British frigate *Rainbow*, had written the day before the evacuation that he and his fellow captains were "in constant expectation of being ordered" to cut off their escape route by sailing to the East River. But Admiral Howe never issued the order, even when a British patrol boat discovered the retreat in progress and reported it to him. Although Captain Collier could not have known Lord Howe's motives for allowing his enemy to escape, he could sense the possible consequences, as he confided to his diary

his "inexpressible astonishment and concern [that] the rebel army have all escaped across the river to New York! ... Now I foresee they will give us trouble enough, and protract the war, Heaven knows how long."

CHAPTER SEVEN
AN ADMIRAL SEEKS PEACE
AND NEARLY LOSES HIS LIFE

"The enemy, after approaching within fifty or sixty yards of the machine ... began to suspect a yankee trick, took alarm, and returned to the island."

> *- An American describing the British discovery of David Bushnell's "sub-marine."*

While Washington was busy ushering the Long Island division of his army across the East River, the division still on Manhattan was on alert for a possible British landing. North of the city, young Private Samuel DeForest and 300 others were spaced forty feet apart, forming a continuous "line of sentries from the North River to the East River." His recollection of that night:

> As soon as the sentries were set, an officer on horse-back rid close to me and says to me, "Let no man pass you this night. Take no countersign nor watchword. If any man come to you, see that he is put under guard. You must keep your station here till morning." There was no more through the night.
>
> The fog thickened, and all was silent as death. At about twelve o'clock and so on, the dogs began to bark, the cattle to low, the Indians to howl and yell. All these noises was from Long Island, by reason of the thick and heavy fog, and all the other dense qualities which con-

spired to tune the air like an organ. It was said later that the Indians was set to yelling that night by the counsel of General Putnam.

About day, the noise was all still, and about sun an hour high the fog began to go off. At this instant a man in the appearance of an officer came up to the guard-house. One of the officers asked him where he was from. He replied, "From Long Island, sir." "What's the word from there?" "Our army has all came off the night past." The [sentry] officer says, "Gentlemen, this man ought to be put under guard." The gentleman who had just came up said, "You can put me under guard if you please, sir, but I presume that in less than forty minutes you will find what I tell you is true." The officer of the guard now says, "Gentlemen, if this is true, we shall be all sacrificed. What can hinder the whole British army now on Long Island? Flushed with conquest, thirty or forty thousand can march their army up the island till they get opposite Kingsbridge in four hours, and their fleet can send them the boats [to] cross their army."

So thought many in the demoralized army of perhaps 20,000 men in New York and nearby points, such as Kings Bridge, which connected northern Manhattan and the mainland. With control of the East River now firmly in British hands, everyone, including Washington himself, felt sure that Howe would cross over at or near Kings Bridge and trap the Continental Army on Manhattan. Surely Washington would now evacuate the city. It made sense to any soldier who took a minute to reason it out, or listen to those who already had. One such man was Noyes Palmer, Jr., who wrote home to his parents on August 30, "expect every hour to leave the City."

Despite the painstaking fortifications built in and around the city during the preceding months, the position was now untenable. The only sane thing to do was give it up and fight Howe somewhere else

some other day. It was already early September - a busy time for these citizen soldiers - they must get in the harvest and cordwood, so their families would not starve or freeze come winter.

So thousands of Washington's soldiers "got the cannon fever and very prudently skulked home." Perhaps they would come back in the spring to fight the British, who would surely be content to spend their winter peaceably in hospitable New York. The arms and ammunition these deserters took away with them, according to a Pennsylvanian who stayed, were a "greater loss than themselves." One man was arrested for trying to carry off a bag stuffed with "notions, among them a cannon ball which, he said, he was taking home to his mother for the purpose of pounding mustard." Within a week after the evacuation from Long Island, 6,000 of the 8,000 Connecticut levies went home. Washington reported to John Hancock, President of Congress:

> Great numbers of them have gone off, in some instances almost by whole regiments. [Their] refusal of almost every kind of subordination has infected another part of the army [the Continental troops].
>
> All these circumstances fully confirm the opinion I ever entertained, and which I more than once in my letters took the liberty of mentioning to Congress, that no dependence could be put in a militia. Men, who have been free and subject to no control, cannot be reduced to order in an instant; and the privileges and exemptions, which they claim and will have, influence the conduct of others; and the aid derived from them is nearly counterbalanced by the disorder, irregularity and confusion they occasion.

Washington recommended that the Congress use the promise of land to entice "permanent enlistment" in a "standing army, to exist during the war." But Congress was still wary of a standing army, and Washington would have to continue for a while longer with a mixture

of one year Continentals, supplemented by shorter term state levies and militia.

He went on in the letter to raise a more immediate question:

> If we should be obliged to abandon the town, ought it to stand as winter quarters for the enemy? They would derive great conveniences from it on one hand; and much property would be destroyed on the other.

Always reluctant to act without authority derived from government, the Commander-in-Chief was asking Congress for permission to burn New York, the third largest city in America. He realized now his chances of successfully defending the city were not good. Congress immediately responded to his inquiry:

> Resolved, that General Washington be acquainted that Congress would have special care taken, in case he should find it necessary to quit New York, that no damage be done to said city by his troops on their leaving it; the Congress having no doubt of their being able to recover the same, though the enemy should for a time obtain possession of it.

So Washington ruled out burning the city. But should he remove the army, rather than risk being trapped? The longer Washington held New York, the longer he could delay Howe's Hudson River rendezvous with the other British army coming south from Canada. But George Washington was no fool - he had barely escaped entrapment on Long Island, and he did not want to risk a similar entrapment on Manhattan. So he began making plans for a withdrawal to Kings Bridge. He wrote to John Hancock, who informed Congress of Washington's plans:

> That the enemy mean to winter in New York, there

can be no doubt; that, with such an armament, they can drive us out is equally clear. The Congress having resolved that it not be destroyed, nothing seems to remain but to determine the time of their taking possession. It is our intent to prolong it as much as possible. ...

[I am] ordering our stores away, except such as may be absolutely necessary to keep as long as any troops remain; that if an evacuation of the city becomes inevitable, which certainly must be the case, there may be as little to remove as possible.

* * * * *

Washington was fortunate that he was left undisturbed by the British for these two weeks following his retreat from Long Island. George Collier, the British naval captain, recorded his own opinion:

[Washington was] certainly very deficient in not expressing his gratitude to General Howe for his <u>kind</u> behaviour towards him. Far from taking the rash resolution of <u>hastily passing</u> over the East River ... and <u>crushing at once</u> a frightened, trembling enemy, he generously gave them time to recover from their panic, to throw up <u>fresh works,</u> to make new arrangements, and to recover from the torpid state the rebellion appeared in from its late shock.

For <u>many succeeding</u> days did our brave veterans, consisting of twenty-two thousand men, stand on the banks of the East River, like Moses on Mount Pisgah, looking at the promised land, little more than half a mile distant. The rebels' standards waved insolently in the air from many diferent quarters of New York. The British troops could scarcely contain their indignation at the

sight and at their own <u>inactivity</u>; the officers were <u>dis-pleased and amazed</u>, not being able to account for the strange delay.

Unbeknownst to all but the highest ranking officers, "the strange delay" was caused by another peace initiative on the part of the brothers Howe. They sent the captured General Sullivan, himself a former Congressman, to deliver an invitation to Congress to send a committee to hear the Howes' peace proposals. The Howes hoped that, after their army's defeat on Long Island, the rebel Congress would be ready to renounce their resolutions on independence.

So, on September 11, while General William Howe was preoccupied with planning his invasion of Manhattan, his brother, Admiral Lord Richard Howe, met on Staten Island with a committee of three from the Continental Congress: John Adams, Benjamin Franklin and Edward Rutledge. Franklin had already written to Lord Howe, back in July, rejecting his first attempt at scheduling such a meeting:

> Directing pardons to be offered the Colonies, who are the very parties injured, can have no other effect than that of increasing our resentment. It is impossible that we should think of submission to a government that has with the most wanton barbarity burnt our defenseless towns in the midst of winter, excited the savages to massacre our farmers, and our slaves to murder their masters, and is even now bringing foreign mercenaries to deluge our settlements with blood.

That was on July 20th, when the Congress was still in the flush of pride and determination that swept the new nation, after passage of the Declaration. Since then, Congress's "Grand American Army" had been routed. More significant than that day's casualties were the desertions and loss of morale since then. William Williams, one of the signers, wrote that if the Declaration had not been passed before the defeat on

Long Island it probably would never have been passed.

Howe and the three Congressmen met at a British guardhouse on Staten Island. In his autobiography, John Adams recalled the meeting:

> The house had been the habitation of military guards and was as dirty as a stable; but his lordship had pre-pared a large handsome room by spreading a carpet of moss and green sprigs from bushes and shrubs in the neighborhood, till he had made it not only wholesome, but romantically elegant; and he entertained us with good claret, good bread, cold ham, tongues.
>
> Lord Howe was profuse in his expressions of grati-tude to the state of Massachusetts for erecting a marble monument in Westminster Abbey to his elder brother, killed in America in the last French war ... [Howe said] "such was his gratitude and affection to this country, on that account, that he felt for America as for a brother, and, if America should fall, he should feel and lament it like the loss of a brother."
>
> Dr. Franklin, with an easy air, replied, "My Lord, we will do our utmost endeavors to save your lordship that mortification."
>
> His lordship appeared to feel this with more sensibility than I could expect; but he only returned, "I suppose you will endeavor to give us employment in Europe" [a Franco-American alliance]. To this observation, not a word, nor a look, from which he could draw any infer-ence escaped any of the committee.

Howe's secretary, in his lengthy notes on the meeting, mentions an important, though delicate, point that Howe then had to make: "If matters could be so settled that the King's government should be re-established, the Congress would of course cease to exist, upon restoration of legal government." Therefore, Lord Howe suggested, at

this meeting he would not deal with Franklin, Adams and Rutledge as members of that illegal body, but rather as "private gentlemen of influence." Franklin, ever the diplomat, "said that His Lordship might consider the gentlemen present in any view he thought proper, and that the conversation might be held as amongst friends." John Adams, not content to be quiet for too long, quickly spoke up. From his auto-biography again:

> "Your lordship may consider me in what light you please, and indeed, I should be willing to consider myself, for a few moments, in any character which would be agreable to your lordship, <u>except that of a British subject</u>."
>
> His lordship, at these words, turned to Dr. Franklin and Mr. Rutledge and said, "Mr. Adams is a decided character," with so much gravity and solemnity that I now believe it meant more than either of my colleagues, or myself, understood at the time.

Perhaps it did, for years later Adams learned that he was on a list Howe brought from England of Americans to be excluded from the general amnesty. Howe went on with his opening remarks, mentioning "that his powers were, generally, to restore peace and grant pardons, and to confer upon means of establishing a re-union," but the real substance of a settlement would be handled by Parliament. He made it clear, too, that Parliament would not deal with the colonies until they renounced independence. He then asked for Franklin, Adams and Rutledge to speak their views.

Franklin started by pointing out that Congress's Petition to the King the year before had been answered with the Prohibitory Act, foreign mercenaries, coastal cities burnt, slaves and Indians aroused, etc. All "former attachment was <u>obliterated</u> ... America could not return again to the domination of Great Britain."

Adams spoke next and emphasized that the members of Congress

had not acted "upon their own authority" in passing the Declaration of Independence, but "that they had been instructed so to do by all the Colonies and that it was not in their power to treat otherwise than as independent States."

Rutledge, in his turn, expressed his conviction that Britain would benefit greatly from a healthy commerce and an alliance with an independent United States, for "the people were now settled and happy under that government and would not (even if they, the Congress, could desire it) return to the King's government."

The meeting then came to a close, both parties disappointed, but not surprised, at the outcome. Franklin urged Howe "to get fresh instructions from home," but "Lord Howe replied it was in vain to think of his receiving instructions to treat upon that ground" (independence).

The three Congressmen returned to Philadelphia to tell an anxious Congress that "America is to expect nothing but upon total unconditional submission," and Lord Howe "has no propositions to make us." John Penn, of North Carolina, summed up the mood in Congress: "we have no alternitive for our safety but our spirit as soldiers." Rutledge wrote to General Washington, "Our reliance continues, therefore, to be, under God, on your wisdom and fortitude and that of your forces."

* * * * *

Admiral Howe was fortunate to be alive to hold this September 11th conference, for just four nights before there had been an attempt on his life and that of everyone else aboard his 64-gun flagship *Eagle* in New York harbor. The attempt to blow the flagship out of the water was made by a single man, in the world's first workable "sub-marine."

For more than a year, young David Bushnell, of Connecticut, with the assistance of his brother, had been building and testing David's invention on a secluded island in the lower Connecticut River between Saybrook and Lyme. Made of wood and metal, it was shaped like a clam and navigated by its single occupant, who propelled and steered it by turning cranks. Years later, Charles Griswold, who came to

know the pilot of this "famous water machine," described its offensive capability in a letter to a Yale College professor:

> [A gunpowder] magazine was attached to the back of the machine by means of a screw. This screw could be withdrawn from the magazine, by which the latter was immediately detached, and a clock commenced going.
>
> But the most difficult point of all to be gained was to fasten this magazine to the bottom of a ship. A very sharp iron screw was provided with a crank, by which the engineer was to force it into the ship's bottom. This screw was next to be disengaged from the machine, and left adhering to the ship's bottom.

By August, the Bushnell brothers had successfully blown up a useless old merchant ship donated for testing purposes. They hauled the submarine overland to Manhattan and waited for a calm night with the right tide conditions. On September 7th, conditions were right and the submarine, by now dubbed the *Turtle*, was ready. With the Bushnell brothers both sick, Sergeant Ezra Lee would make the attempt, which was also described in the letter quoted from earlier:

> At 11 o'clock a party embarked in two or three whale boats, with Bushnell's machine in tow. They rowed down as near the fleet as they dared, when Sergeant Lee entered the machine, was cast off, and the boats returned.
>
> Lee now found the ebb tide rather too strong and, before he was aware, [it] had drifted him down past the men of war. He however immediately got the machine about, and by hard labour at the crank for the space of five glasses by the ship's bells, or two and a half hours, he arrived under the stern of one of the ships at about slack water. Day had now dawned, and by the light of

the moon he could see the people on board, and heard their conversation. This was the moment for diving: he accordingly closed up overhead, let in water, and descended under the ship's bottom.

He now applied the screw, and did all in his power to make it enter, but owing probably in part to the ship's copper, and the want of adequate pressure to enable the screw to get a hold upon the bottom, his attempts all failed; at each ... [turn of the crank] the machine rebounded from the ship's bottom.

Frustrated by not being able to penetrate the copper plating, Lee frequently came up to the surface "searching for exposed plank. Once, he was discovered by the watch on deck and heard them speculate upon him, but concluded a drifted log had paid them a visit." Finally, "the increasing light of the morning" making his discovery certain, he "concluded that the best generalship would be to commence an immediate retreat." The letter goes on to describe Ezra Lee's retreat:

He now had before him a distance of more than four miles to traverse, but the tide was favourable. His compass having got out of order, he was under the necessity of looking out from the top of the machine very frequently to ascertain his course, and at best made a very zigzag track.

The [British] soldiers at Governor's Island espied the machine, and curiosity drew several hundreds upon the parapet to watch its motions. At last a party came down to the beach, shoved off a barge, and rowed towards it. At that moment, Sergeant Lee thought he saw his certain destruction, and as a last act of defence, let go the magazine, expecting that they would seize that likewise, and thus all would be blown to atoms together.

Providence, however, otherwise directed it: the en-

emy, after approaching within fifty or sixty yards of the machine, and seeing the magazine detached, began to suspect a <u>yankee trick</u>, took alarm and returned to the island.

Approaching the city, he soon made a signal, the boats came to him and brought him safe and sound to the shore. The magazine in the mean time had drifted past Governor's Island into the East River, where it exploded with tremendous violence, throwing large columns of water and pieces of wood that composed it into the air. Gen. Putnam, with many officers, stood on the shore spectators of this explosion.

"That'll do it for 'em!" shouted Old Put. The world's first workable submarine ceased to exist a few weeks later, when the British sailed up the Hudson and destroyed all the rebel ships near Kings Bridge, among them the sloop that was home base for the little *Turtle*. The submarine went down while still aboard the ship. Lacking funds, Bushnell waited "for a more favorable opportunity" to build another, but it never came. He soon enlisted and continued in the service through the end of the war, enoying some success with another invention - water mines - at the Battle of the Kegs, on the Delaware River in 1778.

Admiral Lord Richard Howe had survived the attempt on his life, and was able to hold his fruitless peace conference. Nothing coming of his attempt to win back the colonies peacefully, he told his brother, General William Howe, to go ahead with the plans to invade Manhattan. Ambrose Serle, the admiral's secretary, summed up the Staten Island Conference: "They met, they talked, they parted, and now nothing remains but to fight it out."

CHAPTER EIGHT
HOWE TAKES NEW YORK

"Are these the men with which I am to defend America!"

> - General Washington, watching
> his troops flee from the British.

By September 12, the day after the fruitless Staten Island Conference, General Howe had his troops in place to cross the East River and take the city by storm. If he waited a few more days he would have been able to take the city without a fight, for Washington was making plans to evacuate New York. But Howe did not know that. He spread his army out along Long Island's shore north of Brooklyn, as well as on some of the islands in the East River. Facing some of the troops on Blackwell's Island were some Connecticut levies on the Manhattan shore at Turtle Bay. Among them was Private Joseph Plumb Martin:

> These British soldiers seemed to be very busy in chasing some scattering sheep that happened to be so unlucky as to fall in their way. One of the soldiers, however, thinking perhaps he could do more mischief by killing some of us, had posted himself on a point of rocks at the southern extremity of the island and kept firing at us as we passed along the bank. Several of his shots passed between our files, but we took little notice of him, thinking he was so far off that he could do us but little hurt and that we could do him none at all, until one of the guard asked the officers if he might discharge his

piece at him. As it was charged and would not hinder us long, the officer gave his consent. He rested his old six-feet barrel across a fence and sent an express to him. The man dropped, but as we then thought it was only to amuse us, we took no further notice of it but passed on. In the morning, upon our return, we saw the brick colored coat still lying in the same position. It was a long distance to hit a single man.

Washington was convinced that Howe would land above Kings Bridge or just below it, near the village of Harlem. On the fourteenth he moved his headquarters to the Morris House on Harlem Heights. Howe's recent maneuvers had indicated the invasion would be at that end of the island. The first frigate up the East River two days before had bombarded Horne's Hook, trying to silence the American batteries there, presumably to facilitate movement up the East River. Also, from Harlem a large encampment of troops could be seen across the river on the northwestern tip of Long Island. Washington sent some of his best regiments to Harlem, Smallwood's Marylanders and Knowlton's Connecticut Rangers.

Howe did, in fact, plan on landing at Harlem, but changed the target to Kip's Bay, closer to New York, after the unsuccessful attempt to silence the rebel battery at Horne's Hook. And the captains of the ships which would provide covering fire made it known they were reluctant to sail so close to the swirling waters of Hell Gate, at the convergence of the East River and Long Island Sound. Kip's Bay was a promising site for a landing: the rebel lines there had no cannon, were sparsely manned, and were only 600 yards from the Post Road - the vital artery of Manhattan, running its entire length from New York to Kings Bridge. Between the Kip's Bay shore and the Post Road was a large V-shaped meadow. The meadow would be a good assembly area for the troops after they landed, and it was surrounded by rising ground which would serve as a good defensive perimeter.

Guarding the lengthy middle sector of the East River shore, which

included Kip's Bay, was Nathanael Greene's division of Connecticut and Massachusetts levies. General Greene was still suffering from the fever that had forced him to give up his command on Long Island three days before that disastrous battle. His command on the East River devolved to Joseph Spencer, a 60-year-old militia general from Connecticut. His troops were spread quite thinly over the five mile sector from New York's outskirts to Horne's Hook. Most of them had never been tested under battle conditions. The men were on 12-hour shifts, which meant that if Howe attacked he would meet only half of any given point's defenders, unless Spencer quickly sent in reserves from another point in his sector. Spencer was not likely to do that, being a general that kept very loose control of his regiments and let each of his colonels decide for themselves how best to defend in case of attack.

The same barges that had carried the Regulars from Staten Island to Long Island the month before were moved up the coast after dark. Now they were hidden in coves where Newtown Creek emptied into the East River. In his journal, Major Carl Leopold Bauermeister notes that General Howe had scheduled the invasion for September 13

> because it was the eighteenth anniversary of General Wulff's victory at Quebec. Consequently the watchword was "Quebec" and the countersign "Wulff." However, the frigates were too dilatory for this attack. Not until five o'clock in the evening of the 14th did [they] leave the fleet to sail up the East River.

That evening, the five frigates anchored in the East River opposite Kip's Bay. The invasion they would support with covering fire was now scheduled for the next morning, Sunday the fifteenth. That same night, on the Manhattan shore, Private Martin's company was shifted from Turtle Bay to Kip's Bay. He couldn't sleep much that night and heard his company's sentinels making their rounds.

Every half hour [they] passed the watchword to each other, "All is well." I heard the British on board their shipping answer, "We will alter your tune before tomorrow night." And they were as good as their word for once.

Thirteen thousand British and Hessians would take part in the invasion. The advance division of 4,500 rose at 2 a.m. to break camp and march to the assembly points for the dawn embarkation. General Howe had earlier given them final instructions:

An attack upon the enemy being shortly intended, the soldiers are reminded of their evident superiority on the 27th August, by charging the rebels with their bayonets even in woods where they had thought themselves invincible. The General therefore recommends to the troops an entire dependence upon their bayonets, with which they will ever command that success which their bravery so well deserves.

Bartholomew James, a midshipman on the frigate *Orpheus*, noted that "at six in the morning we anchored about fifty yards from the enemy's entrenchments." When Private Martin arose that morning, the long cannon barrels of one of those five ships were "within musket shot of us," so close he could "read her name as distinctly as though I had been directly under her stern. They appeared to be very busy on shipboard, but we lay still and showed our good breeding by not interfering with them." A few minutes later, he saw eighty-four flatboats, each carrying fifty soldiers, "coming out of a creek or cove on the Long Island side of the water, filled with British soldiers. They appeared like a large clover field in full bloom."

Leading the first division was General Henry Clinton, who had spent most of the evening before trying in vain to talk Howe out of the Kip's Bay site. His recommendation had been for a landing above Kings

Bridge, to trap all the rebel troops on Manhattan. Clinton could picture in his mind the Regulars floundering in the muddy riverbank "entirely exposed to the enemy's fire." He saw "little prospect of victory without buying it dear."

The Americans onshore watched their enemy being slowly rowed across the mile-wide East River. Some of those watching, perhaps to release the tension of silence, shouted insults, waved their muskets overhead, and challenged the sailors on the five frigates "to come on shore." The sailors ignored them and methodically went about loading their cannon and preparing their ships for action. Already, diversionary fire could be heard from the south, where warships were bombarding the city's shoreline batteries.

The Kip's Bay "lines" were "nothing more than a ditch dug along the bank of the river with the dirt thrown out towards the water." Most of the defenders had just arrived from Connecticut within the last few days, having never before faced an enemy, white or Indian, intent on killing them. They must have wondered at the injustice of Howe choosing this very spot for his invasion, when the 13-mile length of Manhattan Island must have offered so many other landing sites. Ironically, Washington had scheduled Kip's Bay for evacuation before nightfall this very day!

The Yankees onshore were not the only men with queasy stomachs as the flat-bottomed boats slowly "paraded" on the East River. The Hessian troops in some of those boats may have begun to wonder why the five warships were still silent. By now, the 16 sailors in each barge had rowed them almost within musket range of those "breastworks filled with men" with muskets levelled directly at them. A British officer, Lord Francis Rawdon, recalled:

> The Hessians, who were not used to this water business and who conceived that it must be exceedingly uncomfortable to be shot at whilst they were quite defenceless and jammed so close together, began to sing hymns immediately. Our men expressed their feelings as

strongly, though in a different manner, by damning themselves and the enemy indiscrimanently with wonderful fervency.

Suddenly, the five frigates let go almost simultaneously with 86 guns. Private Martin thought his "head would go with the sound. I made a frog's leap for the ditch and lay as still as I possibly could and began to consider which part of my carcass was to go first." Midshipman Bartholomew James recalled the ships keeping up "a tremendous fire for fifty-nine minutes, in which time we fired away in the *Orpheus* alone 5,376 pounds of powder."

The meticulous William Howe had planned this invasion well. A militia chaplain named Benjamin Trumbull noticed the leading barges make a last minute change of direction.

> The ships about 10 o'clock began from the mouths of near an 100 cannon a most furious cannonade [which overshot the trenches, and] buried our men with sand and sods of earth and made such a dust and smoke that there was no possibility of firing on the enemy to any advantage. The ships from their round tops kept up a smart fire with swivels loaded with grape shot which they were able to fire almost into the entrenchments they were so near. The boats [barges] all this time kept out of the reach of the musketry and finally, turning off a little north of the lines, in the smoke of the ships they made good their landing without receiving any annoyance from our troops.

Chaplain Trumbull noted in his journal that there had been "no general order given how to support each other in a general attack, or any disposition made for it." So the men at Kip's Bay, and those to their north at Turtle Bay and to their south at Stuyvesant's Point, "attempted an escape" toward Harlem. The British and Hessians, after

landing, swung around with the precision of trained soldiers and, with bayonets levelled, marched at double time to cut off their escape.

From the *Orpheus*, Bartholomew James was sent with a few other sailors to help "tow on shore the flat boats," where they would remain until the sailors that had rowed them rested enough to start the trip back across. James recalled his adventures on shore, where he stayed for a while after helping beach the boats:

> Curiosity led me to follow the army through the works, where I saw a Hessian sever a rebel's head from his body and clap it on a pole in the entrenchments. While I was amusing myself with these sights, and picking up some curious trifles, several volleys of musketry was fired from a boat belonging to the *Orpheus* at us, who had, in rowing along shore, taken us for rebels. As I knew the boat, I made signs of friendship, but all in vain; and I was obliged to throw away my little affairs and take to my heels as the enemy had done before.
>
> On my arrival on board, I found the second lieutenant amusing the captain with an account of his attack on a body of rebels, which I gave him to understand was myself, by which I lost some valuable swords, [etc.] ... Captain Hudson permitted me to go again on shore with the above lieutenant [Mr. Barton] but all our little matters were taken and we procured only nine drums and some fusees.
>
> Mr. Barton leaving me by accident on shore, I rambled into the woods with one of the midshipmen of the *Phoenix* who had with him the gunner and seven men. On our entrance into an orchard we took a rebel prisoner who had lain concealed there for some time. From this man we learned there had been a skirmish in the woods with the rebels and a body of the Hessians and that the former was dispersed all round the woods.

Having consulted each other on the consequences of advancing further from the ships, and pleased in some measure with the success of taking the above man, we determined to go in quest of some more and shortly after heard several voices in an orchard. We assembled with our muskets presented to the gate and levelling at some men we saw in the grass were about to fire, when up start two or three hundred Hessians with flaming large brass caps on, and with charged bayonets advanced rapidly towards us.

The sudden unexpected surprise of such a visit alarmed us prodigiously, and we made signs of being friends, which had little or no effect in our favour, as on their coming close to us they knocked us down with their muskets, frequently using the word "rebel," for which they really took us. In vain I assured them with signs that we were part of the British navy and pointed to my white cuff, having changed my clothes on going on board, that I might not a second time be taken for an American.

But I was much surprised, and in fact at a loss how to act, when they pointed out a rebel officer who lay there with a leg shot off, who had on the very exact uniform of a midshipman, which having explained to each other, they again beat us unmercifully and would undoubtedly have put their bayonets through us had not General Pigot come to our relief, when they made a thousand ridiculous apologies for their treatment, and we returned to our ships in need of both cook and doctor, and totally weary of our expedition.

Four miles to the north, on Harlem Heights, George Washington heard the thunder of the frigates and, with some other generals, rode "with all possible despatch towards the place of landing." On the west

side of Inclenberg Height, or Murray Hill, he came upon the defenders fleeing west on the Cross Road (approximately where 42nd Street is today). General Parsons, whose brigade it was that was fleeing in disorder, helped Washington try to rally them to form and make a stand. The Commander-in-Chief, himself, barked out orders to the troops: "Take the walls! Take the cornfield!" Though most kept moving north, others obediently took up positions behind the stone walls and corn shocks. Some of these men stayed only until the Virginian turned his back. When the enemy was soon spotted on the crest of Inclenberg Height, the panic proved too contagious and everyone resumed their flight. Washington later recalled the scene:

> I used every means in my power to rally and get them into some order; but my attempts were fruitless and ineffectual; and on the appearance of a small party of the enemy, not more than sixty or seventy, their disorder increased, and they ran away in the greatest confusion, without firing a single shot.

At this moment of extreme frustration and anger, Washington showed a rare example of that legendary temper which he usually worked so hard to keep under control. After these troops had fled upon sight of the enemy, Washington was left "in a hazardous situation, so that his attendants, to extricate him out of it, caught the bridle of his horse, and gave him a different direction." General Greene wrote that Washington "was so vexed at the infamous conduct of the troops, that he sought death rather than life." General Weedon of Virginia recalled that Washington "struck several officers in their flight, three times dashed his hatt on the ground and at last exclaimed 'Good God, have I got such troops as those!' It was with difficulty his friends could get him to quit the field, so great was his emotions." Another officer claimed he threw his hat on the ground, exclaiming, "Are these the men with which I am to defend America!"

* * * * *

Two of the men fleeing were fifteen-year-old Private Joseph Plumb Martin and a sickly former neighbor of his. Like everyone else, they were trying "to escape from death or captivity, which at that period of the war was almost certain death." Private Martin:

> In retreating we had to cross a level, clear spot of ground. ... The grapeshot ... served to quicken our motions. A little out of the reach of their combustibles, we went into a house by the highway in which were two women and some small children, all crying most bitterly. We each of us drank a glass and, bidding them good-by, betook ourselves to the highway again.
>
> We had not gone far before we saw a party of men, apparently hurrying on in the same direction with ourselves. We endeavored hard to overtake them, but on approaching them we found they were not of our way of thinking: they were Hessians. We immediately altered our course and took the main [Post] road leading to Kings Bridge. We had not long been on this road before we saw another party, just ahead of us, whom we knew to be Americans. They were fired upon by a party of British from a cornfield and all was immediately in confusion again. I believe the enemy's party was small, but our people were militia, and the demons of fear and disorder seemed to take full possession of all and everything that day. When I came to the spot where the militia were fired upon, the ground was literally covered with arms, knapsacks, [etc.] ... All I picked up of the plunder was a block-tin syringe, which afterwards helped to procure a Thanksgiving dinner.
>
> We had to advance slowly, for my comrade having been some time unwell was now so overcome by heat,

hunger, and fatigue that he became suddenly and violently sick. I took his musket and endeavored to encourage him on. I was loathe to leave him behind, although I was anxious to find the main part of the regiment. We soon came in sight of a large party of Americans ahead of us who appeared to have come into this road by some other route. We were within sight of them when they were fired upon by another party of the enemy. They returned but a very few shots and then scampered off as fast as their legs would carry them.

... [Later] we found a wounded man and some of his comrades endeavoring to get him off. I stopped to assist them in constructing a sort of litter to lay him upon, when my sick companion growing impatient moved on. We had proceeded but a short distance before we found our retreat cut off by a party of the enemy stretched across the island. I immediately quitted the road and went into the fields, where there happened to be a small spot of boggy land covered with low brushes and weeds. Into these I ran, and squatting down concealed myself from their sight. Several of the British came so near to me that I could see the buttons on their clothes. They, however, soon withdrew and left the coast clear for me again.

What had become of my sick comrade or the rest of my companions I knew not. I still kept the sick man's musket. I was unwilling to leave it, for it was his own property and I knew he valued it highly and I had a great esteem for him. I had indeed enough to do to take care of my own concerns; it was exceeding hot weather, and I was faint, having slept but little the preceding night, nor had I eaten a mouthful of victuals for more than twenty-four hours.

Private Martin continued on, and came upon a brook where he saw one man drown himself. Martin "waddled on as fast as I could" and, after crossing more fields, came upon some men resting under some trees. Among them

> was my sick friend. I was exceeding glad to find him, for I had but little hope of ever seeing him again. He was sitting near the fence with his head between his knees. I tapped him upon the shoulder and asked him to get up and go on with me. "No," said he, at the same time regarding me with a most pitiful look, "I must die here." I endeavored to argue the case with him, but all to no purpose; he insisted upon dying there. I told him he should not die there nor anywhere else that day if I could help it, and at length with more persuasion and some force I succeeded in getting him upon his feet again and to moving on.

After a drenching rain, Martin and the man stumbled upon a group of two or three hundred American soldiers, who would not let them pass.

> I remonstrated with the officer who detained us. I told him that our regiment was just ahead. He asked me how I knew that. I could not tell him, but I told him I had a sick man with me who was wet and would die if exposed all night to the damp cold air, hoping by this to move his compassion. I shall not soon forget the answer he gave me. "Well," said he, "if he dies the country will be rid of one who can do it no good."

Martin and his sick friend eventually slipped away in the night and the next day found their regiment, where they finally got some food.

* * * * *

Within an hour after the landing had started, Clinton's advance force of 4,500 was completely ashore and had already secured the meadow's wooded perimeter. Despite his desire to move all the way to the Hudson, and thus seal off those rebels still in the city, Clinton knew better than to disobey Howe's strict order to secure the meadow area and wait for him to bring over the next wave of barges.

The nearly 4,000 troops still in New York were General Israel Putnam's division. He rode up the Bloomingdale Road and met with Washington on the Cross Road to discuss their extrication from the trap. "Old Put" quickly returned to the city and ordered his young aides-de-camp, including Aaron Burr, to ride to the widely dispersed posts and tell the officers to form columns for a forced march to Harlem Heights. Sixty-seven cannon, tons of gunpowder, ammunition and provisions, as well as precious blankets and spare clothes would all have to be left behind. The swift, somewhat disorderly retreat was a risky move: Putnam suspected that Howe might be waiting in ambush anywhere between New York and Harlem.

Putnam kept his two-mile long column moving through pastures and fields west of the Bloomingdale Road, with scouts moving amongst the trees looking for signs of the enemy. Old Put was seen constantly flying back and forth along the column, his horse covered with foam, wherever his presence was needed to spur the men on, or to direct the scouts. Colonel Humphreys noted, "Without his extraordinary exertions, it is probable the entire corps would have been cut in pieces." Much of the credit, too, belonged to his aide, Aaron Burr, whose leadership and knowledge of the terrain proved invaluable. When they passed directly west of Inclenberg Height, there was not an enemy soldier in sight. Where was Howe?

General Howe had by now crossed over the river to Kip's Bay and, among other things, was "looking for comfortable quarters for himself." Frederick Mackenzie, of the Royal Welsh Fusiliers, boldly urged the Commander-in-Chief to send a brigade west of Inclenberg Height

and seal off the escape of any rebel troops still in the city. Mackenzie noted Howe's reaction in his diary:

> He is slow and not inclined to attend to whatever may be considered as advice. ... Upon my urging the matter with some earnestness ... he grew angry and said I hurried him, and that he would place the brigade as he thought proper.

Howe was sticking to his plan: land the first wave and secure the area, but do not risk a general engagement until the remaining troops were safely across. Howe had arrived at 2 p.m., but it took until 5 p.m. to land all the troops. While he waited for the second and third waves to arrive, Howe spent a good part of the afternoon with his generals and the exiled governor in the house of a Quaker merchant named Murray, on Inclenberg Height. Putnam's escape was widely attributed to the hospitality of Mrs. Murray, such as in this British account:

> Mrs. Murray treated them with cake and wine, and they were induced to tarry two hours or more, Governor Tryon frequently joking her about her American friends. By this happy incident, General Putnam, by continuing his march, escaped a rencounter with a greatly superior force, which must have proved fatal to his whole party. Ten minutes, it is said, would have been sufficient for the enemy to have secured the road at the turn and entirely cut off General Putnam's retreat. It has since become almost a common saying among our officers, that Mrs. Murray saved this part of the American army.

Overall, the invasion had been almost a bloodless affair. The British suffered only one wounded man, and the Hessians about fifteen casualties, the Americans perhaps sixty. However, about 300 American

soldiers were captured. Late in the day, General Howe sent a brigade down the Post Road to secure the city. But his brother beat him to it. When it became apparent that Putnam was abandoning the city, Admiral Lord Howe sent a large party of marines to take possession of Fort George at the tip of the island (present day Battery Park). Lord Howe's secretary, Ambrose Serle, observed New York's long awaited liberation:

> The King's forces took possession of the place, incredible as it may seem, without the loss of a man. Nothing could equal the expressions of joy shewn by the inhabitants upon the arrival of the King's officers among them. They even carried some of them upon their shoulders about the streets and behaved in all respects, women as well as men, like overjoyed Bedlamites. A woman pulled down the rebel standard upon the fort, and a[nother] woman hoisted up in its stead His Majesty's flag, after trampling the other under foot with the most contemptuous indignation.

The next morning, the exiled governor and a brigade of the King's soldiers marched triumphantly down Broad Way. The soldiers almost immediately proceeded to identify deserted rebel houses, marking the doors with "a broad R" so the properties could be confiscated. Most of the plundering was done by the Hessians, who had no trouble with confiscation, but some with identification. Ebenezer Hazard reports:

> The Hessian and British troops disagree and are kept entirely separate. The latter do not like the former's being allowed to plunder, while they are prohibited from doing it. Those rascals plunder all indiscriminately; if they see any thing they like, they say, "Rebel, good for Hesse-mans," and seize it for their own use. They have no idea of the distinction of Whig and Tory.

CHAPTER NINE
THE YANKEES SHOW THEIR COURAGE:
HARLEM HEIGHTS AND NATHAN HALE

"I do not value my life if we do but get the day."
                                        - Lt.-Colonel Thomas Knowlton.

"I only regret that I have but one life to lose for my country."
                                        - Captain Nathan Hale.

Once his entire invasion force of 13,000 was ashore, General Howe moved north and camped his army for the night between Horne's Hook and Bloomingdale. Lieutenant George Harris, of the Fifth Regiment of Foot, described his own accomodations that evening in a letter to his uncle:

> After landing in York Island, we drove the Americans into their works beyond the eighth mile stone from New York, and thus got possession of the best half of the island. We placed our picquets, borrowed a sheep, killed, cooked and ate some of it, and then went up to sleep on a gate, which we took the liberty of throwing off its hinges, covering our feet with an American tent, for which we should have cut poles and pitched, had it not been so dark. Give me such living as we enjoy at present, such a hut and such company, and I would not care three farthings if we stayed all the winter.

George Washington returned to Harlem Heights to speed up the intrenching there, as he expected Howe to take advantage of the

confusion and attack in the next day or two. The lines there ran for over a mile from the Harlem River to the Hudson, and consisted of a double row of breastworks and intrenchments with abatis sticking out in front - all atop steep hills. On his way there, Washington regained the composure he had lost on seeing the rout west of Kip's Bay. A story was soon after printed in the newspapers that he stopped his horse on the Bloomingdale Road, not far from the Cross Road, to ask a lone soldier why he was sitting there when the enemy was not far behind. The man answered, he'd "rather be killed or taken by the enemy than be trodden to death by cowards."

The day after Kip's Bay, Monday, September 16th, George Washington rose at 5 a.m., as was his habit, to work on correspondence and orders for a few hours. He sent off an express rider to Philadelphia to report the disastrous "Kip's Bay affair" to Congress.

> We are now encamped with the main body of the
> army upon the heights of Harlem, where I should hope
> the enemy will meet with a retreat in case [they] attack,
> if our troops would behave with tolerable bravery. But
> experience has convinced me that this is a matter to be
> wished, rather than expected.

The Yankee troops awoke to taunts of "Kips Bay cowards" and "dastards" from the Pennsylvanians, Marylanders, and a Virginia regiment that had just arrived the day before. All these troops had been safe on Harlem Heights, far from the enemy's fire. This reputation, now applied freely to all New Englanders, was somewhat but not entirely lessened later that day by the actions of 36-year-old Lieutenant Colonel Thomas Knowlton, of Connecticut.

Knowlton, a veteran of the French and Indian War, had commanded the Connecticut militia behind the rail fence at Bunker Hill, on June 17, 1775. General Howe's flanking maneuver, the key to his battle plan that day, had been stopped cold by Knowlton's men and others. Tall, handsome and courageous, Thomas Knowlton was greatly ad-

mired by his own troops and his fellow officers. Aaron Burr acknowledged that it was "impossible to promote such men too quickly."

After Howe's stunning surprise night march through Jamaica Pass that had led to the rout on Long Island, Washington had decided he absolutely must have better intelligence about his adversary's movements. He asked Knowlton to form and lead a battalion of "Rangers" to perform scouting and other hazardous intelligence gathering duties. Knowlton selected volunteers from Connecticut's Continental regiments.

From the Point of Rocks - the steep bluff that formed the southeastern tip of Harlem Heights - a man with a spyglass might look down on Harlem Plains to observe not only the village of Harlem but also the Post Road where it disappeared into the woods at McGowan's Pass (today, a northern boundary of Central Park). Toward the Hudson, the Plains narrowed to what was called the Hollow Way, where the low land contrasted sharply with the steep bluffs of Harlem Heights on the north and Vandewater's Heights on the south (today's Morningside Heights). These latter heights were largely wooded and, therefore, could conceal troop movements from the direction of Bloomingdale, making it the most likely route for an attack by Howe.

Washington ordered Knowlton to take his Rangers across the Hollow Way and scout toward Bloomingdale. They advanced past Hoaglandt's farm nearly to Jones's house, only two or three hundred yards from Clinton's camp on the Bloomingdale Road. There, British pickets sighted them through the trees and gave the alarm. Two "companies of light infantry were sent to dislodge them," according to a British Captain Harris, and were soon reinforced by grenadiers. The following excerpt, printed in the Connecticut Gazette, was taken from a letter Captain Stephen Brown, of the Rangers, wrote to a friend:

> On Monday morning the General ordered us to go
> and take the enemy's advanced guard; accordingly we
> set out just before day and found where they were; at

day-brake we were discovered by the enemy, who were 400 strong, and we were 120. They marched up within six rods of us and there formed to give us battle, which we were ready for; and Colonel Knowlton gave orders to fire, which we did, and stood theirs till we perceived they were getting their flank-guards round us. After giving them eight rounds apiece, the Colonel gave orders for retreating, which we performed very well, without the loss of a man while retreating, though we lost about 10 while in action.

Another Ranger, Oliver Burnham, told it as follows:

The Colonel marked a place about eight or ten rods from the wall, and charged us not to rise or fire a gun until the enemy reached that place. The British followed in solid column, and soon were on the ground designated when we gave them nine rounds and retreated.

While Knowlton was thus engaged, Washington had finished his letter writing at the Morris House and was riding down to the Point of Rocks to reconnoiter the Plains. He could distinctly hear musket fire toward Bloomingdale and was told that Knowlton had not yet come in. Should he send reinforcements to cover Knowlton's retreat? He did not want to be lured into a trap, and he could not be sure how the troops would behave if he sent them out, based on their scandalous showing the day before. Yet, even the smallest victory might be a tremendous morale boost to the despondent army. First, he must know whether the enemy was approaching in strength. So he dispatched his adjutant, Colonel Joseph Reed, of Philadelphia, to go "down to our most advanced guard" (the Rangers) then quickly ride back and report.

Reed found them near the Vandewater farmhouse. The Rangers were falling back rapidly but in good order, pressured by a superior force of light infantry. From Claremont Hill, where the British pursuit

stopped (site of present-day Grant's Tomb), they could look down and see Knowlton's men crossing the part of the Hollow Way near the Hudson, known locally as Martje David's Fly. It was the third time in three weeks that they had seen the Yankees flee before them. Mockingly, a British drummer put a trumpet to his lips and blew the huntsman's call of "Gone to Earth," meaning the fox was dead and the chase was over. Reed recorded the moment:

> Finding how things were going I went over to the General to get some support for the brave fellows who had behaved so well. By the time I got to him the enemy appeared in open view and in the most insulting manner sounded their bugle horns as is usual after a fox chase. I never felt such a sensation before; it seemed to crown our disgrace.

Reed urged Washington to teach the British a lesson for this display of arrogance. He reported that he had not seen any enemy forces other than this party, which had advanced dangerously far from the British lines. While Washington was mulling over Reed's report, Knowlton came in with information confirming the enemy strength. The Commander-in-Chief now felt it safe to give battle. Here was an opportunity, as he later told Patrick Henry, for his troops "to recover that military ardour which is of the utmost moment to an army." Tench Tilghman, an aide-de-camp, wrote the following account:

> When our men came in they informed the General that there was a party of about 300 behind a woody hill, tho' they only showed a very small party to us. Upon this the General laid a plan for attacking them in the rear and cutting off their retreat, which was to be effected in the following manner: Major Leitch with three [rifle] companies of Colonel Weedon's Virginia regiment, and Colonel Knowlton with his Rangers, were to steal round

while a party [of Rhode Islanders] were to march towards them and seem as if they intended to attack in front, but not to make any real attack till they saw our men fairly in their rear. The bait took as to one part; as soon as they saw our party in front the enemy ran down the hill [into the Hollow Way] and took possession of some fences and began to fire at them.

The Rhode Islanders who had so eagerly volunteered to be "the bait" had crossed the Hollow Way and started up Vandewater's Heights. Upon the enemy's charge, they acted the part of Kip's Bay cowards and fell back, luring the pursuing light infantry into the open ground of the Hollow Way. While this was taking place, Knowlton's Rangers and Leitch's riflemen were moving forward, east of the action, screened by a woody ridge. The Rhode Islanders could wait no longer to see if Knowlton and Leitch had reached the enemy's rear, but vigorously returned the light infantry's fire.

[They] let the enemy advance until they arrived at the fence, when they arose and poured in a volley upon them. How many of the enemy were killed and wounded could not be known, as the British were always as careful as Indians to conceal their losses. There were, doubtless, some killed, as I myself counted nineteen ball-holes through a single rail of the fence.

Knowlton and Leitch, moving in one long column, were making good progress and might have got in the enemy's rear, but for a few imprudent riflemen who could not resist taking some shots at the unsuspecting redcoats who seemed so close, and were already engaged with the Rhode Island troops. As soon as these few fired, the column instinctively stopped and other men began shooting. The attempt to get in the enemy's rear was abandoned and a flank attack began from the top of the ridge.

The British light infantry, who had expected the Rhode Islanders to either flee or surrender, found themselves confronted with resistance in their front and on their right flank. But these Regulars were trained for situations like this. An order was given for part of the force to wheel to the right and defend against the flank attack. They hit the riflemen and Rangers with mass volleys. One of the first to fall, with three bullets in him, was Major Leitch, who had been standing atop the ridge directing his men. Less than three minutes later, Colonel Knowlton also fell, as he too stood giving orders, fully exposed to the enemy's fire. Captain Brown relates:

> My poor Colonel, in the second attack, was shot just by my side, the ball entered the small of his back - I took hold of him, asked him if he was badly wounded? He told me he was; but, says he, "I do not value my life if we do but get the day." I then ordered two men to carry him off. He desired me by all means to keep up his flank. He seemed as unconcern'd and calm as tho' nothing had happened to him.

Joseph Reed, who had covered this same ground earlier on his search for Knowlton, had gone out with the column as a guide. He joined the party carrying the wounded Knowlton back to camp, noting of Knowlton, "when gasping in the agonies of death, all his inquiry was if we had drove the enemy."

The flank attack was now commanded by only captains, but they stood firm and soon were pursuing the enemy up Vandewater's Heights. Atop the Point of Rocks, Colonel David Humphrey observed that the men, "stimulated with the thirst of revenge for the loss of their leaders, and conscious of acting under the eye of the commander-in-chief, maintained the conflict with uncommon spirit and perseverence."

At the same time, Washington was sending forward 800 more men, mostly Marylanders, to join the action down in the Hollow Way. Lieutenant Joseph Hodgkins wrote to his wife, "Our brigade marched

out of the woods, then a very hot fire began on both sides and lasted for upward of an hour." The Americans were battling "European style" with good results. The double attack finally was too much for the British, and they retreated up the steep hillside to some woods.

The Marylanders led a spirited charge that drove the enemy out of the woods to the edge of Vandewater's buckwheat field. There the British were reinforced from Bloomingdale by two additional battalions of light infantry, as well as the famed 42nd Highlander regiment, some other British and Hessian grenadier regiments, and some jagers. One captain remembers that his grenadiers were "trotted about three miles without a halt to draw breath." A pair of three-pounders were also frantically "hauled by hand" from McGowan's Pass.

Washington now sent forward some of the New England levies that had fled from Kip's Bay the day before. The battle became quite hot for another hour, the two parties of perhaps 2,000 apiece moving back and forth, trampling Vandewater's buckwheat. The day before, the Regulars had been instructed to "receive the Rebels' first fire, and then rush on them before they had recovered [reloaded] their arms, with the bayonets" to throw them into "utmost disorder and confusion." The plan, a standard European open field tactic, did not work this time, as repeatedly the Americans fired, then fell back quickly, only to regroup and come on again.

The British and Hessians were pushed all the way to Jones's farm, near the Bloomingdale Road, where the action had begun at dawn, ten hours before. British ships in the Hudson tried in vain to cover their retreat. Howe was dispatching two more regiments in an effort to stem the tide, when Tench Tilghman galloped up to the Americans with Washington's order to call off the pursuit. The troops were getting too close to the main British Army. Though the Americans gave no fox call, Tilghman did note that they "gave a hurra and left the field in good order."

Among the British reinforcements which "found that they had not the milisha to deal with this time" was Lieutenant George Harris, of the Fifth Regiment of Foot.

A man in my company had his hat shot through, but the ball merely raised the skin. And in the battalion on our left, a man was shot so dead when lying on the ground, that the next man did not perceive it. But when he got up to stand to his arms, kicked his comrade, thinking he was asleep, [he] found, to his great surprise, that he was quite dead, a ball having entered under the ear, and very little blood having issued from it.

Casualties on the American side had been about 25 killed and 70 wounded, while their enemy's, according to Bauermeister, had been 70 killed and 200 wounded. But the real significance of the Battle of Harlem Heights (Vandewater's Farm would have been a more accurate name for it) was the tremendous boost in morale it provided the American cause. New York's General George Clinton:

It has animated our troops, given them new spirits and erased every bad impression the retreat from Long Island, etc., had left on their minds. They find they are able with inferior numbers to drive the enemy - and think of nothing now but conquest.

Lt. Joseph Hodgkins wrote home, "I dout not if we should have another oppertunity but we should give them another dressing." The new spirit in the army after the battle, a grim determination to persevere, is revealed in the following incident, as told by Private Joseph Plumb Martin:

The men were very much fatigued and faint, having had nothing to eat for forty-eight hours. After the action had ceased, one of the men complained of being hungry. The colonel, putting his hand into his coat pocket, took out a piece of an ear of Indian corn burnt as black as a

coal. "Here," said he to the man complaining, "eat this and learn to be a soldier."

In his journal, Captain Frederick Mackenzie, of the Royal Welsh Fusiliers, recorded that this "unfortunate business" gave General Howe "a good deal of concern." Howe knew from personal experience at Bunker Hill how the rebels would fight if behind breastworks and well officered. Now it appeared that some could also fight in the open field. Howe gave up any idea he might have had about storming their strong position on Harlem Heights, and ordered his own army to intrench from Bloomingdale to Horne's Hook. One American soldier, doing picket duty, wrote:

> They are greatly mortified at their disappointment & have ever since been exceedingly modest & quiet, not having even patroling parties beyond their lines. I lay within a mile of them the night after the battle & never heard men work harder. I believe they thought we intended to pursue our advantage & attack them next morning.

Washington was certainly not strong enough or foolish enough to follow up this minor success with a general attack. His policy throughout the war was to stay on the defensive and avoid general engagements unless he had the advantage of numbers, position or surprise. Washington spent the days following the Battle of Harlem Heights strengthening his lines and preparing for Howe's next move.

* * * * *

General Howe issued strict orders against plundering the inhabitants on Manhattan, even specifying that the soldiers should not "pull roots or enter gardens without the owner's leave." Loyalist families returned from their New Jersey and Long Island refuges to occupy their homes

again. A Hessian lieutenant named Heinrichs had taken possession of some abandoned houses south of Harlem on September 15th. The next day, in the Battle of Harlem Heights, he was "shot by a rifle-ball in the left side of the breast 4 fingers distant from the heart." He was carried back to one of these houses to recover. The occupants, he wrote, returned later that day and "joyful tears rolled down the faces when they found again their houses delivered back to their hands." Heinrichs continued: "the emotion I felt on seeing mother and children, grandfather and grandchildren, &c., down to the black children of the slaves, hugging and kissing each other, so affected my wound that I got a fever in the night."

With all but the northern end of Manhattan under British control, and the memory of the Kip's Bay rout still fresh in American minds, the Howe brothers tried another peace initiative. Having earlier found both Washington and the Congress determined to fight for independence, the Howes this time went directly to the people. On September 19th, the admiral and general issued a joint proclamation urging Americans to come forward and confer with them on "the means of restoring public tranquillity and establishing a permanent union." They urged Americans "to reflect seriously upon their present conditions and expectations, the unjust and precarious cause in which they are engaged, to return to their allegiance, accept the blessings of peace, and to be secured in a free enjoyment of their liberty and properties upon the true principles of the constitution." The proclamation was ignored by Congress, and ridiculed by the rebel press. Even the loyalists criticized it for offering no specific proposals. William Smith, a leading proponent of reconciliation, stated in Congress, "This paper confirms the assertion of the [Staten Island] committee that his Lordship had nothing to offer."

* * * * *

Writing copies of the proclamation had kept Admiral Howe's secretary, Ambrose Serle, busy that September 19th. The next night, Serle

wrote in his journal: "Preparations were made this evening for the attack on Powley's Hook to-morrow - a post of the rebels on the North River almost opposite the town." However, the early hours of that next morning, September 21st, would find the sailors preoccupied with a more urgent matter.

Shortly after midnight, Admiral Howe had to order his sailors to row their longboats to the city. The cause of all this nighttime activity is explained by John Joseph Henry, a Pennsylvania rifleman who had been captured at Quebec and was now on board a British transport in New York harbor, waiting to be exchanged. Henry's slumber below decks was interrupted by a deck sentry's cry of "Fire!"

> Running upon deck, we could perceive a light. In a moment we saw another light at a great distance from the first. The flames were fanned by the briskness of the breeze. We observed many boats putting off from the fleet, rowing speedily towards the city. Our [ship's] boat was of the number. This circumstance repelled the idea that our enemies were the incendiaries. The boat returned about daylight. The sailors told us that they had seen one American hanging by the heels dead, having a bayonet wound through his breast. They averred he was caught in the act of firing the houses. They told us also that they had seen one person who was taken in the [act and] tossed into the fire.

British soldiers quartered in the city began a house by house search, and several Americans, "suspected as incendiaries, were bayonetted." The man hung up by his heels had been caught "cutting the handles off water buckets" and stabbing a woman, said to be his wife, who insisted on carrying water to the engines. Captain Frederick Mackenzie was in the city that night, and the next day wrote:

> The sick, the aged, women and children, half naked

were seen going they knew not where, and taking refuge in houses which were at a distance from the fire, but from whence they were in several instances driven a second and even a third time by the devouring element, and at last in a state of despair laying themselves down on the Common. The terror was encreased by the horrid noise of the burning and falling houses, the pulling down of such wooden buildings as served to conduct the fire, the rattling of above 100 waggons, sent in from the army, and which were constantly employed in conveying to the Common such goods and effects as could be saved. ...

The appearance of Trinity Church, when completely in flames was a very grand sight, for the spire being entirely framed of wood and covered with shingles, a lofty pyramid of fire appeared, and as soon as the shingles were burnt away the frame appeared with every separate piece of timber burning, until the principle timbers were burnt through, then the whole fell with a great noise.

During the night, General Howe had kept his troops at their stations, for fear of an attack, and left it up to the sailors to put out the fire. At dawn, however, he sent a regiment into town to assist the exhausted sailors in tearing down houses to form a firebreak and thus halt the progress of the fire, which was still raging. Early response to the outbreak had been hampered by the lack of church bells - they had earlier been taken out of the steeples and melted to make weapons for the rebel army.

Altogether, about 500 dwellings, or one-fourth of the city, were destroyed. George Washington, although innocent of any connection with the sabotage, was not unhappy upon learning of it that morning. "Providence or some good honest fellow," he wrote, "has done more for us than we were disposed to do for ourselves." General Howe would now find it a more difficult task to shelter his huge army and the

thousands of loyalist refugees that were pouring into the city for the army's protection. By 1778, more than 40,000 people would be crammed into a city which in 1775 housed only 22,000.

* * * * *

Infuriated by the still-smoldering fire, reportedly of Yankee origin, General Howe was not likely to be lenient that morning of September 21st, when a rebel spy from Connecticut was brought before him. Caught the evening before carrying "drawings of the works" upon his body, 21-year-old Nathan Hale freely admitted to gathering intelligence behind British lines on both Long Island and Manhattan. Dispensing with the formality of a trial, Howe immediately ordered Hale to be executed the next morning.

The story of Hale's mission began on September 1. That day, Washington wrote to two of his generals about his desire for a volunteer to be a "channel of information" about the enemy's "intended operations." Where would Howe land next? If no such patriot could be found to go behind enemy lines on Long Island, perhaps some Tory might be bribed to spy "for a reasonable reward." But no one could be found to perform such a hazardous assignment. Four days later, the worried commander told the same two generals to "not stick at expense to bring this to pass, as I never was more uneasy than on account of my want of knowledge on this score."

Finally, on September 8th, Washington ordered Lieutenant-Colonel Thomas Knowlton to find a solitary volunteer for the mission. Knowlton held a council of his most trusted officers. Lieutenant James Sprague, a veteran of the French and Indian War, spoke what was probably the consensus. "I am willing," he declared, "to go and fight them, but as far as going among them and being taken and hung up like a dog, I will not do it." Just as the meeting appeared to be breaking up, young Captain Nathan Hale rose and said, "I will undertake it."

In retrospect, it was indeed a suicidal mission. Hale was not given any standard tools of the spying trade - proper training, safe houses

and contacts on Long Island, "sympathetic" ink, or even a code to disguise his observations. He would have to rely on his own ingenuity. If caught, any notes he committed to paper would surely betray him.

Before leaving, he went to see his close friend, Captain William Hull. They had been classmates at Yale and later were in Webb's regiment together until Hale transferred to Knowlton's Rangers. Hull was shocked when Nathan told him what he proposed to do. Hull pleaded with him to refuse the dangerous mission. Hale pointed out that it was for the good of the country, the Commander-in-Chief desired it, and there was no other way to know where the enemy would strike.

Hull then pointed out the disgrace of being a spy: "Who," he asked, "respects the character of a spy?" Hale replied, "For a year I have been attached to the army and have not rendered any material service. Every kind of service, necessary to the public good, becomes honorable by being necessary." All Hale would promise his friend was to "reflect, and do nothing but what duty demands."

After some reflection, Nathan Hale decided to go through with it. He set out on September 12th with Sergeant Stephen Hempstead, who would see that Hale crossed safely over to Long Island, then wait for his return. Hale carried "a general order to all armed vessels to take him to any place he should designate." They rode north to Norwalk, Connecticut, where they found a ship's captain willing to risk crossing Long Island Sound.

While on board, Hale changed from his frock, "made of white linen, & fringed, such as officers used to wear," into his disguise. After his graduation from Yale in 1773 at the age of 18, he had taught school for two years before enlisting in the army, so it was natural for him to now assume that occupation. And the time of year was right, too, for an unemployed schoolmaster to be traveling the countryside seeking work. Sergeant Hempstead watched Hale put on

a plain suit of citizens brown clothes, with a round broad-brimmed hat, leaving all his other clothes, commission, public and private papers, with me, and also his

silver shoe buckles, saying they would not comport with his character of school-master, and retaining nothing but his college diploma as an introduction to his assumed calling. Thus equipped, we parted.

His actions, from the time of his landing on Long Island to his capture by sailors along the East River south of Harlem, remain a mystery. We do know that he was not able to send any word to Washington about when and where Howe would attack Manhattan. After Kip's Bay, Hale's mission effectively cancelled, he could have returned "to Connecticut Main" and then south to the army. But, instead, he crossed over from Long Island to British-occupied New York, perhaps by helping a farmer transport vegetables to the city.

Hale was caught on Manhattan trying to make his way around the British lines south of Harlem. "They stopped him, searched & found drawings of the works, with descriptions in Latin, under the inner sole of the pumps which he wore." He spent the night before his death in the greenhouse adjoining the Beekman Mansion, Howe's headquarters near Kip's Bay. One officer present at the questioning by Howe the day before noted that Hale's "manly bearing" under the circumstances touched the general. Nevertheless, Howe ordered the death sentence - "the stern rules of war concerning such offenses" left no room for mercy. The condemned man was then entrusted to the care of William Cunningham, Provost Marshall of prisoners, a sadistic Tory refugee who during the war would order the secret torture and execution of hundreds of Americans.

Several British officers were among the crowd that witnessed the hanging "at 11 o'clock in front of the park of artillery" (present day Grand Central Station). Captain Frederick Mackenzie noted the execution in his diary that night:

He behaved with great composure and resolution, saying he thought it the duty of every good officer to obey any orders given him by his Commander in Chief; and

desired the spectators to be at all times prepared to meet death in whatever shape it might appear.

Captain John Montresor had also been present at Nathan Hale's execution. The next day, Montresor accompanied a flag of truce to discuss exchanging the Quebec prisoners. Among the Americans meeting the flag were an artillery captain named Alexander Hamilton and Captain William Hull, Hale's friend. Montresor described to them Hale's last hour. From Hull's memoirs:

> I learned the melancholy particulars from this officer, who was present at his execution and seemed touched by the circumstances attending it. Captain Hale, on the near approach of death, asked for a clergyman to attend him. It was refused. He then requested a Bible; that too was refused by his inhuman jailor.
>
> "On the morning of his execution," continued the officer, "my station was near the fatal spot, and I requested the Provost Marshall to permit the prisoner to sit in my marquee, while he was making the necessary preparations. Captain Hale entered: he was calm, and bore himself with gentle dignity. He asked for writing materials, which I furnished him. He wrote two letters, one to his brother and one to a brother officer."
>
> He was shortly after summoned to the gallows. But a few persons were around him, yet his characteristic dying words were remembered. He said, "I only regret that I have but one life to lose for my country."

A noose had been thrown over a tree limb, and now the executioner, a mulatto named Richmond, bound Nathan Hale and guided him as he stumbled up a ladder leaning against the tree. Upon Cunningham's command "Swing him off!" Richmond pushed Hale off the ladder. His body was left hanging to serve as a warning to others. Some British

soldiers found "in a rebel gentleman's garden, a painted soldier on a board." This they hung up beside the swinging corpse and labeled it "George Washington."

The two letters Hale wrote never reached their destinations. Cunningham kept them, so that "the rebels should never know they had a man who could die with so much firmness." Many years later, in London, Cunningham himself died at the end of a rope, convicted of forgery. Nathan Hale's fate did not become widely known during the war, for spying was considered too disgraceful a profession to be made public.

* * * * *

Alexander Hamilton brought back another message from that prisoner exchange parley. This one was a personal message to Washington from General Howe. It read:

> My aid-de-camp will present to you a ball cut and fixed to the end of a nail, taken from a number of the same kind, found in the encampment quitted by your troops on the 15th instant. I do not make any comment upon such unwarrantable and malicious practices, being well assured the contrivance has not come to your knowledge.

The American commander replied in writing, assuring Howe that it was "the first of the kind I ever saw or heard of. You may depend the contrivance is highly abhorred by me, and every measure shall be taken to prevent so wicked and infamous a practice being adopted in this army."

Washington's army was again withering down to a skeleton force. Double sentries were posted every night now, in a vain effort to stop the "abominable desertions." On the 23rd, the commander stole some time "from the hours allotted to sleep" to write a very long letter to

John Hancock, again pleading with him to end the dependence on short term enlistments. He urged Congress to promise each soldier 150 acres of land after the war, and immediately upon enlistment give him "a suit of clothes and blanket" to induce him to enlist for the duration of the war. It was obvious that the war would not be over this year, so it "must be carried on systematically, and to do it you must have good officers. Giving your officers good pay will induce gentlemen and men of character to engage."

Too many officers were being "driven by a scanty pittance to low and dirty arts, to filch the public." Washington went on to give Hancock an account of one officer who had robbed a house of everything valuable, including "looking glasses, women's cloaths and other articles which one would think could be of no earthly use to him. He was met by a major of brigade who ordered him to return the goods." The officer refused, and with the aid of some thieving companions, swore he would defend his spoils of war "at the hazard of his life." The major called out a full company of troops and subdued the thieves. The officer was court-martialled and cashiered from the army.

Colonel Henry Knox, chief artillery officer of the army, probably echoed Washington's own sentiments when he labeled most of the army's officers "a parcel of ignorant stupid men who might make tolerable soldiers, but are bad officers. As the army now stands, it is only a receptacle for ragamuffins."

As for the Commander-in-Chief, Knox wrote, "The general is as worthy a man as breathes, but he cannot do every thing nor be every where." Washington described his burden in a letter to his brother, John Augustine Washington: "it is not in the power of words to describe the tasks I have to perform. Fifty thousand pounds would not induce me again to undergo what I have done."

Washington and his generals needed a supporting cast of quality colonels, majors, captains, sergeants and lieutenants in order to have any chance of making an army out of this "receptacle for ragamuffins." Joseph Reed wrote to his wife that he was planning to resign (and he eventually did), because it seemed impossible to produce the proper

subordination in the army. "Either no discipline can be established, or he who attempts it must become odious and detestable, a position no one will choose." The real problem was not the soldiers themselves, but their officers. Colonel Smallwood explained it in a letter to the Maryland Council of Safety:

> Could our <u>officers</u> be brought to a proper sense of their duty and dignity, the enemy might be checked in their course. [The Regulars] are as much afraid and cautious of us as we can be of them. <u>Their officers alone give the superiority</u>.

A crisis now reached its climax in the camp on Harlem Heights. During the recent Battle of Harlem Heights, a Connecticut sergeant, Ebenezer Leffingwell, had been sent to the rear to get more ammunition. He was stopped by Colonel Joseph Reed, Washington's adjutant from Philadelphia. Reed accused the Yankee of deserting, and ordered him back to the fight. Leffingwell argued his case in vain. Reed drew a sword and threatened to kill the Yankee. Leffingwell cocked his musket and fired at Reed, but the gun misfired. Reed then grabbed the musket of a nearby soldier and fired at Leffingwell, but this gun also misfired. So Reed then rushed upon Leffingwell, and with his sword cut off the man's thumb before the Yankee finally surrendered. Leffingwell was court-martialled and condemned to be executed by firing squad.

Washington reluctantly approved the sentence and set the date for September 22. By then, "the resentment of the [Connecticut] troops" had been "raised to a high pitch" and they "showed what their feelings were by secret and open threats." A soldier describes the execution proceeding:

> The Connecticut troops were drawn out and formed in a square, and the prisoner brought forth. After being blindfolded and pinioned, he knelt upon the ground. The

corporal with his six executioners were then brought up before him. But the sergeant was reprieved, and I believe it was well that he was, for his blood would not have been the only blood that would have been spilt.

Concerned about the Yankee threats, Reed had at the last minute swallowed his pride and asked Washington to pardon the Yankee. Leffingwell and Washington were not the only men having a hard time these days. Life in the "Grand American Army" was not too grand. What better soldier to go to for an account of these trying times than the ever descriptive fifteen-year-old, Private Joseph Plumb Martin?

We remained here [Harlem Heights] until sometime in the month of October without anything very material transpiring, excepting starvation, and that had by this time become quite a secondary matter; hard duty and nakedness were considered the prime evil, for the reader will recollect that we lost all our clothing in the Kip's Bay affair.

It now began to be cool weather, especially the nights. To have to lie as I did almost every night, on the cold and often wet ground without a blanket and with nothing but thin summer clothing, was tedious. I have often ... lain on one side until the upper side smarted with cold, then turned that side down to the place warmed by my body and let the other take its turn at smarting, while the one on the ground warmed. Thus, alternately turning for four to six hours till called upon to go on sentry, as the soldiers term it, and when relieved from a tour of two long hours at that business and returned to the guard again, have had to go through the operation of freezing and thawing for four or six hours more. In the morning the ground as white as snow with hoar frost.

Or perhaps it would rain all night like a flood; all that

could be done in that case was to lie down (if one could lie down), take our musket in our arms, and place the lock between our thighs and "weather it out."

We kept a long chain of sentinels placed almost within speaking distance of each other, and being in close neighborhood with the enemy we were necessitated to be pretty alert. I was upon my post as sentinel about the middle of the night. Thinking we had overgone the time in which we ought to have been relieved, I stepped a little off my post towards one of the next sentries, it being quite dark, and asked him in a low voice how long he had been on sentry. He started as if attacked by the enemy and roared out "Who comes there?" I saw I had alarmed him and stole back to my post as quick as possible. He still kept up his cry, "Who comes there?" and receiving no answer, he discharged his piece, which alarmed the whole guard, who immediately formed and prepared for action and sent off a non-commissioned officer and file of men to ascertain the cause of alarm.

They came first to the man who had fired and asked him what was the matter. He said that someone had made an abrupt advance upon his premises ... They next came to me, inquiring what I had seen. I told them that I had not seen or heard anything to alarm me but what the other sentinel had caused. The men returned to the guard, and we were soon relieved, which was all I had wanted.

Upon our return to the guard I found, as was to be expected, that the alarm was the subject of general conversation among them. They were confident that a spy or something worse had been amongst us and consequently greater vigilance was necessary. We were accordingly kept the rest of the night under arms, and I cursed my indiscretion for causing the disturbance, as I

could get no more rest during the night.

* * * * *

On September 29th, Captain Mackenzie wrote in his journal: "I am of opinion Genl Howe will never attack them in front in their present position. He certainly intends something very different, if we may judge from his fortifying the narrow part of the Island so strongly, and other preparations which are making for a movement." Frederick Mackenzie was right - Howe recognized a strong position when he saw one. He intended to land part of his army north of Manhattan and flank Washington once again, as he had on Long Island and at Kip's Bay. But first, he would secure New York by finishing his own intrenchments.

And he would await a large reinforcement that he had learned was now crossing the Atlantic, due to arrive in early October. He wrote to Lord Germain to ask for even more troops and ships: "I have not the smallest prospect of finishing the contest this campaign, not until the Rebels see preparations in the Spring that may preclude all thoughts of further resistance."

This year's campaign was rapidly coming to a close. What had General Howe accomplished? When he had arrived in New York harbor back in June, his aim had been to destroy Washington's army and take that key city. His admiral brother, however, soon arrived with their joint commission as peacemakers and persuaded the younger brother to not make a martyr out of Washington by annihilating his army. Creating martyrs does not win back the allegiance of colonists who see themselves as oppressed. The Howe brothers, who themselves had reluctantly agreed to participate in this war, felt that they could return to England as saviors of the empire only if they arranged America's reconciliation with the mother country. Therefore, General Howe was apparently ignoring opportunities to trap and capture the rebel army. He was content each time to beat them, but not destroy them, while he gained more territory and waited for the American people to grow dis-

illusioned with the rebellion

So far, this humane approach to war had resulted in nothing more than the capture of New York. The rebel army had simply moved back a few miles to a stronger position, and neither Congress nor the American people were yet crying out for peace.

CHAPTER TEN
WASHINGTON'S ARMY ESCAPES AGAIN
OCTOBER 1776

"If I were to wish the bitterest curse to an enemy on this side of the grave, I should put him in my stead."

- General George Washington,
October, 1776.

After the rout at Kip's Bay on September 15, 1776, the British were in possession of New York City, but Washington's ragged, depleted army still clung to the northern end of Manhattan. From mid-September to the second week of October, both armies dug in. George Washington strengthened his lines atop Harlem Heights, while his adversary, William Howe, built redoubts and breastworks of his own on Vandewater's Heights and at McGowan's Pass, just south of Harlem village. Howe knew that not until these lines were finished, securing New York from recapture, would he be free to put most of his army on the offensive again.

Though the opposing lines were about one mile apart, the advance scouts or "picquets" often came within shouting distance of each other. In his memoirs, the American General William Heath relates an incident from this period of relative inactivity:

> They were so civil to each other, on their posts, that one day, at a part of the creek where it was practicable, the British sentinel asked the American, who was nearly opposite to him, if he could give him a chew of tobacco. The latter, having in his pocket a piece of thick twisted

roll, sent it across the creek to the British sentinel, who after taking off his bite sent the remainder back again.

But such isolated incidents are contrary to the inhumanity of war. Two soldiers could feel moved to exchange a chew of tobacco one day, but the very next day they might meet again in a life or death struggle.

Washington was still anxious for "early intelligence" of the next British movement. As he put it to two of his subordinate generals, "I should much approve of small harassing parties, as they might keep the enemy alarmed, and more than probably bring off a prisoner, from whom some valuable intelligence may be obtained." An attack was ordered on September 23rd upon a party of British camped on an island in the East River, just offshore from Harlem village. The raid proved to be a tragic failure, due to inconsistent leadership. Colonel John Glover, of Massachusetts, described the raid in a letter to his mother:

> On the 23d, a detachment from several corps commanded by Lieut. Col. Jackson, consisting of 240 men, were sent off to dislodge the enemy from Montresor's Island, for which purpose six boats were provided to carry 40 men each. Col. Jackson led, Major Hendly of Charlestown with him. They were met by the enemy at the water's edge before they landed, who gave them a heavy fire. Notwithstanding this, the Colonel landed with the party in his boat, gave them battle and compelled them to retreat, called to the other boats to push and land.
>
> But the scoundrels, coward-like, retreated back and left him and his party to fall a sacrifice. The enemy seeing this, 150 of them rushed out of the woods and attacked them again at 30 yards distance. Jackson with his little party nobly defended the ground until every man but eight was killed on the spot, and himself

wounded, before he ordered a retreat. Major Hendly carrying off Colonel Jackson was shot dead as he was putting him into a boat, and not a single man of the 8 but what was wounded. One of them died at the oar before they landed.

The officers who commanded the other boats are all under arrest and will be tried for their lives. In short, if some example is not made of such rascally conduct, there will be no encouragement for men of spirit to exert themselves. As the case now is, they will always fall a sacrifice, while such low-lived scoundrels, that have neither honour nor the good of their country at heart, will skulk behind and get off clear.

On October 7th, the British lines were declared complete. And, with the arrival of 9,000 more Hessians expected any day now, the brothers Howe set in motion their plan for the final act in the capture of Manhattan. Like the Long Island and Kip's Bay actions, this too would be a flanking maneuver, forcing Washington to retreat again.

Two main roads led from southern New England to Manhattan and Washington's army. William Howe intended to seal off both roads. He readied 20,000 troops for another flatboat ride. This time they would move up the East River, past the whirlpool of Hell Gate, and land in Westchester County. After securing the coastal road, a quick march north to the village of White Plains would gain control of the other road.

If Washington stayed put at Harlem Heights, Howe could close in on Kings Bridge, trapping Washington (or at least forcing him to flee again). Admiral Richard Howe's warships already roamed the lower Hudson, preventing supplies from reaching the rebel army by water. General Howe now sought to also gain control of the land routes leading to Kings Bridge. Washington's army would be strangled. And if Washington became desperate enough to try to stop Howe, Howe's army should be well intrenched on the heights above White Plains by

the time the rebel army arrived.

Just before dawn on October 12th, the first wave - nearly 5,000 soldiers - set off in flatboats up the East River toward Hell Gate, where the waters of the Harlem River, Long Island Sound and that arm of the ocean called the East River all merged in a whirl commonly and "vulgarly called The Pot." A British sea captain noted that "very few people in the flat boats [had] ever been through or knew anything of the passage of Hell Gate. This made the danger much the greater." Initially, they were mainly concerned with some rebel batteries on the Westchester shore, but these fears were soon replaced with others, as the lead boats "came on a fog equal to pitch darkness."

Admiral Howe accompanied and personally directed the operation from a sloop. Despite the fog, he insisted on proceeding, because it would be more dangerous for the fogbound boats to anchor or turn around, as "the boats that followed would in all probability run foul of them, sinking each other." Captain Frederick Mackenzie, who earlier had expected "one or two hundred men" would be drowned, described the trip through Hell Gate in his diary:

> Fortune, however, favored the bold: only one boat, having on board an officer and 25 artillery men and three 6-pounders, was sunk. All but four men and the guns were saved ... In one place, if the stream catches a boat or vessel, it is drawn into a kind of whirlpool or eddy, where it is carried round several times with great violence, and then, if not sucked in, is thrown on the adjacent rocks and dashed to pieces. One boat with a detachment of grenadiers was caught into this place, and after some turns round was thrown upon the shore, but fortunately the men got out safe, and soon after got into another boat and followed the army.

By 9 a.m., the leading boats were nearing their destination - Throg's Neck (a Westchester peninsula known originally as Throckmorton's,

then Throck's, and finally Throg's or Frog's Neck). On shore, a handful of rebel sharpshooters opened fire, but hastily fled when a British frigate cruising in Long Island Sound to cover the landing opened fire. The advance division of 5,000 troops landed safely at what is today Fort Schuyler Park in the Bronx.

As General Howe's second in command, General Sir Henry Clinton was leading the expedition. Clinton was pleased with the results so far: "the landing was effected without loss. As soon as the troops could be formed, we pushed for Westchester Bridge in hopes of securing it." The peninsula of Throg's Neck was virtually an island, being separated from the mainland by a brook in the middle of a marsh. A long narrow causeway, called Westchester Bridge, spanned this "morass." Near its northern end, the Americans had constructed a redoubt to block any attempt by Howe to move inland and get in the army's rear.

Colonel William Prescott, the year before, had valiantly directed the defense of another redoubt atop Breed's Hill, in the misnamed Battle of Bunker Hill. Now he was in command inside this little redoubt, which boasted two light field pieces. Also on the northern side of the bridge was a long stack of cordwood, and hidden behind it were twenty-five of Hand's Pennsylvania riflemen. On their retreat from the shore earlier that morning they had stopped to take up the planks in the bridge.

The vanguard of the British-Hessian force cautiously approached the bridge, looking for snipers. When they reached the southern end of the bridge they were met by a sudden well-aimed fire from the woodpile on the other side. They broke, and ran back to the main body of the army to alert General Clinton.

It took several hours for the advance division to land and form. This gave Clinton time to consider his options. He could storm the rebel position, forcing his disciplined troops to wade the marsh while under concentrated fire from the woodpile and redoubt. The light field pieces he brought along would probably silence the woodpile, but not the redoubt. The rebels would still have their artillery. Clinton's su-

periority of numbers was rapidly becoming less overwhelming as rebel reinforcements began arriving. The rebel position could be taken, but only by paying a heavy price in casualties if the rebels put up a determined resistance.

This predicament was proof to Clinton that he had been right all along - he had tried in vain to talk Howe into landing at Myer's Point a few miles northeast, near New Rochelle. Clinton made up his mind: rather than risk an engagement on disadvantageous terrain, he would sit tight and let the Commander-in-Chief accept that responsibility or order the troops transferred to another landing site. The cautious William Howe opted for the latter, but high winds and heavy downpours delayed the move until the 18th, six days after the Throg's Neck landing. However, this delay gave Howe time to move up to Throg's Neck some additional artillery and other supplies, plus 10,000 more British and 5,000 more Hessian troops, thus giving him 20,000 men for the Westchester campaign.

Howe's delay at Throg's Neck gave Washington six days to react. The Virginian personally rode the fifteen miles to White Plains, so he could select the best locations for fortifications should a decision be made to move the army there. On October 16th, he called a council of war. Included now was General Charles Lee, the army's highest ranking general next to Washington. Haughty and eccentric, but having much experience in the British and Prussian armies, Lee was enjoying the high point of his popularity, having received credit for the victory at Charleston (credit that should have gone to Colonel Moultrie alone).

After the Long Island and Kip's Bay disasters, there were some in both the army and Congress who felt that Lee should supplant Washington as Commander-in-Chief. But the Congress made no move to replace him. Washington was so discouraged he probably would have welcomed such a move. He wrote to a confidant back in Virginia, "if I were to wish the bitterest curse to an enemy on this side of the grave, I should put him in my stead." Washington had contemplated resigning, but was persuaded to see it through. He was told "that if I quit the

command, inevitable ruin will follow from the distraction that will ensue."

At Washington's October 16th council of war, it was decided that, because nearly "the enemy's whole force is in our rear at Frog's Point," the strong American position on Harlem Heights was no longer tenable. The army should be moved to White Plains. General Spencer was assigned the task of building a series of interim fortifications along the Bronx River to protect the army on its slow march to White Plains. General Greene would oversee the defense of the lower Hudson, with 3,500 men in Fort Lee and Fort Washington and the rear guard in the Harlem lines. General Heath was assigned the defense of the upper Hudson, with 4,000 men at the Highlands near Peekskill. Washington, with Putnam and the newly returned Sullivan and Stirling (both captured at Long Island, but recently exchanged) would oversee the main army's transfer from Harlem and Kings Bridge to White Plains.

General Lee was assigned defense of Westchester County's shore, including Throg's Neck and points east. According to Washington's aide, Tench Tilghman, Lee "will have the flower of the army with him, as our lines in front [Harlem Heights] are so strong that we can trust them to troops [militia] who would not stand in the field."

Forts Washington and Lee were located atop cliffs on either side of the Hudson River at a point about a mile north of the Harlem lines. Below the two forts, the Hudson was only about forty feet deep. Here the patriots had sunk several ships to form a *chevaux-de-frise* (hidden barrier) "to obstruct navigation of the North River" between the two forts. Twice already, British ship captains had proven the river passable, despite the *chevaux-de-frise* and a hail of cannon balls from the forts. So defense of the river at that point was no longer practicable, and Washington could have justifiably evacuated Forts Washington and Lee. But, at the October 16th council, the majority of his generals voted to hold the forts "as long as possible" - a decision they would later regret.

Movement of more than 10,000 men with all their camp equipage and artillery is quite a logistics feat with almost no horses and wagons.

Most of the cannon had to be pushed and pulled by hand the entire fifteen miles. The few wagons had to cover each stretch of ground countless times: barrels of gunpowder, provisions, etc. would be hauled short distances, then the wagons sent back for more. Thus, the army progressed in a leapfrog fashion. And all the time, work went on feverishly to build temporary fortifications along the route, to protect against a swift attack from Howe's army only a few miles down the coast road. It was a very exhausting and disillusioning time for half-starved, half-naked soldiers, like Joseph Plumb Martin:

We crossed King's Bridge and directed our course toward the White Plains. We saw parties of the enemy foraging in the country, but they were generally too alert for us. We encamped on the heights called Valentine's Hill where we continued some days keeping up the old system of starving. A sheep's head which I begged of the butchers who were killing some for the "gentlemen officers" was all the provisions I had for two or three days. ...

[Our sergeant] warned me to prepare for a two-days command. What is termed going on command is what is generally called going on a scouting party or something similar. I told the sergeant I was sick and could not go. He said I must go to the doctor and if he said I was unfit for duty he must excuse me. I saw our surgeon's mate close by, endeavoring to cook his supper, blowing the fire and scratching his eyes. We both stepped up to him and he felt my pulse. He very gravely told the sergeant that I was unfit for duty. I was as well as he was; all the medicine I needed was a bellyful of victuals. The sergeant turned to go off for another man when I told him that I would go, for I meant to go; I only felt a little cross and did not know how to vent my spleen in any other way. I had much rather go on such an expedition

than stay in camp, as I stood some chance while in the country to get something to eat.

We marched from Valentine's Hill for the White Plains in the night. We had our cooking utensils (at that time the most useless things in the army) to carry in our hands. They were made of cast iron and consequently very heavy. I was so beat out before morning with hunger and fatigue that I could hardly move one foot before the other. I told my messmates that I could not carry it any further. They said they would not carry it any further. Of what use was it? They had nothing to cook and [therefore] did not want anything to cook with. We were sitting down on the ascent of a hill when the discourse happened. We got up to proceed when I took up the kettle, sat it down in the road, and one of the others gave it a shove with his foot and it rolled down against the fence, and that was the last I ever saw of it. When we got through the night's march, we found our mess was not the only one that was rid of their iron bondage.

On October 18th, the same day that Washington's army started on their march, Howe moved his army from Throg's Neck a few miles northeast to Pell's Point. From there, good roads on firm ground - easy marching - led to White Plains. These roads were guarded by four skeleton American regiments, totalling only 750 men all together, under the command of Colonel John Glover. Early on that morning of the 18th, Glover took his spyglass and ascended a hill in the little village of Eastchester. He saw off the Point "upwards of two hundred [flatboats], all manned and formed in four grand divisions." Glover ran down the hill to turn out his men and to send a dispatch to General Lee, headquartered a few miles to the north.

Tench Tilghman had noted that Lee's arrival four days earlier "made our people feel bold" and, with Lee now in charge of Westchester County's defense, he predicted "a considerable slaughter ... let the en-

emy advance by what road they will, they cannot elude him." According to Tilghman, the soldiers were all "in good spirits and determined to dispute every inch of ground." But Lee was not on the spot, and it looked like Clinton's Hessian jagers and British light infantry were not going to halt their rapid advance from Pell's Point to wait for any rebel general to arrive.

If Clinton could overwhelm Glover's 750 Massachusetts Continentals and push north to White Plains, Howe's plan to cut Washington's communication lines would be realized. Short, stocky John Glover, whose regiment of Marblehead fishermen had allowed the army to escape from Long Island in a night crossing of the East River seven weeks earlier, was once again given the task of saving the army. But this time he would direct men with guns, not oars. From Colonel Glover's memoirs:

> Oh! the anxiety of mind I was then in for the fate of the day - the lives of seven hundred and fifty men depended on their being well disposed of. Besides this, my country, my honour, my own life, and every thing that was dear appeared at this critical moment to be at stake. I would have given a thousand worlds to have had General Lee or some other experienced officer present. ... [I] looked around, but could see none, they all being three miles from me, and the action came on so sudden it was out of their power to be with me.

The terrain between Eastchester and Pell's Point was very similar to that found in Massachusetts - "roads lined with stone fences and the adjacent hills divided off with stones likewise." This was the ideal setting for Glover's troops, considering their lack of skill in open field European style combat. As Israel Putnam had said before the Battle of Bunker Hill, "The militia are not afraid for their heads, only their legs. If their legs are protected, they will fight forever."

Glover placed his three regiments of farmers behind three successive

stone walls, and kept his field pieces and his own regiment of fishermen and dock workers in reserve on a hill behind a creek in the rear. He instructed his subordinate colonels to have the lead regiment defend their respective wall as long as possible, then leap-frog past the hiding troops in their rear and stop behind a distant wall to rest and reload. Fairly dense brush and woods made the road leading from the Point the only feasible route of advance. This would subject the enemy to a funnel-like concentration of musket fire from the walls.

Glover, himself, would move back and forth to help direct whichever regiment happened to be the front line at any point in time. If pushed back past the last stone wall, the rendezvous for a last stand would be the hill across the creek, where the reserve and the three cannon were placed. This ideal use of tactics, so obvious and natural to Americans, would probably not have been selected if the European-trained General Lee had arrived in time to take command.

As the enemy's vanguard, mostly "jagers," the riflemen from Germany's Black Forest, approached the first stone wall, they could not see Colonel Reed's regiment lying behind it. Glover rode forward and ordered a small advance party of his own to move past Reed's wall and engage the enemy's vanguard. Returning to Glover's account, his advance party primed their muskets and marched to

> within fifty yards, and received their fire without the loss of a man; we returned it and fell four of them, and kept the ground till we exchanged five rounds.
>
> ... having two men killed and several wounded, which weakened my party, the enemy pushing forward not more than thirty yards distant, I ordered a retreat, which was masterly well done by the captain that commanded the party. The enemy gave a shout and advanced. Colonel Reed's laying under cover of a stone wall undiscovered till they came within thirty yards, then rose up and gave them the whole charge; the enemy broke and retreated for the main body to come up.

In this situation we remained about an hour and a half when they appeared about four thousand, with seven pieces of artillery. They now advanced, keeping up a constant fire of artillery. We kept our post under cover of the stone wall before mentioned till they came within fifty yards of us, rose up and gave them the whole charge of the battalion. They halted and returned the fire with showers of musketry and cannon balls. We exchanged seven rounds at this post, retreated, and formed in the rear of Colonel Shepherd and on his left.

They then shouted and pushed on till they came on Shepherd, posted behind a fine double stone wall. He rose up and fired by grand divsions, by which he kept up a constant fire and maintained his part till he exchanged seventeen rounds with them, and caused them to retreat several times, once in particular so far that a soldier of Colonel Shepherd's leaped over the wall and took a hat and canteen off of a captain that lay dead on the ground they retreated from.

Badly outnumbered, the defenders of the last stone wall were finally by late afternoon forced to retreat across the brook to the position on the hill. The enemy did not pursue any further, but both sides "played away their artillery till night." During the night, Glover's force was relieved and the position strongly reinforced. Surprised to find such a setback, Howe resorted to his usual caution and did not immediately advance to White Plains, but chose a circuitous route via New Rochelle and Mamaroneck to the east.

The day's casualty figures were lopsided, with less than fifty Americans killed or wounded, and estimates ranging from 800 to 1000 on the other side, according to British deserters. Being the Hessians' first encounter against firm resistance, the casualties were not officially published, in order to save them embarassment in Europe. Perhaps because the larger Battle of White Plains followed soon after, the Battle

of Pell's Point has been virtually ignored by most historians of the Revolution, even though Glover's courageous Yankees, outnumbered five to one, held off the enemy for a full day and perhaps saved Washington's army in the process.

Washington, overseeing the partial evacuation of upper Manhattan, sent Colonel Rufus Putnam to reconnoiter the enemy position around Eastchester, between Kings Bridge and New Rochelle. With Washington's adjutant, Joseph Reed, and a guard of twenty men, Putnam reached Eastchester, but could find no sign of the enemy. And he could gather no intelligence as to their whereabouts, because the villagers had fled during the action at nearby Pell's Point two days before. Reed insisted on returning to Kings Bridge "to attend to issuing general orders," and took the guard with him. Putnam decided to continue on, despite the danger of traveling alone through predominantly loyalist territory. And he was ignorant of "where the road I had taken would carry me." He disguised himself as best he could as a civilian. Here is Rufus Putnam's story:

I had gone about two and a half miles when a road turned off to the right. I followed it perhaps half a mile and came to a house where I learned from the woman that this road led to New Rochelle, that the British were there and that they had a guard at a house in sight. On this information I turned and pursued my route toward White-plains. The houses on the way were all deserted, until I came within three or four miles of the place. Here I discovered a house a little ahead with men about it. By my glass I found they were not British soldiers; however, I approached them with caution.

I called for some oats for my horse, sat down and heard them chat some little time, when I found they were friends to the cause of America, and then I began to make the necessary enquiries, and on the whole I found that the main body of the British lay near New

Rochelle, from thence to White-plains about nine miles, good roads and in general level open country, that at White-plains was a large quantity of stores, with only about three hundred militia to guard them, that the British had a detachment at Mamaraneck only six miles from White-plains.

Putnam returned and reported to Washington, who sent General Stirling's division on a forced night march to reach White Plains before the enemy. The British detachment that Putnam had learned was at Mamaraneck was led by the famed French and Indian War hero, Robert Rogers. Rogers was encamped with 500 armed loyalists, a regiment known as "The Queen's American Rangers." Well supplied by Howe, they had spent the past several weeks attacking and defeating militia companies, and capturing supplies in the countryside from New Jersey to Connecticut.

General Stirling chose "the redoubtable Colonel Haslet" to conduct a raid on this band of "renegades" and hopefully capture them. As one soldier commented, Haslet's Delawares, "since the bravery [they] exhibited on Long Island [at Gowanus Pass] have been chosen for all feats of peculiar danger." Reinforced by some Virginia and Maryland volunteer companies, Haslet led a select force of 750 on this mission.

Late in the night they set out from White Plains on a silent march of five miles to Mamaraneck. They knew exactly where Rogers was encamped, and approached from a direction where only a single sentry was posted. They seized and silenced him, apparently clearing the way for a complete surprise attack on the hated Tory regiment.

But Rogers had that very day decided to start posting sixty men between the sentry and his main camp. Haslet's vanguard stumbled into these sixty in the dark. A hand-to-hand battle ensued. Soon Haslet's main body rushed forward and overwhelmed the sixty, but the Tories deceived Haslet's men by echoing their cries of "Surrender you Tory dogs! Surrender!" It was too dark to distinguish friend from foe. In the melee, twenty of the Tories escaped to their main camp.

Haslet pushed on, but Rogers was now ready for him. The skirmish became a standoff. Being so near the enemy camps, Haslet wisely contented himself with a partial victory and returned to White Plains with 36 prisoners, 60 muskets, two flags and, perhaps most important, 60 blankets. Like Glover's defense near Pell's Point, this affair was a much needed boost for the retreating army's fighting spirit.

On October 23th, the long awaited reinforcements from Europe splashed ashore at New Rochelle. During the next few days, as Howe made plans for the march to White Plains, the Hessians looted almost every house for miles around, those of Tory and Whig alike. Their officers insisted that it was a tradition for all conquering armies, and quite necessary to maintain morale.

Each day, patrols of dragoons clashed with advance rebel parties sent forward to harass Howe's army. The dragoons enjoyed much success, since the rebels were unaccustomed to opposing troops on horseback, and they had none of their own. Washington addressed the problem in his general orders of October 27th:

> The General, observing that the army seems unacquainted with the enemy's horse, and that when any parties meet with them they do not oppose them with the same alacrity which they show in other cases, thinks it necessary to inform the officers and soldiers that, in such a broken country full of stone walls, no enemy is more to be despised, as they cannot leave the road.
>
> And that any party attacking them may be sure to do it to advantage by taking post in the woods by the roads, or along the stone walls, where they will not venture to follow them. And, as an encouragement, the General offers one hundred dollars for every trooper, with his horse and accoutrements, who shall be brought in.

By October 27th, Howe had sent two brigades west to seize Kings Bridge, preventing the 2,000 rebel troops left on Manhattan from join-

ing Washington. Then he ordered the advance division on to White Plains. Clinton would lead the avant-garde, or vanguard, while Howe brought up the main body from New Rochelle, a few miles behind him.

Before dawn on the 28th, Clinton's foremost troops, a Hessian unit, progressed slowly toward a detachment of rebels posted one and a half miles south of White Plains. These were some of the Connecticut troops that had fled in the Kip's Bay rout the month before. However, on this day, they were more advantageously posted behind stone walls, and were not facing a covering artillery barrage from British frigates.

Major Carl Bauermeister later recalled that the "narrow and poor road necessitated marching in file." For a while, it was Pell's Point all over again, as the Americans fired volley after volley, slowly falling back from one stone wall to the next. Colonel Rufus Putnam noted that one "rail and stone fence behind which our troops were posted proved as fatal to the enemy as Knowlton's rail and hay fence had at Bunkers Hill." An American officer remembered that at one point a volley delivered at close range scattered the Hessians "like leaves in a whirlwind; and they ran off so far that some of the Americans ran out to the ground where they were and brought off ... [the dead Hessians'] rum, which we had time to drink rounds with before they came on again."

After a while, Clinton sent General Lord Cornwallis and a few field pieces around a knoll to come up behind the rebel party. Just as he was getting in their rear, the Americans spotted him and quickly ran west to the Bronx River, waded across, and made it safely back to the main American lines near White Plains.

Howe had taken his time moving his troops to White Plains, expecting Washington to keep retreating northward to the Hudson Highlands around Peekskill. Now, to his surprise, Howe found his foe intrenched and prepared to give battle on the hills just south of the tiny village of White Plains. Washington's position appeared strong, since he had had almost a week to fortify his lines, which stretched for three miles along the ridge. His flanks were secure, too. On his left (east), was a lake and an inaccessibly steep hill; while, on his right, was the Bronx River.

Also, he had belatedly sent Rufus Putnam forward to oversee construction of advance works on Chatterton Hill, about half a mile in front and to the right of Washington's lines.

But, shortly after dawn and before Putnam could accomplish much on Chatterton Hill, the enemy "hove in sight." The Americans looked down and saw 13,000 beautifully uniformed and equipped European Regulars advancing in perfect formations to give battle. Otto Hufeland, an officer in Webb's Connecticut levies, was impressed with the sight.

> [Their] appearance was truly magnificent. A bright autumnal sun shed its lustre on the polished arms; and the rich array of dress and military equipage gave an imposing gandeur to the scene as they advanced in all the pomp and circumstance of war.

From the top of Chatterton Hill, Colonel John Haslet observed "their general officers on horse back assemble in council." In this council of war, Howe politely listened to his generals' suggestions, then decided for himself how to meet Washington's challenge. Unlike American commanders, Howe asked for no votes in his councils. Howe decided to first capture Chatterton Hill. From there, a covering cannonade would soften the rebel lines if he should decide to risk a frontal assault on their main lines.

Howe and his second in command, Henry Clinton, stood together now to watch the only action that took place that day. Brigadier-General Alexander Leslie was asked to cross the narrow Bronx River and take the hill. To accomplish this, he was given twelve cannon, some cavalry, and two regiments of British infantry and three of Hessians, about 4,000 men altogether. The rest of the army "all sat down in the same order in which they stood," to watch the action.

From the main lines on the hills in the rear, Washington observed this deployment in his spyglass. He quickly ordered Chatterton Hill reinforced. It soon boasted 1,600 men, but no fortifications. Brigadier-

General Alexander McDougall, of New York, had overall command of these forces, composed of his own 1st New York regiment, Ritzema's 3rd New York, Smallwood's Marylanders, and Haslet's Delawares (all Continentals), as well as Webb's Connecticut levies, and two militia regiments from Connecticut and Massachusetts.

Chatterton Hill was a ridge 180 feet high, running in a north-south direction for about three-fourths of a mile. The top half of the ridge was composed of fields and pastures separated by stone walls. The lower slopes were wooded down to the Bronx River, which ran along the hill's eastern front.

The fight for Chatterton Hill, which would become known as the Battle of White Plains, started on a discouraging note for the Americans. The British General Leslie had made good use of his plentiful horses to pull his dozen cannon up a steep hill that faced Chatterton Hill from the southwest. "They commenced a severe cannonade" on the Americans, who were moving into position behind the stone walls near the top of the ridge.

Colonel Haslet described the noise of the British bombardment as "a continual peal of reiterated thunder" as it echoed off the hills. The first volley wounded a militiaman in the thigh, and the sight of the gaping wound, the blood, and his groans were too much for the undisciplined militia. "The whole regiment broke and fled immediately and were not rallied without much difficulty." Haslet, trying to rally them back to their positions, fired on one man, but his gun only "flashed in the pan" without igniting its powder.

A request for artillery brought only one piece, which Haslet helped drag forward himself until it was struck by a British cannon ball. The carriage was shattered and a wad of padding was set afire. The artillerymen fled, except for one who stayed to put out the fire and managed to get off a few rounds, despite the gun's condition. Later that morning, Captain Alexander Hamilton's artillery company would arrive with two guns and distinguish themselves in the battle.

General Leslie sent his two British regiments and the cavalry against the American center and left, and two of his three Hessian regiments

against the American right. The other Hessian regiment he held in reserve. The Hessians reached the Bronx River, but they refused to wade across. Although it was so narrow here as to be a creek, it was deep and swift from recent heavy rains. So they felled trees along the riverbank and laid planks across them to form a makeshift bridge. Seeing this, General McDougall sent Smallwood and Ritzema more than half way down the hill, where they opened fire, throwing the Hessians into disorder.

At this point, a British officer doing reconnaisance galloped up to General Leslie and informed him of a fording place to the left. Leslie then called on the British infantry to show their allies what British courage can do. Cheering lustily, they followed him to the ford and crossed it. As they marched by, the British soldiers taunted the Hessians, telling them to stand out of the way of real fighting men. Before ordering a bayonet charge, Leslie sent back word to have the artillery silenced.

As the British moved up the slope, "they were exposed to very severe small-arms and grapeshot fire," and were compelled to retreat almost to the river. But they formed and came on again.

By now, all Leslie's forces had either forded the river or crossed the bridge, except the third Hessian regiment held in reserve. They were hidden from American view by the woods on the lower slopes, and by smoke from a bushfire around the British artillery that had been set off by their discharges. Scouting the riverbank, this reserve regiment had located another fording place further to the west, which they would utilize as soon as Leslie gave the word to advance.

Now that Leslie's main body had crossed, they formed two columns and marched to the right along the riverbank. Eventually, they stopped and formed battle lines parallel to the rebels, before proceeding up the slope with that grim courage so typical of European armies. They were trained to not stop to fire, but keep moving forward into a hail of bullets until they reached the enemy. Then they could put their bayonets to work. The Americans, lacking bayonets, would be forced to flee, or else risk ending their lives like so many had done on Long

Island two months before, pinned to trees by the long blades.

Johann Ries, a captain in one of the two Hessian regiments that had followed the British regiments across the Bronx River, later described the difficulties of the advance:

> We advanced and found a little river before us, through which we had to wade, the water going into the cartouche [ammunition] pouches of most of the men. Scarcely were we through the water, than a rain of shot fell upon us, by which many were wounded. Besides that, the left wing had to march through a wood that had been set alight, so that many men burnt the shoes on their feet. Notwithstanding all these difficulties, we scaled the heights.

Ritzema and Smallwood slowly fell back to their hilltop positions, firing as they went. The European Regulars continued moving up the wooded slope, despite the Americans' fire. They reached the open fields above, formed ranks, and then resumed their advance in perfect formations. The sight must have reminded Howe and Clinton of a similar advance the year before up Breed's Hill. Learning from Howe's mistake that day, the British officers now ordered their wide lines compressed into narrow columns, thus reducing the number of men exposed to the enemy's fire.

There was another lesson, though, that the officer at the head of one of these columns apparently had not learned. Clinton later recalled the scene, in his narrative of the war:

> Two British regiments, having very spiritedly passed the river, suddenly found themselves exposed to a heavy fire. The officer who led them immediately formed in columns for attack and advanced; the instant I saw the move I declared it decisive.
>
> But when the officer had marched about twenty paces

he halted, fired his fuzee and began to reload (his column remaining during the time under the enemy's fire), upon which I pronounced it a *coup manque* [tactical error] foretelling at the same time that they would break.

It happened as I said, and I could not help remarking to Sir William Howe that, if the battle should be lost, that officer was the occasion of it. I had scarcely done speaking when Lord Cornwallis came up with the same observation.

The British column broke and ran back down the hill. Clinton for years had argued that officers should not be allowed to carry the short little muskets - not much longer than pistols - called "fuzees." Their only effecive use was for having something on which to affix a bayonet if it became necessary to force one's own troops back in line when panic set in and the men attempted to break ranks and flee.

By now, the party of British light horse were on the Americans' left flank and trying to do their part. But it was not yet time for a flanking charge, since the infantry had obviously not arrived. They consequently found themselves opposed by Webb's entire regiment, whose close fire forced them to retreat. The horsemen then used the cover of the woods to switch direction - their next attempt would be against the rebels' other flank, defended by militia.

Repeatedly, the advance of the British and Hessian infantry was repulsed. Finally, Howe ordered Colonel Johann Rall to bring forward his third regiment, the reserve. These grenadiers forded the river at a point further west than where the other regiments had crossed. Hidden from American view by the woods on the lower slopes, they moved quickly uphill and burst into the open fields leading to the extreme American right, not allowing General McDougall time to reinforce it. They screamed at the rebels as they charged across the fields with fixed bayonets pointed forward, their brass mitred helmets making them appear deceptively tall and formidable. The surprised and frightened militia turned to face them, fired one mass volley, then

fled over the top of the hill and down the other side toward the main lines, half a mile away.

These fearsome Hessian grenadiers were not the only surprise for the Yankees. Also out of the woods came the British light horse, their kettle drums and trumpets sounding the charge. Dozens of drawn sabers slashed through the air as their steeds pounded across the turf. Most of the fleeing militia were chased down and hacked apart as the razor sharp sabers did their bloody work. The militia's flight also exposed the regiment next to them - Haslet's Delawares - to the fury of the Hessians, and the cavalry when they returned from the chase. Some of Haslet's men also fled, but he quickly posted the rest behind the militia's abandoned wall and "twice repulsed the light troops and horse of the enemy," before ordering a retreat. Captain Johann Ewald credited the victory to the Hessians' discipline (in contrast to the British), enabling them to attack "with the bayonet without firing first."

In the center and left portions of the American line, General McDougall was finally forced back by sheer weight of numbers. However, as they fell back, they managed to cover both Haslet's retreat and Alexander Hamilton's men hauling away their two field pieces. The retreating troops met reinforcements who had been sent out too late from the main lines. Washington had not wanted to commit too many troops to Chatterton Hill, because he still felt Howe would assault the main lines that day. Besides, being on the other side of the hill, he could not see the action.

General Leslie soon "arrived at the summit, formed and dressed his line without the least attempt to pursue the Americans." Leslie had accomplished his mission; Chatterton Hill was firmly in British hands. The battle had ended about 5 p.m. Howe ordered crews to work all night building battery emplacements and breastworks atop the hill. Soon the artillery crews were put to work, bombarding the rebel lines. As one American soldier put it, "they entertained us with their music all evening."

Including the preliminary vanguard action before dawn, south of Chatterton Hill, the day's toll was 28 Americans killed, 126 wounded,

and at least as many captured; and, on the other side, about 350 killed and wounded. The Maryland and Delaware Continentals "had again confirmed their reputation." The young artillery captain from New York, Alexander Hamilton, also had performed admirably. The behavior of the 3rd New York was especially satisfying to its commander, Lieutenant-Colonel Rudolphus Ritzema. During a night march in the Canadian woods the year before, his entire regiment had deserted him, mistaking their own vanguard's gunfire for that of bloodthirsty Indians who existed only in their minds.

With enemy artillery now atop Chatterton Hill, Washington moved his army back the night after the battle to a ridge one mile farther to the north, just on the other side of the crossroads village of White Plains. Meanwhile, Howe had his army spend the next two days intrenching until more reinforcements were due to arrive. Heavy rains all day on Halloween wet much of the army's gunpowder, causing Howe to postpone the assault he had planned for that day. The rain surely must have wet the rebel powder, too, but Howe did not take advantage of this and order a bayonet charge, despite the rebels' almost total lack of bayonets.

Washington was now even more strongly positioned than before, prompting Clinton and others to advise against a frontal assault. The Americans on Chatterton Hill had inflicted heavy casualties upon the advancing British and Hessian infantry. Nevertheless, against the advice of his generals, William Howe ordered an attack for dawn the next morning. He had come all this way, and he must not lose face by backing down now.

Shortly after dawn, Howe's leading troops reached the rebel intrenchments. They found them empty! During the night, Washington had moved his army again, this time five miles north to North Castle Heights. Mistakenly informed that the location was in Connecticut, General Percy wrote from Manhattan to a friend in England, "General Howe has gone to the continent & has sent the Rebels to the Devil, or at least the next thing to it, into New England."

CHAPTER ELEVEN
HOWE OUTMANEUVERS WASHINGTON
NOVEMBER 1776

"This garrison must stand, because it has been hitherto too fashionable to run away."

> - *An American soldier at Fort Washington, on upper Manhattan.*

William Howe was now somewhat frustrated, but still bent on accepting his adversary's challenge to fight, if Washington would only hold still long enough. On November 3rd, he sent a detachment to the right in an attempt to get in the American rear at North Castle Heights. If successful, it would have made a subsequent frontal assault much easier. But the attempt was repulsed by effective American artillery fire. This finally convinced Howe to take the advice of his generals and revert back to his normal cautious nature; he called off the attack. Some of the "very formidable" rebel breastworks were actually an illusion: cornstalks pulled from nearby fields had been piled up, tops inward, then covered with dirt. Each plant's roots, still with "a large lump of earth" clinging to it, pointed towards Howe's army.

During the night of November 4th, American sentries heard the rumble and clank of wheels and the clip-clop of horses' hooves coming from the direction of the enemy camp. The army was immediately placed on full alert for the expected attack, but when dawn arrived the sentries found that the enemy had retreated. Howe had moved his army five miles west to the village of Dobb's Ferry, on the Hudson.

The next night, some Massachusetts troops celebrated the enemy's

retreat by looting and burning the village of White Plains. This raid could only worsen the already poor relations between the Yankee regiments and those from New York and the other "southern" states. Mrs. Nathaniel Adams, wife of a loyalist, begged Major Austin, the leader of the looters, to spare her home. Austin replied, "You are all damn Tories!" and drove Mrs. Adams and her children into the November night without allowing them time to change clothes. After the house was looted, he ordered it set afire like the other fourteen houses and the courthouse. The next day, a furious General Washington ordered an immediate court-martial and, based largely on Mrs. Adams's testimony, Major Austin was cashiered from the army.

These were not the only Yankees making a habit of stealing and terrorizing the New York inhabitants. Two weeks before, in his general orders of the day, Washington had condemned some Rhode Island officers who were seizing horses from nearby farms: "Can it be possible, that persons bearing commissions, and fighting in such a Cause, can degrade themselves into plunderers of horses?"

* * * * *

From Dobb's Ferry, Howe could quickly proceed on a good road that led north toward Albany or south to Kings Bridge. Would he move south and lay siege to Fort Washington? Or would he cross over the Hudson into New Jersey, and march inland to Philadelphia? As Washington put it, Howe's plans were now "a matter of conjecture and speculation." To Captain Mackenzie, of the Royal Welsh Fusiliers, however, it was obvious what Howe should do:

> It is probable that the moment Fort Washington is taken General Howe will land a body of troops in Jersey ... [and march] towards Philadelphia ... rout the Congress, and establish quarters in that city.
> Numberless advantages would arise from the execution of this plan, which does not appear difficult to

effect, as the Rebels have very few troops that way, and it would be impossible for them to receive any succours from Washington's army or that above Albany time enough to prevent our arrival at Philadelphia.

The appearance of a formidable force in Pennsylvania, where the measures of Congress are now much condemned, would induce numbers of the deluded inhabitants to seize the favorable opportunity of returning to their allegiance, and the enjoyment of their former ease, peace and happiness. Many of the leading men in Congress might also take the opportunity of making their peace by an early submission. If anything of this nature should happen, the strength of the Rebellion is at an end, and Washington's army would disperse.

But Philadelphia was not in General Howe's plans yet. Now that he had forced the main rebel army off Manhattan, he planned to take Forts Washington and Lee, and perhaps some New Jersey territory as well. He would quarter his army for the winter at Brooklyn, Manhattan, Staten Island, and New Jersey. And, in order to establish a naval base in New England, Howe would have his annoying second in command, Clinton, set sail for Rhode Island. This plan would prevent congestion and provision problems, while providing a test of his brother's pacification program. The big push to end the rebellion by joining with the army from Canada could wait until spring.

Washington informed Congress of his own opinion, that Howe would "make a descent with a part of his troops into New Jersey, and with another part invest Fort Washington." Just in case Howe should choose to push north in an attempt to unite with the British army still on Lake Champlain, Washington sent General Heath with 4,000 troops to fortify the Highlands, where the Hudson narrowed near Peekskill. General Lee would keep another 7,000, mostly New Englanders, in the White Plains area to protect New England. Washington, himself, would lead the remaining 2,000 troops across the Hudson near Stony

Point, and march to New Jersey to join General Nathanael Greene to block Howe's path to Philadephia. Greene's division of the army consisted of 3,500 men spread between upper Manhattan, Fort Lee on the Jersey shore, and "The Flying Camp" of militia held in reserve at Amboy, New Jersey.

During the past week, the Commander-in-Chief had been corresponding with Greene. From his headquarters outside Fort Lee, Greene wrote to Washington on November 7th, informing him that, just that morning, three British frigates had sailed up the Hudson, past the underwater *chevaux-de-frise*. A spirited barrage from Forts Washington and Lee did little damage to the passing warships. This was the British Navy's third sucessful passage in three tries since July. Despite Congress's repeated desire to defend the passage at all costs, it was now obvious, at least to Washington, that the forts no longer served their only intended purpose, and therefore should be abandoned. General Lee had been outvoted in council when he had called for evacuating Fort Washington, saying it was "almost a certainty" to be captured. Washington was beginning to believe Lee's prediction of doom for the Fort Washington garrison. But he had the highest esteem for Greene, the youngest and perhaps the brightest of his brigadiers. Washington's response to Greene's letter, therefore, was more of a strong suggestion than an order:

> The late passage of the 3 vessels up the North River is so plain a proof of the inefficacy of all the obstructions we have thrown into it, that I cannot but think it will fully justify a change in the disposition [of troops] which has been made. If we cannot prevent vessels passing up, and the enemy are possessed of the surrounding country, what valuable purpose can it answer to attempt to hold a post from which the expected benefit cannot be had?
>
> I am therefore inclined to think that it will not be prudent to hazard the men and stores at Mount Washington, but as you are on the spot, leave it to you to give such

orders as to evacuating Mount Washington as you judge best.

Greene wrote back, acknowledging that yes, the British had proven the river passable. But, he argued, Fort Washington and the Harlem lines were still "of an advantage," because they controlled the Kings Bridge Road, thus forcing Howe's communications between Westchester County and New York to go by water through treacherous Hell Gate. A Hessian officer felt the same way and later cited this as the reason why the fort had to be attacked.

Greene and his commanding officer on Manhattan, Colonel Robert Magaw, were both confident that any attempt to force the Americans from upper Manhattan would occupy several thousand of Howe's best troops for two months. Anyway, Greene assured Washington, "the men may be brought off [across the Hudson] at any time." Earlier, Greene had stated, "I would not evacuate one foot of ground, as it will tend to encourage the enemy and dispirit our people." As one soldier still on Manhattan put it, "This garrison must stand, because it had been hitherto too fashionable to run away."

General Greene, a Quaker anchorsmith from Rhode Island, and Colonel Magaw, a lawyer from Pennsylvania, each lacked a thorough knowledge of military science, and neither one had any military experience prior to this war. Their judgement being influenced by their zeal, they overrated the fort's defenses. Captain Alexander Graydon, of Philadelphia, noted that "there were no barracks or casemates [bombproofs], or fuel, or water within the body of the place." Water had to be carried up 230 feet from the Hudson. There was no protection from cannon balls coming over the walls, or from European troops, trained to charge while under fire, climbing over the short walls and putting their bayonets to use. Graydon went on:

In addition, there was not found in it ammunition adequate to the shortest defence. Yet, it was to be defended, as will soon appear. Colonel Magaw had

heard of sieges being protracted for months and even
years; he had a good opinion of the spirit of the garrison;
and, as the place he had to defend was called a fort, and
had cannon in it, he thought the deuce was in it if he
could not hold out a few weeks.

The decision whether to evacuate or defend was further complicated
by the disposition of the troops on upper Manhattan. Some were at
the old Harlem Heights lines, some at minor works near the Harlem
River, some in Fort Washington, and still others near Kings Bridge.
Before the main army left for White Plains, a council of war had estimated a successful defense of all this territory would require 8,000
men, four times the number Greene had on Manhattan. So, on
Halloween, he wrote to Washington, asking for direction as to how
much territory should be defended if the enemy was seen preparing to
launch an attack. Greene reminded Washington of the fort's small capacity: "If we attempt to hold the [entire] ground, the garrison must
still be reinforced, but if the garrison is only to draw into Mount
Washington and keep that, the number of troops is too large." But
Washington was preoccupied with Howe at White Plains. One of his
aides finally wrote back on November 5, "the holding or not holding
the grounds between Kingsbridge and the lower lines depends upon so
many circumstances that it is impossible for him to determine the
point. He submits it entirely to your discretion."

On November 10th, Washington led his division of 2,000 soldiers
and its small train of artillery and supplies across the Hudson. Over
the next four days they slowly made their way to Hackensack, New
Jersey, via a circuitous 65-mile march around The Great Cedar
Swamp. Off and on, these half-naked, shoeless men were pelted by icy
rain as they marched over muddy country roads.

After personally overseeing the crossing, Washington rode ahead to
establish his temporary headquarters at Hackensack, arriving there on
the thirteenth. Though this part of New Jersey was predominantly loyalist, a staunch Whig named Peter Zabriskie offered to put the general

up in his house for as long as he wished. Zabriskie warned Washington that numerous armed Tories were ready to rise up, just as soon as Howe crossed the Hudson. Retreat through this country would be hazardous.

Washington was particularly upset to learn that the militia were not turning out to defend their home state. New Jersey's system of monthly rotation was not working, as fewer men were turning out with each rotation Washington had expected to find at least 5,000 New Jersey militia awaiting his arrival, ready to fight for their home soil. Instead, there were only a handful. This meant that the 2,000 he had brought with him, and Greene's 3,500, comprised the only resources immediately available to stop a British invasion of New Jersey. Furthermore, the enlistments of most of the 7,000 left at White Plains under Lee were due to expire before December.

Washington did not stay long at Zabriskie's that afternoon. He wanted to go on to Fort Lee, five and a half miles to the east, to see how Nathanael Greene was making out. At 5:30, mud-splattered and grim, he arrived at the nearby farm house serving as headquarters. Greene and his staff came out on the porch to greet Washington, who dismounted and walked stiffly up the steps. He took off his large three-cornered hat, revealing a head of reddish-brown hair now well sprinkled with gray. It had been a typically long day in the saddle for the 44-year-old Washington, having ridden thirty miles since morning. If not directing a major move of his army, he was almost constantly riding from one point to another to inspect new troops, supplies or positions.

Cold and weary, almost too exhausted to think, Washington sat down with his friend Greene in front of the fireplace. Reviewing the overall military situation, they agreed on one point - they could expect Howe to first capture upper Manhattan, then cross the Hudson and head for Philadelphia.

When the conversation shifted to more specific concerns, Greene vigorously defended his actions in not ordering the evacuation there. He expected Howe to make a methodical siege against the fort and its

outworks. He pointed out that the fiery Irishman in charge there, Colonel Magaw, was confident the garrison could hold out until "at least the end of December." When the pressure became too great, they could call on Colonel Glover's regiment of fishermen for a night crossing of the Hudson, just as Washington had escaped across the East River after the Battle of Long Island. By the time that became necessary, it would be early winter - too late for any British move against Philadelphia. It was common knowledge that British generals almost never marched their armies in winter. Campaigning in cold, wet weather more often than not resulted in an army being decimated by illness.

Greene also felt strongly that another retreat would be devastating to the army's morale, especially that of the unstable militia. Just the week before, Greene had had his hands full putting down a near mutiny by an entire regiment of New York militia posted at Kings Bridge. They claimed that Admiral Lord Richard Howe "promised them peace, liberty and safety," and that was all they wanted. The time had now come, Greene told Washington, to make a stand. Or else the army, and with it resistance to Parliament, would all but disappear.

Washington was not totally convinced by Greene's arguments, and weighed them against his own feelings in what he later called "that warfare in my mind." They ended the conference with "nothing concluded upon." Bone-weary, Washington rode off into the dark to Hackensack to catch a few hours of sleep. He told Greene that he would spend the next two days settling his division in Hackensack, and meeting with civilian and militia leaders to discuss how to defend the roads leading to Philadelphia, then he would return on the sixteenth and go over to Manhattan with Greene "to see the situation of things."

Greene knew that a British attack was imminent, thanks to his own observations and those offered by a British deserter. Many years later, Captain Graydon recalled the desertion incident in his memoirs. It was a "raw, rainy and tempestuous" night in the first week of November. Graydon was in charge of a chain of guard posts at The Point of Rocks, "our most advanced picket towards New York and only sepa-

rated from that of the enemy by a valley of a few hundred yards."
Captain Graydon and his lieutenant sought shelter from the icy rain by
spending the rest of the night in a deserted house slightly closer to the
enemy. After extending "the line of sentinels round the building," the
two officers went in and made "a good fire." The lieutenant soon fell
asleep, but Graydon remained in front of the fireplace, drying his
clothes. His account of what followed:

> A sudden noise of feet and voices reached the door.
> The latch was lifted, and as I rose up, not without con-
> siderable alarm, the first object that presented itself was
> a British soldier, with his musket and fixed bayonet in his
> hand.
>
> "Who are you," said I, "a deserter?" "No deserter!"
> was the answer. My first impression was that we were
> surprised, and should be bayonetted out of hand. But
> this idea was scarcely formed, when the appearance of
> one of my own men behind the British soldier changed it
> to a more pleasing one. In fact, he was a deserter; but,
> though in the very act of committing the crime, he re-
> volted against its opprobrium. I understood him, and
> softened down the ungraciousness of my salutation, by
> asking if he had come over to us. He answered, "yes."
> He informed us that we might expect to be attacked in
> six or eight days at farthest, as the preparations for the
> assault were nearly completed.

Now was the time to order either an evacuation or a reinforcement.
Greene chose the latter, sending over half of his 1,500 men from Fort
Lee. This made Colonel Magaw's strength on Manhattan well over
two thousand. Major Carl Leopold Bauermeister, adjutant to the Hessian General von Knyphausen, noted on November 14th the arrival of
"considerable reinforcements" of rebels. "General Howe," he wrote,
"who had supposed all along that the enemy would evacuate the fort,

now realized that they were determined to defend it."

The Americans guarding Kings Bridge had been beaten back by von Knyphausen on November 2nd, so defense of the northern approach would have to be handled much closer to the fort. Colonel Moses Rawlings and his 250 Maryland and Virginia riflemen took positions at the northern end of Mount Washington, half a mile from the fort. At the very top of this almost clifflike northern slope, the small Forest Hill Redoubt, with a battery of two guns, was in position to command the Kings Bridge Road. Below this, on the slope itself, were three successive breastworks. And between each of these, sticking out of the ground, was a sharp wooden abatis. Altogether, these defenses composed a pretty formidable set of obstacles for a distance of "200 paces." The slope itself was so steep and rugged that a British officer contemptuously claimed only such cowardly "poltroons as the Americans would think to fortify it." The Hessian Captain Johann Ewald later remembered the steep hill, a difficult climb under normal conditions, much worse in the face of grapeshot and the well-aimed musketry of hundreds of riflemen:

> The road runs up the hill through a wood which is cut
> through with rocks and deep ravines, and which has
> been made completely impassable by many abatis. Sev-
> eral small works lie in the wood, one behind the other,
> which can fire upon the entire road.

Any attack from the east would have to be an amphibious one, the troops landing on the Harlem River's marshy west bank, then climbing up a ridge called Laurel Hill while under fire from Americans posted above them. Atop Laurel Hill, a couple of small "fleches" (two-sided breastworks) were far from adequate cover for the nearly 500 Pennsylvania militia posted there, under Colonel William Baxter. These troops had recently been brought over from the "Flying Camp" at Amboy, New Jersey - reserves ready to fly wherever most needed. Whether these men would stand firm under fire was doubted by many

who held the common belief that "the Flying Camp was too literally such." Not all of these 500 men were untested, however. Colonel Baxter and some others had seen plenty of action at Gowanus Pass, on Long Island.

Two miles south of Fort Washington, Lieutenant-Colonel Lambert Cadwalader commanded 800 men, mainly Pennsylvania Continentals, as well as the Connecticut Rangers formerly under Knowlton. They occupied the front line of the old Harlem Heights works, which now boasted an artillery force of one puny six-pounder. Magaw posted minor detachments at other locations, and himself kept a small reserve and the sick inside Fort Washington.

All told, it was a very ambitious plan, an attempt to hold more than three square miles of territory with small detachments against vastly superior numbers of well-equipped, trained Regulars. Ensign Thomas Glyn, one of the British soldiers who would attack Laurel Hill, later wrote that he was not surprised at the rebels' works being "too extensive for the number of troops, as was generally the case with the Americans, who were indefatigable in constructing redoubts."

After the battle, one of the American officers stated that, given the precision of their assault, the British "must have had a perfect knowledge of the ground we occupied." In fact, that was exactly the case. Colonel Magaw's adjutant, Major William Demont, had secretly copied the positions and strengths of the fort and its outworks. Then, during the night of November 2nd, he had deserted "and joined Lord Percy [and] brought in with me the plans." Demont made public his defection many years later when, as a penniless petitioner before Parliament, he asked for compensation. He claimed that by deserting "I sacrificed all I was worth in the world" and "from my knowledge of the works I saved the lives of many of his Majesty's subjects." According to a British officer's diary, Demont gave General Percy other intelligence, too:

> There are great dissensions in the rebel army, everybody finding fault with the mode of proceeding, and the

inferior officers, even ensigns, insisting that, in such a Cause, every man has a right to assist in council and to give his opinion. They are much distressed for clothing. The people from the southern colonies declare they will not go into New England, and the others that they will not march to the southward. If this account is true in any degree, they must soon go to pieces.

The evening of the fourteenth (the day after Washington and Greene discussed evacuating the fort), Howe made his first move. Thirty empty flatboats were rowed up the Hudson, past the rebel forts. At Spuyten Duyvil, where the Harlem River starts at Manhattan's northwestern tip, they turned right and rowed down that river until they reached the British and Hessian camps on its east bank. Each of these thirty empty flatboats was capable of transporting fifty Regulars down the Harlem to a favorable landing place.

On the fifteenth, the 32-gun *Repulse* sailed up the Hudson from New York and anchored near the American lines on Harlem Heights. Another 32-gun frigate, the *Pearl*, one of the three ships that had sailed upriver on the seventh, was now on its way back down to take up a position just north of Fort Washington. These two ships would cover the attacking columns' western flanks, and also ensure that no Americans would escape by crossing the Hudson.

Captain Frederick Mackenzie, a confidant of General Percy, recorded in his diary Howe's plan for a three-pronged attack on Fort Washington:

The disposition of the several attacks was nearly as follows. General Knyphausen, with the Hessian brigades under his command, was to advance from Kingsbridge, and drive the enemy from their advanced posts, and then to take post on a hill which was within half cannon shot of the fort, with his right to the N. River.

The Brigade of Guards were to cross Haerlem Creek

and join Genl Knyphausen's left. The 1st Light Infantry were to cross the creek on the left of the Guards; the 2d Light Infantry in another place on the left of the 1st, and the 42d Regiment to pass it under Col Morris's house. ...

Lord Percy, with the 3rd brigade of British Infantry, & Stirn's brigade of Hessians were to advance from the lines at McGowan's [Pass], drive the enemy from their most advanced posts, & wait, with his left to the N. River, until he heard or saw that the troops which were to cross Haerlem Creek had gained the summit of the [Laurel] hill.

Every column was then to push forward, force all the enemy's posts, and unite as near as possible to Fort Washington.

* * * * *

At five p.m. on November 15th, a lathered horse galloped into the Zabriskie yard in Hackensack. The rider reined in his horse, quickly dismounted, and announced he had an urgent message for General Washington from General Greene. In a classic understatement, Greene had written, "Dear Sir: Enclosed you have a letter from Colonel Magaw; the contents will require your Excellency's attention." In the enclosed letter to Greene, Magaw had explained that Howe was in position to attack, and demanded complete and immediate surrender. Magaw then finished, "You'll I dare say, do what is best. We are determined to defend this post or die." In Greene's own note, he informed Washington that he was sending over more reinforcements and would cross over himself with General Israel Putnam.

After hastily writing that letter to Greene, Colonel Magaw had written a response for the British messenger to take back to Howe:

Sir: If I rightly understood ... your message ... this post is to be immediately surrendered, or the garrison

put to the sword. I rather think it a mistake than a settled resolution in General Howe to act a part so unworthy of himself and the British nation. But give me leave to assure His Excellency that, actuated by the most glorious cause that mankind ever fought in, I am determined to defend this post to the very last extremity.

Washington called for his horse and raced to Fort Lee, only to find that Greene and Putnam had already gone across the Hudson to meet with Magaw. So Washington spurred his horse again and proceeded down the steep farm road that led to the river landing below. By now it was dark; it would be difficult to spot enemy patrol boats in the water. But the Commander-in-Chief was willing to run that risk; he ordered two soldiers at the landing to row him across.

In mid-stream, other oars could be heard but not seen up ahead, the sounds coming closer and closer. The two soldiers in Washington's boat put down their oars and picked up their muskets. When the approaching boat came alongside, it proved to be carrying Greene and Putnam, returning to Fort Lee. The oarsmen in each boat used their hands and arms to hold the two boats together as the three generals talked over the sound of gunwales creaking and waves lapping against the sides. Greene and Old Put informed Washington that "the troops were in high spirits and would make a good defense" whenever the assault should begin, probably the next morning. Since it was now too late to accomplish any more that night, Washington instructed his two oarsmen to turn the boat around and follow the other generals back to Fort Lee.

* * * * *

General von Knyphausen, just north of Kings Bridge, had his division of 5,000 men up at 3 a.m. By 5:30, they were marching across a pontoon bridge onto Manhattan, the wooden Kings Bridge and Dyckmans Bridge having recently been burned by the Americans. The

sun would rise on this sixteenth of November at 6:48 a.m.

Leading the vanguard of 100 light troops was Lieutenant Andreas Wiederhold. He had been commended for bravery fourteen years before, but had never received his captaincy, because he was a commoner. Like the British Army, commissions in the German military were purchased at great expense, and usually only by those with influence at court. Lieutenant Wiederhold's orders this morning were to silently climb up the mountain as far as possible without being observed. The veteran knew many of his men would die this day; he thought the rebel position at Forest Hill was "a hard nut to crack."

Now, as dawn approached, his men were laboriously advancing up the steep incline, the ground covered with wet maple leaves and tangled bushes. He was within sight of Rawlings's pickets. Suddenly, an out-of-breath messenger came scrambling up at a very fast pace, finally reaching Wiederhold at the very front of the long column. Between gasps, he managed to whisper an urgent message: "General von Knyphausen ... orders to come back." Lt. Wiederhold, somewhat disappointed as well as relieved, motioned for his men to return as silently as they had come.

Above them, atop Mount Washington's northern face, John and Margaret Corbin had not seen the enemy advancing through the darkness, and perhaps did not see them retreating either. But this husband and wife team, working one of the Forest Hill Redoubt's two field pieces, would have a fateful meeting with these foreign mercenaries when they returned a few hours later.

The dawn attack had been postponed because of "some neglect not foreseen" when Howe had made his plans. The Harlem River, often called Harlem Creek, would not be deep enough at low tide for the flatboats to come right up to the east bank for the British troops to be loaded. The tide would not "serve" until several hours later. Therefore, the amphibious assault against Laurel Hill would not be launched until almost 11 o'clock.

At 10 o'clock, all was quiet at the Harlem Heights lines south of the fort, where Captain Alexander Graydon had been on full alert since be-

fore dawn. He and several others from his company were shielding their eyes from the eastern sun, as they gazed at the British position atop a hill across the Harlem. What caught their attention was a flurry of activity around the artillery there. Suddenly, they saw red-gold flashes of light, followed by rings of smoke, emanating from those big guns. Graydon and the others quickly scattered, some of them jumping into the trench, as the thundering booms reached their ears. A moment later, a cannon ball "fell short by about ten or fifteen yards and bounded over the spot we had precipitately abandoned."

Those big guns across the Harlem were soon not the only British batteries firing at the American outposts. Lord Percy's guns opened up south of the Harlem Heights lines, and so did von Knyphausen's lighter field pieces north of Forest Hill Redoubt, to support the advancing infantry. In the Hudson River below, the two frigates opened up, elevating their guns as best they could. Altogether, for two hours it would be "a furious cannonade from all the batteries which were within reach of the works."

As planned, Percy's British and Hessian forces were able to "drive the enemy from their most advanced posts" - the Point of Rocks above Harlem Plains. Graydon's memoirs provide a detailed account:

> At ten o'clock in the morning, a large body of the enemy appeared on Harlaem plains, preceded by their field pieces, and advanced with their whole body towards a rocky point of the height ... and commencing a brisk fire on the small work constructed there, drove out the party which held it, consisting of twenty men, and took possession of it, the men retiring with the picket guard to the first line. The enemy, having gained the heights, advanced in column on open ground towards the first line; whilst a party of their troops pushed forward and took possession of a small unoccupied work in front of the first line; from whence they opened their fire with some field pieces and a howitzer, upon the line, but

without effect.

When the column came within proper distance, a fire from the six-pounder was directed against it; on which, the whole column inclined to their left and took post behind a piece of woods, where they remained. As it was suspected that they would make an attempt on the right of the line, under cover of the wood, that part was strengthened.

Graydon's company was shifted to become part of the reinforcement for the western end of the line. There he was annoyed by cannon fire from the *Repulse* in the Hudson River.

Also in the Harlem Heights trenches was 18-year-old Private Ichabod Perry, of Connecticut, whose only previous experience under fire had been the past summer while alone in an orchard atop a bluff near Powle's Hook, New Jersey. On that day, Perry, while climbing a plum tree, was spotted by sailors aboard a British warship in the Hudson River. Permission was given to one gun's crew to practice their skill. On their second shot, the cannon ball knocked a branch out of the tree. The young private scrambled down the tree, grabbed the fruit from the fallen branch, and bowed his thanks to the enemy before running off.

Now, in the trench on Harlem Heights, there were many more cannon balls flying at him, but not solid shot this time. Percy's gunners were using howitzers to send up shells - hollow cannon balls filled with gunpowder. A fuse slowly burned as the ball sailed through the air, then kept burning for a short time after it landed. Finally it would burn through to the powder, exploding the metal casing. This was an early form of what would be called "shrapnel" in the Civil War. Private Ichabod Perry later wrote of this anxious time:

We had a small dog that would watch them, and whenever he saw one strike the ground he would run and catch the fuse in his mouth and hold it with his feet on the shell, till he pull'd it out and so stopp'd it from ex-

ploding. He had the good luck to serve several that way which made some amusement to the spectators, but at length he failed. While he was in the act of trying to get out the fuse, the shell exploded and the poor dog went to atoms.

At this time, Generals Washington, Greene, Putnam and Mercer were being rowed across the Hudson. Greene noted in a letter to Colonel Henry Knox the next day, "just at the instant we stepped on board the boat, the enemy [Percy's men] made their appearance on the hill and began a severe cannonade." It was 11:30 by the time the American generals arrived at the fort and rode with Colonel Magaw to the Morris House.

They made their observations from that vantage point. Percy was still threatening the Harlem Heights lines, but holding back, waiting for a sign that the amphibious expedition was succeeding, below Laurel Hill. Heavy firing could also be heard from north of the fort, where the Forest Hill Redoubt was under attack by von Knyphausen. Looking northeast from the Morris House, Washington and the others could see the Laurel Hill defenders firing down its steep east bank. Just what they were firing at the generals could not tell from this angle. Greene later wrote of this meeting at the Morris House:

> There we all stood, in a very awkward position. As the disposition [of troops] was made, and the enemy advancing, we durst not attempt any new disposition, indeed we saw nothing amiss. We all urged his Excellency to come off - I offered to stay, General Putnam did the same, and so did General Mercer, but his Excellency thought it best for us all to come off together.

Colonel Magaw returned to Fort Washington, and the four generals to Fort Lee. Captain Graydon later learned that "the British troops

took possession of the very spot, fifteen minutes after they left it."

Generals Matthews and Cornwallis, accompanied later by Howe himself, were landing the amphibious expedition at the bottom of Laurel Hill. Two thousand Regulars, led by the elite light infantry, splashed ashore, waded the marshy riverbank while under heavy fire from above, and were now rapidly proceeding up the steep hill. Early that morning, Greene had sent over more Pennsylvania militia from the Flying Camp and Magaw had used them to reinforce Laurel Hill. But even with these, Colonel Baxter had little more than 500 men to oppose the 2,000 crack British Regulars.

Covered by a heavy bombardment from the hilltop across the Harlem River, the British were making good progress up Laurel Hill. The militia, behind rocks and some minor breastworks, had only a few light field pieces to assist them, and these could not be angled enough to fire down the steep slope. Virtually none of the American muskets were equipped with bayonets. In front of them, hundreds of Regulars with fixed bayonets kept on coming, despite the militia's musket fire. When the British were within fifty yards, most of the militia turned and headed down the west side of Laurel Hill and across the narrow valley toward Fort Washington. Those who tarried on Laurel Hill suffered for their courage. Colonel Baxter died falling face forward, a British officer's sword thrust through his body. As promised, he had not turned his back on his country's enemy.

The British troops that reached the Morris House fifteen minutes after Washington left it were not those that overran Baxter's militia on Laurel Hill. They were another amphibious expedition - the 42nd Regiment of Highlanders, the famed Black Watch. Howe had originally planned to use them as a feint attack, threatening to land below the Morris House, but not actually doing so. This would draw off a detachment from Cadwalader's division, weakening the Harlem Heights lines, at which time Percy would push forward with his attack. But the attempt on Laurel Hill was going so well that Cornwallis sent an order down to immediately land the flatboats and have the more than 800 kilted Scotsmen scale the pathless bluff below this unde-

fended sector around the Morris House. If they could overcome whatever resistance they met there, and get behind Cadwalader, he would be caught between two fires. This was a particularly vulnerable area, since the nearby third line of fortifications on the Heights had never been extended to the Harlem cliffs as planned.

Almost immediately after Washington left the Morris House, a runner came up to Colonel Cadwalader and informed him that flatboats full of enemy troops were approaching the shore a few hundred yards north of the Morris House. Cadwalader dispatched a captain with fifty men to oppose them from the clifftop. A few minutes later, word came that the enemy troops were at least 800 Highlanders. He sent off another 100, though he felt he could not spare them. These troops laid down on the ground at the cliff's edge and had target practice against the Highlanders, who were sitting ducks, crowded fifty men to a flatboat. In their attempt to land, and climb up a gorge formed by a stream falling to the Harlem, they suffered 80 casualties. When these kilted grenadiers, famed for their courage and ferocity in battle, reached the top they found the 150 defenders falling back, firing as they went, to a farmhouse south of the Morris House. Thirty of them were not fast enough and were captured.

Meanwhile, Colonel Magaw had sent 150 of the reserve from Fort Washington. These militia, recent arrivals from the Flying Camp, were unfamiliar with the terrain and took positions near the Morris House, not seeing the others who had just retreated. Within minutes, seventy-five of them, in a trench, found themselves completely surrounded by the Highlanders and wisely put up no resistance. The Scottish leader, Colonel Stirling, assigned a detachment to guard the prisoners, then ordered the remainder, nearly 700 men, to head for the Harlem Heights lines.

As planned, Percy was now pressing forward with his 4,200 British and Hessian troops against Cadwalader's remaining 650, spread out to cover nearly a mile of breastworks. And, now in Cadwalader's rear, were the approaching Highlanders. A rider came galloping up to Cadwalader, with an order from Magaw to fall back to the fort. From his

vantage point on Mount Washington, Magaw had seen Cadwalader's danger. Cadwalader ordered his troops to make a run for Fort Washington, two miles in the rear.

Percy's left column of Hessian grenadiers chased Ichabod Perry's company on top of the slope that led down to the Hudson. They had not received the order to retreat until the last possible moment and now were almost surrounded by swarms of these fearsome foreign mercenaries they had heard so many stories about. The only hope of escape was to run down the path to the shore, then follow it nearly two miles to the path that led up to Fort Washington. Private Perry rushed down the narrow path, just behind his lieutenant. They were among those at the head of the column. Looking to the side as he ran, he saw the enemy crashing through the woods, trying to reach the shore first and cut off their escape. Ichabod Perry's account of those last few yards:

> When I passt them (we had to go in single file) there was a Hessian that had got within eight feet of us who fired off his gun, the contents of which went through the leg of Lieutenant Meade. I discovered the Hessian behind a cedar bush. I immediately dropp't my gun with the muzzle to the bush and fired. I saw him pitch forward but did not stop to pick him up. There was few that got past after me.

Running on, Ichabod Perry saw a brook up ahead and next to it a demijohn - a large glass bottle encased in wicker. He let his comrades continue on without him, as he stopped to drink from the stream and fill the bottle. It would be invaluable once he reached the fort, which he knew had no water supply of its own. He climbed out of the ravine through which the stream ran, and, looking back, spotted the enemy reaching the opposite bank.

> They calld to me to stop, but I thought it was no place

for me to stop. They then began to fire at me. I could see the dust rise all round me, where the balls hit the ground, and several went through my clothes, and two hit the stock of my gun, which about split it. There was one which took off most of the skin of one arm, but the grass did not grow under my feet. I got safe into the Fort with the botol of water where there was many begging for a sip at it, but I refus'd giving any of it, telling them that I had been in jeopardy of my life to procure it.

When we last left Captain Alexander Graydon, he was on the extreme west end of Cadwalader's line, near the Hudson. Graydon's account of his retreat:

The line of entrenchment was too extensive to be manned without leaving intervals. Some of these were large, and intervening hillocks cut off the communication in some parts; otherwise, the whole of us under the command of Colonel Cadwalader must have retreated at the same time. The first notice that I had of the entrenchment being given up was from an officer I did not know, posted at some distance from me, going off with his men. I called to him to know what he meant. He answered, that he was making the best of his way to the fort, as the rest of the troops had retreated long since. I immediately formed my company, and began to retire in good order.

After proceeding some hundred paces, I reflected that I had no orders for what I was doing, my movement might be premature. I knew nothing of what had passed in the centre, or of the enemy being master of the high grounds in my rear about Colonel Morris's house. To be entirely correct in my conduct, I here halted my men, and went myself to a rising ground at some distance,

from which I might have a view of the lines ... I ordered them [the company], under the command of my ensign, to make the best of their way and join the body of men, which none doubted being our own, on the heights beyond the inner lines; and that I would follow them as fast as I could, for I was a good deal out of breath. I walked on, accompanied by Forrest who did not choose to leave me alone.

The troops on the heights, which Graydon thought were Cadwalader's, "turned out to be the British, consisting of Colonel Stirling's division of Highlanders." The rest of Graydon's company managed to elude them by going around toward the Hudson, but Graydon and Forrest did not discover their mistake until they almost reached the height. By then, they "had no chance of escape." Continuing with Graydon's account:

We clubbed our fusees in token of surrender, and continued to advance toward them. They either did not or would not take the signal; and though there were but two of us, from whom they could not possibly expect a design to attack, they did not cease firing at us. I may venture to say, that not less than ten guns were discharged with their muzzles towards us, within the distance of forty or fifty yards.

Luckily for us, it was not our riflemen to whom we were targets; and it is astonishing how even these blunt shooters could have missed us. But as we were ascending a considerable hill, they shot over us. I observed they took no aim, and that the moment of presenting and firing was the same. I took off my hat with such a sweep of the arm as could not but be observed, without ceasing however to advance. This had the intended effect: a loud voice proceeded from the breast-work, and

the firing immediately ceased.

An officer of the forty-second regiment advanced towards us; and as I was foremost, he civilly accosted me by asking my rank. Being informed of this, as also of Forrest's, he inquired where the fort lay and where Colonel Magaw was. I pointed in the direction of the fort, and told him I had not seen Colonel Magaw during the day. Upon this, he put us under the care of a sergeant and a few men, and left us. The sergeant was a decent looking man, who, on taking us into custody, bestowed upon us in broad Scotch the friendly admonition of "Young men, ye should never fight against your king."

The little bustle produced by our surrender was scarcely over, when a British officer on horseback, apparently of high rank, rode up at full gallop, exclaiming, "What! taking prisoners! Kill them, kill every man of them." Turning to him, I took off my hat, saying, "Sir I put myself under your protection." No man was ever more effectually rebuked. His manner was instantly softened. After a civil question or two, he rode off towards the fort, to which he had inquired the way.

Most of Cadwalader's men made it safely back to the fort, partly because Colonel Stirling's Highlanders hesitated when they neared the second Harlem Heights line, not realizing immediately that the trenches were empty. But Stirling and also General Percy, who was accompanied by Captain Mackenzie and Admiral Howe, made it an interesting chase, as the rebels were "briskly pursued for near two miles." Mackenzie noted that "the ardour of the troops was only checked by a smart fire which the most advanced received from some Rebels who had thrown themselves into a small wood very near the fort."

Yes, off to the fort. The separate commands under Percy, Stirling and Mathews were all rapidly closing in on the fort. While these

actions already described were taking place, a much more bloody encounter was being fought north of the fort. After word arrived at Kings Bridge that the British flatboats were finally under way, von Knyphausen had set out again toward the north face of Mount Washington, defended by Colonel Moses Rawlings. His 250 riflemen were posted behind three breastworks on the steep slope, as well as the Forest Hill Redoubt on top. Sixty-year-old General Wilhelm von Knyphausen led the left column of 2,800 men, while fifty-year-old Colonel Johann Rall led the right column of 1,200. Just three weeks before, Rall had led the decisive charge, sweeping the rebels off Chatterton Hill, at the Battle of White Plains.

Many an advancing soldier was undoubtedly cursing Howe in German for calling off their pre-dawn attack. Because of the postponement, they no longer could count on surprising their enemy. Inside the hilltop redoubt, the Americans manning their pair of six-pounders looked down and plainly saw hundreds of blue-coated soldiers marching toward them. They sent the King's mercenaries a welcoming barrage of solid round shot.

Young Lieutenant Philipp Waldeck was in his first battle. Later he remembered how "the cannon balls howled terribly" overhead as he marched. Suddenly, he spotted a fellow officer he had last seen back in the fatherland. His friend was in the advance party, about to start up the mountain for the second time that morning. As Waldeck's friend marched by,

> he reached out his hand to me. We were each very happy to see that the other had arrived healthy and well in America. A quarter of an hour later I saw him dead - white, and being carried away. Once more, I looked at him, with tears in my eyes, that noble and courageous man, and with heartfelt sadness I left him.

Philipp Waldeck and hundreds more like him continued on, coming to a hill so steep they had to sling their muskets on their backs and use

both hands to grab hold of the wall of rock to pull themselves and each other up. Even the musicians were going forward, some with big drums sticking out on top of their knapsacks. When they reached flat ground on top of the hill they would be expected to play while the regiments formed ranks and marched against the rebels.

When this first cliff was surmounted, the soldiers were disgusted to find a swamp between them and the next cliff. They sloshed on, as now hundreds of half-ounce balls rained down on them, shot from Pennsylvania rifles made, ironically, by German immigrants. Many of these rifle balls found their mark; many a man fell into the water and didn't stand up. But still they kept on wading, and finally reached the last cliff to scale before they could get at the rebels. Private Johannes Reuber, just seventeen, later remembered the tortuous climb: "We were obliged to creep along up the rocks, one falling down alive, another shot dead." With his musket slung on his back, he had both hands free to grab "the beech tree bushes" and pull himself "up the height."

In the lead, Lieutenant Weiderhold was seemingly advancing in the face of death, as he looked up and saw not the Americans, but trees, which seemed to spout continuous flashes of orange fire and clouds of blue-grey smoke. Panicky soldiers were now coming up to him, telling him that their captain and the other lieutenant had been hit and killed. Two more men who would never see Germany again. As might be expected, the American riflemen were aiming at the officers. The flower of this elite corps was now gone, and Weiderhold found himself in charge of the company, the very spearhead of this insane, suicidal assault. A bullet hit a branch above him, severing a twig which scratched his face - the only wound he would suffer this day. His good fortune not to be hit, while his superiors were being shot down around him, made an old proverb come to his mind: "Weeds never die."

Four times they were repulsed, falling back to the cover of trees and boulders, only to come on again. By now, their artillery crews in the rear had dragged their 12-pounders up the intermediate hill before the swamp. They directed a heavy fire of grapeshot at the clifftop redoubt

where the two rebel guns were hampering the infantry's advance. The rebel gunners, for their part, shifted from solid round shot to grapeshot for what was now close range fire.

Unlike the riflemen in the breastworks below, protected by the cliff wall, the gunners in the little horseshoe-shaped Forest Hill Redoubt on top were exposed to fire from the *Pearl* far below in the Hudson. Despite suffering damage from the fort's guns, the *Pearl* was persisting in its mission of supporting von Knyphausen's attack. Its guns were firing "barshot" (iron dumbbells) that tumbled as they sailed through the air. Fortunately for the Americans, the barshot merely hissed over their heads as it flew by, landing in the valley to the east, where British infantry were advancing on Fort Washington from Laurel Hill.

Von Knyphausen's eight field pieces were more effective than the frigate's bigger guns in their attempts to put the two American guns out of action. One by one, the American artillerists were struck down by the grapeshot. John Corbin fell beside the wheel of his cannon. His wife, Margaret, dropped her water bucket and ran to kneel beside him and offer comfort. After a few moments, she looked up and saw that there were no more men able or willing to take his place loading the cannon. So she did it herself. First, she stuck the pole with its sponge end down the long barrel to expunge any leftover sparks. Next, she used the ramrod to push down a new cartridge. When she brought the linstock to the touch-hole, the gun fired off another charge of lead pellets. Then, as she dipped the sponge in the bucket again, answering grapeshot came hurtling up and knocked her to the ground. Two pellets tore open her breast and another ripped apart one arm. She lay on the ground now, bleeding beside her dying husband.

The "old lions," General von Knyphausen and Colonel Rall, were personally leading their troops. Lieutenant Weiderhold recalled the general's performance:

> He was at all times to be found where the resistance
> and the attack were hottest. He himself laid hold of the
> fences to take some of them down and to spur on the

men. He was exposed to the terrible cannonade and musketry as well as to the rifle shots, like a common soldier. It is to be wondered at, that he came off without being killed or wounded.

With the redoubt's artillery out of action and many of their rifles fouled from too much firing, the riflemen were forced to fall back to the top of the cliff, where they took cover behind boulders and fallen logs. They would roll some of these boulders off the edge in the next charge. Sharpshooting jagers had been exchanging fire with their American counterparts in an effort to cover their advancing comrades. Now, von Knyphausen realized, was the time for the final charge to exploit the enemy's retreat and temporary disorder. For this fifth charge he "forbid firing."

Above them, Pennsylvanian Lieutenant Henry Bedinger, son of German immigrants, overheard these orders and quickly passed the word: they have been ordered to not fire in this next charge, so hold your own until they are on top and in point-blank range. The Americans knew they could not stop their enemy from at least reaching the top; the point now was to make the most effective use of their limited firepower.

A few yards away from Lieutenant Henry Bedinger was his fifteen-year-old brother, Daniel. Despite the minute or more it took to properly reload his long rifle, Daniel managed to get off 27 shots in this battle, shouting after each one, "There! Take that, you -------!"

Now, for the last time, General von Knyphausen gave the battle cry, *"Drauf! Drauf!"* (At them! At them!) and led hundreds of blue coats from their cover. Henry Bedinger crouched behind his boulder and waited until he heard them come over the rim and run toward him. Then he stood up and met a charging Hessian officer with murder in his eyes. Both of them quickly levelled their pieces and fired. The Hessian was faster. His bullet hit a finger on Henry's firing hand just as Henry pulled the trigger. Continuing on, the bullet chopped off a lock of Henry's hair. But Henry's bullet found its mark, blasting a hole

through the man's forehead and sending him tumbling back down that hill he had endured so much to climb.

On von Knyphausen's right, Colonel Rall was leading his smaller division, shouting *"Hoch! Hoch!"* (Up! Up!). Finally, both divisions reached the level ground on top where they would have the advantage of numbers and equipment - bayonets. Earlier, Colonel Moses Rawlings had fallen with a wound in his thigh. His place had been taken by Major Otho Holland Williams, of Maryland, who himself soon fell with a bullet in his groin. As he lay on the ground, his blood soaked his commission, signed "Delegates of the United Colonies, Philadelphia." Still, despite these losses and their inability to stop the enemy from gaining the summit, the Americans would not yield. Private Johannes Reuber, of Rall's regiment, describes the action:

> At last, however, we got on the top of the hill where there were trees and great stones. We had a hard time of it there together. Because they now had no idea of yielding, Colonel Rall gave the word of command thus: "All who are my grenadiers, march forwards!" All the drummers struck up the march, the hautboy [oboe] players blew. At once all that were yet alive shouted, "Hurrah!" Immediately all were mingled together, Americans and Hessians.

The "mingling together" saw the swift thrusts of bayonets. The Hessians were finally paying the Americans back for the hundreds of casualties they had suffered on the way up. Those riflemen still alive and able to run turned and headed for the fort. A half-mile chase ensued. Most of the Americans made it, and clambered up and over the earth walls. The British troops were now also converging on the fort, one of them derisively yelling, "Make room for the soldiers!"

Outside the fort, the Hessians stopped and sat down, taking cover beneath a ledge "to protect ourselves from the cannonade from the fort." Colonel Rall turned to one of his captains and said, "We can still

lose a lot of people, Hohenstein. You speak English and French. Take a drummer, tie a white rag on a gun, and go into the fort and demand their surrender." The drummer began beating the call for a parley, and the two men starting walking toward the fort, Hohenstein slowly waving his improvised flag back and forth as he went. His account of the parley:

> I did this at once, but they kept firing at me and the drummer, until we came to the glacis [ground immediately in front] where the rebels led us off with our eyes bound. They sent me to a colonel [Cadwalader] who was second in command, to whom I made the following proposal:
> He should immediately march out of the fort with the garrison, and they should lay down their arms before General von Knyphausen. All ammunition, provisions, and whatever belonged to Congress should be faithfully made known. On the other hand, I gave my word that all, from the commanding officer down, should retain their private property. Finally, a white flag should be immediately hoisted to put a stop to all hostilities.
> The commander asked for four hours time to consider, which I refused, and allowed him half an hour to speak with his officers.

It was now after 3 o'clock. Four hours to consider the terms would allow enough time for a possible escape attempt under the cover of darkness ... if the garrison could sneak down or fight their way down to the riverbank and if Washington could have boats waiting there. In fact, this is exactly what Washington had in mind, and he sent off a volunteer to cross over, elude the enemy, and get word to Magaw. The message: hold out until darkness, when an attempt would be made "to endeavor to bring off the garrison." Magaw sent the messenger back to tell Washington that, regrettably, it was not possible

this time; General Howe had come up and "insisted they should surrender immediately." The messenger had to go through a German picket line, "dodging their bayonets," but made it to his hidden boat and rowed back to the Jersey side to give Washington the bad news.

For Robert Magaw, the backwoods lawyer with only seventeen months military experience, "the last extremity" had come after only a few hours, not several weeks. Hohenstein noted that the American's "fate seemed hard to him." Magaw said to him, "The Hessians make impossibilities possible." The half-hour up, Cadwalader stayed in the fort this time and Magaw went to talk with von Knyphausen himself. Magaw had the audacity to ask for the "Honors of War" - surrender of the fort, all weapons, and supplies, but freedom for the garrison. He even requested permission to take two of the field pieces with him! Von Knyphausen, a crusty old veteran of 42 years in the military, restrained his temper and instucted Hohenstein to translate a reply to the upstart rebel: surrender the fort and garrison, or shelling would commence in thirty minutes!

In a fort with no bombproofs, and holding three times the number of men it was built for, the shelling would be a massacre. Magaw, realizing he had no bargaining power, acquiesced, but asked for one last request - could the wounded Americans be paroled and sent over to New Jersey? Von Knyphausen agreed to release only the most seriously wounded - they would be more of a hindrance as prisoners than a threat as free men. Colonel Magaw returned to his fort and three minutes later a white flag ran up its pole. General von Knyphausen "put up his watch, lighted his pipe," and accepted the congratulations of his staff. Thousands of shouts in English, Gaelic and German went up from the victors. The shouting was heard a mile away at Fort Lee, where eyewitnesses saw Washington "in agony." Earlier, watching the Forest Hill Redoubt being overrun, Washington's aides had seen tears roll down his cheeks.

The Americans had suffered only 54 killed and 93 wounded during the action, compared to their enemy's 59 dead and 335 wounded, mostly Hessians. But an astounding total of more than 2,800 Ameri-

cans were captured in the futile defense of this post that should have been abandoned long before. The day after the battle, Howe renamed Fort Washington "Fort Knyphausen." With the addition of barracks, a hospital and a bakery, it would serve as headquarters for various Hessian regiments for the next six and a half years. Today, the site is marked by a flagpole on Fort Washington Avenue between 183rd and 185th Streets.

Sixteen-year-old John Adlum, of Pennsylvania, was one of the Americans captured that day. Inside the fort, he noticed several American officers' faces had "tears trickling down." Many of the men had come over from New Jersey that very morning, or the day before. Others had toiled during the hot, humid summer, building what they naively thought was an impregnable fortress. Young Private Adlum was now marched off to New York to be confined as a prisoner of war. On this march, escorted by "a guard of Hessians," Adlum's company passed between a considerable number of British soldiers and camp followers.

> Some of the women observed that it was a shame to let our troops carry off their packs. Some of the Hessian soldiers began to cut the knapsacks off the backs of our men with their swords. Some of our soldiers was severely cut with the swords of the Hessians.
>
> There was great numbers of people collected on various parts of the road, very few of whom seemed to sympathize with us, saying that we ought to be or would be hanged, and called us by opprobrious names of rebel, with a damn added to it by some.
>
> The Hessian women were particularly abusive. When we got to the environs of the city we were assailed by a number of soldiers' trulls and others who the soldiers called Holy Ground Ladies. Numbers were calling out, "Which is Washington? Where is he?" and treated us with volleys of indecent language.

Alexander Graydon and Ichabod Perry experienced much the same treatment. Graydon found the label "damned rebel" "extremely offensive to my ear, however appropriate it might be." Perry did not long keep possession of his precious "water botol." During a stop in the march, he persuaded a British private guarding him to fill it for him at a nearby pump, "but one of the Hessians, who was at the pump, found out who it belong'd to, struck it with the breach of his gun, and broke it." The prisoners were deliberately detoured "to a place calld Gallows hill and causd to march throu, under the gallows."

Being a captain, Graydon was one of the lucky ones - officers were granted parole, allowing them to remain in New York or in the British occupied villages on Long Island. They enjoyed relative freedom until their eventual exchange.

Ichabod Perry and John Adlum, however, being enlisted men, were packed into makeshift prisons - converted warehouses in the city, and the hulls of the infamous prison ships in the harbor. During the war, an estimated 10,000 prisoners died slow deaths in and around New York.

Ichabod Perry and his Connecticut company were marched down to board a ship far too small for the number of prisoners assigned to it. When the hold was filled with so many men that there was no more room to stand, the guards began to "punch them down with the breeches of their guns, and their boots." Finally, the hatches were shut, leaving the prisoners in total darkness, with virtually no air to breathe. Then the ship got under way, sailing to what Perry would later learn was a cove near Brooklyn, where the sails were removed and the ship permanently anchored.

The motion of the ship was too much for the men to keep standing, packed solid and having nothing to hold onto for balance. "We stood," recalled one prisoner, "on our feet as long as we could, then like a heavy piece of wheat in a wet time, we sallied away one on top of another, and he that was the best fellow kept atop." When the hatches were opened the next morning, the guards found that one third

of the prisoners had died of suffocation.

> It took us the bigger part of the day to pull out the
> dead, and the boatmen to carry them ashore and bury
> them. We was then a little thinnd out, but not much re-
> lievd, for we had nothing to eat in four days after we
> went on board. ... This was only the beginning of
> sorrow.

Eighteen months after the surrender of Fort Washington, 800 of these prisoners (all that were still alive) were exchanged. Colonel Magaw would have to wait five years for Congress to arrange for his release from parole - no one wanted to have back in the army an officer who had surrendered over 2,800 men. The Battle of Fort Washington "was a cursed affair" and the released captives were a painful reminder of it. Captain Graydon had planned on re-enlisting but, finding himself undesirable ("militarily dead" as he put it), he married and let the war go on without him.

Ichabod Perry was exchanged and, after his parole expired, he re-enlisted. Margaret Corbin went home to live thirteen more years, a bitter widow with a crippled arm. She was buried at West Point. Daniel Bedinger re-enlisted, with a promotion to lieutenant based on the testimony of his comrades from Forest Hill Redoubt. He was soon captured and imprisoned again, this time for two more years. Upon his release, he joined the army once again and served in some decisive battles under General Nathanael Greene. Greene's successful direction of the southern campaign in 1781 restored his reputation, though it could not eradicate the hardships caused by his insistence that Fort Washington be defended - a guilt he and Washington would share the rest of their lives.

Three days after the surrender of Fort Washington, Howe sent Cornwallis and 4,000 crack troops across the Hudson and forced the remaining American troops to precipitately abandon eastern New Jersey. The invasion was executed so swiftly that Fort Lee was

evacuated with hardly a minute to spare. Between the two forts, 146 cannon were captured (almost the entire American supply), along with 12,000 shot and shell, 2,800 muskets, and 400,000 cartridges. Besides the munitions, much of the army's tents, intrenching tools, and provisions, including 1,000 barrels of flour, were also taken. But the most important loss was the soldiers themselves.

Washington's pitiful little army, dwindling to only a few thousand men by the end of November, was now on the run and an early end for the fledgeling United States of America seemed inevitable. Perhaps the Congress had erred when it appointed George Washington as Commander-in-Chief of its armed forces. General Charles Lee, the European-trained second in command, whom many considered better suited for the job, now wrote to his friends in Congress, offering himself as a replacement. Lee also sent a letter of condolences to Washington, shrewdly couching a reprimand within it for his "fatal indecision." Even Washington's friend, Colonel Joseph Reed, began to doubt George Washington was capable of the task given him. Reed wrote confidentially to Lee, "An indecisive mind is one of the greatest misfortunes that can befall an army. How often I lamented it this campaign."

CHAPTER TWELVE
RETREAT THROUGH NEW JERSEY
NOVEMBER 1776

"Tis almost impossible to catch them. They will neither fight nor totally run away ... We seem to be playing at Bo Peep."

- British officer.

"Turn out! Turn out! We are all surrounded. Leave everything but your blankets. You must fight your way through or be prisoners." The Fort Lee garrison was fortunate that a sympathetic farmer, up before dawn, had heard creaking wheels and marching boots, suspected it to be the British Army, and warned a Continental Army patrol. The British had apparently climbed a path up the cliffs known as the Palisades, a few miles north of the fort, in the darkness of night. Now they were threatening to capture Fort Lee even faster than they had Fort Washington just four days earlier.

Because Fort Lee was at the end of a narrow peninsula, its garrison would be cut off if the British reached the one bridge over the Hackensack River. After consulting with Washington, Greene ordered an immediate evacuation. The men were "on the march in about ten minutes, taking what baggage we could with us, which was very little compared to what we left behind." With no wagons, all that could be brought off was what each man could carry, little more than his musket and a blanket. Left behind, still standing, were over two hundred tents, destined to be slept in that evening by British and Hessian soldiers. Also left was the army's winter food supply: more than one thousand barrels of flour, and thousands of cattle in nearby pastures that could not be rounded up in time.

Not all 2,000 men, however, escaped with Greene and Washington. "Near a hundred remained hid about the woods, a set of rascals that skulked out of the way, for fear of fighting." About another hundred simply stayed in the fort, telling their officers they would not risk their lives by staying with the army. As soon as the troops marched off, these lingerers "nocked the heads ought of the hogsheads" and "got drunk with the sutlers liquir."

After the recent defeat just across the Hudson, Greene's sentries and patrols had been doubly careful in watching for any approach by the enemy. The ferry landings at the base of the Palisades had been guarded, so how could this surprise attack have happened?

A New Jersey Tory named John Aldington had been seeking revenge against the rebel army ever since they had commandeered his brewery for a military storehouse. After the fall of Fort Washington he saw his chance, and managed to reach British headquarters on Manhattan to offer his services as a guide, should Howe decide to invade New Jersey.

So, before dawn on November 20th, British sailors rowed General Lord Cornwallis and 5,000 British and Hessian troops in flatboats across the Hudson, about six miles north of Fort Lee. With Aldington pointing the way, they landed at a little known spot, Lower Closter Dock Landing. From there, a concealed, nearly vertical path led up the face of the Palisades. The four foot wide "rocky, bushy path" was "impassable for horses," so the seamen had to use ropes to drag up the eight field pieces that Cornwallis brought along. These sailors, wrote Howe, "distinguished themselves remarkably upon this occasion by their readiness to drag the cannon."

Leading the way were the British light infantry and the jagers, or huntsmen, from Germany's Black Forest. Soldiers of German descent in the Continental Army were familiar with the jagers, and called them "foresters from Hell." These "greencoats" carried long octagonal barrelled rifles more accurate than the Brown Bess, the British Army's smooth-bore musket. The jagers proved to be expert scouts and sharpshooters, protecting the long columns of infantry from ambush.

Three months before, on Long Island, the German troops had established a fearsome reputation in their first battle on American soil. Survivors of the Battle of Long Island came away with horror stories about Americans who had thrown down their arms, only to be bayonetted mercilessly by these "Hessians." (Because the majority of the German troops were from the principalities of Hesse-Hanau and Hesse-Cassel, all the Germans were collectively called Hessians by the British and the Americans.)

There were actually three versions of the same gruesome story. The first had the victims being bayonetted in the back as they tried to run away. The second had the defenseless Americans receiving the bayonet through the genitals and up through the intestines. The third version, corroborated by a German officer's letter, had the trapped Americans "spitted to trees" by the long bayonets, like papers tacked to a wall.

Such tales spread like wildfire through the American camps and were widely printed in the newspapers, making it natural for soldiers and civilians alike to panic whenever it was rumored that Hessians were approaching. Admiral Richard Howe's secretary, Ambrose Serle, noted during the New Jersey campaign, "The dread which the Rebels have of these Hessians is inconceivable. They almost run away at [mention of] their name."

However, the jager company that was leading Cornwallis's advance toward Fort Lee had not participated in the bloody work on Long Island. Instead, they had arrived with several regiments of infantry and grenadiers at New Rochelle, New York, a few days before the Battle of White Plains. After surviving scurvy and other diseases that had ravaged the troops in the holds of the transports during the nearly five month voyage from Europe, they were determined to make the most of their chances. Plundering of civilians was an accepted part of European warfare, and both the German and British troops would successfully ignore the British generals' death threats for those caught in the act. These death threats were almost never carried out. As one officer named de Saxe explained, "A soldier caught pillaging is hanged.

277

The result is that no one arrests him because they do not want to cause the death of a poor fellow who is only trying to live." Trained soldiers were very difficult to replace, so it was not surprising that the generals sympathized more with their men than the civilians.

The jager company leading the way up the Palisades and through the forests to Fort Lee was under the command of Captain Johann Ewald. At age 32, he was already a veteran of sixteen years of campaigning. When his company had landed at New Rochelle in October, Ewald's men had wasted no time in showing their worth:

> No sooner had several fires blazed than we heard the cries of chickens, geese and pigs which our resourceful soldiers had discovered. Within that hour, several roasts hung from long sticks before each fire. The whole camp was busy as an anthill. From this one can see how easily a good soldier knows his way about.

The very next day they had partaken in their first skirmish against the rebels with great spirit. They did not give up the fight, though greatly outnumbered, until Colonel von Donop came up to cover their retreat. Afterwards, the exasperated colonel shouted at the zealous Captain Ewald, "You want to conquer America in one day!"

Returning to the 20th of November: Captain Ewald's company, safely atop the Palisades, progressed through the woods and came to a house by a road. The owner informed the captain that this road led to the bridge over the Hackensack. From Captain Ewald's account:

> During this conversation I discovered ... a cloud of dust in the distance. - Who is that? - That must be the garrison of Fort Lee! - Can't we cut them off from the bridge? - Yes you have only two English miles from here to there! ...
>
> I began to skirmish with them, and sent back a jager to fetch more men; but instead received an order from

278

Lord Cornwallis to return at once. I had to obey, and informed him what I had discovered. - "Let them go, my dear Ewald, and stay here. We do not want to lose any men. One jager is worth more than ten rebels."

A few days later, after being called off yet another chase, Ewald confided to his journal: "Now I perceived what was afoot. We wanted to spare the King's subjects and hoped to terminate the war amicably, in which assumption I was strengthened the next day by several English officers."

But Lord Cornwallis was not deliberately letting the rebels escape. He was only following Howe's orders to the letter, by pushing on to Fort Lee as fast as possible. When he arrived at the fort, he rounded up the skulkers in the woods and those who had remained in the fort to drink their miseries away. When the storehouse was entered, the British were greeted with, "Brother soldier, we'll have a dram." In the officers' quarters, the pots were still boiling the noonday meal, and the tables were set. One British soldier noted:

> They have left some poor pork, a few greasy proclamations, and some of that scoundrel *Common Sense* man's letters, which we can read at our leisure, now that we have got one of the "impregnable redoubts" of Mr. Washington's to quarter in. We intend to push on after the long-faces [Yankees] in a few days.

What was left of Greene's division reached the village of Hackensack, where they joined Washington's own equally small division that had arrived there a few days before. A resident of the village noted the arrival of the Fort Lee garrison:

> It was about dusk when the head of the troops entered Hackensack. The night was dark, cold and rainy, but I had a fair view of them from the windows as they passed

on our side of the street. They marched two abreast, looked ragged, some without a shoe to their feet, and most of them wrapped in their blankets. That night the British encamped on the opposite side of the river.

In the morning, before the General left, he rode down to the dock, viewed the enemy's encampment about ten or fifteen minutes, and then returned to Mr. Campbell's door and called for some wine and water. After he had drank and Mr. Campbell had taken the glass from him, the latter, with tears streaming down his face, said "General, what shall I do? I have a family of small children and a little property here. Shall I leave them?" Washington kindly took his hand and replied, "Mr. Campbell, stay by your family and keep neutral." Then, bidding him goodbye, rode off.

The proud general from Virginia, looking dignified on his horse despite the despair of another defeat and retreat, led his wretched army away from this defenseless land. The landscape - "almost a dead flat" - provided no natural fortifications from which to make a stand, and the army had almost no intrenching tools left to create man-made ones. Washington could not help feeling for his soldiers, who were "much broken and dispirited, not only with our ill-success, but the loss of their tents and baggage." His goal now was to outmarch the enemy and try to consolidate his own forces into a large enough army to offer some resistance to what he foresaw as Howe's objective - a march to Philadelphia.

Part of the small division that Washington had brought to New Jersey, and that he now planned to join on this march from Hackensack, was at Brunswick under General Lord Stirling. In the few days that Stirling's brigade had been there, some of the troops had suffered an interesting malady, as explained by one of them:

Here our soldiers drank freely of spiritous liquors.

They have chiefly got a disorder which at camp is called the "Barrel Fever," which differs in its effects from any other fever - its concomitants are black eyes and bloody noses.

Washington now realized that he should not have left Charles Lee at North Castle with 7,000 men to guard the roads to New England. He wrote to Lee from Hackensack the morning after the evacuation of Fort Lee, "I am of opinion, and the gentlemen about me concur in it, that the public interest requires your coming." It is "of the utmost importance that at least an appearance of force should be made to keep this province in connection with the others."

When the retreat had begun the day before, Washington's adjutant, Colonel Joseph Reed, had scribbled a hasty note to General Lee, "We are flying before the British. I pray -" Reed told the express rider to deliver the rest of the message verbally: Lee must come to New Jersey to save the country. Before sealing Washington's letter, Joseph Reed slipped into the packet a letter of his own he had written that morning to his friend, Charles Lee:

> I do not mean to flatter or praise you at the expense of any other, but I confess I think it is entirely owing to you that this army, and the liberties of America so far as they are dependent on it, are not totally cut off. You have decision, a quality often wanted [lacking] in minds otherwise valuable ... [I] have no doubt had you been here the garrison of Mount Washington would now have composed part of this army. Every gentleman of the family [Washington's aides], and the officers and soldiers generally, have a confidence in you.

On November 29th, a messenger arrived with a dispatch from Lee. His answer to Washington's request was that it would not be wise for his division to go over to New Jersey at this time, because it would

leave the roads to New England weakly defended. Also, his men did not have enough shoes, clothing, blankets and tents, and he was planning an attack on the nearby Tory regiment under Robert Rogers.

The packet from Lee contained letters for both Washington and Reed. Because Reed was not there to open it for him - Reed was in Burlington, trying to persuade New Jersey's governor to call out the militia - Washington opened the packet. He inadvertently read the letter addressed to Reed. In it, Lee thanked Joseph Reed for "your most obliging, flattering letter," and went on to state his agreement with Reed in lamenting "that fatal indecision of mind which in war is a much greater disqualification than stupidity, or even want of personal courage." Lee finished by promising to "fly to you, for to confess a truth, I really think our chief will do better with me than without me."

Washington was deeply hurt by this accidental revelation of his closest aide's lack of confidence in him. He was most hurt, as he wrote to Reed many years later when they would first discuss it, by the fact that "the same sentiments were not communicated immediately to myself." After reading the letters, Washington forwarded to Reed the personal letter, enclosing a note explaining that it was read by accident, but not making any other comment. The next day, an embarrassed Colonel Reed submitted his resignation to Congress, but a few days later was coaxed into staying on by Washington. Within a few months, though, he would return to his law practice in Philadelphia, and twenty-year-old Alexander Hamilton would take his place as Washington's most trusted aide.

With no commitment from Lee, Washington sent General Mifflin, a politician from Pennsylvania, to visit the Congress and tell them in terms they could understand what a crisis the army was in. And he sent Colonel Smallwood, known now as "the bullet stopper" for his heroics in battle, to Maryland to recruit there. Washington also personally wrote to each governor and council in the states. And he asked Congress for permission to order General Schuyler to send a portion of his northern army at Ticonderoga south to New Jersey.

These pleas for reinforcements would not have been necessary if the

states were not so slow in raising their quotas of new enlistments. Back in September, Congress had authorized a new army of 88 regiments, with enlistments for the duration of the war. So far, none of these new regiments had been raised. In January, Congress would change the enlistment period to three years, and have a better response. The states were authorized to commission their own colonels and lower ranking officers, who were responsible for recruiting men to fill out their paper regiments. Just the appointment of officers would take months in some of the states. Enthusiasm for joining Washington's losing army was a rare thing in the fall of 1776. Gone was the spirit of June 1775, when a British officer had observed, "the *Rage Militaire*, as the French call a passion for arms, has taken possession of the whole Continent."

With the enlistments of much of his army due to expire on either the last day of November or December, George Washington calculated that, by January 1st, he might be left with only 1,400 men to oppose over 30,000 trained European Regulars at Howe's disposal. Washington would then have to rely on whatever militia could be raised by stirring, patriotic calls to arms, such as the ones that New Jersey's Governor Livingston was now issuing. But Washington desperately needed men right now, even undependable militia.

To his surprise and disgust, however, he found that the New Jersey militia failed to come forward and defend their homeland. And, on November 30th, 2,000 New Jersey and Maryland state levies, their enlistments up, left for home, despite personal pleas from Washington and other officers. Washington wearily sat down that night and wrote of the contagion of desertion that was menacing his army:

> Being applied to, they refused to continue longer in the service. But what is still worse, altho' most of the Pennsylvanians are inlisted till the first of January, I am informed that they are deserting in great numbers.

So Washington was forced to continue retreating. He sent a colonel

and fifty men to gather boats along the Delaware and hold them under guard at Trenton. He knew his meager army, down to 3,400 now, would have to put a sizable river between it and the enemy. But what defense is a river alone in a country where the people are not willing to rise up in defense of their homes?

Lord Cornwallis, not content to merely take Fort Lee, followed on Washington's heels, trying to catch him and force him to fight on open ground. At one point, he forced his Regulars to march 20 miles of muddy roads in a day-long rainstorm, only to see the rebels elude him again. There were almost daily skirmishes, as the rebel rear guard "pioneers" from western Virginia endeavored to "tear up bridges and fell trees" to slow down the enemy's advance. The Hessian jagers and British light infantry, in turn, tried to stop them. One British captain wrote home, describing the chase:

> As we go forward into the country the Rebels fly before us and when we come back they always follow us; 'tis almost impossible to catch them. They will neither fight nor totally run away, but they keep at such a distance that we are always above a day's march from them. We seem to be playing at Bo Peep.

Cornwallis tried to increase his speed by ordering his men to leave their tents and other baggage behind, despite the almost constant rain and sleet. However, the Americans, due to their lack of almost every necessity of an army on the march, moved too fast for the heavily burdened Regulars, each of whom had nearly one hundred pounds of clothing, boots, musket, etc. on his person. Samuel Webb, of Connecticut, wrote home to Governor Trumbull, "Our soldiers are the best fellows in the world at this business" of retreating.

But their trail was marked with the blood from their shoeless feet, and they had to huddle front-to-back at night as they lay on the wet ground, often while being rained on, hoping that their own body heat would prevent frostbite, pneumonia, and other ailments that steadily

weakened the army. Sergeant Joseph White, years later, recalled the march: "The sufferings we endured is beyond description - no tent to cover us at night - exposed to cold and rains day and night - no food of any kind but a little raw flour."

On December 1, what Washington called "the wretched remains of a broken army" set out from Brunswick, reaching Trenton six days later. Lieutenant Enoch Anderson was one of Haslet's Delaware Continentals, "the flower of the army." They were posted at the rear to provide cover for the pioneers as they worked feverishly to destroy the bridges over the Raritan River.

> The British appeared on the bank of the Raritan River. We were now under the command of Lord Stirling. He ordered his brigade in front of the barracks. A severe cannonading took place on both sides, and several were killed and wounded on our side. Orders were now given for a retreat. Our regiment was in the rear. It was near sundown. Colonel Haslet came to me and told me to take as many men as I thought proper, and go back and burn all the tents. "We have no wagons," said he, "to carry them off, and it is better to burn them than they should fall into the hands of the enemy." Then I went and burned them - about one hundred tents.
>
> When we saw them reduced to ashes, it was night and the army far ahead. We made a double quick-step and came up with the army about eight o'clock. We encamped in the woods, with no victuals, no tents, no blankets. The night was cold and we all suffered much, especially those who had no shoes.

The rebel army's precipitous retreat made for good conversation amongst the Tories. Judge Thomas Jones, a New York loyalist, recorded one tale making the rounds: "So great was the panic among the rebels that a captain of theirs, with about fifty men, near

Hackensack, took to their heels upon the approach of six wagoneers dressed in red coats." Another tale was recorded in the journal of Lieutenant Andreas Wiederholdt:

> It happened that the silly Americans had an odd impression and fear of us Hessians. They did not believe that we looked like other human beings, but thought that we had a strange language and that we were a raw, wild, and barbaric nation.
>
> Some Light Dragoons of the enemy were sent on patrol to reconnoiter ... This patrol had to pass a forest at night, and they followed their route quietly and full of fear. They believed that they soon would approach our Hessian advance posts. Suddenly, a bull frog croaked loudly. In dismay, they answered, "Friend." At this answer, the frog croaked a second time. They now believed that it was a Hessian picket, whereupon they stopped and cried out, "Yes, yes, gentlemen, we are your prisoners." They got off their horses and waited for somebody to advance and take them prisoners. Finally, they realized their mistake and were ashamed and said: "God damn, it is only a bullfrog."

Over in the American camp, stories with a rather different perspective abounded, such as the one about the Tory who mistook some American officers in the vanguard as British and ran up to offer his services as a guide. He was given an "absolution" by having his britches pulled down and being forced to sit on the ice "to cool his loyalty. He seems pleased, knowing that he got off easy."

Another story circulating in camp concerned a conversation the Commander-in-Chief had with Joseph Reed. General Washington asked, "Should we retreat to the back parts of Pennsylvania, will the Pennsylvanians support us?" Reed answered, "If the lower [eastern] counties will not come forward, the others will do the same." The

storyteller then described Washington passing his hand over his throat and saying, "My neck does not feel as though it was made for a halter. We must retire to Augusta County in Virginia, and, if overpowered, we must pass the Allegheny Mountains."

Meanwhile, at British headquarters in New York City, General Howe's second in command, Henry Clinton, was about to set out on what would be an almost useless expedition to Rhode Island. The Commander-in-Chief's brother, Admiral Howe, was responsible for patrolling the coastal waters and needed one more ice-free harbor for the winter. Newport, Rhode Island, provided the perfect base for a large portion of his fleet, and Clinton's 6,000 man force could more than adequately provide the necessary protection and foraging parties. Best of all for William Howe, it was a perfect excuse for getting rid of Clinton and his constant advice.

When Howe had turned the army around after White Plains and headed back to Manhattan - instead of attacking Washington at North Castle Heights - Clinton had exploded in anger in front of Cornwallis. "I cannot bear to serve under him, and had rather command three companies by myself than hold my post [as] I have done last campaign in his army!" Cornwallis, perhaps out of a desire to supplant Clinton as the primary field officer, mentioned Clinton's outburst to Howe. A few days later, when Fort Washington was attacked, it was Cornwallis, not Clinton, who was given the active role. And now, it was Cornwallis that was pursuing Washington, and Clinton who was being banished to Rhode Island with Admiral Sir Peter Parker.

The only real effect of the Rhode Island expedition would be to take a few thousand Regulars out of the war for three years. By 1778, though, both King and Parliament would be disenchanted with Howe's performance. Howe would be recalled, and Clinton put in his place.

General Howe probably could have ended the war that winter if he had taken Clinton's last advice, offered while Clinton's troops were aboard the ships, waiting to sail to Rhode Island. "I proposed," Clinton wrote, "that my detachment should be thrown on shore in the Jersies. Failing likewise in this, I finally proposed [sailing to] ...

Philadelphia." Howe refused the unsolicited, annoying proposals.

Clinton was not the only one with such ideas. The diaries of other officers reflect the general feeling that it was time to end the war - by capturing Washington's broken, dispirited army and swiftly marching on Philadelphia. After that, the rebellion would surely fall to pieces, and the rebels "never make head again."

But the capture of Washington's army was not in the Howe brothers' secret master plan for ending the rebellion. Washington's army must be forced into frequent embarrassing (but not total) defeats and be pushed back, again and again, giving up more and more territory. Under this pacification plan, the inhabitants of "liberated" territories must be treated fairly in order to coax them into renouncing their congresses and committees, and return to their former allegiance. For this reason, Admiral Howe refused to issue "letters of marque," which would have authorized Tory shipowners to act as privateers, raiding rebel shipping. Admiral Howe believed that raids against American ports and shipping would serve no useful purpose, and only make reconciliation more difficult.

He was harshly criticized for this by the more vocal loyalists. To one such critic, the admiral exclaimed, "Will you never have done oppressing these poor people? Will you never give them an opportunity of seeing their error?" Admiral Howe instructed his naval captains "to allow the inhabitants dwelling upon the coasts the use of their ordinary fishing craft or other means of providing for their daily subsistence, in order to conciliate their friendly dispositions and detach them from the prejudices they have imbibed." Naval gunpowder should be expended only on American ships carrying munitions, trying to run the blockade.

The Howes also refused to issue muskets to any loyalists except those in Tory regiments under the direction of the regular British Army. The Howes wanted to avoid an intensification of partisan warfare, and the brother against brother hatreds that they had observed in New York's Westchester County.

The most visible step in the Howes' pacification program, though, was their November 30th proclamation, offering "protection papers"

to anyone who would appear before a British official within sixty days and sign a statement renouncing the Congress and promising to "remain in a peaceful obedience to His Majesty." During the first half of December, as the British Army completed its march across New Jersey, thousands of citizens signed this loyalty oath. They naively trusted that, when British and Hessian soldiers entered their homes and barns to take everything they could carry off, they would simply show these protection papers and the plunderers would meekly go away empty-handed. The soldiers, however, proved them wrong, as they ravaged the properties and (if newspaper reports were correct) the wives and daughters, too, of Whig and Tory alike.

General Clinton predicted the resulting backlash effect that soon followed. The soldiers' plundering quickly reversed most of the good will that the Howes' proclamation had won. Clinton believed that, "Unless we refrained from plundering, we had no business to take up winter quarters in a district we wished to preserve loyal." Another British officer lamented "the licentious ravages of our soldiery (both British and foreign) who were shamefully permitted to pillage friend and foe."

Joseph Galloway, the most influential loyalist in the first Continental Congress, had authored the "Plan of Union with Britain," a compromise intended to avert war. It had fallen one vote short of passage in the fall of 1774. By the next session of Congress, in the spring of 1775, war had broken out and the Congress had turned more radical. Disillusioned, Galloway gave up his seat and retired to his rural Pennsylvania estate, only to suffer harassment by hotheaded patriots. In November 1776, after barely eluding an assasination attempt, he decided to join the loyalist exodus to New York. On his way to New York, Galloway passed the retreating Continental Army going the other way.

He arrived at Brunswick, New Jersey, where Lord Cornwallis was waiting for Howe to reverse his earlier order to halt the pursuit there. The diary of the jager Captain Johann Ewald notes what he heard of the meeting that Galloway and some other loyalists had with Corn-

wallis at Brunswick. The loyalists were quite disgusted with the excuses General Cornwallis offered for Howe's slow pursuit.

> [They] implored the general to press General Washington as closely as possible so that we might overtake him in the vicinity of the Delaware River, by which his retreat would be cut off. There we could surely destroy or capture his disheartened army. ... Mr. Galloway was so enraged over the delay of the English, that he said out loud, "I see, they don't want to finish the war!"

After several days of waiting, Cornwallis was joined at Brunswick by Howe, who arrived with reinforcements and personally led the subsequent march to Trenton. It was not the swift march of a pursuer, but rather the slow one of a liberator, as he took pains to ensure wide distribution of his proclamation. The days he spent holding Cornwallis back allowed Washington enough time to cross the Delaware into Pennsylvania with his remaining baggage and the eleven field pieces that he had managed to retain. By the time Howe and Cornwallis reached the Delaware River, on December 8th, they found that all boats had been removed from the Jersey shore for a stretch of eighty miles.

By now, Congress had decided to join many of Philadelphia's citizens and leave town. Before they "resolved to retire to Baltimore in Maryland" they ordered handbills circulated throughout the states, again urging the swift recruitment of those 88 new regiments. As a token of support to Washington, Congress sent him the Philadelphia Associators, a gentlemen's company of cavalry, which he put to use right away, scouting the west bank of the Delaware. After all, it would be no great feat for Howe to construct a few dozen rafts and cross at almost any point along the river.

Congress also resolved "that it be recommended to all the United States as soon as possible to appoint a day of fasting and humiliation." This, Doctor Thacher noted, "is according to the custom of our pious

ancestors in times of imminent dangers and difficulties." It must have seemed ironic to the half-starved soldiers that, instead of provisioning them, Congress was declaring a day of fasting.

Finally, because they were going to be on the move, Congress resolved that, until further notice, "Washington possessed full power to order and direct all things relative to the department and to the operations of war." This was to save the Commander-in-Chief much valuable time waiting for permission from Congress before making major military decisions. George Washington could have used this resolution to exercise dictatorial powers, but he did not. Throughout the war, he continued to let Congress dictate to him on military matters. Washington remained a firm believer in the supremacy of civilian government over the military.

* * * * *

In this and other respects, Washington was a stark contrast to his second in command, General Charles Lee. Lee wrote to James Bowdoin, president of the council of Massachusetts:

> The resolves of Congress must no longer too nicely weigh with us. We must save the community in spite of the ordinances of the Legislature. There are times when we must commit treason against the laws of the State for the salvation of the State. The idea of detaching and reinforcing from one side [of the Hudson] to the other on every motion of the enemy is absolute insanity. We must therefore depend upon ourselves. To Connecticut and Massachusetts I shall look for assistance.

He asked that new recruits be sent to him for use in his division of the army, promising that he (not Washington) would "answer for their success." Lee looked upon Washington with disdain, and resisted wherever possible submitting his own will to that of the Virginian who,

so far, had nothing but a string of defeats to show for his tenure as the Commander-in-Chief.

Upon receiving Washington's request to come with most of his troops and join him, Lee wrote to General William Heath. Heath's division of 4,000 was fortifying the Hudson Highlands further north, near Peekskill. Lee, being the higher ranking general, ordered Heath to detach 2,000 of his troops from Peekskill and send them to Washington's aid. Heath refused. In his response to Lee, Heath explained that, when the army had divided up in early November, Washington's orders to him had not allowed "moving any part of the troops from the posts assigned to me, unless it be by express order from his Excellency, or to support you in case you are attacked."

Lee had not expected to be stonewalled by this mild-mannered, bald-headed, old farmer from Massachusetts. In his own reply, Lee ranted and raved profusely that "the Commander-in-Chief is now separated from us." And that Lee, therefore, commanded "on this side of the water [and] I must & will be obeyed." Nevertheless, Heath did not give in.

Unable to convince Heath to go, Charles Lee finally left for New Jersey, after all. On December 4th, he took part of his forces and set out. He intended to incorporate the 800 men General Schuyler had detached, at Washington's request, from the northern army near Ticonderoga. Lee had been told that these 800, led by Horatio Gates and Benedict Arnold, were already on their way south. A friend of Lee's on the New York Council of Safety had met with Gates two days before and urged him to place his troops under Lee's command instead of pushing on directly for New Jersey. The wary Gates, though a friend of Lee, refused. He, like Lee, may have been thinking of himself as a possible replacement for Washington, and it would therefore not be wise to subordinate himself to Lee at this time.

Lee wrote to Washington, telling him that he would soon arrive in New Jersey with "five thousand good troops in good spirits." He urged Washington "to communicate this to the corps immediately under your command. It may encourage them." Lee was boldly

condescending in this and other letters he would soon be writing to the Commander-in-Chief. He ended the letter by asking Washington to "take out of the way of danger my favorite mare," stabled at Princeton.

He also mentioned that on the march through New Jersey he planned "to clothe my people at the expense of the Tories, which has a double good effect - it puts them in spirits and comfort, and is a correction of the iniquity of the foes of liberty." (This is something Washington would not do, lest the general population begin to view the army as tyrannical.) Lee gave the following order to his foraging parties on the march:

> Proceed to Harrington Township, where they are to collect all the serviceable horses, all the spare blankets (that is, to leave a sufficient number to cover the people), they are to collect any spare shoes, greatcoats ... The people from whom they are taken are not to be insulted either by actions or language; but told that the urgent necessity of the troop obliges us to the measure. That unless we adopt it, their liberties must perish. That they must make an estimate of what is taken and the publick shall pay them.

The New England troops under Lee's command at North Castle were not enthusiastic about venturing so far from New England, to suffer and perhaps die for New Jersey. Nearly all of those whose enlistment expired on November 30th went home. Many others, whose time was not yet up, decided to desert, rather than march to another "country." Still others used different tactics to avoid marching to New Jersey. Lieutenant Joseph Hodgkins, of Massachusetts, noted that in his regiment three fourths of the men, including the colonel, had declined to join the expedition, claiming illness or some other excuse. So many New Englanders were among what one termed "the lame & lazy & the faint hearted" that the skeleton state regiments were consolidated into a New England brigade headed by a Rhode Island colonel,

Daniel Hitchcock. Though Hitchcock was coughing up blood and slowly but surely dying of consumption, he was one of those patriotic few whose refusal to quit the Cause kept the army going.

Most of those who marched with Lee to New Jersey planned to make the long walk back to New England just as soon as their enlistments expired on January 1, 1777. Lieutenant Hodgkins wrote to his wife that he was looking forward "to the pleasure of facing you & all friends in a fue weaks." When he arrived in New Jersey, he wrote to her again: "This march whas very unexpected to us all & the traveling verry bad. The contry is full of them cursed creaturs called Torys." Sergeant John Smith, of Rhode Island, wrote in his diary, "The inhabitents abused us caling us Damd Rebels & would not sell us any thing for [Continental] money. The soldiers killd their fowles & one stole a hive of bees & caried it off with him."

General Lee stopped at Peekskill to cross the Hudson there and to pick up some of the troops he had assured Washington he would be leading into New Jersey. Lee presumed that General Heath, when confronted in person, would back down and release the 2,000 he had requested. Heath's memoirs provide us with a detailed account of that face to face meeting:

> Upon coming into the house, before he sat down, he wished to speak in private, which being instantly granted, he told our General [Heath] that, in a military view, or, to use his own words exactly, "In point of law, you are right; but in point of policy, I think you are wrong. I am going into the Jerseys for the salvation of America; I wish to take with me a larger force than I now have, and request you to order 2,000 of your men to march with me." Our General answered that he could not spare that number. He was then asked to order 1,000; to which he replied that the business might be as well brought to a point at once - that not a single man should march from the post by his order.

Gen Lee replied, that he would then order them himself. He was answered that Gen Lee was acknowledged by our General to be his senior; but as he had received positive written instructions from him who was superior to both, he would not <u>himself</u> break those orders. And that he knew the Commander in Chief did not intend any of the troops should be removed from that post - having expressed it not only in his instructions, but also in a letter just received from him.

On the letter being shewn to Gen Lee, he observed, "The Commander in Chief is now at a distance, and does not know what is necessary here so well as I do." [Lee] asked if he might be favoured with the return-book of the division. Major Huntington, the Deputy Adjutant-General, was directed to hand it. Gen Lee ran his eye over it and said, "I will take Prescott's and Wyllis's regiments" - and turning to Major Huntington, said, "You will order those two regiments to march early tomorrow morning to join me."

Our General, turning to the Major, said, "Issue such orders at your peril!" and then turning to Gen Lee, addressed him: "Sir, if you come to this post, and mean to issue orders here, which will break those positive ones which I have received, I pray you to do it completely yourself and through your own Deputy Adjutant General, who is present, and not draw me, or any of my family, in as partners in the guilt."

So Lee had his own adjutant issue the order to the two regiments. But only after Heath insisted that he write "a certificate" testifying that he had taken command there and personally ordered the troops to march. At first, the haughty Englishman refused to write it, but then reluctantly agreed after another general who was present interjected, "General Lee, you cannot refuse a request so reasonable." Heath goes

on to finish his account of the incident:

> Early the next morning, the regiments moved from their cantonments towards Peekskill; but before they had reached it, Gen Lee, now ready to pass into the Jerseys, rode up to our General's door, and calling him, observed, "Upon further consideration, I have concluded not to take the two regiments with me - you may order them to return to their former posts.

The Yankee farmer watched the aristocratic Englishman, who "could scarcely brook being crossed in any thing in the line of his profession," head south. Heath must have wondered whether the war could continue much longer, as he observed Lee's men:

> Gen Lee took with him into the Jerseys some as good troops as any in the service; but many of them were so destitute of shoes that the blood left on the rugged frozen ground, in many places, marked the route they had taken; and a considerable number, unable to march, were left at Peek's Kill.

With each new letter Washington wrote to Lee, he tried to be more persuasive, telling him that it was "beyond all question" that Howe intended to march for Philadelphia, "whose loss must prove of the most fatal consequences to the cause of America." Washington, perhaps suffering from an inferiority complex when dealing with the more experienced Lee, could not bring himself to be forceful enough with him. When he informed Congress that he had written to Lee "and ordered him to come over the Hudson" Washington told his aide to cross out the words "and ordered him" before rewriting the final draft of the letter. From Hackensack, Washington had written to Lee, "the public interest requires your coming." By the time he reached Trenton, Washington was practically begging Lee to leave North Castle, using

words such as "I entreat you." He was careful to mention that his own opinion was not his alone, but was "by the advice of all the general officers with me."

On December 10th and 11th, Lee was at Morristown, in northwestern New Jersey, "obliged to halt these two days for want of shoes." Sergeant John Smith noted the temporary solution: "Many of our soldiers had no shoes to wear, was obliged to lace on their feet the hide of cattle we had killed the day before."

Lee sent messengers to find Gates and tell him to join him at Morristown. Lee seemed determined to act on his own, as head of a separate command. He wrote to Washington, "I could wish you would bind me as little as possible. Detached generals cannot have too great latitude, unless they are very incompetent indeed." Lee certainly felt he was competent to take independent action, informing Washington that he could do him "more service by beating up and harassing their detached parties," taking advantage of the extended British supply line from New York. Any victory, no matter how small, would boost morale. Perhaps it was no secret to Lee, who had many friends in Congress, that almost every week now a new motion was being made to replace Washington. None had yet passed, but a signal victory by Lee at this time might propel him from second in command to Commander-in-Chief.

On December 12th, Washington gave in and granted Lee permission to harass the enemy's rear and flank, rather than join the main army near Trenton. Washington wrote to Lee, urging him to consult with Gates and Arnold, and work out "what probable mode of attack can be attempted."

> Weigh every circumstance of attack and retreat properly [so] that nothing that can be guarded against may be unprovided for. I do not mean to tie you down to any rule, but leave you free to exercise your own judgements, of which I only want timely advice.

For the good of the country, George Washington was giving his chief rival the power to outshine him. Fortunately for America, Lee never received that letter. That same day, Lee led his army out of Morristown and marched them eight miles to Vealtown. There he instructed his second, New Hampshire's General John Sullivan, to supervise the making of a temporary camp. Lee then examined a few houses in Vealtown, looking for quarters for the night, and rejected them as "pious holes," the houses of God-fearing Methodists and Lutherans. He wanted to spend the night with the comfort of a bottle and a woman, away from the righteous Yankees he had for officers. So, with only a guard of six men, he set off for the next town - Basking Ridge - three miles away, where he took his quarters at a tavern.

Lee was disturbed twice that night: once, while he was still drinking, and once while asleep. The first interruption was by a local Tory who came to the inn to complain to the general that his horse had been stolen by Continental Army deserters. Lee cursed him soundly and threw him out. Later, Lee was awakened by twenty-year-old Major James Wilkinson, an aide to General Gates. Gates had instructed Wilkinson to ride to Trenton and get directions from Washington for a safe route around the enemy, but to stop and interview Lee on the way. Lee read Gates's dispatch addressed to Washington, made some disparaging remarks about the Commander-in-Chief, and then told Wilkinson to stay the rest of the night downstairs with the guard, and wait in the morning until Lee was ready to give him some dispatches of his own.

In the morning, a patrol of British Light Dragoons, led by Cornet Banastre Tarleton arrived at the inn. Years ago, Lee had commanded this same regiment. Therefore, its present officers considered his treason all the more damnable. Before coming with the army to America, 22-year-old Banastre Tarleton had stopped at a London gentlemen's club and, tapping his sword, had vowed, "With this sword I will cut off General Lee's head!" Now, patrolling the roads near Basking Ridge, Tarleton had "found by some people that General Lee was not above four or five miles distant," staying the night away from his camp. Cornet Banastre Tarleton and his thirty raiders spurred their

horses and rode further on. Tarleton's account:

> I observed a Yankee light-horseman, at whom I rushed and made prisoner. I brought him in to Colonel Harcourt; the fear of the sabre extorted great intelligence and he told me he had just left General Lee.

Major Wilkinson's memoirs relate what happened next:

> I had risen from the table and was looking out of an end window down a lane about one hundred yards in length which led to the house from the main road, when I discovered a party of British dragoons turn a corner of the avenue at a full charge. Startled at this unexpected spectacle, I exclaimed, "Here, Sir, are the British cavalry!" "<u>Where?</u>" replied the general, who had signed his letter in the instant. "Around the house" for they had opened files and encompassed the building.
>
> General Lee appeared alarmed, yet collected ... "Where is the guard? Damn the guard, why don't they fire?" and after a momentary pause, he turned to me and said, "Do, Sir, see what has become of the guard."
>
> The women of the house at this moment entered the room and proposed to him to conceal himself in a bed, which he rejected with evident disgust. I caught up my pistols which lay on the table, thrust the letter he had been writing into my pocket, and passed into a room at the opposite end of the house, where I had seen the guard in the morning. Here I discovered their arms; but the men were absent. I stepped out of the door and perceived the dragoons chasing them in different directions and, receiving a very uncivil salutation, I returned into the house. ...
>
> "<u>If the general does not surrender in five minutes, I</u>

will set fire to the house!" After a short pause [this] was repeated with a solemn oath; and within two minutes I heard it proclaimed, "Here is the general. He has surrendered." A general shout ensued, the trumpet sounded the assembly, and the unfortunate Lee, mounted on my horse, which stood ready at the door, was hurried off in triumph, bareheaded, in his slippers and blanket coat, his collar open, and his shirt very much soiled from several days' use.

Upon hearing this "melancholy intelligence," Washington remarked, "Our cause has received a severe blow." The jubilant Colonel Harcourt wrote home to his brother in England, telling him that he had taken the "most active and most enterprising of the enemy's generals." Now, "it seems to be the universal opinion the rebels will no longer refuse treating upon the terms which have been offered them."

However, a patriot newspaper, the Freeman's Journal, reported the event from a different perspective:

> The enemy showed an ungenerous - nay, boyish triumph - after they had got him secure at Brunswick, by making his horse drunk while they toasted their King till they were in the same condition. A bank or two of music played all night to proclaim their joy for this important acquisition. They say we cannot now stand another campaign. Mistaken fools! To think the fate of America depended on one man. They will find ere long that it has no other effect than to urge us on to a noble revenge.

* * * * *

As soon as Lee's second in command, General Sullivan, was informed by Wilkinson about Lee's fate, Sullivan marched Lee's division

west to Delaware Gap, brought it across, and then marched south to join Washington. Within 24 hours of learning of Lee's capture, nearly one thousand of Lee's former soldiers lost heart and deserted, leaving Sullivan with only 2,000 men. A day behind Sullivan's column were Gates and the 800 he was bringing from Ticonderoga. Gates had intended to bring 2,300 men, but 1,500 new levies from New York refused to march with him when they learned they would have to leave their home state.

As they marched down the Pennsylvania side of the Delaware River, they found the villagers "cold and indisposed to show kindness to the army. The Quaker conscience will not allow of their treating those well who are engaged in war." The good people of Bethlehem and Nazareth, however, were more hospitable. These were Moravians, a Protestant sect from Germany that came to America in the 1730's to evangelize the Indians and whites. Their religious beliefs would not allow them to bear arms, but they were willing to bear their share of "the burdens of the country." They consented to George Washington's request to establish a temporary hospital there, and care for the hundreds of sick soldiers.

Some illnesses were less severe, allowing the soldiers to remain with the army. Such was the case with one of Sullivan's soldiers, Private John Greenwood, from Boston. Only 16 years old, Greenwood was already an 18 month veteran in the army. On this march, he was hampered with two of the least deadly, but most common, ailments in the army.

> I had the itch then so bad that my breeches stuck to my thighs, all the skin being off, and there were hundreds of vermin upon me, owing to a whole month's march and having been obliged, for the sake of keeping warm, to lie down at night among the soldiers who were huddled close together like hogs.

CHAPTER THIRTEEN
THE CRISIS
DECEMBER 1776

"I think the game is pretty nearly up."

> *- George Washington,*
> *writing to his brother.*

"These are the times that try men's souls."

> *- Thomas Paine.*

In this hour of darkness, the burden placed on Washington was almost overpowering. On December 16th, one of his aides, Colonel Tench Tilghman, wrote, "Business seems to multiply upon him as the campaign draws to an end; indeed the weight of the whole war may justly be said to lay upon his shoulders." Earlier, Washington had confided in a letter to his brother, "I am wearied almost to death."

He was truly alone in the crisis now. Congress had fled to Baltimore. Lee had first rebelled against him, then foolishly allowed himself to be captured. Washington's most trusted aide and confidant, Reed, had proven unfaithful. The debacle at Fort Washington had shown that the advice of Greene and Putnam was not to be taken. Gates, like Lee, was disdainful toward him and was no help in the crisis. The states had virtually ignored both his pleas and those of Congress for reinforcements. New Jersey had all but given up the struggle. In nearby Delaware, the assembly was petitioning Congress to accept Howe's terms.

Equally appalling, farmers on both sides of the Delaware were refusing to accept Continental currency for provisions desperately needed by the army. Not surprisingly, they felt the government that backed

the paper money would cease to exist in a few more weeks. Pennsylvania farmers were going to extraordinary efforts to elude Continental Army patrols and get their produce across the river, to sell to the enemy for hard currency.

However, even the provision problem, bad as it was, was not as distressing as the shortage of shoes and clothing. The Pennsylvania Committee of Safety took up a collection of "old clothes for the use of the army," for which Washington humbly thanked them. Those who benefitted from its distribution were a lucky few compared to the many in need. A Burlington, New Jersey, widow named Margaret Morris noted in her diary on December 22nd:

> A peaceable man ventured to prophesy to-day that, if the war is continued through the winter, the British troops will be scared at the sight of our men; for, as they never fought with naked men, the novelty of it will terrify them, and make them retreat. From the appearance of our ragged troops, he thinks it probable they will not have clothes to cover them a month or two hence.

Congress appeared almost ready to give up, as the following account indicates. On December 14th, while leading a company of new recruits north from Delaware, Captain Thomas Rodney met Thomas McKean and a few other members of Congress, who were on their way south to Baltimore. McKean and the captain's brother, Caesar Rodney, had both voted for independence back in July. The Congressmen "sat late" with Captain Rodney that night and told him the news, observing that "everything was very gloomy and doubtful." They held out some hope that General Charles Lee would provide the answer to the crisis - they had not yet heard that he had been captured by the British the day before. From Captain Rodney's account:

> The chief hope that remained was that Gen. Lee, who was on the mountains in the rear of the enemy, would be

able to effect some lucky stroke that would prevent the enemys crossing the Delaware, but if nothing of the sort happened, Congress would be obliged to authorize the Commander-in-Chief to obtain the best terms that could be had from the enemy.

Like the Congressmen, the soldiers, too, were understandably downcast. One of them noted that "despair was seen in almost every countenance." Wrote another, "Such is now the gloomy aspect of our affairs, that strong apprehensions are entertained that the British will soon have it in their power to vanquish the whole remains of the Continental Army."

As for George Washington himself, earlier he had told New Jersey's governor, "I will not despair." But, by December 16th, he was truly dismayed at "the spirit of disaffection" in eastern Pennsylvania. He wrote now to the Council of Safety, telling them that the militia was not only refusing to come out and reinforce the army, "but, I am told, exult at the approach of the enemy, and on our misfortune." Washington confided his deepest feelings, in writing, to his brother:

> We are in a very disaffected part of the province; and between you and me, I think our affairs are in a very bad condition; not so much from the apprehension of General Howe's army, as from the defection of New York, the Jerseys and Pennsylvania. In short, the conduct of the Jerseys has been most infamous. Instead of turning out to defend their country, and affording aid to our army, they are making their submissions as fast as they can. ... In a word, my dear Sir, if every nerve is not strained to recruit the new army with all possible expedition, I think the game is pretty nearly up.

But the situation started to turn around on the 20th, a few days after Washington wrote that depressing letter to his brother. Amidst a

snowstorm, Sullivan arrived in camp with Lee's 2,000 men, and marching right behind him were Gates and the 800 he had brought from the northern army. Benedict Arnold was not with him, having just the day before received orders from Washington to return home to Connecticut to help organize a defense against Clinton, who was now in Rhode Island. The men now had something to cheer about as they renewed old acquaintances and were heartened by these reinforcements. Word spread quickly along the Delaware and to Philadelphia that reinforcements had arrived in camp.

The sagging morale of the troops, and the rebellion in general, was also given a boost in the days just before Christmas with the publication of the first in a series of essays, collectively titled *The Crisis*. The author was Thomas Paine, whose *Common Sense* had set the whole country astir the previous winter. Now the pen that had worked a miracle before was being put to work again, at the urging of General George Washington. Thomas Paine had been with the army, as an "assistant aide-de-camp" under General Greene, during the retreat from Fort Lee. He had started his latest work, writing on paper that he placed on the head of a drum, while the army stopped for a few days at Newark. Washington then sent him off to Philadelphia to finish it, and have it printed as soon as possible.

In this first installment of *The Crisis*, Paine urged Americans not to give up hope, but to actively participate in the revolution, and secure the independence that had been declared with such high hopes in July. The essay started with stirring words that have since become some of the most famous in American history:

> These are the times that try men's souls. The summer soldier and the sunshine patriot will, in this crisis, shrink from the service of their country; but he that stands it now deserves the love and thanks of man and woman. Tyranny, like hell, is not easily conquered; yet we have this consolation with us, that the harder the conflict, the more glorious the triumph.

Heaven, according to Thomas Paine, puts a heavy price on freedom. He went on to argue that "God Almighty will not forsake a people who so earnestly and so repeatedly sought to avoid" this war; and that the King of Britain has no more right to look up to heaven against us than "a common murderer, a highwayman or a house-breaker."

Paine's essay, first published on December 19th in the weekly Pennsylvania Journal, was reprinted and available in pamphlet form just four days later. It "flew like wildfire through all the villages and towns." Washington read the essay as soon as it arrived in camp on the 19th, liked it, and immediately ordered enough copies be made so it could be read aloud in front of every soldier.

The men Sullivan and Gates brought into camp were not the only new arrivals. General Smallwood returned from his recruiting mission to Maryland with over a hundred men. Major Sheldon, of the Connecticut Light Horse, was actively recruiting new cavalry companies on Washington's authorization. In Philadelphia, Putnam and Mifflin had issued a decree on the 20th "requiring all able bodied men in the city to report in the State House yard the next day with their arms and equipment." All who had arms "which they can not or do not mean to employ in the defense of America" were ordered to sell them to the army or be "severely punished."

Washington was putting to use at least some of the new powers Congress had granted him for directing the "department of war." He suspected an entirely new army would have to be raised, for "you may as well attempt to stop the winds from blowing, as the regiments from going when their time is expired." In addition to the 88 new regiments Congress was requesting from the states, he personally authorized the raising of 16 more by "any good officers" who are able "to raise men upon Continental pay and establishment." He promised a bounty for both the recruiting officer and the recruits. He also ordered all his brigade commanders to personally plead with their troops to stay six more weeks. Otherwise, as he wrote to Congress on the 20th, "ten more days will see the end of the existence of the army." Each man

that stayed on was promised a bounty of $10 and a 25% raise in pay, though Congress had not authorized such payments. If Congress refused to honor Washington's promises, he would have to exhaust his personal fortune to pay it, but he was willing to take that risk. He informed the Congress of his new recruiting methods:

> It may be thought that I am going a good deal out of the line of my duty to adopt these measures. A character to lose, and a state to forfeit, the inestimable blessings at stake, and a life devoted, must be my excuse.

On December 20 and 21, nearly 1,500 Pennsylvanian militia, newly enlisted for a period of six weeks, arrived in camp. The recruiting was helped by "authenticated" reports in the newspapers, describing the enemy's advance across New Jersey. Typical was this report:

> On Monday morning, they entered the house of Samuel Stout, Esq., in Hopewell, where they destroyed his deeds, papers, furniture, and effects of every kind, except what they plundered. They took every horse away, left his house and farm in ruins, injuring him to the value of three thousand pounds in less than three hours. Old Mr. Phillips, his neighbour, they pillaged in the same manner, and then cruelly beat him.
>
> On Wednesday past, three women came down to the Jersey shore in great distress. It appeared that they all had been very much abused, and the youngest of them, a girl about fifteen years of age, had been ravished that morning by a British officer.
>
> A number of young women in Hopewell to the amount of sixteen, flying before the ravaging and cruel enemy, took refuge on a mountain near Ralph Hary's, but information being given of their retreat, they were

soon brought down into the British camp, where they have been kept ever since.

Hundreds of families are reduced from comfort and affluence to poverty and ruin, left at this inclement season to wander through the woods without house or clothing.

If those scenes of desolation, ruin, and distress do not rouse and animate every man of spirit to revenge their much-injured countrymen and countrywomen, all virtue, honour and courage must have left this country, and we deserve all that we shall meet with, as there can be no doubt the same scene will be acted in this province [Pennsylvania] upon our property, and our beloved wives and daughters.

Washington put the new arrivals to good use, helping the rest of the army guard "every suspicious part of the river." He did not want a repeat of the surprise Howe had given him on Long Island.

Leading one of these new companies was a Philadelphia painter named Charles Willson Peale. Four years earlier, a Virginia planter named George Washington had sat for the first of many portraits that would later make Peale famous. To Peale's surprise, he was elected a lieutenant by his fellow Philadelphians, despite being "but a stranger to them," having recently moved there from Maryland. Short and frail, he described himself as "totally unfit to endure the fatigues of long marches and lying on the cold wet ground," but he confidently predicted that he would manage even "better than many others whose appearance was more robust." One way he planned to do this was by "temperance." He brought along a canteen filled with water, a drink he claimed was "better than rum" for soldiers on the march.

When the call for his militia company was heard in early December, Peale was determined to do his duty, though he had to leave a houseful of three women and two children without a breadwinner. He visited the house of each member of the company and wrote down the

needs of each household. He promised the men that if they enlisted for six weeks they would "get everything they should want, and told their wives that they would be supplied with necessaries while their husbands were doing their duty in the field." When Peale and his men arrived at Trenton, after a two-day sail up the Delaware, he was shocked by the condition of the army.

> The sick and half naked veterans of the long retreat streamed past. I thought it the most hellish scene I have ever beheld. Suddenly a man staggered out of the line and came toward me. He had lost all his clothes. He was in an old dirty blanketjacket, his beard long and his face full of sores, which so disfigured him that he was not known by me on first sight. Only when he spoke did I recognize my brother James.

One member of Charles Willson Peale's company, an elderly sergeant named William Young, had a habit of quoting passages from the bible. Sergeant Young was shocked by the behavior of the men in his own company and others. He confided to his diary:

> It is melancholy to think what looseness prevails among all our men. A great deal of swearing and taking the Holy Name of God in vain. If salvation comes to our guilty land it will be through the tender mercies of God, and not through the virtue of her people. So much swearing and profane living is nowhere else to be found.

Profanity was not the only vice of the American soldiers. At times they resembled the British or Hessians, taking from the inhabitants what they wanted to fill up their bellies or their haversacks. Though most reports of plundering during the war focused on the King's forces, the American soldiers were guilty of the practice, too. On the retreat through Princeton, a few hundred soldiers stayed overnight in

Nassau Hall. The largest building in America, this was the main structure of the College of New Jersey (now Princeton University). What the Continentals started, the British finished a few days later - the near complete destruction of the college's famed library and planetarium.

When the Continentals crossed over into Pennsylvania, Joseph White, a nineteen-year-old sergeant from Massachusetts, was fortunate to be billeted in "the back part of a tavern." This was great news to his men, for they would be able to sleep out of the wind and buy at least one solid meal each day. However, White soon learned that the tavernkeeper, a Quaker, "refused to take rebel money, as he called it." A few months earlier, young Joseph had faced a similar situation. He had been staying in a Quaker barn while recuperating from "a dangerous sickness." The farmer had refused to sell him milk, but his wife had agreed to give White "half a pint each morning" when he offered "to milk the cows." "My health," he soon wrote, "gained fast."

But the tavernkeeper he now faced was adamant: no rebel money. Sergeant White brought the situation to the attention of General Israel Putnam. White told "Old Put" that the tavernkeeper had "everything we wanted, but he will not take paper money, he calls it 'rebel money.'" Putnam was furious: "You go and tell him, from me, that if he refuses to take our money, [you can] take what you want, without any pay." Sergeant White returned to the tavern.

> [I] told the man what the General said. "Your Yankee general dare not give such orders," says he. I placed two men at the cellar door as sentries. "Let nobody whatever go down," I said. I called for a light and two men to go down cellar with me. We found it full of good things: a large pile of cheeses, hams of bacon, a large tub of honey, barrels of cider and one barrel marked "cider-royal," which was very strong; also all kinds of spirits.
>
> The owner went to the General to complain. "The sergeant told me," said the General, "that you refused to

take paper money." "So I did," said he. The General flew round like a top. He called for a file of men. A corporal and four men came. "Take this Tory rascal to the main guard house!"

White's company feasted themselves, after sending "a ham of bacon, one large cheese and a blanket full of cider-royal" to Old Put as a token of their gratitude. Sergeant White's example of plundering was one where he had the official sanction of a general officer. More common was unsanctioned "foraging." Typical was the experience Rhode Island's Sergeant John Smith recorded in his journal, on a march through Norwalk, Connecticut, a few months before:

> I was awaked by something pulling me and a voice crying, "Turn out, damn you! Look here, see and behold!" I looked and saw five fat geese. I eat a hearty meal, asking no questions with the rest of my brother soldiers who seemed hearty in the cause of liberty of taking what came by their industry. By the road in the morning we eat the fragments and rested in our hut, or Den of Thiefs.

* * * * *

Let us return to the progress of Howe's army. Washington's army finished crossing the Delaware just as Howe and Cornwallis arrived on the outskirts of Trenton. Charles Stedman, an officer in Howe's army who later wrote a history of the war, charged in his book, "General Howe appeared to have calculated with the greatest accuracy the exact time necessary for the enemy to make his escape." Captain Johann Ewald, whose jagers tried "to seize the rear guard of the enemy at the crossing," was too late. "Their last boats were already leaving the shore when we were still about 300 paces away." Ewald later reflected on the march from Brunswick to Trenton:

On this two-day march, which could have been done in twelve hours, it became clearly evident that the march took place so slowly for no other reason than to permit Washington to cross the Delaware safely and peacefully. The two Howe brothers belong to the Opposition Party [in Parliament]. Therefore no more need be said. They will not, and dare not, act otherwise.

Howe left the main column on the outskirts of "Trent Town" and went forward with his aides to where the jagers and light infantry had halted their pursuit, near the riverbank. There he was welcomed by "a very heavy cannonade from the opposite side of the river." One of Howes's aides, Captain "Fritz" von Muenchhausen, employed as a translator of orders, was as usual at Howe's side. Muenchhausen later recorded this reconnaisance in his diary:

> Howe rode with us all around, stopping from time to time. He stayed there with the greatest of coolness and calm for at least an hour, while the rebels kept their strongest fire going. Wherever we turned, the cannon balls hit the ground, and I can hardly understand, even now, why all of us were not crushed by the many balls. Just as General Howe was about to move into the town, a ball landed so close to him in soft ground that dirt splattered his body and face.
>
> I had the honor to receive a small contusion on my knee. We were just standing still when a ball took away the hind leg of my horse, and hit some stones on the ground, one of which hit me in the knee and caused my knee to swell up. I was lucky, for my horse fell to the ground with me, with great force, and feeling the blow on my knee just then, I believed that I was really severely wounded. Afterwards, General Howe gave me a

superb English horse to replace mine.

[Later that evening] ... the rebels must know the
house where our General is staying, for they have
thrown several shells at our house. But so far none have
come very close.

Shortly after midnight, the drums sounded and the redcoats groaned
as they prepared for a night march. Their destination: Coryell's Ferry,
sixteen miles upriver. With the spirited Cornwallis in command of the
detachment, the exhausted troops arrived on the New Jersey side,
opposite the ferry, around daybreak. However, their mission was
frustrated - they "could find neither boats nor a ferry." Scouting
parties searched the whole day while being fired at by rebel riflemen
across the river. By evening, Cornwallis gave up the search and established camp at Pennington, a village five miles north of Trenton.
Howe also sent parties south of Trenton. But they, too, found, in
Muenchhausen's words, no boats "or any other means to cross this
cursed river."

A British captain named Hall thought the ordnance department committed "a capital oversight" by not bringing along "pontoons or boats
on carriages, essentially necessary for the service in this country." But
he blamed Howe even more, "for want of vigor and decisiveness" during the march through New Jersey.

In the catalogue of military errors and misconduct, I
will venture to assert, this appears so singular that it
almost stands without example. Yet this march was
extolled in the publick papers, and drew applause from
the deceived and credulous multitude.

However, it would not draw applause two years later, during a Parliamentary inquiry into Howe's conduct of the war.

General Howe decided that his long, "very unsafe" supply line, and
the weather's being "too severe to keep the field," justified removing

the army to New York. Some of his officers had thought he would wait until the river froze over, then "cross the river and capture Philadelphia to end the war." Or, he could have utilized the "48,000 feet of boards" at the "board yard directly back of his headquarters and which he must have seen every time he looked out his bedroom window." With this lumber, his army could have built rafts "in the space of two days sufficient to have transported the whole Britsh army."

But Howe knew from his informants that the rebel army was nearly naked, dispirited, and scheduled to all but disappear on January first. Deserters had told him that almost to a man the Continental troops had declared "that they will not serve longer than the term of their enlistment." By spring, there might no longer be a rebellion. Muenchhausen noted in his diary that Howe gave Cornwallis leave to return to England to be with his ailing wife. He was supposed to return to New York in the spring - "that is, if there is to be another campaign, which we doubt."

Howe also knew that his mistress, a buxom "flashing blonde" named Mrs. Elizabeth Loring, was in New York waiting for him. On Friday, the thirteenth of December, he announced the close of the campaign of 1776 and headed back to New York. He was subsequently ridiculed in Whig and Tory press alike for spending the winter in New York, instead of destroying the rebel army and taking Philadelphia.

> Awake, arouse, Sir Billy.
> There's forage in the plain.
> Ah! leave your little filly,
> And open the campaign.
> Heed not a woman's prattle,
> Which tickles in the ear.
> But give the word for battle,
> And grasp the warlike spear.

During a later campaign, Francis Hopkinson would be more to the point in another poem:

Sir William, he, snug as a flea,
Lay all this while a-snoring;
Nor dream'd of harm as he lay warm,
In bed with Mrs. Loring.

So William Howe returned to New York. Good news was awaiting him there. After his arrival, Muenchhausen proudly recorded in his diary:

> We met Major Cuyler, adjutant general to our General. He had gone from here to England on September 6 to bring the King news of the first successful feat of our campaign, the affair at Flatbush, etc. He brought back with him the Baronet or Sir William title and the Order of the Bath for our General.

With Cornwallis about to leave for London, Howe left the less capable General James Grant in charge of a string of fourteen cantonments from Hackensack southward to the Trenton area. Howe admitted in his report to Secretary of State Germain that his chain of outposts, or "cantonments," in New Jersey was "too extensive." But, he explained, it was necessary to reassure "the friends of government" in New Jersey. Howe concluded his report, "trusting to the almost general submission, and to the strength of the corps placed in the advanced posts, I conclude the troops will be in perfect security." Clinton, before embarking for Rhode Island, had advised Howe about the possibility of the cantonments "being broken in upon in the winter, as he knew the Americans were trained to strategem and enterprise, that they knew every trick of that country of chicane and would quickly catch at any opportunity that might offer." But Howe did not make a habit of accepting the advice of his irritating second in command.

CHAPTER FOURTEEN
WASHINGTON STRIKES BACK AT TRENTON

"Fiddlesticks! These clodhoppers will not attack us; and should they do so, we will simply fall on them and rout them!"

> \- Colonel Rall, ignoring
> orders to fortify Trenton.

"They make a great deal of Christmas in Germany, and no doubt the Hessians will drink a great deal of beer and have a dance tonight. Washington will set the tune for them about daybreak."

> \- American officer's diary,
> December 25, 1776.

Washington expected Howe to return from New York "so soon as the ice will afford the means of conveyance." General Lord Stirling had been Surveyor General of New Jersey before the war. So George Washington sat with him now and studied maps. They concluded that Howe would not have to return by the same route. Instead, he could cross the Delaware farther north, and be in Philadelphia before any defenses could be thrown in the way. Washington was not content to sit and wait for that to happen.

Now was the opportunity for the counterattack that Washington had been looking for, ever since the retreat began. He wrote to Connecticut's Governor Trumbull that he hoped soon to "attempt a stroke," since the enemy "lay a good deal scattered and to all appearance in a state of security. A lucky blow in this quarter would be fatal to them, and would most certainly raise the spirits of the people." By December 21st, he had formulated his plan of attack. That day, Major Wilkinson thought the commander's countenance was "always grave

and thoughtful, pensive and solemn in the extreme."

Colonel Joseph Reed was at Bristol, several miles south of the New-town, Pennsylvania, headquarters and unaware that Washington had already determined upon an attack on the Hessian posts at Trenton and Bordentown. Reed wrote to him on the 22nd, suggesting "a diversion at or around Trenton:"

> Allow me to hope you will consult your own good judgment and spirit, and not let the goodness of your heart subject you to the influence of opinions from men in every respect your inferiors [as he had done at Fort Washington]. Something must be attempted before the sixty days expire which the commissioners [the Howes] have allowed [for signing the oath of allegiance]... unless some more favourable appearance attends our arms and cause before that time, a very large number of the militia officers here will [sign].

Washington answered Reed's letter the next day, the 23rd, addressing it to Reed "or, in his absence, to John Cadwalader, Esq., only." A militia colonel from Pennsylvania, Cadwalader was in charge of the growing militia forces at Bristol. Washington wrote:

> Christmas day at night, one hour before [sunrise of the next] day, is the time fixed upon for our attempt on Trenton. For Heaven's sake keep this to yourself, as the discovery of it may prove fatal to us. Dire necessity will, nay must, justify an attempt. Prepare and, in concert with Griffin, attack as many of their posts as you possibly can with a prospect of success. The more we can attack at the same instant, the more confusion we shall spread and the greater good will result.

It was a desperate venture, and Washington knew it. He would

have nearly every man in the army who was at all fit for duty, 5,000 all told, cross the river. They would attack the 1,400 Hessians at Trenton under Colonel Rall, and a like number at Bordentown, to the south, under Colonel von Donop. Once across, there would be no turning back if they were discovered en route. They would have to fight and be victorious, or else be pinned to the river. If the plan succeeded, he would push on and also attack the British posts at Princeton and Brunswick, then head northwest for a winter encampment in the hills near Morristown. There his army would be secure and in a position to watch for any move from New York toward Philadelphia.

Washington had an additional incentive for attempting a surprise attack at this time: he had just been informed by one of his most reliable spies that Colonel Rall would most likely be ill-prepared for such an assault. John Honeyman was a recent Scotch-Irish immigrant and a weaver by trade. However, when he had offered his services to Washington, at Hackensack back in November, the general had persuaded him to assume the guise of a cattle dealer. His instructions had been to fall in with the British Army, provide it with cattle and intelligence so as to be in their favor, and learn as much as he could about the daily routine, picket and artillery locations, regimental strengths, troop movements, etc., of some of their camps.

On the afternoon of December 22, Honeyman allowed himself to be captured outside Trenton by a militia patrol. They recognized him as that "notorious Tory and British spy." After a struggle they managed to tie him up and bring him over the river to headquarters. Washington looked stern and told the guards to leave him alone with this Tory rascal, who might want to save his neck by telling all he knew. After a half hour of hushed conversation, Washington called the guards again and told them to lock the prisoner up and shoot to kill if he tried to escape, for there would be a courtmartial and hanging in the morning.

Later that night, a haystack near the farmhouse he was confined in mysteriously caught fire. When the guards rushed to put it out, Honeyman used the key Washington had given him to let himself out. As he ran for the river a sentry's bullet whizzed by his head. After wading

and walking across the ice-choked river, he arrived, drenched and exhausted, at the feet of a Hessian sentry.

Recognized as one of Colonel Rall's Tory informers, he was brought to headquarters. While drying off and warming up, he told Rall of his capture, interrogation and narrow escape. Then he described what he had seen and heard of the rebel "soldiers" huddled around their camp-fires, trying to keep their feet from freezing: suppliers were refusing to accept the Congress's paper money; the army was hopelessly disorganized; its leaders were cowards; and the men were on the verge of mutiny over the lack of pay, food and clothing, etc. Rall believed every word of it, since it confirmed everything he had been led to believe from his other informers. He decided to go ahead with his plans for a big Christmas celebration. The men deserved it after their costly assaults at White Plains and Fort Washington, their foul weather march across New Jersey, and their duty here in this miserable little village.

Despite the reassuring report from Honeyman, Washington could not be sure that Trenton would be unprepared. He worried that rumors of the planned attack might reach Rall. Indeed they did. On December 23rd, three different persons arrived at Rall's headquarters and told him the same story: the rebel troops were being given three days' cooked provisions and were ordered to be ready to march. But Rall dismissed the reports as "idle woman's talk."

* * * * *

During their occupation, the British and Hessian soldiers found the people of New Jersey were becoming increasingly hostile. A Hessian officer noted, "when they see one person or only a few who belong to our army, they shoot at their heads." The gentlemen officers from Europe were outraged by such uncivilized conduct. Accustomed to the formal rules of warfare, as played out by professional armies in what historians call The Age of Limited Warfare, it was incomprehenisble that civilians would take up arms against a regular army.

General Howe tried to discourage these ambushes. In a December 14th proclamation, he warned that "small straggling parties not dressed like soldiers who presume to molest or fire upon soldiers or peaceable inhabitants of the country" would be apprehended and "immediately hanged without trial, as assassins." But the warning was not heeded; in fact, the guerrilla warfare increased. A few days before Christmas, a Hessian officer named von Jungkenn wrote in his diary:

> [The Light Dragoons] were so frightened when they were to patrol, that hardly any of them were willing to venture it without infantry, for they never went out patrolling without being fired upon, or having one wounded or even shot dead. We have not slept one night in peace since we came to this place.

One day Colonel Rall sent out two mounted men from Trenton to deliver messages to General Leslie at Princeton. After one of them returned with the message undelivered, and said the other rider had been shot dead, Rall decided to give these snipers a show of force. This time the message bearer had an escort of 100 infantry and a field piece! Many years later, Lieutenant Wiederholdt could still recall the humiliating two day mission. The weather was "exceedingly bad," the men had to spend the night "on the bare ground," and when this huge detachment arrived in Princeton, just to deliver a few letters, "the English laughed at us."

Why were the inhabitants so inhospitable to Howe's army? The answer lies in the behavior of the occupation forces. Howe's pacification program had become a cruel joke, as his soldiers, British and Hessian alike, ignored the inhabitants' protection papers and plundered as they pleased. Some people fled, to live with distant relatives or friends; some stayed, and suffered for their courage. Though both Whigs and Tories suffered from the pillaging, Tory informers gladly identified the houses of rebel families needing special attention. In this way, the Tories could avenge past persecutions at the hands of Whig

committeemen.

An example of what it was like having the King's soldiers billeted in your house is provided by a Trenton woman. Her ten-year-old daughter, Martha Reed, years later recollected the cold mid-December night, when "the dreaded Hessians" arrived:

> Mother and we two children were gathered in the family room; a great fire blazed in the chimney place, and mother sat with her feet on the low fender talking to us about father who was away with the army. Suddenly there was a noise outside, and the sound of many feet. The room door opened and in stalked several strange men and a couple of women who looked like giants and giantesses to us they were so tall. These were the dreaded Hessians surely come. They jabbered away in harsh guttural tones and, coming to the fire, spread out their hands to the blaze.
>
> We children jumped up screaming and clung to our mother. She was a brave little woman and, standing up, pointed to the door telling them to go out. They understood the gesture, if not the words, and shook their heads doggedly. As they crouched about the fire, one of the women caught sight of the large silver buckles which mother wore in her shoes ... and made signs for her to take off the shoes. Seeing her hesitate, the woman snatched at the buckle and, pulling off the shoe, rapped my mother in the face with the heel.
>
> The next morning mother was obliged to open her store room and they helped themselves. They killed a hog and cut it up on the mahogany table; pickles and preserves and our winter stores vanished. We looked on in fear and trembling, thankful that our lives were spared and that we were permitted to remain in our own house.

For the next several days, Mrs. Reed, her ten-year-old daughter and eight-year-old son were allowed to remain in a tiny room upstairs, so long as they didn't disturb the new residents. Although her husband was an officer in the Continental Army across the river, Mrs. Reed convinced the Hessians who invaded her house that she was the wife of an officer in a Tory regiment. However, this deception did not last long.

> To please my little brother, my mother had made for him an officer's coat of the rebel buff and blue, in which he delighted to strut and fight imaginary battles. The coat was carefully folded away in the linen chest, and one day when the women were tossing about its contents, they came across the rebel coat. It was a revelation. What a storm broke around us! They shook the little coat in our faces, jabbering and threatening, and we understood by their gestures that they only awaited the orders of their captain to punish us.
>
> Mother hurried us into our room, but we were all too much frightened to feel any longer safe. We kept out of sight until the angry hubbub died away and when it grew dark we crept softly down the stairs and out of the back door to the hen house. There were no cackling hens to betray us, for our enemies had killed them all. We ascended the ladder, which mother pulled up after us, and here in this loft we remained all night, trembling with cold and fear. The Hessians [during the days] built fires in the barnyard and cooked in huge pots, in the manner of gypsies. In the cold grey of the morning, mother crept down the ladder and brought up her apron full of warm ashes to try and warm our numbed feet and hands.

Mrs. Reed soon decided to risk Hessian retribution rather than spend the winter outdoors, so she and her children slipped back into

the house. To their surprise and relief, no orders were issued to punish them for the deception.

* * * * *

From Brunswick, General Grant sent some new intelligence to Colonel Rall. It arrived in Trenton early on Christmas morning:

> Washington has been informed that our troops have marched into winter quarters and has been told that we are weak at Trenton and Princeton, and Lord Stirling expressed a wish to make an attack on these two places. I don't believe he will attempt it, but be assured that my information is undoubtedly true. Be upon your guard against an unexpected attack at Trenton.

Apparently, someone close to Washington was keeping the enemy very well informed. However, Rall ignored the advice, just as he had an earlier order to build redoubts at all the vulnerable approaches to the town. Major von Dechow later testified that Colonel Rall replied to these advices: "Fiddlesticks! These clod-hoppers will not attack us, and should they do so, we will simply fall on them and rout them!"

Colonel Johann Gottlieb Rall, at age 50 already a veteran of 36 years in the army, was known as "The Lion" for his aggressiveness and durability in battle. He had followed up his impressive flank attack at White Plains a few weeks later with a courageous and bloody frontal assault up the north face of Mount Washington. Because of these heroics, Rall had persuaded Howe that he deserved the command at Trenton, which was the army's "post of honor" (most advanced post) in the string of winter cantonments.

According to one of his officers, Rall "was made for a soldier but not a general." He had never been in sole command of so many men before - three regiments at Trenton, totalling 1,400 men. Rall was enjoying every minute of it. Every morning he slept until nine, and then

often soaked in the bath until 11 o'clock, keeping the men who were standing outside "waiting a half hour for the changing of the guard." Instead of constructing redoubts for the artillery, he had all the cannon "drawn up in front of his quarters." Major von Dechow had asked Rall to send a request to headquarters at New York for more winter clothing for the troops. The men needed the extra clothes, because they were doing a tremendous amount of guard duty, necessitated by the lack of earthworks. Rall scoffed at the idea. Lieutenant Wiederholdt's diary reflects the general disgust of the troops:

> It was no concern whatever to [Rall] whether the off duty soldiers were sloppily dressed or not, and it was of little moment whether or not they kept their muskets cleaned, polished, and in good repair, and kept their ammunition ready. He never even asked about things like that. But the music, the band! That was his affair! The officer in charge of the guard had to march around the church with his guards and musicians. The colonel would always follow the parade as far as the guard house just to hear the music during the changing of the guard. Around 2 in the afternoon, the guards were relieved and at 4 o'clock the pickets. All the officers had to participate, and to be around his quarters, so that it might look grand and like a real headquarters.

Colonel Francis Scheffer commanded one of the three regiments under Rall. He wrote, "Colonel Rall's behavior was inexcusable, it made me sick." Scheffer and von Dechow recorded their complaints in a letter to General von Heister, head of all German troops in America. It reached his headquarters at New York on Christmas Day. Before von Heister had time to consider their complaints, though, Rall had to answer to another general - George Washington.

* * * * *

Sunset, December 25th. The Hessians were celebrating Christmas by eating, drinking and singing in their quarters throughout the town, some of them reminiscing around small evergreen trees they had cut while on patrol. Americans in 1776 had not yet adopted the Christmas tree, holly wreath, St. Nicholas, and other German customs. One of Washington's aides noted in his diary, "They make a great deal of Christmas in Germany, and no doubt the Hessians will drink a great deal of beer and have a dance tonight. Washington will set the tune for them about daybreak."

Across the river and several miles north of Trenton, 2,400 American troops were gathering at McKonkey's Ferry. (Today the site is part of Washington Crossing State Park, Pennsylvania.) Sixteen-year-old John Greenwood, the fifer from Boston, was one of those who received orders that afternoon to march to the ferry.

> None but the first officers knew where we were going
> or what we were going about, for it was a secret expedi-
> tion ... [the soldiers did not] trouble themselves as to
> where they were led, owing to the impossibility of being
> in a worse condition than their present one. The men al-
> ways liked to be kept moving in expectation of bettering
> themselves.

Private Greenwood was still suffering from "the camp itch," but it was not as painful as it had been while on the march from Ticondero-ga. An ointment had eased the pain, but his thighs were still raw and all scabbed over now. However, he limped along with the others, carrying not only his fife but also a musket, sixty cartridges in his car-tridge box and pockets, and three days' cooked provisions (heavily salted meat and hard bread) in his haversack.

It had been a much colder December than normal in the Delaware Valley. Large sheets of ice were floating in the river already, three or four weeks earlier than most years. But this Christmas Day had been

relatively mild, the thermometer reaching all the way up to 32 degrees. By late afternoon, however, the wind picked up and the thermometer began to drop sharply. In McKonkey's house, a roaring fire was kept up all day and night for the many officers who stopped in to escape from the cold wind for a few minutes, and to consume countless mugs of hot buttered rum. One such officer, believed to be Colonel John Fitzgerald, took the time to record his thoughts in his diary:

> 6:00 p.m. The regiments have had their evening parade, but instead of returning to their quarters are marching toward the ferry. It is fearfully cold and raw and a snow storm is setting in. The wind is north-east and beats in the faces of the men. It will be a terrible night for the men who have no shoes. Some of them have tied old rags around their feet, others are barefoot.

It was time, once again, for Colonel John Glover's regiment of fishermen from Marblehead, Massachusetts, to be unsung heroes. They had rescued the army after the defeat on Long Island by bringing it across the East River at night, practically underneath the guns of the British fleet. Eight weeks later, they had stood their ground on Pell's Point and held off a much larger force under General Henry Clinton, thus allowing Washington enough time to reach White Plains safely. Since then, they had crossed the army over the Hudson and many other rivers during the retreat across New Jersey. Glover's regiment had one of the lowest desertion rates in the army, despite the fact that almost every letter arriving from home brought news of friends and relatives who were making their fortunes as crewmen on privateers, taking British supply ships as prizes of war. The men had already stayed past their enlistments, hoping for the frigates that Congress had promised them. Glover pointed all these things out to Washington. And just as Gates had, he reminded Washington what would happen to the defenseless men in the boats during the slow crossing if the Hessians, with their artillery, got wind of what was happening.

Like many New England officers, John Glover had no love for the aristocratic Virginian who was known to disdain New Englanders, because of their lack of class consciousness. He was not fully won over to helping Washington again until the 23rd, when Colonel John Stark arrived. Stark, one of the heroes of Bunker Hill, was not about to be left out of any significant action. He had come all the way from the New Hampshire Grants with six rough backwoodsmen, members of the "Bennington Rifles." As soon as he arrived, he freely expressed his opinion to Washington that the soldiers struggling to put up earthworks at the ferry crossings should not be doing such work. He stated emphatically that soldiers are meant for fighting, and he boldly demanded to know when Washington would order an attack. Stark coaxed his fellow New Englander, Glover, into doing what he knew only his men could do.

So, after dark on December 25, 1776, George Washington crossed the Delaware again, this time from west to east. But, not in the tiny boat in which, years later, the painter Emmanuel Leutze would place him, and certainly not standing up with one foot on the bow. With the darkness, the high winds, and the sheets of ice crashing into the sides of the boats, he would have gone head first into the water. The vessels actually used were called Durham Boats, from 40 to 66 feet long and eight feet wide. Normally used for hauling iron ore and grain down to Philadelphia, they could carry 20 tons apiece. Even when fully loaded, they drew only 24 to 30 inches of water, so the men would not have very far to wade to shore in the icy water when the boats struck bottom. They were navigated by a steersman, and by two men on each side who moved along a walkway with 20-foot poles.

The 2,400 men were brought across first, then the 150 or so horses, and finally the eighteen field pieces, mostly three-pounders. These were nearly all that remained of the hundreds of cannon the army had boasted just a few months ago. The heavy guns proved the most troublesome cargo, with the petulant Colonel Knox constantly berating, and at times enraging, Glover's overworked seamen. George Washington directed the crossing, with the help of Henry Knox's "stentorian

lungs." Knox, the six-foot-three, 280-pound colonel of artillery, had "a deep bass" voice easily "heard above the crash of the ice which filled the river." The "floating ice made the labor almost incredible," as it piled up against the boats, pushing them downstream. The polemen had to struggle to push away the ice, and pole upriver against the current to the landing place.

Incredibly, however, the crossing came off perfectly, without the loss of a single man, horse or cannon, or discovery by the enemy. The Yankee fishermen performed commendably. The aristocratic Philadelphian, Captain Alexander Graydon, was impressed by "the regiment's apparent aptitude for the purpose" at hand, but he was somewhat disturbed by its makeup. He noted that "in this regiment, there were a number of negroes, which, to persons unaccustomed to such associations, had a disagreeable, degrading effect."

In the midst of all this commotion, twenty-year-old Major James Wilkinson arrived from Philadelphia, where he had left General Gates that morning. Gates had refused to partake in the attack, and had requested an "illness leave." Now he was on his way to Baltimore to try to persuade Congress to replace Washington with himself.

On the way to McKonkey's Ferry, Wilkinson oberved "there was a little snow on the ground, which was tinged here and there with blood from the feet of the men." He found Washington "with his whip in his hand, prepared to mount his horse." Wilkinson handed him a letter from Gates. Washington was annoyed by the distraction. "What a time is this to hand me letters!" Wilkinson answered that he had been ordered by Gates to deliver it. "By General Gates! Where is he?" "I left him this morning in Philadelphia." "What was he doing there?" asked Washington. "I understood him that he was on his way to Congress," replied the major. Exasperated with Gates's refusal to do his duty, Washington could only repeat, "On his way to Congress!" He then broke the seal of the letter, read it, and quickly returned to directing the crossing.

The Commander-in-Chief's strict orders for the march were passed along: "profound silence ... no man to quit his ranks on pain of death

... march eight men abreast ... each officer to provide himself with a piece of white paper stuck in his hat." The vanguard, a Virginia regiment, crossed first and spread out in a semi-circle to secure a landing area and stop all traffic on the roads. Then Washington, himself, crossed in the next boat.

The wet snow was now changing to sleet that "cut like a knife" and sapped the men's strength. Those waiting on either side of the river stood for hours, shivering in the cold and the wind. Many of them were already weak from poor diet, exposure, and heavy duty on the retreat through New Jersey. Washington rejected with violent rebukes the suggestions by some of his officers that the crossing be postponed until the next night.

He also broke the despondent mood, perhaps intentionally, with a remark he made to oversized Colonel Henry Knox while climbing into the boat. As Washington edged past the other men in the boat, he nudged Knox with his toe and said, loud enough for all to hear, "Shift that fat ass, Harry - but slowly, or you'll swamp the --- ---- boat." This timely remark was greeted with laughter that was heard by the men in the other boats and those waiting on shore. The story quickly spread through the ranks and gave the men something to talk about and take their minds off their misery.

After waiting several hours for its turn, Private Greenwood's company was poled across the river, and waded onto New Jersey soil.

> [We] began to pull down the fences and make fires to warm ourselves, for the storm was increasing rapidly. When I turned my face toward the fire, my back would be freezing. By turning round and round I kept myself from perishing.
>
> The noise of the soldiers coming over and clearing away the ice, the rattling of the cannon wheels on the frozen ground, and the cheerfulness of my fellow comrades encouraged me beyond expression, and big coward as I acknowledge myself to be, I felt great

pleasure.

* * * * *

Around six p.m., just as Washington had started his crossing, he had received word from Colonel Reed that Cadwalader's division was not going to attempt the planned crossing at Kirkbright's Ferry to Borden-town, south of Trenton. The reason: "it was supposed the enemy had too many friends" there who would send word to Colonel Donop. Instead, Cadwalader's 1,500 men would march several miles further south and cross at Dunk's Ferry. From there, they would have a five mile march through wooded, sparsely inhabited territory and, hope-fully, surprise Donop's Mount Holly camp at dawn.

With Cadwalader and Reed were Captain Thomas Rodney, of Delaware, and Lieutenant Charles Willson Peale, of Philadelphia. Peale almost missed going on the expedition, having been a few miles from camp buying milk and butter for his men when the marching or-ders arrived that afternoon. Some of his men "were unwilling to turn out, as it was a day [Christmas] they wished to enjoy themselves."

The river was wider here than where Washington was crossing, and nearly frozen near the New Jersey shore. And they did not have any-one like Glover's seamen to man the boats. Nevertheless, the attempt was made. Rodney's company of Delaware militia was part of the advance guard that crossed first. Because of the thick ice, they "were obliged to land on the ice 150 yards from the shore" and walk the rest of the way. Once ashore, they set out pickets in a semi-circle that extended 200 yards from the river. Colonel Reed later described the tortuous crossing:

> It had been attempted to keep the troops from kin-
> dling any fires, but this was found impossible, and we
> were obliged to take our chance of giving the enemy the
> alarm. The ice had drifted in such great quantities upon
> the Jersey shore that it was absolutely impossible to land

the artillery. An attempt was made by them to land their horses which was effected with such difficulty as excluded all hope of debarking the field pieces. Advice of this being sent over to the other shore, the troops which by this time were nearly all transported were ordered to return.

Cadwalader ordered the troops to return because, he felt, the artillery was absolutely necessary for the attack. The muskets would be almost useless in such wet weather. Captain Rodney noted that the militia already across had "waited three hours" for the others and did not take too kindly to this order to abort the mission. They were "greatly irritated and they proposed making the attack without both the generals and the artillery." But they were coaxed into returning by the argument that "if General Washington should be unsuccessful and we also, the cause would be lost, but if our force remained intact it would still keep up the spirit of America."

At Colvin's Ferry, just across from the southern end of Trenton, General Ewing failed to cross any of his division. He was supposed to secure the bridge over Assunpink Creek, sealing off Rall's possible escape route to Bordentown. However, Ewing's officers told him that the men were very reluctant to go out onto the river, which was wider and more turbulent here than at McKonkey's Ferry. Also, like Cadwalader, Ewing had none of Glover's seamen to man the boats. Unwilling to force the issue, Ewing called off the crossing.

The three-pronged attack was now down to a single prong: Washington's division would have to do it all.

* * * * *

Meanwhile, back at McKonkey's Ferry, the crossing was taking nearly three hours longer than Washington expected. He had planned to be on the march by one o'clock, so as to arrive in Trenton about five, while the garrison was still asleep. He later wrote to Congress:

> [The delay] made me despair of surprising the town,
> as I well knew we could not reach it before day was
> fairly broke. But, as I was certain there was no making
> a retreat without being discovered and harassed on re-
> passing the river, I determined to push on at all events.

Though Washington did not know it, Colonel Rall already had in his possession a message stating that the attack was under way. Hours before, a Tory had arrived at Abraham Hunt's house to inform Rall that a large rebel party was on the march toward Trenton. However, he had not been allowed admittance, since Rall had left strict instructions that no one was to disturb him while he enjoyed his cards and liquor. So the Tory had written down his message and left, after being assured that the note would be immediately given to the commander. When Colonel Rall was handed the note, he snorted contemptuously and stuffed it in his waistcoat pocket without reading it.

Shortly before four a.m., Washington led the long column forward, not knowing whether Rall was at that moment sleeping or preparing for their arrival. The watchword for the night, "Victory or Death," had been chosen well. Perhaps, with the army three hours behind schedule, death seemed more likely than victory. By 6 a.m., when they stopped at the hamlet of Birmingham for a brief rest, the sleet had changed to hail, but the wind had not lessened. One soldier thought it "as severe a night as I ever saw." The sleet and snow made the road very slippery. At one point, one soldier observed "his Excellency's horse's hind feet slipped from under him, and he seized his horse's mane and the horse recovered." Many of the tired, sleepy marchers slipped and fell down. Once on the ground, some of them found sleep too tempting to resist. Two were found the next day, frozen to death.

Private Greenwood almost came to the same end, having sat down on a stump and fallen asleep when the column had halted. Fortunately, his sergeant noticed he was missing, went back, roused him, and made him walk about until fully awake. They then hurried on to catch up with their company. Though sworn to silence on this march, some of

the men could not help but grumble; contrary to normal marching procedure, they were allowed "not a drop of liquor" to warm themselves. Private Greenwood recalled that the whole army marched "not only sober but nearly half dead with cold for the want of clothing." These men were not going to let this suffering go for naught; they would make the best of their encounter with the hated Hessians. As Captain Alexander Hamilton put it, the men were "ready, every devil of them, to storm Hell's battlements."

At Birmingham, five miles from Trenton, the road split and so did the army. One column of 1,300 men and ten cannon, under General Greene and accompanied by Washington, took the Pennington Road to approach Trenton from the north. The other column of 1,100 men and eight cannon, under General Sullivan, continued along the River Road heading for the town's western edge. Sergeant Elisha Bostwick, of Connecticut, marching in Sullivan's largely New England division, noted that "the torches of our fieldpieces stuck in the exhalters. They sparkled and blazed in the storm all night." From this light the men could look up at the trees as they passed underneath them, their ice-covered branches looking like huge, diamond studded chandeliers. Sergeant Bostwick also recalled Washington riding back and forth "speaking to and encouraging the men in a deep and solemn voice" to keep their eyes open so as not to fall asleep while marching, and to "keep by your officers" once the battle began.

Each column was led by local men "in plain farmer's habit." One of them, David Laning, had escaped from the Hessians on Christmas Eve, breaking out of the building in which he had been confined and spending the night hidden in a friend's house. On Christmas morning, he "dressed in an old ragged coat and flapped hat, put an axe under his arm and went with his head down, limping along, and so passed in safety the enemy's sentries in the character of a wood chopper."

Between Birmingham and Trenton, both columns met up with the contingents of cavalry that Washington had sent on ahead with orders to "post themselves on the road about three miles from Trenton and make prisoners of all going in or coming out." One of these cavalry

units was led by George Washington's distant cousin, Captain William Washington, and his lieutenant, eighteen-year-old James Monroe, the future president.

Earlier that night, Monroe had an encounter with an inhabitant who came out of his house to see why his dogs were barking. At first, the man thought Monroe was a British officer and ordered him off the property. "He was violent and determined," Monroe would write, "and very profane and wanted to know what we were doing there on such a stormy night." Monroe advised the man to return to his house and be quiet, or face arrest. As Monroe talked, the man gradually realized that he was a Continental Army officer. The man changed his tone, and invited Monroe in for something to eat. Monroe declined, saying he must do his duty and stop all traffic on the road. The man hurried back to his house and soon returned with food for the men. He told Monroe, "I know something is to be done, and I'm going with you. I'm a doctor and I may be of help to some poor fellow."

As the two columns continued marching toward Trenton, a rider approached George Washington with a message from General Sullivan. Despite every effort being made to cover the muskets' firelocks, they were wet and would certainly misfire. "Tell your general," Washington replied, "to use the bayonet and penetrate into the town. The town must be taken. I am resolved to take it."

Just before Greene's column reached Trenton around dawn, its vanguard saw a force of men up ahead, marching toward them. An order was issued to prime and load muskets. However, after a few anxious moments, they discovered it was an American raiding party from General Adam Stephen's brigade of Virginians. Though the rest of Stephen's brigade was marching with Washington, Stephen had ordered this party across the Delaware the day before, without Washington's knowledge or consent. Though the group was only supposed to do reconnaisance without engaging the enemy, they had unwittingly fired on a Hessian outpost on the Pennington Road. An account of the incident is provided by their Captain Richard Anderson:

The party came close upon the Hessian sentinel, who was marching on his post, bending his head down as he met the storm. He saw them about the same time he was seen, and as he brought his gun to a charge and challenged, he was shot down.

Captain Anderson had then quickly ordered his patrol to turn around and march back to camp. However, "much to his surprise," he soon "encountered Washington's army." Anderson "never saw General Washington exhibit so much anger as he did when he told him where he had been and what he had done." The Commander-in-Chief turned to General Stephen in a rage and demanded to know how he dared authorize such a mission without his authority. "You, sir, may have ruined all my plans by having them put on their guard." After calming down, Washington instructed Anderson and his men to fall in and march with the vanguard. It appeared that the army would now need every available man.

Greene's column reached the northern outskirts of Trenton about 8 a.m. Just before they did, Colonel Charles Scott gave his Virginians his usual battle instructions:

> Take care now and fire low. Bring down your pieces. Fire at their legs. One man wounded in the leg is better than a dead one, for it takes two more to carry him off, and there is three gone. Leg them, damn 'em. I say, leg them!

Washington and one of his aides were among the first to discover the Hessian outpost on the Pennington Road. According to his aide:

> It was broad daylight when we came to a house where a man was chopping wood. He was very much surprised when he saw us. "Can you tell me where the Hessian picket is?" Washington asked. The man hes-

itated, but I said, "You need not be frightened; it is General Washington who asks the question." His face brightened and he pointed toward the house of Mr. Covell.

Looking down the road, I saw a Hessian running out from the house. He yelled in Dutch *"Der feind! Heraus! Heraus!"* ["The enemy! Turn out! Turn out!"] and swung his arms. Three or four others came out with their guns. Two of them fired at us, but the bullets whistled over our heads. Some of General Stephen's men rushed forward and captured two. The others took to their heels, running toward Mr. Calhoun's house, where the guard was stationed, about twenty men under Captain Altenbrockum. They came running out of the house. The captain flourished his sword and tried to form his men. Some of them fired at us, others ran toward the village.

A captain of the Philadelphia Light Horse, which was serving as Washington's escort, noticed a Hessian bleeding profusely on the snowy ground and groaning in agony. He dismounted and ran to the dying man's side to comfort him. General Greene, observing this, shouted, "No time for that, get back on your horse!" The column "pushed on with resolution and firmness," the retreat of the enemy's picket instilling the troops with "universal animation and spirit."

Colonel Knox recalled that the wind was now their ally. "The storm continued with great violence, but was in our backs and consequently in the faces of the enemy." The column had been able to approach so close to their picket without being observed, because the storm had muffled the noises normally heard from an army on the march, and the swirling snow and rain had reduced visibility to only a few yards. The storm had also caused the scheduled dawn patrols to be cancelled. Certainly no half-naked army would venture out of its quarters on a night like this.

Washington's aide continues his account: Within a few minutes, "from the West came the boom of a cannon. General Washington's face lighted up instantly for he knew that it was one of Sullivan's guns." Actually, the artillery Washington heard was not Sullivan's, but a battery on the Pennsylvania shore. The vanguard of Sullivan's column had encountered enemy guards at a small house on the River Road. They had rushed the house, put the guards to flight, and then done the same to a company of jagers posted in a mansion a bit farther called The Hermitage. Philemon Dickinson, a general of New Jersey militia, on hearing the musket fire, had ordered his artillerists to fire on the house. For General Dickinson, this was a personal sacrifice, since The Hermitage was his home.

Sullivan's three brigades pushed on, down the River Road. Their adrenaline flowing now, they charged into town, led by Colonel John Stark, of New Hampshire. He came galloping up to the front and, despite being subordinate in rank to Sullivan, St. Clair and Glover, screamed like an Indian and yelled to the New Englanders to follow him. A moment later, hundreds of Yankees were howling war whoops and racing as fast as their tired legs could carry them into the town. Major Wilkinson described the scene: "The enemy made a momentary shew of resistance by a wild and undirected fire from the windows of their quarters, which they abandoned as we advanced. ... the dauntless Stark dealt death wherever he found resistance and broke down all the opposition before him." The attacking troops had a temporary advantage of numbers, since the Hessians were spread out, billeted in houses all over town.

While Sullivan's troops were taking the western end of town, it was time for the American artillery to do their part at the northern end. The horses were unharnessed, and the field pieces were unplugged and swung around at the junction of King and Queen Streets. Ironically, this was the exact spot where Rall's superior had ordered him to build a redoubt - an order he had ignored. These were the town's two main streets, which ran downhill through most of town.

As the Hessians came out of the houses and tried to form in the

streets, they were met with bounding cannon balls and exploding shells from the Queen Street battery under Captain Forrest, and the King Street battery under Captain Alexander Hamilton. The only British troops in town, a company of Light Dragoons, who might have been a major factor in the battle if they stayed, managed to quickly mount up and escape to Princeton.

The bewildered Hessians could not even see their enemy, because the wind whipped them full in the face with hail and sleet. "From their motions," General Washington would later write, "they seemed undetermined how to act." They would have done better to act individually, taking cover and firing, or to charge in groups with their bayonets, instead of trying to form and wait for orders. But they were trained in the European style. Finding it impossible to form ranks and fight in unison, some sought cover in the houses. Others ran into the alleys to escape the withering fire. About 400 made their escape across Assunpink Bridge before it was secured by Sullivan's division.

Colonel Rall, at his headquarters on King Street, had been awakened by Lieutenant Piel soon after the Americans entered the town. According to an American officer who talked with Piel the next day:

> He had been in bed but a short time when the battle began. Piel shook him, but found it hard work to wake him up. Supposing he was wide awake, Piel went out to help rally the men, but Rall not appearing, he went back and found him in his nightshirt. "What's the matter?" Rall asked. Piel informed him that a battle was going on. That seemed to bring him to his senses. He dressed himself, rushed out, and mounted his horse.

When Rall came out of the house, he found the artillery company gathering in the street. He ordered them to bring their horses from the stable to the artillery park, fifty yards away, hitch them up, and move them into a position to take out the American artillery. "My God!" Rall yelled, "the picket is already coming in. Push your cannon

ahead!" Responding well to this order, they suffered for their bravery, as American firepower concentrated on them. They managed to fire off only thirteen rounds before losing five horses and eight men.

Colonel Henry Knox suspected that, if the two Hessian guns were not put out of action soon, they might provide a rallying point for the enemy and perhaps turn the tide of the battle. He asked Virginia's Colonel George Weedon if he thought any of his men could do the job. Weedon ordered Captain William Washington to race down the street and take the battery. At the same time, Colonel Knox saw that Sergeant Joseph White was standing idle with his company of artillerists. After firing only three rounds, their cannon's axletree had broken, taking the piece out of action. Knox rode up to them and ordered them to assist Captain Washington. "My brave lads, take your swords and go up there and take those two pieces they're holding! There is a party going; you must go and join them." Then the colonel rode off as quickly as he had come. The men hesitated. Then White's captain, John Allen, broke the awkward silence. "You heard what the colonel said, Sergeant White. Now take your men and join the others in the attack!" So White, in his first experience leading an infantry attack, "hallowed as loud as I could scream to the men to run for their lives right up to the pieces."

Ahead of them, Captain Washington and Lieutenant James Monroe were reaching their objective. Monroe describes the action, referring to himself in the third person:

> Captain Washington rushed forward, attacked and put the troops around the cannon to flight and took possession of them. Moving on afterwards, he received a severe wound and was taken from the field. The command then devolved to Lieutenant Monroe, who advanced in like manner at the head of the corps, and was shot down by a musket ball which passed through his breast and shoulder. He also was carried from the field.

Sergeant White was the first of his party to reach the two artillery pieces after Monroe's party had moved on. All the Hessian artillerists by now had either been shot or run away except one. "Run, you dog!" yelled White as he held his sword over the man's head. The Hessian "looked up and saw it, then run. We put in a cannister of shot and fired."

After ordering the artillery forward, Rall's next move had been to go down King Street toward the old barracks. Before reaching it, he found his men forming in the street. He took charge of them and a contingent from the southern part of town near Assunpink Creek. Resorting to proven tactics, he ordered a bayonet charge up King Street. But the charge went only about forty yards when it was met by artillery fire from the upper end of the street, sending Rall's ranks into disorder.

According to Lieutenant Engelhardt, Rall was bewildered by the situation, as he heard firing on all sides. "Lord, Lord, what is it, what is it?" he kept repeating. Finally, he composed himself enough to realize the most probable chance for escape lay in retreating through the orchard on the eastern edge of town, which led to the Princeton Road. He therefore set out in that direction, the brigade band playing to give the men heart, even though American lead was flying at them from musketmen in second floor windows, in cellarways, and behind fences.

At the southern end of town, Sullivan had by now sent Glover's regiment forward to Assunpink Creek. Not finding General Ewing's division there as expected, Glover crossed the bridge and set up his field pieces on the other side of the creek.

Private John Greenwood was in the other part of Sullivan's force that was making its way through the town. His account:

> As we advanced, it being dark and stormy so that we
> could not see very far ahead, we got within 200 yards of
> about 300 or 400 Hessians who were paraded, two deep
> in a straight line, with Colonel Rall, their commander, on
> horseback, to the right of them. They made a full fire at

us, but I did not see that they killed anyone.

Our brave Major Shelburne ordered us to fall back about 300 yards and pull off our packs, which we accordingly did and piled them by the roadside. "Now, my boys," says he, "pass the word through the ranks that he who is afraid to follow me, let him stand behind and take care of the packs!" Not a man offered to leave ranks, and as we never went back that way, we all lost our packs.

As we had been in the storm all night we were not only wet through and through ourselves, but our guns and powder were wet also, so that I do not believe that one would go off, and I saw none fired by our party. When we were all ready we advanced and, although there was not more than one bayonet to five men, orders were given to "Charge bayonets and rush on!" and rush on we did.

Within pistol shot they again fired point-blank at us. We dodged and they did not hit a man. Before they had time to reload we were within three feet of them, when they broke in an instant and ran ... [and] we after them pell-mell.

Meanwhile, Colonel Rall's men were making their way to the orchard, harassed by parties of Americans as they marched through the town, and fired on by Glover's artillery across the creek. Soon there were about 600 gathered in the orchard. Washington had anticipated this escape route and placed two-thirds of Greene's men and artillery, under Generals Stirling and Fermoy, just north of the orchard to block their escape to Princeton. As the Hessians tried to make their way through the orchard, Colonel Hand's Pennsylvania riflemen and a recently recruited regiment of German immigrants from Pennsylvania were ordered forward to stop them. "This they did with spirit and rapidity and immediately checked them. The [Hessian] officers tried

342

to rally them, but our men kept advancing and picking off the officers."

Rall and his officers then turned the troops around and headed back to the town, in a desperate effort to retake it, Rall shouting, "All who are my Grenadiers, forward!" In the attempt, they were blasted from nearly every direction by musket fire and even some inhabitants who had hidden their weapons during the occupation. One woman, firing out her window at point-blank range, mortally wounded Major von Scheffer. By now, the Hessian muskets were incapable of firing, due to the continuing storm. Milling around in confusion, they were easy targets for sheltered American marksmen who had been inside houses long enough to dry their firelocks.

The two cannon at the northern end of Queen Street had been moved forward to where they could fire grapeshot at point-blank range at Rall's party. Rall was hit by several pieces of lead and carried into a Methodist Church on Queen Street. A few moments before he was hit, he'd issued orders to return to the orchard.

Major von Scheffer, though wounded in the hip, led the troops back to the orchard and held a conference there with the other officers. They decided to make a run for the upper fords of Assunpink Creek. If they could get across, they might have a chance of sending word to the British post at Princeton. But, before they could start out toward the creek, they were hit by grapeshot from the artillery of Stirling and Fermoy at the northern edge of the orchard. The lead flew into their ranks "like a swarm of bees." Scheffer, before he died a few days later, would report, "It rained cannon balls and grapeshot here, and snow, rain and sleet came constantly into our faces. None of our muskets would fire any longer." Through the swirling haze of rain and snow, they saw a long line of Americans marching toward them, then stop at fifty paces to fire. The Americans were shouting to them now, in English and German, to throw down their guns and surrender.

Scheffer called to an American officer and asked for quarter. A cease-fire was called and one of Washington's aides rode up to talk with Scheffer and an interpreter. Soon he was riding off to Washing-

ton, on the high ground near the junction of King and Queen Streets, to inform him that two of the three Hessian regiments had surrendered.

The colors of the Rall and Lossberg Regiments were lowered and the men stacked their muskets and swords on the ground, a few of the officers slamming them down, as tears of rage and frustration streamed down their cheeks. Several of the officers put their hats on their sword tips and raised their swords high over their heads to signal their surrender. The jubilant American troops threw their own hats high in the air and shouted so loud they were heard all over town. General Lord Stirling rode forward and accepted the swords of the regimental commanders. Several American soldiers then ran forward and mixed with the captured Hessians "and after satisfying their curiosity a little, they began to converse familiarly in broken English and German."

Meanwhile, the last of the three Hessian regiments, the Knyphausen regiment, was trying to reach Assunpink Creek. But they lost much valuable time trying to bring along two field pieces. The heavy wheels sunk in the marshy ground near the creek. They finally dropped the drag lines and abandoned the guns. By the time they reached the bridge, they found it heavily guarded by General Arthur St. Clair's regiment with two cannon. They were being fired at now from nearly every direction. They moved north along the creek bank, frantically searching for a fording place. They found one, but Colonel Glover's regiment was on the other side, also with two field pieces. Glover had even sent a detachment of his infantry wading into the icy water up to "about mid-thigh in order to cut off the enemy's retreat."

The Knyphausen Regiment now had no choice but to surrender. The regimental commander, Major von Dechow, had received a bullet in his hip, and turned over the command to Captain Bernhard von Biesenrodt. Aware that the other two regiments had already struck their colors, Dechow advised him to surrender. However, the captain, fiercely proud like all Hessian veterans, would not give up so easily to irregular troops. He led all those who would follow him into the creek and swam or waded up to their chins in the swiftly running, ice-cold water. A larger group headed further up the bank, looking for a shal-

lower spot, but they were stopped by some of Glover's waders, who had now crossed over to cut them off.

Captain von Biesenrodt and his followers staggered up the bank, only to find themselves being surrounded. St. Clair had moved up his two field pieces and placed the guns forty paces in their front. Major James Wilkinson walked out in front of the lines and tried to attract the attention of the Hessian captain. Through his interpreter, Lieutenant Wiederholdt, Captain von Biesenrodt warned Wilkinson to halt or he would fire. Wiederholdt then went forward to parley with the young rebel officer, and soon returned to tell von Biesenrodt that the rebel general had ordered him to surrender. The captain refused. Once again, Wiederholdt went forward to parley, this time with General St. Clair, who described to him the hopelessness of his situation, and stated bluntly, "Tell your commanding officer that if you do not surrender immediately I will blow you to pieces." That did it. The captain and his interpreter came forward and said he would surrender if his men could keep their swords and baggage. St. Clair agreed, and the two men shook hands.

Washington's complex and difficult amphibious expedition had not totally come off as hoped. But, due in large part to good luck, the pieces of the plan that did work met with more than satisfactory results. After a 45 minute battle, the American forces had taken the enemy cantonment at Trenton, including nearly 1,000 prisoners of war. Another four hundred had managed to escape across the Assunpink Creek bridge at the beginning of the battle. The much heralded and feared Hessians had been soundly beaten. The only American casualties were the two men who froze to death on the march, and the wounded William Washington and James Monroe. This shocking victory would prove to be the spark of life that the dying revolution needed.

Wilkinson raced down to the bridge, crossed it, and located Washington to tell him the good news. The Commander-in-Chief took his hand, smiled, and said, "Major Wilkinson, this is a glorious day for our country."

CHAPTER FIFTEEN
ONE MORE CRISIS FOR WASHINGTON

"The drums beat the second time. The soldiers felt the force of the appeal. One said to another, 'I will remain if you will.'"

> - *A soldier recalling Washington's personal appeal to his regiment.*

"The Hessians are coming!" These were words that ordinarily created instant panic, causing many to abandon their homes and flee for their lives. But not on this day, December 30, 1776, for the citizens of Philadelphia. Marching into the city, "all fine hearty looking men and well clad" in their impressive uniforms, were over 900 of the hated and feared mercenaries that King George III had hired from various German princes. Marching alongside, and guarding the Hessian prisoners closely, were the proud Continentals, "mostly in summer dress and some without shoes."

During the trip to Philadelphia, the prisoners crossed the Delaware River and encountered some of the hazards the Americans had a few nights before. Lieutenant Elisha Bostwick, in one of the boats with them, was amused by the sight of the Hessians' long black hair pinned so tightly in queues that looked "like handles of frying pans."

> The ice continually stuck to the boats, driving them downstream. The boatmen endevering to clear off the ice pounded the boat, and stamping with their feet beckoned to the prisoners to do the same, and they all set to jumping at once with their cues flying up and down.

347

Many of the boats could not get all the way to shore, due to the shallow water being frozen over. This forced the men to wade up to their middles, breaking the ice with their muskets as they went. Private John Greenwood observed that "some of the poor fellows were so cold that their underjaws quivered like an aspen leaf."

Along the route of the night march, many of the prisoners appeared to be terrified about their possible fate. They had been told that Americans were "a race of cannibals who would not only tomahawk a poor Hessian and haul off his hide for a drum's head, but barbecue and eat him." Greenwood noticed that a few Hessians, seeing how much their American guards admired their brass caps, gave them up out of sheer fear. "It was laughable to see how our soldiers would strut" with these brass helmets on, "elbows out, some without a collar for their half-a-shirt, no shoes, etc."

The night before arriving in Philadelphia, the Hessians stayed in "a miserable prison" in Newtown, Pennsylvania. The diary of a Hessian officer noted that when the guards arrived with loaves of bread that would serve as the evening meal, "they dumped it out of baskets into the snow. This was terrible to see. Hardly anyone could imagine how miserable we felt, and how cold. It was said that we would leave this valley of tears and would have regular barracks when we reached Philadelphia." Indeed, by the next night he was writing from the relative comfort of militia barracks in Philadelphia:

> Early in the morning we left Newtown and marched to the big and beautiful city of Philadelphia. As we marched through the city many people, big and little, young and old, stood there watching sharply, seeing what kind of people we were. Some of them came up very close to us. The old women screamed fearfully and started to threaten us. They cried out that we ought to be hanged for coming to America to rob them of their freedom. Others, however, brought us liquor and bread

but they were not allowed by the old women to give them to us. At one time the people pressed on us with such force as to nearly break the guard over us. The old women were the worst. If the American guards had not protected us, the women would have killed us.

Later, General Washington of the Americans made a proclamation and it was posted all over the city: the Hessians were without blame and had been forced into this war. The Hessians had not come of their own free will. They should not be regarded as enemies but as friends of the American people and should be treated as such. Because General Washington had full authority and gave his honest word, it became better for us.

At Washington's urging, Congress soon had the Hessian officers sent to Virginia, and the rank and file to German-American farming and mining communities in Pennsylvania, to work as indentured servants until their exchange (in 1778). According to one observer, "this kind treatment, so contrary to their expectations, excited their gratitude and veneration for their amiable conqueror, whom they styled 'a very good rebel.'" Nine of the prisoners, the musicians, remained in captivity in Philadelphia, and were called upon quite often to perform, most notably the next July at the first anniversary celebration of the Declaration of Independence!

* * * * *

Searching Trenton for hidden Hessians and supplies, one group of men discovered the Hessian stores of rum and immediately came down with a well-earned case of "barrel fever." They dumped one cask of rum and one of sugar into a rain barrel, stirred it with a fence rail, and celebrated the victory with homemade "punch," using shoes for cups. Washington quickly ordered the remaining forty hogsheads of rum staved in and dumped onto the snowy ground. Christmas cheer had

been the downfall of the Hessians; it could be for the Americans, too, if they were allowed to become incapacitated and enemy troops from other cantonments in western New Jersey marched on Trenton.

The next day, the 27th, Washington sent his official report to John Hancock, President of the Congress, praising the troops and pointing out that not a single man had turned his back. Rather, "when they came to the charge each seemed to vie with the other in pressing forward, and were I to give a preference to any particular corps, I should do great injustice to the others." To the troops, he promised that the monetary value of "the field pieces, the arms and accoutrements, horses and everything else which was taken" would be divided proportionally among them all.

Washington was anxious to cross the river again and "beat up more of their quarters," especially Brunswick, where his spies had reported a huge army depot. He wanted to take advantage of the enemy's panic and drive them "entirely from, or at least to the extremity of New Jersey." With New Jersey recaptured, Howe would have only two towns - New York and Newport - to show for all his troubles after more than a year and a half of war.

But Washington was in a time bind. On the one hand, he would have to wait until at least the 29th, when food was due to arrive from Philadelphia. For no amount of praise and promises could make men with empty stomachs repeat what they had done during the two previous days. But, on the other hand, New Year's Day was fast approaching, and with it the expiration of the New England regiments' one year enlistments. Any offensive moves in New Jersey would have to be started before the new year arrived.

To the soldiers, however, the victory at Trenton, and Howe's retiring to New York for the winter, meant the end of this year's campaigning. The New Englanders, in particular, were in good spirits because of their prospect of heading home in just a few more days. On the 28th, a young private in camp noted in his diary, "This day we have been washing our things." But, on December 30th, his regiment was ordered to march, once again, to New Jersey. A soldier who only

referred to himself in his journal as "Sergeant R." recalled his regiment being addressed by the Commander-in-Chief that day:

At this trying time, General Washington, having now but a handful of men and many of them new recruits in which he could place but little confidence, ordered our regiment to be paraded and personally addressed us, urging that we should stay a month longer.

He alluded to our recent victory at Trenton, told us that our services were greatly needed, and that we could now do more for our country than we ever could at any future period, and in the most affectionate manner entreated us to stay. The drums beat for volunteers, but not a man turned out. The soldiers, worn down with fatigue and privations, had their hearts fixed on home.

The General wheeled his horse about, rode in front of the regiment and, addressing us again, said, "My brave fellows, you have done all I asked you to do and more than could be reasonably expected. But your country is at stake, your wives, your houses, and all that you hold dear. You have worn yourselves out with fatigues and hardships, but we know not how to spare you. If you will consent to stay only one month longer, you will render that service to the cause of liberty and to your country which you probably never can do under any other circumstances. The present is emphatically the crisis which is to decide our destiny."

The drums beat the second time. The soldiers felt the force of the appeal. One said to another, "I will remain if you will." Others remarked, "We cannot go home under such circumstances." A few stepped forth, and their example was immediately followed by nearly all who were fit for duty in the regiment, amounting to about two hundred volunteers.

Washington's appeal also included a promise of ten dollars bounty per man. Not having had time to seek prior Congressional approval, he pledged his personal fortune to cover the promise, in the event that Congress refused. Ultimately, Congress did honor the bounty. To John Hancock, he explained that "Pennsylvania had allowed the same to her militia" now being recruited. To Congressional Treasurer Robert Morris, he wrote, "I thought it no time to stand upon trifles, when a body of firm troops inured to danger were absolutely necessary to lead on the more raw and undisciplined." Besides, Washington had good reason to assume that if the New England veterans departed on New Year's Day, most of the recent recruits from Pennsylvania would follow.

Washington did not have time to personally address all the New England regiments. General Thomas Mifflin, who had already raised a few thousand militia, spoke to the Rhode Islanders. Sergeant John Smith later recalled the scene:

> In the afternoon our brigade was sent for into the field where we paraded befor the General who was present with all the feild officers & after meaking many fair promises to them he begged them to tarey one month longer in the service. Almost every man consented to stay longer who received 10 doler bounty as soon as signd their names. Then the Genll with the soldiers gave three huzzas & was with claping of hands for joy amongst the specttators. As soon as that was over the Genll ordrd us to heave a gill of rum pr man. We was dismisd to goe to our quarters with great applause the inhabitents & others saying we had done honour to our country viz New England.

Unfortunately, besides the bounty, Mifflin used half truths and out-right lies to entice the men to re-enlist. Among other things, he told

them that they would be allowed to keep any booty they captured, and that reinforcements, warm clothing, and better food were on the way. Altogether, a little more than half of all the New Englanders agreed to stay. Washington would be left with 1,600 veteran Continentals and about 4,000 militia, almost all of the latter recruited from New Jersey and Pennsylvania within the last ten days. Among those who would depart on New Year's Day was Colonel Glover's regiment. They had served well in battle and in transporting the army across rivers, and now decided it was about time they joined many of their fellow fishermen in seeking their fortunes aboard privateers.

* * * * *

Slightly more than half of the army was several miles southeast, at Crosswicks under Colonel Cadwalader, and south, at Bordentown under General Mifflin. It was Cadwalader's division, back on the night of December 25-26, that had failed to cross the Delaware 20 miles below Trenton to provide a diversionary attack against Mount Holly and Bordentown while Washington was attacking Trenton. The militia colonel had written to Washington on the morning of the 26th, "I imagine the badness of the night must have prevented you from passing over as you intended." However, just minutes after he dispatched a rider with that letter, another had arrived informing him that Washington had indeed made it across and captured Trenton. Cadwalader, eager to do his part, had responded by crossing over the next morning, only to learn that afternoon that Washington had returned to Pennsylvania.

This left Cadwalader's unsupported force of 1,800 in a precarious position. Should the enemy gather their remaining forces in western New Jersey and march against him, he could easily be overwhelmed. Therefore, Cadwalader called a council of war to discuss the options with his officers. "Long and pretty warm debates ensued." Some were in favor of returning to the safety of Pennsylvania. Cadwalader, however, was not in favor of crossing back. His reasons: 1) the

victorious troops at Trenton "should be emulated" and the victory "followed up" before the enemy "recovered the panick"; 2) "Jersey must be recovered to save Pennsylvania" from invasion; and 3) without action, he thought the militia might go home. The militia, he later wrote, "being taken from their families and kept out a long time without action, began to grow uneasy ... this was the third time they had been drawn out and, if they should again return without attempting anything, a general desertion might be apprehended."

A compromise was finally settled upon: rather than march against the Hessians at Bordentown, they would assault the smaller enemy force reported to be at Burlington. They marched to Burlington, only to find that it had been deserted by the enemy. However, an officer on reconnaisance duty "returned with an account that he had seen some of the enemy's jagers." A party under Colonel Joseph Reed was immediately dispatched. Though they did not catch the German riflemen, Reed's detachment did reach Bordentown, and subsequently informed the council of what they had learned from the inhabitants there: "that upon the runaways from Trenton coming in on the 26th, the Hessians and their followers the [Tory] refugees fled in the greatest confusion, leaving the sick behind them."

Evidently, as each enemy post south of Trenton received word of the disaster at Trenton, they quickly moved out of danger. Perhaps the Hessians, if not the British, were beginning to respect this "rabble in arms" that was showing signs of becoming a real fighting force. One of Cadwalader's officers, Thomas Rodney, was told by an inhabitant that the Hessians "curse and imprecate this war, and swear they were sent here to be slaughtered." Many years later, Captain Johann Ewald of the jagers remembered that after Trenton "such a fright came over the army that if Washington used the opportunity we would have flown to our ships and let him have all of America."

Riding into Bordentown, Colonel Reed observed that the local turncoats were becoming patriots again, "Almost every house along the road had a red rag nailed up on the door, which the inhabitants, upon this reverse of affairs, were now busily pulling down." Reed spent the

night of the 27th in Burlington. There, a widow named Margaret Morris noted in her diary, "An officer spent the evening with us and appeared to be in high spirits, and talked of engaging the English as a very trifling affair - 'nothing so easy as to drive them over the North River.'" But she knew it would not be so easy. Early the next morning, after she watched the troops march out of town "in high spirits," she wrote, "My heart sinks when I think of the numbers unprepared for death, who will probably be sent to appear before the Judge of Heaven."

On December 30th, Colonel Joseph Reed left Colonel Cadwalader and returned to Trenton. He knew that General Washington needed intelligence about the enemy - their whereabouts, strength and intentions. He volunteered to go "to the neighbourhood of Princeton" to seek out such information. Joseph Reed was a good choice for the mission, having been raised in Trenton and attended the College of New Jersey, at Princeton. He set off with a handful of newly arrived Philadelphia Light Horse.

As they approached the town, Reed asked some friends of his among the inhabitants "to go into Princeton on this errand." But he found that "the arms and ravages of the enemy had struck such terror that no rewards would tempt the inhabitants." However, Reed and his six cavalrymen, none of whom had any prior military experience, were "fully resolved not to return while there was a chance of success." So, despite the risk of being detected and taken prisoner, they rode on.

Four miles south of Princeton, they spotted a British soldier (perhaps a plunderer, they thought) walking from a barn to a stone house. Reed ordered two men to chase him down and take him prisoner. Just then a second Regular came into view, and then a third. Reed did not know it, but there were a full dozen Regulars inside the house, "attacking and conquering a parcel of mince pyes." Reed and his six horsemen spurred their horses and surrounded the house. What happened next surprised them. "Twelve British soldiers, equipped as dragoons and well armed, their pieces all loaded and having the advantage of the house, surrendered." Although the British sergeant fled

through the back door, the others were all taken. One of Reed's men noted:

> [They] came out of the house and formed in the yard with muskets in hand. We compelled them to surrender and lay down their arms. A prisoner was mounted behind [each] trooper, whose horse would carry double, and the rest were marched towards Trenton. We found they were a party of the Queen's Light Dragoons, late from Ireland, fine looking fellows.

After questioning his prisoners, Colonel Reed was able to bring back to Trenton news that the British were advancing across New Jersey again.

* * * * *

When word of "the unfortunate Trenton affair" had reached New York, Howe had cancelled Cornwallis's scheduled December 27th departure for London (his baggage, however, went on without him). Cornwallis lost no time in gathering all the New Jersey forces together at Princeton, and with the addition of reinforcements from New York, was now bringing nearly 8,000 Regulars and a train of artillery with him in hot pursuit of Washington. Three weeks before, having chased the Continental Army all the way across New Jersey, Cornwallis had entered Trenton just in time to see them scurry across the Delaware River. This time, he was determined not to let the rebels escape again.

The intelligence that Reed delivered was corroborated by a report arriving that same day, December 31st, from Colonel Cadwalader. From Crosswicks, southeast of Trenton, he had sent forward a "very intelligent young gentleman" who had managed to sneak into Princeton about noon on the 30th, and had been captured while reconnoitering. He had escaped the next morning, and reached Crosswicks to inform Cadwalader that "about five thousand men" were already in

town. He rattled off an amazing amount of detail from memory, reciting the exact location and strength of the enemy's various posts in Princeton, the number of cannon at each place, etc.

He also mentioned that there were "no sentries on the back, or east, side of town." From all these bits of information, Cadwalader drew up a map of the town, showing its defenses and a little known offshoot of a "Quaker Road" which paralleled the main road to Trenton, farther to the east. The spy assured him that this side road and the Quaker Road itself were totally unguarded. This map would soon prove extremely useful to Washington.

Early on New Year's Eve, Washington held a council of war. Though not included in that council, Major James Wilkinson could easily guess what was being discussed, as he later explained in his memoirs:

> The information received from the prisoners left no doubt of the enemy's superiority and his intention to advance upon us, which put General Washington in a critical situation. To make a safe retreat was impracticable, should the enemy act with energy; and if it could be effected at all it would depreciate the influence of antecedent successes and check the rising spirit of the community. On the other hand, to give battle would be to hazard the annihilation of the grand army.

The council decided to concentrate all the American troops at Trenton. Orders went out to Cadwalader at Crosswicks, and Mifflin at Bordentown, to join Washington on the south bank of Assunpink Creek. Once they arrived, the army would total nearly 5,500 men. There, they would dig in and await the enemy, or maneuver around him, if necessary. Washington wanted to stay in New Jersey, hanging near the enemy's flank, in case they should make a move toward Philadelphia. This would also give him the opportunity to make his own bold moves, if the opportunity arose, to attack the British rear at

Princeton and Brunswick. Yet he could not ignore the fact that more than two thirds of his army was inexperienced, undisciplined militia - just the kind of "soldiers" who were likely to drop their muskets and run home when things got tight during a battle. Washington was playing a dangerous game.

The first priority was to stall Cornwallis long enough to allow the scattered American forces to come together and prepare for whatever might come next. To that end, General Mathias Alexis de Fermoy's brigade was sent forward along the road to Princeton. This brigade, all Continentals, consisted of the remnants of two Virginia regiments and one from Pennsylvania - the so-called "German" regiment, since everyone in it was of German descent. The Virginians took up defensive positions along the south bank of Five Mile Run, a stream that crossed the main road about a mile and a half south of Maidenhead, which lay between Trenton and Princeton.

However, the German regiment, led by Colonel Nicholas Hausegger, proceeded farther along the road, toward Princeton. Hausegger and his regiment had come south from Canada after that disastrous campaign, and had joined the main army just in time for the equally disheartening retreat across New Jersey. Now he was leading his regiment's survivors - about 400 men - precariously close to the enemy's camp. He had already marched through Maidenhead and was about half a mile from Princeton when his second in command, Major Weltner, decided to stop him before it was too late. Private Conrad Housman provides us with this account:

> Major Weltner rode up to Colonel Housacker [Hausegger] and immediately a smart altercation took place between them. The Major ordered the regiment to halt. Housacker ordered them to march, when the Major said, "The enemy are in the town." Housacker said they were not. The regiment halted during the altercation and most of the officers of the regiment came [forward] ... The Major said, "They shall not march until

358

the town is reconnoitered and then we can act according to circumstances."

The Colonel replied he would go and reconnoiter the town himself. He ordered out ten men and Lieutenant Bernard Hubley to go with him. The Major ordered the Lieutenant to stand by his platoon. Housacker said it was mutiny and that he would have him punished. The Major replied that prudence was not mutiny and that he knew the enemy were in the town and that the Colonel also knew it, and that it was highly improper to go into a place occupied by the enemy. Housacker said there was no enemy there, and he set out for Princeton, taking ten men with him and went directly to the Hessian quarters.

Private Conrad Housman, one of the ten men that Colonel Hausegger took with him into Princeton, finishes his account:

> ... [Colonel von Donop] came to the door and took him by the hand and asked him where his regiment was. The Colonel replied that the Major mutinied and usurped the command, and these ten men was all he could bring with him. "Well, says [von Donop], I am sorry you did not bring in your regiment. I had ordered all the troops to keep close in their quarters. You see, I have not even a sentinel at my own door and if they had come in we could have taken them with little or no bloodshed."

Colonel Hausegger spent his time as a "prisoner" in New York trying to persuade captured American officers to renounce the rebel cause and join the British. He was unsuccessful in his efforts, and was soon released on parole. He spent the remaining years of his life at his home in Pennsylvania, and never came before a court-martial.

The next morning, January 2nd, Lord Cornwallis was on the road to Trenton with 7,000 troops and a complement of 28 field pieces. After

having ridden fifty miles on New Year's Day, arriving in Princeton at 1 a.m., Cornwallis had napped for a few hours and then set out with the army before dawn. This kind of celerity was most uncharacteristic of British generals. It indicated his determination, as Captain Ewald put it, "to give the enemy a beating and thereby repair the damage done at Trenton." Leading the long column were the Hessian troops, set on avenging the defeat suffered by their brethren in this same town just one week before. From the diary of Sergeant Thomas Sullivan, of the British Forty-ninth Regiment of Foot:

> [Colonel von Donop] was so exasperated against the enemy, especially for the Rall corps being taken prisoner by them, that he resolved to be revenged. He therefore went thro the ranks and declared openly to his men that any of them who would take a Rebel prisoner would receive fifty stripes, signifying to them they were to kill all the Rebels they could, without mercy.

The army was not progressing toward Trenton as fast as Cornwallis had hoped. By noon, they had only reached Maidenhead, despite encountering no resistance other than some snipers that shot one Hessian officer from his horse. The march was slow because, on the previous day, the weather "began to break," after having been "exceptionally severe" most of December. A warm front arrived on New Year's Day, resulting in a reading of 51 degrees in Philadelphia. By 11 o'clock that night, "it was raining heavily in Prince Town." The next morning, the roads were deep mud, in some places up to the soldiers' knees.

The scattered American regiments, on their way to Trenton, faced similar road conditions. Sergeant William Young recalled marching, during that night of January 1-2, from Crosswicks:

> It rained when we set out. On account of the thaw, the road was very muddy and deep. Though we had but

eight miles to go, it was 9 o'clock [a.m.] before we reached Trenton. I was a good deal fatigued on account of the deepness of the road, and its being night I could not see my way. The moon gave some light, but it being on my back I could not see the best road.

When the militia company of 18-year-old James Johnston arrived at Trenton that morning they were ordered to take quarters in a greenhouse on the River Road, a mile past the center of town. They had barely arrived there - exhausted, tired and hungry - when, "whilst preparing breakfast, the alarm was given of the approach of the enemy." They had to forego both breakfast and sleep, and hustle off to the other side of Assunpink Creek, where they were paraded with the other regiments.

Dr. Benjamin Rush, of the Continental Congress, had come across the river to Trenton with the Philadelphia militia that morning. He immediately went to the house of a friend in town "and begged the favor of his bed for a few hours." But he was soon "awakened by a black woman who came into the room, crying and wringing her hands." Then General Arthur St. Clair, who was staying at the house, walked into the room and "with a composed countenance" began carefully strapping on his sword belt. Alarmed, Dr. Rush asked, "What is the matter?" St. Clair answered, "The enemy are on their way here." "What," Rush asked, "do you intend to do?" St. Clair, surprised at such a question, calmly answered, "Why, fight them."

The Congressman was not used to being so close to this war that he and his colleagues had been directing from a room in Philadelphia. He left the house to search for the Philadelphia militia. Outside, he found "all was now hurry, confusion and noise," but the troops appeared to be energetic and eager, rather than frightened. Dr. Rush located his Philadelphia company and asked one of the men, "How do you feel?" The private answered, "As if I were going to sit down to a good breakfast."

Meanwhile, out on the road from Princeton, the Americans at Five

Mile Creek fired off one round, then turned and fell back a mile to take up new positions along Shabbakonk Creek. The Hessian Captain Ewald, who was leading the vanguard of the army, noted the effect of that first American fire: "Lieutenant von Grothausen - fortunately for him - was shot dead along with several jagers." Von Grothausen thus escaped being court martialed for his part in the disaster of December 26th, when he had been in charge of the outpost a mile north of Trenton on the River Road. His sentries had been the ones completely surprised by Sullivan's column that morning.

As the enemy approached Shabbakonk Creek, General Fermoy suddenly wheeled his horse around and rode back to Trenton. The Frenchman was one of several Europeans who had talked Congress into giving them generals' commissions based on exaggerated (and, in some cases, fictitious) achievements on European battlefieds. No explanation was given for why Fermoy left his post this day. He would be involved in another questionable incident a few months later, at Fort Ticonderoga. Eventually, in 1778, Fermoy would resign his commission in protest, after Congress refused the last of his many requests for promotion to major-general. Like some of the other European "professionals," he would turn out to be, in Major James Wilkinson's words, "another worthless drunkard."

Ironically, Fermoy's disappearance this day was fortunate for the American cause, since command of the advance party of 1,000 now fell to Colonel Edward Hand, a capable veteran. Back in 1775, upon hearing the Lexington alarm, Hand and his rifle regiment had marched from Pennsylvania to join the blockade of Boston. Since then, they had performed well in several encounters with the enemy. Now here was another opportunity for Hand to lead men in the Indian style of fighting that Americans preferred. Wilkinson provides this account:

> [Hand] secreted his men some distance within the wood on the flanks of the road. In this position he waited for the enemy until they came within point-blank shot, and then he opened a deadly fire from his ambush,

which broke and forced them back in great confusion on the main body, closely pursued by the riflemen. The boldness of this maneouver menacing a general attack, induced the enemy to form in order of battle and bring up his artillery.

During this action, General Washington rode up with General Nathanael Greene and General Henry Knox (recently promoted to brigadier for his brilliant use of artillery at Trenton). Washington wanted to personally encourage the men holding off the enemy and to emphasize to them how important it was "to retard the march of the enemy until nightfall." He talked to the men, giving them "orders for as obstinate a stand as could be made on that ground without hazarding the [field] pieces," then he "retired to marshal the troops for action behind the Assunpink."

Seventeen-year-old Ensign Robert Beale explains how Hand soon lost nearly half his strength: "There was to our left the German regiment. Just as the enemy appeared in column this regiment ran away." The remaining troops, perhaps only 600, but all seasoned Continentals, did not panic at this sight. They stayed on, despite the odds of 10 to 1 they were now up against.

Under increasingly devastating fire, the riflemen began grudgingly giving ground - firing, falling back, reloading, and firing again. Colonel Hand ordered a detachment to leave the road and retreat obliquely to the southeast, toward the Assunpink. This was to prevent the enemy from outflanking them before they could fall back to Trenton. The main body continued to slowly fall back in good order, finally stopping on some high ground just north of town and overlooking a ravine. Here they "made their last stand, in which they distinguished themselves." They were supported by the two field pieces that Knox had placed there. When the enemy came up, the battle was resumed for "twenty-five minutes" with both musketry and artillery fire on each side.

Finally, Hand was forced to turn and head for the bridge and the

relative safety of the American lines on the other side of the Assun-pink. Hessian journals note that the retreating Americans "withdrew in the most perfect order." In Trenton, the advancing Hessians "found the wounded belonging to the Rall Brigade who had been treated very well" since their capture on December 26th. Washington had left it up to the townspeople to tend the prisoners who were too severely wounded to march to Philadelphia.

The "perfect order" of Hand's retreat was not maintained for long, though, due to the charge of the Hessian jagers and British light infantry. Robert Beale explains:

> [The major] in a very audible and distinct voice, or-dered to the right and about face on and off in order. We had not taken more than regular steps until the word "Shift for yourselves, boys, get over the bridge as quick as you can." There was running, followed by a tremen-dous fire from the British. Mr. Livingston, a very clever young man, who had but a few days before been made an ensign by Colonel Parker, carried the colors. He was shot down in the street with his thigh broken, but the colors were brought off.

As Colonel Hand's troops came streaming into the town, Colonel Hitchcock's Rhode Islanders hurried forward to provide a covering fire for their retreat. One of them, John Howland, noted that his regiment opened ranks to let Hand's men through.

> [We] then closed in a compact and rather solid col-umn as the street through which we were to retreat to the bridge was rather narrow. The British made a quick advance in an oblique direction to cut us off from the bridge. In this they did not succeed, as we had a shorter distance in a direct line to the bridge than they had, and our artillery which was posted on the south side of the

brook played into the front and flank of their column, which induced them to fall back. The bridge was narrow and our platoons were, in passing it, crowded into a dense and solid mass, in the rear of which the enemy was making their best efforts.

The noble horse of General Washington stood with his breast pressed close against the end of the west rail of the bridge, and the firm, composed, and majestic countenance of the General inspired confidence and assurance in a moment so important and critical. In this passage across the bridge it was my fortune to be next to the west rail and, arriving at the end of the bridge rail, I pressed against the shoulder of the General's horse and in contact with the boot of the General. The horse stood as firm as the rider and seemed to understand that he must not quit his post and station.

When I was about half way across the bridge, the General addressed himself to Colonel Hitchcock, directing him to march his men to that field and form them immediately.

One American who did not make it safely across the bridge was John Rosbrugh, a 62-year-old Presbyterian minister from Pennsylvania. In late December, John had kissed his young wife and five children goodbye and set off, accompanying some of his parishioners who were answering the call for short term militia to supplement the army. He had crossed the Delaware with Cadwalader on December 27th and, while waiting for his turn in the boat, had written a quick note to his wife:

Friday morning, 10 o'clock at Bristol Ferry. I haven't a minute to tell you that by God's grace our company are all well. We are going over to New Jersey. You would think [it] strange to see your husband, an old man, riding

365

with a French fusee slung at his back.

This may be the last letter ye shall receive from your husband. I have counted myself yours, and have been enlarged of our mutual love of God. As I am out of doors I cannot at present write more. I send my compliments to you, my dear, and children. Friends, pray for us. From your loving husband, Jno. Rosbrugh

On the afternoon of this Second Battle of Trenton, the Reverend Rosbrugh had been catching up on his sleep in a house on Queen Street when the alarm sounded that the enemy was approaching the town. Rosbrugh rose and went outside to mount his horse and return to the safety of the lines across the creek. To his dismay, he found that the horse had been stolen while he was asleep. After searching for a while, he gave up and started running toward the bridge. However, it was unapproachable, for the retreating American troops by now had made it across, and Knox's artillerists were firing their first rounds at point-blank range into the jagers and light infantry coming down the streets.

So the old man changed direction, away from the bridge, and tried to find a place to wade across the Assunpink. Alas! he was too late again. Before he could find a fording place, he was discovered by a party of Hessians. Quickly overpowering him, they first took away his fusee, then his purse and gold watch. He "fell down on his knees and begged his life," to no avail. They were jagers, equipped with sabers instead of bayonets, which they now used to slash at his head, cutting through his horsehair wig into his scalp, then stuck him in seventeen places. "After he was thus massacred," the newspaper account read, "he was stripped naked and left lying in an open field."

The Reverend John Witherspoon - radical Congressman and president of the nearby College of New Jersey, who had been burned in effigy by the enemy troops on Staten Island - later wrote to his son what the people in Princeton told him about Reverend Rosbrugh's death. When the Hessians returned to that town, Witherspoon

learned, they told someone "they thought they were killing me, and boasted that they had done it."

Like the Reverend Rosbrugh, a militiaman from New Jersey was also caught between the two opposing forces. He tells his story:

> [We had] orders to collect as many men as we could in the country [south of] Princeton, and then unite our-selves with the company of riflemen who had remained in that neighborhood. We advanced nearly to Shab-bakonk Creek when we were met by a little negro on horseback, galloping down the hill, who called to us that the British army was before us. One of our party ran a little way up the hill and jumped upon a fence, from whence he beheld the British army within less than half a mile of us.
>
> And now commenced a race for Trenton. We fortu-nately escaped capture; yet the enemy were so near that before we crossed the bridge over the Assunpink, some of our troops on the Trenton side of the creek, with a field piece, motioned to us to get out of the street while they fired at the British at the upper end of it.
>
> Washington's army was drawn up on the side of the Assunpink. The troops were placed one above the other so that they appeared to cover the whole slope from bot-tom to top, which brought a great many muskets within shot of the bridge. Within 70 or 80 yards of the bridge as many pieces of artillery as could be managed were stationed.

The bridge itself was now clear of retreating Americans. They were all in positions either along the slope near the bridge or at the fording places upstream. Disdaining caution, Cornwallis allowed his advance force of about 1,500 British and Hessians to go forward and test the American position along the creek. A militiaman provides this account:

[The enemy] moved slowly down the street with their choicest troops in front. When within sixty yards of the bridge they raised a shout and rushed to the charge. It was then that our men poured upon them from musketry and artillery a shower of bullets under which, however, they continued to advance, though their speed was diminished. And, as the column reached the bridge, it moved slower and slower until the head of it was gradually pressed nearly over, when our fire became so destructive that they broke their ranks and fled.

It was then that our army raised a shout, and such a shout I never since heard; by what signal or word of command, I know not. The line was more than a mile in length and from the nature of the ground the extremes were not in sight of each other, yet they shouted as one man.

The British column halted instantly. The officers restored the ranks and again they rushed the bridge, and again was the shower of bullets poured upon them with redoubled fury. This time the column broke before it reached the centre of the bridge, and their retreat was again followed by the same hearty shout from our line.

They returned a third time to the charge but it was in vain. We shouted after them again but they had had enough of it.

The British and Hessians were not totally unsupported by their own artillery. One American noted that during these attempts at the bridge several militia were killed by British cannon balls. But the Americans held firm. Delaware's Captain Thomas Rodney noted that, "In their third and final attempt, the British came down in a very heavy column to force the bridge." Some of the officers were driving the men forward by swatting them with the flat of their swords.

Lieutenant Charles Willson Peale, the portraitist, was with his Philadelphia company near the bridge. He observed that, "some of the artillery stood their ground till the enemy advanced within 40 yards, and they were very near losing the field piece." Sergeant Joseph White, working one of the guns, "let them come on some ways. Then, by a signal given, we all fired together." For the third charge, they "loaded with canister shot and let them come nearer. We fired all together again, and such destruction it made, you cannot conceive. The bridge looked red as blood, with their killed and wounded and their red coats."

After their unsuccessful attempts at the bridge, the British tried to cross at a fording place upstream, but were held off by Colonel Hitchcock's Rhode Island regiment. So Cornwallis ordered an end to such attempts and spread out his army near the high ground at the north end of town. General Henry Knox later wrote to his wife, telling her that the exchange of artillery fire "continued till dark, when of course it ceased, except for a few shells we now and then chucked into town to prevent their enjoying their new quarters securely."

CHAPTER SIXTEEN
CLOSE OF THE CAMPAIGN OF 1776

"The enemy was despised, and as usual we had to pay for it."

- *Captain Johann Ewald,*
of the Hessian jagers.

Lord Cornwallis knew his army was tired after their difficult march from Princeton. Allow them a good night's sleep, and they would be fresh for the attack next morning. He consulted with his generals that evening. Sir William Erskine proposed a night attack: "My lord, if Washington is the general I take him to be, and you trust these people tonight, you will see nothing of them in the morning." Cornwallis answered, "Nonsense, my dear fellow. We've got the old fox safe now. We'll go over and bag him in the morning. The damned rebels are cornered at last!" To ensure it, Cornwallis stationed two regiments on the north bank of Assunpink Creek, at points one mile and two miles from the bridge. This would also guard against a surprise attack on his own camp. Before retiring for the night, he sent a dispatch to Lieutenant-Colonel Charles Mawhood, ordering him to bring up two-thirds of his 1,500 men from Princeton in the morning as reinforcements.

Meanwhile, Dr. Benjamin Rush's skill as a surgeon was proving to be very useful to the Continental Army. He had set up a temporary hospital in a house not far from the bridge, and it quickly filled up with wounded men. The first man carried in was a New Englander hit by a cannon ball. His right hand was hanging "a little above the wrist by nothing but a piece of skin." Rush and one other doctor treated over twenty men that night, then lay down to rest sometime after midnight.

We all lay down with some straw in the same room with our wounded patients. It was now for the first time war appeared to me in its awful plentitude of horrors. I want words to describe the anguish of my soul, excited by the cries and groans and convulsions of the men who lay by my side. I slept two or three hours.

Despite the success of his army that day, Washington was impressed by the size and discipline of the army Cornwallis had brought to do battle with him. And he knew that this adversary, unlike Howe, would not hesitate to attack in the morning. Washington was not the only one concerned about the outcome of such a square-off. Captain Stephen Olney was one of several soldiers who remembered that anxious night:

It appeared to me then that our army was in the most desperate situation I had ever known it. We had no boats to carry us across the Delaware, and if we had, so powerful an enemy would certainly destroy the better half before we could embark. To cross the enemy's line of march between this and Princeton seemed impracticable; and when we thought of retreating into the south part of New Jersey, where there was no support for the army, that was discouraging. Notwithstanding all this, the men and officers seemed cheerful and in good spirits. I asked Lieutenant Bridges what he thought now of our independence. He answered cheerfully, "I don't know; the Lord must help us."

Ensign Robert Beale later reflected, "if the British had attacked us that evening the war would have ended." Another lieutenant: "The most sanguine among us could not flatter himself with any hopes of victory. The fate of this extensive continent seemed suspended by a single thread."

Though Washington's next move would subsequently be labeled brilliant by some, he really had little choice. His army (seventy percent of it inexperienced and undependable militia) was fewer in numbers and vastly outclassed in ability. It would be easy enough for Cornwallis to reposition the British artillery in the morning to cover a crossing by his army at one of the many fording places upstream. If Washington retreated to southern New Jersey with no prospects of crossing the Delaware, Cornwallis would eventually catch up and destroy him.

On the other hand, now that the enemy had overextended themselves, Washington had his chance to inflict the kind of damage he had intended when he had recrossed the Delaware three days before. It was thus hardly surprising that "there was not a single dissenting voice" in the council of war he called at sunset, once he outlined his strategy:

> Having by this time discovered that the enemy were greatly superior in numbers and that their drift was to surround us, I ordered all our baggage to be removed silently to Burlington soon after dark, and at twelve o'clock (after renewing our fires and leaving guards at the bridge in Trenton and other passes on the same stream above) marched by a roundabout road to Princeton, where I knew they could not have much force left and might have stores.

As so often seemed to happen at critical times, "a providential change of weather" occurred. During the afternoon battle, the wind had shifted to the northwest, and the thermometer began to drop rapidly. By early the next morning it would drop to 21 degrees. This was good news. It meant fast marching, since the muddy roads froze hard. The wagons, carrying the army's food and other supplies, left for Burlington at 7 p.m. General Israel Putnam would meet them there with new recruits from Philadelphia. Doing without these supplies would make life even more miserable for the army, but the march must

be swift and as quiet as possible. The forty artillery pieces, of course, stayed with the army. But first, their metal wheels were wrapped in rags.

The march to Princeton began shortly before 1 a.m. on this chilly morning of January 3, 1777. No one under the rank of brigadier-general knew its purpose or destination. No one, that is, except Colonel Joseph Reed, the Trenton native. He and the New Jersey militia general, Philemon Dickinson, led the way in the darkness.

Sergeant White remembered that "orders came by whispering (not a loud word must be spoken) to form the line and march." And Captain Rodney recalled that "no one knew what the General meant to do. Some thought we were going to attack the enemy in the rear; some thought we were going to Princeton."

Four hundred men were left to keep the fires going, continue guard duty, and otherwise make it appear that the entire army remained in place. This rear guard had orders to continue the deception until two hours before dawn, then to follow the trail of the main body and catch up as fast as they could. To prevent deserters or captives from alerting the enemy, only the rear guard's commander was told where the main army was headed. Ensign Beale, the young Virginian, recalled that, "every endeavor was made to convince the enemy we occupied our ground by making an immense number of fires and throwing ourselves before first one, then the other, to make them believe we were numerous." Major Wilkinson noted that Washington, to "more effectually mask the movement, ordered the guards to be doubled, [and] a strong fatigue party to be set to work [with intrenching tools] ... within distinct hearing of the sentinels of the enemy."

At the house near the river where Dr. Rush and the other doctor were napping, Rush's colleague awoke before sunrise and went out to inquire for orders. However, he soon came hustling back to announce that the army "was not to be found!" They must leave immediately or risk capture. As quickly as possible, they hitched up the horses, helped the wounded into the wagons, and rode off toward Bordentown, where they assumed Washington had taken the army. Rush would

later criticize him for not notifying them, observing that "a general should be great in minute things."

Captain Rodney's company from Dover, Delaware, was in the vanguard of the main army's long column. He relates a common hazard of attempting night maneuvers with green troops:

> The van moved on all night in the most cool and determined order, but on the march great confusion happened in the rear. There was a cry that they were surrounded by the Hessians and several corps of militia broke and fled towards Bordentown. The rest of the column remained firm and pursued their march without disorder, but those who were frightened and fled did not recover from their panic until they reached Burlington.

There, some of them received the hospitality of the widow Margaret Morris, as she noted in her diary:

> Jan 3d. At noon a number of soldiers, upwards of 1000, came into town in great confusion. They were again quartered on the inhabitants and we again exempt from the cumber of having them lodged in our house. Several of those who lodged in Colonel Cox's house last week returned to night, and asked for the key, which I gave them. About bed time, I went into the next house to see if the fires were safe, and my heart was melted to see such a number of my fellow-creatures, lying like swine on the floor fast asleep, and many of them without even a blanket to cover them. It seems very strange to me, that such a number should be allowed to come from the camp at the very time of the engagements, and I shrewdly suspect they have run away - for they can give no account why they came, nor where they are to march next.

Jan 4th.   The accounts hourly coming in are so contradictory and various, that we know not which to give credit to. A number of sick and wounded brought into town - calls upon me to extend a hand of charity towards them.   Several of <u>my</u> soldiers left the next house, and returned to the place from whence they came.   Upon my questioning them pretty close, I brought several to confess they had run away, being scared. There were several pretty innocent-looking lads among them, and I sympathised with their mothers, when I saw them preparing to return to the army.

Meanwhile, the Continental Army, now down to about 4,000 men, continued to slip quietly eastward along the Sandtown Road. As Lieutenant Peale noted, "after some time" they changed direction to "northerly. By this I expected we were going to surround the enemy." However, Washington had no intention of attacking Cornwallis. The change in direction that Peale noticed was the army's leaving "the direct road" and taking a freshly cut road that ran northward.

The stubs, two to five inches high, left after cutting the brush and small trees when this new road was made, posed quite a hazard for men marching in the dark. These stubs also "stopped the movement of the guns and caused many a fall and severe bruise to some of the over-weary, sleepy men." For some of the troops this was their second night march in a row. One of them remembered:

We moved so slow, on account of the artillery, frequently coming to a halt. When ordered forward again one, two or three men in each platoon would [be] stand[ing] fast asleep; a platoon next in the rear advancing on them, they, in walking or attempting to move, would strike and fall.

This rough byroad which led to the Quaker Road was not on any

map, and in later years would disappear altogether, swallowed up by forest and field. Parts of it were mere shortcuts from one farm to another. The night before, four members of the Philadelphia Light Horse had discovered the byroad while on patrol and explored it and the Quaker Road "as far as Quaker Bridge," they had reported. "We found that the enemy had no patrols there, and that apparently they had no knowledge of it."

Actually, the British did know about the Quaker Road, though probably not the uncharted byroad. They also knew that the Americans conceivably could go east from Trenton to Allenstown, then take the northwest running Allenstown-Maidenhead Road until they reached the beginning of the Quaker Road, which would lead them north to Princeton. So the British commander in Princeton had stationed 100 Regulars at the Quaker Meeting House. For three consecutive nights, they had patroled the Quaker Road. They simply must have missed the Philadelphia Light Horse on the third night. Ironically, on the fourth night (which saw Washington march his army down the Quaker Road) the British patrols stayed in Quaker Meeting House. They needed their sleep - they were scheduled to leave before dawn the next morning as part of the reinforcements ordered to Trenton. Ensign Thomas Glyn wrote in his journal, "Had our Light Dragoons patroled during the night of the 2nd, the enemys movement round the left of Lord Cornwallis's corps would not have taken place without our notice."

What's surprising is that Cornwallis had not learned from Howe's previous mistakes, when Washington had twice pulled off silent nocturnal marches to avoid battles the next day. After the debacle at Long Island, when his army was nearly captured, Washington had settled more firmly on his fundamental strategy for winning the war: harass the enemy at every possible point, but never risk a general engagement that might result in the destruction of an entire American army.

Cornwallis's refusal to swing part of his army east of the Assunpink on January second to surround Washington's army was labeled by Sir

Henry Clinton "the most consummate ignorance I have ever heard of [in] any officer above a corporal." As Captain Ewald put it, writing in his diary, "the enemy was despised, and as usual we had to pay for it."

According to a Captain Hall and a few other British officers, Cornwallis was even alerted during the night that the rebels were on the march, but he chose to ignore the reports.

> The sentries who were advanced heard the rattling of carriage and uncommon hurry in the enemy's camp that indicated they were in motion, which was visible at times thro the glimmering of their fires. These reports though confirmed and carried to headquarters were disregarded.

The discovery was made the next morning, according to Johann Ewald:

> At daybreak on the morning of the 3d we suddenly learned that Washington had abandoned his position. At the same time we heard a heavy cannonade in our rear, which surprised everyone. Instantly we marched back at quick step to Princetown, where we found the entire field of action, covered with corpses.

Sunrise came at 7:35, and for the Americans marching on the Quaker Bridge Road it was "bright, serene, and extremely cold, with a hoar frost which spangled every object." Two miles from the center of Princeton, the road veered to the left, following Stony Brook, while the "back road" shown on Cadwalader's spy map split off to the right. Here, Washington divided his forces. He sent General Nathanael Greene's division down the Quaker Road. General Hugh Mercer, leading Greene's vanguard, was instructed to "break down the bridge and post a party at the mill on the main [Post] road, to oppose the enemy's main army if they should pursue us from Trenton." Greene was to take the rest of his division along the Post Road into Princeton,

attacking it from the west.

Washington, himself, would lead the other division, under General John Sullivan, down the back road. Hidden from the Post Road by a slight rise, it would lead into the east part of town, and thus allow Sullivan's troops to mount a flank attack from the east.

This strategy seemed sound, especially since - thanks to Colonel Cadwalader's spy map - the locations of British troops and stores in Princeton were known. Unfortunately, things would not go that smoothly, thanks primarily to the British Lieutenant-Colonel Charles Mawhood. Mawhood's regiment, the 17th Foot, before being transferred to Princeton on January 2nd, had been stationed several miles away at Somerset Courthouse. There, Mawhood had taken quarters in the house of a physician, who noted some of Mawhood's conversations in his diary. Like Cornwallis, the Howe brothers, and several other British officers, Mawhood had opposed the Administration's hard line against the colonies. But, as an officer loyal to King George III, he had not hesitated when asked to help put down the rebellion.

According to his physician host, Mawhood "often expressed himself very freely, lamenting the American contest very much and pronouncing Lord North a villain for being the cause of it." He also had his opinions about how the war was being run. On Christmas night, discussing strategy with some subordinate officers in the physician's house, Mawhood had been "blaming the English generals for dispersing their army so much, and said that if he was in General Washington's place he would make an attack on several posts at the same time ... and be in possession of all Jersey in a few days." The next day, an express rider carrying news of the capture of Trenton had come through town. "Well, Colonel," one of his subordinate officers said, "Washington has executed your last night's plan already."

In Princeton, Mawhood had been put in charge of the three regiments still there: his own 17th, plus the 55th and 40th. These British soldiers, unused to winter campaigns before this year, were tired of the almost constant marches, as reflected in Ensign George Inman's journal:

The season of the year being severe, snow on the ground and for nights having no other bed than hard frozen earth or ice and no covering than a cloak oftentimes induced me to reflect on past times when I used to sleep on soft downy beds and with every comfortable necessary around me, amongst them friends whom I left, and which, perhaps, if I had remained, might still have enjoyed.

Dawn on January 3rd saw Mawhood crossing the Stony Brook bridge on the Post Road. He was on his way to Trenton with the reinforcements Cornwallis had requested. Trotting alongside him, as usual, were his two cocker spaniels. Mawhood was leading the 17th Regiment, with the 55th following about a mile behind. After crossing Stony Brook, the Post Road continued south up a steep hill a quarter mile in length. Near the crest of it, a mounted scout, riding ahead of the foot soldiers, looked to his left and spotted a column of men in the distance moving along the back road. In the foreground, the forest prevented him from seeing Mercer's brigade on the Quaker Road heading for the bridge. Captain Hall would later report:

As this was in the grey of morning, at their first appearance they were mistaken for Hessians; but their movements and other circumstances soon proved the mistake. Colonel Mawhood, who on the first intelligence rode forwards to reconnoitre, presently perceived that it was part of the rebel army making for Prince Town, and as readily suggested that the enemy had slipt past Lord Cornwallis in the night and by stealing a march meant to surprize that place.

Mawhood sent a rider back to the 55th Regiment, instructing all of them except their vanguard to return to Princeton and join the 40th

Regiment in preparing the town's defense. Then, with his own 17th Regiment and the 55th's vanguard - a total of about 300 men - Mawhood started back along the Post Road. Once out of the woods, he moved to the right, seeking to reach the high ground (known today as Mercer's Heights).

Robert Lawrence and some neighbors had observed Mawhood's regiment from the window of Lawrence's house near the Post Road, when they passed by earlier, on their way to Trenton.

> In about half an hour's time we saw them coming back faster than they went. A party of them came into our field and laid their packs there and formed at the corner of our garden about sixty yards from the door and then marched away immediately.

Meanwhile, Mercer's brigade was proceeding along the Quaker Road toward the Post Road. The surrounding forest temporarily protected them from detection by the British. However, Mercer soon observed Mawhood's column marching back on the Post Road. One of Mercer's Continentals - "Sergeant R." - noted the discovery in his journal:

> About sunrise, reaching the summit of a hill near Princeton, we observed a light-horseman looking towards us as we view an object when the sun shines directly in our faces. General Mercer, observing him, gave orders to the riflemen who were posted on the right to pick him off. Several made ready, but at that instant, he wheeled about and was out of their reach.

Mercer decided to leave the Quaker Road, head overland toward Princeton, and thus cut off the British retreat. However, from the crest of a hill, he soon perceived that his men would be too late to stop them. So he ordered the column to turn farther to the right and head

uphill, to catch up with Washington and the rest of the army on the other side of the ridge.

After spotting the American column on the Quaker Road, Mawhood had judged it would be a race for the high ground between the Post Road and Quaker Road. So, to give his infantry time to reach it, Mawhood sent ahead his fifty dragoons. They would never make it that far. On the way, scouts sighted another American column. It was Mercer, leading "100 Pennsylvanians and 20 Virginians." The rest of his brigade of 350 was further back on the Quaker Road.

The British dragoons quickly dismounted in an apple orchard and lay down behind a rail fence to wait in ambush for the Americans. Captain Rodney states that Mercer's small force "never discovered the enemy until not more than fifty yards off. Sergeant R. recorded the ensuing action, the beginning of the Battle of Princeton:

> As we were descending a hill through an orchard, a party of the enemy, entrenched behind a bank and fence, rose and fired upon us. Their first shot passed over our heads, cutting the limbs of the trees under which we were marching. At this moment we were ordered to wheel. As the platoon which I commanded were obeying the order, the corporal who stood at my left shoulder received a ball and fell dead on the spot. He seemed to bend forward to receive the ball, which otherwise might have ended my life.
>
> We formed, advanced, and fired upon the enemy. They retreated eight rods to their packs, which were laid in a line. I advanced to the fence on the opposite side of the ditch which the enemy had just left, fell on one knee and loaded my musket with ball and buckshot. Our fire was most destructive. Their ranks grew thin and the victory seemed nearly complete, when the British were reinforced.

Mawhood brought up his infantry; and the rest of Mercer's brigade - mostly Colonel Hand's riflemen - also arrived about the same time. A general engagement ensued, with about 300 on each side facing each other forty yards apart. The two British field pieces were engaged early on, as were two American guns. The latter were positioned atop a steep 35-foot bank above the orchard directly facing their British counterpart. Sergeant Joseph White, in command of one American cannon, had his crew frantically drag it up the bank with ropes. He then took a moment to observe the enemy, before commencing fire. The low morning sun shone "upon them, and their arms glistened bright," he wrote. "It seemed to strike an awe upon us." But not for long. White's men started firing round shot, then switched to canisters loaded with grapeshot, which "made a terrible squeaking noise" as it flew through the air.

Each side fired off round after round for a few minutes. Then Mawhood sensed the moment was right for a bayonet charge and gave the order. The American riflemen, lacking bayonets and requiring nearly a full minute to reload, fought well. But again, as on Long Island, British bayonets destroyed the riflemen's myth of invincibility. Those tenacious enough to stand their ground were overwhelmed by the charging British. Captain John Fleming, rallying his company of 20 Virginians, shouted at them, "Gentlemen, dress the line before you make ready!" "We will dress you!" yelled a British soldier, as he shot Fleming dead. At this point, Sergeant R. heard "General Mercer command, in a tone of distress, 'Retreat!'"

Several wounded Americans lying on the ground received bayonets instead of mercy from the charging Regulars, at last having a chance to avenge the harassment of local snipers, who as recently as the day before had shot "a captain and his servant as they travelled unarmed." General Mercer was one of the first victims of this British bayonet charge. Moments after he gave the order to retreat, his horse was shot in the foreleg and went down. "Unable to extricate himself" quickly enough to get away, he was surrounded by the enemy. One of them shouted at him, "Call for quarter, you damned rebel!" By now on his

feet, Mercer refused to obey the insult and, drawing his sword, attempted to defend himself. He was stunned by the stroke of a musket butt, then bayoneted seven times. Finally, after feigning death, he heard one of his attackers say, "Damn him, he is dead. Let us leave him." After the battle, he was carried into the Clark house, where he died several days later.

Mercer's death would be a severe blow to George Washington, his friend since their days together in the French and Indian War. According to Major Wilkinson, two nights earlier in Trenton, several officers had been debating the merits of serving in the army. Hugh Mercer had expressed his devotion to the Cause and added, "God can witness how cheerfully I would lay down my life to secure it."

With Mercer captured, command of the brigade fell to Colonel John Haslet. During the Battle of Long Island, Haslet's 1st Delaware regiment had been decimated as they courageously held off a much larger enemy force so other, nearly surrounded Americans could escape. Since then, the survivors had served well in several engagements, but by January 3 death, disease, and expired enlistments had whittled the once strong regiment down to just Haslet and five men. After Mercer fell, "Haslet retired some small distance and endeavored to rally them but, receiving a bullet through his head, dropt dead on the spot and ... [the rest] fled in confusion." After the battle, Haslet's burial party found in one of his pockets a week-old order from Washington to immediately return home on recruiting duty - an order Haslet had made known to no one and had, tragically, chosen to ignore.

Ironically, one of the first casualties of the battle was a non-combatant. The leg of a Princeton woman "was shot off at her ankle by a cannon ball. She was in one of the houses near the bridge on the main road. It was thought to be done by one of General Washington's field pieces." From another house, Robert Lawrence (who had earlier seen the British drop their packs in his garden) lingered in his doorway long enough to see the battle begin, before deciding to seek a safer place.

The battle was plainly seen from our door. Before any gun was heard a man was seen to fall and immediately the report and smoke of a gun was seen and heard, and the guns went off so quick and many together that they could not be numbered. We presently went down into the cellar to keep out of the way of the shot. There was a neighbour woman down in the cellar with us that was so affrighted that she imagined that the field was covered with blood, and when we came out of the cellar she called earnestly to us to look out and see how all the field was quite red with blood, when none was to be seen at that distance. This I mention only to show into what strange frights the fear of death may put us.

The remains of Mercer's brigade fled up the western side of the hill, toward Thomas Clark's house, pursued by charging Regulars. At about the same time, Cadwalader's militia were coming up the eastern side from the Quaker Road. Cresting the rise, they ran straight into the fleeing veterans. Suddenly, British lead whistled through the air all around the raw recruits. They were also engulfed in the other terrifying sounds of battle - the booming of guns, the screams of wounded men and horses. Plus the anguished cries of those presently being hit by flying lead or pierced by steel bayonets. It all added up to pure terror for these inexperienced militia, fresh off the Philadelphia streets. Many of them immediately turned and ran back over the hill. Others stayed long enough to be sent forward into the melee. Captain Thomas Rodney describes the action on the slope below the Thomas Clark house:

> Cadwalader led up the head of the column with the greatest bravery to within fifty yards of the enemy. But this was rashly done, for he was obliged to recoil and, leaving one piece of his artillery, he fell back about forty yards and endeavored to form the brigade. ... [He] rode

in front of the column and ordered the second divisions to double up to the right, the third to the left, and so on alternately. This was done in the face of the enemy and under a shower of grape shot. About half the first battalion was formed when they broke, fell back upon the column, [and] threw the whole into confusion.

Mawhood's single regiment had so far routed two different American brigades. Washington's "bold stroke" was turning into a disaster. General Greene now hurried forward two field pieces that were coming up Quaker Road. They were quickly put into position by artillery Captain Joseph Moulder and twenty rough and ready boys he had recruited among Philadelphia's dock workers. Placed on the American right, next to the Thomas Clark house at the top of the hill, these cannon were for a few minutes the only opposition to Mawhood's further progress up the slope.

Captain Thomas Rodney was ordered to go to Moulder's support while Cadwalader tried desperately to reform his frightened militia. Rodney and fifteen of his men took cover behind some stacks of firewood and a few outbuildings to the right of Moulder's battery and commenced supporting Moulder with musket fire. Rodney's account:

> I could not keep them all there for the enemy's fire was dreadful and very thick. ... [Three balls] had grazed me. One passed within my elbow, nicking my great coat, and carried away the breech of Sergeant McKnatt's gun, he being close behind me. Another carried away the inside edge of one of my shoe soles; another had nicked my hat, and indeed they seemed thick as hail.
>
> From these stacks [of firewood] and [out]buildings, we with two pieces of artillery, kept up a continuous fire on the enemy, and in all probability it was this circumstance that prevented the enemy from advancing, for they could not tell the number we had posted behind

these covers, and were afraid to attempt passing them. But if they had known how few we were, they might easily have advanced while the two brigades were in confusion and routed the whole body, for it was a long time before they could be reorganized again, and indeed many that were panic struck ran quite off.

At last, Greene's final brigade - the New Englanders - came up. Colonel Daniel Hitchcock, who would die of consumption within a few days, was by now so ill that he let Major Israel Angell lead these veterans from Rhode Island and Massachusetts against Mawhood's Regulars. Rhode Islander Captain Stephen Olney noted in his journal that, earlier that morning, Major Angell had "made a short speech to the regiment, encouraging them to act the part that became brave soldiers worthy of the Cause for which we were contending." Some of Cadwalader's troops, Stephen Olney wrote,

> broke and came running through our ranks. This had like to have disconcerted our march, but Captain Jeremiah Olney in a peremptory manner ordered them to join our platoon. I seconded the motion in earnest, so that with some persuasion and a few hard words, some ten or twelve of them complied, and the rest made off into the woods.
>
> When clear of the woods and other obstructions, our column displayed and marched in line. At this instant the enemy made a full discharge of musketry and field pieces loaded with grape shot, which made the most horrible music about our ears I had ever heard ... [nearly all] continued the march, looking ahead at the colors, which were carried steady by Ensign Oliver Jencks ... no fool of a job to carry colors steady at such a time.

Washington, meanwhile, was still with Sullivan's division on the

crest of the slope about a mile farther along the back road, toward Princeton. He had been observing the battle through his spyglass and had seen the rout of Mercer's brigade (probably cursing Cadwalder's slowness in coming up to assist Mercer). The British 55th Regiment was also watching, from the rise now known as Mercer's Heights. Neither they nor Washington wanted to risk sending a large party to assist their comrades, for fear they would weaken themselves. But Washington could clearly see that the Continentals needed help. So, leaving Sullivan to oppose the 55th, and telling his aides and the Philadelphia Light Horse to follow, Washington galloped off toward the rear as fast as his horse could carry him.

Following the back road, he soon arrived on the east side of the slope, in back of the Clark house, where he found hundreds of militia and the remains of Mercer's Continentals milling around in confusion. Washington reined in his white horse and began shouting at them, "Parade with us! There is but a handful of the enemy and we will have them directly." Encouraged by their charismatic leader, the men took heart, scurried around looking for their respective units and began forming. Washington personally led forward the remnants of Cadwalader's brigade and Mercer's. The Commander-in-Chief, with no regard for his own safety, rode back and forth along the front lines, using his hat to wave the men into position.

At the top of the little hill, Sergeant Joseph White's artillery crew, and Hitchcock's men behind the stacked firewood, were still holding off Mawhood. Now White turned and saw the reformed brigades coming on. "I never saw men looked so furious as they did."

Washington had given the order for absolutely no firing until he gave the signal. Under his leadership, they marched forward into the enemy's fire until within thirty yards, when Washington yelled, "Halt!" and then, "Fire!" He "was exposed to both firings for some time," one of the astonished men remembered, and hidden from view by a cloud of smoke. Colonel John Fitzgerald, one of Washington's aides, covered his eyes with his tricorne, not bearing to witness his commander's death. But, miraculously, Washington soon rode back out of the

smoke, unharmed, yelling to Fitzgerald, "Away, my dear colonel, and bring up the troops!"

Mawhood's troops were outnumbered now, and the American fire was so hot and delivered at such close range that they could hear the British being hit - they "screamed as if so many devils had got hold of them." The British were unable to withstand the attack for long, and after "a few minutes they threw down their arms and ran." Colonel Cadwalader "pressed my party forward, huzzaed, and cried out 'They fly, the day is ours!' and it passed right and left." Another soldier noted, "Their lines were broken and our troops followed them so close that they could not form again." A jubilant George Washington rode alongside the pursuing troops, yelling, "It's a fine fox chase, my boys!"

Sergeant R., one of Mercer's vanguard that had suffered in the orchard, now "marched over the ground again" and saw the results of the early fighting there:

> O, the barbarity of man! On our retreat we had left a comrade of ours whose name was Loomis from Lebanon, Ct., whose leg was broken by a musket ball, under a cart in a yard; but on our return he was dead, having received several wounds from a British bayonet. My old associates were scattered about groaning, dying and dead. One officer who was shot from his horse lay in a hollow place in the ground rolling and writhing in his blood, unconscious of anything around him. The ground was frozen and all the blood which had been shed remained on the surface, which added to the horror of the scene of carnage.
>
> In this battle my pack, which was made fast by leather strings, was shot from my back, and with it went what little clothing I had. It was, however, soon replaced by one which had belonged to a British officer and was well furnished. It was not mine long, for it was stolen shortly after.

Immediately after the battle, an officer observing blood on my clothes, said, "Sergeant R---, you are wounded?" I replied, "No," as I never expected to be injured in battle. On examination, I found the end of my forefinger gone, and bleeding profusely. When and how it happened I never knew; I found also bullet holes in the skirts of my coat, but, excepting the slight wound of my finger, was not injured.

In this battle, and that of Trenton, the excitement of rum had nothing to do in obtaining the victories. As I had tried [it] on Long Island to promote courage, and engaged here without it, I can say that I was none the less courageous here than there.

Mawhood's regiment had performed well. They had routed their American foes twice, and not retreated until overwhelmed by superior numbers. This 17th Regiment (also known as the Royal Leicestershires) soon became known as "The Heroes of Prince Town" back in England and were for many years glorified on recruiting posters. They were also nicknamed the Tigers, a name later adopted as mascot by the college at Princeton because of their valor there.

Mawhood and his survivors managed to escape to Maidenhead, thanks to the dragoons, who covered their retreat in a rear guard action. Some of Hand's riflemen pursued stragglers for several miles along Stony Brook, not returning to the Continental Army until the next morning.

Robert Lawrence had by now become too curious to stay in his cellar. He therefore came up and witnessed Americans pursuing the British along the Post Road. In fact, at one point, "seven Regulars was seen from our door to fall at once." Lawrence continues his account:

Immediately after the battle Genl Washingtons men came into our house. Though they were bo[th] hungry

and thirsty some of them [were] laughing out right, others smileing, and not a man among them but showed joy in his countenance. It really animated my old blood with love to those men that, but a few minutes before, had been couragiously looking death in the face.

Washington ordered an artillery company to tear up Stony Brook bridge and temporarily hold off the enemy when they came down the Post Road from the direction of Maidenhead and Trenton. He then rode off, and soon came upon a British Regular lying on the frozen ground. The soldier later recalled his encounter with the rebel general:

[Washington,] after enquiring into the nature of his wound, commended him for his gallant behaviour, and assured him that he should want for nothing and that his camp could furnish him. After the General left, an American soldier who thought he was dead came up in order to strip him. The General, seeing it, bid the soldier be gone, and ordered a sentry to stand over the wounded prisoner till he was carried to a convenient house to be dressed.

* * * * *

The commander of the 55th Regiment, on Mercer's Heights one mile northeast of the battle, observed the rout of the 17th. Then he turned his regiment around and headed toward Princeton to join the 40th Regiment. On the way, however, he found the 40th already lined up on the far bank of a ravine known as Frog Hollow. He had his regiment fall in on their left. About this time, Sullivan had decided to force the action and sent forward several regiments to attack Mercer's Heights. By the time they arrived, though, the 55th had moved to Frog Hollow.

The men of the 55th and 40th Regiments were some of Britain's

finest. They knew that often in the face of superior numbers a highly disciplined force of Regulars could win the day. But they had just witnessed the rout of Mawhood's equally renowned regiment, and it took the heart out of them. Thus, when they saw Sullivan's troops advancing toward Frog Hollow, they panicked and ran. Some didn't stop until they reached Brunswick. Seventeen-year-old Ensign Robert Beale, of the Virginia Continentals, describes the advance and pursuit:

> Colonel Scott observed - "Boys, there are two hundred and fifty Red Coats on yonder hill [Mercer's Heights] and about two hundred and fifty of us. We can beat them. Huzza, come on" and down the hill we went, but when we got to the top of the hill there was not one man to be seen. A small battery stood to our left and the college to the right. Twas said, "They are in the battery," then up to the battery we went and no one was there. Then they were in the college, but when we passed the college we looked down the hill and saw them running in confusion. We broke directly and every man ran with all speed in pursuit. Lieutenant Eggleston, Ensign Smith and myself out-ran all and came up with a party that had halted and formed near a wood as if to make battle, but seeing us followed by all our men they grounded their arms and surrendered.

Nearly 200 British, finding themselves surrounded by Sullivan's men, took shelter in Nassau Hall, the 52-room building that served as the College of New Jersey. They smashed windows with their muskets and fired out them at the Americans outside. Captain Alexander Hamilton then brought up his two artillery pieces and fired solid shot, at point blank range, at the building. One of the cannon balls bounced off an outside wall and barely missed the horse ridden by Major Wilkinson. Another went in a window and, passing through a painting of King George III hanging on the wall, "took off the King's head."

Tradition has it that when George Washington later heard about this, he offered to personally pay for a new portrait of the King. However, the college's Board of Trustees refused the offer. What they did was commission Charles Willson Peale to paint a portrait of Washington to hang in the same spot.

The two or three rounds of artillery fire were immediately followed by a charge on Nassau Hall's front doors, led by Captain James Moore, a local resident whose house and business had been recently ruined by plundering British and Hessians. The doors were broken down and Moore's men charged into the building, but found no resistance - for, by then, a white flag was hanging out a window. The captured Regulars cursed themselves for seeking refuge inside the building. Sergeant R. thought they were "a haughty, crabbed set of men."

With Princeton taken, Washington now considered his next move. He had planned to continue marching northeast some sixteen miles to Brunswick, where a small enemy force was known to be guarding a huge supply depot and the captured Charles Lee, the second highest ranking general in the Continental Army. However, the lateness of the day, the closeness of the enemy's pursuit, and the condition of the army ruled out that mission. The army had been through battles and marches without "rest, rum or provision for two nights and days," and were not capable of any more.

So, instead of heading for Brunswick, Washington led his exhausted army north to Morristown, where they would set to work building cabins and establishing winter quarters. Reflecting on the Brunswick opportunity, on January 5th Washington regretfully wrote to Congress that, in his judgment, "six or seven hundred fresh troops, upon a forced march, would have destroyed all their stores and magazines, taken (as we have since learned) their military chest containing seventy thousand pounds, and put an end to the war."

The American troops lacked sufficient horses and wagons to transport most of the barrels of gunpowder captured at Princeton. So they put most of it to the torch, sending into the sky huge clouds of smoke which lingered above the town the rest of the afternoon. Not all the

British artillery had to be left, though. One American artillery officer made a good exchange: "He left an iron three-pounder and brought a brass six-pounder."

To some of the Americans, the order to march came all too soon. A major noted that his troops, who had been taking charge of "their prisoners, [and] taking paroles of two or three sick officers, had not time even to distribute the rum found in store, tho much wanted, before a firing was heard on the Trenton Road."

Back in Nassau Hall, Sergeant Joseph White was doing some post-battle scavenging. He sat down to enjoy some unknown British officers' breakfast which had been served but not eaten that morning. After heartily gorging himself, he discovered the flour supply and determined to put it to good use. He went to a nearby house and asked the mistress there if she would be willing to bake him a few cakes if he paid her in flour. She agreed. When the order came to march, White "ran to see if the cakes were done. The woman said the oven was heating. I could have some in an hour's time." He told her where the staved in flour barrels were and that she and her daughters should scoop up as much as they could in their aprons. An hour later, the cakes were done, but White was already on the march, with an empty knapsack.

That night, the army - exhausted, cold and hungry, but "in high spirits" - camped at Somerset Courthouse, fifteen miles north of Princeton, having arrived there at "ten or eleven o'clock." For many of the men, this had been the third night march in a row. At one point, Washington, watching them march by, saw the marks left in the road by the bare and bloody feet of one William Lyon. "My boy," the general said, "you deserve a better fate." Lyon reassured him, "There is no danger of my feet freezing as long as the blood runs."

The prisoners were locked up in the courthouse, to the envy of the American soldiers who had to sleep outside without their blankets or tents.

There were barely houses sufficient for quarters of the

generals and their attendants. The troops took up their abode for the rest of the night on frozen ground. All the fences and everything that would burn was piled in different heaps and burnt, and he was the most fortunate who could get nigh enough to smell the fire.

Tired as he was, Lieutenant Elisha Bostwick had to stay awake, though thankfully out of the wind, guarding the prisoners in the courthouse. About midnight, when all was still, one of the prisoners, a Scot, arose and softly sang a song called "The Gypsy Laddie." Bostwick memorized the lyrics, some of which were: "Will you leave your houses, will you leave your lands, And will you leave your little children a-a-h, ..." When he finished the song, Bostwick remembered, the prisoner "lay down again. The tune was of a plaintive cast and I always retained it and sung it to my children."

* * * * *

Just after the last of Washington's victorious army had left Princeton, the British had entered the town, according to one inhabitant, "in a most infernal sweat - running, puffing and blowing, and swearing at being so outwitted." These troops were part of General Leslie's brigade, which had been posted at Maidenhead. The general's nephew, Captain William Leslie, had been wounded in the battle and treated by an American doctor. Taken along with the American wounded, Captain Leslie died the next day in Pluckemin, near Morristown, and was buried with full military honors.

The Continental Army's exit was covered by the rear guard left at Stony Brook bridge. An exchange of artillery fire resulted in the capture of Major John Kelly, the officer in charge of demolishing the bridge. Determined to finish the job of prying up the wooden planks, he stayed on after his men had left, while all about him the artillery fired on both sides. A British cannon ball hit the plank he was squatting on, catapulting him into the icy stream. He climbed out, but his

clothes quickly froze stiff as boards, preventing him from running. He was the only member of the rear guard captured.

Cornwallis's main army, hurrying back from Trenton, arrived shortly after Leslie's troops from Maidenhead. Captain Johann Ewald led the way with his jagers.

> [I] found the entire field of action ... covered with corpses. In the afternoon, the entire army reached Princeton, marching in and around the town like an army that is thoroughly beaten. Everyone was so frightened that it was completely forgotton even to obtain information about where the Americans had gone. But the enemy now had wings, and it was believed that he had flown toward Brunswick.

Cornwallis, horrified at the prospect of all those supplies <u>and</u> the war chest of 70,000 pounds sterling falling into enemy hands, pushed his men on with "haste toward Brunswick." They arrived there at nine the next morning, after a 25-hour march. One of the Hessians wrote that the soldiers were so fatigued "they could barely totter." Cornwallis must have breathed a huge sigh of relief when he found the depot untouched.

After "the coup at Princeton," General Howe, never one for winter campaigning, called off the war until spring. The British were thus left holding only the northeast corner of New Jersey, close to New York. The two principal towns there - Amboy and Brunswick - were both on the Raritan River and could be supplied by water from Staten Island. Howe placed a garrison of 5,000 men at each post to discourage any more raids like those on Trenton and Princeton.

The reversals at Trenton on December 26th and Princeton January 3rd were particularly distressing to William Howe, who had worked so diligently and patiently to pacify New Jersey and win it back for the crown. In the space of just nine days, Washington and his dispirited, destitute "rabble in arms" had not only refused to disintegrate with the

expiration of enlistments, but had pulled off two stunning victories and revived the dying rebellion. William Harcourt, the dragoon officer who, just three weeks before, had predicted the rebel army's imminent demise, now wrote to his father, "Though it was once the fashion of this army to treat them in the most contemptible light, they are now become a formidable army."

General Howe had the unenviable task of informing his superior, Secretary of State Germain, that the pacification plan for winning the war by territorial acquisition had failed. On January 20th, he reported that the enemy's recent successes had

> thrown us further back than was at first apprehended, from the great encouragement it has given the rebels. I do not now see a prospect of terminating the war but by a general action, and I am aware of the difficulties in our way to obtain it, as the enemy moves with so much more celerity than we possibly can.

For the patriot cause, the darkest hour of the revolution had passed. Though five more years of bloodshed and suffering lay ahead, never again would America's prospects look as bleak as they did in December of 1776. The Continental Congress, which in December had seriously considered suing for peace, now was confident enough to publish, for the first time, the fully signed version of the Declaration of Independence. Unlike the July 4th version, which had only Hancock's signature, the official parchment copy had been carefully hidden since August 2nd, when every member of Congress had signed it. Washington's leadership had restored so much confidence that they were now willing to openly risk their lives and fortunes. Nicholas Cresswell, an English gentleman and non-combatant traveling in America, described the new spirit in his journal:

> The minds of the people are much altered. A few days ago they had given up the cause for lost. Their late

successes have turned the scale and now they are all liberty mad again. Their recruiting parties could not get a man. Now the men are coming in by companies. They have recovered their panic and it will not be an easy matter to throw them into confusion again. Even the parsons, some of them, have turned out as volunteers, and [in] pulpits summoning all to arms in this cursed babble. Damn them all.

CAMPAIGN OF '76

(a drinking song by G. Edgar)

Pray listen my friend and I'll tell you herein,
Of the campaign of seventy-six.
Black Dick and Sir Billy, the two brothers Howe,
Thought now they would get in their licks.
Ri tour ra li a, ri tour ra li o,
Thought now they would get in their licks.

Old Putnam did try to fortify high,
All the passes on Long Island.
But Clinton found out when he searched about,
One pass that Putnam left open.
Ri tour ra li a, ri tour ra li o,
One pass that Putnam left open.

So the British set out for Jamaica Road,
A long night's march to Flatbush.
Come morning the Hessians kept Putnam tied down,
While the British came up behind him.
Ri tour ra li a, ri tour ra li o,
While the British came up behind him.

George Washington's army appeared to be trapped,
Then Glover's seamen stepped forward.
Under cover of night they rowed them right past,
Black Dick's thirty-two pounders.
Ri tour ra li a, ri tour ra li o,
Black Dick's thirty-two pounders.

The fight for New York was put off for three weeks,
While Congress was baited with pardons.
But Franklin rejected their offers and said,
"We'll never submit to the crown!"
Ri tour ra li a, ri tour ra li o,
"We'll never submit to the crown!"

Peacemaking they failed at, the Howes must admit,
They were very much better at war.
So Black Dick provided the cover at Kip's Bay,
When Sir Billy sent thousands ashore.
Ri tour ra li a, ri tour ra li o,
When Sir Billy sent thousands ashore.

But Knowlton showed them that Yankees can fight,
As he lured the Highlanders out.
And Washington sent in the "Kip's Bay Cowards"
To help him finish the rout.
Ri tour ra li a, ri tour ra li o,
To help him finish the rout.

Harlem Heights was too strong for the British,
So they went around by Hell Gate.
But when they landed at Pelham,
Glover's seamen refused to be moved.
Ri tour ra li a, ri tour ra li o,
Glover's seamen refused to be moved.

When Sir Billy arrived at White Plains,
He found rebels already intrenched.
So he set up his guns on Chatterton Hill,
To win the battle next morning.
Ri tour ra li a, ri tour ra li o,
To win the battle next morning.

That night Howe prepared his army,
For the battle to end the war.
But when he awoke ... he found it a joke,
For the rebel army had gone!
Ri tour ra li a, ri tour ra li o,
For the rebel army had gone!

"When will that rebel let me get at him!"
Sir Billy cried out in anger.
So he gave up the chase, turned round about,
And headed back to New York.
Ri tour ra li a, ri tour ra li o,
And headed back to New York.

Fort Washington back on Manhattan,
Sir Billy found easy prey.
Three thousand pris'ners he took there,
With Washington's army away.
Ri tour ra li a, ri tour ra li o,
With Washington's army away.

The stage was now set for Cornwallis,
To chase rebels all over the map.
With Washington out of New Jersey,
Sir Billy laid down for a nap.
Ri tour ra li a, ri tour ra li o,
Sir Billy laid down for a nap.

"Wake up and fight, I'm not licked yet!"
Washington cried to Sir Billy.
At Trenton and Princeton ... he got in the last licks,
Of this campaign of seventy-six.
Ri tour ra li a, ri tour ra li o,
Of this campaign of seventy-six.

CANNON BALLS

(A whimsical song by G. Edgar, inspired by
the Battle of Long Island, August 27, 1776.)

Washington will know, the news we redcoats bring,
That cannon shells and musket balls, soon in the air will sing.
Buttons on red coats shine, making our march grand,
Oh what fun it will be, to conquer this great land.

Oh, ... cannon balls, cannon balls, shot off by the ton,
Oh what fun it will be, to see those Yankees ru-un.
Cannon balls, cannon balls, shot off by the ton,
Oh what fun it will be, to see those Yankees run.

A year ago last June, back in seventy-five,
Swift sailing ships to London Town, did hurriedly arrive.
The news they brought of war, could none of us believe,
So with Lord Howe we soon set sail, to make those Yankees grieve.

Oh, ... cannon balls, cannon balls, shot off by the ton,
Oh what fun it will be, to see those Yankees ru-un.
Cannon balls, cannon balls, shot off by the ton,
Oh what fun it will be, to see those Yankees run.

To New York we come, to meet their boastful best,
At Flatbush Pass and Brooklyn Heights, we'll put them to the test.
Their riflemen do hide, and like a savage fight,
With bay'nets fixed we'll march right up, and put them all to flight!

Oh, ... cannon balls, cannon balls, shot off by the ton,
Oh what fun it will be, to see those Yankees ru-un.
Cannon balls, cannon balls, shot off by the ton,
Oh what fun it will be, to see those Yankees run!

SELECTED BIBLIOGRAPHY

Author's Note: Many of the sources, both primary and secondary, listed below were first published in the late eighteenth or nineteenth century, and later reprinted in the twentieth century. I have listed here not necessarily the original edition, nor the most recent reprint, but rather the edition that I consulted.

Primary Sources

Adams, John, *The Works of John Adams*, v. 2. Edited by Charles Francis Adams. New York: Little, Brown, 1850.

Anderson, Enoch, *Personal Recollections of Captain Enoch Anderson, an officer of the Delaware Regiments in the Revolutionary War*. Edited by Henry Hobart Bellas. Historical and Biographical Papers of the Historical Society of Delaware, v. 2, no. 16, 1896.

Anonymous, *Letters From America 1776-1779, Being Letters of Brunswick, Hessian and Waldeck Officers with the British Armies During the Revolution*. Ray W. Pettengill, translator. Boston: Houghton Mifflin, 1924.

Balderston, Marion, and David Syrett, ed., *The Lost War, Letters from British Officers during the American Revolution*. New York: Horizon Press, 1975.

Baldwin, Jeduthan, *The Revolutionary Journal of Colonel Jeduthan Baldwin 1775-1778*. Edited by Thomas William Baldwin. Bangor, Maine: The DeBurians, 1906.

Bauermeister, Carl Leopold, *Revolution in America, Confidential Letters and Journals 1776-1784 of Adjutant General Major Bauermeister of the Hessian Forces*. Edited by Bernhard A. Uhlendorf. New Brunswick, N.J.: Rutgers University Press, 1957.

Beard, Mary R., ed., *America Through Women's Eyes*. New York: MacMillan, 1933.

Bloomfield, Joseph, *Citizen Soldier, The Revolutionary War Journal of Joseph Bloomfield*. Edited by Mark E. Lender and James Kirby

Martin. Newark, N.J.: New Jersey Historical Society, 1982.

Butterfield, L.H., and Marc Friedlander and Mary-Jo Kline, ed., *The Book of Abigail and John, Selected Letters of the Adams Family 1762-1784*. Cambridge, Mass.: Harvard University Press, 1975.

Clinton, Henry, *The American Rebellion, Sir Henry Clinton's Narrative of his Campaigns, 1775-1782, with an Appendix of Original Documents*. Edited by William B. Wilcox. New Haven: Yale University Press, 1954.

Commager, Henry Steele, and Richard B. Morris, ed., *The Spirit of 'Seventy-Six, The Story of the American Revolution as told by the Participants*. New York: Harper & Row, 1975.

Commager, Henry Steele, and Allan Nevins, ed., *The Heritage of America*. Boston: Little, Brown, 1939.

Crary, Catherine S., ed., *The Price of Loyalty, Tory Writings from the Revolutionary Era*. New York: McGraw-Hill, 1973.

Dann, John C., *The Revolution Remebered, Eyewitness Accounts of the War for Independence*. Chicago: University of Chicago Press, 1980.

David, Ebenezer, *A Rhode Island Chaplain in the Revolution, Letters of Ebenezer David to Nicholas Brown 1775-1778*. Edited by Jeannette D. Black and William Greene Roelker. Providence: The Rhode Island Society of the Cincinnati, 1949.

Eelking, Max von, *The German Allies in the American Revolution, 1776-1783*. Baltimore: Genealogical Publishing Co., 1969.

Evans, Elizabeth, ed., *Weathering the Storm, Women of the American Revolution*. New York: Scribner's Sons, 1975.

Ewald, Johann, *Diary of the American War, A Hessian Journal*. Translated and edited by Joseph P. Tustin. New Haven: Yale University Press, 1979.

Gallup, Isaac, *Letter* from Roxbury, Mass., dated March 27, 1775, to his parents in Groton, Conn. Unpublished. Hartford: Connecticut State Archives Collection, Connecticut State Library.

Graydon, Alexander, *Alexander Graydon's Memoirs of His Own Time, with Reminiscences of the Men and Events of the Revolution.*

Edited by John Stockton Littell. New York: New York Times & Arno Press, 1969.

Greenwood, John, *The Revolutionary Services of John Greenwood of Boston and New York 1775-1783*. Edited by Isaac Greenwood. New York: DeVinne Press, 1922.

Gutman, William H., ed., *The Correspondence of Captain Nathan and Lois Peters, April 25, 1775 - February 5, 1777*. Hartford: Connecticut Historical Society, 1980.

Hart, Albert Bushnell, ed., *American History Told By Contemporaries*, v. 2. New York: MacMillan, 1898.

Heath, William, *Heath's Memoirs of the American War*. Edited by Rufus Rockwell. New York: A. Wessels, 1904.

Hinman, Royal R., ed., *Historical Collection, From Official Records, Files, etc. of the Part Sustained by Connecticut During the War of the Revolution*. Hartford: E. Gleason, 1842.

Huntington, Jedidiah, *Letters* home from Roxbury, Mass., during the blockade of Boston, 1775-1776. Connecticut Historical Society *Collections*, v. XX.

Lee, Henry, *The American Revolution in the South*. Edited by Robert E. Lee. New York: Arno Press, 1969.

Mackenzie, Frederick, *Diary of Frederick Mackenzie, Giving a Daily Narrative of his Military Service as an Officer of the Regiment of Royal Welsh Fusiliers During the Years 1775-1781 in Massachusetts, Rhode Island and New York*. Cambridge, Mass.: Harvard University Press, 1930.

Martin, Joseph Plumb, *Private Yankee Doodle*. Edited by George F. Scheer. New York: Little, Brown, 1962.

McDonald, Hugh, *A Teen-ager in the Revolution, Being the recollections of a high-spirited boy who left his Tory family at the age of fourteen and joined the Continental Army*. Harrisburg, Penn.: Historical Times, 1966.

Moore, Frank, ed., *Diary of the Revolution, from Newspapers and Original Documents*. New York: Scribner, 1860.

Morris, Margaret, *Private Journal Kept During the Revolutionary*

War. New York: New York Times and Arno Press, 1969.

Muenchhausen, Friedrich Ernst von, *At General Howe's Side 1776-1778*. Translated and edited by Ernst Kipping and annotated by Samuel Smith. Monmouth Beach, N.J.: Philip Freneau Press, 1974.

Murray, James, *Letters from America 1773-1780, Being letters of a Scots officer, Sir James Murray, to his home during the War of American Independence*. Edited by Eric Robson. Manchester, England: Manchester University Press, 1951.

Niles, Hezekiah, *Principles and Acts of the Revolution in America*. New York: A. S. Barnes, 1876.

Thomas Paine, *The American Crisis, and a Letter to Sir Guy Carleton on the Murder of Captain Huddley, and the Intended Retaliation on Captain Asgill of the Guards*. Edited by Daniel Isaac Eaton. London: D. I. Eaton, 1796.

Palmer, Noyes Jr., *Letter*, from New York, dated August 30, 1776, to his parents in Stonington, Conn., describing the retreat from Long Island. Unpublished. Hartford: Conn. State Archives Collection, Connecticut State Library.

Peckham, Howard H., ed., *Sources of American Independence, Selected Manuscripts from the Collections of the William L. Clements Library*, v. I and II. Chicago: University of Chicago Press, 1978.

Percy, Hugh, *Letters of Hugh Earl Percy from Boston and New York, 1774-1776*. Edited by Charles Knowles Bolton. Boston: Gregg Press, 1972.

Perry, Ichabod, *Reminiscences of the Revolution*. Lima, N.Y.: Ska-Hase-Ga-O Chapter, Daughters of the American Revolution, 1915.

Pole, J. R., ed., *The Revolution in America, 1754-1788*. Stanford, California: Stanford University Press, 1970.

Rankin, Hugh F., *The American Revolution*. New York: Putnam's Sons, 1964.

Ryan, Dennis P., ed., *A Salute To Courage, The American Revolution as seen through Wartime Writings of Officers of the Continental Army and Navy*. New York: Columbia University Press, 1979.

Scheer, George F., and Hugh F. Rankin, *Rebels and Redcoats*. Cleveland: World Publishing Co., 1957.

Scull, G. D., ed., *Memoir and Letters of Captain W. Glanville Evelyn, of the 4th Regiment ("King's Own") from North America, 1774-1776*. Oxford, England: James Parker & Co., 1879.

Serle, Ambrose, *The American Journal of Ambrose Serle, Secretary to Lord Howe 1776-1778*. Edited by Edward H. Tatum. San Marino, California: Huntington Library, 1940.

Tallmadge, Benjamin, *Memoir of Col. Benjamin Tallmadge, Prepared by Himself at the Request of his Children*. New York: Thomas Holman, 1858.

Thacher, James, *A Military Journal During the American Revolutionary War, from 1775-1783*. Boston: Cottons & Barnard, 1827.

Tilghman, Tench, *Memoir of Lt. Col. Tench Tilghman, Secretary and Aid to Washington, together with an appendix containing revolutionary journals and letters, hitherto unpublished*. Albany, N.Y.: J. Munsell, 1876.

Washington, George, *The Writings of George Washington*, v. IV. Edited by Jared Sparks. Boston: Russell, Odiorne and Metcalf, 1834.

Weedon, George, *Orderly Book of General George Weedon of the Continental Army under Command of Gen'l George Washington in the Campaign of 1777-8*. New York: Dodd, Mead & Co., 1902.

Wheeler, Richard, *Voices of 1776*. New York: Crowell, 1972.

White, Joseph, "A Narrative of Events, as They Occurred from Time to Time, in the Revolutionary War; with an Account of the Battles of Trenton, Trenton Bridge and Princeton." *American Heritage*, v. VII, no. 4, June, 1956.

Willard, Margaret Wheeler, *Letters On The American Revolution, 1774-1776*. Port Washington, N.Y.: Kennikat Press, 1968.

Wright, Esmond, *The Fire of Liberty*. London: The Folio Society, 1983.

Secondary Sources

Adams, James Truslow, *History of the United States*, v. 1. New York: Scribners, 1933.

Albanese, Catherine L., *Sons of the Fathers, The Civil Religion of the American Revolution*. Philadelphia: Temple University Press, 1976.

Alden, John R., *The American Revolution 1775-1783*. New York: Harper, 1954.

Alden, John R., *History of the American Revolution*. New York: Knopf, 1969.

Anderson, Troyer Steele, *The Command of the Howe Brothers During the American Revolution*. New York: Oxford University Press, 1936.

Atwood, Rodney, *The Hessians, Mercenaries from Hessen-Kassel in the American Revolution*. Cambridge, England: Cambridge University Press, 1980.

Bakeless, John, *Turncoats, Traitors and Heroes*. Philadelphia: Lippincott, 1959.

Bancroft, George, *History of the United States of America*, v. 4. New York: Appleton, 1893.

Becker, Carl, *The Spirit of '76 and Other Essays*. New York: Augustus M. Kelley, 1966.

Billias, George Athan, *General John Glover and his Marblehead Mariners*. New York: Henry Holt and Co., 1960.

Bishop, Jim, *The Birth of the United States*. New York: Morrow, 1976.

Bissell, Richard, *New Light On 1776 And All That*. Boston: Little, Brown, 1975.

Blivens, Bruce Jr., *Battle For Manhattan*. New York: Henry Holt and Co., 1955.

Blumenthal, Walter Hart, *Women Camp Followers of the American Revolution*. Philadelphia: George S. MacManus Co., 1952.

Boatner, Alexander, *Encyclopedia of the American Revolution*.

Boorstin, Daniel J., *The Americans: The Colonial Experience*.

Volume one in a three volume series, *The Americans.* New York: Vintage Books, 1958.

Bowie, Lucie Leigh, "The German Prisoners in the American Revolution," *Maryland Historical Magazine*, v. XL, 1945.

Bowman, Allen, *The Morale of the American Revolutionary Army.* Port Washington, N.Y.: Kennikat Press, 1964.

Bradley, Francis, *The American Proposition, A New Type of Man.* New York: Moral Re-Armament, 1977.

Buel, Joy Day, and Richard Buel, Jr., *The Way of Duty, A woman and her family in Revolutionary America.* New York: Norton, 1984.

Burnett, Edmund Cody, *The Continental Congress.* New York: MacMillan, 1941.

Calhoon, Robert McCluer, *Revolutionary America: An Interpretive Overview.* New York: Harcourt, Brace, Johanovich, 1976.

Carrington, Henry B., *Battles of the American Revolution, 1775-1781, including Battle Maps and charts of the American Revolution.* New York: Promontory Press, 1973.

Chidsey, Donald Barr, *July 4, 1776, The dramatic story of the first four days of July 1, 1776.* New York: Crown, 1958.

Chidsey, Donald Barr, *The Siege of Boston.* New York: Crown, 1966.

Chidsey, Donald Barr, *The Tide Turns, the Campaign of 1776.* New York: Crown, 1966.

Christie, Ian R., and Benjamin W. Labaree, *Empire or Independence 1760-1776.* New York: Norton, 1976.

Coakley, Robert W., and Stetson Conn, *The War of the American Revolution.* Washington, D.C.: Center of Military History, U.S. Army, 1975.

Collier, Christopher, *Connecticut In The Continental Congress.* Connecticut Bicentennial Series, v. 2. Chester, CT: Pequot Press, 1973.

Cumming, William P., and Hugh Rankin, *The Fate of a Nation, The American Revolution through contemporary eyes.* London, England: Phaidon Press, 1975.

Davis, Burke, *George Washington and the American Revolution.* New York: Random House, 1975.

Donovan, Frank, *Mr. Jefferson's Declaration, The Story Behind the Declaration of Independence.* New York: Dodd, Mead, 1968.

Dupuy, Trevor N., and Gay M. Hammerman, ed., *People & Events of the American Revolution.* Dunn Loring, Va.: Bowker Co./Dupuy Associates, 1974.

Dwyer, William M., *The Day Is Ours! November 1776-January 1777: An Inside View of the Battles of Trenton and Princeton.* New York: Viking, 1983.

Falkner, Leonard, "A Spy for Washington," *American Heritage*, v. VIII, no. 5, August 1957.

Fisher, Sydney George, *The Struggle for American Independence*, v. 1. Philadelphia: Lippincott, 1908.

Fleming, Thomas J., *1776 Year of Illusions.* New York: Norton, 1975.

Flexner, James Thomas, *George Washington in the Revolution.* Boston: Little, Brown, 1965. Volume 4 of a 5 volume set.

Flood, Charles Bracelen, *Rise, And Fight Again, Perilous Times Along the Road to Independence.* New York: Dodd, Mead, 1976.

Ford, Corey, *A Peculiar Service, A Narrative of Espionage in and around New York during the American Revolution.* Boston: Little, Brown, 1965.

Freeman, Douglas Southall, *George Washington, A Biography. Volume 4: Leader of the Revolution.* New York: Scribner's Sons, 1951.

French, Allen, *The First Year Of The American Revolution.* Cambridge, Mass.: Riverside Press, 1934.

Frothingham, Richard, *History of the Siege of Boston, and of the Battles of Lexington, Concord, and Bunker Hill.* New York: DaCapo Press, 1970.

Furneaux, Rupert, *The Pictorial History of the American Revolution as told by Eyewitnesses and Participants.* Chicago: J.G. Ferguson Pub. Co., 1973.

Gelb, Norman, *Less than Glory, A Revisionist's View of the American Revolution.* New York: G. P. Putnam's Sons, 1984.

Griffith, Samuel B. II, *In Defense of the Public Liberty, Britain America and the Struggle for independence from 1760 to the surrender at Yorktown in 1781.* Garden City, N.Y.: Doubleday, 1976.

Gruber, Ira D., *The Howe Brothers and the American Revolution.* New York: Atheneum, 1972.

Handlin, Oscar, and Lilian Handlin, *A Restless People, Americans In Rebellion 1770-1787.* Garden City, N.Y.: Anchor Press/Doubleday, 1982.

Hargreaves, Reginald, *The Bloodybacks, The British Serviceman in North America and the Carribbean 1655-1783.* New York: Walker and Co., 1968.

Hibbert, Christopher, *Redcoats and Rebels, The American Revolution Through British Eyes.* New York: Norton, 1990.

Higginbotham, Don, *The War of American Independence, Military Attitudes, Policies, and Practice, 1763-1789.* New York: MacMillan, 1971.

Hughes, Rupert, *George Washington.* New York: William Morrow Co., 1930.

Hutchins, Jack Randolph, *Jacob Hutchins of Athol, Massachusetts, Revolutionary Soldier, and Accounts of other Hutchins who served in the Revolutionary War.* Washington, D.C.: Goetz Press, 1976.

Jensen, Merrill, *The Founding of a Nation, A History of the American Revolution, 1763-1776.* New York: Oxford University Press, 1968.

Johnson, Curt, *Battles of the American Revolution.* New York: Rand McNally, 1975.

Johnson, William, *Sketches of the Life and Correspondence of Nathanael Greene.* New York: Da Capo Press, 1973.

Johnston, Henry P., *The Battle of Harlem Heights.* New York: MacMillan, 1897.

Johnston, Henry P., *The Campaign of 1776 Around New York and Brooklyn.* Brooklyn: Long Island Historical Society, 1878.

Jones, Maldwyn A., "Sir William Howe: Conventional Strategist." In *George Washington's Opponents*, edited by George Athan Billias. New York: William Morrow Co., 1969.

Ketchum, Richard M., *The Winter Soldiers*. Garden City, N.Y.: Doubleday, 1973.

Lancaster, Bruce, *From Lexington to Liberty, The Story of the American Revolution*. Garden City, N.Y.: Doubleday, 1955.

Leckie, Robert, *George Washington's War, The Saga of the American Revolution*. New York: Harper Collins, 1992.

Lengyel, Cornel, *Four Days in July, The Story Behind the Declaration of Independence*. Garden City, N.Y.: Doubleday, 1958.

Lowell, Edward J., *The Hessians and the other German Auxiliaries of Great Britain in the Revolutionary War*. New York: Harper Brothers, 1884.

Ludlum, David M., "The Weather of American Independence - 2: The Siege of Boston," *Weatherwise*, v. 27, no. 4, August 1974.

Lundin, Leonard, *Cockpit of the Revolution, The War for Independence in New Jersey*. Princeton, N.J.: Princeton University Press, 1940.

Maier, Pauline, *The Old Revolutionaries, Political Lives in the Age of Samuel Adams*. New York: Knopf, 1980.

Main, Jackson Turner, *The Sovereign States, 1775-1783*. New York: New Viewpoints, 1973.

Malone, Dumas, *Jefferson The Virginian*. Volume one of a six volume set, *Jefferson and His Time*. Boston: Little, Brown, 1948.

Malone, Dumas, *The Story of the Declaration of Independence*. New York: Oxford University Press, 1954.

Marshall, Douglas W., and Howard H. Peckham, *Campaigns of the American Revolution, An Atlas of Manuscripts and Maps*. Ann Arbor, MI: University of Michigan Press and Hammond, Inc., 1976.

McCrady, Edward, *The History of South Carolina in the Revolution, 1775-1780*. New York: Russell & Russell, 1969.

McNitt, V. V., *Chain of Error and the Mecklenburg Declarations of Independence, A New Study of Manuscripts: Their Use, Abuse, and Neglect*. Palmer, Mass.: Hampden Hills Press, 1960.

Meigs, Cornelia, *The Violent Men, A Study of Human Relations in the First American Congress*. New York: Macmillan, 1949.

Middlekauff, Robert, *The Glorious Cause, The American Revolution, 1763-1789*. New York: Oxford University Press, 1982.

Miers, Earl Schenck, *Crossroads of Freedom, The American Revolution and the Rise of a New Nation*. New Brunswick, N.J.: Rutgers University Press, 1971.

Miller, John C., *Triumph of Freedom 1775-1783*. Boston: Little, Brown, 1948.

Mitchell, Joseph B., *Discipline and Bayonets, The Armies and Leaders in the War of the American Revolution*. New York: Putnam's Sons, 1967.

Montross, Lynn, *Rag, Tag and Bobtail, The Story of the Continental Army 1775-1783*. New York: Harper & Brothers, 1952.

Montross, Lynn, *The Reluctant Rebels, The Story of the Continental Congress, 1774-1789*. New York: Harper & Brothers, 1950.

New York Historical Society, *Commemoration of the Battle of Harlem Plains on its 100th Anniversary*. New York: New York Historical Society, 1876.

Pancake, John S., *1777, Year of the Hangman*. University, AL: University of Alabama Press, 1977.

Palmer, Dave Richard, *The Way of the Fox, American Strategy in the War for America 1775-1783*. Westport, Conn.: Greenwood Press, 1975.

Pearson, Michael, *Those Damned Rebels: The American Revolution As Seen Through British Eyes*. New York: Putnam's Sons, 1972.

Peckham, Howard H., *The War For Independence, A Military History*. Chicago: University of Chicago Press, 1958.

Peterson, Merrill D., "Adams and Jefferson, A Revolutionary Dialogue." *Mercer University Lamar Memorial Lectures No. 19*. Athens, Georgia: University of Georgia Press, 1976.

Rawson, Jonathan, *1776, A Day-by-Day Story*. New York: Frederick A. Stokes Co, 1927.

Roberts, Robert B., *New York's Forts in the Revolution*. Rutherford, N.J.: Fairleigh Dickinson University Press, 1980.

Robson, Eric, *The American Revolution In Its Political and Military*

Aspects. New York: Norton, 1966.

Royster, Charles, *A Revolutionary People at War, The Continental Army and American Character, 1775-1783*. New York: Norton, 1979.

Scott, John Anthony, *Trumpet of a Prophecy, Revolutionary America 1763-1783*. New York: Knopf, 1969.

Shy, John, *A People Numerous And Armed, Reflections on the Military Struggle for American Independence*. New York: Oxford University Press, 1976.

Smith, George, *An Universal Military Dictionary, A Copious Explanation of the Technical Terms &c. used in the Equipment, Machinery, Movements and Military Operations of an Army*. Ottawa, Ontario: Museum Restoration Service, 1969.

Smith, Page, *A New Age Now Begins, A People's History of the American Revolution*. New York: McGraw-Hill, 1976.

Thompson, Charles O. F., *A History of The Declaration of Independence, A Story of the American Patriots who brought about the Birth of our Nation*. Bristol, R.I.: Charles O. F. Thompson, 1947.

Wade, Herbert T., and Robert A. Lively, *this glorious cause ... The Adventures of Two Company Officers in Washington's Army*. Princeton, N.J.: Princeton University Press, 1958.

Ward, Christopher L., *The Delaware Continentals 1776-1783*. Wilmington: Historical Society of Delaware, 1941.

Ward, Christopher L., *The War of the Revolution*. New York: MacMillan, 1952.

Ward, Harry M., *Duty, Honor or Country, General George Weedon*. Philadelphia: American Philosophical Society, 1979.

Wilson, Ellen Gibson, *The Loyal Blacks*. New York: Putnam's Sons, 1976.

Wright, Esmond, *Fabric of Freedom, 1763-1800*. New York: Hill and Wang, 1961.

Young, Norwood, *George Washington, Soul of the Revolution*. New York: Robert M. McBride & Co., 1932.

EVERY-NAME INDEX

CALLENDER, John 145
CAMPBELL, 78 Capt 82 John 81
    Mr 280
CARLETON, Gov Gen 75
CARPENTER, Capt 139
CASWELL, 82 Col 83 Richard 80
CHARLIE, Bonnie Prince 76
    Young Pretender 76
CHASE, 61 Samuel 55
CHESTER, Col 142 144
CLARK, 384 388 Abraham 68 Col
    90 Thomas 385 386
CLINTON, 83 87 91 92 96 97 112
    127-133 139 142 144-146 152
    179 187 193 220 224 230 234
    235 237 241 288 306 316 399
    Gen 85 86 89 101 219 289
    George 199 Henry 178 231 287
    327 Sir Henry 78 84 126 219
    377 378
COLLIER, Capt 161 George 161
    167
COOKE, Gov 5
CORBIN, John 253 265 Margaret
    253 265 272
CORNWALLIS, 130 144 147 148
    272 277 287 312 314-316 356
    358 360 367 369 372 373 376
    378 379 396 401 Gen 129 150
    257 290 Lord 78 150 230 235
    276 279 284 289 359 371 377
    380
COVELL, Mr 337
COX, Col 375
CRESSWELL, Nicholas 397
CUNNINGHAM, 207 208 William
    206
CUYLER, Maj 316
DARTMOUTH, Lord 14 18 77 Sec
    Of State 117
DEANE, Silas 4 43 73
DECHOW, Maj 324 325 344

DEFOREST, Samuel 134 158 163
DELANCEY, 131 Oliver Jr 130
    Oliver Sr 129
DEMONT, William 249
DESAXE, 277
DICKINSON, 56 60 61 68 Gen
    338 John 30 48 55 59 67 Messr
    42 Philemon 338 374
DONOP, 144 152 Col 278 319 331
    359 360
DUNMORE, Gov 86
EDEN, Gov 85
EGGLESTON, Lt 392
ELLIOT, Barnard 98
ENGELHARDT, Lt 341
ERSKINE, Sir William 371
EUSTIS, William 108
EVELYN, 131 Capt 132 William
    Glanville 130
EWALD, 279 Capt 278 360 362
    378 Johann 236 248 278 289
    312 354 371 378 396
EWING, Gen 332 341
FERMOY, 343 Gen 342 362
    Mathias Alexis 358
FITZGERALD, 389 John 327 388
FLEMING, John 383
FORREST, 261 262 Capt 339
FRANKLIN, 48 50 52 55 56 58
    171 400 Benjamin 28 33 37 43
    49 54 117 120 168 Dr 38 42 43
    64 69 169 170
FRASER, Simon 146
GADSDEN, Christopher 42 43 54
    56 87
GAGE, Gen 2 17 78
GALLOWAY, Joseph 289 Mr 290
GALLUP, Isaac 23
GATES, 297 301 303 306 307 327
    Gen 35 298 329 Horatio 34 292
GEORGE III, King Of England 2
    29 31 33 34 52 68 70 73 77 82

GEORGE III (cont.) 347 379 392

GERMAIN, 116 117 152 George 85 Lord 213 Lord George 77 Sec Of State 76 316 397

GERRY, Elbridge 62 68

GIST, Maj 149 150 Mordecai 149

GLOVER, 225-227 229 331 332 338 341 342 345 399 400 Col 224 246 344 353 John 157 216 223 224 327 328

GLYN, Thomas 249 377

GORDON, David 16

GRANT, 133 141 142 144 148 Gen 129 134 138 139 147 324 James 128 316

GRAYDON, 254 255 261 Alexander 8 70 243 253 260 271 329 Capt 246 247 256 271 272

GREENE, 127 243 244 246 247 250 252 257 275 276 279 303 335 336 342 387 Gen 35 108 110 177 183 221 243 251 256 306 334 337 386 Nathanael 7 107 125 177 242 245 272 363 378

GREENWOOD, John 12 16 301 326 341 348 Pvt 326 330 333 334

GRIDLEY, Col 16

GRIFFIN, 318

GRISWOLD, Charles 171

GROTHAUSEN, Lt 362

HALE, 206 Capt 207 Nathan 191 204 205 207 208

HALL, 314 Capt 378 380

HAMILTON, Alexander 207 208 232 236 237 282 334 339 392

HANCOCK, 59 60 63 67-70 109 397 John 1 15 66 104 165 166 209 350 352 Pres 62

HAND, 219 390 Col 123 159 342 363 364 383 Edward 362

HARCOURT, Col 299 300 William 397

HARNEY, Lt 140

HARRIS, Capt 193 George 191 198

HARRISON, Benjamin 60 62 66 68

HARY, Ralph 308

HASLET, 138 141 229 236 Col 228 232 285 John 231 384

HAUSEGGER, Col 358 359 Nicholas 358

HAWLEY, Joseph 44

HAZARD, Ebenezer 70 189

HEATH, 295 296 Gen 17 124 221 241 294 William 10 215 292

HEERINGEN, Col 145 160

HEINRICHS, Lt 201

HEISTER, 129 133 134 145 147 Gen 142 151 325 Philip 123

HEMPSTEAD, Sgt 205 Stephen 205

HENDLY, Maj 216 217

HENRY, John Joseph 202 Patrick 44 46 56 195

HEWES, Joseph 31 47 63

HITCHCOCK, 388 Col 364 365 369 Daniel 294 387

HOAGLANDT, 193

HODGKINS, Joseph 154 197 199 293 Lt 294

HOHENSTEIN, 268 269

HONEYMAN, 320 John 319

HOOPER, Lisa 13

HOPKINS, Stephen 62

HOPKINSON, Francis 315

HOUSMAN, Conrad 358 359

HOWARD, 132

HOWE, 10 15 16 18-21 24 25 32 59 84 86 101 107 115 128 130

417

SHERMAN, 52 Roger 48 50 57
SHEWKIRK, Rev 113 114
SHULDHAM, Adm 22 118
SMALLWOOD, 138 141 150 176
    232-234 Col 149 210 282 Gen
    307
SMITH, Ensign 392 Francis 17
    John 294 297 312 352 William
    201
SPENCER, Gen 221 Joseph 177
SPRAGUE, James 204
STARK, John 328 338
STEDMAN, Capt 139 140 Charles
    312
STEPHEN, Adam 335 Gen 336
    337
STEWART, 78 Lt 140
STIRLING, 142 144 148 149 161
    221 343 Col 258 261 262 Earl
    105 Gen 106 138 147 150 228
    342 Lord 105 138 139 141 147
    280 285 317 324 344
STIRN, 251
STOUT, Samuel Esq 308
STUART, Charles 16
SUFFOLK, Lord 31
SULLIVAN, 127 133 134 142 144
    145 147 161 221 301 306 307
    338 339 341 362 387 388 391
    392 Gen 110 111 146 168 300
    334 335 John 125 298 379
    Thomas 360
TALLMADGE, Benjamin 159
TARLETON, 299 Banastre 298
    Cornet Banastre 298
THACHER, Dr 18 290
THOMAS, John 16
THOMPSON, 97 Col 91 John 64
    65 William 7
THOMSON, 68 69 Charles 31 53
    Secretary 35 57 59 62 63 66
TILGHMAN, 224 Tench 195 198

TILGHMAN (cont.)
    221 223 303
TOWNSHEND, Lord 70
TRUMBULL, Benjamin 180
    Chaplain 180 Gov 7 104 284
    317
TRYON, Gov 62 84 108 188
VANDEWATER, 194 198
VAUGHN, Gen 152
VERGENNES, Foreign Minister 73
WALDECK, Philipp 263
WARD, Artemas 24
WARREN, Joseph 28 Mercy Otis
    28
WASHINGTON, 5 9 10 13-15 18
    20-24 35 37 58 75 83 84 100
    101 104-107 109 110 112 114-
    116 120 122 124-128 132 135
    138 145 153-156 158 160 163-
    165 167 176 179 183 187 193-
    195 197 198 200 201 204 206
    210 211 213 216 217 220 221
    223 224 227-231 236 237 239
    241-246 250 252 257 258 268-
    270 272 275 276 280-282 284
    285 287 288 292-294 296 297
    300 304 307 308 312 313 318-
    320 324 326 327 329-331 333
    334 342-345 347 350 352-354
    356 358 364 367 372-374 376-
    378 382 386-388 391 394-397
    400-402 Capt 340 Gen 2 4 7 8
    11 19 34 53 59 62 63 66 69 85
    108 119 121 151 159 166 171
    175 240 251 256 286 290 332
    336-339 349 351 355 357 363
    365 371 379 384 390 George 28
    32 42 103 108 119 161 166 182
    191 192 203 208 215 273 283
    291 298 301 303 305 306 309
    317 325 328 335 384 389 393
    399 George Esq 12 119 John

421